IN THE MATTER OF THE HEARING

IN RELATION TO

"THE GREATER NEW YORK,"

HELD BEFORE THE

Sub-Committee of the Joint Committee on the Affairs of Cities.

TRANSMITTED TO THE LEGISLATURE FEBRUARY 25, 1896.

WYNKOOP HALLENBECK CRAWFORD CO.,
STATE PRINTERS,
ALBANY AND NEW YORK.
1896.

STATE OF NEW YORK.

No. 44.

IN SENATE,

FEBRUARY 25, 1896.

MATTER OF THE HEARING

IN RELATION TO

"THE GREATER NEW YORK," HELD BEFORE THE SUB-COMMITTEE OF THE JOINT COMMITTEE ON THE AFFAIRS OF CITIES.

The subcommittee appointed by the joint committee on the affairs of cities of Senate and Assembly by virtue of concurrent resolution, as follows:

WHEREAS, Under and by virtue of chapter 311 of the Laws of 1890, a commission was created, known as the "Municipal Consolidation Commission," to inquire into the expediency of consolidating into one municipality the various municipal corporations and parts of municipal corporations contiguous to the port of New York, said commission, after inquiry and examination, did, by memorial to the Governor and the Legislature of the State, report in favor of consolidation; and,

WHEREAS, Pursuant to such report an act was thereupon passed, being chapter 64 of the Laws of 1894, entitled "An act providing for the submission of the question of consolidation of the city of New York with certain territory under a single municipal administration to the vote of the people." Such question of consolidation was submitted to the vote of the fully qualified electors of the territory embraced within the limits of the proposed greater city, and a majority in each locality voted in favor of consolidation, the aggregate of such majority being 44,464; and,

WHEREAS, A bill was thereupon introduced in the Legislature of 1894 designed to carry into effect said popular vote by providing for a commission to prepare a charter and laws for the government as one municipality of the territory embraced within the limits of the proposed greater city, but said bill failed of passage; and,

WHEREAS, The said municipal consolidation commission, by reason of the premises, being unable to present to this Legislature any adequate kind of government for said proposed greater city in form to enable this Legislature intelligently to consider and determine the important question involved; and,

WHEREAS, A just and considerate treatment of the questions connected with and arising from the creation of the greater city, and the consolidation of the various local governments into one municipality, is of vital consequence to the people, not alone of the territories immediately affected, but of the whole State, and concerns so deeply the moral and material interests, the well-being, security and convenience of more than three millions, and the principles of government and administration to be applied, require deliberation and care commensurate with the complexity and magnitude of the undertaking, and should suggest a practical solution of many of the problems of municipal government and administration, and afford relief from evils now existing, and a full, fair and deliberate consideration of the whole subject is deemed advisable and expedient; therefore,

Resolved (if the Assembly concur), That the committee on the affairs of cities of the Senate and the committee on the affairs of cities of the Assembly be and they are hereby appointed a joint committee of this Legislature, and are authorized and empowered fully and diligently to investigate and inquire into all and singular the matters set forth and related to the questions hereinbefore mentioned, with full power and authority to prosecute their inquiries in any and all directions in their judgment necessary and expedient to enable them to obtain and report the information required by these resolutions;

Resolved, further, and for the purposes aforesaid, That said committee may employ a stenographer, and one or more counsel, and such other assistants as may be necessary, and may send for persons, books, records and papers, call and subpoena witnesses and administer oaths;

Resolved, further, That said committee be authorized and empowered to appoint a subcommittee, consisting of four Senators and five Members of Assembly, which subcommittee (when appointed) shall have the same power and authority hereunder in all respects as are possessed by said joint committee, and whose duty it shall be to proceed with the inquiry and investigation into the matters aforesaid with all reasonable diligence; and to that end, full power and authority are hereby conferred upon such subcommittee (when appointed) to perform and exercise all and singular the functions and duties of said joint committee; to send for persons, books, records and papers; call or subpoena witnesses and administer oaths, with the same force and effect to all intents and purposes as though done by said joint committee and for the convenience of the public, and, in order to secure as full and complete an inquiry as may be practicable, to hold sessions in the city of New York, Brooklyn and Albany;

Resolved, further, and for the purposes aforesaid, That said joint committee and said subcommittee thereof (when appointed) be and they hereby are authorized and empowered to call to their aid and assistance in an advisory capacity the president and associate members of the municipal consolidation commission hereinbefore referred to, and also the Attorney-General of the State and the corporation counsel of the cities of New York, Brooklyn and Long Island City to aid and facilitate the acquisition of the information required by these resolutions and the report of said committee;

Resolved, further, That said committee shall make a preliminary report as soon as practicable and not later than the 1st day of March, 1896, to the end that proper legislation may be enacted in the premises.

Hereby make the following report of the proceedings had before it and the conclusions reached thereon:

In conformity with the permission expressed in said resolutions, it was decided to hold public meetings in the cities of New York, Brooklyn and Albany, in order to give the citizens abundant opportunity to make their views and opinions known to the Legislature through the medium of this committee.

In order that the situation may be fully understood, it will be useful to call attention to the history of the movement, which culminated in the consolidation legislation, which is the subject-matter of inquiry. It is conceded that for almost half a century a well defined movement toward the unification of the populations at the mouth of the Hudson into one municipality had been in operation. This movement existed at the time of the creation of the city of Brooklyn.

Even then large bodies of people residing on both sides of the river appreciated the logic of the situation, and realized the importance from every point of view, material, moral and governmental, of union between those enjoying closely related privileges, in order that one should not compete with the other, but rather act together, in working out their manifest destiny. At that early day opposition was made to a divided municipal existence and a segregation of commercial advantages. The movement then initiated waned at times, and at others pressed itself into the fore front, until in 1890 its culmination was reached by the appointment of a commission known as the "Consolidation Inquiry Commission" pursuant to chapter 311 of the Laws of 1890.

This commission was the creature of the Legislature of this State, the result of many years of agitation of the consolidation question, and was the first step taken by the Legislature, looking to the erection of the greater municipality. Reference to that act indicates the purpose of the Legislature as then expressed distinctly in favor of the general principle of consolidation, leaving it to the commission, provided under that act to dilimit the boundaries of the proposed greater city, and suggest legislation for the attainment of the proposed result. From the time of the passage of that act until the passage of the so-called referendum of 1894, (chapter 64, of the Laws of 1894) municipal consolidation became one of the burning questions of the hour. The commission during that period were pursuing its inquiry, the public prints were discussing the questions involved, and through their medium the people were kept informed of the progress of events. It was at this time, in the fall of 1893, and the early spring of 1894, that concerted action against consolidation assumed palpable form, and in order that, upon a subject of such stupenduous magnitude, due consideration should be had of the sentiments of each one of the localities affected and that violence should be done to the sentiments of none, the commission proposed a reference of the subject to popular vote, and memoralized the Legislature accordingly. This resulted in the passage of chapter 64 of the Laws of 1894, providing for a popular vote on the question of consolidation, at the next ensuing November election. It is proper to remark here, that organized opposition to consolidation had by this time assumed so aggressive a shape, that even this act referring the matter to a vote of the people was strenuously resisted, especially in the Senate, where an abortive attempt was made to create hostility to the bill, by the insertion of an amendment providing for immediate, equal, and uniform taxation and valuation for the purposes of taxation.

This recital is important in the subsequent consideration of the effect to be given to the vote of 1894, because it is conceded that the question of equal taxation is one lying so close to the hearts of the people of Brooklyn, that even the most pronounced opponents of consolidation admit the existence of an overwhelming sentiment in favor of municipal unification, provided equal taxation is unqualifiedly guaranteed. And the attitude of the Legislature in refusing to embody an equal taxation provision in the referendum bill of 1894, was turned to good account by the anti-consolidationists as indicating legislative hostility to equal taxation, but even this did not deter the people of Brooklyn from rolling up a majority in favor of consolidation, pure and simple.

It points, moreover, the conclusion that consolidation was an exceedingly live issue before the people, and that Brooklyn and her representatives in the Legislature were fully aroused to the importance of the questions involved.

It was under the mandate of this act of 1894 that the people of the various localities cast the referendum vote, which so far as relates to Brooklyn, has been so persistently criticised and the binding effect of which has been so ably repudiated by some, and as ably championed by others of the most eloquent and representative citizens of Brooklyn.

We come, therefore, to the consideration of that vote and what it signifies to this Legislature.

The proposition is presented by three bills now in committee, embodying three different views of the subject:

First. The bill prepared by the consolidation inquiry commission, which gives effect to the popular vote of 1894 by ordaining consolidation to take effect on the first day of January, 1898, provides for the continuance of all existing local governments until changed by future legislative action, and for an appropriation to enable the commission to prepare and submit to the Legislature necessary legislation with the specific direction to prepare a plan for the attainment of equal taxation and valuation.

Second. The resubmission bill, which substantially provides for a new vote on the question of consolidation.

Third. The referendum bill, which substantially provides for an epitome of the proposed charter of the greater city, to be prepared and submitted to popular vote, and makes its adoption a prerequisite to consolidation.

The result of the investigation indicates that those of the people of Brooklyn who manifest a public interest in this question are not divided merely into consolidationists and anti-consolidationists; but rather into three groups, of which the consolidationists, and the anti-consolidationists are the two extremes; while those who stand for a referendum of the proposed charter occupy a middle position. The great majority of the latter seem to desire consolidation sincerely, but for one reason or another, wish to be informed of the terms and conditions upon which consolidation shall take place, before consenting to the final step. This classification is important.

It appears that the resubmissionists insist upon another opportunity to vote, in order to defeat consolidation, while the referendists desire to secure another vote, not for the purpose of defeating consolidation, but of securing those terms and conditions which they deem important; and that for all purposes of the main inquiry consolidationists and referendists may be grouped together opposed only by the resubmissionists, pure and simple.

If this is conceded, and it is difficult to see how this proposition may be successfully disputed, then the opposition to consolidation in the city of Brooklyn is confined to comparatively few, who, for a variety of reasons, personal and sentimental, prefer the maintenance of existing conditions.

It would be strange indeed, if any change however beneficial, should meet with no opposition.

Conservatism is a predominant characteristic of some, and others from time immemorial have opposed every advance along the lines of progress.

The situation here considered is no exception to the rule. Opposition was encountered to the building of the Brooklyn bridge, which has added so enormously to the population of Brooklyn and has so prodigiously increased her private and public wealth.

The water supply was introduced only as the result of most determined and public spirited effort, while her public park system, which was successfully carried through by the efforts of the vice-president of the Consolidation Inquiry Commission, Hon. J. S. T. Stranahan, met with most persistent and embittered opposition. The elevated railroad and trolley system, the extension of boundary lines, all these incidents in Brooklyn's march to the front, point as many mile stones in the contest of progress against that conservatism, which, while well meaning and disinterested, is reactionary and retarding.

It is claimed that very many of those who desire resubmission were found in the front rank of the battle against the improvements just enumerated; and such statement publicly made has not been denied.

While the terms of the concurrent resolution did not directly empower the committee to consider any question connected with the popular vote of 1894, it was unanimously decided in consideration of the magnitude of the question presented, to permit full scope of inquiry and debate, allowing the widest latitude in the treatment of the entire subject; and in order to completely cover any and all objections that had been urged, the opponents of consolidation were permitted to question the result of the popular vote of 1894, and show any reason why it might be ignored by this Legislature.

The resubmissionists relied upon the following propositions:

First. That the question of consolidation in 1894 was not understood by the people. That it was lost in the consideration of many other questions then before the people.

Second. That the vote of 1894 was based upon alleged misrepresentation as to effect, and as to the conditions under which it was given.

Third. That the majority in favor of consolidation in 1894, was too insignificant to be deemed binding or authoritative.

Fourth. That the vote of 1894 was not determinative of any question, but was at best a mere expression of the then prevailing opinion and that its force was spent with the failure of the Legislature of 1895 to act upon it.

Fifth. That the sentiment of Brooklyn has undergone a radical change, and was now opposed to consolidation.

Sixth. That municipal government was a failure on the whole, that consolidation would lead to larger perplexities, and that until the problems of municipal government had been solved, larger concentrations of populations should be avoided.

Seventh. That if resubmission could not be secured in any

event, a referendum of the terms and conditions should be first had.

Enough has been said in the recital of the history of the greater New York movement to indicate that the position assumed by the resubmissionists is untenable; and the nearer we approach the day when the vote was actually cast, the more clearly does this become apparent. The failure of the Legislature in the spring of 1894 to insert the equal taxation clause into the bill providing for referendum, at the following election thoroughly disheartened consolidationists. Those opposed to consolidation insisted that this was declaratory of legislative opposition to equal taxation. Many of the most pronounced advocates of consolidation became either neutral or openly hostile, while with one exception every newspaper in the city of Brooklyn opposed consolidation.

The most important local organ of public opinion contained strong assaults upon the proposition, both by word and picture, contending for many days before election that it was the burning question of the hour upon the lip of every citizen, everywhere throughout the city. Enough will be found spread upon the record to indicate beyond peradventure the accuracy of the statement of those who appeared before the committee, and insisted that of all questions that of consolidation occupied the most prominent position in the Brooklyn mind, that for years before it had been agitated, and for weeks before the November election it was the one all important, and much discussed public subject. And that consolidation was successful in spite of the opposition of a united press, in spite of the untoward conditions under which it was presented, in spite of the ammunition furnished its opponents by reason of legislative refusal to insert an equal taxation clause, and in spite of the aggressive opposition of those, either sentimentally or materially interested in its defeat, is a remarkable evidence of the independence of the citizen, which has no parallel in the history of the State.

A consideration of the vote cast emphasizes this conclusion. At the same election the revised constitution, the legislative apportionment provision, the canal appropriations, and municipal consolidation were all considered by separate ballot.

The vote stood as follows:

Question.	For.	Against.	Total.
Consolidation..................	64,744	64,467	129,211
New Constitution................	58,961	48,201	107,162
Apportionment..................	54,533	54,237	108,770
Canal amendment...............	66,065	46,703	112,768

It thus appears that so deep was the interest of the people of Brooklyn in the question of consolidation that, notwithstanding the circumstances stated, 22,049 more votes were polled upon that question than upon the revised Constitution, the supreme organic law of the State, and 20,441 more than on the legislative apportionment, which was so vehemently attacked in every part of the state. It is doubtful whether a statement of circumstances may be conceived of more strongly corroborative of the unusually binding character of that vote of 1894. May it be claimed that the constitutional revision and apportionment were not sufficiently understood or considered by the people; or that the apportionment provision should be resubmitted to the people of Brooklyn, because forsooth it was approved by 296 majority, only.

If lack of public interest may be argued from the popular vote on the organic law of the State, it must be an argument against the whole theory of popular suffrage, hence equally against resubmission, but if, as must be admitted, a popular vote upon the organic law radically revised should serve as a proper measure of comparision then the vote upon consolidation in the city of Brooklyn demonstrated beyond cavil the overshadowing interest attached to that question by the people of that city.

It was argued on the part of the resubmissionists as evidencing lack of interest, that only 129,211, of a total of about 200,000 electors, voted upon the question of consolidation; but we point to the fact that 22,000 less voted on the constitutional revision, about 20,000 less on legislative apportionment and 16,443 less on the canal appropriation. Again, in what column are the 70,000 who did not vote to be placed. Certainly under the theory of our institutions, they should go into the column of those who were either in favor of the proposition or at least not opposed to it.

On the Second Point.

The committee is unable to find any warrant or authority for the proposition "that the vote of 1894 was based upon alleged misrepresentation as to its effect and as to the conditions under which it was given." The argument made that the people were led to believe that the vote was not a finality but simply an expression of opinion is disingenious, and yet an accurate exposition of the true principle governing the referendum.

It was not a finality. It simply was an expression of opinion upon a subject with reference to which the citizens of Brooklyn could only express an opinion, which would in no sense be final.

The ultimate decision must, of constitutional necessity, rest with the Legislature. The literature introduced to substantiate the claim of misrepresentation contains what we believe to be a candid statement of the principle underlying popular representative government, that with reference to all questions of legislation the people have delegated their powers to their chosen representatives, and that a popular vote upon a matter which is within the scope of legislative prerogative can not have any force except as it may be held to be a declaration of public opinion and a command to the Legislature. It was remarkable that some of the distinguished speakers appearing before the committee insisted that they had just reached the conclusion that the Legislature possessed the inherent power to decree consolidation, without a popular vote, and yet it must be self-evident that the popular vote ordered in 1894 was a concession made by the Legislature to those who opposed consolidation, and not because of any inherent right of suffrage upon that question. The vote itself was not a finality, because it determined nothing, and could determine nothing specially committed by the Constitution to legislative action; and whatever might be argued as to the power of the Legislature to take action in derogation of any of the ancient rights and privileges of the municipality of New York conferred by grants and charters antedating the erection of the State government, there is certainly no limitation upon the power of the Legislature with reference to the municipalities created by act of the Legislature, except as imposed by the organic law of the State. On the other hand, so far as the Constitution permitted, the result of the referendum of 1894 was as much a determination of the subject as the people themselves, under the limitations which they themselves have imposed, could make. In the absence of a claim of fraud, dishonest ballot or an unfair count, and none of these are even indirectly charged, it was a determination of the sentiment of Brooklyn, and a final conclusion of the question presented by the act of referendum, so far as legally any determination or conclusion might be made. It was not final only because it could not be final; it required ex-necessitate rei subsequent legislative action to give it the sanction of law. The statutory declaration of consolidation, and the terms and conditions, i. e., the bills or charter embodying them, rest within the exclusive province of the Legislature, and the finality referred to remained in abeyance until legislative action upon the subject.

On the Third Point.

The third contention presents a proposition novel in American political economy. To depart now from that axiom of our political faith, which prescribes that a majority, no matter how small shall be as conclusive as one no matter how large, would be a dangerous and unprofitable experiment. It goes to the very essence of majority rule and popular institutions, and if here conceded would be in contradiction of all known precedents.

It was urged that resubmission of certain constitutional amendments had been had, but it is claimed with convincing force that this procedure occurred only where a proposition had been negatived, and in no instance where a majority had declared in favor of it. To resubmit a question once determined would be to open the door to a series of resubmissions, without prospect of any ultimately binding decision. In the absence of fraud, or other inherent infirmity in the ballot, such a precedent does not receive the sanction of reason; such a precedent once established would be urged in favor of another resubmission, if upon a new vote consolidation was defeated by a slender majority, and so on ad infinitum.

We who hold our offices by the will of a majority of the people, however small, can not consistently advocate any other proposition than that a majority of one, honestly cast and fairly counted, is, for all purposes, a final determination, and one as binding and potential as a majority of thousands and tens of thousands.

The majority in favor of the legislative apportionment was but a few votes larger on a much smaller aggregate of ballots cast, and yet nobody would dream of resubmitting that question again to the people of Brooklyn in order to ascertain whether or not that majority represented the true sentiment of the people. The considerations urged above apply in this connection with great force and should be considered conclusive.

On the Fourth Point.

" That the vote of 1894 was not determinative, but was at best a mere expression of the then prevailing opinion, which spent its force with the Legislature of 1895."

The first part of this proposition has been already considered. The argument that the mandate of that vote spent its force with the Legislature of 1895 can not be seriously entertained; it might be otherwise, if the Legislature of 1895 had affirmatively disapproved the sanction of the vote of 1894.

The Assembly of 1895 passed a bill giving effect to the vote of 1894; and that the opposition of the anti-consolidationists carried from the polls into the Legislature was successful in preventing the bill from receiving a constitutional majority is rather an argument against the proposition now urged, than in favor of it. Assuming as we do, that the vote of 1894 was a final determination of the question submitted to the people then as could be constitutionally made, it is clear that a successful effort to prevent or obstruct the Legislature from giving due effect to the popular vote was nothing more or less than an attempt to defeat the will of the people as expressed at the polls. That which remained open for discussion, for agitation and opposition, or advocacy was not the main proposition which had been decided, subject to legislative sanction, but the terms and conditions which the consolidated communities should carry on the work of local government; upon all such questions, and their method of treatment the citizens were not concluded by the voice of the people; these were left expressly open for future consideration and decision. The opposition, however, in the Legislature of 1895 concentrated its efforts to negative legislation that had been affirmatively commanded by the people of the various localities, including Brooklyn; the fact that the insistence and ability of the opposition prevented the Senate of 1895 from carrying into effect the popular voice, furnishing no logical reason why the Legislature of the next year should not deem itself bound to execute the mandate of 1894. The force of a public judgment is not spent until the judgment itself has been reversed by like authority and until such time is just as obligatory upon this Legislature as upon the preceding one.

On the Fifth Point.

"That the sentiment of Brooklyn had undergone a radical change, which should be considered by the Legislature."

Assuming that we were authorized to consider a plea of this kind, the character of which is in conflict with many of the propositions hereinbefore laid down, it would present itself largely as a question of fact to be determined as all such questions are by a preponderance of evidence. We have not taken testimony in the sense of the examination of witnesses under oath, but we have listened to all the statements and arguments made pro and con, and have reached the conclusion that if any change in sentiment has occurred it is one more favorable to consolidation; and some of the speakers who appeared before the committee to urge consolidation admitted that they had vigorously opposed it in 1894, by speech and work at the polls, while a very large majority of the great institutions of Brooklyn, the leaders in those great enterprises that go far toward making up the prosperity and grandeur of that city, including the banks, railroad and trust companies, and mercantile establishments by representation and petition placed themselves on record as in favor of municipal unification. A very large majority of these agreed that consolidation was not only desirable from every point of view, but absolutely imperative from many view points, and concurred in the conclusion that a resubmission would find not less than from seventy to eighty per cent. of the people of Brooklyn voting in favor of municipal union. The committee spared neither time nor effort to possess itself of all information attainable on this question, and did not adjourn its hearings in Brooklyn until both sides agreed that the investigation had been completed. It was sought to convey the impression that the advocates of consolidation were largely estate owners or speculators, who saw in municipal union the promise of an increase in the value of real estate, but this suggestion was not carried out by the arguments. Those advocating consolidation were not confined to the ranks of real estate speculators, but were largely of the character above alluded to, whose arguments, as spread upon the record, demonstrated the faith that was in them sustained by the most cogent reasons from every standpoint of domestic and political economy. In any event the burden of proof was upon those who questioned the vote of 1894 to show what a change of heart had taken place. This they fell far short of accomplishing. There is, however, another and potent reason why, in view of the situation as found by the committee, resubmission should not be recommended.

It was conceded by all that the vote of 1894, was a purely non-political vote — an ideal vote with reference to a question of municipal unification. It was admitted that neither party took stand upon the question, and that political affiliation did not color the sentiment of the voter, or determine his ballot. It became plain during the progress of the hearing that in this regard the situation had undergone a radical change.

Questions of political exigency have intruded themselves. It follows that upon resubmission, this great question of municipal unification might not be determined, as it was in 1894, free from all party and partisan consideration, but would be made the football of party strife, or factional contention inflamed by prejudices engendered and stimulated by those who avail of these as the last straws to defeat this great and matchless project.

The true merits have by many been lost sight of in the conjecture as to what will be the political result of union. Party and factional passions, which have no place in the consideration of such a subject have been appealed to in order to obscure the one all-important issue, that of the well being and prosperity of the people as a whole, without regard to the advantage of any strictly political or partisan interest. Fears have been sedulously fostered as to the impending domination of this or the other party organization. Opposition has been stimulated by appeals to prejudice founded upon such catch words as the "destruction" of Brooklyn, the "effacement" of the city, the "extinction" of her charter, until it would be strange indeed for the average citizen to believe that consolidation meant anything more or less than impending disaster of some occult character, including the total denial of self-government. It is strange and at the same time significant that with every newspaper, but one, raising this ghost of coming calamity, and flaunting it daily in the eyes of Brooklyn's citizenship with an organized opposition, superb in its efficiency, using every effort to change public sentiment naturally susceptible to such arguments, the citizenship of Brooklyn, nevertheless firmly adheres to its faith in consolidation.

It seems obvious that were consolidation not an abiding consciousness on the part of a majority of the people of Brooklyn, such aggressive opposition as it has encountered would have completely annihilated any movement, less deep seated.

It is urged by the consolidationists, and with much force, that a resubmission would be tantamount to a declaration that no matter what the decision may be it would have no binding force, and would discourage all efforts for municipal union, and serve only as an encouragement to the opponents of the greater city. To sum this branch of the subject up it seems to us that upon the showing made, the sentiment of Brooklyn has undergone no change, except in favor of consolidation. That resubmission would cause the question now to be considered, on political lines and not on its merits, but clouded by fears and misgivings which we believe have no foundation in fact, but which have been carefully fostered for interested purposes.

On the Sixth Point.

This would involve the admission that municipal government is a complete failure. If the conclusions of the committee hereinbefore made are justifiable, it is unnecessary to consider this objection in detail. It is no compliment either to the ability of the representatives of the people, or to the sagacity and capacity of the people residing within the limits of the greater city, to suggest that they will be unable to govern themselves according to their wishes. When the city of New York comprises a half million people it was a mooted question whether a city of its present size and population could be well governed. A few years ago comparatively, Brooklyn was in the same category. The union of the various localities presents no stronger argument against the probability of good government, than does their separate and independent existence. The march of progress is in the direction of concentration on every hand. The larger demands of civilized existence require increased economies, which may be attained only by concentration. The voice of the representatives of the various localities will have a very potent influence in moulding the rules of municipal government and life in any bill or charter to be hereafter enacted.

The argument used before the committee that the demand of some and a majority of Brooklyn's representatives for resubmission or referendum being overslaughed now, implies like treatment hereafter has no just application, because the Legislature here is concerned with a direct mandate from the people upon this special subject superior to any authority which is possessed by any representative in the Legislature. If, as is claimed by some of the speakers, Brooklyn's charter is the best that has ever been framed, there is no valid reason why the Legislature should not adapt it to the requirements of government of the greater city. It may, however, not have occurred to those making that particular statement, that for years past the time of the Legislature has been very largely engrossed in considering amendments to that same charter, which, like that of every other city of the State, is a mere series of bills consolidated or independent, prescribing the rules and methods of government procedure and machinery.

The Final Point.

The final point of the resubmissionists is in line with that made by the referendists, but presumably for the diametrically opposite purpose. We have reached the conclusion that resubmission is sought with the hope thereby to defeat consolidation and obviously unless for such a purpose it would be worse than useless and unnecessary. It is equally our conclusion that referendum as demanded by resubmissionists will defeat consolidation. We consider a referendum of the terms and conditions of a municipal charter as more objectionable than a resubmission of the main proposition.

The bill introduced for a referendum provides for a general statement or synopsis of the proposed charter, and for a vote of the people upon it. It is a serious question whether such a bill would be constitutional, and certainly it would have no more binding effect in any event than has the vote of 1894. It seems the very climax of absurdity to provide for a referendum of the charter before giving effect to the vote of 1894, thereby indirectly discrediting the authority which is again appealed to, either upon the same proposition or one closely related thereto.

We are convinced that those who desire a referendum apart from resubmission, are earnestly in favor of consolidation, but we are equally convinced that the method proposed would be more perilous to consolidation than would resubmission.

In the first place, it must be assumed that every resubmissionist desirous of defeating consolidation would vote against any charter or laws, or synopsis of laws, that might be framed by human ingenuity. Then, again, inasmuch as every scheme of local or general government embodies and is largely composed of a system of rules which prescribe such limitations upon personal liberty as experience has demonstrated to be necessary, affecting the citizen in his daily vocation and in his relation to his fellow citizen, and the municipality at large, from the street vender up to the man of wealth, it follows that in a vote upon a charter personal considerations, opposition to personal limitations, hostility to encroachments upon business and traffic privileges would be entertained in the determination of the great question at issue.

Comparatively few comprehend the limitations and disabilities which the law, whether of local or general government, imposes upon them, and any system of laws outlined crudely or otherwise, which fairly treats the questions referred to, would be rejected by a vote of the people, if submitted to them.

This principle has undergone experiment in the framing and submission of the organic law resulting in the exclusion of any subject which may properly be left to legislative action.

The main proposition, that of consolidation, would hang in the balance indirectly in a referendum of the charter, and yet it would be lost sight of in considering the special and peculiar provisions of the charter itself, which because of its necessary limitations and disabilities would probably fail of adoption, a result from which would be inferred the defeat of consolidation itself. Admitting all that might be said in favor of the present charter of Brooklyn, it might be well to query whether if submitted to a popular vote it would be approved by the people. When we consider the difficulties which hedge in the consideration of this great question, the gradual steps that are necessary in order to secure its full and perfect development, the care and deliberation which should mark every step in the progress towards a complete result, the enemies that would seize upon every vantage point to incite those upon whom at present limitations and disabilities exist, and are necessary in any well regulated and progressive community, to rise in revolt against conditions, which surround them now, but of which they know little and care less, the failure of a referendum is a self-evident proposition. The true purpose of the referendists would be defeated and the plans of those who would prevent consolidation would succeed.

We have here considered and answered the main objections made to the declaration of consolidation. We have not attempted to discuss questions of necessity, or of advantage, or that concern the people of the state, as well as the people of the localities immediately interested.

It is very clear to us that the situation of the city of Brooklyn imperatively demands municipal unification. Inasmuch as under the terms of the present bill such union or consolidation shall not take effect until the first day of January, 1898, it is not necessary to consider in this preliminary report any plan or system to be recommended for the government of the greater city. The claim upon which so much stress has been laid of extinction, destruction, or annihilation of Brooklyn's identity and government is premature and unsupported by any fact. We believe it to be without the slightest foundation. We are confident that the Legislature will securely guard the interests of the respective localities. A system measurably preserving local identity and giving full effect to the principle of home rule as applied to the various localities retaining for Brooklyn both her identity and local influence as a district of the greater city, doing violence neither to her traditions nor to the sentiments of her people, can not be difficult of attainment.

It seems to your committee that the interests of Brooklyn are served by consolidation to a greater degree even than are the interests of that city, which will give name and prestige to the greater metropolis. Brooklyn occupies to that part of the city of New York which lies south of Fourteenth street relatively the same position as the remainder of the city of New York lying to the north of Fourteenth street. Both portions contribute their manhood, intelligence and thrift to building up the enormous taxable values which are to be found south of Fourteenth street on Manhattan Island. To the east and north are the homes of those who create the prodigious wealth located in the business part of the city. Both sections have the same right to share in the prosperity they have jointly created. As it is Brooklyn is isolated and acting alone without means to procure that interchange of persons and property, which is necessary to her ideal development. Even the water front is not her own, and the commerce of the world under the restrictions imposed seek the shores of the State of New Jersey, because of the absence of necessary facilities that unity of action and possession would bring. The financial condition of Brooklyn is such as to warrant the conclusion that the work of development must soon be brought to a close.

Her debt limit has been reached, her present contractural engagements are in excess of the limit of constitutional bond issue, her people are groaning under a burden of oppressive taxation, which falls with equal severity on both the owner and the occupier. Competition between the distinct municipalities is turning the tide of home-seekers, who do business in the city of New York, towards the New Jersey shore, and the only remedy seems to be consolidation.

It was at first our intention to give hearings on these questions, in the city of New York, equal in number and duration to those allowed to the city of Brooklyn. During the progress of the investigation, however, no demand for a hearing manifested itself, and it was only after public announcement that the hearings would be declared closed when a demand was made for a hearing in the metropolis.

This was no sooner made than conceded, and upon the investigation held there no expressly anti-consolidation sentiment disclosed itself. Some citizens, members of the West Side Taxpayers' Association, filed protests and made arguments on the subject of equal and uniform taxation and valuation, maintaining that each locality should bear its own expense, at least so far as concerned local improvements. All appeared in favor of consolidation in the abstract. Some, however, objected to that part of the phraseology of the bill referring to equal taxation. Citizens representing labor and trades unions and other interests appeared and argued in favor of the measure and we discovered absolutely no sentiment against consolidation in the city of New York. We cannot understand on what principle New York could suffer even temporarily from consolidation.

The question of taxation is one to be carefully considered in its relation to each locality and to the whole greater municipality. Even those who lay particular stress upon the question of uniform taxation did not contend that the burden upon the greater city, as a whole, or the city of New York as an integral portion of that greater city, would be oppressive or unduly increased.

The contention was made that upon a plan of equal taxation New York city would be constrained to bear the whole burden of equalization, that if done at once and now a considerable amount of tax would be added to the city budget. But they fail to take into consideration the stimulus and impetus given to progress in each of the annexed localities, they fail to consider the added wealth of the greater city, its larger facilities, its greater commercial energies, its higher developments, its increased opportunities, and the resulting improvement of all interests. They fail to take into account the value of undisputed commercial supremacy, and the concentration of larger business opportunities, and greater financial resources within the boundaries of the greater city, all of which will co-operate to adjust taxation so as to weigh less heavily on the individual citizen. They fail finally to estimate the reduction of expenditures which always proceeds from concentration and the numerous results that will flow from a unity of action between local sovereignties now competing against each other. Once union is perfected the people of that greater city may be relied upon to work out their manifest destiny with a due regard to the rights of the individual.

In conclusion we will consider the objections of a legal character that have been urged upon the attention of the committee. It might be inferred from the introductory and conservative nature of the consolidation bill, that only a few objections could be made and that these, if tenable, would substantially render consolidation on any lines of action impracticable, because it is inconceivable how any legislation could be suggested presenting fewer vulnerable points, because making so little change in existing conditions. Most, if not all of the objections urged, may fairly be attributed to a misconstruction of the bill. However timely they may be at later stages and in regard to other measures they certainly are premature here if urged against the present bill. It was contended last year before the Legislature that this same measure was unconstitutional because no provision was made for the election of a board of supervisors in the county of New York, whose revival it was claimed became necessary under the provisions of article 3, section 26 of the Revised Constitution. Apparently now this contention of unconstitutionality has been wholly abandoned and inconvenience and undesirability are the objective phrases that have been substituted in the place of unconstitutionality. The possibility of the resurrection of the board of supervisors in the counties of New York and Kings is held up as "an awful warning" and an unanswerable barrier to the creation of the greater metropolis. If this objection were valid it would obviously be an insuperable bar to any legislation whatever until the Constitution could be amended. It is a sufficient answer, however, to say, first, that if necessary there is ample time prior to 1898 to provide for the contingency referred to; second, that if the duty to revive a board of supervisors thereafter should be cast upon the Legislature by the enactment of the Consolidation bill, even the failure to perform that duty would not leave the communities of New York and Kings despoiled of an instrument essential to the execution of the governmental power now vested in their common councils as boards of supervisors. These powers will be presumed to exist where now lodged and to continue for all essential public purposes, until some new agency has been expressly substituted.

Then it was objected that the bill, if passed, would permit not only the greater city but each of the counties embraced within it to contract indebtedness up to the constitutional limit.

It seems to us that this can constitute no valid objection. If, for the sake of argument, we assume the proposition to be true, there is adequate power in the Legislature, by proper limitation, to forestall any such predicted abuse.

Another objection has been founded upon the constitutional necessity for the continuance of the county officers as prescribed in article 10, section 1, of the Revised Constitution. The point of any such objection is not easily intelligible, when directed against this bill. It would seem answer sufficient that the mere fact of declared consolidation does not render it imperative that the present condition of affairs, so far as it relates to such officers, shall at all be disturbed. The bill expressly provides for the maintenance of existing conditions absolutely undisturbed until further legislation. What inconvenience can possibly result from the obliteration of invisible city boundaries? There may be details of treatment and adjustment that remain to be considered; but these are only such as may be completely covered by legislative action. These comprise the least of even plausible legal objections to the bill.

All these questions may be fully considered and determined when methods and systems are devised. It is enough for this purpose to report that in our judgment they present no barrier to consolidation and apply not to the naked question of consolidation, but to future legislation which will be necessary in order to fully accomplish the complete unification of the distinct localities.

There is one objection, however, to the consolidation bill proposed by the inquiry commission which, in our judgment, merits serious consideration. Those in the city of Brooklyn who appeared in opposition to the bill claimed that the commission, as at present constituted, was not appointed for any other purposes than those enumerated in the act of their origin, chapter

311 of the Laws of 1890; and that in their selection, peculiar fitness and ability to frame laws which shall govern the affairs of the greater metropolis, with all its complex interests, were not necessarily considered by the appointing power.

It was claimed, moreover, that the various localities were unequally represented with reference to both population and influence, and that a new commission, especially selected to adequately perform the difficult and delicate mission should be provided. We believe that there is much force in this position, and that a new commission, appointed with special reference to the work, should be created, selected with a due regard to the interests of the respective localities.

We have treated the objections raised by citizens of Brooklyn in detail, and confine this report largely to their consideration, for the reason that none of the other districts proposed to be consolidated have raised their voice in protest against the execution of the mandate of 1894. It is true that one appeal was made by a citizen of Richmond county, to exclude that territory from the proposed consolidation, and that the corporation counsel of the city of New York suggested the advisability of pursuing that course. On the other hand, there appears to be an overwhelming preponderance of sentiment in favor of consolidation, and it is not deemed advisable to pay heed to this solitary demand.

All the districts combined cast a majority vote in favor of consolidation of 44,464; one which we believe reflects the sentiment of the people and emphasizes the duty of the Legislature to carry the proposition to its legitimate conclusion.

We, therefore, recommend, the passage of the consolidation bill so amended, first, as to provide for the appointment by the Governor, by and with the advice and consent of the Senate, of a new commission, consisting of fifteen members, of which the present president of the inquiry commission and the mayors of the cities of New York, Brooklyn and Long Island City, the State Engineer and Surveyor and the Attorney-General shall, ex-officio, be members.

Finally, in making this preliminary report, the committee attach the testimony, exhibits and other documentary evidence upon which this report is based.

All of which is respectfully submitted.

CLARENCE LEXOW,
Chairman.

CHARLES B. PAGE,
GEORGE C. AUSTIN,
JAMES M. E. O'GRADY,
EDWIN M. WELLS,
JAMES KEENHOLTS.

I favor not only the " consolidation " herein recommended, but the consolidation decreed by popular vote in its entirety.

THOS. F. GRADY.

HEARINGS

HAD IN RELATION TO

AN ACT CONSOLIDATING THE LOCAL GOVERNMENTS OF THE TERRITORY WITHIN THE CITY AND COUNTY OF NEW YORK, THE COUNTIES OF KINGS AND RICHMOND, THE TOWNS OF NEWTOWN, FLUSHING AND JAMAICA, AND PART OF THE TOWN OF HEMPSTEAD, IN THE COUNTY OF QUEENS.

Resolution appointing Senate and Assembly Committees on Cities a joint committee to confer upon the question of the proposed Greater New York:

WHEREAS, Under and by virtue of chapter 311 of the Laws of 1890, a commission was created known as the "Municipal Consolidation Commission," to inquire into the expediency of consolidating into one municipality, the various municipal corporations, and parts of municipal corporations, contiguous to the Port of New York, said commission after inquiry and examination did, by memorial to the Governor and Legislature of the State, report in favor of consolidation; and,

WHEREAS, Pursuant to such report an act was thereupon passed, being chapter 64 of the Laws of 1894, entitled "An act providing for the submission of the question of consolidation of the city of New York with certain territory under a single municipal administration to the vote of the people;" such question of consolidation was submitted to a vote of the duly qualified electors of the territory embraced within the limits of the proposed greater city, and a majority in each locality voted in favor of consolidation; the aggregate of such majorities being 44,464; and,

WHEREAS, A bill was thereupon introduced in the Legislature of 1895, designed to carry into effect said popular vote, by providing for a commission to prepare a charter and laws for the government as one municipality of the territories embraced within the limits of the proposed greater city, but said bill failed of passage; and,

WHEREAS, The said municipal consolidation commission has, by reason of the premises been unable to present to this Legislature any adequate kind of government for said proposed greater city in form to enable this Legislature intelligently to consider and determine the important question involved; and,

WHEREAS, A just and considerate treatment of the questions connected with and arising from the creation of the greater city, and the consolidation of the various local governments into one municipality, is of vital consequence to the people, not alone to the territories immediately affected but to the whole State, and concerns so deeply the moral and material interests, the well being, security and convenience of more than three millions, and the principles of government and administration to be applied require deliberation and care commensurate with the complexity and magnitude of the undertaking, and should suggest a practical solution of many of the problems of municipal government and administration, and afford relief for evils now existing, and a full, fair and deliberate consideration of the whole subject is deemed advisable and expedient; therefore,

Resolved, (If the Assembly concur), That the committee on the affairs of cities of the Senate, and the committee on affairs of cities of the Assembly, be and they are hereby appointed a joint committee of this Legislature, and are authorized and empowered fully and diligently to investigate and inquire into all and singular the matter set forth and relating to the questions hereinbefore mentioned, with full power and authority to prosecute their inquiries in any and all directions in their judgment necessary and expedient to enable them to obtain and report the information required by these resolutions;

Resolved, Further, and for the purpose aforesaid, that said committee may employ a stenographer and one or more counsel, and such other assistants as may be necessary, and may send for persons, books, records and papers, call and subpoena witnesses and administer oaths.

Resolved, Further, that said committee be authorized and empowered to appoint a sub-committee consisting of four Senators and five Members of Assembly, which sub-committee (when appointed) shall have the same power and authority hereunder in all respects as are possessed by said joint committee, and whose duty it shall be to proceed with the inquiry and investigation into the matter aforesaid, with all reasonable diligence; and to that end, full power and authority are hereby conferred on such sub-committee when appointed, to perform and exercise all and singular, the functions and duties of said joint committee, to send for persons, books, records and papers, call or subpoena witnesses, and administer oaths, with the same force and effect to all intents and purposes as though done by said joint committee, and for the convenience of the public, and in order to secure as full and complete inquiry as may be practicable, to hold sessions in the cities of New York, Brooklyn and Albany.

Resolved, Further, and for the purpose aforesaid, that said joint committee and said sub-committee thereof, when appointed, be and they hereby are authorized and empowered to call to their aid and assistance, in an advisory capacity, the President and Associate Members of the Municipal Consolidated Commission, hereinbefore referred to, and also the Attorney-General of the State, and the corporation counsel of the cities of New York, Brooklyn and Long Island City, to aid and facilitate the acquisition of the information required by these resolutions and the report of said committee.

Resolved, Further, that said committee shall make a preliminary report as soon as practicable, and not later than the first day of March, 1896, to the end that proper legislation may be enacted in the premises.

Pursuant to the above resolution, the Senate and Assembly joint committee appointed the following sub-committee:

Senate.— Messrs. Lexow, Brush, Page and Grady.

Assembly.— Messrs. O'Grady, Austin, Wells, Keenholts and McKeon.

Common Council Chamber, Brooklyn, N. Y.,

January 17, 1896, at 11 a. m.

Mr. Lexow:

The committee on inquiry for consolidation will now begin its session. We have determined to follow the usual legislative course and give those opposed to the bill of consolidation the first opportunity to be heard in opposition to the bill. In order to serve the convenience of everybody we will divide the sessions of to-day and to-morrow into two parts, the morning session to those in opposition to the bill. I will say, incidentally, that the opposition to the bill will raise all the questions of referendum resubmission, as well as that of simple consolidation. The afternoon hearing will be devoted to those in favor of the bill, and the same course will be followed to-morrow. I would suggest, however, that inasmuch as those who are to speak in favor of the bill will be expected to answer those who speak in opposition to the bill, that at least some of the champions of consolidation listen to the arguments of those who are opposed to it. Mr. Redfield, do you represent the organized movement against it?

MR. REDFIELD:

I did not come here to-day, Mr. Chairman, as an official representative, but I am willing to speak for the organized opposition if you desire.

MR. LEXOW:

While it is not the desire of the committee to change any of the plans of those who favor or oppose consolidation, they must choose their champions and we will give them abundant opportunity to be heard. Each man who rises now will speak against the bill and against consolidation.

MR. DYKMAN:

Pardon me, Mr. Chairman, but are you referring to a bill and opposition to that bill? We do not quite understand what bill is referred to?

MR. LEXOW:

The bill which gave rise to this resolution. The bill providing for consolidation, either immediately or to take effect January 1, 1898.

MR. DYKMAN:

Do you refer to the bill of Mr. Green, of New York, and his associates, introduced by yourself?

MR. LEXOW:

Yes. In order to be absolutely fair we will admit at this stage the arguments of those in favor of resubmission and referendum as well as simply arguments against the bill.

MR. DYKMAN:

Is this to be the last session in which opposition to the bill may be heard?

MR. LEXOW:

To-morrow's session will be the same as to-day; in the morning those opposing may speak; in the afternoon, those in favor will be heard.

MR. DYKMAN:

How long will the morning session continue? We are quite unprepared for this announcement, and would like to know just how much time we will have to-morrow.

MR. LEXOW:

Assuming that we sit two hours now in hearing arguments against consolidation we will sit two hours this afternoon hearing arguments in favor of consolidation. To-morrow the same course will be pursued. It may be just as well to state here that in addition to those who present an organized front against consolidation we are prepared to hear the people as well. I mean those who belong to neither one nor the other organization for or against consolidation.

MR. REDFIELD:

May I ask that some limit be put on the time that each speaker may occupy?

MR. LEXOW:

We are prepared to give this important question all the time that it requires. (Applause.) The audience will please not applaud. No amount of applause is going to change our opinions or make any difference in our legislative course.

ROBERT D. BENEDICT:

Mr. Chairman and Gentlemen of the Committee: I had not expected to be called upon to begin this matter. I can give, however, some views which are very clear in my mind in opposition to the bill which proposes a consolidation and in favor of the proposition of resubmission of the question to the popular vote of the people of the city of Brooklyn. I am opposed to the consolidation of the two cities of New York and Brooklyn for many reasons.

First. It is impossible under the present Constitution of the State of New York to abolish county lines. Hence the county lines of Kings and of New York must remain preserved, and if those cities are to be consolidated they will form the anomalous creation of a city different parts of which lie in different counties.

MR. LEXOW:

In order that the committee may be able to hear the words of Mr. Benedict, will not the audience remain quiet?

MR. BENEDICT:

That being the condition, Mr. Chairman, of the situation, it follows as a necessary result from the Constitution, which provides that there shall be a board of supervisors in every county of the State, that the result of consolidation would be to re-establish the board of supervisors of Kings county, which has just been abolished and to re-establish a board of supervisors in New York county, which was abolished some years back. And the result would be necessarily that all the financial concerns of the two counties, which, by the laws of the State, are under the control of the supervisors of the two counties must necessarily be committed to the board of supervisors in the two counties mentioned. That condition of things is, in my opinion, dangerous to good government, to economical government; it has proved to be such in the past, and the results of that situation in the past have been such that the desirability of abolishing the power of the board of supervisors in the two cities has been, I think I may say, considered by everybody for two years. I do not know whether the committee desire me to state the legal grounds on which I make the statement that the boards of supervisors in the two counties shall be re-established, and, therefore, I do not propose to go into that matter unless requested to do so.

MR. GRADY:

Do you mean, Mr. Benedict, that under the Constitution there will be a necessity in New York for any other body than the board of aldermen which exercises the powers of a board of supervisors?

MR. BENEDICT:

Certainly, the words of the Constitution are distinct that there shall be in every county of the State a board of supervisors.

MR. GRADY:

I understand that. But that provision of the Constitution is covered by the fact that the board of aldermen in New York have a certain power as supervisors which would make such an additional body unnecessary. Is that not so?

MR. BENEDICT:

There would be that necessity.

MR. LEXOW:

Why?

MR. BENEDICT:

Because the Constitution provides that where there is a city whose limits are of more than one county there shall be a board of supervisors made to govern the question of the finances of said counties.

MR. GRADY:

I desire to know whether your contention is that a board of supervisors distinct from a board of aldermen would be necessary?

MR. BENEDICT:

There are other matters connected with this question. The Constitution provides for a board of supervisors for every county and also provides that the Legislature may confer upon those boards of supervisors, by general law that provision will govern the case in my opinion.

MR. LEXOW:

Have you changed your opinion that this bill would be unconstitutional because of that fact?

MR. BENEDICT:

I have never said that the bill would be unconstitutional. I have always said that a city of that kind could be made under the Constitution. But I have also said I did not believe that anybody who understood that that was a necessary result of an attempt to make a city under the Constitution would be in favor of the establishment of such a city.

Another provision of the Constitution exists and that is the provision that relates to the limitation of debt. The Constitution provides that the limit of the debt-creating power of a city shall be ten per cent. on the assessed valuation of the real estate. It also provides that the limitation of any county to make a debt shall be the same, but it also provides where the limits of a city and county are the same the limits of the county to make a debt shall cease. It necessarily follows, therefore, that if the limits of a city and county are not the same, that both the city and county can create a debt to the extent of ten per cent. of the assessed value of the real estate of the city on the one hand and a county on the other hand; and it would therefore follow that if the city so undertaken to be set up which was composed of the county of New York and the county of Kings, the county of Kings could create a debt upon the county of Kings and the county of New York which would be equal to the ten per cent. of the property and the real estate of the county, and the cities could do likewise; hence, the peculiar result of a consolidation of the two cities would be to double the debt-contracting power of each.

That, as it seems to me, is a result which good citizens in neither city could desire; the limitation of the debt-creating power of the city and county was put in the Constitution of the State for wise purposes. It was accepted by the people who considered it wise, and the plan which would result in defeating the provision of the Constitution would, in my opinion, be not only unwise, but would be subject to severe criticism.

Again, there is another provision of the Constitution which points out a great danger to the people which would be produced by consolidation. The Constitution has provided that any legislation which related to a city shall be referred to the mayor of that city for approval, and he shall have particular and qualified veto power. As it is now, matters of legislation which relate to Brooklyn must be submitted to the mayor for his approval, and the same applies to New York. This bill which proposes, as I understand it, to establish one city, which, if I recollect rightly, under the law is to be created on the 1st of January, 1898, and the bill also provides for the appointment of a commission which is to frame, not a charter for the new city — not a word concerning a charter as I remember it — but to frame bills whereby the new territory which is to be made one city is to be governed. In my opinion, if that bill would become a law, the extent of the city of Brooklyn and the city of New York, as now constituted, would cease on January 1, 1898. Therefore, a bill relating to the government of any part of that city would not longer have to be submitted to the mayor of Brooklyn. I do not know who would be mayor of that city under that bill. As I recollect it, there is no provision in the bill for an election of a mayor to whom the rights of the citizen shall be intrusted and to whom he may look for protection.

Mr. Lexow:

Do you not believe that this can be cared for by future legislation. That a mayor could be elected for the greater city in 1897?

Mr. Benedict:

Yes, but to whom would that bill be submitted if it is to be fulfilled before any such election? Who would be the mayor of that city until there had been an election, and therefore, it seems to me that those who favor it are in this dilemma, namely: That they must say that either the question of the mayor of this greater city which is to be formed is a matter outside of the Constitution and not to be submitted to any mayor or else there is no mayor to submit the question to.

MR. LEXOW:

Why not submit it to both?

MR. BENEDICT:

There is no provision in the Constitution. It would have to be before a constitutional submission. There is no clause in the bill to cover this question.

MR. LEXOW:

Why does it not come under the constitutional provision?

MR. BENEDICT:

Because the Constitution, as I recollect the words, requires that legislation relating to the city has to be submitted to the mayor of that city. You can not have a mayor of Brooklyn if you wipe out the corporate existence of Brooklyn.

MR. LEXOW:

Yes, but this bill makes the date of such consolidation January 1, 1898.

MR. BENEDICT:

It may be provided before that time that any bills relating to Brooklyn, as long as the existence of the corporate city continues, shall be submitted to the mayor of Brooklyn. But the point in this case is that all bills that have got to be prepared for this whole government must be prepared and proposed before January 1, 1898, or else there is no provision, no mayor, to whom those bills could be submitted under the Constitution.

Mr. Lexow:

I desire to ask you if all the legislation which referred to Brooklyn and New York could not be submitted to the two cities of New York and Brooklyn.

Mr. Benedict:

As long as the cities were in existence, all right. But after the 1st of January any bill that was passed would not be submitted to the mayor of Brooklyn or of New York, and I know of no reason myself why bills passed in 1897, should be required to be submitted to the mayor of Brooklyn for his approval and another bill should not be required to be submitted to such officers, simply because passed in 1898.

Mr. Lexow:

Why could not there be a mayor of the greater city? So that until the 1st of January, 1898, there would be a mayor of each city, and after the bill could be presented to the mayor of the greater city.

Mr. Benedict:

I am aware of that but so far as the matter relates to Brooklyn it ought to be submitted to the mayor of Brooklyn, and, therefore, unless you can be certain that all your bills shall be passed and your whole system and scheme be put in full working order by the 1st of January, you are acting against the principles and purposes of the constitutional provisions. I wish to say, and I am backed by the best authority of the State, that it will be a matter of more than ten years before the various legislative works which will be necessary to put in full operation to create a new city like this can be put in full operation.

Mr. Lexow:

Don't you think the less government you have the better?

Mr. Benedict:

That brings me to another point which I desire to make. I think that, as far as I have been able to see, the great problem in our American republic is the government of the great cities. There are the difficulties which we are to meet. There are the great dangers which we are to taste. In my opinion those dangers have recently become very much greater. Those difficulties have increased to a very much greater extent than our ability to meet them. In my opinion, it would seem wiser for us to learn more about the government of these great cities and be better able to govern a city of a million or a million and a half before we try the dangerous experiment of creating a city of over three millions of people, not by growth, but by one stroke. (Applause.)

MR. LEXOW:

I request that if there be any further applause the sergeant-at-arms remove the offenders.

MR. BENEDICT:

I think that such a thing would be a monstrous mistake. It would therefore seem unwise to me, gentlemen, for us to bring upon ourselves the difficulties which are inherent in the government of a city of over three million people. If we are in the course of years to meet the difficulties arising from the government of a city which by gradual growth increases to the extent of such a population, it may very well be assumed that our ability to assume such responsibility and to face the dangers and difficulties of such a situation will have increased, and the exigencies of the case will be met by greater experience. But I think it unwise to crowd all those dangers into one and force it upon the people of these two cities. We appreciate well the difficulty of governing cities of the present size. Setting aside New York, I am not speaking about that, we appreciate the difficulty of governing a city the size of Brooklyn. We say that it would not be wise to substitute for the two governments of these two cities a government of one city by all the people of the territory. This territory which is now embraced in Brooklyn is large enough to have men within it of all classes, to have their interests all represented by their own officers and looked after by them. We think that they are assured of much better government under the present conditions than under the vastly enlarged territory. We do not deem it wise to add a city of double the amount to our present difficulties; we also say, Mr. Chairman, that the experience of the world and of civilization is against bringing so many people under one government, and we point to Boston, where there is Cambridge, Brookline, and they are not consolidated.

MR. LEXOW:

Are they not now taking steps toward consolidation?

MR. BENEDICT:

I do not know that they are, but we will pass that, as it is a subject that requires much information. I say that the civilization of the world and of wise-thinking men of the world are against the tendency of bringing too many people under one government. But there is another question that I wish to discuss. That, Mr. Chairman, is in reference to the bill which has been proposed in favor of resubmission; to answer the suggestion that the question has been once submitted to the popular vote and therefore should not be sent again. I wish to say, Mr. Chairman, that any man who is fair and who raises that objection to a resubmission of the question to a vote of the people is ignorant of the law under which that vote was taken, or he is ignorant of the difference between opinion and determination. Election under our form of government is a determination. We ask the people, "Whom are you determined shall be mayor of Brooklyn?" Not "Who do you think ought to be mayor?" The vote of the people to elect is not an expression of opinion, it is an expression of determination. The vote on this question was merely a request for an opinion.

MR. LEXOW:

You don't claim anything else than that this was an expression of opinion? There is no way under our laws for the people themselves to determine this question in the form of a determination, because it is a matter of legislative action and not of the popular vote.

MR. BENEDICT:

All that I am claiming is that is was not a determination, and those who say that any resubmission of this question is taking a second vote on the question do not understand it.

MR. LEXOW:

Do you mean to dispute that it is any less a determination than it could have been under the law. It could not be an absolute determination for the reason that legislative action is necessary to procure a determination. The law did not in any way permit a determination. It simply permitted an expression of opinion. It was so stated in the bill.

MR. BENEDICT:

The people expressed an opinion in reference to that. What opinion did they express? Supposing there was a committee, we will say of thirteen, who were to express their opinion upon a certain subject, and five of that committee voted aye and four voted no, and four did not vote at all, would you say that the expression made by the five represented the sentiment of the whole thirteen? No. All you can say is, that there was a divided opinion, and no statement can be made that this represents the expression of the whole thirteen. Now that, Mr. Chairman, is substantially the situation of a popular vote. There was just about a third voted for aye, a third voted for no,. and a third did not vote at all. It did not decide what was then the opinion of the people of Brooklyn. And it comes very far from deciding or expressing the opinion of the people to-day. There has been no expression of anything, save an opinion, and that does not constitute a vote. I know, and I speak what I know, that during the fall campaign which resulted in the vote of indecisive expression of opinion the question of consolidation was not discussed by the city. Neither party desired to discuss it, and everyone who wished to find out anything about it had to get what information he could by his own efforts. The matter, so far as an expression of opinion was concerned, was given without popular discussion and without popular information, and it was largely due to that that there was so many people who did not vote one way or the other. I can't believe, Mr. Chairman, that if the question had been understood that there would have been one-tenth of the voters who would have refrained from voting. If the Legislature will submit that question again, not as an expression of opinion but as a determination, in my opinion, there would not be a man in Brooklyn who would fail to vote.

Mr. Lexow:

You don't mean to argue that the Legislature should delegate its legislation to the convictions of the people?

Mr. Benedict:

I don't know whether, under the Constitution, it could be provided that a law should go into effect on a popular vote or not. I know that the Constitution itself goes into effect on a popular vote, and I know no reason why, if the Constitution, which is over all laws, can go into effect on such a vote, another law should not be passed upon in the same manner.

Mr. Grady:

It has been accepted in the Legislature that they can't pass a statute which will become operative only in event of an affirmative vote of the citizens, and it was because of the character of the vote taken in 1894 that it has been regarded of as solemn or decisive character as could well be taken.

Mr. Benedict:

I say I have not examined the provisions of the new Constitution or of the old one either. If that is so, if there is no probability of submitting the question to a popular vote as to a determination, then, of course, all you can have is an expression of opinion. But it ought to be clearly understood, as it was not at that time, that an expression was all that could be had. The circumstances have so largely changed that there is a very widespread feeling that the question was not properly submitted, was not so submitted as to make that vote the expression of the calm, judicial voice of the people, and it ought, therefore, to be submitted again. I pledge myself for one, that if the people of Brooklyn are given an opportunity to vote, and after a fair discussion shall then vote and say that in their opinion Brooklyn ought to be wiped out of existence and consolidated with New York, I am done on that subject.

MR. LEXOW:

We have heard Senator Grady's statement that the Legislature can not delegate its legislative power. All we can do is to resubmit this question for another expression of opinion, and then in three or four months, if there is another change of feeling, submit it again.

MR. BENEDICT:

If that is the law and if it can't be submitted to the popular vote, then, of course, there is nothing left but to submit to the expression of popular opinion. I say, however, that if the circumstances have changed there is no reason why another expression of opinion should not be offered them. I say, without hesitation, that the circumstances and the feeling, the knowledge of the facts and the knowledge of the principles involved have so changed as to make it reasonable for us to ask that that question shall be submitted to the people of Brooklyn again, and to say that our reasonable request shall be refused because hereafter some men shall make an unreasonable request is entirely illogical. If it is submitted again, and if circumstances change so as to make it reasonable to submit it again, why not? I say the question ought to be resubmitted for three reasons: First, it was a completely indecisive vote and expressed nothing; second, it was a vote taken without full and fair discussion, without knowledge and information, and that so important a matter as the civic existence of the city of Brooklyn should never be allowed to be wiped out out, except with the full consent of the people expressed on full information and full knowledge.

A. T. White:

Mr. Chairman, and gentlemen of both houses of the Legislature: I do not come to you as commissioner of the city works, but as a private citizen, born in Brooklyn, having lived all my life here, but likewise all my life a merchant in New York, and still nominally a merchant there, although giving my actual time here. I am very decided in my opinions as to the interest of both cities in these questions. Let me first of all point out that, while at Albany the issue of consolidation appears to be paramount, in Brooklyn it is the issue of resubmission that is most discussed. The people here recognize that in the registered vote of 1894, a little over one-third of the voters voted for consolidation. A couple of hundred less were against and almost an equal number did not vote at all. That, in itself, was an evidence that the question was not understood and that the vote was not as full nor as reliable as it should have been. I am frank to say that I voted no, because I wished to speak for others who voted the other way. It is a matter perfectly well known in Brooklyn and perhaps, to some extent known in Albany as the Senator from Brooklyn has witnessed thereto, that numerous voters who voted for consolidation in 1894 either have changed their views in the meantime, or without having changed their views, regard that vote as inconclusive and desire that the whole question shall be resubmitted to the people. Beside the Senator, there is ex-Mayor Schieren; there is a gentleman whom I met at the foot of the stairs, Alderman Leich, the representative of the twenty-third ward, which cast the largest vote in favor of consolidation in this city, are now ardently in favor of resubmission and, I believe, would vote against consolidation. Let me say, also, inasmuch as real estate interests are to be represented here, that I am a considerable taxpayer myself, that I represent other taxpayers here, near to me in interests and in blood, and as taxpayers we are opposed to consolidation and in favor of resubmission. On that subject it is, perhaps, not improper if I should say a word of the resources of Brooklyn as I have found them after two years in the office of the department of city works. I confess that when I took that office in the financial condition in which the city was placed, I had my doubts whether Brooklyn could make the improvements necessary in a long term of years. It is right and proper for me to say that with reasonable care all reasonable and necessary improvements will be made in proper and reasonable time, much more quickly than if the city of Brooklyn were joined to the larger city of New York. Two years ago I had my doubts whether we could inaugurate in a reasonable time the improvements which have already been completed. We have completed the Wallabout Market for $1,200,000, have wiped off several hundred thousand dollars of arrears, besides three million of indebtedness to the government. We have paved more streets in a year than are to be found in New York, below the Harlem; we have built more school-houses than the city of Brooklyn ever saw before. In one year we have added 11,000 sittings. The amount already appropriated and available for 1896, will secure a still greater increase. In every respect we are far ahead of New York. In the park department we are far ahead of New York city. I have come to the conclusion, which I am perfectly frank to state as a citizen and as a taxpayer, the necessary improvements on this side of the river will progress more lively if we remain independent than if we were joined. I said that the people of Brooklyn did not feel that the verdict of 1894 was either a fair or a final verdict. I know, personally, a number of men and know of many others out of my immediate acquaintances whose opinions I know on this subject, but who feel that they voted under a misapprehension and have changed their minds. On that point, let me say that some conclusion should be submitted to them. The people of Brooklyn do not desire that this question should be left open from year to year. They are ready to take the chance to vote for it at a special election or at the presidential election. Enough interest has been excited during the last year and the issues have become perfectly understood. Without exception they are quite ready that it should be put to its ultimate conclusion if it be the desire of the Legislature at a popular election in November or in which way the Legislature may decide. Now this question, as I stated in my speech at the Academy of Music meeting, was involved in the choice of several members of the Legislature in the last election. If it was not understood in 1894, it was thoroughly understood in the fall of 1895. In every election district the issue was discussed, and among the legislators at Albany there is not a single advocate of the consolidation bill without resubmission to the people.

MR. LEXOW:

You desire resubmission for the purpose of defeating consolidation?

MR. WHITE:

No, sir; but because more than two-thirds of the people of Brooklyn desire it. I voted against it before and should again.

MR. LEXOW:

Do you mean to say that the desire of resubmission is not a desire to defeat, but simply a sentimental desire.

MR. WHITE:

Not only do the people who previously voted against consolidation desire to record their votes in the same way again at an election when a full vote could be had, but in addition to that, at least one-third of those who voted for consolidation in 1894, desire that the question be resubmitted in order that there may be no doubt that the will of the majority of the people has been expressed. Some ask for it because they have changed their minds and some want it simply because they wish to see fair play.

MR. LEXOW:

It comes right down to the proposition that you and those who have changed their minds desire resubmission for the purpose of defeating consolidation.

MR. WHITE:

If I had changed my mind, I should, certainly.

A VOICE:

Is it not the fact that the people of Brooklyn want this resubmission in order that the Legislature should know the opinion of the people of Brooklyn?

MR. WHITE:

That is a fact.

MR. LEXOW:

When you entered upon your office you had concluded that Brooklyn could not carry on her own improvements, that is the statement you made.

MR. WHITE:

I said I was in doubt as to whether Brooklyn could carry on it. own improvements.

MR. LEXOW:

Had you not expressed yourself as being of that opinion?

MR. WHITE:

No, sir; I never held an opinion that was conclusive. I voted against consolidation in 1894. I desire resubmission because I believe that more than two-thirds of the voters desire it. I voted against consolidation before and I shall vote against consolidation again, if I had an opportunity to vote to-day. No man closes his ears to argument.

MR. LEXOW:

Do you mean to be understood that the desire for resubmission is not a desire for defeat, but simply the desire to express an opinion without having in any way a desire to defeat the proposition. Is that not the sentiment of the people of the city of Brooklyn, as you would have us understand it?

MR. WHITE:

The sentiment, as I endeavored to construe it, is this: That nearly all the people who previously voted against consolidation desire to record their votes in the same way again at an election when a full vote on the question might be had instead of partial vote. I also believe that one-half of the gentlemen who voted for consolidation in 1894 desire that the question shall be resubmitted in order that there may be an issue, and that the will of the majority of the people shall be expressed. Some of them ask for resubmission because they have changed their minds. But from my acquaintance with those who voted I should say that fully one-half of them are for resubmission to-day.

MR. BRUSH:

Is it not, from your observation, the fact that the sentiment on this matter has very largely changed within the last year?

MR. WHITE:

I think so, decidedly; I think that the gentlemen whose names I have already mentioned, ex-Mayor Schieren and Alderman Leich and a number of others whose names I might mention, are living testimony of these facts.

GEORGE C. REYNOLDS:

Mr. Chairman and Gentlemen of the Committee: I am here upon only a very few moments' notice. I had not expected to be able to come before the committee to-day, but I am very glad of the opportunity to express my views upon one single point and it is a point which has been discussed to a considerable extent and which evidently has a very important bearing upon the whole subject. I do not propose to discuss the advisability or desirability of consolidation as an abstract question upon its merits. I would be glad of the opportunity to do so if I had the opportunity. I have the most decided and absolute opinion in regard to it, but what I want to say bears upon the question of resubmission to the people of Brooklyn for final determination. I ought to take it for granted that the committee assume that the people of Brooklyn have the right to express an opinion as to whether their municipality would be extinguished or not. It would be contrary to our American ideas to take away the charter of the city of Brooklyn without the well considered approval of its citizens. Charters of corporations are sometimes forfeited by law, by the law officers of the State when they have so grossly violated their charters that they are not considered worthy to hold them In such cases the Attorney-General of the State may institute proceedings for the purpose of taking away the charter. I do not apprehend that the members of this committee desire to assume the office of Attorney-General and use their influence against the city of Brooklyn for the purpose of forfeiting its charter on the ground of misconduct, although sometimes we have made mistakes in our elections, but that should not deprive us of the right of existence. Now, the point which the committee seem to have in mind — some members of it — that this consent of the city of Brooklyn has been secured. If not, the questions that have been put have no meaning. I take it that the members of the committee bow to the universally accepted opinion that the city of Brooklyn has a right to be heard on the subject as to whether she shall be deprived of her charter or not. It is assumed that this opinion has been expressed. I say that it never was. I want to stop here to discuss whether the result of that vote was an expression of opinion, whether it is to be regarded and treated afterwards in its results as a mere opinion with binding force. It is said that the opinion has been expressed and that the charter can be taken away. I have no doubt that the vote of 1894 was merely an expression of opinion. I don't care what force or what degree of force you attribute to that vote, my point is that that vote has no force beyond the Legislature of 1894. It was for them to say that that expression of opinion was of sufficient force to pass an act consolidating these two cities. I say plainly, when your Legislature declined to do it or failed to do it, the vote had spent its force and had no other force whatever. If the vote taken that year can be considered by this Legislature the same thing may be continued for half a century. It is easy to put an extreme case to show the alleged absurdity of any particular position. It may be easy to say that you will have a resubmission, and it seems to me that is the wise thing to do, for why should a vote taken ten years ago be binding now? You must give a reasonable, practicable operation in a measure, and the question must be determined upon common sense principles. I may try to argue before this committee that when a vote was taken for the purpose of determining a question that the Legislature would have the right to throw it aside and leave it entirely open for any subsequent Legislature. The question is, what do the people of Brooklyn want to-day? But as I just said, 1894 was not an expression of the general sentiment of Brooklyn. I said that only one-third of the people were in favor of consolidation. I confess I voted against it on instinct; to-day I would vote against it on well-matured judgment. Shall we be responsible for the vote of 1894? It would be as sensible to hang a man now because he had determined in 1894 to commit suicide, when, as a matter of fact, only one-third of him resolved to commit suicide. That shouldn't send Brooklyn to the electric chair. The joint committee should be very careful how it recommends the union of New York and Brooklyn. Is there any harm in a community like this to let the people have a chance for their life? You can have the vote at a special election in the spring. This is not a party question. It is a question of existence. To say that you will take up that raveled thread and blot us out is not right or just, and the people will, if extinguished by the exercise of arbitrary power, appeal for another hearing to the authorities. As I took occasion to say the other night, my own judgment would be that we should have the charter submitted to us; that we ought to have a chance to know under what conditions we are to be taken into another city when we lose our own existence. We should have the right to say whether we would commit ourselves to any commission for the purpose of claiming a charter. I am willing to admit that I am in favor of resubmission for the purpose of voting again. I want an opportunity to vote, because I believe that the people of the city of Brooklyn to-day, a large majority of them, are opposed to consolidation. It is right that the question should be resubmitted. Is there any harm in granting to anybody that wants the right to vote that concession, in accordance with the rights, the wishes, the sentiment, the judgment of the community? If they vote in favor of it the Legislature will enact it; undoubtedly the only question is, whether you will give them a chance or not. You can have the election as quickly as you please. Let the people be called upon to vote upon it. In denying them this privilege you would be trampling upon the commonest rights conceded in a republican form of government like this, to say that after such a vote as that of 1894, after such a length of time, and after the Legislature has passed upon the question, to go back to that vote and blot us out. The sentiment of the people is so strong upon this subject that they shall look upon any action of the kind as a very great wrong. That the city of Brooklyn has been extinguished, which is entirely inconsistent with the principles of free government. I have nothing further to say.

MR. GRADY:

Do you seek to settle the question by a popular vote?

MR. REYNOLDS:

I understand that the committee take the ground that no such vote can have legal and binding force. My preference is that if we are to have annexation I would like to know under what condition it is to be done.

MR. LEXOW:

Do you mean to be understood in your argument as expressing the opinion that the people of the city of Brooklyn are opposed to consolidation upon any basis?

MR. REYNOLDS:

Yes, sir; that is my well-settled opinion to-day.

W. R. WALKLEY:

Mr. Chairman and Gentlemen of the Committee: I am in Brooklyn this morning for the first time in a year and I have not heard all the arguments pro and con in regard to this question of consolidation. But I understand your committee are here with the determination to hear an expression of the people on the bill that proposes to unite these two cities without the city of Brooklyn having anything to say about it. You are to force a consolidation of these two cities and the destruction of the city of Brooklyn as a city because two years ago some vote was taken which indicated an expression of opinion in favor of consolidation. Now, I want to say for myself that I think I voted upon that question, but it was not an issue, it was not a defined issue in that campaign and, though I ought to be ashamed of myself to say it, I could not state to-day whether I voted for or against it. It was not a defined issue. To-day, I have an opinion because Brooklyn is in the dawn of a new era of prosperity — it has interests vital to itself, as a city; it has been laying miles and miles of streets; it is to-day one of the best governed municipalities in the country. We have our own interests and I believe I voice the expression of the people when I say that three-quarters are against consolidation. They believe in Brooklyn as a city of their own. They believe in Brooklyn as a city distinct by itself. There has been much said about the question of taxation, and now the terms of this consolidation are not understood by the citizens of Brooklyn. As Judge Reynolds just said, if we are to be united are we not to know under what conditions? Have we no voice in the matter; does the honorable Legislature propose to take the city of over a million inhabitants and annex it to New York without giving the people a chance to vote upon that question, without giving them full opportunity for discussion? Let the voice of the people signify their desires. Are not the people of Brooklyn entitled to say whether they will unite in this greater municipality or not? It is certainly not allowed to do it as it now exists. It is not the desire of the Republican Legislature to destroy the city of Brooklyn without the consent of the voters. I only plead, gentlemen, that the citizens here may have a chance to vote and say whether they are willing to consolidate with New York or not. Let the people express themselves by a vote on this question. After the issue is presented and a discussion had I think the people will be willing to vote readily and quickly. I do not care how soon it comes, but they are certainly entitled to consider the question and to express their opinion — whether that expression be an opinion or a determination.

FRED. W. HINRICHS:

Mr. Chairman and Gentlemen of the Committee: I did not expect to speak here, but after two years' experience I have something to say on this question. I remember that you, Mr. Chairman, sat with me in the school room in Brooklyn, when you laid the foundation for that career which has been of so much honor to you. I remember that we used to read books of fiction together in those old days when your early career was started in Brooklyn schools. One, " The Trapper's Secret " or " Bloody Gulch." Had we expressed then an opinion on the question of the literature that should be given to the young for their information we would have voted for Beadle's "Dime Novel " (laughter). We would not, now, indorse that class of literature, of which, I believe, you had a circulating library. (Great laughter, in which Senator Lexow joined.) I believe there is no question that Brooklyn people do not wish consolidation. They have learned better — they have passed through the juvenile period of education.

Now, I would speak of consolidation generally. I occupy the office of collector of arrears of taxes and we found, after consolidation of country towns and the city, that three officers are selling the same property — the county treasurer, the State Treasurer, and I, myself — want to sell it for arrears of taxes. Now one sale wipes out all the others. When it comes to this proposed imperial combination matters will still be more confused. There was no consolidation ever proposed like it. You can not effect it in one, two or three years. You want a commission with knowledge of law, a commission that will sit for several years and will be well paid. The present commission have not the experience. It is not paid and can not devote the time and attention the great subject needs. Even Mayor Schieren, who has studied the question, saw this point. Mr. J. S. T. Stranahan of Brooklyn, who is just approaching the end of his career, is a member of this commission. Just so with Mr. Green, who is also on the commission. Both have been very useful men, but it needs younger men. I ask you to pause before recommending legislation. Study taxes. You couldn't reach a knowledge of this particular subject in six months. Lack of information and complexities might cause a loss of millions of dollars to New York and Brooklyn. The present bill must be repudiated.

MR. LEXOW:

The bill leaves out all these questions. It provides only for a sentimental union of the two municipalities.

MR. HINRICHS:

I am glad of the interruption. If sentimentalism is to rule, then let the people of Brooklyn vote. It is as sure as that the sun will rise to-morrow that the people will vote against consolidation. We honor New York, but we love Brooklyn. There is more artificiality across the river. There is more extravagance, there is more of the glitter, there is more of so-called society. We have grown up in an atmosphere entirely separate and apart from that sort of thing. We believe in the old traditions of home, of wife and children. Our clubs are distinguishable from the clubs across the river.

MR. LEXOW:

How will the declaration of legal union of the municipalities affect any of those questions?

MR. HINRICHS:

It is like two lovers who have concluded to marry, but who have concluded, after knowing each other's faults and virtues that they had better live apart.

JESSE JOHNSON:

Mr. Chairman and gentlemen of the committee: Though I had hoped to say something sometime on this subject, I came here this morning to sympathize. I want to say to you, gentlemen of the committee, that I for one, and I believe every man here receives as a friendly tender, as a considerate act, this coming of your committee to listen to us and we hope to meet in that spirit of fair and temperate statement and argument which befits such a commission as you bear. There has been no larger question, no greater political problem, submitted in this union since the constitutional amendments, growing out of the civil war, than this problem of merging the two largest cities of the State, two of the largest cities in the United States, and making it, with one or two exceptions, the largest now or that will ever be known in the history of the world. There is no precedent for it. Great cities of the world have been governed by imperialism, but not by popular suffrage as in America. To merge into a great proposed city two such cities as New York and Brooklyn, demands careful, considerate attention. Such a gigantic system is a problem and an experiment worth demanding the fullest, the most careful, the highest consideration. I will say a word which I believe no one here will deny: We love Brooklyn. Men have ridden to their death for the guidon of their regiment. We bear Brooklyn as our guidon; if Brooklyn is blotted out against the will of the people — I am going to make a strong statement — it will be one of the political crimes, or blunders which amounts to a crime, in this generation. If it is believed that it was not a fair union, then the blunder will be almost as great. Brooklyn must know and feel that it is a heartfelt union. If it will be a union with and by juggling, it will not be heartfelt.

MR. LEXOW:

On what basis do you make that statement?

MR. JOHNSON:

Because the vote taken in 1894 was not considered a finality. It was understood that it would not be final. What I say is this: That is was so submitted that it was not understood to be a finality, and it was presented in words that have at least left that impression. The vote shows that it was not understood.

MR. LEXOW:

Why do you say that the vote shows that?

Mr. Johnson:

Because over one-third of the votes were against consolidation.

Mr. Lexow:

You admit that the organic law of the State is probably the most important thing that the voter can possibly vote upon or that can be submitted to him. Is it not a fact that 20,000 more or thereabouts in the city of Brooklyn voted upon the question of consolidation than voted upon the question of the constitutional amendments then submitted, or rather the whole revised Constitution.

Mr. Johnson.

It has so been stated and I doubt it not. That was submitted with the knowledge that it would be a finality; I think it diverted the attention of the people and made them believe that it did not have the efficacy which is now claimed for it. That is my thought, that is my sentiment as to the question of that vote. But I am not here to argue it. That vote is two years old. In thirty days you can find out what this city wants, and there is no appeal from that — yes, in fifteen days if necessary.

I say to you that a law blotting out Brooklyn would be felt as being an unfriendly act. I do not propose to say anything about the merits of consolidation. I will say, however, that bringing Staten Island into the city I can see no reason for that. It is larger than the city of Brooklyn and New York before the recent addition, and has but 51,000 population and is over five miles from the city. Why consolidate that? I want to see first the consolidation of bridges, that shall carry our cars right into the heart of New York, as was provided by the Legislature for the eastern district last year. Last year the Legislature gave us a bill to build such a bridge connecting the eastern district. One bridge here will consolidate Brooklyn more than any paper record. I believe paper records can no more effect consolidation than we can make paper money with gold.

Mr. Lexow:

Why not legal consolidation as well as physical consolidation.

MR. JOHNSON:

For the same reason that we desire communication between Albany and New York. For the same reason that we desire quick rapid transit between all the great cities. We believe that government is not necessarily connected with traffic or transit. We believe that government is a matter of the wishes, the heart, the sentiment, the patriotic feeling of the people and we do not believe that these sentiments will be nourished by any consolidation which is brought about. But, gentlemen of the commission, I desire to pass to another branch of the subject, a branch of the subject as to which I feel very deeply, and that is this bill which is presented by the commission.

I do not regard it as a bill of consolidation, but a bill of effacement, a bill effacing Brooklyn in order, as the bill itself says, to pave the way for other bills that shall build up a new municipality. I am sure this committee has thought much both upon the bill presented by the commission and upon the bill presented by Senator Brush. I ask what will be the condition of Brooklyn if that bill passes? What will be its condition when the first section takes effect? Will this be a city or will it not? You will then simply have enacted that it shall be consolidated with New York. Is it consolidated? Is there one or two corporations? Does the city hall, in which we sit, remain the property of the city of Brooklyn? Is Brooklyn a corporation of the municipal government or is it not? I do not know how those that drew the bill consider it. If Brooklyn is not a municipal corporation what then is it?

MR. GRADY:

Do you mean before or after consolidation takes effect?

MR. JOHNSON:

I mean after two years. You have said that Brooklyn is consolidated with the corporation known as the mayor, aldermen and commonalty of New York. But for the purpose of local government all her officers and all her elections shall proceed as now. If we are a part of New York, if Brooklyn is wiped out as a corporation we are a mere borough, with a local government administered temporarily and during the will of the Legislature. The dignity, the name, the constitutional safeguard to protect this city will be no more. We are not a city. We are to be something which is unknown in the history of the world and unknown to the constitution, a mere temporary makeshift until it shall be provided where we shall go and what we shall do by the Legislature. If, on the other hand, we are not consolidated, if the city of Brooklyn remains with its corporate rights, its corporate existence, its corporate functions — whatever you do, don't do this, don't take away its name. Don't pass an act which the city doesn't want, an act that will leave it without its name and without its history, but leaves all the prodigious responsibilities with its representatives.

But it seems to me that it will not and can not claim that this act of consolidation is intended to be an act of consolidation in name only, that it is only consolidation in name; if it is then you take away our name and our rallying point while we have the responsibility. You have told us that we have the responsibility and yet are liable to come into the other city. You have left no rallying point from which to effect its consolidation, then, I say, you have taken away all the constitutional safeguards that protect us. Every one. You have taken away the provision that we shall elect and appoint our own officers, you have taken away the provision under which we elect our mayor, you simply make us a temporary commission, disgraced, discrowned — responsibilities that might appall the most daring. I submit, gentlemen of the committee, I am criticising that provision of the bill, but nothing that I may say is intended in criticism of the responsible offices of that commission, after their six years, but what have they done? They have prepared a bill fixing the territorial boundaries of the proposed greater city, and providing for an appropriation of $25,000 to defray the expense of the commission to prepare laws, bills — which when enacted into laws will govern this municipality. In the bill of last year they asked to be directed to prepare a charter. This year they have left that out. They do not propose to prepare a charter. They not only failed to propose it, but their failure is marked, in that they have omitted the proposition that was in last year's bill, that there should be a charter. They have simply asked that they be authorized to prepare bills.

MR. LEXOW:

Is it true that there is no such thing as a charter known to the law — that whatever a city operates under must be a bill, or an act of the Legislature?

MR. JOHNSON:

I am very glad that you presented that question. While a definition from a lawyer's standpoint is true, this is true: That every city in the State, I think, has an act which embraces a system of laws under which it is governed, and which is called and recognized as its charter.

MR. LEXOW:

Were you not one of the distinguished leaders in the Constitutional Convention who placed his feet upon the charters and demanded that uniform laws should be enacted for the government of the cities, and that cities of the first, second and third class should not have charters as heretofore, but be governed by uniform charters, established by the Legislature.

MR. JOHNSON:

I am very glad that the very minor work that I did in the Constitutional Convention has been called to my attention. I was opposed from first to last to the proposition that there could or might be unity of charters in this State. I had the pleasure of an interview with Judge Earl, who is at the head of the uniform charter commission, and I told him that it was as impossible to make the charters of the cities uniform as it is impossible to make the trees grow uniform; but what I did say was that the great principle of home rule for cities should be embodied in the supreme law. I also said that if the Legislature undertook to legislate as to matters that were purely local, that affected the sovereignty and the dignity of the city, that it should not be done without placing upon the bill a record that it had been done at or against the wish of the city. My thought was this, that in general legislation for cities, the cities should have nothing to say; that in matters pertaining to special legislation, the cities should be heard, and what they said as to it should be recorded and given prominence, as a stimulus to prosperity and city patriotism. What we must have in this State is this brief mandate. "That as we make our bed we shall lie on it;" that if we build for the good it will remain and not be taken away, that if we build for the bad we must take the responsibility. Let me say to you, and I never meditated anything longer in my life: The cities have grown so large that you can not have good government in the State if you do not have it in the cities. It is different than it was thirty years ago, when a third of the population was in the cities; now, seventy-one per cent. is in the cities.

A charter has a recognized meaning. It is a body of law uniting territory of a municipality in the form of government. It was used in that sense in the bill of last year. It is omitted this year. If this city is put under the government of a commission it will be a great wrong. I want to say that if it is done, I believe the greatest blow possible will be struck at the independent and patriotic feeling of this city. It takes away all there is of aspiration for better politics. It takes all there is away of thoughtful care for good government. If the people are told that they are to be disfranchised of their governmental power, that they are to be made different from other municipalities, made different in being plunged in with this city of New York—the government of which some of us do not love — I believe that it will be something that will break down the municipal spirit here and will be an injury of great magnitude. These cities must live in and by themselves and for themselves. And if the principle of government by commission is imperfect and corrupt it will grow and germinate for many years. I want to say to this commission that it was a patriotic uprising of the people that changed the politics of Brooklyn. The people did not like the way things were being run — perhaps they were unreasonable. They wanted home rule. And it was because a minority party came forward and planted itself upon the principle of abolishing those corrupt influences, and, under the leadership of Mayor Scheiren, demanded immediate responsibility, that the minority party came out from behind the clouds. That is the very alphabet of politics in Brooklyn. I have acted on this principle for ten or twenty years, and I hope the party to which I belong will act on it, that that party will not wipe out our existence and that that party will leave to us the principle of home rule, which some of us helped plant in the Constitution. That is the sentiment of to-day; I speak as a citizen of Brooklyn. I speak as a man that loves Brooklyn, and what has been done in Brooklyn. I ask as a citizen, as a member of the party to which some of you belong, that you will not take away our charter rights and give them to a commission which may be appointed under this bill.

MR. LEXOW:

The sessions of to-morrow will be held in Part IV of the Supreme Court, room 23, in the court-house. We will now take a recess for one hour. The afternoon session will be given to those who will speak in favor of the bill.

AFTERNOON SESSION.

COMMON COUNCIL CHAMBER,

BROOKLYN, N. Y., *January* 17, 2.30 P. M.

A. ABRAHAM:

Mr. Chairman and Gentlemen of the Committee: I have been requested by the merchants of the city of Brooklyn to present to you their views on this question of consolidation. I do so with the conviction that almost the entire mercantile community of this city favors consolidation with New York, provided the unification takes place on a basis of equal taxation. The names appended to this petition were hurriedly procured, and the canvasser informed me that among the merchants the limited time at his command permitted him to visit, comparatively speaking, only a few objected to sign the petition. The names on this list represent the largest concerns in this city, with many millions of dollars invested in capital and property and employing many thousands of people in their various vocations, and are, therefore, well qualified to judge, from a practical business standpoint, what are the best interests of the city. Brooklyn is near its debt limit, her taxable resources are about exhausted, real estate being in many instances assessed at higher figures than the actual value, and, nothwithstanding the high rate of taxation, the revenue derived is insufficient for actual requirements and improvements necessary to a city covering so much territory as does Brooklyn. While New York is annually adding to its boundless resources, Brooklyn is practically stagnated. The comparative small amount added the past few years to the assessed valuation of real estate, is owing principally to increases on existing property, thus adding to our burdens now almost unbearable, while New York city, notwithstanding the depression in business, will, I am informed, add this year alone more than eighty millions of dollars which represent but fifty per cent. of the value of the new buildings and improvements erected in New York. The opposition to this movement seems to be confined to a coterie of sentimentalists who, aside from social reasons, have not advanced a single, solid reason wherein it will be detrimental to Brooklyn, provided consolidation takes place on a basis of equality so far as taxation is concerned. While I have the greatest admiration for our local press, I believe their fear that amalgamation with New York will affect them injuriously, is groundless. If they exercise the same enterprising spirit after the cities are made one, their influence will not be confined as it is at present, to Brooklyn alone, but will expand and they can enter the field for supremacy on their merits and can cope successfully with the great metropolitan papers in New York. It is a base libel on the intelligence of the voters to assume that those who voted for consolidation, did not understand its import. The question had been agitated for a long period prior to the election, and it is a monumental and impertinent assumption on the part of the opposition to claim that those who did not vote for or against consolidation, were against the union. Is it not reasonable to suppose that those who oppose consolidation would have voted against the scheme? I believe that it is the wish of our citizens that the Legislature should speedily ratify the action of the people as expressed by the majority vote then cast by the various districts affected. The people have no misgivings but that the Legislature will enact a just and consistent charter equitable to every district in the union. We have confidence in our representatives and our Brooklyn legislators will have the co-operation of all fair-minded confreres throughout the State, and if not, I claim that Brooklyn holds the balance of power and now that the municipal elections are divorced form national elections, party lines will be abolished and on home matters, the Democrat and Republican who may differ in national politics, will unite and exact such pledges from either party and the respective candidates which can not and will not be ignored; so Brooklyn with its 1,100,000 people need not fear the result. Confidence and faith should go together.

I have given the question of consolidation considerable thought and in my opinion, should it take place, Brooklyn will enter into an era of prosperity which will eclipse and sink into insignificance any past experience in her history. It is true we have grown to be a large city, so far as size and population, but bigness is not always greatness. Brooklyn can be likened very much to a merchant who has a large store with an insufficient capital to run his business. The size of the plant requires a large force of clerks and to be equipped with a stock commensurate with its proportions; but, alas! the capital is inadequate and to avoid bankruptcy, the merchant wisely takes in a rich partner. This is analogous to Brooklyn's condition. We have as many miles of streets to police and clean; we have all the incidental expenses of a large city, but our taxable resources are not sufficient for the necessary requirements, and this condition is likely to continue in the same ratio until annexation taxes place.

Brooklyn, in turn, will give New York a city naturally endowed, and not exceded by any other in the land, with a boundless territory for a large population, washed by the waves of the ocean and its numerous bays thus insuring healthfulness and salubrious air. New York can only grow vertically and the natural expansion is in our direction, which has made Brooklyn particularly attractive with its near proximity to the ocean beaches and its limitless capacity of growth in every direction and yet be within easy and quick accessibility to the business district of the enlarged metropolis. This gives this side of the river the natural advantage over the upper part of New York.

Real estate in Brooklyn, should the union be affected, will never be as valuable as in New York. New York, owing to its narrow conformation, is now congested, while over here there is practically no limit to a healthy expansion. Rents will always be comparatively low on Long Island, and houses will be built so long as the demand makes the investment a profitable venture and competition will keep down the rental of houses as it does in merchandise or any other commodity. Aside from all material interest, we are in reality a part of New York, why not be with it? New York and Brooklyn are one city in all that is essential to unity, they ought to be one city in form as well as in fact; a great metropolis with but a single opinion, a single, common prosperity. The artificial and arbitrary division of the city into a number of separate municipalities is hurtful in many ways. It deprives the metropolis of its proper rank among the great cities of the world. It is wasteful of public revenues. It tends to high taxes and worse service; it embarrasses efforts for improvement. It confuses council and it breeds indifference and antagonism, where combination of effort is most necessary for the public welfare.

What a picture for the imagination to dwell upon is this mighty coming unified metropolis. Its vast army of workmen, its mighty accumulation of capital, its public works surpassing all known wonders of man's ingenuity; its numerous bridges sure to follow: its chain of parks rivalling in beauty the most famous of the world; its hum and roar of ceaseless traffic; its broad domain packed with homes limited on one side only by the broad Atlantic. And its churches and great schools; its palaces of trade and huge dives of industry. This will be a sight to quicken the blood and make us proud citizens of the second city of the world.

BROOKLYN, N. Y., *January* 15, 1896.

To His Excellency, the Governor, and the Legislature of the State of New York:

The undersigned, merchants of the city of Brooklyn, respectfully urge the passage of a bill consolidating Brooklyn city with New York city, providing, among other things, for attaining an equal and uniform rate of taxation and uniform valuations for the purpose of taxation:

A. D. Matthews & Sons.
Henry Offermall.
Abraham & Straus.
The Liebman Company.
Samuel Koch & Sons.
Slater & Co.
Harding Manufacturing Company.
L. Manne & Co.
Brooklyn Furniture Company.
Anderson & Co.
Keating & Co., 573 Fulton street.
James Morton, 581 Fulton street.
The Singer Manufacturing Company, Winch, Agent.
W. H. Hooper, Jr., 593 Fulton street.
John Wood, 609 Fulton street.
Alfred F. Wise, Flatbush avenue and Fulton street.
Theodore T. Ovington, Flatbush avenue and Fulton street.
Hardenbergh & Co., Flatbush avenue and Fulten street.
John C. Grennell & Co., 19-21 Flatbush avenue.
Pet. Schmitz, 1-11 Flatbush avenue.

Charrot & Henry, 58 Flatbush avenue.

Dayton & Montgomery, 69-73 Flatbush avenue.

James Levine, 74 Flatbush avenue.

Luther H. Potter & Bro., 97 Flatbush avenue.

Richard Knox, 152 and 154 Flatbush avenue.

John Herrmann, firm of Herrmann & Grace, Flatbush and Fifth avenues.

Wm. H. Bennett, 448 Dean street, corner Flatbush avenue.

Cameron & Co., 203 Flatbush avenue.

Cameron, 209 Flatbush avenue.

Philip F. Cassidy, 471 Dean street.

Thos. E. Langton, 196½ Flatbush avenue.

Edward Bull, 253 Flatbush avenue.

Horatio S. Stewart, 261 Flatbush avenue.

Henry Batterman, 747-749 Broadway.

S. B. Kraus, 657 Broadway.

Boynton & Co., 658 and 660 Broadway.

William Baterman.

Philip Ritter, 674 Broadway.

Murzesheimer Bros., 676 Broadway.

A. Westheim, 687 Broadway.

Geo. P. Schneider, 689 Broadway.

John Schulthers, 709-711 Broadway.

Blasius Allgeier, 714 Broadway.

B. Ollricht, 730 Broadway.

John Mayer, 734 Broadway.

Stultz & Bauer, 738 Broadway.

James Healy, Broadway and Flushing avenue.

Charles Lyon, 769 Broadway.

M. Barkas, 779 Broadway.

J. H. Deskau, 783 Broadway.

M. Descau, 797 Broadway.

Wolf Bros., 831 Broadway.

John A. Schwarz & Brother, 834 and 840 Broadway.

Bernhard Monneuse, 893 Broadway.

William Gohringer, 895 Broadway.

Fred. H. Levy, 929 Broadway.

Black & Fische, Broadway, corner Myrtle avenue.

John H. Thielman, 890 Broadway.

Miller & Son, 878 Broadway.

Joseph O'Brien & Co., 151 to 159 Atlantic avenue.

Standard Shoe Company, 139 Atlantic avenue.

Brooklyn Clothing Company, 141 and 143 Atlantic avenue.

L. Manne & Co.

W. H. Mumford.

Nell & Scott.

Charles M. Gage, of Gage & Toller.

Moses Genung, 370 Fulton street.

John Ferguson, 362 Fulton street.

Wm. H. Patton, 575 Baltic street.

John H. Peters, 360 Fulton street.

Erastus Gulick & Co., 350 Fulton street.

Julius Miller, 414 Fulton street.

C. C. Adams & Co.

Thomas Keeley.

P. George W. Hall.

Hydeman & Co.

James Cassidy.

A. I. Nanna.

Charles K. Ash.

Herman A. Rothschild, manager for J. Rothschild, 450 Fulton street.

Wm. H. Voorhees, secretary Bolton Drug Company.

Cousins & Urner.

W. Schrieder, manager for the Fulton Cloak and Suit Company, 520 Fulton street.

M. E. Keogh, 522 Fulton street.

E. J. Ergens, manager for J. M. Chauntskis, 486 Fulton street.

Johnston Bros., Nevins street and Flatbush avenue.

William Irvine, 814 Carroll street.

Mr. Bailey:

Mr. Chairman and gentlemen of the committee: I should like briefly to call to your attention why the material interests of Brooklyn demand consolidation, and to beseech you to advise the granting of the relief necessary, which can come only with assistance from the boundless wealth of the city across the river.

In 1883, the present Brooklyn bridge was opened to the public. The assessed value of Brooklyn at that time was $299,000,000, a gain in ten years previous of $65,800,000. In 1895, the assessed value of Brooklyn was $566,000,000, again since the opening of the bridge of $267,000,000, an average gain for the thirteen years since 1883, of over $20,000,000, per year, while previous to 1883, the annual gain was only six and three quarter millions. This immense yearly increase is now at an end. The gain of 1895 over 1894 was $14,500,000. Of this $6,500,000 came by the addition of the new wards. From this source there will be no such immense gain in 1896. In 1895, the assessments in four wards were decreased over $1,000,000, and should have been decreased $2,000,000, and as the Brooklyn "Eagle" most justly says, "the increase of the assessed value in Brooklyn during 1895, below 1894, is $2,785,709, less than the aggregate increase due to known causes, such as new buildings, the increase in value of real estate in new wards, the increased assessment on personal property and increase in mileage assessment on the railroad." From these sources there should have been an aggregate increase of $17,303,000, but was in reality less than that by $2,785,709. This loss in 1895 in comparison with 1894, is due to the inadequacy of the present bridge accommodations. Brooklyn most justly attributes its $20,000,000 annual increased enlargement in wealth from 1883 to 1894, directly to the improved facilities of access to New York, caused by the construction of the present bridge, and the vitality and future growth of the city are entirely dependent upon increased rapid transit facilities between the two cities. Our present bridge is now taxed to its utmost, and more bridges should be built at once. New bridges require large expenditures of money and immense issue of bonds must be forthcoming to provide the funds.

The most ardent or the most visionary member of the so-called League of Loyal Citizens, can not by any possibility demonstrate how Brooklyn is to pay her share of the cost of the construction of two more bridges within the next decade.

The assessed value of Brooklyn is now eighty per cent. of the real value, and you can buy to-day hundreds of pieces of property at less than their assessment. The gain in aggregate assessment in the city in 1896 over 1895, can not be over $6,000,000, and the increase of the bond issuing capacity will therefore, not increase over $6,000,000. Six hundred thousand dollars per year for ten years will be $6,000,000, which is less than one-half the cost of the present bridge. To be sure the city can now issue $3,000,000 of bonds, but after paying balances due on existing contracts, and providing for but very few of the extra expenditures yearly necessary, the $3,000,000, will certainly be absorbed in two years.

How Brooklyn can devote all of its future resources to the construction of bridges, is certainly not apparent. Ten million dollars, if not more, must be spent immediately after the close of the century for the enlargement of Brooklyn's water supply. Bonds can be issued for enlargement of water facilities, to be sure, but after the debt limit has once been passed, money for bridges will no longer be available. The congestion on Fulton street must be relieved. That will cost $2,000,000. New sewers and water mains must be laid during the next decade, at a cost of not less than $5,000,000. Can you, gentlemen of the committee, see how Brooklyn can do all of this without help?

If Brooklyn does not have another bridge to New York in five years, instead of an annual gain of $6,000,000, it will lose $10,000,000 in assessed value each year for the next ten years.

If you gainsay what the bridge means to Brooklyn, and why its growth has now stopped, cross the bridge from Brooklyn to New York between 7.30 and 9 A. M. on any week day, and ask yourself if you would live in a city where twice a day your life would be endangered in order to reach your business in the morning and home at night.

Annexation would mean not only the speedy completion of

the bridge now under contemplation, but also additional bridges at once started and speedily finished. Then Brooklyn would contiue to grow as it did from 1883 to 1895. Its immense growth in population and increased taxable value, mostly at the expense of New Jersey, would soon turn present Brooklyn into the most prosperous wards of the Greater New York.

New York is generous to her newly annexed territiories, so generous that the most earnest opponents of consolidation are to be found in the remaining portions of Westchester county. The twenty-third and twenty-fourth wards of New York city, that portion beyond the Harlem river, the nearest part of which is further from the City Hall, New York, than Coney Island, have increased in assessed value since 1883, $23,937,703, and is now assessed at about thirty per cent. of its actual value. Does that look like bad treatment? New York certainly would take even better care of that part of its territory so much nearer the seat of government as Brooklyn would be, if annexed.

That Brooklyn's position and its lack of resources for proper development, is thoroughly understood by financiers, as I have endeavored to state, is well reflected by the market price of its bonds, which is below the market price of New York city bonds bearing the same rate of interest, and by the difference in the rate of interest which must be paid by the home owner in Brooklyn to his mortgagee.

The average rate of interest on bonds and mortgages in Brooklyn is over five per cent. The average rate of interest on mortgages in New York is four and one-half per cent. Brooklyn owes on bond and mortgage not less than $300,000,000, and this difference in the rate of interest means an annual loss of at least $1,500,000, which is all paid by the struggling owners of small homes and the small merchants on the business streets in this city. The following institutions, with headquarters in New York, all large lenders of moneys on bond and mortgage, will lend, practically, no money in Brooklyn: The Equitable Life Insurance Company, the Germania Life Insurance Company, the Manhattan Life Insurance Company, the Washington Life Insurance Company, the United

States Life Insurance Company, to say nothing of the large trust funds and endowment moneys, custodians of which absolutely refuse to lend one dollar on Brooklyn property. These large insurance companies alone have outstanding on bond and mortgage at the present time $56,985,000.

The following savings banks in New York city exclude Brooklyn as a place of investment on bond and mortgage: The bank for savings known as the Bleecker Street Bank, the Bowery Savings Bank, the Citizens' Savings Bank, the Drydock Savings Bank, the Franklin Savings Bank, the German Savings Bank, the Greenwich Savings Bank, the Institution for the Savings of Merchants' Clerks, the Irving Savings Institution, the Manhattan Savings Institution, the New York Savings Bank, the North River Savings Bank. These institutions have outstanding on bond and mortgage $103,879,804.70. Even two Brooklyn institutions hold upwards of $2,000,000 on bond and mortgage in the city of New York at four per cent., where they have not loaned one dollar at that rate in Brooklyn.

These New York savings banks and kindred institutions loaned during the last year in New York city $8,000,000 at four per cent. During the same year, one loan was made in Brooklyn at that rate, and that was for $100,000, and was made by an institution outside of New York and Brooklyn.

Consolidation increase at once the supply of money available for bond and mortgage in Brooklyn. With increased supply, the rate must of necessity decrease. Let me appeal to you, gentlemen, to report to the honorable Legislature of the State that this measure is demanded to protect the homes of the struggling house-owner in Brooklyn. It is for his fireside that sentiment should be shown, not that sentiment which would stifle this measure because the light of many now prominent by comparison would be hid under the bushel of Greater New York (and I can not blame them in their opposition, for self-preservation is a law of nature); but that sentiment which will say to the owner of a home, The people of your city have voted for consolidation. You should have it, and all it brings. Reduced taxation, reduced rates of interest on your borrowed money, better streets, better transit, enlarged police force, enlarged fire department, and above all, more bridges, and a certainty of money enough to bring water even from Lake Superior, if necessary. What does your sentiment tell you to-day? If you fail in your duty, it means ruin to many a home.

To you, as citizens of the State of New York, I now appeal. Think for a moment how many trains daily carry commuters to their homes in New Jersey from their business in New York city. Think how many those commuters represent. Not less than 250,000 souls. If Brooklyn could have had the facilities which it should have had over the East river, 100,000 of these people, house-owners, and the best citizens, would now be residents of Brooklyn. I ask you, gentlemen of the committee, to apply the great Republican principle of protection, and stop this growth of the towns in New Jersey.

The citizens of New York State, from the general tax levy, could afford to build bridges over the East river, to conserve its resources, and stop the growth of New Jersey at the expense of Brooklyn.

Give to the people of the Empire State the largest city on the continent, and save the future of Brooklyn from its real enemies, who, under the guise of patriotism, are the real Tories of the contest. There is no doubt, gentlemen, how Brooklyn would vote were she to vote again. The taxpayer would come and vote for less taxes, for lower assessment, and lower rates of interest. But would New York? I am fearful she would not again offer us the benefits of her wealth if it were once declined.

In conclusion, let me ask you, gentlemen, if every one of your opponents at the last election does not now think that there was not a fair election. I will wager that each one would talk for hours if opportunity offered, to show that he and not you were elected. Is there any doubt in your mind who was elected? I think not. So it is with the vote on consolidation. The next vote, if it should be in favor of consolidation, would likewise be unfair in the minds of nearly every member of the Loyal Legion, because they would not win. May you not be numbered among those who are false to the will of the people, as expressed by the ballot, solemnly and deliberately, after two years of discussion, for remember that it was by that power that you have been exalted to the high offices you now hold.

MR. LEXOW:

Do you think that the declaration of union would be sufficient to raise this embargo upon Brooklyn property?

MR. BAILEY:

The loaning of money on bonds and mortgages is one of tne large lines of business engaged in by the corporation with which I am connected, and I think it would, to a great extent.

MR. LEXOW:

You find great trouble in inducing money to come to Brooklyn?

MR. BAILEY:

When it comes it is because the banks guarantee the payment of the interest; that is why we have been able to bring New York money to Brooklyn. I know of two Brooklyn institutions that have upwards of $2,000,000, but they will not loan one dollar of it in Brooklyn at New York rates. New York savings banks and kindred institutions during the last year in New York city loaned $8,000,000 at four per cent.; during the same year but one loan was made in Brooklyn, and that was made by an institution up in the country that didn't know any better.

MR. GRADY:

Brooklyn has reached the end of its purse, and you expect New York to take whatever steps may be necessary to continue it in a progressive way. How would that affect New York?

MR. BAILEY:

She has expressed her willingness and I am afraid New York will vote against it if she had another opportunity.

Mr. Brush:

How, in your judgment, would consolidation affect rents in the city of Brooklyn?

Mr. Bailey:

The rent question is governed by the laws of supply and demand as every other production is.

Mr. Lexow:

Would consolidation necessarily increase the value of real estate in Brooklyn, or would it be more likely to make the value stable?

Mr. Bailey:

It would make the value stable. I do not believe, as the consolidationists seem to think, that annexation would make any marvellous increase in the value of real estate in Brooklyn. But I do believe that when a man's house was sold under foreclosure, there would be somebody there to buy it. There is no sustaining public here to buy up property because they are fearful of the financial future of the city.

Mr. Brush:

Do you believe that the mere act of the declaration of union would lead to an increase of the rental in Brooklyn?

Mr. Bailey:

I am tempted to answer by saying that I believe that rents are governed entirely by supply and demand.

Mr. Brush:

Would it make any difference, in your judgment?

Mr. Bailey:

It would not.

Mr. Lexow:

It seems to me that the logical result of your argument is that consolidation would bring a large part of the population in certain parts of New York over to this side of the river?

MR. BAILEY:

That is my belief based upon the experience of the people with whom I have done business. In the condition in which the Brooklyn bridge now is, it is absolutely impossible to take care of the people.

MR. BRUSH:

Is it not you contention that consolidation would increase the value of real estate?

MR. BAILEY:

Yes, sir.

MR. BRUSH:

How can you expect the value of real estate to increase without the rents increasing?

MR. BAILEY:

The taxes are reduced without an increase of rent.

DAVID A. BOODY:

Mr. Chairman and Gentlemen of the Committee: I can not doubt, gentlemen, that your minds are already filled with the arguments that have already been presented, bearing upon this very important question. I can not presume to detain you long with any remarks that I may make, particularly as I am unfortunate in not having had the privilege of listening to the arguments that have been made on the other side. And not having had the privilege either of listening to the remarks which have been made in favor of consolidation, I may very easily drift into the way of repeating what has already been said. I am not surprised, gentlemen, and I presume that you are not surprised, in finding here a diversity of opinion, in finding what you may call strong opposition to the proposition which is before you. I have never known — and I believe that you will agree with me that you have never known of any movement for a great purpose, for a larger effort, for a higher experience, that has not met with opposition. It seems to be a condition of life, individual and national. We have many of us heard of the story of the opposition which was presented to the furnishing of this city with a water plant. There was opposition when one of Brooklyn's first citizens declared the necessity of providing public parks. We all remember the opposition which we met and the indignation which was aroused against the efforts which he then made. The same wisdom which guided him then, the same sense of civic pride and civic duty which influenced him then has guided him in the efforts which he has made to bring about the consolidation of these two communities and if he were a younger man and could to-day devote the efforts to this question to this purpose which he devoted years ago in providing the citizens of Brooklyn with beautiful Prospect park, the time would come when he would be successful in his efforts for the Greater New York. I regret that time is upon him and that his work is done. But the efforts which he has made in the past should make a strong appeal to all the citizens of Broooklyn.

Now, gentlemen, this is not a sentimental question which you are to consider. It is not a theory which confronts us. it is a condition. It is a condition of vital importance. Why, gentlemen, we are tired of living thus divided, unnatural, unproductive life which these two cities are living to-day. One gentleman who recently spoke upon this question declared that the bride who is to be united should be a willing bride. I say to you, gentlemen, that we are — those two communities —living to-day together in all the important relations of love which ought to be consumated by honorable wedlock. What are the conditions which confront us to-day? They are simply business conditions. They are conditions which we must meet one way or the other. We are a city of over a million of people. The longer we live under the present system the worse will be our condition and the greater will be our burden. What are these peculiar conditions? They are these: We live by the side of a greater city and we must have the institutions of a greater city. We must have those institutions within our own borders or we must unite with the people on the other side of the river and have them and enjoy them together. And I take it, gentlemen, that in this union we propose, we seek only our own rights, we seek only that which we have produced. We seek the wealth which our own efforts have helped to create. It is not a new proposition. It is not an unnatural proposition in any way. Day after day and year after year hundreds and thousands of the citizens of Brooklyn cross the river and in doing so attend to business which calls them there. In attending to that business they build up the wealth and the greatness and the honor of that city, and we simply want that which we create and nothing more. Let me repeat again that the city of Brooklyn must do one of two things, we must have all the institutions of a great city; we must have a custom-house, a clearing-house, a chamber of commerce, we must have a stock exchange, a cotton exchange, a produce exchange and a metal exchange. We must have all the institutions which belong to a great city, or else we must unite with the city that has them. Remember that we sustain them, and we make them and create them. Who to-day is the president of the chamber of commerce? Our own-honored citizen, Alexander Orr. Who is president of the stock exchange? Another of our citizens, within a stone's throw of where we are sitting. Who are the presidents of the banks and leaders in commercial enterprise — who has built her up? The citizens of Brooklyn. Whatever she represents to-day has come into existence through our and their efforts. Let our brains and our hearts be united. Let our homes and our occupations be united. Let it not be said that the only division between these communities is simply a stream of water running between them. The older cities of the world in times past have not allowed such impediments to stand in their way. It is true of the Thames river and the same may be said of the Seine. I say first that it is not entirely present conditions that confront Brooklyn, it is the future conditions that will confront us. It has been insisted and repeated that we are suffering because the taxes are excessive and why? It is not because our resources are wasted. It is not because any administration has been bad, but it is plainly and simply, because we have not the taxable property, the taxable property which brings the great institutions. It does not come from the dwellings of the people, it comes from the great institutions of business. It comes from those business places that concerns the great marts of trade. You cannot get it here in Brooklyn. You go on and year after year your burdens increase and the difficulties which I have referred to will grow larger, to-morrow you will be poorer than you are to-day. Then I say let us unite the products of our work. Let us unite in reality under a form of government which will give us justice, which will simply return that which we have created, and what will be the result? It will result in the extension of transportation facilities in order to make it comfortable for those who pass between the two great cities to transact their business and return to their homes. The consolidation of these two cities would modify or largely decrease or remove that question of over-crowded thoroughfares which carry us to the other side of the river. One quarter of the sum which they propose to spend in tunneling Broadway, into putting into operation an underground railway, would place three bridges across this river and then you will have practical and beneficial consolidation and these communities will feel that they are one, that their interests are united and the people will be filled with strength and hope and courage and the union would be such that you will see these bridges in the course of construction sooner than your imagination can conceive of. What may not these two communities united, produce? What hardships may they not produce living, divided as they are to-day? I wish instead of coming here and listening to these speeches that you could stand upon some pinnacle from morning until night and observe the crowd that struggles backward and forward, then you would realize where you interests mingle to day. You would see that there is no place where you could draw a dividing line. Give us consolidation, and New York city instead of spending millions for tunnels will be able to find homes for all her inhabitants. Remember that New York city wants men and needs them every day, and these men want homes on this side of the river which they can reach easily.

I am sure that if I could go on I should weary you, but I am as sure as I am sure of any other thing in life that no greater question has ever confronted you since you have been clothed with official authority. You are considering a question which not only interests the citizens of Brooklyn, the citizens of New York; you are considering a question which interests this whole country. I hope that you will aid in bringing into existence a city which shall have as a competitor only one city in the known world, and that you will be instrumental in bringing into the condition of cityhood two communities united, which, within the life of many who stand here to-day will be the empire city of the world; and then, gentlemen of the committee, as you look forward to the results of your labors not only in removing the difficulties from which we suffer to-day, not only as to the advantages which will come to our sister on the other side of the river, but when you think of that proud city, that grand city of the future which will result from this consolidation you will feel that you have been instrumental in creating the grandest metropolis that the world has ever known, whose power, whose greatness, whose institutions, whose glory, shall outstrip the imagination of to-day.

MR. LEXOW:

What do you consider the sentiment of Brooklyn in regard to the question of consolidation?

MR. BOODY:

I have always believed, and I believe to-day, that the people are in favor of that which is best and right. I believe they are in favor of consolidation.

RUFUS L. SCOTT:

Mr. Chairman and Gentlemen of the Committee: In the very brief remarks that I shall make I shall confine myself principally to the vote of 1894 and the public sentiment of Brooklyn, as I understand it, on this question. You would think to hear what was said this morning that the question was sprung up in Brooklyn without notice and without argument. The contrary is the fact. There was never a question in Brooklyn or anywhere else discussed, more understood by the people of any place, than was this question. The newspapers were full of the question for months before the election took place. The people were discussing it everywhere. Lawyers, merchants, ministers, all hands. The press of the city of Brooklyn, consisting of five daily newspapers — and I may say that they are as ably conducted newspapers as there are in the United States — they were against consolidation. They all used their utmost efforts to defeat consolidation. There was not a single newspaper in Brooklyn that took the side of consolidation. In addition to that, the leader of the Democracy was against it; men in office were against it. The common people alone were for it; they worked for it; they met the question, and with all these difficulties in the way the question was carried. It was the most remarkable victory that ever was accomplished in any locality under such diverse circumstances. To show you how fully this matter was considered I must refer to one of the leading newspapers of Brooklyn —

Mr. Lexow:

Is the statement correct that every newspaper was against it at the time?

Mr. Scott:

Yes, sir; every newspaper was against it at the time. And not only that, but the Anti-Consolidation League was not satisfied with the newspapers working in their behalf, but organized another newspaper, but it had a short life and soon passed out of existence. I take the Eagle of October 30, 1894. When I confine myself to the Eagle I wish to be understood as not disparaging any other paper, as that paper is the recognized organ of the anti-consolidation movement. The Consolidation League, of which I am a member, had the audacity to issue a card, and in that card they undertook to show some of the advantages of consolidation. The Brooklyn Eagle took up that card as follows: "Twelve reasons that are twelve frauds." That is the language they used; that shows certainly that there was some interest taken in that question; you may judge by this forcible language that the Eagle is not a common paper; it is one of the ablest papers in the country. Its editorials are like those of the late Horace Greeley. It makes every word tell. "Twelve reasons that are twelve frauds;" that is the way they undertook to defeat consolidation. The people of Brooklyn did not understand it that way and they voted in favor of consolidation. It is pretty easy to make arguments in cold type; it is a very hard thing to meet pictures. On November 4th, two or three days before election, we have the Brooklyn Eagle in a picture. It is called the "Beauties of consolidation."

MR. LEXOW:

Do I understand that the Eagle stated that consolidation or no consolidation was the burning question of the hour — that that question was being discussed on the public streets every day by everybody?

MR. SCOTT:

Yes, sir; I said that. I will read it to you as it is here.

[Reads from the Brooklyn Eagle of November 4, 1894, as follows:]

(Brooklyn Eagle, November 4, 1894.)

Consolidation or no consolidation? That is the question which the Rambler hears asked on every side. The artist to-day answers it in the negative by showing what would be the consequences of adopting it. That lovely woman, Miss Brooklyn, her beautiful face within her shapely hands, her regal form suffused with grief and wrung with emotion, is "like Niobe, all tears." She is sitting on the statue of James S. T. Stranahan, our First Citizen, which has been rudely thrown from its pedestal into the dirt, while where it stood before will be seen a lifelike effigy of Tweed, the freebooter, the malefactor, the convict, and the boss, to whose pious memory the Tammany braves drink unto this day, and whom they regard as their patron saint and lasting model. In a lower part of the picture the statue of Henry Ward Beecher, some of whose creed was in every church, and all of it in none, the man who helped free America and the slave, the lover of Brooklyn because the lover of humanity, has been thrown in the mire with the companion figures that attested the largeness and the liberality of his soul in the mire with him. In his place and in theirs will be seen the typical representation of the Tammany Indian of whom the feet are fondly licked by the carniverous chops of the typical Tammany Tiger.

More havoc has been wrought around Prospect Park than the demolition of the monument of our First Citizen. The statue of the great Lincoln, erected by the pennies of the people, has been cast from its place. The statue of Mayor Gilroy, the latest, but not the last evolution of Tammanyism and political turpitude, is erected where stood that of the martyr of liberty. A representative Tammany policeman is mercilessly clubbing an inoffensive and vainly protesting citizen of Brooklyn, for the nameless crime of being a Brooklynite. The bust of Charles A. Schieren, which admiring citizens of the second and last reform mayor of the city of Brooklyn that was, had erected in the park, has been thrown into the mud, and its upturned, immobile face pathetically suggests the argument which the artist would enforce. Surrounding Tweed is a statue of Peter B. Sweeney, the brains of the old Tammany combine, who is still in the flesh, and whose interest in public affairs is not only real, but apparent. There are other evidences of the fruits of consolidation brought out with skill and point by the cartoonist's pencil. They speak for themselves to the brains and the hearts of all who have loved Brooklyn, who love her still, and who would keep Brooklyn as she is, the City of Churches, and of homes as distinct from New York, the City of Tammany and of criminal government, as if an ocean instead of a river rolled between them.

The Rambler does not consider our First Citizen either consistent or grateful in his leadership of the movement for the effacement of Brooklyn. Brooklyn has greatly honored him. She has placed his statue in her noblest park. She has done so in his lifetime. She has set him not only in enduring bronze, but in more enduring song and story. The city thought that its honors to him were a recognition of his labors for Brooklyn. The idea was not entertained that these labors, large, luminous and lasting as they are, were put forth out of any other love than the love of Brooklyn, which in turn commanded Brooklyn's love for him. Alas! It now seems as if they were put forth for some shadowy, immense and inchoate municipality of the future, the Greater New York, if you please, whereof Brooklyn is to be a political appendicitis or a social wart, or an unregarded pustule, or a geographical button. The Rambler is satisfied that our First Citizen should repent ere it is too late. Other men might be able to justify their support of this consolidation movement, but for James S. T. Stranahan to advocate and to lead in the movement to wipe out Brooklyn seems as wrong as it would be to suggest Washington as a tory or Jefferson as a courtier or Grant as a rebel, or Lincoln as a slaveholder, or Dr. Parkhurst as a sachem of Tammany Hall, or John W. Goff as a dive-keeper, or John Y. McKane as a reformer.

This picture should be neutralized. What it suggests should not be brought about. The Rambler has but one vote, but he intends to cast that next Tuesday against consolidation with New York, he intends to get all those he can influence to vote the same way. Brooklyn must be preserved. Mr. Stranahan must be saved. The fame and the name of the statue of Henry Ward Beecher must not be swallowed up by Tammany Hall. The baby carriages, which are the ornament, the argument and the increment of the city of homes which keeps them well and periodically filled, must not be attacked by the ferocious beast of Fourteenth street. Better the goat of Gowanus than the tiger of Tammany. Vote consolidation down. Save Brooklyn. Keep rents low by keeping Brooklyn to herself. Continue home government here and do not invite the blackmail, the bloodmail, the bulldozing and the highway robbery of New York into our life. Make impossible the substitution of Tweed for Stranahan, of Gilroy for Lincoln, or of any smirched sachem for Henry Ward Beecher, in this beautiful city by the sea.

(Brooklyn Eagle, November 5, 1894.)

The way to deal with consolidation is to vote it down. Not to vote at all on the matter will be half a vote for it. The expression will be made up from the votes cast on the subject, whether for or against, not from the votes cast either way. Each voter will get two ballots relating to the matter. Inside of one will be "Against Consolidation." Inside the other will be "For Consolidation." The friends of Brooklyn should vote the one which has the word "against" inside of it. The reasons for this are plain. If you want to see them, look at the cartoon in to-day's Eagle. That tells the story to the eye and the eye should tell it to the soul of every true Brooklynite.

The reasons against consolidation now are absolute. The government of this city is getting better. The government of New York is the worst in the world. In Brooklyn reform is on top in the City Hall. In New York reform is in the mud and Tammany Hall controls every part of the government. A generation ago and more Tammany Hall was a temple of principle and of honor. It is now a den of thieves. The high places of New York are in possession of those thieves. All the powers of New York government are theirs. Brooklyn is clean, pure and progressive. New York is foul and in the mire. The moral reasons for opposing consolidation now are exactly the same as those which should lead a self-respecting man or woman to avoid vile associations.

The material reasons are not few. Our debt is less than $50,000,000. The debt of New York is many millions more than a hundred. Government here costs per person less than half it costs in New York. Our people here know their officials and can call them to account. Brooklyn would be of no account governed from the City Hall of New York or from the Tammany den of scoundrelism on Fourteenth street. The officials over there would laugh at our wants. They would jeer us down when we demanded our rights. They would regard Brooklyn as a fresh field to loot and ravage. There would be fine pickings over here for the New York spoilsmen. That city has twice as many votes as Brooklyn and against Brooklyn it could work its wickedest will with ease.

Brooklyn is a city of homes. New York is a city of palaces and tenements. The very rich and the very poor make up its characteristic population. The very rich are robbed with their own consent by its political thieves. The very poor are oppressed by those political thieves. The men in middling circumstances in New York have no more chance for comfort and for betterment in existing political conditions over there than a cat without claws has in Hades.

The consolidationists tell us that valuations in Brooklyn would go up. They might, and they might not. If they did rents would go up and Brooklyn people, especially the poor and moderately well-to-do, are not anxious that rents should go up. Imagine a tenant going to a landlord, hat in hand and humbly saying: " Dear sir, please increase my rent; I will be very much obliged to you if you will." Such a man would have to be taken care of by his friends, yet if Brooklyn votes for consolidation it is a vote to put up rents, and every rentpayer should, therefore, be sure to vote against the proposition.

Now, why is this consolidation matter pressed? There are a few large property-holders with big water privileges who would like to increase their value and decrease the tax which they have to pay for them. New York, under an old charter, has jurisdiction to the Brooklyn water line. If Brooklyn became New York, then the sums due under that old charter could either be compounded, reduced or removed. That accounts, perhaps, for the popularity of consolidation along the Atlantic docks. More on this head need not be said.

Then there are a lot of socially ambitious people who live in Brooklyn, but are ashamed to say so. They would like to be called New Yorkers. They apologize for being Brooklynites. They have property in some cases earned, in other cases inherited, and in still others neither earned nor inherited, and they would like to subscribe themselves as New Yorkers and to be regarded as New Yorkers here and elsewhere. There is nothing in that feeling but vanity, and it's a miserably small vanity.

Then there are our always esteemed friends, the real estate boomers, who buy what they do not own and sell what does not belong to them, and who make a thrifty living by the deft manipulation of that gaseous exudation called commissions. If they could run Brooklyn houses up to a New York valuation, then they could demand New York rentals for them, and their commissions would correspondingly swell, at least they think so, and life is so much of a boom and so little of an actuality to them that they would rather vibrate in a bubble than live in solid comfort in a castle.

They say that the Eagle is against consolidation " because this paper has the corporation printing." A fig for corporation printing! The Eagle would be better off without it. The law puts it into this paper, and this paper obeys the law. If we were rid of it, commercial advertisements twice its value would take its place. This paper is money out for opposing consolidation and until consolidation may occur. But it is principle in and conviction in through opposing it, and the good Lord has been kind enough to the Eagle to enable it to put right above revenue and to oppose wrong, not for revenue only, but to oppose it as a duty and a delight. There may be papers that would go off and die if they lost the corporation printing. If so, they are not live enough now to take into consideration. The insult, however, of raising this corporation printing issue against the Eagle's views on this subject is in one sense as large and in another sense as contemptible as if A. L. Low's patriotic opposition to consolidation was ascribed to sordid instead of to noble motives. This paper is not buying or selling anybody, but it could buy up and sell out the creatures that thus seek to insult it, and if they have learned from these words what we think about them, they have been brought into association with something that ought to do them good.

Consolidation, if it made the rich richer, would certainly here make the poor poorer. The rich are rich enough now. The poor are too poor now. The middle classes have in Brooklyn an ideal home. They should preserve it from Tammany and from Tammanyism. The New York Times says that " The Eagle is opposing the relief and expansion of New York." Not at all. Bless your dear heart, come over and grow up with our country wards, if Park Row is too straight for you. Tell your tenement-folk to come over here and settle in our outlying districts. There they can have real homes. Tell your half-rich and would-be richer folk to drop the tenements which they call flats, or the flats which they call apartments, and come over here and get a house with a yard to it big enough for the children and the dog. The children could root around and enjoy themselves, scratch their faces, eat candy and be happy, while the dog would be able to wag his tail from side to side instead of up and down, lest he knock the bric-a-brac off the tables. Let all New York come over here. The ferries are open. Walking on the bridge is good. We have a better transit system, in air and on the ground, than New York has. Let them all come over here and be welcomed, if only to save our esteemed contemporary from being so silly.

If ever the time for consolidation comes, now is not the time. When New York has cleaned house and put on better clothes, driven its thieves away and started on a career of honesty, come over here and we'll talk about it. Meanwhile, as consolidation could be legislated without a vote, so no vote whatever for it will be effective for legislation in its behalf. But the attack on the integrity of Brooklyn should receive a smash right between the eyes, and the Eagle hopes the splendid home-keeping, rent-paying and home-loving people of Brooklyn will administer the smash next Tuesday.

(Brooklyn Eagle, November 11, 1894.)

If a small majority of those voting on the subject in Brooklyn have favored consolidation, the formulation of a bill for consideration by the Legislature will be in order. The Legislature should give to the terms of any such measure the most careful consideration. They should be terms which will not disadvantage Brooklyn, but which will be to Brooklyn's fair and just advantage as much as possible.

Those who have not favored consolidation should labor with those who have favored it, to see that such a bill is made what it ought to be. If the bill is objectionable it should be beaten and it will be beaten, until it is made substantially unobjectionable. It can not be made perfect and no one should carpingly insist on such an impossible proposition. But it can be made just, or, if it can not, it can be defeated and the proposition can be deferred until time itself relieves the disparities under which Brooklyn, in the Eagle's opinion, is placed at present with regard to consolidation at all.

The Legislature had all the power last year that the Legislature will have this year to enact anything on this subject. The Legislature recently elected, however, may have a warrant to act upon the matter which previous Legislatures did not possess. The number, value, complexity and magnitude of the interests involved require their most careful study. The project is entitled to the best thought alike of those who opposed it and of those who supported it. We do not think there is any need for haste, and we shall be surprised if the coming Legislature does not find too many purely partisan or political duties laid upon it to complete or even to make much progress in the attention which should be given to this subject in the ensuing session.

(Mr. Scott exhibits cartoon from the Brooklyn Eagle, representing a tiger.)

Mr. Grady:

The tiger has been perfectly harmless since that election.

Mr. Scott:

If we had known that before the vote on consolidation, we would have carried it in Brooklyn by about 50,000. According to the statements of some of the speakers you would think that there was no vote at all. The fact is that the vote on consolidation was 22,049 more than on the general constitutional provisions — 22,049 more. It was 16,446 more than the total vote on the canal amendment, which received the largest vote of any of the constitutional provisions. It had the enormous comparative vote of 77 per cent. of the total number of votes polled, a fact which never occurred before in the adoption of any similar measure in any election in the state of New York. If you will look back to the various constitutional amendments when a vote on the Constitution was taken you will see that it never reached 77 per cent. of the total vote. The nearest vote, I believe, was in the constitutional amendment of 1884, that came after a series of troubles — it was on the question of the power of limiting municipal indebtedness. It is the most valuable amendment that was ever attached to any constitution, in my judgment. It saved many of the cities from bankruptcy. At that time some of the cities had run up to 24 per cent. of the assessed valuation. The vote taken at that time — when excitement was running high, was only 46 per cent of the total vote cast. The vote on all the other constitutional amendments have fallen below that. I repeat what I said in the beginning, that it was the most remarkable victory, after the most thorough canvass, that was ever had under any similar question under the most adverse circumstances. When the vote was taken the will of the people on that matter was stated. Of course we never had any discussion over what a vote meant. We all thought it meant an expression of opinion. That was all the people could do on a question of that kind. The Legislature did not surrender its powers. It simply asked the people to express their wishes, to give their opinion. We thought it was very well understood, we simply thought it was an expression of opinion. We thought, however, as an expression of opinion that it was final, and that the next work would be for the Legislature to frame an act and carry out the will of the people. When the people expressed their views have them enacted into law.

I make this second proposition, Mr. Chairman and Gentlemen of the Committee, it is this: There is absolutely no considerable sentiment in Brooklyn against consolidation. Men may deceive themselves, and Loyal Leaguers may think that the sounding of a trumpet both far and wide, but it remains simply right around its own locality — the first ward of Brooklyn. Some few of those who voted against consolidation got up a petition against it and wanted to make another fight, and they did so. They hunted all over Brooklyn and found seventy men who signed a petition calling for a public meeting. They are all very respectable, excellent gentlemen. I believe they call themselves "The Ancient and Honorable Aristocracy of Brooklyn,"— they called a public meeting. That meeting was held on November 21, 1895. How many do you think was there? The New York World has by actual count, 124 people. The Brooklyn Eagle says "probably about 200." After the most earnest and vigilant efforts these seventy men could not bring but 200 to that meeting.

I was requested to limit myself to this question or to the question of the vote, but I realize there are many here that want to talk.

A Voice:

Go on.

Mr. Scott:

I desire to talk about resubmission. If there is any difference between a resubmission of a question of opinion and a resubmission of a question of candidate, I don't know what it is. Of course the one executes itself; the other is to be executed afterward. The bill serves the purpose. The one is carried just as much as the other. There would be just as much reason in resubmission of a vote given a candidate for office as there would be in a resubmission of a question of opinion. I can not see the difference. I know my Tammany friends would like very much to have a resubmission on some of the constitutional amendments, especially the apportionment one. I did not vote for the apportionment myself, but I thank the Republican party for giving it to us. On the question of the apportionment I think Tammany would take another vote if we would give it to them.

Mr. Grady:

That was only an incidental question.

Mr. Scott:

I believe that the constitutional amendment was carried in Brooklyn by 196 votes. That is ten or eleven votes more in plurality than the consolidation received. The total was far less, but the majority was that.

There is some strange logic in the action of those Loyal Leaguers. The chairman of the committee at the meeting the other night was ex-Mayor Schieren, and I want to say that he made an excellent mayor — he always indicated that he was in favor of consolidation, but since he got into office he has been at work endeavoring to defeat consolidation, and did defeat the bill last year. There is a strange logic about his action. He did a very good thing in forcing in all the towns of Kings county, he did not ask them whether they voted or not; he said they must come in without any vote at all. His influence in the Legislature brought them into Brooklyn, and they are here to-day. I do not see the consistency of these gentlemen coming here and asking for resubmission, and at the same time forcing these country towns without any submission at all. As the chairman of your committee very appropriately asked one of the gentlemen speaking on this question of resubmission, we might go on and on voting, and never stop. There must be a limit to it. Not submit another and then ask for another submission. There would be a good reason, according to their logic, to have another vote, and then go on indefinitely. Judge Reyonlds did make one very good point that I had not thought of before. He said there has been a lapse of time; the bill should have been passed last winter. If our representatives from the Legislature had carried out the wishes of the people we would have had consolidation. I don't think that Judge Reynolds would impose the same logic in a suit before him — because he is one of the fairest of our judges. I have occupied more time than I ought to, a little more than I had license to.

MR. BRUSH:

I understand Mr. Scott to say that he does not think there is any sentiment against consolidation?

MR. SCOTT:

Yes, sir.

MR. BRUSH:

Is it not a fact that during the last canvass for mayor in this city one of the Democratic candidates was an avowed consolidationist, and the Republican candidate was an avowed resubmissionist?

Mr. Scott:

It is a fact that one of the candidates was an avowed consolidationist, and it is a fact that the other was as mum as an oyster. He said it was bound to come and the people rested on that. It is also a fact that two of the candidates for mayor in the last election voted for consolidation in 1894.

Mr. Brush:

I think you will find in the letter of acceptance of Mayor Wurster that he did state that he was in favor of resubmission of a vote to the people. He did say that he was in favor of resubmission.

Mr. Lexow:

What was the position of Mr. Shepherd with reference to consolidation?

Mr. Scott:

If anybody can find out, I can not. All I can say is, that he voted for consolidation, as he says himself. There is no considerable sentiment against consolidation; there is not a society in Brooklyn who dare to call a meeting against consolidation. They know that they could not carry it at all. In the preliminary meeting of a few days ago a gentleman, in discussing the question, said, "Gentlemen, don't ask for resubmission; if you do it will be carried overwhelmingly against a referendum in the charter." It was Mr. George Foster Peabody, so they undertook by referendum to deceive the people; they tried to make them believe that you gentlemen from Albany, you politicians, are going to impose upon them something that is not right, and they undertook to deceive the people and make them believe that they are only looking for a proper charter. We are looking for it in a direct way.

Mr. Grady:

You said the common people were in favor of consolidation; how did you arrive at that.

MR. SCOTT:

Because they were the men who took a strong position on the subject. The people were left with the discussion on the subject — anti-consolidationists and the newspapers on the other side. The leading politicians kept mum, and the people were not led by anybody except their own good judgment, and the arguments presented to them carried the question.

MR. BRUSH:

Are you aware, Mr. Scott, that the board of aldermen recently passed a resolution in favor of the submission?

MR. SCOTT:

If the gentlemen had listened to my remarks he would have understood that. I never knew of an officeholder who wanted to vote himself out of office, and I never expect to find but a very few. We do not care to take the views of the board of aldermen, the people of Brooklyn know their own mind on the subject.

MR. BRUSH:

How do you account for the fact that every one of the members of the Legislature are in favor of resubmission in some form?

MR. SCOTT:

The Legislature who went to Albany from this city to the Legislature of 1894 were almost unanimously pledged for consolidation, and when they got up there they were almost unanimously against it. If you will explain that I will explain the other.

MR. GRADY:

Do you mean the present legislators?

MR. SCOTT:

No, sir. The consolidation league sent them letters and they had to answer, and the answers were published in the newspapers. It was at the election following the adoption of the constitutional amendment. I may mention Senator Reynolds' name; he signed his name to a petition and said that he would endeavor to pass the consolidation bill. He was a leading spirit against it when it got up there.

MR. GRADY:

I ask whether the press and the candidates for the Legislature in 1895 took sides upon the question.

MR. BRUSH:

If you thing there is no change in sentiment in the city of Brooklyn why do you oppose a resubmission of the question?

MR. SCOTT:

In the first place, you assume that I think there is no change. That is not true, there is a vast change in favor of consolidation. I oppose a resubmission on the same principle that I would oppose a resubmission of your election to the Legislature. It is against all principles of government. It is against common sense. It is revolutionary. It would destroy any government on the face of the earth. If you take the position that a vote is not a vote, or not an expression of the people, you have nothing left under God's heavens but revolution.

MR. BRUSH:

The point is to get the sentiment of the people. Is it not a fact that since a vote was taken that more than 50,000 more people have become inhabitants of this city. If this vote is taken as final they will have no voice in the matter whatever.

MR. SCOTT:

We can not legislate for all the people. We legislate for those who are here.

MR. H. G. SCHUMANN:

Mr. Chairman and Gentlemen of the Committee: I am somewhat interested in this question for the following reasons: First, we voted upon this question and the citizens of Brooklyn have declared that they are in favor of consolidation. I believe that we are not fair to our old friend Stranahan, who, when he heard that the farmers were complaining because he had given us our beautiful park system, he said: "Gentlemen, I must beg the pardon of those men for having made them rich." New York is in the position of Mr. Stranahan. You gentlemen from New York ought to beg our pardon for trying to make your city large and prosperous. That is the standpoint that I take. I take the standpoint that New Yorkers desire consolidation. If you resubmit this question you can resubmit anything. I have never seen a poker player yet, who, when he had a bad hand, would not ask for another deal. You ask the citizens again if you dare so to do — because if you do, that principle that Mr. Scott told you about, that principle of government would be lost and we would suffer great injury. We are in favor of consolidation to-day; and you will find that the main agitators own the buildings — those opposed to consolidation are the owners of the buildings surrounding this spot. They believe that if the City Hall should vanish they would lose millions. If you ask my friends from the eastern district, you will find another question there. You will find that there are hundreds and thousands of rooms for rent. We have the accommodations and we want the people in New York to come over here. We want the working people to come over here and we will make them comfortable. We want consolidation so that we can have bridges that will enable the people to come over here. If we are consolidated we will surely get a bridge. Again you will find that the politicans are against consolidation. They fear that they will lose their prestige. Then, there are the newspapers. A few days ago I had a discussion with Colonel Roerer, the newspaper editor; he gets $16,000 a year for advertising. The Eagle gets, probably, twice that amount. There are others in politics who fear the loss of patronage. The newspapers are afraid that they will lose a little patronage. We are not afraid, we have made our living heretofore and we will make our living after consolidation takes effect. We want to be one of the largest families in the world. Again it has been said that in a few years hence — probably eight or nine years — we must consolidate. We will need an additional water supply. We will need consolidation upon that point. If you take another view of the case there is hardly one of the western district families when they go to Europe that register from Brooklyn, but I register from Brooklyn and I am proud of my city. I have often seen those citizens register "Van Dusenberg." Senator Brush has asked a question whether the Assemblymen and Senators were not asked to vote for resubmission when they were candidates. I have before me my old friend, Senator Grady. I have been for many years president of the Brewers' association, and in years gone by would ask every Senator and Assemblyman whether he was going to vote for liberal excise laws. Every one of them said yes — yes, in such a way that every-one of them turned out against it. If this question were voted upon to-day two-thirds of the people would vote in favor of consolidation. Mr. Peabody was quite correct, when he said "don't resubmit." We would wipe the floor with the anti-consolidationists. That is all I want to say now. I thank you very much.

MR. BRUSH:

Is it not a fact that a large proportion of the eastern district voted against consolidation.

MR. SCHUMANN:

The question at that time had not won the hearts of the working people, but to-day, in consequence of its adoption, the working people are in favor of it. I took a vote the other day of fourteen persons, and found twelve were in favor of annexation and two against.

J. G. JENKINS:

Mr. Chairman and Gentlemen of the Committee: I do not represent the banks of Brooklyn here before you, but I represent my own views and the views of my neighbors. It is true that the banks have many sources of information, through different channels. In the banks and in the trust companies we have opportunities of knowing the pulse of the people on various subjects, and in that way, perhaps, I represent the financial people in favor of consolidation. In the eastern district, where I live, I have been somewhat prominent for forty years. I believe the sentiment in that district is 75 per cent. in favor of consolidation. In this city the means of assessing are limited, and the property is of small valuation. We have no river docks to rent, no carriages to license, no peanut venders to tax; we have nothing but real estate and the tax falls so heavily upon it that we are mere collectors of rents. That is the condition in which we seem to be now. If we get a greater city we will build another bridge. We are now within $3,000,000 limit of our bonded valuation, and a bridge would cost $8,000,000 or $10,000,000. How is it to be built? That is the puzzle in our finances that we can not answer. If we were annexed to New York, you gentlemen in New York would be kind enough to build 75 per cent. of the bridge, leaving 25 per cent. to Brooklyn. I present to you a proposition in relation to the East river. The city of Brooklyn has no right or authority over the East river. If a man commits a murder on the waters of the East river, he must be tried in the city of New York. That is queer, is it not? Every time you cross the bridge you have to pay your fare. Every time you cross the ferry, you pay two cents. You pay that into the treasury of the city of New York. What would you do if we were joined to that city? A certain part of this money would go towards paying your own taxes. The building of bridges across the East river would wipe us out unless we get some help. The officials of the city of Brooklyn are not to blame for our condition. They have been reasonably economical. You simply hadn't the income from taxation. If you go through the streets of the city of Brooklyn to-day you will find signs "For Sale or To Rent." You must let your property go for the mortgages upon it, because we have certain taxes to meet and somebody must pay them. Nothing could be worse. The will of the people was in favor of consolidation, and it should be carried out. If the question of consolidation was resubmitted, I am sure there would be a still greater majority in favor of consolidation. I believe 75 per cent. of the people are in favor of consolidation.

I desire to present the following petition in favor of consolidation, signed by all of the banks in Brooklyn except three.

A Voice:

May I ask whether that document was signed by the stockholders of the various banks before the signatures of the bank officers were attached?

Mr. Jenkins:

I think the stockholders authorized it.

Mr. Lexow:

Do I understand you to say that from your knowledge of the situation 75 per cent. of the voters are in favor of consolidation?

Mr. Jenkins:

I speak for the eastern district. In the great population of that district I think 75 per cent. of the voters are in favor of consolidation.

Mr. Lexow:

What percentage of the Brooklyn financial institutions does this petition comprise?

Mr. Jenkins:

I should say all but two or three — the Nassau, the City and the National.

Mr. Lexow:

Was your petition presented to those banks?

Mr. Jenkins:

The petition was circulated.

Mr. Lexow:

Signature was refused?

Mr. Jenkins:

The president of one of the banks said he was personally in favor of consolidation, but that he would rather not sign, as he did not want to bring the bank into the matter at all. I believe the other banks have signed a petition in opposition.

MR. BRUSH:

Are you certain that this petition was signed by all but three or four of the banking institutions?

MR. JENKINS:

Yes, sir.

MR. LEXOW:

Is not the introductory of your petition taken from the bill that was introduced? A. It is taken from the bill now being considered.

MR. BRUSH:

Don't the people in Brooklyn who are favoring consolidation want a prior ascertainment of the terms of consolidation further than this bill goes?

MR. JENKINS:

I could not answer that question. These things, like water, will find their own level and adjust their own difficulties.

MR. LEXOW:

If the consolidationists will take one more speaker for to-day, then each side will have been represented by the same number of speakers; and the same order will be followed to-morrow. Those who appear to-morrow morning before this committee will be expected to answer the arguments of those who spoke in favor of consolidation this afternoon, and in the afternoon those who favor consolidation will be expected to answer the arguments made by the opposition in the forenoon. I desire to announce that the session of to-morrow will be held in Part V of the Supreme Court, room 23, in the court-house.

The following is a copy of the petition, presented by Mr. Jenkins:

BROOKLYN, N. Y. *January* 15, 1896.

To His Excellency, the Governor, and the Legislature of the State of New York:

The undersigned bankers of the city of Brooklyn respectfully urge the passage of a bill consolidating Brooklyn city with New York city, providing among other things, for attaining an equal and uniform rate of taxation and uniform valuations for the purpose of taxation:

Felix Campbell, President People's Trust Company.

C. T. Christenoon, President Brooklyn Trust Company.

S. B. Dutcher, President Hamilton Trust Company.

G. W. White, President Mechanics' Bank.

M. H. Hazzard, President Fulton Bank.

Julian D. Fairchild, President Kings County Trust Company.

B. M. Maloy, Vice-President Title Guarantee and Trust Company.

W. H. Palmer, Cashier Schermerhorn Bank.

M. S. Sprague, President Sprague National Bank.

James T. Ashley, Cashier Union Bank of Brooklyn.

Howard M. Smith, Vice-President Bedford Bank.

John Loughran, President M. F. R. S. Bank.

J. G. Jenkins, First National Bank, Brooklyn.

Charles A. Sackett, North Side Bank, Brooklyn.

Ditmas Jewell, President Twenty-sixth Ward Bank.

James Gascoine, President People's Bank of Brooklyn.

John C. Kelley, President Eighth Ward Bank of Brooklyn.

N. A. Conklin, Hamilton Bank of Brooklyn.

MARSHALL S. DRIGGS:

Mr. Chairman and Gentlemen of the Committee: In politics I am a Democrat; in religion I am a believer in the survival of the fittest. I have resided in the city of Brooklyn for forty-eight years, and as an old Brooklynite I feel a patriotic interest in all matters which concern her social advancement. I believe great good can come by uniting in one great municipality these two great cities and making it the Empire City of the Nation. In the city of Williamsburgh we had a population of about 50,000, and you could pass from one boundary to another in a few hours. It had a mayor and an official family, a board of aldermen, devoted to business and public duty; it became important to do something to improve the condition of the city of Williamsburgh, and we did so by getting the city out of debt. When the subject of consolidation was under discussion there were certain influential gentlemen, loyal citizens of Williamsburgh, who were fearful that taxation would not be properly adjusted; that they would lose their identity. They feared that they were about to engage in the painful process of absorption, but the union was effected, the marriage was consummated, and it turned out a very important and a very prosperous one. Now we furnish you a mayor, district attorney, a corporation counsel and a fire commissioner, and a new bridge commissioner, and almost everybody who is anybody in power and influence in the city of Brooklyn comes from the splendid old city of Williamsburgh.

In conclusion, I pray that you and your committee may recommend such legislation as will raise this proud city out of the dust and consolidate it with the magnificent city of New York, and thus place it on the roll as the greatest city on the earth.

MR. GEORGE W. WINGATE:

Mr. Chairman and Gentlemen of the Committee: I do not propose to make anything in the nature of a speech. I am not here for that purpose. I am not here as a paid attorney. I am simply here to represent myself. I have certain interests to represent, but in representing myself and in representing my own personal interests in certain things, I am satisfied that I represent a very large number of my associates in the city of Brooklyn. I come here as a convert, because, when the original question of annexation to New York was brought up I was opposed to it. I have studied fully both the arguments which have been made against it by the newspapers and by those who have spoken for and against consolidation before your committee. Many arguments have been considered here; some of them have no merit at all; I was of the opinion — and I retained that opinion for some considerable time that consolidation was not a wise thing for the city of Brooklyn. But after deliberation and reflection and after conversing with those who are interested in different branches of business and in my associations with bank presidents and the official trust companies; association with gentlemen who are connected with mercantile matters, and conversations had with people who are the best authorities on real estate, and my own observations and my own business relations, have convinced me that consolidation is not only a good thing but an indispensable thing for the future prosperity of Brooklyn. To-day, Mr. Chairman, as has been said, it is practically impossible to get New York capitalists to loan one single cent of money on Brooklyn property. To-day with the Brooklyn capitalists who loan money in Brooklyn, it is practically impossible for you to foreclose a mortgage and get anything like what the property is worth. I have in my office at the present time, property which has been covered by a mortgage for twenty years, which was based upon valuations made in good faith by the best real estate experts in the city of New York. The money belongs to infants and I have been withholding the property for eighteen months simply because the infants are not able to protect themselves, and I do not want to sacrifice the property for $15,000. If the city of New York and Brooklyn are annexed under the bill — and mark you I am only discussing the bill which is here before you — this bill which annexes upon equal taxation and upon equal valuation, nothing else — if Brooklyn is annexed under this bill we will prosper. My judgment is that the arguments which are made to-day against consolidation are simply based upon the theory that we are not to be annexed upon equal taxation. I am confident that seventy-five per cent. of the people who have any interest in the prosperity of the city of Brooklyn are in favor of this bill.

MR. LEXOW:

You have read the bill.

MR. WINGATE:

Yes, sir.

MR. LEXOW:

You have considered the items and the points that you made, and the bill is satisfactory to you?

MR. WINGATE:

Yes, sir. My judgment is that it is impossible to frame a bill which when complete will be satisfactory to all the citizens, but I think the idea contained in the bill is a sound one — to say first that we will be annexed under a uniform system of taxation, and then let the Legislature look after administration matters, such as police and health, the cleaning of streets and the building of sewers. In this way consolidation can be effected and decided and put into operation in proper form. If you undertake to make a general charter you will be sure to have antagonism.

MR. LEXOW:

Several of the candidates that were before the people last fall stated in their platform, as I understand it, that consolidation was inevitable, but that they were nevertheless in favor of resubmission, is that true?

MR. WINGATE:

Yes, sir; that is true.

MR. LEXOW:

If it is inevitable, why should there be resubmission?

MR. WINGATE:

A good reason for it is this, the anti-consolidationists have a compact and strong organization. They were prepared to deliver or make votes for or against any candidate who might be in favor or them. The consolidationsists were not organized, and held out no threat. They would vote for a man even if he did say he was in favor of resubmission; that is why they are in favor of consolidation, and having made that pledge they are willing to stand by it. The idea of resubmission is a perfect farce. We have no referendum in this country like Switzerland. This idea that a bill of a political nature must necessarily be submitted to the people is absurd. This question was carefully considered by the people of Brooklyn and the territory that voted upon it, and their wishes ought to be enacted into law. The matter was thoroughly discussed and was carried. If that does not settle the question what is the use of having any election.

Dr. Brush:

I would like to ask the speaker whether the original city of Brooklyn gave the majority in favor of consolidation or whether it was Gravesend and other towns that gave the majority in favor of consolidation?

Mr. Wingate:

My impression is that Senator Brush is right. That it was the votes of the county towns that made up the majority in favor of consolidation. I am simply speaking from recollection.

Mr. Lexow:

I ask whether or not the city as it existed at the time of the bill was passed did not give a majority in favor of consolidation.

Mr. Wingate:

It is a fact that it did give a majority of some 1,034; whatever fact Senator Brush states must be correct; that the majority of 1,034 was against consolidation. The county towns to-day are in the city of Brooklyn and their vote is just as important as that of any other ward in the city of Brooklyn. I am heartily in favor of consolidation.

Court House, Brooklyn, *January* 18, 1896, 11 a. m.

Arguments in Favor of Consolidation.

Mr. Lexow:

Instead of holding two sessions to-day we will have one continuous session of four hours, two hours to each side. My attention has been called to the fact that a communication which came to the chairman of the committee yesterday was not made public. I find a letter addressed to me as chairman of this committee in print, in this morning's paper, signed by William C. Bryant. I purposely withheld that letter both from publication and from mention because it has exclusively to do with the political side of this question and I take it that the question of politics will not enter into the consideration of a question of this great importance — one that so deeply concerns the people; and that neither Republican or Democratic policy would be considered, but that the good of the people of the cities, alone, would enter into our consideration of this question. It was for that reason that I did not publish the letter.

The following is a copy of the letter above referred to:

January 17, 1896.

To Hon. Clarence E. Lexow and Gentlemen of the Committee:

I regret exceedingly that a most urgent business engagement at the very hour at which you are to meet prevents my being present at your hearing, but that my voice may not be entirely unheard I take this method of presenting briefly my views on the subject of consolidation of the cities of New York and Brooklyn.

I shall not waste your time by going over the arguments that others who will be present can more effectually lay before you, but as a Republican, desirous of the continued success of my party in city, state and national elections, I say to you that if consolidation is brought about without referring the matter to the citizens of Brooklyn, the party guilty of such legislation may expect and will receive such a condemnation at the polls at the next election as will seriously affect the chances of their candidate for the presidency carrying this State.

Kings county went against Folger by upward of 45,000 majority. Governor Morton, or whoever is the standard bearer of the Republican party this year, will lose the county by over 50,000 if this unwise legislation is brought about, which, added to New York county's Democratic majority, will wipe out the Republican majorities in the other counties and give the State to the Democrats.

Very respectfully,

WILLIAM C. BRYANT.

W. C. REDFIELD:

Mr. Chairman and Gentlemen of the Committee: Understanding, unofficially, that the committee intend to hold sessions elsewhere after to-day, we beg respectfully to announce that we have present here this morning, desirous of addressing your committee, twenty-one speakers, and we respectfully ask, before we proceed for some definite knowledge as to whether further sessions will be had, and if so, when and where.

Mr. Lexow:

We have had no consultation on that subject, and we are to have no executive session of the committee until we reach Albany again. Hence, it will be impossible now for us to determine just when other hearings of the committee will be had. You better present your two hours' discussion to-day; and then we can consider in executive session how much longer, if at all, we will consider this question in Brooklyn.

Mr. Redfield:

It is upon the words "if at all" that I desire to place some emphasis. I understood the chairman to say that there would be no time limit and that everybody would have the fullest opportunity to be heard. I claim, on behalf of the citizens who favor resubmission, that everybody who desires to speak should be given an opportunity, and I ask that for the other side also. (Applause.)

Mr. Lexow:

The sergeant-at-arms will see that no further demonstrations are heard in this room. They are not going to affect the judgment of the committee. The sergeant-at-arms will see that this order is obeyed.

Mr. Redfield:

Are we to understand that the question as to whether we shall all be allowed to speak is to be left undetermined?

Mr. Lexow:

Certainly. There is no objection to you all being allowed to speak before this committee. I believe that the judgment of the committee is to give the fullest and fairest hearing; you will understand, however, that there are limits upon endurance and time; that we have our duties to perform at Albany, not only with reference to this legislation, but also with reference to general legislation. And this matter must be considered in connection with those. We have given special prominence to this question and propose to devote as much time as possible to it. I can readily see that those opposed to the passage of the bill or any legislation upon this question might readily marshal 10,000 speakers before this committee and absolutely prevent the determination of any question at this session of the Legislature. This question must be determined one way or another, and I believe that it is the judgment of the committee that the legal principles applicable to expert testimony should be introduced here and that each side should have as many speakers as the other, so that absolute equality shall exist in that sense and after hearing the arguments we will then endeavor to ascertain the true sentiment of Brooklyn on the question.

MR. REDFIELD:

Relying upon the statement of the chairman, yesterday, that full time would be given to everybody, I desire officially, to file with this committee the names of the following gentlemen who here appear before this committee and claim the right to be heard. I will read the names and request that the official stenographer take them down.

MR. LEXOW:

The chair announced as the decision of the committee, yesterday, that each side should have two hours to-day. If, instead of taking the two hours of time to-day in discussing the merits of the proposition before this committee you desire to waste the time of this committee in putting upon record something that is not going to appeal to our judgment you will have to take that time from the time allowed to your side.

MR. REDFIELD:

Does the committee refuse to have the names inserted?

MR. LEXOW:

You can do that after your two hours have expired.

MR. REDFIELD:

I hand the list of names to the stenographer for insertion here.

John S. McKeon.	Franklin Woodruff.
Dr. T. J. Backus.	S. L. Woodhouse.
Charles A. Moore.	S. V. White.
Frederick E. Crane.	Dr. Robert Boocock.
William C. Redfield.	Judge D. G. Harriman.
Superintendent Maxwell.	W. J. Coombs.
Henry Hentz.	A. G. McDonald.
George W. Mead.	C. C. Skilton.

MR. DYKMAN:

Mr. Chairman and Gentlemen of the Committee: I have spoken before the chairman and some members of the committee before. The circumstances have changed, largely changed, since then. That may be my excuse for speaking again. The organization of which I am a member is as much opposed to the bill of this year as it was to the bill of last year. If the limits of time allow, I shall undertake to criticise some of the details of the bill. I should like to ask the gentleman who drew the bill what is to be the situation of the officers of the towns of Richmond county under this legislation. Are the towns of Richmond county to be consolidated and to go out of existence? And if they are, as they would seem to be under this bill, merged in a greater New York, what have you left of Richmond county? Many questions of that kind have occurred to me, but they are of least importance in comparison with the other questions to which I shall address myself.

MR. LEXOW:

You just made the statement that you were prepared to criticise that bill. I noticed yesterday that none of the speakers criticised that bill itself — none of the arguments were addressed to the merits of the bill.

MR. DYKMAN:

It is far easier to point out the demerits of the bill, and I am going to try and do it. We are opposed to the bill, because in the first section we are made to make a leap into the future without knowing where we are going. We are made to take a leap in the dark such as no community, certainly no city in this State, ever took before in our history. It is enacted that we shall be consolidated on the 1st day of January, 1898 — consolidated in a way to be left to the discretion of a gentleman whom we all honor, but who is at the point of death or nearing his end — to a gentleman who deals in vacant lots in East New York, and to some other gentlemen. No matter what comes from their brains, no matter what may be their wisdom or unwisdom, no matter whether they keep their promise as we hope they will, or break their promise as we know they have, is it right to take this community of over a million inhabitants and consolidate it with the city of New York without our knowing something about their plans? Ought we not to know now what they have in their brains? No one ever heard of such a proposition before. Why should we not know what they intend to do. What is their excuse? The chairman says there is a sentiment. There is no sentiment of that kind there. These gentlemen love sentiment. There is no sentiment in Mr. Chauncey or in the other gentlemen who are pushing this measure of consolidation. They are dealing in facts. They are not dealing in sentiment. We are opposed to the first section of the bill because it deprives us of our existence, but when you read the second and the fifth section there is no force to extract from the first section. Those sections contain the sting and venom that is in the bill. It provides that Mr. Green and these gentlemen shall have office and money to carry on their work. That is all there is in the bill. We ask you in the first place, if it is your proposition to entrust our municipality to Mr. Green and Mr. Stranhan to wipe us out under the first section of the bill. Why, sir, these gentlemen who drew this bill promised us in a pamphlet which they issued on the eve of election — and the League of Loyal Citizens has had it reprinted in order that no one shall mistake the promises that were made on the eve of election and what they said we have had put in red type — we have red-lettered it that every one may read what we voted for. This bill is not what we voted for. I read from Mr. Green's pamphlet, "If every ballot in every city and town were cast in favor of consolidation there would be no finalty about it. No consolidation would result until further action by the Legislature prescribed the terms and conditions. I say these gentlemen have been false, false as ever men could be — in handing this bill to us after making those promises. Your judgment may approve of the bill and no one can criticise it. No one does criticise you, but I am speaking for the interests of Brooklyn and her destiny. This commission made a solemn promise and now make haste to break that promise if ever man broke a promise in the world. This first section of the bill does exactly what they promised should not be done. Why should we trust them again. Shall we enact that in 1898 there shall be consolidation when everybody admits that all we know on the subject is that it is full of the most profound questions, when we are confronted with difficulties greater than ever man assumed to face. No problem like this ever before confronted a Legislature. Every man who has even thought over the seriousness of the question is appalled by the magnitude of its difficulties and will you enact the first section no matter what the difficulties are? Must we accept what this commission gives us? Is that good consolidation? Did you ever in your experience know of even a little question being treated as this is? I have known of bills enacted to take effect at some future time, but those bills stated what was sought to be accomplished. When we changed our whole system of procedure in 1846 or 1848 it was not done in this way. There were great men, there were giants in those days, but did the Legislature entrust to Mr. Field and his associates the power to enact laws without the public knowing anything about them? Does anybody pretend that the difficulties which Mr. Field and his associates then met are to be compared with the difficulties that now stare us in the face?

MR. LEXOW:

The Legislature will have to pass upon the work of the commission and if it is not done properly the Legislature will take a hand in it themselves.

MR. DYKMAN:

Speaking of section 2; there comes down to us in Brooklyn remarks from Albany that we are unwilling to entrust our interests to the Legislature until we know what the Legislature is going to do. This section of the bill says there shall be bills — many of them, and among them a bill for equal taxation.

MR. LEXOW:

How are you going to legislate for any city except by bills?

MR. DYKMAN:

Of course we must legislate by bills, but we want to know what the bills are to be. We may have a police bill passed by the majority, and we may have an equal taxation bill rejected by the majority. We have been fooled by these promises, and many of my friends on this side, active and zealous citizens who love Brooklyn speaking from their heart what they believe for the advantage of Brooklyn, are fearful that you will give us a series of bills this year which we will all be opposed to. I distrust this commission and I distrust this bill. I believe this bill has in it infinite power for harm. We don't know what we are going to get, no one but the Almighty can read human hearts. We finite beings can not do it. We must judge this intended commission by what we know of them. I must judge what you men would give us, not what is promised. Our fear is founded upon the remarks that have come down to us from Albany. I say that that charter, by a series of bills, is the worst possible way of consolidating this community.

MR. LEXOW:

Is there any charter that does not consist in a series of bills?

MR. DYKMAN:

Brooklyn's charter was enacted in 1883 as a whole, and again in 1888. New York's charter was enacted as a whole.

Mr. Lexow:

When you speak as enacting as a whole was it not composed of a series of bills?

Mr. Dykman:

Yes; but the public knew something about it. How can we judge from one little piece of a charter which you may present next week, or the week after, or on March first? How can we tell whether the interest of our city will be best served by the bills which you may introduce. It may be that no matter how much we might dislike a consolidated police district I think these gentlemen would swallow it. But who in Brooklyn can say that we will have equal taxation, because Senator Lexow introduces and the majority passes a police bill? If these gentlemen mean what they say why don't they write in this bill a section providing for equal taxation. Let the first bill be a measure of equal taxation. Is there anybody bold enough to do that? Why not, why don't we hear that the first thing that will be done will be to give us a bill of equal taxation. I don't question for a moment but that these gentlemen who are in favor of consolidation in Brooklyn are for equal taxation, but the point that I am striving to make is that we have no assurance that we will be given an equal tax rate. Why give us the police and other bills without first enacting a bill for equal taxation? We do not want the police and other bills this year and then be left struggling for the benefits of consolidation in the future. That seems to be the purpose of this bill.

There has been introduced by Dr. Brush another bill and the vital principle of that is resubmission. That bill provides for a final determination of the question. I undertake to say, sir, and I have had something to do with the preparation of this bill and after consultation with very eminent lawyers, I am prepared to say that under the decision of the Court of Appeals and under the Constitution of the State of New York, we can make that question final so far as the vote of the people and the voice of the people is a finalty, an absolute determination as to whether any further steps shall be taken under that bill.

MR. LEXOW:

That is all it can determine?

MR. DYKMAN:

Yes, sir.

MR. LEXOW:

It can not determine any legislative proposition.

MR. DYKMAN:

I mean to say that there may be put into this bill these words: That if the people vote no, that bill has spent its force and no further can it go. I mean to say that this proposition has been upheld by the Court of Appeals. Why are you here? Why does the committee come down to Brooklyn. I do not believe it is to go through the form and procedure of giving somebody at this end a chance to speak before his head comes off. I do not think that it is a mere courtesy. I think that you are trying to find out what Brooklyn sentiment is. It cannot be done here. It can not be done in this room. It can not be found in the heat and passion of debate. I recall the words of Garfield in a Republican convention when he warned the delegates of the Republican party that not in the heat and strife of debate in that convention would the questions at issue be settled, but in the quiet and still of a November day, and then only could the question be settled.

We have asked that this question be settled. What stands in the way of it? I say, sir, and I answered the question that you put yesterday, "Why do you want resubmission; do you want to consolidation?" For myself, I want resubmission to kill consolidation, and I believe resubmission will kill it. I believe the vote will be adverse by a large majority, but if it shall not be adverse why then we will all join Tammany Hall and try to bring her future rulers up to the Brooklyn standpoint. I believe it will kill consolidation. But if we are in the end to be governed by New York we will try and raise her rulers to our Brooklyn standard. The vote of 1894 is not an expression of the opinon of Brooklyn to-day. I do not believe that we should be consolidated in 1896 when we are not in favor of it. But you argue that we are in favor of it to-day because we were in 1894. I understand that to be your argument.

MR. LEXOW:

That is not the argument. The situation shifts the burden of proof, and you will have to satisfy us beyond peradventure that that sentiment has changed so that it may not be regarded as a finality.

MR. DYKMAN:

I confess that I do not believe that any approval can be absolutely final except by the passage of this bill. You can have a vote on that bill and ascertain the sentiment in two months, if you are honestly desirous of settling the question. You can not ascertain it from the hundreds that come here out of mere curiosity, but by the silent 1,000,000 people alone. They can settle this question. Give us a chance to discuss the question in every fireside and in every home in Brooklyn, and then you will have a determination that you can not get otherwise. If you refuse us that, you are not, I submit, desirous of learning what Brooklyn wants, and of getting a full expression of Brooklyn's opinion. You can not get it otherwise. I can tell you that my friends have changed. I can tell you that I prefer to take the vote of last fall, which shows that almost without exception every member of the Legislature from this city is against this bill. Is that not a change in public sentiment? Why, in the year 1894 we did not know what Mr. White, our commissioner of public works, could accomplish. We did not know that there was in Brooklyn the power that has proved to be in Brooklyn, and that has changed the mayor, who was in favor of consolidation. It has changed the opinion of the commissioner. The new mayor which comes in is against your bill. The new fire commissioner has written a letter that you said something about this morning. The old corporation counsel is against the bill. The new corporation counsel is against the bill. All of the Assemblymen, all of the Senators, the whole board of aldermen; and I ask you, also, to consider the

League of Loyal Citizens, and the work they have done, which was started and almost wholly sustained by my friend Low, and contrast those with the people who are against consolidation.

MR. LEXOW:

You do not dispute the general political proposition that a small, compact, aggressive opposition will coerce many men into assenting to at least some part of their platform, in order that they may be in a position to defeat the main proposition at the polls.

MR. DYKMAN:

But if you find every member of the Legislature, if you find every member of Assembly and every member of the Senate, if you find the mayor and his cabinet, if you find the leaders of public thought in the city of Brooklyn against the bill, it might at least be sufficient evidence that they want another chance to vote.

MR. LEXOW:

Without reflecting upon them, is it not a fact that they have a peculiar interest in preserving the city as it is,because they are officeholders under the present government.

MR. DYKMAN:

Is Mayor Schieren an officeholder? Will not Mayor Wurster be out of office before this bill takes effect?

MR. LEXOW:

Did not ex-Mayor Schieren say that consolidation was inevitable?

MR. DYKMAN:

I think he did.

MR. LEXOW:

If it is inevitable, why not have it now?

Mr. Dykman:

I do not think it is inevitable. I think if it were not for the exigencies of the politics of to-day there would be no sentiment in favor of consolidation. I do not yield to your proposition that there is a large sentiment in favor of consolidation. As long as there is such a dividing line as the East river between New York and Brooklyn, consolidation is not inevitable.

Mr. Lexow:

How can you criticize the bill as being political, when the author of it is a Democrat in the city of New York, Mr. Green, and when the drafter of the bill is one of the Democratic police commissioners of the city of New York, how can you then question that it has any political bearing?

Mr. Dykman:

We do not know the intricacies of New York politics here. We find strange alliances in New York city, and it is impossible for us in Brooklyn to tell just what the politics of a man are when he is drafting bills that provide offices.

Mr. Lexow:

But your criticism was that everybody might be legislated out of office.

Mr. Dykman:

I don't know the gentleman that drafted the bill.

Mr. Lexow:

Police Commissioner Parker, of New York, is the drafter of the bill.

Mr. Dykman:

I understand that Mr. Parker stays in office until the 1st of January, 1898; he is not legislated out of office.

Mr. Lexow:

You said that some remarks that had come to you from Albany had caused you to take this position?

MR. DYKMAN:

It may be that my friend Parker is abundantly provided for in the measure that is in the chairman's brain.

MR. LEXOW:

What assurance have we that you will not be standing before some legislative committee in 1897, making the same arguments for resubmission that you are making to-day, if we finally conclude to resubmit this question to the people?

MR. DYKMAN:

The answer must be found in the bill that I have something to do in drafting, and if the verdict of the people should be in favor of that bill, the League of Loyal Citizens — all of us — would abide by the verdict. If the vote is aye, and the commission is to be at once appointed by the Governor to draft a bill, all right. We pledge ourselves as good citizens to help make a charter — the best possible charter — if the vote of this locality shall favor consolidation.

MR. LEXOW:

Is that not practicable under the provisions of the bill that was voted upon in 1894?

MR. DYKMAN:

I hope the chairman will not subtract the time allotted to me, the time he occupies; the chairman might use up the whole time of the opposition.

MR. GRADY:

Whom do you represent when you say, "We pledge ourselves?"

MR. DYKMAN:

I speak for the League of Loyal Citizens. I have heard them say that if the vote shall be in favor of consolidation that they will pledge their best work to the framing of the charter to be drawn. Our conditions since 1894 have changed. We have a new constitution. We have a new city boundary. We have abolished the board of supervisors. We have a ten per cent. limit of debt; we did not have that in 1894. We did not vote under this condition of affairs in 1894; that changed condition, it seems to me, sufficient to justify our demand that we be given another opportunity to vote as Brooklyn is to-day.

MR. LEXOW:

Is it not the fact that the 10 per cent limitation is a trouble in Brooklyn to-day — that you cannot make the necessary improvements and that there is no money with which to make improvements?

MR. DYKMAN:

You have heard Mr. White, the commissioner of public works. I do not pretend to answer that question. I believe that Brooklyn can make all the necessary improvements.

A VOICE:

Do you represent the Brooklyn Eagle? I understand that the gentleman is counsel for the Brooklyn Eagle.

MR. LEXOW:

I do not think that any personal allusions are in order.

MR. DYKMAN:

I have many clients in Brooklyn and I find among them an overwhelming majority opposed to consolidation.

JOSEPH R. CLARK:

Mr. Chairman and Gentlemen of the Committee: I am going to speak as a politician this morning, and as an officeholder who does not desire to be turned out of office as was spoken of yesterday. The gentleman making the remark is an ex-official himself, and perhaps he is in favor of consolidation, because he expects to be returned to office under the greater city. I want to call the attention of the committee as a man who has been identified with the city government as an officeholder to the fact that politicians are natural cowards, in that they do not want to do anything that the people are alarmed at in order that they may be retained in their position. I do not, and I do not think the Greater New York would have that effect as there would still be politicians. Two years ago when this vote was taken what was the object of the politicians in this city? I said to all in my district to make sure and vote everything so that we would get a new constitution, which would make the State of New York Republican for some time to come, it is because of that reason that so many voted in favor of consolidation two years ago; and it is for that reason that I speak here this morning in favor of resubmission. At that time our party was desirous of putting through everything and were anxious that no votes should go astray, and the Republicans in the different districts were asked to vote everything. Since that time what has been the result in the city of Brooklyn? A great many people who voted at that time now feel that they would be better off than if they were joined to New York and Tammany Hall.

MR. LEXOW:

How do you account for the fact that 22,000 more votes were cast for consolidation than on the constitutional amendment?

MR. CLARK:

Because there was a body of men that were organized and determined that this thing should be carried.

MR. LEXOW:

Have you ever known in your experience as a politician — devoting your time to politics — that any proposition was ever before carried by the people in opposition to united press against it.

MR. CLARK:

I think that this case is an exception to your question.

MR. LEXOW:

Is it not astonishing?

Mr. Clark:

I don't think it is. Our district organizations simply said, go on and vote all, and they all voted for consolidation.

Mr. Lexow:

Your argument would be convincing if it were not for this difference of 22,000 votes between the constitutional amendments and consolidation. Can you explain to us how it is that with the united opposition of the press of the city of Brooklyn against this proposition that the people were able to get votes enough into the ballot box to carry the proposition?

Mr. Clark:

If you will take the results of the election of that year and study them carefully you will find that in the Republican wards at that time they received the largest amount for consolidation. Now, the situation, as I understand it, has changed. I am free to say that there was a time when I had not made up my mind, even after election. I never made any public expression of opinion on the matter, but last fall when I saw the two great parties in this city arrayed one against the other, and one candidate a pronounced consolidationist before the people as unreservedly in favor of consolidation, and the other in favor of resubmission, then I began to study the question. One of the candidates said he was in favor of resubmission, if the people wanted it, and that he would not oppose a bill of that kind if he was elected mayor. Don't this show that there was a change of sentiment after the vote of 1894 was taken? One candidate said, "Gentlemen, I am for consolidation and vote for me on that issue." The other candidate did not do that nor do I know of a single other candidate in the city of Brooklyn who took that position. Simply because they knew that there was a great feeling among the people in Brooklyn against consolidation and in favor of resubmitting this question and every one of them "ran to cover" and said, "We are for resubmission." There are twenty-eight men in the board of aldermen, sixteen Republicans and the balance Democrats, and every one are in favor of resubmission. I claim,

Mr. Chairman, coming as we do, direct from the people, that we ought to know something as to the sentiment of the people in our respective districts on this question, and knowing their desires and their wishes, we take this position in favor of the bill, resubmitting this question to them. I think that that should have some weight with this committee in determining this question. The people should be given another opportunity to vote, and then you can see if there is any change of opinion on this question. I believe that there is a very great change. I believe it would be a great wrong for the Republican Senate to assume to pass a bill which will annex the city of Brooklyn to the city of New York without once more giving the people a chance to express themselves on this question.

MR. REDFIELD:

The following resolutions have just been handed to me, and I desire their insertion in the record of your committee.

MR. REDFIELD:

A gentleman appeared here this morning intending to address your committee, but illness preventing he requested me to present to your committee the communication which I now read. I desire that it be made a part of your record:

At a regular meeting of the Brooklyn Republican Club, held at its club-house No. 146 Pierpont street, Brooklyn, on January 16, 1896, the following resolution was unanimously adopted:

Resolved, That it is the sense of this club that the best interests of this city will be subserved by giving its citizens an opportunity to fully discuss this great question of consolidation that it may be intelligently voted upon, and that the question be again submitted to the people.

WM. L. GERRISH,
President.

WM. H. WELWOOD,
Recording Secretary.

Copy of resolution adopted at a meeting of the citizens of Brooklyn, held in the Art building, January 7, 1896:

WHEREAS, Several bills have been and are being prepared for introduction in the present session of the Legislature of New

York, the purposes of which are to seriously modify, abridge and supplant the present charter of the city of Brooklyn and existing laws affecting the public interests of the city; therefore,

Resolved, That it is the sense of this meeting that whatever legislation is proposed, no law should be enacted which will deprive the people of Brooklyn of the right to determine by popular vote whether they will accept or reject any charter or other measure which shall be intended to replace the present charter, or terminate in any way the corporate existence of the city of Brooklyn.

Adopted by unanimous consent.

Among those present at the meeting were:

Ex-Mayor Charles A. Schieren, *Chairman.*

Ex-Mayor David A. Boody.	Rev. Dr. Richard S. Storrs.
Hon. John Winslow.	George Foster Peabody.
Henry K. Sheldon,	Elijah Kennedy.
Henry Hentz.	Hon. W. J. Coombs.
Isaac H. Cary.	Janes D. Bell.
Prof. Franklin W. Hooper.	Robert D. Benedict.
A. D. Wheelock.	S. L. Woodhouse.
Henry D. Atwater.	Henry W. Maxwell.

Henry Sanger Snow, *Secretary.*

---

80 Pierpont Street, Brooklyn. N. Y.,
January 18, 1896.

Hon. Geo. W. Brush, M. D.:

My Dear Sir.— I thank you for your kind suggestion that I present my views on the urgent question of resubmission to the Legislative committee now in session in this city. I have earnestly desired to do so to-day, but a serious and threatening cold confines me to my house, and forbids me to meet the committee. I can not forbear, however, to call your attention and that of the committee, to one fact pertinent to your inquiry, which seems of quite controlling importance.

The people of Brooklyn, whom I meet, and I meet them familiarly and widely, do not accept the opportunity which they had in 1894, of expressing their opinion and feeling in regard to consolidation with New York as having had a fair opportunity, no general discussion having preceded it. Even the gravity of the question being at that time but vaguely apprehended. Whether they are right or wrong in the feeling need not now be debated. With my knowledge of the confusing circumstances attending the expression at the ballot-boxes at that time, I think that they are right. That a large majority of them are agreed in the feeling, I have no doubt whatever. Many of those who favor consolidation openly declare or freely concede it.

It is this general and very strong feeling which your committee will decisively antagonize if you fail to recommend a resubmission of the preliminary question to a popular vote in this city, before further legislative action is taken. How the majority may turn on that vote, "for consolidation" or "against consolidation," I have no other means of judging than are open to all. I have never, myself, been finally committed against consolidation, though expressing my preference against it fourteen months ago, because, feeling the need of further information and the generally lax maxim, quieta non —. But at the same time that I appreciate some arguments for it, perhaps more fully than they, I sympathise earnestly, even intensely, with the vast number of our citizens — I am sure the great majority of our voting citizens — who insist that our city rights shall not be taken from us without our previous deliberate consent. The Legislature may do many things which we shall regret, but not passionately resent, but if it strikes our city pride full in the face by treating us as a community not capable of maturing our thoughts, or intelligently expressing them on a question which involves the life of the city, it seems to me as certain as are the processes of nature, that a detonation force will here be evolved, before which parties will be shattered and political plans be overwhelmed to an extent not probably fully expected. We, who have lived in Brooklyn for half a century, who have seen it growing in that period four times as fast as New York, with a more homogeneous population, who have done whatever we could to make it noble and beautiful, and to set it forth before other cities of the land as an example of wise and wholesome life and government, can hardly be expected to contemplate with equanimity any action at Albany, which shall propose to strike it from the list of American cities, without its own previous decisive assent. Thanking you again for your courtesy, I am

Very truly and respectfully yours.

(Signed) RICHARD S. STORRS.

Rev. Dr. Cuyler:

Mr. Chairman and Members of the Committee: My remarks will be very brief. I understand that the issue now is clearly joined between a proposal for resubmission and a proposal to proceed to active and aggressive steps for the consolidation of the two cities. As you know, nearly two years ago, we, the people of Brooklyn, were allowed to express an opinon. Sixty-four thousand of our voters expressed a preference for consolidation. Sixty-four thousand expressed an opinion in opposition to consolidation. Therefore, for all the moral purposes for ascertaining public sentiment, it was practically a tie, a drawn battle. To-day there are 200,000 legal voters in the city of Brooklyn, 200,000 citizens demanding the right to be heard on this question, and it is a piece of sublime audacity to claim that the opinion of 64,000 people expressed nearly two years ago is a binding mandate upon 200,000 before the Legislature of the State of New York. This simple, solid fact, sir, is a good argument for fair dealing and justice and the right of resubmission. The more you look at the other proposition, the proposition that I think means to enforce consolidation without the privilege of being heard, the more practicable the difficulties become and the more rapidly they accumulate. Why, gentlemen, it can not be impressed upon you too strongly that to-day Brooklyn is a homogeneous city, happy and contented, thank God. At the other end of the bridge is a city largely agitated with serious questions of local government, and that agitation is not likely to end soon. An attempt to combine these two cities would only produce a heterogeneous and discordant mixture. What can a man that lives in Flatbush or Jamaica know about the interests of the people about the Harlem? What municipal relation is there between the residents of

Staten Island and the residents of Green Point? The more you increase the dimensions of a great city the more you decrease the probability for wise, thorough and honest municipal government. Every city must have a head. You know that it taxes all the time and all the mental powers of one of our best citizens to be mayor of Brooklyn. There is a still heavier strain on the mayor of New York city. What must be the physical strength and mental equipment of the man who asumes the colossal task of governing a colossal city thirty-one miles in length and twenty miles wide with three or four millions of people soon to become five millions. This would be a great risk and a very doubtful experiment. If in fairness consolidation is to be perpetrated endless confusion will arise, I suppose that the new consolidated, confabulated, concatenated, conglomeration will be called New York. But for all purposes of distinction this side of the river will be called Brooklyn, and we shall have the hollow memory of a name instead of the precious right of self-government. And more than that many of the streets and avenues of the two cities are of the same name and after consolidation comes the confusion will be great, but we will never give up our grand old historic name of Fulton, of Washington, of Madison, Lincoln, and Jefferson. Finally, after the vast array of arguments that were presented yesterday, I solemnly assert that the strongest argument of all is the argument founded on the loyal love of the people of Brooklyn, the love of their firesides and their homes, the buried ashes of their fathers and the peace of their children. You may call it sentiment. I would have you know that the world is ruled by sentiment, your mother's love is sentiment, noble sentiments make noble works. Behind me stands the great army of Brooklynites that are speaking through humble lips this morning, with heart cords bound fast to this beauiful and beloved city, protesting against any rash and reckless proposal to assassinate Brooklyn. To protest against the destruction of our organic and civic life—a destruction which would be before Heaven a monstrous crime of civic assassination. Therefore, gentlemen, I have in a few words given a few of the arguments against the monstrous crime, and, sir, woe be to the political leader of any party that has our blood upon his hands.

Mr. Redfield:

It was asserted here yesterday that the opposition to consolidation comes from around the Heighths. I call your attention to the fact that no speaker who addressed the committee this morning comes from that district, and that very few of the speakers that addressed you yesterday were from that district.

William Cullen Bryant:

Mr. Chairman and Gentlemen of the Committee: It is not my purpose to go into any lengthy argument on the pros and cons of the bill before you. If I am correctly informed, there were three gentlemen here yesterday, claiming to represent the sentiment of the eastern district of the city of Brooklyn. It may not be out of the way for me to say that, if I have been correctly informed, that neither of the three gentlemen live in the eastern district. I think I may say with propriety and without egotism that I may come here as a representative of that section of the city, on the theory that a burnt child fears the fire. I may say to you, so far as my knowledge goes, that the sentiment of that district is decidedly against consolidation. On my way to the office this morning, for the purpose of getting the sentiment on this question, I took occasion to speak to every man with whom I had even a passing acquaintance. I must say that before speaking to them, I never heard any expression of opinion from them in regard to their position on this matter. Altogether, I spoke to ten persons. The result was as follows: Of the ten, eight were against consolidation, the other two were for it, each as positive on one side as the other. Without any desire to drag politics into the question at all, I may say that the two who favored consolidation were Democrats.

Mr. Brush:

You live in the eastern district, and you know something of the sentiment of that district?

Mr. Bryant:

Yes, sir.

MR. BRUSH:

Was the statement that was made yesterday by some of the gentlemen present, that 75 per cent. of the people in the eastern district were in favor of consolidation, a correct statement?

MR. BRYANT:

If they had placed the question the other way, I should say they were correct. I think that fully 75 per cent. of the people in the eastern district are against consolidation.

MR. REDFIELD:

It was stated in your presence yesterday that the voters of the eastern district were 75 per cent. in favor of consolidation. The wards composing the eastern district cast 10,500 votes in favor of consolidation. I offer, Mr. Chairman, to produce to this committee the original signatures of 16,000 citizens of the eastern district wards who are in favor of resubmission; and I offer to produce with them, before this committee, the registration rolls of 1895 for the purpose of comparison.

MR. LEXOW:

You can put in evidence any papers you desire.

MR. BRUSH:

I authorize you to turn over to this committee the enrolled signatures of the wards composing the old city of Williamsburgh.

MR. LEXOW:

Do you mean those that were presented to the Senate?

MR. BRUSH:

Yes, sir. They are now in the possession of the Senate.

MR. REDFIELD:

I desire to say, concerning this, that it contains 6,000 more voters in Williamsburgh than favored consolidation in 1894. It is made up by wards and election districts, and it will be easy for you to have a comparison made with the registration-rolls which we have filed, and we would respectfully request that such comparison be made.

George H. Roberts:

Mr. Chairman and Gentlemen of the Committee: As the newly-elected chairman of the county organization of the Republican party of Kings county, I wish to bear the testimony that it is my humble opinion that at least 90 per cent. of that committee are against consolidation. Personally, I am one of those who opposed consolidation from the start. I voted against it. I plead now for resubmission. The city proper did not vote for consolidation. The bare 277 majority that you had in the county was obtained from a section of our city that had recently been annexed. There was 192,000 registered. Over 73,000 did not vote on the question at all. Now, Mr. Chairman, I simply come here to bear my personal witness. I know of a district of 160 Republicans and thirty Democrats, and there are not five consolidationists in that district. I am in favor of cheap homes for Brooklyn, as strange as that assertion may be to you. In my observation of the gentlemen who are in favor of consolidation, a vast majority will take a narrow and selfish view of looking to enhance the value of property, because many of them have told me, "If you were abroad and registered from Brooklyn, the people over there would think you came from a wilderness." Such an argument has very little effect upon me.

Mr. Lexow:

Do you mean to claim that the mere fact of consolidation would enhance value?

Mr. Roberts:

They claim that. They claim that it will make the value of real estate more stable. In other words that a piece of property, the estimated value of which is $20,000 to-day will bring that price where it now goes begging. I am in the flour business in the city of New York, and I have made some observations of real estate transactions in both cities. There are sections in New York city where property is unsalable to-day, as in East New York, where it is the most depressed of any portion of the city. I believe that from all my heart; and I believe another assertion; that $10,000 judicially invested in the city of Brooklyn will yield as big an interest as the same amount of money in the city of New York. The consolidationists say that property that is now worth $10,000 will be worth $20,000 if we consolidate ourselves with New York. I do not believe that. There is nothing in the world that will enhance property unless there is a supply and demand. There has been a supply and demand for property both in New York and in Brooklyn in the past. But to-day there is no demand in either city. There is not in the United States, on account of the poliical complexion of our government. We have a city of homes. We have a beautiful city here and we want to retain its political automony. It has been said that there are no politics in this question, but it has its political side. It is the opinion of hundreds of Republicans that are taking an active interest, as every Christian man should, in the welfare of his government, that if we are annexed to the city of New York that Tammany Hall influence in New York will so influence the city of Brooklyn that instead of it being a city about equally divided, it will become 25,000 to 50,000 Democratic.

MR. LEXOW:

How do you account for the fact that every Democratic representative in the Legislature from the city of Brooklyn is an anti-consolidationist?

MR. ROBERTS:

I will answer that the regular Democratic standard bearer at the last election pronounced himself a consolidationist, and on that one issue he got his vote, and my Democratic friends know it is true.

MR. LEXOW:

We have thus far conducted this investigation without bringing politics into prominence, and I think the consolidation question should be decided without reference to politics. It a question of a greater city. It is not a question of the supremacy of any political organization. I hope that the Republican party is strong enough and able enough to rise to any crisis that might be directed against it because it had done its duty to the people.

Mr. Roberts:

As an American citizen and a citizen of the city of Brooklyn, as a pronounced Republican of the radical type, I come here to you, sir, to say that higher in the interests of the Republican party is the interest of the city of Brooklyn to my heart to-day. All we ask of you, gentlemen of the Legislature, is to resubmit this question to the intelligence of the people in order that they may vote on it understandingly. In my district the issue was not understood. We are in a tremendous political strife. We had been in the minority. The issue was not fairly before the people. You can readily understand that. Let me give you a parallel. In a very few of our political meetings during the last campaign was the question of the deepening and widening of the Erie canal and the spending of $9,000,000 discussed at all. It was hardly mentioned; our average voter gave it very little attention; it was a very rare thing that the question came up before them for debate, and yet it was one of the most important issues at stake at the last election. Under this Greater New York I can not see that our taxes will be reduced or that the expense of living will be reduced and our property will not materially advance. The moral influence of the Greater New York will be depressing. We have provided, up to the present time, for all that have come here for the simple reason that we have cheap homes. A man with a small income can buy a little home here, we give him school and churches, clean streets, and we have been able to the present time to clean our own house, politically.

Mr. Redfield:

I beg to answer that question relating to real estate. I hold in my hand a pamphlet containing the names of the entire consolidation commission, issued by that body. I call your attention to page 27, "Greater New York," "Reasons Why." Signed by Edward C. Green, and bearing the imprint of the consolidation commission.

MR. LEXOW:

You do not object to a boom in Brooklyn real estate?

MR. REDFIELD:

No, sir. Some of them claim that it will increase property, and others claim that it will make it more stable.

MR. LEXOW:

The one is inconsistent with the other. If a piece of property sells under a forced sale to-day for $10,000, when it is worth $20,000, and if consolidation has the effect of keeping it at $20,000, it is practically for all business purposes an increase in the value of the property. It makes it more valuable for loaning and other purposes. Is not that true?

MR. REDFIELD:

I think it may be.

MR. LEXOW:

Do you agree with the statement made by Mr. Roberts, that at the last election, the question of consolidation made up the votes given to the candidate who was defeated?

MR. REDFIELD:

I am greatly indebted to you for asking that question. I read an advertisement from the Brooklyn Eagle, November 7, 1895, signed by the Consolidation League of Brooklyn: "The only way to express an opinion on the question of consolidation is to vote for Edward M. Grout for mayor." In the aggregate total he was in the minority of 12,000.

MR. LEXOW:

He was in the minority of 2,000?

Mr. Redfield:

No, sir; not in the total vote for mayor.

Mr. Lexow:

The successful candidate received only 2,000 more votes.

Mr. Redfield:

There were three candidates for mayor; Republican, Independent Democrat and Regular Democrat. The Republican and Independent Democrat both favored openly over their signatures a resubmission of the matter to the people before final determination. Those two men had together united as they were on that question, a majority in the total of 12,000 over the man who was openly supported by the consolidation league. Mr. Wurster, the Republican candidate was elected a member of the executive committee at the league meeting, and he is a loyal friend of Brooklyn. He is in favor of resubmission, and so declared himself. I call attention to the fact that of the eleven men from Brooklyn who stood by us in Albany last year six were nominated to the Senate and two went back to the Assembly, five men who favored it, four of them stayed at home.

Mr. Lexow:

Is it not a fact that prior to the election guarantees were demanded by the Loyal League?

Mr. Redfield:

I will read you the letter that we sent out: The League of Loyal Citizens desired if possible that the question of consolidation should not enter political conflicts. We never did enter the mayoralty conflict. The people of Brooklyn defeated consolidation without our help.

Mr. Lexow:

Is it not a fact, a remarkable fact, that if the issue was met on one side, that the sentiment in Brooklyn does not seem to be so unanimously against consolidation as you would have it appear yesterday? It was claimed yesterday on one side that seventy-five per cent. were in favor of consolidation; on the other it was claimed that the percentage was on the other side. Now, if you admit that consolidation entered into the vote cast for the Democratic candidate for mayor, it certainly does not show that seventy-five per cent. of the people are opposed to consolidation.

MR. REDFIELD:

It shows that on a question met by that candidate and enforced by the entire power of the Consolidation League, that in a vote where 45,000 of our citizens did not register, there was a majority against consolidation of 12,000 and over. I will furnish the committee a copy of the letter sent out by the League of Loyal Citizens.

MR. LEXOW:

Your ranks are divided into a number of factions, are they not?

MR. REDFIELD:

No, sir.

MR. LEXOW:

Some are in favor of resubmission; others are in favor of a referendum.

MR. REDFIELD:

I do not know about that; in speaking of the Loyal League, I speak of the anti-consolidation sentiment.

MR. LEXOW:

Is it not true that the league consists of two factions that are about as strongly divided between each other as are the consolidationists from the anti-consolidationists.

MR. REDFIELD:

I know of no faction that favors referendum as opposed to resubmission.

MR. LEXOW:

You don't mean to suggest that there are no people in the city of Brooklyn who take that position?

Mr. Redfield:

Some favor referendum because they say they can not get a resubmission.

Foster L. Backus:

Mr. Chairman and Gentlemen of the Committee: I do not appear here as a consolidationist or an anti-consolidationist. I do not appear here as a politician. It was stated yesterday that the poor men of Brooklyn favor consolidation. The man who made that statement is rich enough to say that "I am the thirteenth child of the forefather in one of those families that could buy the whole of our estates." If I stand for anything in the city of Brooklyn, I stand as the representative of the poor men, the workingmen, the common men, some of them who own their own homes, humble homes they may be, but they are their own homes. They are the ones who, with their wages, pay the expenses of the city; the rich do not have to pay the expenses of the governments of our cities. It may be said that there should be no politics in this question. Every one of your committee is a politician. I think that every one of your committee is an exception, in my sense, of the term of being a politician. It may be possible that in the Legislature there are men who are politicians in the lower sense. But I confidently believe that when men are selected from any district they are selected as the higher type of citizens. I am not a politician myself though I hold a public office. It has been said of the men who are in favor of consolidation, the anti-consolidationists or the resubmissionists that they are in this for the purpose of political gain. I differ from a lawyer who is a consolidationist when he made a statement at a dinner the other night that when we had consolidation that the present district attorney of Kings county should be district attorney of the whole city. I ask Senator Wray, who was at that dinner, how it was that a lawyer could so far forget the Constitution as to make such a statement as that, and he said it only illustrated how some of the consolidationists are so eager for consolidation that they forget all rules of law and all principles of jurisprudence. It would not make any difference to me, so far as the office is concerned, except the Legislature should decide that if I favor a resubmission or anything else that they would not pass the bill to extend my term of office to four years. I do not care whether the Legislature fixes it at four years or two years. I want to call your attention to one or two propositions — and if we discuss the question at all, if there is any politics in it, we might as well talk politics; if there is any politics in it, let us discuss politics. Brooklyn is listening to the discussion; the city of New York is listening to it, why should we not discuss its political side? You have started on the theory that it is a business proposition; that is undoubtedly true, but there are two great political parties, the Democratic party upon principle and the Republican party upon principle, and in both of these cities are political rings, cancers that are eating into the body politic of these two cities. I do not say that for the purpose of attacking either party; but if you show me a great city where either party has control of its departments, and I will show you a history of selfish men united for the purpose of making money. And the danger is, therefore, that the young men in any great city where either party has a sufficiently safe majority, those young men flock to that party. What is the use of a young lawyer in a city where all the officials are Democrats seeking to establish a business and standing in a minority party?

MR. LEXOW:

They have done it, just the same.

MR. BACKUS:

I will tell you why they have done it. They have done it wherever there is a gleam of hope that good citizenship shall finally be recognized. They have done it in some of our great cities when the body politic have become so rotten that those in power were indicted and dethroned. Once in a while there would be a spasm so great that the young men, the old men, the fathers and the mothers will rise up and dethrone those who are corrupt. It would be a good thing for the Democracy in the city of New York if once in a while the people would strike a blow that would stagger them, if the surgeon would cut out the cancer. In the city of Brooklyn the people watch the politicians closely, and the people are in close contact with our mayor. Mayor Schieren will tell you that his relations to all the citizens has been very intimate, a sort of family relation. In this city the people can reach our mayor — the rich and poor alike. When the politicians here become corrupt and greedy the Democrats and Republicans unite against that ring and we change the administration. We stand to-day in this position. The Democrats and Republicans alike, are petitioning you to resubmit this question. I believe that these citizens of Brooklyn desire another opportunity to vote upon the subject of consolidation. My observation in the city of Brooklyn leads me to believe that it will be a great misfortune if to-day the Legislature should decide to draw the lines and deny the people the right to again vote upon this question.

MR. LEXOW:

I have been told that our political throats will be cut if we declare consolidation, and then again if we do not declare it.

MR. BACKUS:

What do those who are opposed to consolidation ask? That you shall kill consolidation? No. What they do ask is that you shall give those who are opposed to consolidation an opportunity to show their strength. The consolidationists say, that we, having been allowed to vote once, should not be allowed to vote again. I think it is a good thing that this representative body has come to Brooklyn to feel the pulse of the people. If the Legislature shall agree to resubmit this question to a vote of the people, and they vote upon it, whatever the result may be, the people will abide by it. Nobody will cut your throats. I am glad that that question has come up, because I believe that when a voter has once had an opportunity to vote and is given notice that is to have another chance, and that it will be his last chance, I believe that he should be bound by it. There is no constitutional provision that will prevent the people voting again upon this question. I do not think that the voters of the city of Brooklyn will blame either party if the question is resubmitted.

I do not believe in the real estate boom business. What I would like to see is a steady growth in the outlying wards of the city. I think it would be a most unfortunate thing to have a boom in real estate, for who would be benefited? The real estate speculators. I believe in steady growth in the city of Brooklyn. Real estate in the city of Brooklyn is stable enough under normal conditions. One of the things that makes uncertainty is this constant fret to take from the voters of the city of Brooklyn the question whether Brooklyn shall remain as it is. I say to you that it must be for the best interests of all the people if there were a steady growth instead of a boom. Confidence will make real estate values steady. Booms result in large profits to real estate speculators.

MR. LEXOW:

Is it not a fact that every great improvement in the city had met with like opposition? The elevated railroads, the Brooklyn bridge, the parks — have they not met with this same opposition?

MR. BACKUS:

I do not know that I am willing to make any statements about facts that I do not know. I know that the people were opposed to elevated railroads in front of their houses. There were many influences that opposed the elevated railroad system; there were many who opposed it for selfish reasons. I do not see what that has to do with the question. Look at the history of the great cities that have been combined, and you will see that they desire to return to home government, that they want to resume the responsibility of self-government. There are certain departments right here in the city of Brooklyn that can best be managed right here on this side of the river. This great change could not be made without giving the people an opportunity to pass final judgment upon this important subject. Give us a chance to discuss the question. I do not claim that when I voted on this question, that I was prepared to cast my vote intelligently. All that we were called upon to do was to express such an opinion as we had, with the notice that it was not to be final. I would like an opportunity to talk with my neighbors about it. I know many people who have changed their minds upon the subject. I do not know that it is important whether they have changed their mind one way or the other. If the consolidationists are afraid that the result will be defeat, I do not blame them for opposing a resubmission. But what harm can come to pass, what good reason is there for not letting the voters of the city of Brooklyn pass their judgment upon this important subject?

MR. BRUSH:

In view of what you have said about the vote on this question at the general election, would you not think it better to have a special election to express an opinion on the subject?

MR. BACKUS:

It seems to me that the people should not be confused by political considerations. I think the question should be voted upon separately. I do not think it was fair to say that Mr. Grout was defeated because he was a consolidationist for there is a strange thing about politics in this city as elsewhere. You can not draw lines that will get Democrats to vote the Republican ticket, and you can not draw lines that will get Republicans to vote the Democratic ticket, no matter what you mix in with it. I do not think it would be quite right to say that he was defeated because he was a consolidationist.

MR. LEXOW:

You do not believe in nonpartisan municipal government?

MR. BACKUS:

I believe in honest municipal government. I believe there are honest Democrats and honest Republicans. We went to the people on straight political lines. There were Democrats and Republicans running on straight lines. I believe in honest government. It would be a blessed thing for all the cities of the country if State and National politics could be separated from municipal politics.

Mr. Lexow:

Then you mean to draw the inference from the last election that Brooklyn is a Democratic city by upwards of 6,000 majority?

Mr. Backus:

I mean to say this; that the results of the last election show this: and I believe it from the bottom of my heart, that among the mass of voters there is a large number of intelligent men that will vote for a certain man no matter what their interests are, that will vote because their party organization is behind them. The city of Brooklyn is neither a Republican nor a Democratic city. It is so nearly balanced so that when either party gets intrenched and thinks it can run the government independent of the voters of the city of Brooklyn, it arises the next morning after election and finds that the people of the city of Brooklyn have taken their interests from its hand. The city of Brooklyn is Republican to-day, for certain reasons. I think it will remain Republican for several years if those in office give a fair, honest and nonpartisan administration of the business affairs of the city, and it will be Democratic as soon as the independent voters get the suspicion that they are under a selfish and corrupt ring. Wait until next election and do not mix consolidation up and divide our lines, and then we can tell whether this city is Democratic or Republican.

Mr. Redfield:

Before introducing our honored ex-mayor, Mr. Schieren, I desire to state that at the request of Assemblyman Forrester, representing the Thirteenth Assembly district of this city, I went to Greenpoint a week ago to-night. That district gave quite a large majority for consolidation. They had a meeting and 10,000 circulars were circulated, and the meeting was advertised in the evening papers. The evening was inclement, the attendance was about one hundred and fifty, as nearly as I could judge. Mr. Forrester called upon that meeting to inquire if there was anybody there who desired to speak for consolidation, or against resubmission. There was nobody who showed a desire to speak. After a dozen gentlemen spoke for resubmission a resolution since placed in the hands of the Legislature, was unanimously adopted in favor of resubmission. This was in Williamsburgh, where seventy-five per cent. of the voters are said to be in favor of consolidation; and on the following Monday evening the Nassau Republican club passed this same resolution.

MR. SCHIEREN:

Mr. Chairman and Gentlemen of the Committee: I have the honor to present to you as chairman of the meeting of the citizens of Brooklyn, held in the city of Brooklyn on January 7, 1896, the following resolution:

"WHEREAS, Several bills have been, and are being prepared for introduction in the present session of the Legislature of New York, the purposes of which are to be seriously modified, abridged and supplant the present charter of the city of Brooklyn, and existing laws affecting the public interest of the city; therefore,

"*Resolved,* That this is the sense of this meeting, that whatever legislation is proposed, no law should be enacted which will deprive the people of Brooklyn of the right to determine by popular vote whether they will accept or reject any charter or other measure which shall be intended to replace the present charter, or terminate in any way the corporate existence of the city of Brooklyn."

This resolution was adopted by unanimous vote.

Mr. Chairman, this clearly defined my opposition on this great question. And certainly it is a grave question. It means the effacement of the fourth largest city in this country. The effacement of it means the effacement of more than 1,000,000 people. Has there been up to to-day, any man who would submit an idea for a charter for the Greater New York? Has ever such a thing been outlined? I am a merchant of the city of New York, and have been such for the past twenty-five or thirty years. I believed in annexation all that time. And when the people of Brooklyn sent me to be mayor of this great city, then I had a practical knowledge of it; then I could look into the question in a practical way, and then I found that it is one of the most serious things that can be done. What are you going to replace? What charter are you going to give us? The charter of this city, the city of Brooklyn, is in demand all over the country. From all over the country demand for copies of that charter have been received, and we have been compelled to print several hundred more copies to supply the demand.

MR. LEXOW:

We could, if consolidated, pass as a charter that of the city of Brooklyn.

MR. SCHIEREN:

The people of Brooklyn will consider that and will rejoice. But, Mr. Chairman, one thing I will say to you — I will tell you that that was an annexation, to annex to unite Brooklyn and New York; it does not mean the annexing of 250 square miles of cabbage fields; it does not mean that Brooklyn and New York will be benefited by this great consolidation, because it will make demands upon the resources of Brooklyn and New York. I am a property holder in the city of New York. I have more real estate and property in New York than I have in this city; therefore, I am just as much interested in the city of New York as I am in the city of Brooklyn. (Applause and laughter.) And I say to you, sirs, it is a very important question and one that should be clearly looked into, that before any act is passed a charter should be prepared for this immense city and should be submitted to the people by a popular vote.

MR. LEXOW:

Do you think any charter could be formulated that would be satisfactory to all the people?

MR. SCHIEREN:

The Constitution of the United States (applause) is satisfactory to all the people.

MR. LEXOW:

Do you believe any charter that would be formulated would receive the assent of all the people?

MR. SCHIEREN:

There is no such a thing as unanimity, but such a thing can be framed to which a majority of the people would consent. But several districts should be represented and should have their interests guarded. I believe in fair representation of all districts to be taken into consideration, but otherwise it is a serious mistake. I am firmly convinced of it to-day, having had the practical experience of governing the city of Brooklyn. You have in question a city of three million and a half. Our population is larger than other parts of the city, and are we to be in the hands of these people who are in the minority? Is that justice? I appeal to you and I appeal to you and all the people. Submit to us the question; submit to us the charter, and we will give you then our voice whether we are in favor or not. (Applause.)

MR. LEXOW:

You stated that the Constitution of the United States was satisfactory to the people, but do you recollect how many years it took before they would agree to this Constitution?

MR. SCHIEREN:

Mr. President, such a prominent speaker as Chauncey M. Depew made an address on the subject of the greater New York. He said that the great city, if it were formed, would be a great honor, and it took almost a greater man to be mayor of that city than to be President of the United States. In that he wished to imply that it would be more difficult to govern such a large city than simply to be President of the United States. That is Chauncey M. Depew's opinion. I don't belong to any rank. Whatever is in the mind of the Legislature I will take into consideration, whether it be resubmission or referendum.

MR. BRUSH:

You have been the mayor of Brooklyn and know something about its financial ability?

MR. SCHIEREN:

I do; yes, sir.

MR. BRUSH:

Can you state whether Brooklyn is practically bankrupt?

MR. SCHIEREN:

The last sale of the bonds sold at eight per cent. premium. (Applause.)

MR. BRUSH:

Do you think from your observation of the affairs of Brooklyn that she has had a good prospect of taking care of her financial state in the future?

MR. SCHIEREN:

Brooklyn had to economize, because Brooklyn is larger than New York. New York has 250 miles, while Brooklyn has 560 miles. Brooklyn is larger than New York.

MR. BRUSH:

What per cent. do these bonds carry that you say brought a premium of eight per cent. — what annual per cent.?

MR. SCHIEREN:

Four per cent.; excuse me, three and one-half per cent.

MR. BRUSH:

Is it a fact that the estimated valuation has increased very rapidly within the last ten and a half years?

MR. SCHIEREN:

It has.

MR. BRUSH:

That is since the building of the Brooklyn bridge?

MR. SCHIEREN:

Certainly.

Mr. Brush:

Brooklyn has increased $38,000,000 in ten years?

Mr. Schieren:

Yes, sir. Let me say to you in connection with this that the conversation with Mayor Strong in respect to Williamsburgh, the eastern district — I beg your pardon — Mr. Strong made this assertion, that in New York city, after the completion of the Brooklyn bridge, property below Chambers street had more than doubled in valuation. That is the opinion of a man who ought to know.

Mr. Brush:

How much increase in the present annual increase?

Mr. Brush:

Is it $15,000,000?

Mr. Schieren:

I have not looked at the statistics enough to exactly state it.

Mr. Lexow:

Why is it you don't see the benefit of that valuation yourself if Brooklyn adds so much to the benefit.

Mr. Schieren:

I am a New Yorker. My real estate is below Chambers street (Laughter.)

Mr. Brush:

Nothing can be taken from us in the future if we are increased in valuation of property that give us over a million dollars increase of it in the tax levy?

Mr. Schieren:

When I took hold of the finances of the city, the people said, "You can get no money," and there are hardly any surplus, but somehow we managed to do things and we left a surplus of $3,000,-000, and had less than $1,000,000 to start with.

MR. LEXOW:

How did you do it?

MR. SCHIEREN:

I don't know. It came over night. (Laughter.)

MR. BRUSH:

Is it not largely due to good government?

MR. SCHIEREN:

You have just touched it. That is just where it is. (Applause.)

MR. LEXOW:

The greater city might be equally as well governed.

MR. SCHIEREN:

I dispute that. No one has ever attempted to outline a charter for this vast territory, but permit me in a few words to outline to you the enormity of it. Say that we will divide this enormous territory into five departments: The Manhattan department, comprising New York up to the Harlem river; then another division, and call it Westchester department, extending from the Hudson river way up to the sound; then Long Island City, call it the Flushing department, and in a way to illustrate it all, the other from that point way down to Newtown creek; the next department, the Brooklyn department, and then all that territory south, and call it the Richmond department; call it five departments. Each department is larger than Manhattan; each department has a greater territory than Manhattan. What do you think could be accomplished in the Flushing department? You have got a vast territory to govern. How is a man to know who sits in the mayor's chair whether a bill is justifiable in Flushing? How is he to know what they need there? Do you think that you can find a man who can listen to the complaints of those five departments and live? (Great applause and laughter.) I would rather sit in your chair, sir. If you must take in all this cabbage field and that material it will cost a great deal of money, and I, as a real estate owner of New York and Brooklyn, will predict this, if they unite that large district, that the tax rate will be enormous.

MR. LEXOW:

We are not, under the terms of this bill, taking in any more cabbage fields than you took in years ago.

MR. SCHIEREN:

We have got the experience. We don't want any more of it.

MR. LEXOW:

You would not separate this district now as a Brooklynite, studying the interests of the city?

MR. SCHIEREN:

I think that the city of Brooklyn may in time benefit by that annexation, but before that she will have to spend an enormous amount of money for things that are demanded for improvement of that section.

MR. LEXOW:

Were you not in favor of it?

MR. SCHIEREN:

I represented the interests of the people of Brooklyn and as mayor of that city I used by best judgment to represent the interests of the people. (Applause.)

MR. LEXOW:

You consider that that interest was in the annexation of those outlying districts at the time?

MR. SCHIEREN:

It is a very long question that you would have me answer,

sir; because very many interests enter into it. There was bad local government in those town, and the people were burdened down, and they cried to us, " Take us in." It was a call of salvation, to get right at it. I lived in one of the outlying districts myself in the summer. During 1881 or 1883 a friend of mine bought a piece of property there. He has that property to-day and he paid 10 per cent. of its valuation for taxes.

AFTERNOON SESSION.

SUPERIOR COURT, PART IV, ROOM 23,

January 18, 1896.

Speakers in Favor of Consolidation.

JOHN WINSLOW:

The gentlemen of the Loyal League have come here to present their views. Why, just consider their name. The imputation is that every man who does not take their name is a disloyal citizen. (Laughter.) The real truth is that the gentlemen of the Loyal League are loyal to their notions and the gentlemen who favor consolidation are loyal to their opinions, and so we are loyal all around. The argument has been made that there was no popular discussion before the vote was taken in 1894. How a man who speaks the truth or ever expects to speak it and says that, is past my comprehension. Mr. Scott showed yesterday where the press had fired away on the subject. But the press are afraid their little nest will be disturbed. Judge Reynolds has had the unfairness to say that the majority of 277 came from Gravesend. He ought to remember that when that vote was taken Gravesend had been fumigated and that its chief was in Sing Sing. There is no politics in such legislation as that. I happen to live in the thirteenth ward and own a few lots there. (If anybody wants to buy them he can have them.) We were jerked into Brooklyn nolens volens. (Laughter.) Not a man of the people demanded that a vote should be taken. We were just jerked in head over heels.

I have heard a great deal about change of sentiment. The opposition might have been able to discover it; he had not. The responsibility for the entire matter was in the Legislature. There is no such thing as referendum. All great questions of life and law are cared for by the Legislature. It was a good-natured act on the part of the Legislature of 1894 to sound the people. There was one idea referred to by the ex-mayor, looking as solemn as possible, that the floor was to be wiped with Brooklyn, that the city was to be wiped out. The speaker had a friend much worked up on the subject of annihilation. He might be destroyed after death. He finally announced himself as follows: " If I'm going to be annihilated, if he was, he wanted to go to ——, there he would have something to say." (Laughter.) There was no doubt that in the charter the people of Brooklyn would be provided for. There could be a Brooklyn department for taxes, another for water-works. If he had the framing of the charter, the aldermen might sit alternately in Brooklyn and New York. The people need not be effaced. It would be a good thing if the New York mayor should come to Brooklyn. There was no doubt that Brooklyn is in trouble. The vast taxable property is in New York, and New York should help Brooklyn because it is rich and because Brooklyn had helped to create the wealth. The ex-mayor, Mr. Schieren, and all Brooklynites having business interests in New York, are emasculated citizens. It leads to indifference. Thousands of citizens don't register here; New York ought to help Brooklyn on the tax question. This city has a right to participate in the affairs of the city of New York. It might be that every alternate mayor should come from Brooklyn; one of the members of the Loyal League might be made mayor.

Arguments in Favor of Consolidation.

MR. MATTHEWS:

In behalf of the consolidationists, may I ask the same privilege to be heard by any number of speakers that you might designate. We will furnish any number that the committee might desire to hear. It was stated that you were to have a recess, and for that reason a number of our speakers are not here at this time.

This petition was read by Mr. Matthews:

BROOKLYN, N. Y., *January* 15, 1896.

To His Excellency, the Governor, and the Legislature of the State of New York:

The undersigned, representing the railroad companies of the city of Brooklyn respectfully urge the passage of a bill consolidating Brooklyn city with New York city, provided, among other things, for attaining an equal and uniform rate of taxation and uniform valuations for the purpose of taxation.

The Kings County Elevated Railroad company.

The Brooklyn and Brighton Beach Railroad company, by James Jourdan, president.

In case the provisions of the Cantor Railroad Act do not apply to the territory of Brooklyn, the Nassau Railroad company, by P. H. Flynn, president. (Laughter.)

The Brooklyn Elevated Railroad company, by Elisha Dyer, Jr., treasurer.

Van Brunt Street and Erie Railroad company, by Michael Murphy, president.

Coney Island and Brooklyn Railroad company, by W. Vanderhoef, treasurer.

MR. LEXOW:

That phraseology was in the bill?

MR. MATTHEWS:

Yes.

MEMBER OF LOYAL LEAGUE:

Were those names representative of the stockholders of the railroad companies?

I understand that the names represent nine-tenths of the stockholders.

LOYAL LEAGUE:

Was any action taken by the stockholders?

Mr. Matthews:

I don't know that.

Member of Loyal League:

Then I protest that this is a false representation here.

Mr. Grout:

Mr. Chairman and Gentlemen of the Committee: It was not my wish to make any statement here to-day, because I have so often discussed this question in the past before your committee; but when I remember that you, Mr. Chairman, have sat on this question many times; that this is the third time that you have listened to this argument; I think, perhaps, that the very fact of my speaking may remind you that the question is not one of the moment; that the question is not one suddenly developed, but that it has been discussed for years and years; that it has been brought to Albany and discussed there with the same opposition before the Senate and Assembly committees. There is no new question involved. I have listened to the arguments for the past two days, many of which I but hear over again, and it seems to me that the speakers, or many of them, misapprehend the situation of the question before you. They misrepresent, or, at least, misunderstand the position of the committee in this question. The Legislature of the State of New York is the sole power to deal finally with this question; the people of Brooklyn, the people of the State, the people of New York city, have no power, except as through their representatives in the Senate and Assembly, regarding this case. Years ago the movement became active in Brooklyn for a vote on this question of consolidation of the two cities, and it was urged upon the Legislature by petition and by voice. For two or three years that proposition was pressed upon the people at Albany. In the third year it at last succeeded, and your members kindly acceded to the request and gave us the right to voice our sentiment upon the subject by ballot. The act of 1894, which touched upon the consolidation question, was vigorously opposed. You provided for us a vote for the expression of opinion of the voters. If anything was said during that time that that vote was simply an expression of opinion, certainly I did not know of it. Yet it has been said here that the people had no chance to know anything about what they were doing at the time. It has been said here, that the vote was, in effect, not a vote. The charges made by Mr. Dykman here this morning are untrue and unfair. There was no false representation of the question. The people knew just what they were voting for. By that expression of the people were you asked to carry the consolidation into effect. The Legislature has failed before to do its duty because of these same people. Then they say that because this question was voted upon last year and you did not do your duty then and put consolidation through, that it shall not be done this year. A vote is a vote whenever it is made or however long after it is made, and consolidation having been voted for should be put into effect whether it is three or four years afterward or simply a month. They know that the details of such a thing can not be done in a night. It will take two or three, possibly three or four, years to effect consolidation. When anybody voted on that question he knew, if he had the intelligence requisite for the enfranchisement of a citizen, that that vote must stand as a guide to the people of the state of New York for years to come. Stale? No, no; it is not stale until the object for which it was cast is accomplished. The question has been submitted. Simply because a year has passed since the answer in the affirmative has been given is no reason to say that the decision of that vote shall not stand.

Now, what is the purpose of your inquiry? It must be limited to two things. The vote that is taken is a vote that must stand. If you find that this is the case that is the thing for which you have come here. If you are at all uncertain on that question, you may turn to the question of consolidation itself.

This question was fully presented to the people before a vote was taken. Judge Gaynor made a statement at a meeting at the Academy to the effect that the taxation of Brooklyn was in proportion twice that of New York.

That, gentlemen, is the basis of the turn of sentiment in favor of consolidation in this community. The tax of Brooklyn is just twice that of New York. Meetings were held and letters were written upon that subject. Yet they say this question has not been placed before the people. Carloads of Brooklynites went to Albany a year or so ago urging the Legislature to give us a vote upon the question. They say this morning that the question has become one of politics. There was not a politician who took a stand upon it or wanted to make it a party issue. It has never been heard until now that it is one for any political organization or that any political organization wishes to make it a party issue. It is not a matter of politics, and never was. It is a matter of purely municipal effect and welfare. Certainly your committee do not wish to call it a party measure. They tell us the registration was 192,000 and speak of the small number who voted upon consolidation and try to make us believe the people did not vote upon it to any extent. There are thousands who register who do not vote.

The people do not vote upon measures as they do upon men. See the small majority that won the apportionment bill last time. I was bitterly opposed to this measure as I considered it wrong. It is impossible to get the people to vote upon a question of that kind as they would for a candidate.

I do not believe that to-day you could get eighty per cent. of the voters to vote aye or nay on a special measure and yet we had seventy-seven per cent. who vote a year ago on consolidation. There can not be any question raised upon the size of that vote, except the size of the majority. Is there any American citizen who will question that the vote was not decisive, simply because it was settled by hundreds instead of thousands? Is there any citizen of this great republic who will say that a majority of one is not just as effective in a vote as a majority of a thousand? For the election of a man one is enough and as good as one million. There is no way to test this question of the vote for and against. Do you propose to examine and compare the registration list with all the petitions presented by the anti-consolidationists? You certainly can not waste time in matters of this kind. They had their vote that they clambered for. It was taken as an expression of the people here. It went against them. Their pleading for a resubmission is an act that can only be expressed as the greatest baby act on record. They have been defeated and now they ask you to let them try it again. They want you to let them have the advantages of the possible mistakes that have been made since this measure was voted upon. For that matter I would like a resubmission of the vote of last fall. (Great laughter.) I would like to have a chance to try conclusions with Mr. Wurster again (applause and laughter); perhaps I might be successful. (Applause.) But I am satisfied that I was beaten and do not ask for another try. And their petitions — what do they amount to? I do not know whether Mr. Redfield knows it or not, but one of the men whom he placed upon the list of the citizens calling for the meeting recently held at the Academy by the League of Loyal Citizens, as they call themselves, is a consolidationist. He is a consolidationist of the firmest kind. Now, if they can make a mistake of that kind in a public list of men who call for a meeting of that kind what possibility of mistakes there may lie in their petitions representing the storekeepers, the clerks, the factory hands and the mass of men that have placed upon their other petitions for your consideration.

Mr. Redfield did not ask him who this man was; that probably he knew by this time and the mistake had been rectified.

C. C. SKILTON:

Did this man express his objection to being placed upon that list?

MR. GROUT:

He didn't give his consent. What is more, the New York Tribune printed his picture among his anti-consolidation men. He is going to speak for us, bye and bye, on our side. (Laughter.)

The question had been raised that taxation could not be made equal between the two cities if consolidation was accomplished because the conditions were different. The city of New York, above Fourteenth street, is in the same relative position to the city of New York below Fourteenth street as the city of Brooklyn is to New York below that street. Not only was it physically but financially, and as a business matter the same, because the great wealth of New York city is below Fourteenth street and the great population above. It would be just as difficult to equalize taxation above Fourteenth street with the property below as to equalize it with the property of Brooklyn. And furthermore, it would be unjust to call the great commercial part of New York, below Fourteenth street the whole resource of taxation.

Half the voters of Brooklyn go to New York to attend to business. That means that every foot of space occupied by these Brooklyn men during the day of business is a foot of space for which there would be less demand if those Brooklyn men were not there. Taxable space would be less in such a case. Consequently these men of Brooklyn have more than a little to do with the taxable property in New York. Tax rates are largely due to the Brooklynites who are there. They give value to real estate in New York because there are so many more people to go there. But Brooklyn derives no benefit from this. Brooklyn gets no part of the tax receipts from that. I do not speak of the institutions. I speak of merely the employes of that institution. All that is contributed to New York and Brooklyn gets no benefit from it. And this is the reason why New York should be willing to have Brooklyn to share equally in taxation. I have heard the bill critisised. The bill is a simple declaration that consolidation shall take effect on the first day of January, 1898, and that meanwhile there shall be provision taken to provide for the laws to govern the city then. One provision of the bill is at least an advantage. For years we went to the Legislature and strove to get a bill passed that would provide for equal taxation, the great bugbear of the question. Discouraged at last in this we came home and made up our minds to go in for consolidation anyway. Now the anti-consolidationists use this as a great argument against us. They quoted our own words on the subject. And that shows the great victory which was gained even in the majority in favor of the measure. The vote was for naked consolidation without any terms or conditions. Yet it passed the people. Now, you gentlemen of the Legislature, have given us this bill to-day, the very terms in which we wanted and plead for so long. You have put in this bill the promise of equal taxation. If we had had that to work with when that vote was cast we would have had a majority of tens of thousands. I have exceeded my time and must close. (Applause.)

A. W. TENNEY:

Mr. Chairman and Gentlemen of the Committee: When I heard that this was the last sitting and that you had honored Brooklyn with your presence to-day, I left the court room where I was engaged and hurried here in order to go on record as in favor of consolidation of these two great cities. I shall speak to you, therefore, without any preparation except the thought that comes to me now. I am an old consolidationist. I am a young man, but an old consolidationist. (Laughter.) I have been a resident of Brooklyn for thirty years and for twenty-five of those years I have been a red hot consolidationist of Brooklyn and New York. I believe the interest of these two cities lies in their union and in no other way. I believe it is in the interest of New York that this lovely city of Brooklyn shall be wedded to the great metropolis of New York, and I believe it is in the interest of Brooklyn that the wealth of her nearby neighbor shall be united with her. When the principal merchants of this city, when the banks and great financial institutions, with but two or three exceptions, when the railroads and most important commercial interests of the city come before this committee and state their wishes, it means exactly what this city wants in this matter. We have here in Brooklyn an element that is opposed to everything. They were born in the objective case. (Laughter.) They would take exception to sunrise, if they thought it would have any effect. (Laughter.) They objected to the introduction of water in this city and wanted to keep the old pump, and they take objection to consolidation to-day. It was the same way with gas. They wanted the old lamp and lantern. When they started to introduce the horse railways there was an objection then as sharp and bitter as there is to-day over consolidation. Then the ministers arose in their pulpits and howled against the cars running on Sunday as a desecration of the Sabbath. But she ran just the same. (Laughter.) And now, those very identical ministers use those very same cars; and there was a storm raised when the trolley was introduced. When that magnificent structure that spans the East river, the bridge, was erected, they branded the originators of it as thieves, and those men went to their graves bearing that same objection — at least some of them did. And yet the coming of that bridge has given us millions and millions in valuation and wealth and hundreds of thousands in population. Give us consolidation and we will have three bridges where we have had one. We will have a tunnel under the East river and we will run a line of cars from Montauk Point to New Orleans without a change. (Applause.) That is what consolidation means. This is not a figure of speech but a fact. Those same people objected to the elevated railroads, when they were first projected. Our court calendars are filled with cases of damages and every obstruction known to law and the ingenuity of man. And yet who can estimate the value of these roads and the good they have brought to this city? To-day, when we ask for consolidation, they say: "No; let us look to the eighteenth century instead of the coming twentieth." They say that the vote taken did not amount to anything; and that it was simply a wish. Was it? I understand that was the argument made here to-day and yesterday. Was it? Let us see. This is what the law says: "Shall be submitted and taken as an expression of the voters as the case may be in favor or against the consolidation of the cities of New York and Brooklyn." It was not a wish nor an opinion. It was a desire of the voter whether there should be consolidation here or not. Now, these gentlemen who are against us say the people were not informed upon this question; that they did not know anything about it. That is not much of a compliment to Brooklyn and her people. I say that at that time the question was a live issue here and debated on every hand. I believe in this city. I live in it and have lived in it, and I kind of believe in it. It is my home, and everything I have is here. Because I do believe in it and am a friend of Brooklyn I want consolidation. The five papers of this city published columns on this subject. Look at this bundle of clippings. (The speaker lifted up a large package of clippings from Brooklyn papers.) These papers were discussing the case for weeks and months. They were all against consolidation — for a reason of their own. (Laughter.) It was a question of a nest-egg that they might lose. And I say now that almost everyone of the people on the other side are afraid of losing some little nest-egg of their own if the two cities are consolidated. I discussed the case on platforms all over the city. I remember the meeting referred to by Mr. Grout, and I spoke there with Mr. Gaynor. Perhaps it was because of these speeches the people knew nothing about the subject. (Laughter.) I took it on platform after platform. There was not a question more alive in this city than consolidation. And the people voted on it. If another vote were taken to-day, eighty per cent. of the people, the voters of this city, would go for consolidation. It is not true a change of opinion has taken place against consolidation. But suppose it has. Are elections to be a farce here? Is not our whole government based upon the fact that the majority must rule? That idea found its birth in the cabin of the Mayflower and found its fruitage at the battle of Appomatox. The Civil War decided that majority shall rule, whether the majority is one or 1,000,000. To submit that question back to the people would be un-American, unconstitutional and absolutely revolutionary. It can not be done. It would be establishing a precedent that you must not submit to as the representatives of law and of the people. Whether you favor it or not, whether you believe in consolidation or not, is not in the issue, and I say to you, gentlemen of the committee, if I were one of you, if I were a member of the Legislature of this State, I would rot in my seat before I would ever allow such an example to be set, for this question after once passed upon to go back to the people to be passed upon again. (Loud applause.) Better wipe out Brooklyn from the map of the world than do any such thing as that. It is absurd. It is wrong. It is un-American and revolutionary. It has been said or intimated that the election of Wurster and Grout rested upon this question of consolidation or nonconsolidation. I say that this is not a fair, a true or a rightful statement. If I had thought at that time that such was the case, although I am a Republican right through, I would have voted for Grout. (Applause.) I believe every right-thinking man would have done the same thing. (Applause and cries of "That's right," which was suppressed by the chairman.) This statement is wrong and unfair, because it has a tendency to mislead you, and should not have been made. The issue was a sharp one, clearly and squarely defined between these two parties. In this I am sure I would be substantiated by every man present here to-day. (Cries of "That's so.") It is unkind and ungenerous to make any such assertion as that, and especially unfair to my friend, Mr. Grout. They say they do not believe in putting Brooklyn under Tammany. I do not like Tammany. I do not believe in Tammany. I do not believe in its methods. I do not believe in anything connected with Tammany Hall. And yet I am in favor of consolidation. I do not believe in Tammany, but I am not afraid of Tammany. (Applause.) That is why I am for consolidation, and that is the way I put it. I believe in the people, and if the people want Tammany Hall they can have it. If they do not want it, they need not have it. I believe in the people and I am ready to trust the people. I say that when we undertake to defeat such a magnificent measure as this merely because of a political issue as Tammany Hall or not Tammany Hall, it is unmanly and unworthy of your consideration for a moment in such a case as this. I am willing to put Brooklyn in the hands of the people. Allow these two cities, wedded as they are by the coast of the sea, to be made one. Take in Flushing bay and Jamaica bay, and dig a ship canal from Flushing bay on the north to Jamaica bay on the south. Relieve the harbor of New York of its surplus of commerce. Have your coal, your lumber, flour, grain and all your products carried by this canal; relieve New York harbor and then we will have what we are bound to have — for I tell you that this consolidation is as inevitable as the sun rises — and then we will have not only the grandest city of the country, but have the wealth, trade, commerce, science, literature, philanthropy and everything that tends to benefit man— the grandest city in the world.

MR. GRISWOOD:

Mr. Chairman and Gentlemen of the Committee: I am aware that this hearing is drawing to a close. I came into the room but a few moments ago, supposing that you were to have an intermission. I am aware that your committee and the audience must be weary, and I shall not detain you but a moment. I have been asked to come here as a citizen, as a layman, as a business man, to give my testimony in favor of consolidation, which I do very cheerfully. After the able speeches to which you have listened on both sides of this question, yesterday and to-day, there is nothing new that I can add. I simply say that it must be gratifying to you, Mr. Chairman, who introduced this bill, and to the citizens of this great city who are laboring to bring about a favorite result, the consolidation — it must be a satisfaction, I say, for you to feel that if the results of this shall become a law it would be beneficial to millions of people, not for an hour, for a day, for a year, but for a hundred years. The importance of this bill I am impressed most profoundly with. I do not think we can comprehend the results which are to follow from this movement. I believe that it is the most important bill that has ever been introduced into the Legislature of the State of New York. There are three or four features of the consolidation movement which stand out clear and prominent above all others. The first, as the New York Tribune asked the other day, "Do the people of Brooklyn want it?" You know what the people of Brooklyn want; this is not a new question. A great many people did not understand it, but out of a vote of 144,000, 129,000 voted for and against this measure, showing that 14,000 did not really understand it, or did not care to vote, and therefore, did not vote at all upon the question. The natural inference would be, judging from past experience, that if this vote were taken to-day a large majority, I believe that fully three-quarters of that vote would be cast for consolidation. I judge this from what I hear talked in business places, on the streets and in the clubs. Among the gentlemen whom I met who voted for that measure, I can call to mind many instances where they have said if they were to vote to-day upon that question they should again vote in favor of consolidation. One prominent gentleman in this city who was in this room a few moments ago, told me that he voted for it and would do it again. I know of one instance in the neighborhood where

I reside, of five men that reside in one house and every one of those gentlemen voted against consolidation and every one of those gentlemen have told me that if they had a chance to vote to-day they would vote in favor of consolidation.

Mr. Lexow:

Do you understand that there has been a change of sentiment in favor of consolidation?

S. M. Griswood:

I do, most sincerely. I believe that there never was a moment, when consolidation was gaining favor more rapidly. The people are beginning to understand it.

The question of taxes must necessarily come in; the city of Brooklyn has had a marvelous growth in the face of many disadvantages. The running expenses of this municipal government and this great city, which are large, have been levied almost entirely upon the real estate of this city. We have not the means and the revenue that the city of New York has, and the consequence has been that the call upon the real estate of this city has been tremendous, as I know by personal experience of twenty-five years. Take the tax assessment for New York, which is fifty per cent. larger than our tax levy, the rate was 191, against our assessed value of seventy per cent. and a rate of 261. In view of this, I do not believe there is a gentleman in the room who will say that our tax rate will not be lowered and the obstructions removed from our property by consolidation.

Third. The increase of population. It goes without saying that it is easier for Brooklynites to go to New York than it is for New Yorkers to come to Brooklyn. There are hundreds of citizens who have lived in New York nearly all their life who have never been to Brooklyn. There are thousands here who have never been to New York over once or twice. If we are consolidated the people will come over here to live, for this is the most beautiful city on the continent; and when they come here and find that our taxes are no higher than in New York, they will buy our property.

When they see our beautiful location, thousands of the citizens of New York will come over here and make Brooklyn their residence. That is my earnest opinion and judgment in the matter.

Lastly, the civic pride, the idea that we are citizens of a great city. We believe in union. In union there is strength. We are taught that from our childhood. If we do not believe it, then let us abolish our national government and let every authority go on its own account. We believe in union. In Brooklyn, during the last year, we took to our arms all the surrounding country, the county towns. Now, let us go on and form a city that will stand far ahead of even London, or Paris, or Berlin, or St. Petersburg. Let us form a city that will not have its parallel on the face of the globe. Let it stand as a monument to the liberality, the genius, and the intelligence of the people of the Greater New York.

A VOICE:

If you are honest and believe what you say in reference to the vote that would be cast in favor of consolidation, why will you not give us a chance to vote on the question?

MR. GRISWOOD:

I am perfectly willing to answer all the questions that may be asked. Personally, I would, because I firmly believe that over three-quarters, yes, eighty per cent. of the voters of the city of Brooklyn would march up and cast their votes in favor of consolidation.

MR. LEXOW:

You have heard the arguments that have been produced against resubmission.

MR. GRISWOOD:

I believe that it would only result in delay and confusion, trouble and expense, which all these things produce; it is all unnecessary.

Mr. Matthews:

I desire to present the names of the following gentlemen who desire to speak in favor of consolidation:

S. B. Dutcher.
J. L. Nostrand.
Nelson G. Carnan.
William Harkness.
A. H. Keiley.
J. V. Neserole.
H. S. Hurley.
John J. Madison.
James D. Lynch.
E. W. Bliss.
M. J. McGrath.
Joseph C. Hendrix.
Nelson J. Gates.
A. H. Dailey.
M. Townsend.
Thomas C. Smith.
Stewart L. Matthews.

Mr. N. T. Sprague:

Mr. Chairman and Gentlemen of the Committee: I am surprised to be called at this time to speak on this subject. I came here but a few moments ago from my place of business expecting to leave in a few moments thereafter. I shall be brief in what I have to say to you on the subject of consolidating the cities of Brooklyn and New York. I shall express the opinion that I believe eight-tenths of the business men, the active successful business men of the city of Brooklyn, are in favor of consolidating these two cities on equal terms. I think there is no doubt of it. The idea of asking to have it referred again to the people is, in my opinion, an absurdity. Those who are opposed to consolidation ask that it be resubmitted for the purpose of gaining more time to see if they can not bring up something that will be prejudicial to the interests of the masses of the people of Brooklyn. I, unfortunately, own a little property in New York, about $25,000 worth. The tax on that house is about $300 per year. I own one in this city worth $20,000, the tax on which is $600 per year. As far as I am individually concerned, I do not care about that. I am speaking in the interest of the poor; for if my interests are better, his are proportionately; and we want to work for the benefit of all and not against their interest. And if this committee, in their judgment, shall find it to be against the interests of the people in the city of Brooklyn, the masses of the people, I should hope that they would report against the bill. I think they would. But if they find, in their judgment, that it is for the benefit of the people, then let them make us the second largest city in the world. I would like to say more if I had time; but I am willing to leave the interests of the people in the city of Brooklyn in the hands of the committee that I see before me. I have confidence in your judgment and good sense.

MR. LEXOW:

You are satisfied that if there has been any change of sentiment it is in favor of consolidation?

MR. SPRAGUE:

Among my friends in business, four-fifths of them speak more heartily in favor of consolidation than they did a year ago. It is growing upon them. They are not politicians, not selfish men, but men working for the benefit of the masses. I believe that nine out of ten of the active, stirring, solid men of the city are in favor of the passage of this bill, that their neighbors, as well as themselves, may be benefited thereby.

MR. BRUSH:

Do you not think that the people of the city of Brooklyn would not prefer to have a vote upon a synopsis of a charter or any terms of consolidation?

MR. SPRAGUE:

I am largely interested in the real estate of the city; I am interested in business affairs; I have confidence, great confidence, perfect confidence, in the gentlemen that will be appointed to do this work, provided they put us on equal terms with New York. The longer you defer consolidation the greater the difficulties will be.

MR. LEXOW:

You would be willing to leave the question of terms to the commission that will be appointed?

Mr. Sprague:

Yes, sir; if they work upon equal basis.

Mr. Grady:

When you speak of equal terms, do you mean that you should have so many commissioners; or do you merely mean that taxation after consolidation shall be equal?

Mr. Sprague:

Yes, sir; that should be in the bill.

Mr. Lexow:

You have read the bill?

Mr. Sprague:

Yes, sir.

Mr. Lexow:

Is that bill satisfactory to you?

Mr. Sprague:

Yes, sir; as I understand it now.

J. M. Snooks:

Mr. Chairman and Gentlemen of the Committee: I have been requested to come here this afternoon to present the case in the name of the Builders' Exchange, or Mechanics and Traders' Exchange, which represents the builders' interest throughout the city. I hold in my hand a petition, which has been hastily got up within the last three days; it contains the names of eighty-seven members of the exchange, which is a little over two-thirds of the membership; and we have no doubt that in a day or two more to be able to complete the petition, which is addressed to the Governor, the Senate and the Assembly of the State, and it will then contain sixteen or twenty additional names. In speaking with reference to this, I desire to say, while it is true that through the action of the Legislature in the fall of 1894, a vote was taken in this city to get at the opinion of the voters of this city, as to the desirability of consolidating the cities of New York and Brooklyn and effecting a Greater New York; in obedience to that law, a vote was taken, and a majority of the voters voted in favor of consolidation, but owing to diverse circumstances there was a large number that did not vote. I heard yesterday the argument brought up that it was not an expression of opinion of the people, because it was not a full vote. I ask you, Mr. Chairman, if you ever knew of an election where you ever had a full vote? Aside from this, I understand that the expression called for represented a majority of those who did vote upon the subject, while perhaps a large minority voted against it. Their claim is that a large majority did not vote at all, and that, therefore, we have no expression of opinion. They simply showed by their failure to vote or express an opinion that they were in doubt. We are not opposed to the idea of another vote, nor are we afraid of the result of that vote, but we are afraid of the result of resubmitting that vote on this principle: We believe that it is the establishment of a dangerous precedent and vicious principle, and on that ground we are opposed to a resubmission for the purpose of getting an opinion. We believe that the vote in that respect should be final. We are not opposed to a referendum when a law has been passed by the Legislature; there will be no objection to that. But that is not the question in point. The question in point seems to bring itself down to this: Your committee is here for the purpose of endeavoring to find out the real sentiment of the people in regard to consolidation. The matter is hedged up and clouded with dust by the idea that we must have resubmission in order to find out what the people want. I am willing to leave it to the intelligence of the committee as well as the people, to their own conscience, as to whether that opinion has not already been expressed, and expressed favorably. I would like to say a few words in reference to another point in favor of consolidation. I understand that there is a large portion of the city outside of the old high-water limits that is taxed and the taxes paid into the city of New York. I want to know if New York city has ever done anything for the improvement of

Brooklyn with those taxes? I believe that if we are consolidated the construction of new bridges and tunnels would soon be at hand.

The following petition was handed to the committee by Mr. Snooks:

To His Excellency, the Governor, and to the Honorable Senators and Members of the Assembly of the State of New York:

The undersigned, members of the Mechanics' and Traders' Exchange of the city of Brooklyn, beg to present this memorial.

The project to consolidate the cities of New York and Brooklyn under one municipal government on conditions equitable to both communities, and with an equal adjustment of the burdens of taxation, meets with our hearty approval as a measure eminently calculated to promote the real estate and building interests of Brooklyn, and the general prosperity and prestige of the communities which it is proposed to unite.

George C. Crawford, 393 Flatbush avenue.

Robert L. Crawford, 393 Flatbush avenue.

W. G. Lee, 216 State street.

George W. Melvin, 414 Lafayette avenue.

J. F. Mickles, 340 Schermerhorn street.

Joseph H. Colyer, foot of Washington street.

P. O'Hara & Son, 225 Sixteenth street.

John W. Moran, 313 Jesse street.

Thomas Monahan, 633 Douglass street.

W. L. Glidden, 220 Pacific street.

George W. Anderson, 950a Greene avenue.

J. W. Johnson, Grand and Metropolitan avenue.

Joseph G. Miller, 280 Kasaush street.

W. E. Quay, 900 Green avenue.

John A. Hughes, administrator estate P. J. Hughes, Douglas street and Gowanus canal.

Hughes & Gray, Douglas street and Gowanus canal.

Francis Conklin, 123 Sixth avenue.

P. F. O'Brien, Jr., 148 Lee avenue.

Volney Rutan, 600 Quincey street.
Thomas B. Miniko, 418 Third avenue.
William D. Anderson, 952 Greene avenue.
I. P. Sutherland, 363 Fulton street.
James D. Hawkins, 608 Fifth avenue.
John Morton & Sons, Carroll street and Gowanus canal.
Thomas W. A. Castle, 54 Lott street.
E. F. Nicoll, 2216 Fulton street.
M. M. Canda, Third street and Gowanus canal.
T. G. Christmas, Myrtle avenue and Rutledge street.
John J. Curran & Bros., Third street, near Third avenue.
John C. Austin, 129 Reid avenue, Brooklyn.
Owen O'Keefe, 140 Eighteenth street, Brooklyn.
Abraham Rutan, 957 Putnam avenue.
B. C. Miller & Son, 955 Dean street.
Henry Feltmann, 753 Macon street.
Frank Mapes & Son, 63 Patchen avenue.
K. A. Murphy, 96 Linwood avenue.
John J. Hickey, 253 Eighth street.
Maurice F. Hickey, 413 Tenth street.
J. A. Forshew, 608 Hancock street.
John Golden, 787 Franklin avenue.
Frank D. Creamer, 673 St. Marks.
Peter Cleary, 385 Decatur street.
W. C. Williams, 565 Jefferson avenue.
James P. Stevenson, 591 Bergen street.
William J. Moran, 141 South Fifth street.
James Keenan, 948 Fulton street.
Richard Whalen, corner Fortieth street and Fifth avenue.
David McMullan, 363 Fulton street.
John M. Snook, 19 Fenimore street.
Thomas McCann, 853 Douglas street.
John Thatcher, 674 Tenth street.
E. Snedeker, 391 Green avenue.
Samuel W. Cornell, 121 Court street.
Henry Werner, 88 Schermerhorn street.
William H. Boyes, 370 Pearl street.

M. Fitzsimmons, 81 Ninth street.

Thomas G. Carlin, 93 Garfield place.

Hall & Bradford, 363 Fulton street.

T. H. Waterton, 401 Union street.

William M. Gobson, 939 Lafayette avenue.

Thomas Dobbin, 162 Ross street.

Charles A. Klots, 147 Lee avenue.

Charles W. Comins, 45 Waverly avenue.

John Barnes, 243 Carlton avenue.

Jacob Schratweiser, 110, 112 and 114 Navy street.

Ingolf Iverson, 784 Halsey street.

L. A. Lewis, for Kenyon & Newstadt, 528 Lewis street.

John C. Orr & Co., foot of Haven street.

M. R. Thompson, 11 Linden street.

W. C. W. Child, Milton and West streets.

John Demott & Sons, 270 Schermerhorn street.

Emrick Bros., 134 Stockholm street.

George W. Randall, 669 St. Marks avenue.

M. T. Reynolds, 193 Ralph avenue.

Jacob May, 909 Lafayette avenue.

John Pross, of J. M. Snook & Co., 745 Park avenue.

Herman Pross, of J. M. Snook & Co., 56 Floyd street.

George J. Pross, of J. M. Snook & Co., 82 Stocton street.

Owen Nolan, 340 Union street.

A. E. Pelham, Twenty-sixth street, between Ninth and Tenth avenue.

William F. Donovan, 486 Court street.

C. Cameron, 209 Van Buren street.

H. Grasman, 407 Jefferson avenue.

James W. Pettinger, 47 Brevoort place.

F. G. and G. T. Van Riper, 110 Fourth street, Long Island City.

E. P. Waterbury, 240 Cooper street.

George H. Ray, 454 Jefferson avenue.

Henry J. Brown, 389 Herkimer street.

Abram H. Brown, 374 Herkimer street.

John Kennedy & Son, 175 Front street.

W. B. Martin, 24 Polhemus place.

Charles H. Ridgway, 716 Madison street.
Edward Freel, 435 Court square.
James D. Kenney, 399a Union street.
John Davis, 170 Court street.
George M. Miller, 507 Sixth avenue.
E. D. Newman, 15 Ashford street.
Edward Clark, 315 Fourth avenue.
Andrew P. Blist, 577 Caroll street.
Audley Clarke, 16 Fisk place.
W. & F. B. Conklin, De Graw street and Fourth avenue.

MR. LEXOW:

The committee will decide whether Brooklyn will be given any further hearings.

A VOICE:

Mr. Chairman, I desire to ask the last speaker a question. Is is not true that the Builders' Exchange, which this gentleman represents, voted on Friday last, as a body, to postpone the consideration of this question? Did they so vote?

MR. SNOOKS:

On Friday last, at a meeting of the Exchange, the subject was brought up in a resolution, which I did not take the time to read, but which is embodied in this petition. A motion was made to postpone until the next meeting after the report of the committee on the 8th of March. This resolution, I neglected to state, was a petition of the individual members of the Exchange and not of the Exchange as a body. The Exchange was not fully represented at the time. There were a number of members who voted in favor of postponing who afterwards said to me that they did not know that they were voting to postpone, but thought they were voting for the resolution. Hence, as individual members, we thought it right to put it in the form of a petition and present the actual facts of the case before the Governor and the Legislature.

County Court House, Brooklyn, N. Y.

January 24, 1896.

William C. Redfield:

Mr. Chairman and Gentlemen of the Committee: On behalf of the league which I represent we thank you heartily for this further opportunity to be heard. In the list of banks that was filed with you some days ago, it was stated that that represented three-fourths of the banks of this city. Another gentleman on the other side said it was all but three. The first speaker to-day will be the president of the trust company that was not upon that list, nor was it mentioned among the three that were not on it. I desire to introduce Congressman William J. Coombs.

W. J. Coombs:

Mr. Chairman and Gentlemen of the Committee: I understand that it is not expected that I shall spend much time with my little talk this morning. I was in the habit of being limited in time in my speeches in Congress. I was once limited to a half a minute, but to show the expansive powers of Congressional eloquence, when that speech appeared in the Congressional Record, it covered a whole page. I do not wish you to understand that I come here distinctly as president of a trust company. I am, it is true, the president of such an institution, but my company has taken no action upon this matter, and I do not think it legitimate that they should take such action. That is not the business for which a trust company is formed. Even if my board of directors had taken such action upon the matter, I should not think it legitimate, for the basis of authority in a bank or trust company is its stockholders. And until the gentlemen who have represented the banks here show that there has been a meeting of the stockholders of their respective banks and that they have deliberately passed upon that question, I should think that they spoke without authority, and I do not think it is for you to consider such testimony as coming from such institutions. I do not intend to criticise the gentlemen who spoke. They may have thought they were voicing the sentiment of their stockholders. They are simply the servants of the stockholders, and the stockholders embrace the sentiment, the thermometer, or the test tube, that you must consider.

MR. LEXOW:

Do you think that any reputable bank officer in this city or in the city of New York would sign a paper of that kind unless he considered he had the authority of the stockholders?

MR. COOMBS:

I would not care to express a sentiment upon that subject. I do not believe that such an officer would willfully and with intent do wrong. He might, unthinkingly, consider he was expressing the voice of his bank. But every institution of that kind has from 300 to 400 stockholders, and I do not think they would take action on the question.

MR. LEXOW:

I ask for information only, and wish to get down to facts. The committee are asking you for information, as I said; they want facts. I would like to know whether you, as a similar officer, do not consider that these bank officials considered that they had prima facie evidence, and whether it should not be accepted as such?

MR. COOMBS:

They may have thought they had it, in their judgment.

MR. LEXOW:

Would you not assume that they were satisfied that their stockholders favored their signing such a paper?

MR. COOMBS:

No, I should not think so. Bank officers are in the habit of sometimes acting unthinkingly. There are a certain number of men in a bank, as in any other large institution, who give a tone to the bank. They might be mistaken if they went down and got the opinion of their stockholders. I do not say that the gentlemen intentionally misrepresented. I only make the suggestion that if they have the opinion of their stockholders, that they file that information with the committee. If these gentlemen represent their banks when they speak they can make that statement. I only suggest that they make the fact plain that they do represent their banks. I do not come here to criticise the gentlemen themselves. Neither do I come here, Mr. Chairman, as a politician. I do not think this is a question to be discussed politically, although it has a political bearing, but I think the wisest politicians will recognize this fact: That whatever may be the result of this movement, if it should result in consolidation, it will primarily be injurious to the party that introduced it. Any great change of that kind is primarily injurious, no matter what the after effect may be. I am a Democrat. I know of no action on the part of my party that has looked towards opposing or favoring consolidation. If such action has been taken it has not come to me. I simply speak to-day, Mr. Chairman, as a citizen of Brooklyn, who has lived in this community for over forty years, who has been the greater part of his life in the vicinity of Brooklyn, and has always been proud to call it his home, and who has never been ashamed, wherever he has been, whether abroad or at home, to register himself as from Brooklyn. I understand that some gentlemen have felt a little ashamed to register themselves as citizens of Brooklyn, but I have considered it a high honor to register myself as a citizen of that city, that has, of all the cities of this land, been foremost in every effort to improve municipal government. More efforts at reform have been made here and more has been accomplished by the concentration we have been able to bring to bear to effect reform in Brooklyn, than in any other city of the land. I have been trying to find the reasons for this movement in my mind. There must be reasons. The gentlemen who are proposing consolidation are men whose judgment I have confidence in. I would not, for a moment, base this question upon personality. It is a question that should be considered calmly, placidly, patriotically, in the best interests of the future. I think that possibly the spirit that is broad in the land of consolidation for business interests has finally touched the cities themselves. But the same reason that has brought about the consolidation of business interests does not apply here in any sense. Business interests are consolidated for the purpose of doing away with competition, in increasing profits. There is no competition in this case. New York has helped Brooklyn and Brooklyn has helped New York.

MR. LEXOW:

Isn't it also to reduce the expenditures?

MR. COOMBS:

I do not think, Mr. Chairman, you would for a moment believe that, simply the consolidation of these two cities would decrease expenditure, except possibly, in the administration of the mayor's office.

My judgment as a business man is this: A business of $1,000,000 increased to $2,000,000 does not decrease expenditure in proportion at all. The increased responsibilities require, on the contrary, men of a higher class of intelligence to look after the advantages of such a concern, and I am pretty sure that in this consolidation you would have no decrease of administrative expense. Now, Chicago has led the way in this matter. But New York is such a proud city that I am surprised that with its conservatism, with its grand business interests, with its pride of locality as a gateway to the scene of the continent, it should attempt to follow in the footsteps of Chicago. Why, there is no safety in doing that. We are not the same kind of people at all. If we follow Chicago, she might go us one better and take in the whole State of Illinois. What is there to prevent this enormous power in the State Legislature — I was not aware of it until to-day, but do not dispute it — what is to prevent this power from doing this in the State of New York and changing our whole system of government accordingly? It is a most unusual thing. In Chicago they consolidated hamlets and villages that lay near by. They did not have a city of a million inhabitants lying close beside them with all its pursuits, its machinery, its institutions and debts and everything else that constitutes a great city, with its homes and people. It is a very different problem, indeed. New York, in attempting to absorb Brooklyn as a hamlet or a mere village does this grand city an injustice. It is not the same case. It seems to me it is a problem that ought to be entered upon with the best sort of thought and circumstance. We have also an example of consolidation in Boston, and a letter will be read to you by a man high in authority in the city of Charlestown which was consolidated with Boston. This move, I am assured, brought about the result which I had imagined would be the result if Brooklyn were to be consolidated with New York.

I do not want to repeat what will be said here by others, because I know your time is valuable; but, Mr. Chairman, if there is any man in this world who ought to know that the problem of municipal government has not been solved, it is yourself. For weeks you sat as chairman of a committee in New York and had the opportunity to find out the effect of municipal government there. You know, sir, that the problem of municipal government is not solved on the other side of the East river. I should call upon you as a witness, sir, and ask you if, with the apparent advance of New York city in everything that relates to greatness, if you have not recognized along with the corruption and inability to correct it. How much more would both be extended with this vast territory embraced in the same limits and under the same government?

Mr. Lexow:

I will answer that question, Mr. Coombs, if you will permit me. I was very much gratified to find that ability you speak of when Mayor Strong was elected to the administrative office by 53,000 majority.

Mr. Coombs:

That was merely a sporatic correction. No correction in that light is a correction. Reform falls backward there.

Mr. Grady:

Mr. Coombs, all that was discovered in the investigation you refer to was that certain illegitimate enterprises could be blackmailed and were blackmailed and that that has been the case since the world began, and will always be the case. There was not a suggestion of corruption in the government of the city and there can not be. Gamblers may be blackmailed, but —

MR. COOMBS:

It is very unfortunate then that officials can —

MR. GRADY:

It has always been the case since the world was built.

MR. COOMBS:

I should hate to think that such a thing can not be corrected. I hope the time will come when the problem of municipal government will be solved. There is an unfortunate corruption in this world that always combines its forces and is always at work while reform and virtue sleep. Now we have been able to make the experiment in this city because of this, that with great effort we could get the people's attention undivided and concentrated for a time upon certain things. When you can do this, then the reform comes. How would it be in a city twice or three times the size with no local pride, all swallowed up in one big organization? How impossible it would be for the citizens of such a city, with such diverse interests, to combine and correct any political fault. Now, you know this, Mr. Chairman, that the city proposed by consolidation, would be the largest city in the world.

MR. LEXOW:

Excepting one.

MR. COOMBS:

No, there would be no city in the world as large as that under one government. London is a large city, but London is not under one government. London is a collection of governments, each section having certain rights and privileges. It is a combination which has been built up through centuries. This would be the largest city in the world. It would not solve, however, the problem of municipal government.

Mr. Lexow:

Is not that problem solved? If it is not, then the confederation of States and nations, or the confederation of any government, any system or policy is not solved.

Mr. Coombs:

In solving the confederation of States it came about by degrees. At first it was not a success. I wish to make one more point. In a republic the problem of municipal government is much more difficult than it is in a monarchy. In the latter there is more direct power. Here, everything depends upon the expression and will of the people, which veers in one direction, one day, and in another the next day, whereas, in a monarchy there is one power which can be exercised quickly.

Mr. Lexow:

When you speak of the expression of the people, that is the very glory of our institutions. It is the only power and the citizen is the only monarch recognized in this country. The voice of the people is the voice of God. There is hardly any objection to consolidation in that statement.

Mr. Coombs:

The voice of the people is the voice of God. But the people must have time to be instructed in the various experiments they undertake, and I claim that this very experiment has been forced upon the people without the time to properly investigate the question. I will change my expression. They had no experience in the formation of municipal government, which qualifies them to go into this great combination with the city of New York.

Mr. Lexow:

You understand, Mr. Coombs, that the bill in question provides merely for a consolidation after the first of January, 1898, leaving all the local governments intact in exactly the same condition as to-day, and, until further legislation outside of this bill is had, there can be no actual consolidation except such as is contained within the provisions of this measure.

MR. COOMBS:

I understand that. But the moment that step is taken, whether wise or not, the die is cast and it can not be retraced. We have not investigated yet, sir, to see whether a government can be made to practically and fairly govern these two cities.

MR. LEXOW:

You do not surely assume that if consolidation, as an experiment, proves a failure, that the same power that made it can not unmake it?

MR. COOMBS:

The tangle can never be untangled. The financial tangle could not be untangled. The tangle going in would be great, but the tangle getting out would be greater. That step could not be retraced. You can not contemplate such a possibility.

MR. LEXOW:

I do not see how there could be any entanglement in this bill. After the legislation had passed, there would be no entanglement.

MR. COOMBS:

We suddenly find that the Legislature of this State is possessed of an enormous power which we did not suppose, up to the time they were possessed of. I do not suppose there are many citizens of Brooklyn who knew the Legislature was possessed of that power by which a mandate could wipe out the incorporate existence of Brooklyn and bury it in New York. I do not doubt that power now. I did in the beginning. But I appeal to you, gentlemen, influential members of the Legislature of this State that if that power does exist, if it does not call upon you for the exercise of the greatest deliberation, it throws upon you a responsibility which I hope will be appreciated. Brooklyn certainly should have a chance to decide, deliberately, whether she wants to go into this combination or not. You do not want to take her and put a chain around her neck and fasten her to New York against her will. You are not called upon by your duty to do that. There was an expression of opinion. That expression of opinion was technically in favor of consolidation. The balance of votes, two hundred odd, was in favor of consolidation, but you cannot deny that there were certain statements made at the time that this was no more than an expression of opinion. There were lots of us who made up our minds on that subject who did not vote at all. If we had known that that vote meant absolutely the consolidation of the cities of New York and Brooklyn there would have been a much larger vote and a very deliberate vote at that. The vote does not bind you to go ahead, gentlemen. It is still within your discretion, if you have any reasonable doubt that the citizens of Brooklyn have not deliberately considered that question, to give them another opportunity to consider it. Nothing can be lost by giving them that opportunity, and much can be gained. I do not believe that you, gentlemen of the Legislature, and you gentlemen in favor of consolidation, wish to take the citizens of Brooklyn napping. I do not believe you want to be placed in a position where it can be said that a sharp game was practiced upon the city of Brooklyn. Now, if the citizens of Brooklyn are in favor of consolidation, and I do not know but that they are — I am not, I say frankly, though I may be bye and bye — if the citizens of Brooklyn are in favor of consolidation and are given the opportunity to express their views deliberately at the polls, then you would be absolutely justified in exercising that extraordinary power concerning them.

Mr. Grady:

Some of us believe that we are placed in this position. That if your statement is true that the vote was merely a local expression of opinion in New York and Brooklyn, and has no legal binding force upon the Legislature, and that it can not be accepted as a finality, what reason have we to believe that a vote can be taken which would be more of a finalty than the vote just had? For instance, and I do not mean to ridicule the position by stating an extreme case, suppose the vote desired was given to you and the result went contrary to the last, then what is to prevent the consolidationist from saying it was a rainy day, and asking for another chance which would be fairer to them? What would lead us to believe that the case should not be submitted even again? I know that I take an extreme case, but it was merely for example.

MR. COOMBS:

It is not a very probable one.

MR. GRADY:

I know that, but we must take everything into consideration.

MR. COOMBS:

The people will always uphold you in the right. They will always uphold you in being fair. They will never uphold you in being unfair. There is every suspicion that the citizens were caught napping and if the legislature takes advantage of this, you will not recover from it as long as you live.

MR. LEXOW:

In reference to that last statement of yours you say that we must be fair. Now there were five distinct communities entered into this vote upon the direct understanding of fair play that the five would be bound by the expression of popular judgment at that time. Now one of these five distinct communities which actually voted in favor of consolidation, comes forward to see if we will permit another trial to be made of the vote to see if they are still of the same mind. Will you answer the question as to whether it would be fair to the other communities to give that resubmission with the direct and express purpose of defeating the first decision?

MR. COOMBS:

I do not say that the express purpose is to defeat it. I hope it will.

MR. LEXOW:

Well, what is the good, then of resubmission?

Mr. Coombs:

This community did not deliberately vote with the knowledge that they were voting for absolute consolidation. I did not know at all that it was more than an informal expression of opinion. Upon this question would be prepared a bill including a charter upon which we would be permitted to vote. Now, I have only one more thing to say. Imagine this great city to be formed and the government instituted, you will agree with me that there must be a tremendous condension of power in the government head in so disjointed a community. In such a great corporation of power, Brooklyn would be ignored. The power would go to the greater community.

S. L. Woodhouse:

Mr. Chairman and Gentlemen of the Committee: In order that I may keep within my time limit, and get out of the way of the oratory behind me, and in compliment to the committee, I may never have the chance to compliment them again, I shall read what I have to say. I desire it shall be considered a compliment, rather than an imposition.

I think that we all agree that the consolidation of these two great cities is one of the most momentous questions of modern times; even though the willing assent of both cities were at this moment assured, difficulties which palsy the thought would yet beset the pathway of our most gifted thinkers in their contemplation of this stupendous theme; well nigh insolvable problems spring from ambush at every turn; they allure the imagination but stay the judgment. Consolidation is not therefore a question for hasty conclusion nor for certainty of result; in its final outworking it is not a question for the forum but for the statesman's calmest thought; not of politics but of patriotism. But the question is here and demands solution; we cannot avoid it if we would; arguments before this committee by our wisest citizens, have revealed difficulties and dangers which have stirred Brooklyn's thought as never before. To extinguish the corporate life of this great city of a million people is no light thing — a solemn obligation rests upon every participant in this crucial act which he cannot disregard. Palsied be the hand that would destroy Brooklyn's corporate life save for Brooklyn's weal. Mistakes may be irrevocable and errors crimes.

I state my own views though with many misgivings:

1. I favor consolidation.
2. I am against resubmission.
3. I favor a referendum.

By favoring consolidation I do not mean that it must come to-day: Let the terms of consolidation decide that; I do mean, however, that I am compelled to consolidation by forces external to myself and beyond control. Ours is a material age. The law of centripetal force is potent in finance as in physics. Overshadowing New York will be victor at last, and, I think, in the very near future; $6,000,000,000 of wealth in New York against $1,000,000,000 in Brooklyn; $75,000,000 yearly increase in New against a nominal increase in Brooklyn; that is the proposition. One may increase its debt two fold while the other is already within $4,000,000 of its legal debt limit; one has vast resources of income, aggregating $12,000,000 per annum, while the other is dependent on taxation alone. These two cities are separated by a hand breadth in distance. The greater needs the smaller for increase in world renoun and commanding power; the smaller needs the greater for its co-operation and sustaining strength. We may delay consolidation but, it is my abiding conviction, that we can not finally defeat it; better consolidation now than further delay with other complications, provided, the terms of consolidation shall safeguard the interests of Brooklyn.

This question is not new; for a hundred years New York has sought possession of Brooklyn while Brooklyn has steadily resisted. Until three years ago the word consolidation was not used; the word was annexation. The change marks New York's progress of thought toward Brooklyn; it was compelled by Brooklyn's century of successful resistence. Annexation would tack us on to New York and give us as little as it must. Consolidation — that more self-respecting word —would braid these two great cities into a single strand — a unity of interests; if that be not its meaning let us decline it.

I am opposed to resubmission.

First. The people have already voted upon it.

Second. A vote once case should be final; any other course is un-American; the instinct of the people is against it; the voter is responsible for his acts.

Third. A majority of one vote, if honestly cast, is as binding as a thousand. A vote is a vote.

Fourth. To reopen the question would create endless confusion and arouse distrust, and, in the event of a vote adverse to consolidation would embitter the voters therefor; it would also carry the right to a second resubmission, and, why not to a third and a fourth? These considerations, alone, and, apart from all others, dispose me against resubmission.

Fifth. It is said that the vote was merely the expression of a desire, that it had no legal efficiency. That is strictly true, but can the voter solemnly register even his desire, without any responsibility? Are there no equities whatever due the victor? I think there are and that any other theory is perilous and delusive. Besides, both voter and Legislature exhausted their power in the form of the vote as cast; legal efficacy was impossible, for law making can not be delegated.

Sixth. I believe that equitable consolidation is still Brooklyn's desire; if not to-day, then upon her sober second thought.

Seventh. The submission of a charter to the voter would, in effect, be both a resubmission and a referendum.

Eighth. No harm can, therefore, come to Brooklyn by denying a resubmission; for the above reasons I am opposed to resubmission.

I am, however, in favor of a referendum; what is the present apparent intent of the Legislature upon consolidation? It is to immediately and irrevocably decree these two great cities into one gigantic city; that would wipe out Brooklyn's individual corporate life forever. Am I asked, Is not this what Brooklyn voted for? Yes, but is it broad-minded, patriotic statesmanship to assume that by its vote for consolidaation, Brooklyn abandoned her present life to strangers and her resurrection life to Tammany Hall? Shall her hand be stayed in framing the splendid structure in which she is to dwell? Deny her this right and you Brooklyn's self-respect full in the face. You shatter the principle of home rule at a single stroke and you commit a gigantic moral crime. Do this and thenceforth there will be no more consolidationists, nor anti-consolidationsts, only citizens of Brooklyn, proud of their heritage and united in her defense. Withhold your decree and disclose the charter under which Brooklyn is to live and let her vote upon it.

Consider the vast interests involved; though uniformity of taxation and of valuations is among them, others are even more essential. Our social, educational, political and moral welfare are in the balance as well as our financial and industrial, while the question of municipal government dominates them all. How are you to govern a great city of three to four millions of people with every man a voter? Let some wise man tell us. Shall it be by a general council supplemented by local councils with my lord mayor at the top, as in London? or by a multiplicity of mayors and councils as in Paris and other European cities?

Already the government of our great cities is our conspicuous failure. Under Brooklyn's benign charter she has set the pace in good government for the entire land; shall we surrender this charter without controlling voice in its substitute? As compared with New York, Brooklyn's government is purity itself; there is not a notorious brothel in the town. Brooklyn is the best all-around educated city in America; her teachers are better paid by 15 per cent. than those of New York. How are we assured that improvement will go forward; that morals will be conserved; that education will be promoted; that uniformity of taxation and of valuations will be secured, unless we can see the charter? Is it wise to take in all of Staten Island, the whole of Long Island, part of Bronx river and the rest of the Atlantic ocean? Would this reduce taxation and assure good government?

Mr. Chairman, Brooklyn's life is in the balance, her press is not subsidized, her pocket nerves are not mercenary, as a household we differ, but we are all for Brooklyn. I am concluded that we shall stand at last upon this platform — "Brooklyn must be permitted to decide her own destiny." She asks for nothing that is not right, she will submit to nothing that is wrong.

Mr. Lexow:

Is not Brooklyn's charter thought to be the best of any charter of any city in the United States? There is no notion of taking away Brooklyn's charter. Perhaps the speaker referred to personal likes and dislikes.

Mr. Woodhouse:

Yes, it is to the personnel we object to. We fear we will wake up after consolidation, and at the resurrection find ourselves in the grasp of Tammany Hall.

Mr. Lexow:

You understand that the vote of 1894, and nothing further, is in question? Brooklyn will be represented at Albany as ably in the future as in the past, and there is no danger of her not being heard on a charter. I have in two years seen Brooklyn represented, and know that there is no danger of the city suffering at the hands of her representatives. I do not know, in my experience of two years, where all the representatives of a city or of a district were opposed to a bill affecting the interests of that city, where that bill has passed.

Mr. Woodhouse:

Assure me that those who have the interest of Brooklyn make up the charter and I will throw up the sponge.

Mr. Lexow:

How about the other four parties, the representatives from the other districts that are consolidated — shouldn't they have a vote also on the charter?

Mr. Woodhouse:

I must not take up the time of the others. I have tried to avoid all technical questions.

Mr. Lexow:

That is not a technical question.

MR. WOODHOUSE:

The creation of the greater city and the taking of the life of the city of Brooklyn of course is in the power of the Legislature, and nowhere else. If the Legislature approaches the question of a charter in the spirit of patriotism, that will be enough. There is a binding law of morals which should be considered in every question. What I fear is the influence of those whose interests are not concerned so closely as those in this city.

MR. LEXOW:

No one doubts that Brooklyn could get a good charter. A great many of these questions are merely doubts, or they contain a doubt, and it is hard to bring out facts. That is what we are here for.

MR. GRADY:

A good deal has been said here with reference to the position of Tammany Hall. Now, I officially state here that Tammany Hall has not been eager for the annexation of New York and Brooklyn. From my knowledge of Brooklyn politicians, I must say you can not get the best of them very easily. When attention is called to statements made here openly that Tammany Hall, either through voters or its organization, is seeking to control Brooklyn, I desire to say that they never have manifested the slightest desire in that direction. I could satisfy you on that point in five minutes' private conversation.

MR. WOODHOUSE:

Brooklyn has passed judgment upon Tammany Hall.

ALBERT G. MCDONALD:

Mr. Chairman and Gentlemen of the Committee: It seems to me that the transaction of 1894, the legislation and the action under the legislation, had none of the features of a contract. Moreover, it as the purpose of the act that while New York voting "yes," must swallow the entirety of a proposition that the other parts of the territory affected should determine separately for themselves. There were none of the elements of a contract in the transaction. It was simply the polling of the sentiment of the people of the localities on that question. While I am free to say that I am in favor of resubmission, to my mind there has always been great force in the arguments attending to the inconclusiveness of the situation. My experience of two years with the Legislature has taught me how rigid, and for general reasons, how proper is their rule that on local matters the local delegation shall control. Yet on the matter now in question, if the reports of the newspapers are true, the whole Kings county delegation in the Senate and the whole Kings county delegation in the Assembly are opposed to this project. At least they are opposed to it without a reference to the people, either on the broad question of consolidation itself or on the question of a charter. That alone, it seems to me, should make this committee pause. The members of the Legislature constructively speak, and usually actively speak, the sentiments of their locality; yet all of this body is opposed to the absolute consolidation of Brooklyn. Now, the committee came down here again for the purpose of reaching the sentiment of the locality, and they have these hearings for the purpose.

This question is not one which is determinable properly by the action of the people's representatives in the Legislature. The reason of the thing, it seems to me, is very plain that it ought to be submitted to the people, because it touches the whole of their municipal affairs. Was the submission of 1894, such as should now be regarded as in any way conclusive? I submit to you, no, sir. Attaching to the vote of the people, then, there was nothing conclusive. I don't say that the vote, then, should not be submitted to a measure of respect, but it is right to argue to you that the vote then was inconclusive in its character. The act for a submission of it was passed in February, 1894. It related to a territory covering twenty-eight wards. In April and May, 1894, there was annexed to the city of Brooklyn for other purposes, territories so that it geographically doubled the size of the city, and it was by these people that this project was carried by 277 votes. The city of Brooklyn, as contemplated when that act was passed was not the city that passed upon the question of consolidation. Attaching to that vote all the force that you please and all the dignity that you please the question now, I submit, is: What is the sentiment of to-day? Of course, if this were a contract and if common law rules of contract obligation could be applied to it, that would be a different matter. But it was a poll of the sentiment in 1894, and no action was taken by the Legislature on that vote. If it were good to be annexed in 1894, but not good in 1895, then the annexation ought not to take place. It is not that in 1894 277 more people thought annexation should take place, the question is of 1896.

This is a people's question, and I firmly believe the people's wish, if not for a resubmission of the whole question, is, at least, for a submission of the charter.

MR. GRADY:

Of course you don't mean that we shall submit the charter?

MR. McDONALD:

No, sir; not for a moment. The annexation of West Farms was a pretty project along side of this. In that case no question of settlement was raised against it. Of course, if the Legislature of 1895, upon the strength of the argument of 1894, had included consolidation, that was an end of it. But the question was left open. The situation is deferentiated from any situation that ever existed before. Senator Lexow's bill is a proposition and we are discussing that proposition.

MR. GRADY:

As a New York man I am opposed to consolidation from the New York side. I am very free to say, however, that while I voted against consolidation just for the reverse of the reasons I have heard stated here, I have always felt bound that the people having spoken on the subject should have that opinion recognized.

MR. BRUSH:

With reference to the reasonableness of asking for a resubmission of this question in the case of an election which is final that is a case where the people have a chance to remedy it at the next election. But this is final.

Mr. McDonald:

I see no analogy because at an election the people knew that they were voting on a conclusive question. The vote of 1894 decided nothing. It was simply the sentiment of the time. Is there any doubt about what the sentiment of this time is? Twenty-eight representatives of the people are on one side of the proposition. The burden of proof is clearly shifted over to the other side, when all the representatives are on one side.

Mr. Brush:

The sentiment of 1894 is probably not the sentiment of 1896.

Mr. McDonald:

These arguments concerning the advantages to the city of Brooklyn, presuming them to be true, are arguments to be addressed to the locality and not to the Legislature. If Brooklyn is to be consolidated then let Brooklyn decide upon that as a tribunal. There is a dispute about the facts in this case. There is an assertion that much benefit will flow from consolidation, and there is an assertion that no benefit will flow. Who shall determine it but the people of the locality? I say let it be argued that taxation will be less, and that real estate values will be taxed down, but these things are asserted here and denied, and how are you going to pass upon them except through the people? The proposition of the Lexow bill is abhorent because the proposition is that on a certain day consolidation shall take place. And so I say here that this is a people's question, that they are the true tribunal, that arguments for and against should be addressed to them, that in view of the attitude of the local representatives, whatever argument may be drawn from the vote of 1894 is completely overcome.

Mr. Redfield:

Mr. Chairman and Gentlemen of the Committee: I have the pleasure at this time of saying a few words to you. And in commencing I wish to remove certain misapprehensions of fact that exist. A very prominent Senator of the State of New York said to an acquaintance of mine, from the central part of this state, recently, that the sentiment in Brooklyn was manufactured because the league of which I am the head had spent $250,000 working it up. I desire to have the message conveyed through this committee to the Senator who made that statement that if he had said just one-tenth of that sum he would have been more accurate. It is utterly untrue that any such sum or that one-fifth of that sum or anything like it has been spent, directly or indirectly, by the League of Loyal Citizens. I desire to say also that the counsel of this league has never received one penny for services rendered, nor has the gentlemen who has gone to Albany, from time to time to represent this league in Albany, ever received one dollar of compensation, directly or indirectly. It is also true that most of the expenses of traveling back and forth have been borne by the parties going. I desire also to say that there has been no coercion of any legislator in this city or anywhere else. They were addressed an open letter, published freely at the time, in which the league pledged itself never to ask for another resubmission; to accept as final such a vote; and to ask for their sentiments, which they reasonably and honorably gave. If there were coercion it was the coercive force of the public sentiment of the city of Brooklyn which is represented by twenty-eight members of the Senate and Assembly at Albany. No man dare say that those men do not represent our public opinion unless they say also that you do not represent the opinion of your people. Do you, sir? Then do they?

Now, gentlemen, I wish to pass briefly to a discussion of some of the alleged facts that have been presented before you here, and I wish to say—very carefully say—that I impugn no man's veracity. I doubt no man's good intent. I do impugn the accuracy of much that has been said to you. You are bound in honor to follow the truth when you learn it; you have the right to the truth. There was placed before you a list of the names stated to represent, the majority of the large business houses of the city. Undoubtedly there are large concerns upon that list, I have no reason to doubt it. I think that almost, if not all of the men upon that list are doing business in this city. But I object to the alleged representative character of this list, for this reason, there are eighty-four names representing firms doing business. I have myself personally examined the 1896 edition of R. G. Dun & Co.'s Mercantile Agency Report as to these names, in which agency twenty-four of these names do not appear; they are not in the latest edition of the Mercantile Agency. On that list, furthermore, there is one concern doing business under three different names who signed all three. And there are two of the concerns in addition that are owned in New York City. I do not doubt that those gentlemen are all doing business. I do not doubt that they signed the paper, but what I do protest against is its representative character.

MR. MATTHEWS:

Will you give us the names of those men to whom you refer?

MR. REDFIELD:

I will give them to the committee. I will not do anything in public that will injure any man's credit. I further wish to say that the names of at least ten large concerns in this city are conspicuous by absence from that list; therefore, I object on behalf of the truth to your giving that list any weight further than as that of eighty-four individuals.

MR. LEXOW:

Have you got any petition signed by representative concerns in the city of Brooklyn against consolidation?

MR. REDFIELD:

Yes, sir; and representing more than this list does; 170 names since filed. I further notice, Mr. Chairman, that Mr. Abraham in his speech to you said that Brooklyn is near its debt limit, but omitted to mention that it was twice as far away as in 1894. He also stated that Brooklyn's taxable revenues were nearly exhausted, in reply to which I quote Mr. A. T. White's own words: "I have come to the conclusion as a citizen and as a taxpayer that the necessary improvements on this side of the river will progress more rapidly than if we are joined to New York." Mr. Abraham also dwells upon the fact that New York city is to add "$80,000,000 to its assessed valuation this year alone, which represents but 50 per cent of the value of the new buildings and improvements erected in New York." And I hold in my hand the Real Estate Record and Guide which gives the entire number of buildings completed in New York in 1895 up to January, 1896, and shows the estimated value of them to be $84,111,023. This at 50 per cent would add but 42,000,000 to New York's values. Mr. Abraham has made a trifling error of $33,000,000 in his speech. I desire also to say to you that it is a curious thing that Mr. Abraham asserts it is "a base libel on the intelligence of the voters" to say whether they did not vote intelligently when they voted for consolidation, but the Consolidation League published exactly six weeks before the election this statement: "There is scarcely any sign that the voters concerned are adequately informed upon these matters or even interested." That is "the libel" which they themselves cast upon voters of the city of Brooklyn at that time.

I now pass to the speech of my friend, Mr. Rufus L. Scott, in which a similar class of difficulties appears. He said there never was a question more fully discussed than that, and my personal testimony is as good as his, which is simply this: I was on the platform speaking every night for several weeks, several times a night, at different places, and I never heard the subject of consolidation mentioned, nor have I ever heard any man outside of the immediate ranks of the Consolidation League who did hear that subject mentioned in this city in public discussion that fall.

MR. LEXOW:

Wasn't it a fact that prior to the vote of 1894 it was not only discussed but made the subject of debating clubs in the city of Brooklyn?

MR. REDFIELD:

I never heard of any debating club discussing the subject in the city of Brooklyn prior to the election of 1894, nor did I ever hear of any meeting in which that subject was discussed except at one meeting in the Real Estate Exchange, where the only man who attempted to speak against consolidation told me he was fired out of the hall.

Mr. Scott says there was " absolutely no considerable sentiment against consolidation." I wish to ask if you believe that to be true. Is that a truthful statement? If that be true I beg you to explain to me the fact, first, that every legislator in this city opposes consolidation. I beg you to explain to me, if Mr. Scott speaks truly, how it is that our board of aldermen unanimously favor resubmission of this question. If that be true, explain to me the action of the Central Labor Union, the action of every Republican ward association in this city except one, so far as I know; I beg you to explain to me not only our league's first enrollment of 77,000 voters which this gentleman attempts to impugn, but to explain to me the list filed with you of 72,800 voters, by wards and election districts, with registration rolls given to you for the purpose of comparison. I submit to you that the statement that there is " absolutely no considerable sentiment in Brooklyn against consolidation " is proven to be incorrect, and it is proven to be so by the facts which you yourselves have in your own hands. The statement would be amazing if it were not amusing.

And now, very briefly, I wish to take up the facts about the election of 1895. I have never said, though it has been stated as if I had said it, that the question of consolidation was controlling in that election. I do not say that the question of consolidation was prominent in that election, and in evidence of that I offer to file with this committee the advertisement from which I read to you before, of the Consolidation League, in which they said over their own signature published night after night in the Brooklyn Eagle, that the " only way " to express a vote for consolidation was by voting for Mr. Grout. And I ask you to notice the fact that they published special editions of two pamphlets and circulated them widely all over Brooklyn. And I ask you to note the fact that certain men were at the polls upon election day who may have have misrepresented the Consolidation League, but who said to friends of mine that they were there to work for consolidation at the polls. If these men lie six men of six different districts in one ward lie, for they said they were there to work for consolidation. I do not now say that it was controlling. I do say that while our league kept it out and took no action direct or otherwise on the subject, the Consolidation League brought it in and were beaten. They brought it in, they forced it to the front, they kept it to the front, and the other two candidates for mayor were for resubmission. Those two other candidates had a majority over the consolidation candidate of 12,000.

Again, I ask you if, in all your legislative experience, you ever knew of a case where all but four out of something like sixty-one legislative candidates agreed in both parties, and in two factions of one party (three parties in all), on one question? Is there any sentiment opposed to consolidation in Brooklyn? Fifty-seven out of sixty-one of our candidates for Senate and Assembly were absolutely agreed on that question. Can you explain that away? Did you ever hear in your experience Mr. Chairman, that a whole delegation were united on a subject without backing behind them? Those legislators were elected in all the districts on that issue. It may not have been the controlling issue of the mayoralty canvass but it was the issue in the legislative canvass, and you have the results before you; you know they are true.

MR. LEXOW:

How could that be the issue where the candidates represented both parties and where all were apparently agreed? You couldn't get an issue then if they were all agreed on resubmission, there was no way in which the people could have expressed their preference for consolidation.

MR. REDFIELD:

That is apparently a conclusive question, but it is not, because the contest came in the nominating conventions and here is a man who was the victim of it (Edward F. Linton) who says he was the victim of a fraud. I know nothing of the fraud; it may be so, but this I do say, that when in the ninth district senatorial convention it became known that Mr. Linton was a consolidationist he was defeated upon that one question and upon no other.

Mr. Lexow:

He was defeated by one vote, wasn't he?

Mr. Redfield:

No, sir; I pass no judgment upon the facts; Mr. Linton is probably better informed than I. On the first meeting it was reported abroad in that convention that Mr. Linton was a member of our executive committee. The simple fact was made known then that was not true, that Mr. Linton was a consolidationist and he lost it completely when the convention met again.

Mr. Lexow:

Is it possible that the people in this city didn't know that Mr. Linton for five years has been a member of the consolidation commission and one of the most earnest workers for consolidation?

Mr. Redfield:

I will answer that by what the consolidation league said, that the voters were not informed at all and not interested.

Mr. Lexow:

That would seem to imply that to-day, after five years of discussion, the matter is so indifferent to the people of Brooklyn that they do not even know their representative on the consolidation commission.

Mr. Redfield:

I am very much inclined to believe that if you take the city far and wide, you will find comparatively few men who can tell who are the members of the commission.

MR. LEXOW:

Do you consider that as an argument?

MR. REDFIELD:

Not at all, nor on the other side. I think it has no bearing on the case. I think I can find thousands of men who do not know who represents their county in the Senate. I wish to further enforce upon you the fact that in that election, when the matter was made clear to the people, it did not enter into the legislative canvass and practically the unanimous voice of Brooklyn spoke through its aldermen and its legislators. How else could it speak? Supposing Rockland county desired to speak to the State of New York, must it not speak through you and its Assemblymen? How else can it speak? But suppose beside that they said we will back you up with signatures of nearly half the voters of the county, and said, here is the registration roll, compare it; would I dare to say that you didn't represent the real feeling of your people? It is absurd when this city has elected its entire legislators and entire board of aldermen and backed them up with these signatures that no one has dared to challenge; it is absurd to say that the sentiment of Brooklyn is not in favor of resubmission.

But I pass from that to take up the question of resubmission itself. The heart of the difficulty of resubmission lies in the fact that a referendum differs in its essence from all other votes; it is radically unlike that in this respect, that lawfully, of itself, it can decide nothing. The Legislature being the law-making power can not delegate that power. It can ask the people to express their wishes; and it can ask the people to give their opinions. It is as free to act after that opinion as before save for the moral effect of the vote. A vote so taken is only a mandate when its conditions make it mandatory. Of itself it decides, and under the law can decide, nothing. The fact is different with a vote on constitutional amendments; there a majority must decide. Such is not the law with reference to a popular referendum, that is a guide to the Legislature, not a mandate to it. It is, it can be, only an opinion, and like opinion it has weight or weakness according to its conditions. This was made perfectly clear by the consolidation commission, who said, in 1894: "Electors will please observe that this vote amounts to nothing more than a simple expression of opinion. It is merely," they said, "the gathering of the sentiment of the electors." It was not possible for them to say more clearly that this could not be mandatory, that it was simply opinion, and that its whole force lay in its value as opinion. The law always provides for obtaining the mature opinion of the people. Therefore our mayor serves two years and then the question who shall be mayor is resubmitted to the people. And you had the question who shall be Senator of your district resubmitted to the people last fall with the happy result of your election. Every election is a resubmission. It is not revolutionary, but it is wholly in accord with American law and American institutions to say that the mature judgment of the people is to be sought. You, gentlemen, who have passed in the Legislature upon constitutional amendments know that it comes before the Legislature first and again in identically the same form to the people. So that there are two resubmissions of a constitutional amendment, one legislative and one to the vote of the people. Why are terms of office made if votes be final? Why do terms expire? That the question may be resubmitted. The question of obtaining the will of the people is the heart and root of the law, and they are revolutionary who say there should be no resubmission. Besides, Mr. Chairman, and Senator Grady especially, I ask you to find a precedent in law or history where 277 votes or any number of votes in this country ever finally decided anything.

MR. GRADY:

The only trouble that I see in your argument upon that point is this, that the first vote in any election accomplishes the purpose of the vote and the second resubmission has no more force nor finality than the question submitted first. So we may say that the vote taken in 1894 was simply an expression of opinion, and therefore should be given no legislative force whatever. When we take the vote in 1896 why can't the dissatisfied element say that should have no more force than the vote of 1894.

MR. REDFIELD:

They can.

MR. GRADY:

Then what practical result can come from it?

MR. REDFIELD:

This practical result. I believe if the vote were taken a hundred times and showed that by a narrow margin (one-third either way, with one-third silent,) this thing was hanging in the balance, it never should be brought about. It should not be irrevocably settled. The law nor good morals would not sanction its being so settled. But since 1894, new problems have arisen, new light has been shed upon the subject. Our people have been educated. We are willing to abide by a vote if it be in their favor absolutely. And I believe that when a vote is had there will be a preponderating opinion one way or the other. The weight of 277 votes out of 179,000, with 62,000 silent, that is very little. But if resubmitted —

MR. LEXOW:

Suppose the other fellow succeeded this time, how could you, after establishing this precedent, ask the consolidationists to consider that a finality and not resubmit again?

MR. REDFIELD:

I have not asked that. I say that what is right and fair should be had, and that is it. I should say that the other side had the right to prove the righteousness of another vote; why should they not have it? But my plea is (and I think this is all side-play anyhow), that the thing would be morally settled by the weight of opinion either one way or the other. I believe, Mr. Chairman, and Senator Grady, that you would have said before 1894 that if that thing got one-fourth of one per cent. majority, it would give no warrant for taking away our municipal life.

Mr. Grady:

I stand on the position of Mr. Woodhouse; I believe in the principle of representation. I would give the same weight to a majority of one as to a majority of a million.

Mr. Brush:

If I understand it, the object here is to get the sentiment of the people as to their wishes in this matter. The sentiment of 1894, you think, is not the sentiment of 1896.

Mr. Redfield:

I do.

Mr. Austin:

Then we might have to settle a hundred times.

Mr. Redfield:

Not quite; the question was not then discussed as fully as it has been since. Now there is more light. Our friends say the light is all with them, but we believe it is all with us. We are willing to pledge ourselves; are they not willing?

Mr. Austin:

Isn't it true, according to your statement, that the people in Brooklyn to-day are so ignorant that they do not know which way to vote?

Mr. Redfield:

No, sir; I did not say that; what I said was this, that they were not informed as to all members of the consolidation commission. Can you state them all? Can you from memory repeat them all to me? Can you, Senator Page; I ask the gentlemen here how many of them can repeat the names of the consolidation commission?

MR. LEXOW:

That isn't it. I think every Brooklynite who takes any interest in this city knows that Mr. Stranahan and Mr. Linton have, for five years, been at the head of the consolidation movement in this city, and if there is such a strong feeling against consolidation, how is it that no serious obstacle has been put in their way?

MR. REDFIELD:

I can not answer your question. I do know, however, that it is known in Brooklyn that Senator Lexow is interested in this matter and is very intent to establish the consolidation of these two cities.

MR. LEXOW:

You have absolutely no business or authority to make any such statement. It is not becoming your situation as a speaker for the Anti-consolidation League, and you certainly do not either add weight to your argument or show yourself possessed of the qualities of a gentleman in making any such statement. For myself, I can only say this, that as the chairman of this committee I am paying more than usual attention to the speeches and will decide the question, as far as I am concerned, on the merits.

MR. REDFIELD:

As regards my being a gentleman, that does not rest with the committee to say; as regards my business to say what I said that may be a matter of debate; as regards my reasons for what I said, I am satisfied they are correct.

Mr. Chairman: I proceed now to say that resubmission has the very best consolidation authority, for Mr. Edward F. Linton said, in an address before the cities commission of the Senate, on February 20, 1895, that if there had been thirty per cent. of the vote in favor of consolidation it would not have been a reason to abandon the undertaking, "it would have been a very good basis to follow up." Having thus openly proclaimed, in February, 1895, that they would not have stopped if the vote had been three out of seven in their favor, they would have gone on, an argument against resubmission from their lips would seem to come with very slight weight.

I now take up the speech of Mr. Jenkins, and his statement that 75 per cent. of all the people in the eastern district were in favor of consolidation is flatly denied by Mr. Bryant. I offered to produce over 6,000 enrolled voters more than favored consolidation in 1894, from the eastern district, now opposed to consolidation.

But I pass on to another statement, which was made with great eclat. He said, I have a petition which represents "nearly all the banks" of the city of Brooklyn. And it was said later by Mr. Jenkins that there were "but two or three" that were not there, and by Mr. Chauncey, that that list represented "three-quarters of all the banking institutions of this city and county." And yet I have before me a list of fourteen banks that had not signed the petition, and no savings banks are included in that list. I do not doubt that some of these gentlemen in these banks that were not mentioned may favor consolidation, but I do say that when it was said to this committee that they represent "three-quarters," or that it represented "all but two or three," that they deceived this committee, and that the fact should be made clear. This should be done upon a truthful basis, should it not?

Now, the remarkable speech of Mr. Frank Bailey on the same day. He gives a lot of figures about the assessed valuation of Brooklyn, saying that in 1883 it was $229,000,000, it was $280,000,000; a trifling error there of $50,000,000. He says there was a gain in the ten years before of $65,000,000; that is a mistake, it was $82,000,000. And so the whole later gain, stated as $267,000,000, is about $50,000,000 too much. And this same characteristic, to a greater or less degree, passes through his entire argument.

I come now, however, to his statement that Brooklyn's gain in taxable resources during the next year can not possibly be more than $6,000,000, but note from the city records that during 1895 buildings to an estimated value of $12,000,000 have been erected. I offer to show proof to you from the department of buildings that 553 more buildings were completed in 1895 than in 1894, at an estimated cost of almost $12,000,000. And Mr. Bailey's whole deduction, from his $6,000,000 statement, is entirely imaginary. He speaks of New York being "generous to her annexed district." Yes, if to take $1,000,000 in taxes to give back $300,000 out of it, is generosity, so she has. If to give them their first school-house fifteen years after annexation is just, she is just; if to give them one school-house where there was a year ago habitually thirty inches of water in the cellar is generosity, she shows generosity.

But I pass to Mr. Bailey's chief statement and argument for the householders of Brooklyn, to the effect that the "average rate of interest" on mortgages in New York city is 4½ per cent. The statement is not correct. In 1895 more than $48,000,000 was loaned on bond and mortgage in New York at rates exceeding 5 per cent., thus leaving out of a total of $125,000,000 that was loaned in New York city only $58,000,000 that was loaned at less than 5 per cent. It is also true, on the authority of the Record and Guide, that more loans were made in New York, both in number and amount, in 1895 at rates over 5 per cent. than in Kings county. There were 6,431 mortgages in New York and 6,300 in Brooklyn placed at over 5 per cent. I take this from the Real Estate Recorder and Guide; 15,000 mortgages in all, 6,400 at over five per cent., 6,500 at five per cent., and 2,000 at less than five per cent. So the average rate would be about five per cent; quite that if not a fraction more. But inasmuch as Mr. Bailey's whole argument was based upon the alleged difference of interest rate, it is all proven to be entirely imaginary. For the low-priced loans are on the large business buildings, gilt-edged property and in amounts of fifty per cent of values or less, and not as a whole upon the small residences. The rate of interest on the average dwelling-houses in New York, is according to the record, the same as here. And I am authorized to say for two savings banks in this city, in neither is one loan over five per cent., while a number are at four and one-half, and they have several other records of mortgages at from four and one-half to four and three-quarters.

Mr. Grady:

The second mortgage might be placed in New York at over five per cent. and the first mortgage might be placed at five per cent. and that wouldn't show the rate of interest. You have to have the character of the mortgage. The practical situation of New York is, that upon any residential property in New York, you can place a first mortgage of sixty-six per cent. of its value at five per cent. Can you do that in Brooklyn?

Mr. Redfield:

I do not question that; I believe it is possible here to obtain loans of sixty-seven at five per cent. on all first class property. I am told that Mr. Bailey's own company is loaning it every day at that per cent. All I can say now is that it is incorrect to argue from that alleged difference of one per cent. in favor of the home owners in New York as against the home owner here in Brooklyn. As a matter of fact the result has been such that here we have now over 7,000 more dwellings than there are in New York for a population three-fifths the amount. So we can not be so heavily burdened by this alleged difference in mortgage interest as to prevent our housing our people much more comfortably than it has been done over there. It would be perfectly easy to go on with this speech and point out other inaccuracies, but I come down to where Senator Brush said during Mr. Bailey's spech than an increase of ten mills on the New York tax rate would equalize the taxes, and I point out to you that to even the matter up as suggested would bring an additional tax burden on New York city per annum of $15,000,000. I have had an actuary go over the tax levy for 1895 to find out what would be the increased taxes in New York city if they were equalized, as proposed under consolidation, and his report was that if the expenditures were maintained as in that year, and the taxes and rates of assessment made equal, there would be an increase of more than $6,000,000 per annum in New York city taxes.

MR. GRADY:

I don't understand the force of that. Is there any suggestion anywhere that under consolidation the taxes wouldn't be equal?

MR. REDFIELD:

I have never heard anybody from New York city offer the least guaranty or suggestion that they would assume any of Brooklyn's taxes, and I have heard it said that there were senators in the last legislature who said the idea was preposterous and would not be attempted.

MR. GRADY:

I do not understand that there can be any consolidation so that we can take Brooklyn's property and leave Brooklyn's debts; my idea is that these cities are consolidated and that the government becomes one, and there must be equality of taxes. I am not making a declaration that is binding upon New York unless I am supported by law. Is there any suspicion that a debt now existing in Brooklyn is to be left a lien upon Brooklyn's real estate as a part of the city of New York? I want to say that New York may not get in love with consolidation, but she never will enter into any sort of govermental partnership that is not founded upon principles of honor and good faith.

MR. REDFIELD:

And there is nothing in the law, as the committee well know, as it stands now, or in the bill introduced, to prevent unequal taxation hereafter. The law simply says that bills will be prepared which, "when they shall have been enacted," will provide for it. But there is no guarantee that those bills will be enacted and there is nothing after enactment to prevent any improvement being assessed upon any part of the consolidated city, just as Williamsburgh is exempted from Prospect Park assessment. There can be nothing to prevent a continuance of that law. Equal taxation is an impossibility to guarantee; this law does not provide it; this law can not provide it; it does not pretend to. It says bills shall be prepared for it. If this Legislature were to enact laws the next Legislature can repeal them, and if it does not repeal them other laws can be passed, and if it does not repeal them another Legislature may. There is nothing in this bill, and there can be nothing in this bill to guarantee, to warrant equal taxation permanently.

MR. GRADY:

All I can do is to guarantee to you that no citizen of New York city who has anything at stake, either in the present or in the future of the city, will ask for any union that is not based upon making the territory one in fact as well as one in name, and applying the general system of taxation for every purpose from one end of the city to the other, and the rate of assessment equal from one end of the city to the other. I claim for the people of the city of New York, and I am proud to be able to speak for the humblest laborer as well as for the millionaire, that they have no sort of corrupt or debased idea that would allow them to exercise their power for any inequality of taxation, although of course New York could not promise equal taxation now.

MR. REDFIELD:

I am very far from wishing to cast upon the people of New York any aspersion, that is not my thought ; I am simply dealing with the legal aspects of the question, that equal taxation can not be guaranteed in the future.

MR. AUSTIN:

If as you state, in order to equalize the taxation the tax burden of New York city must be increased $6,000,000 and that of Brooklyn relieved to the same extent, how could the people of Brooklyn find fault with it.

MR. REDFIELD:

I don't think they would find fault with it.

I now pass on to say that the natural result of consolidation is an increase in taxation. Mr. Schieren has testified before this committee that the effect of consolidating the county towns with Brooklyn has been to bring heavy burdens upon it. Corporation counsel Scott, of New York, and the comptroller of New York city both are this morning on record as stating publicly that the effect of the annexation of part of Westchester county has been largely to increase her burden, which is six and one-half million more than she paid last year, partly because of the increased territory from Westchester County. Those gentlemen, each for their own city speak of the burdens brought upon those cities by the annexations of the outlying towns. And if you add Long Island City and Queens County, and if you add to that all of Staten Island, the process which the comptroller of New York city has pointed out, and which our mayor has pointed out is simply continued to a larger extent. New York must assume not only her own burden but those of Queens County, Kings County and Richmond County, and the inevitable result of the assumption of such burdens is a large increase of taxation over the present rate. It is perfectly certain, it seems to me, that the assumption by the Greater New York, if it come to be, of the necessity of providing improvements for Staten Island and Queens county will result in a very heavily increased tax rate throughout that city over that which Brooklyn will achieve for herself if she remained independent. And in that I am supported by Mr. Alfred T. White in his statement. I have only time to say that all the assertions made before you of Brooklyn's inability to take care of herself are flatly contradicted by him and by Mayor Schieren. And I would call your attention to this statement published by the Consolidation League and distributed widely in a pamphlet furnished by them. If consolidation be rejected and if municipal rapid transit be ordered the burden of taxation upon New York will yet drive thousands to Brooklyn to escape it.

One final word. If there were no other reason against consolidation it is sufficient reason would be found in the condition of our public schools. It was said by Mr. Jenkins upon this floor, that Brooklyn can not provide schools for her children. The fact is, and the superintendent of public instruction will be here to-morrow to tell you so that during the year 1896 every child over six years of age wanting a sitting in our schools will be given it. The land is already owned by the city, and the buildings are partly under construction to accomplish this, and that statement of Mr. Jenkins is absolutely untrue, and, gentlemen, it should not have any weight in your minds, whatever. On the other hand the city of New York to-day has over 50,000 children who can find no seats in her public schools, by the official statements. I put it very moderately, I may quote the New York Times, which says the condition of the public schools in New York is outrageous, the Forum which says that flesh and blood and one's purse are alike abused by the New York schools. It would be like going from light to darkness to permit our public schools to go under the control of New York.

Mr. Lynch:

Mr. Redfield says that taxation is not equal, but we make a difference between taxes and assessments, and we include some of the taxes in a special assessemnt. The taxes for mayor and all general purposes are equal, I am proud to say, and when special assessments are made they are included in the tax bill.

MR. REDFIELD:

I do not know about the detail of that further, than to say this, that on the back of every Brooklyn tax bill is found a different rate for every ward in the city. And the share of taxes which is paid for Prospect park is not included in the eastern district tax.

MR. LYNCH:

I mean to say that when the idea is given out that the general tax levy of Brooklyn is not equal all over the city, this is a mistake. That when we have a special assessment on a particular district, the amount of that assessment annually is put in the tax bills of property owners in that particular district, and of course it increases the rate of that district over the other.

MR. GRADY:

Is the expense of the maintenance of Prospect park put in the general tax levy?

MR. LYNCH:

I can not answer that direct question. I know of other special assessments that are included in the tax bill. The amount of the assessment is added to the tax list in that district. It is a matter of bookkeeping. We all pay the same amount for the support of the mayor, aldermen, street cleaning and such expenses, but in one district they may want to have a Prospect park or as in one district here, there may be an expense of $100,000 for a street sewer and that particular sewer is added to the taxes of that district.

MR. GRADY:

Does the maintenance of your park constitute a city tax?

MR. MUMFORD:

Perhaps I can make this very clear to you. When the property was purchased for Prospect park, the purchase money for that property was taxed on what was then understood as the western district of Brooklyn, and still continues, and the interest on the bonds still unpaid or being paid from year to year, is taxed on western district of the city, including all the wards from one to twelve. The cost of the maintenance of Prospect park, and of all the departments of the city, is a general tax upon the entire city, including the western and eastern districts. The way that came about, at the time that Prospect park was begun, or the purchase of the property was begun, the mayor of the city was Mr. Kalbfleisch; he was a sturdy old Dutchman. He came from the eastern district and he represented more especially the eastern district. Because by his efforts and his efforts alone, that the eastern district from which he came and which he lived, and in which he was more interested than in the whole city, that this act was put in that the western district, having the benefit from it, that the western district should pay for it, and she is paying for it to-day. It was claimed by Mayor Kalbfleisch at that time, and those who stood with him, that this park was absolutely of no benefit and no use to the wards of the eastern district, and that was the argument put forth why the eastern district should not be taxed for that purpose. But if you will go with me to-day to Bedford avenue which crosses from north to south, you will find that the people of the eastern district are having just as much benefit of that park to-day, and have for years, as the people in the western district.

The following letters from W. J. Gilbert, and one from Henry W. Bragg of Boston, were handed to the commission:

206 Harrison Street, Brooklyn, N. Y.,
January 23, 1896.

To the Chairman of the Legislative Committee on the Matter of Consolidation:

Dear Sir.— Two meetings have been held in this city by the committee appointed in Albany to examine into the question of consolidating the cities of New York and Brooklyn. There is deep interest in the matter and widespread anxiety concerning the result. The committee has listened to the arguments of some of our leaders upon both sides of the question; will you kindly give a few moments' attention to one of the rank and file — one is a rent-payer and who has lived in Brooklyn more than twenty years. I am a Republican, but I wish to speak mainly as a citizen. The question, in itself, is not one of party. There are Republicans and Democrats on both sides.

First, speaking as a citizen, I repeat the statement, "It was not generally understood that the vote of 1894 was to be conclusive." Indeed, we were distinctly assured to the contrary, and many voted on one side or the other — just as they did on the proposed constitutional amendments — because the votes were put in their hands as a part of a large and confusing assortment. Most of the constitutional amendments proposed were of little or no interest to us. I voted against consolidation without having given the matter much consideration, simply because I thought we should altogether lose our independence under the enormous vote of New York. A further and careful study of the matter has led many people who voted for consolidation to change their minds, and they now oppose consolidation on any terms.

The chairman is reported to have asked if the vote of 1894 was to be considered a mere expression of opinion, would not the same argument be used in the event of a resubmission. I am decidedly of opinion that the answer to this inquiry is "No."

I repeat that there was no general knowledge of the purpose of the vote, as it is now claimed. I scarce recollect hearing of the matter until a few days before the election, and had given no special thought to it. Such, I am assured, is exactly the position of many others. Some gentlemen on the other side take a different view, and say that vote was intended to decide the question at once.

It is due to each side to suppose that both were absolutely honest in this matter, and it goes to prove there existed no general knowledge upon the subject.

But now the question has been thoroughly considered in all its bearings, every one knows what will be involved in the result of another vote, and the wish expressed by the majority will, I am confident, be accepted as decisive.

I beg to remind the committee that of the vote of 1894, the majority of the city of Brooklyn — as the city had existed for years — was against consolidation; that only a bare majority of a couple of hundred could be counted by including the vote of two outlying sections that had just moved within the city limits, and that the affirmative vote, all told, scarce included one-third of the legal voters.

But it is contended that the election did, anyhow, show a majority in favor, and therefore the scheme should be carried out. I protest against this as unfair.

In an ordinary election, it is right that the majority, however small, should prevail, for the reason that the people have their remedy at the ensuing election.

But this all-important proviso does not hold here; consolidation once effected will be final — there will be no appeal. No action so grave and important, so far-reaching and irremediable, should be taken by the Legislature except upon the assured majority of the registered vote. Republican government depends upon the will of the governed. We contend that no authority has been given, nor will be given, to break up the city of Brooklyn and merge it in New York. Other gentlemen take the opposite ground. Then, in all fairness and justice, let the matter be tried, now that we all understand it.

Our study of this matter leads us to object, as citizens, to consolidation, because of the extreme difference, now prevailing between the cost of dwellings and of rents, of expenditures and the general condition of the two cities, and we fear higher rents and higher taxes. Gentlemen speak of bridges to be thrown over the East river and other great improvements to be made when the union is accomplished. But I beg respectfully to ask you who is going to pay for them, and how can the amount now collected in Brooklyn for taxes be reduced? Will New York, as now constituted, contribute a single panny? I think not. Now and henceforth, under all circumstances, I suggest as a certainty that all moneys spent on this side of the river must be raised on this side of the river. It has been asked, why are all the Brooklyn representatives opposed to consolidation? It may not be quite right to put the question in this form. They are opposed to consolidation without a full referendum of the people, now that the matter is generally understood. The anti-consolidation feeling was so strong here at election time that this promise was demanded of each, and it is due to them to say that, so far as I know, the promise was given cheerfully as one demanded by common justice.

In this connection I would call your attention to the petition presented by Mr. Abraham on Saturday, and his remarks in the same tone urging consolidation, "providing, among other things, for attaining an equal and uniform rate of taxation and uniform valuations for purposes of taxation."

Now the bill proposed at Albany, does not, as I understand it, secure anything of the kind, and without such security the petition goes for nothing. No man who signed that petition can be held for a moment as supporting a forced consolidation. The terms of which are unknown.

The extreme difference in the conditions prevailing in the two cities will make it almost, if not quite impossible to establish any "uniform valuation for purposes of taxation." The rate can of course be equalized, but I can see but two ways to accomplish this. Although not quite up to those figures, the rate of taxation in New York we may set at 2 per cent. and in Brooklyn 3 per cent.

Equalization can be effected by increasing the rate in New York—which will hardly please the citizens of that locality and will be of no advantage to Brooklyn—or lowering the rate and increasing the assessments in Brooklyn. This we can not accept as a satisfactory solution. A householder who now pays 3 per cent. on a valuation of $10,000 will hardly feel richer when his tax bill is rendered at 2 per cent. on $15,000. The difficulties of selling his property will be greatly enhanced, and increased rents will necessarily follow increased assessments. More than this, with the tax rate once reduced to 2 per cent. there will be continual temptation before the party in power to venture upon expenditures under which the rate will steadily but surely rise again, and our last condition be worse than now.

We object to losing our name of Brooklyn and what reputation it has acquired. Take away our name and henceforth it is almost inevitable that the maps and the postmaster will describe all the section on this side of the river under the offensive name of "East New York." If the members of the committee were all residents of Brooklyn they would realize that this possibility is unpleasant in the extreme.

With regard to the political side of the question I beg to remind the committee that the adherents of the two great parties in Brooklyn are merely equal in numbers, but neither can claim a majority. To be more particular, about 45 per cent. of the voters are democrats and 40 per cent. Republicans. The remaining 15 per cent. represents the independent vote.

There are perfectly able men in both parties and we can live in peace and comfort which ever side may win in the election. If the evil element which clings to the skirts of every party leads to objectionable measures on the part of those in authority, matters can be reformed when the next election comes by the powerful aid of the independent vote. But if Brooklyn is made a mere suburb of New York we shall be entirely under the control, for taxation and every other purpose, of the Democratic leaders in New York. Brooklyn democrats will object because, in place of the absolute power in their hands, when in control, they will hereafter be wholly under the dominion of the leaders in New York and get only a few crumbs now and then from the political table, while the Republican vote will be entirely useless and its influence in the city obliterated.

It is therefore, for the interests of every citizen in Brooklyn that we shall be let entirely alone—we want no interference—we can manage our own affairs and we demand our right to do it.

Very respectfully yours.

WILLIAM J. GILBERT.

BROOKLYN, N. Y., *January* 23, 1896.

To the Republican Members of the Committee:

Gentlemen.— As a Republican I call your earnest attention to the perilous condition in which the party is now placed in this city — and consequently in the State — there are 70,000 Republican voters here whose right to govern themeselves is threatened with extinction, and the power to accomplish this is in the hands of the leaders of their own party at Albany. Will you not give this matter very earnest consideration. The feeling is far deeper here than some gentlemen seem to imagine.

What reason can be urged that will justify the wiping out of a city with nearly a Republican majority and making political enemies of 70,000 Republicans who will deem themselves outraged by enforced consolidation. I do not say that all these 70,000 are now against consolidation, but I do say it is my firm belief after years of residence here and well knowing the present state of feeling, that the passage of the simplest act looking to consolidation, except one of plain resubmission, will cost 10,000 Republican votes — an actual consolidation bill will increase the disaffected to 30,000 this year imperilling both State and national election — and another year, as the miseries of the case are more distinctly realized the Republican vote may entirely disappear. Why should a people who feel themselves deeply injured and disfranchised do anything to assist the Republican party elsewhere in the State or nation?

It seems to me that the noisy New York World and the Democrats in New York who are clamoring for consolidation, have before them not only the view of absolute control here — to the exclusion of local Democrats — but they count on the sure disaffection in the Republican party to put the State at the ensuing presidential election securely in the Democratic column.

I implore you to consider this matter with care. As political friends and associates we are astonished at the dangerous position we find ourselves in, and that to at the hands of those to whose political protection and assistance we may honestly claim a right. It is hard to believe and we can not believe that the committee will allow this act to be forced upon us. The peril to which the Republican vote in the city of New York is already exposed will require the greatest care on the part of Republican managers to save the State — why incur any additional risk?

The Republicans of Brooklyn ought to have absolute protection from the Republican leaders at Albany. It would seem to be plainly for the interest of the party — without any reference to our personal and political rights — to prevent consolidation under all circumstances so long as it was possible to prevent it.

No one at this time can be regarded as a friend who does not work for and help us. We want actual service — we are dissatisfied with the governor who goes about with his head in the clouds. He can help us, and if he doesn't we will hold him as an accomplice. He will surely be defeated for the presidency, if nominated, as will any State ticket that bears the name of a member of the Senate or Assembly, who does not henceforth work heartily and earnestly for the welfare of Brooklyn. Pass any consolidation act and Republican voters in Brooklyn, disfranchised in all but the right to vote for the benefit of others, can not be expected to go to the polls for that purpose.

If we can not prevent we can punish, and we will do so in November.

Yours very respectfully,

WILLIAM J. GILBERT.

BOSTON, *January* 23, 1896.

WILLIAM C. REDFIELD, ESQ., *President League of Loyal Citizens, Brooklyn, N. Y.:*

Dear Sir.—Yours of the 21st instant is received. Upon so short a notice it is impossible to give you such statistics as could be obtained from the different official records of taxation and valuations upon proper research, but perhaps I can state general facts, based upon personal observation and knowledge, which will be quite as useful for your purpose.

I was city solicitor of Charlestown during the four years first prior to its annexation to Boston, and was necessarily familiar with all the city departments and the general affairs of the city. For thirty years I have also been the solicitor of the Warren Institution for Savings, which has deposits of over eight millions and nearly all of its loans upon real estate have passed through my hands, and thus I have always been familiar with the market values of real estate in this vicinity.

There can be no question but what there has been a steady decline in such values since the date of its annexation in 1874, and that such decline is universal throughout the annexed district, except as to the very cheapest kind of property, which, perhaps, has not changed materially as to value. Residential property has depreciated fully fifty per cent. and the character of the population has greatly changed for the worse. Scarcely one of the old families are now represented in the district, and there has not been erected within the past fifteen years, what would be called a first-class residence, notwithstanding the district was considered an ideal location for residence, by reason of the natural conformation of the land, which afforded perfect drainage, and unrivalled outlook over the Charles and Mystic rivers and Boston harbor, and better than all, it was within fifteen minutes' walk of State street, and the business centers of Boston. These conditions have not been changed except by the increased facilities of transit by electric roads, but these have not staid the decline.

Business property has depreciated at least thirty per cent. notwithstanding the population has increased twenty-five per cent. It is comparatively easy to establish facts of this kind, but usually more difficult to ascertain the causes. It is generally conceded by those whose judgment is entitled to the most consideration, that annexation is the cause of this decline in all that goes to promote the prosperity of a city, and to me that cause appears a perfectly adequate one, for the following reasons:

First. Annexation has swept away every vestige of local pride and spirit. The cry was at once, "A Greater Boston," and all local enterprise was merged and overwhelmed by the desire to improve undeveloped property in the more distant suburbs and a constant wrangling among the city representatives of the different territories to obtain appropriations for local improvements, and the result was combinations whereby the annexed district was practically ignored.

Second. It destroyed all sense of local government and responsibility of representatives to the people. The needs and claims of the district were ignored, and we have had no redress. Whoever we elected from our district, were out-voted, as the original Boston had a much larger representation by reason of its greater population than all the annexed districts combined, and the result is obvious. The people soon lost all interest and either moved to the city proper where their claims would receive consideration, or went into the adjoining towns where their influence would count for something.

Third. The rate of taxation per thousand is a little less than before annexation, but the assessors' valuation is increased so that the burden of taxation remains substantially the same, except as it is affected decreased rentals.

There are other reasons which might be presented showing the direct connection between annexation and the present depression in values and interest, but those reasons are of themselves sufficient to my mind, and I may add that the general consensus of opinion among those who have considered the matter, sustains this view.

Very truly yours.
HENRY W. BRAGG.

January 24, 1896, 2.50 P. M.

NELSON G. CARMAN:

Mr. Chairman, and Gentlemen of the Committee: There are two reasons why I appear here this afternoon. One is because I am a citizen of Brooklyn, taking a deep interest in this question of consolidation, as a considerable property-owner in this town. The main reason why I appear here is to get from the embarrassing position of what might be termed getting astride of the Schomburgh line. I was pictured as an anti-consolidationist in a New York newspaper on the occasion of a big meeting in the Academy of Music on January 13. Owing to a mistake of my own and that of a reporter, I inadvertently got my name on the call of the Academy of Music meeting that took place that night, as going in favor of resubmission. I do not want to face both ways on this subject, and I want to be put on record as for consolidation. As a real estate man, I am utterly opposed to resubmission, as calculated to establish a vicious precedent. Even though the new vote should be for resubmission, I have too much confidence in the judgment of the people to believe that it would be against consolidation. The question has been widely discussed, the local press was a unit against consolidation, and the vote of 1894 was larger than that on the constitutional amendment by 20,000. Nothing shown by the Loyal League convinces me that there is now a great change of sentiment for resubmission. I wonder why the committee come here. They come to feel the pulse; but on any ordinary subject the people could feel the pulse of Brooklyn and go back to Albany as wise as they came. Those arguing against consolidation are men of professional pursuits and sentimentalists, such as lawyers and ministers. The consolidationists are business men, drygoods men, having industrial and financial and commercial interests. The Rev. Dr. Cuyler has said that this was a homogeneous city, and that annexation would be a civic assassination, or something like that. He could not imagine, in 1853, when it was proposed to annex Williamsburgh to Brooklyn, that some venerable man had objected on the same line; it would have been about as sensible. All that was left of Williamsburgh to-day was a more or less fragrant memory. There was always an active and vigilant minority that opposed reform and they were necessary to bring out the real arguments. I will not speak about equal taxation, or of bridge interests, or of the inadequacy of Brooklyn alone to meet the needs of the people. The primacy and prestige of New York should prevail.

Eugene G. Blackford:

Mr. Chairman, and Gentlemen of the Committee: I appear here as a citizen and as a taxpayer of the city of Brooklyn, to place myself on record as being in favor of consolidation and opposed to resubmission. Not that I fear resubmission, because, if I believe that resubmission was proper and right, I think we would have an immensely larger majority in favor of consolidation. In my capacity as president of the Bedford Bank, with 2,000 or more depositors, it is my privilege to come in contact with those people, and it is very rare indeed that we find one of them opposed to consolidation. In forty-four or forty-five stockholders, there are only two, a father and son, that are opposed to consolidation. I am also connected with three other banking institutions, and in all of these I find the sentiment overwhelmingly in favor of consolidation. I am also a taxpayer in the city of New York. I have a fair opportunity to compare the cost of owning property in the two cities and the difference in favor of New York is nearly one-half. Knowing these things, my interests are entirely in the line of consolidation. I believe the taxation will be very much smaller under consolidation. There is a large amount of trust funds in New York in which the holders are restricted, either in real estate or in mortgages, to the city of New York. By consolidation this capital will be released, and we will be able to place the mortgages on our property at moderate rates. We will also get rid of the discrimination against Brooklyn interests and Brooklyn institutions. All of these things have probably been rehearsed to you over and over again. I don't know as I want to say anything more to-day. I simply came here to place myself in favor of consolidation.

Percy G. Williams:

Mr. Chairman, and Gentlemen of the Committee: I am entirely unprepared for this call. I came in merely as a spectator. I am one of those unfortunate individuals known as real estate dealers and landowners, and yet I think the real estate interests make the importance of a town. What are the facts of real estate in Brooklyn to-day? We find there is absolutely no demand for real estate here. There is not one house in the city of Brooklyn that can be sold for the amount of purchase price. Now, the question is, what causes this? Taxes too high? That must be determined. I think something should be said from the standpoint of a person who buys and sells real estate as a means of livelihood. I think the prosperity of the city depends upon the real estate values of that city. Take a city where values are fixed higher, there is no trouble at any time in disposing of a common piece of property; but in this city you can not do that. In this city the real estate interests are stagnant; there is very great trouble in disposing of property. I find there is absolutely no demand for real estate. You can notice signs "For Sale and To Rent" all over the city. I am certain that there is not one house in 100 all over the city of Brooklyn that can be sold for the price for which it was purchased. As an instance, I bought, a few years ago, a very fine brownstone house upon one of the residence streets in the city of Brooklyn, and after holding it for five years, and paying for several improvements in the vicinity, I was obliged to sell it for ten per cent. less than the purchase price.

Another point, it is claimed that this question of consolidation was not properly before the people at the last election. I think it was. We had opposed to it all the newspapers in the city of Brooklyn, with the exception of a little morning daily of very small circulation. All the consolidationists were able to do with the limited means that they had was to distribute a number of pamphlets among the people of the city of Brooklyn. That was all that was done. Yet in spite of the opposition of all the newspapers, the question was carried. It was charged that it was simply a movement of the real estate speculators and land boomers, but instead of all that it was carried by a decisive majority. I think that most of the Loyal Leaguers of Brooklyn that are opposed to consolidation are perfectly honest in their conviction that it is not for the best interests of Brooklyn to have consolidation. I am willing to give them credit for that. I can only say, so far as I have come in contact with all kinds of people, that the sentiment of Brooklyn is overwhelmingly in favor of consolidation. I think if it were voted upon the vote would be decidedly in favor of consolidation.

M. J. McGrath:

Mr. Chairman and Gentlemen of the Committee: I have heard a great deal of this discussion, and I think the most potent argument that has been made against the question of resubmission was made by the first speaker, Mr. Benedict. He said that the election of 1894 was a quiet one and that political parties had taken no part in it. I think that is a great argument for not taking another vote. If another vote were taken it would be carried out on true political principles, and would not be an expression of the will of the people. I think that is what you have come down here to find out — what the will of the people was then, and not what it is now. Even if all of New York and all of Brooklyn are willing that this case should be submitted over again it seems to me that the districts outside would say no. It is a ridiculous proposition to me for the officers of this city to come before the people and ask that this vote be taken over again. I think it would be in the nature of a crime. On the question of a referendum, I think every good subject of Brooklyn would be delighted to have a referendum if it were practicable, but to have this charter framed, put a number of very eminent gentlemen to the trouble of framing a charter, must be cumbersome, and to say that the voters of this city would take up that charter and study it for themselves and then vote upon it intelligently is what I don't believe. Bulky matter, such as this, would not be read by the ordinary layman; it would be unintelligible to three-fourths of the voters, and I don't say anything against the intelligence of the voters of this city. It is practically a legal document; its effect would not be understood and the result would be an ignorant vote. It would be taken up by the politicians of both sides, and whatever their verdict would be would practically be the verdict of this city. In the heat of an election, I do not think that the calm judgment of the people would be represented in any such vote. I do not think that this Legislature or any other Legislature would pass a charter in any such way. A great deal has been said about the effect of this vote and how it has been gained. The argument has been used that Gravesend and that Mr. McKane's subjects voted in favor of consolidation as a little run in on the city of Brooklyn. As a matter of fact, a year before the local election she had repudiated McKane and his methods. It is true that all the county towns voted in favor of consolidation, but the smallest percentage of majority was in that very town of Gravesend, and the largest was in New Utrecht, which certainly had no grudge against Brooklyn. I think that the vote of the county towns was just as intelligent and as much entitled to respect as that of Brooklyn; I contend that their voice has just as much right to be considered as that of the city of Brooklyn. The city of Brooklyn has grown to what it is to-day simply by the addition of Bushwick, Williamsburgh and so forth.

MR. LEXOW:

In each of these acquisitions no vote of the people was taken at all?

MR. MCGRATH:

Oh, no; it was simply that they were taking something in. Notwithstanding that Brooklyn is such a quiet place and such a homely place, it seems to me a very peculiar thing that they should have taken in such a sink of iniquity as Gravesend. I think Brooklyn, in this consolidation, more than any other place, needed consolidation. The county towns have not been any burden. It is plain that Brooklyn has about three and a half millions of a ballot. How did they get that? By annexing the county towns. There is nothing else left in Kings county for Brooklyn to perempt. It has got to the end of its resources; I don't think it will be more than three or four months before they get to the end of their tether. There is a vast amount of money that has been appropriated for improvements which will have to be stopped unless some sort of revenue is discovered. What Brooklyn wants is to be stirred up. It wants to get into active contact with a livelier people. We want a great many new improvements and we especially want better communications with New York. If New York and Brooklyn were consolidated both would have a mutual interest in devoting itself to the improvement of all parts of the city. The point was raised by the registrar of arrears about the county towns and what a vast amount of property was held for taxes. He did not say how much of the property in the newly annexed towns had risen in value. In speaking of his own department the registrar made the point that some of the county towns were in a terrible condition. I think it would be a good thing for Brooklyn to be taken in, because we are in difficulty.

JOHN H. BURTIS:

Mr. Chairman and Gentlemen of the Committee: I have been seized upon as I came into the room to say something of the deepest interest to the people of Brooklyn. I have seen Brooklyn grow from upwards of 300,000 to nearly a million. I was one of the originators of the first elevated road in Brooklyn. It was started in my back parlor, and my wife was in the next room and knew all about it; and I helped start the rapid transit in other ways. In other words, I have believed in the territory on this side of the river as being the most delightful and healthful place for sleeping and eating. I have not believed in it as a business community. We have more cemeteries convenient than you will find in any city on earth. It is a good place to die in. We have been trying to get rapid transit, easy transit, for the laboring men from the grand old city across the river to this city, where they could get cheap homes. Where did the opposition come from against rapid transit here? Public meetings were held everywhere in this vicinity by the same class in Brooklyn that have developed all the interest there is against consolidation here. Has it ever occurred to the Senator chairman from the back woods to ask himself why does White, as fine a man as ever drew breath of life, oppose consolidation; why he lives on the heights? Just one step and he is in New York. Where is his property? Below the City Hall, as near New York as he can get. All the opponents to consolidation live below the City Hall. The most distinguished opponent we have, I don't believe he ever got beyond the City Hall in his life.

MR. BRUSH:

Do you know the districts in which you live and I live gave 500 against consolidation?

MR. BURTIS:

Yes; but they wouldn't do it again. I know what I am talking about. I have seen thousands of citizens who pay taxes. I represent people who own millions.

MR. LEXOW:

Please address the committee.

MR. BURTIS:

I thought you could hear me. I wish I could speak so that people wouldn't laugh, but sometimes I can't. I introduced the bill for that vote and you helped me pass it like a good country hayseed. Senator Brush tells you about the majority against it. If they had known as much as they do to-day they would have come in hoards — masons, plasterers, painters and tinkers. There isn't any work here for them. Why? Go all over the country and you won't find real estate as it is here, dead or dying. I have been here for thirty years and I have seen widows thrown out of their homes, and the most lamentable victims, you might say, but never have I seen such a list of foreclosure sales as are advertised in the columns of the newspapers to-day. I tell you we are on the verge of bankruptcy. In no other year has this depression been as bad as now.

Mr. Brush:

Don't you know that there is a great financial depression extending all over the country?

Mr. Burtis:

Yes, I know that; but there is nothing anywhere like the depression in Brooklyn.

Mr. Brush:

You say this is a nice place to sleep and to be buried in, intimating that there is no life or business here. Do you know that there are 10,583 manufacturing establishments in this city?

Mr. Burtis:

Yes, I know it, and there ought to be 10,000 more of them. I know we have manufacturing places but there should be more — more.

Mr. Brush:

Do you know that there are a hundred and nine thousand persons in the population of Brooklyn that depend on these manufactories for their living? In other words, that one-ninth of the population in this city work in our own manufacturing establishments here.

Mr. Burtis:

Yes. We have a lot of people working in manufacturing places here. We have a lot of them in the penitentiary manufacturing things.

Mr. Brush:

Then this is not altogether a place of sleeping?

Mr. Burtis:

We have manufacturing places here, to be sure. We have Brownsville. Perhaps you counted that in with the other places.

Oh, we have lots of them, we have quite a few manufacturing places in this city. But what we want now is the assistance of New York's wealth. We want help. Help! I say; help! What a stroke of Providence it was that, through the Legislature, New York city was induced to pay half the expense of our new bridge. Could anyone say that Brooklyn would have been able to pay for that bridge? And why can't we pay for a bridge? I tell you we are taxed almost to death as it is; why, I have a house worth $10,500, on which I pay $190 in taxes. Why are we taxed so? Because we must have the money to pay for our new streets, our sewers, our schools and parks and municipal necessity. And yet we have not enough money to provide for sufficient sewers. We have to pray to heaven that we will not have a heavy rain storm which will flood our cellars and deluge our streets. And we need more bridges. But where will we get them unless New York gives us the money? And New York has as much as offered to do it. And I tell you the Brooklynites know this. And, Mr. Chairman, when I think of our representatives from various wards and districts going up before the Governor of this State and deliberately saying that the people of Brooklyn are against consolidation I imagine it is impossible to know where they found that out.

MR. BRUSH:

I would like to interrupt you for a moment to say that within the last two weeks I have received resolution after resolution, letters upon letters from societies and individuals, urging me to stand for the city and against consolidation. And I have had only four or five letters from other parties who favored consolidation, and most of these were from real estate dealers. That is why I went before the Governor.

MR. BURTIS:

Well, I am very glad to know that the real estate dealers have had time enough to write one letter. These real estate men are not disreputable men —

MR. BRUSH:

I did not cast any such imputation or any reflection upon them.

MR. BURTIS:

Oh, I know he did not cast any imputation upon them, Mr. Chairman. He didn't get any letters from doctors? No. He didn't get any from lawyers? No. From journalists? No. They all came from real estate men. Well, I say the interests of a great city are created by its real estate men. They are the men to feel the pulse for the city's condition. I have but one more remark to make. Unite the interests of these great cities, and give to Brooklyn some of that wealth which she has helped to create. Give us a chance to reap a little benefit from the work we have spent there. Unite us legally, as we are naturally.

A VOICE:

Will Mr. Burtis tell us when, in 300 years of the history of Brooklyn, has New York ever had anything other than opposition for Brooklyn's interests?

MR. BURTIS:

I have not lived 300 years and can not answer that question.

A VOICE:

Well, I have lived here half a century and know of many years more, and never once has New York had anything but ridicule and contempt for us here.

MR. GRADY.

I would like to know what the assessment was on that $10,500 residence of yours?

MR. BURTIS:

Seven thousand dollars. That is what they assess a $10,500 house for. Just seventy per cent. And that is not an isolated case. I pay taxes for other people and the assessment is about the same all the way through. And sometimes it is more. And there is a house a few doors from mine, worth $7,000, and assessed for $6,000. Think of that.

J. LOTT VAN NOSTRAND:

Mr. Chairman and Gentlemen of the Committee: I am in favor of this bill of consolidation, and I will give you one or two reasons why. I am a resident of one of the new wards, the Thirtieth, and hold police court at Coney Island. The town of Gravesend gave a very small majority in favor of New York. That was in 1894. In 1893 there would have been three thousand majority against Greater New York, because the conditions were then different. My principal reason in favor of Greater Brooklyn is that I live in a town that was in favor of going into the city of Brooklyn, because our government was so bad. After we got into the city of Brooklyn, we tried to get free delivery, and we used every influence that we knew of to secure that end. We have been unable to get that. Another reason is that the representatives of this county should not control the sentiment of the other legislators. I believe that their opinion was forced from them by the officers of the Loyal League. I think any delay in granting consolidation would be an injury.

MR. BRUSH:

I want to correct the impression that my opinion was forced from me by the League of Loyal Citizens. When they wrote to me I simply gave an honest opinion.

MR. VAN NOSTRAND:

They know that if they gave their opinion for consolidation, the influence of the League would be used against them.

ABRAM J. DAILEY:

Mr. Chairman and Gentlemen of the Committee: It gives me considerable pleasure to appear before you this afternoon and say a few words in behalf of what I deem to be the best interests of these two great municipalities, New York and Brooklyn. I have been a citizen of Brooklyn for upwards of thirty-eight years and during all that time have been in the practice of law. From the time that I first came here, it has always seemed strange to me that two municipalities so related to each other by a community of interest, should be separated as municipalities. But it does not necessarily follow because it seems so to me that I am right in my conclusion; but I am simply giving my views on that question and some reasons why I come to this conclusion. A very pertinent question was asked by a distinguished appearing gentleman of Mr. Burtis, just as he way leaving the room, and it was why New York was persistently opposing what was for the best interests of Brooklyn. It is precisely that reason that causes one municipality to do those things that tend to promote its own interests and confer the least benefit upon the other. In other words, if New York city can get Brooklyn to do—force Brooklyn to do certain things, and bear all the burdens itself, New York will do that every time; that is human nature.

Mr. Grady:

Where is there an illustration?

Mr. Dailey:

The Brooklyn Bridge, in which New York made Brooklyn pay the largest share.

Mr. Grady:

The Brooklyn bridge was demanded entirely by the people of Brooklyn.

Mr. Dailey:

New York would have demanded it if she had not been sulky.

Mr. Grady:

New York might just as well have asked for a bridge from New York to Westchester county. I have been pretty well acquainted with the legislation of twenty years, but I never knew an instance where there has been any blow struck by New York city against Brooklyn.

MR. DAILEY:

The blow consists in a selfish means always taken by a separate municipality looking out for its own interests. Unite these two municipalities and you will see a great improvement—an improvement on a wide scale, no jealousies. The only people that I find in the main, who are opposed to this consolidation are those people, who by a sort of sentiment have got it into their heads that they would not sleep quite as well at night, even though they were in the same house, and in the same streets if this territory was called New York instead of Brooklyn; it is a sort of sentiment for which I have no respect.

Now, it has been repeated here that the vote should stand, as in 1894; others have said that the vote was the conclusive will and desire of the people of Brooklyn. Take the total aggregate vote. There was more than 64,000 votes for and less than 64,000 votes against consolidation, and a little less than 64,000 did not vote at all. Now the argument is repeated over and over again that that is not a fair indication of the feeling of the people on the subject. It seems to me that it is very decisive. What did those 64,000 people mean? They knew what they were about. They knew what was being discussed; the question was before the people, and to say that the people of Brooklyn did not understand this question of consolidation was to be passed upon, and if they were opposed, then and there to cast their vote against it, is to declare the people ignorant to an extent that I will not admit.

MR. LEXOW:

Don't you think that the failure of those 64,000 people to vote was an indication that they did not care which way the matter was decided?

MR. DAILEY:

No, sir; I think it clearly indicated the reverse — that they were not opposed to it, and if you take that and add it to the vote that was cast in favor of consolidation, then you have 128,000 voters who are certainly not opposed to consolidation. That is the way I look at that vote. We need to have these cities consolidated because it is for the best interests of both that they should work together in harmony because their interests are identical. The people of the city of Brooklyn know that we have not the facilities and accommodations that a great city should have. I want to say something that is a little critical of bridge management. It has been such that it will depopulate 50,000 in two years to come. I know it. There is a small class of people opposed to consolidation. I do not find many men that did not vote coming before this committee and saying: "I did not vote on the subject. It is the people that voted and they are coming and asking for an opportunity to vote over again. Now, this consolidation is for the interests of not only these two municipalities, but for the State of New York. I think that the Legislature of the State of New York can well look upon the vote taken so decisive. I am glad that you have come to Brooklyn to get the sense and feeling of the people, but if you were to let them vote again, you would be no more enlightened. Will you send the question back? After you get another vote, won't there be another? Some of the gentlemen say not, but I don't believe them. Let this question be settled and there will be a revival of business. We have had a fair vote and it should be decisive. Let this agitation be stopped. I believe, Mr. Chairman, that this Legislature should respect that vote which has already been taken and pass the bill that is now under consideration and let the two municipalities understand that this subject is settled, and settled forever. As I said before, there will be a great revival of business and there will be better feeling than has existed for ten years past. The people of the city who are working against it are working against their best interests. I believe in a higher patriotism than mere sentiment. I believe in looking to the best interests of the great municipality. I have no sentiment on this subject. Let us look and see what is for the best interests of the whole people. Let us have something that we shall be proud of. Let us have miles of improved streets. Let us have public improvements and beautiful parks and not be in the stagnant condition that we are at present. Consolidation will help us complete and carry on these great improvements.

Some people say: "What is to become of our public property?" We will own it. "What will become of Central park?" We will own it. We will own it with the people of the city of New York. Somebody says that we will be governed by Tammany Hall. I am not afraid of Tammany Hall; no more than I am of certain influences over here. Another thing, if Tammany Hall thinks that they can play any little jobs on the city of Brooklyn they will find their mistakes. Let there be no partiality. This million of people have influence enough and independence enough to wipe out any opposition of that kind. And we will command the respect of the people of the city of New York because we occupy that position. I have no question upon that result. I know New York is very wicked, but we will make it better. Let us consolidate and we will go over and help Brother Parkhurst.

H. B. HUBBARD:

Mr. Chairman and Gentlemen of the Committee: I come before you to discuss this question from a sentimental point of view. Why should we lose the identity of the city of Brooklyn? If I looked at the question in that way my feelings would all be against the union of the two cities. My business is in this city and my property is situated within this city, all my business connections are in this city, and my family have been here for 250 years; so if anybody can speak, sentimentally, I would be one. But as a citizen of this community the first interest to be considered is, whether it is for the interest of the general public, and private interests as well. I am of the opinion that the best interests of the city of Brooklyn will be benefited. It will be of benefit to our business interests if we shall be united with the city of New York; and not only the city of Brooklyn and the city of New York, but the entire State of New York will be benefited.

The city of Brooklyn is in a peculiar situation; she has a very large territory, larger than that of the city of New York; we require sewerage, we require police. We require street lighting and everything appertaining to a large city. For such a large city there is no city in the world that is so little of a city; its business is conducted on the other side of another stream which separates us from New York. People have private interests here but all their business is done on the other side of this river. We of the city of Brooklyn ought to have some of the benefits arising from the work of our own people. Brooklyn is poor in consequence of the enormous expense incurred in her municipal administration by reason of her peculiar position. But she is still able to take care of herself, with time, but we ask to be joined so that we may have the additional credit of a combined city. We can do the business here. We are now reaching our debt limit, and we have found it necessary to raise our valuations so that the taxes are too high. In the city of Brooklyn our tax is about seventy per cent. of the assessed valuation. In New York, I think it averages about fifty per cent. on the assessed valuation. The effect of this is, not that we can not pay but that we pay under difficulties; we are obliged to pay higher rates of interests than New York city. We want the credit to enable us to carry on our business as we want it, and the effect of annexation would be the equalization of the assessed value of property. Some may say that we have different values in this city, as may be seen by the back of the tax bills of 1895, a different value in each ward, but this is because of general improvements for certain localities; they are kept separate and that is why our tax rate is not uniform. It should be uniform throughout. It would be a great benefit if she had increased power to borrow money. She should have the benefit of a tax on personal property that is now largely centered in the city of New York. The city of New York needs our harbor; she needs our wharves, she needs docking; the best docking facilities are on this side of the river. The shipping here of heavy freight is, I believe, larger than in New York. New York has the sea port and is known as the great commercial center of the State of New York, but she needs our docking facilities to preserve her supremacy. Therefore, consolidation would be of benefit to both cities in this respect. In the past there has been great jealousy between the two cities, one growing rapidly. We have great difficulty in getting one bridge. The city of Brooklyn, small as she is in proportion to New York was obliged to pay two-thirds of the expense of that bridge. It is true that it brought a large additional population here. But is it not true that the large additional population earns its money and advances the interests of New York by doing its business there? It is not true that the bridge connecting the lower part of New York has increased the value of property. If there were no rivalries or jealousies between these two cities another bridge would be built, and it would tend to distribute the population in New York city on the Brooklyn side instead of carrying it over to Jersey and the extreme end of Westchester county. New York is a peculiar locality; it is nothing but a narrow strip of land, and it has no ability to spread unless it connects with Brooklyn. We do not want these rivalries and these jealousies to keep us apart any longer. New York has become and is becoming more and more so every year the place of resid:ence of the extremely wealthy and of the extremely poor. The poor live in the tenement-house districts; the wealthy live up town; the great middle class, the safeguard and the protection of humanity are driven from New York and seek their residences here; they seek their residences in New Jersey and in all surrounding counties.

Then comes the question of water supply and everything of that kind, which can be better managed by combination than it can singly.

MR. GRADY:

It was stated when the Brooklyn bridge was being constructed that people from New Jersey and the other outlying districts would come to New York and Brooklyn to live, but they did not come along.

Mr. Hubbard:

I think that the best evidence that they did come along is this: The immense population in the city of Brooklyn since the bridge was completed; also the fact that this bridge is now taxed to the very utmost of its carrying power to take care of the people, with all the ferries that were in existence before the bridge was built still running and still carrying its own passengers.

Mr. Grady:

They come from New York.

Mr. Hubbard:

New York's population has also largely increased before the bridge was built.

Mr. Grady:

Naturally it would.

Mr. Hubbard:

But it could not have taken care of the increased population which has been thrown in part on this side of the river. They do not emigrate from New York. It was the natural growth of New York in its business residents seeking homes in other places than New York city itself. We have saved many from going to New Jersey that would otherwise have gone there.

Mr. Grady:

I remember that it was promised that we would see nothing from early morning until late at night but people coming from New Jersey and finding lodgment in Brooklyn. After the bridge was built, the Jerseymen did not come along, but at the end of the bridge there were a number of houses that gave way to large manufactories, and a good many of the people went over to Brooklyn to take advantage of the cheap rents, advantage of the cheap houses in Brooklyn, and paid their taxes into your treasury, and then after breakfast they came over to New York to see if there was not a little money for them.

MR. HUBBARD:

The most singular thing in reference to that is that New York property, from the bridge to the Battery, is worth from 25 to 100 per cent. more than it was before the bridge was built.

MR. GRADY:

You do not attribute that to the bridge?

MR. HUBBARD:

I attribute it very largely to the fact that the increased population and the people that would have been unable to find comfortable residences in New York city came to Brooklyn.

MR. GRADY:

Property in New York city has not increased. When I was a boy, after a man got on the fourth story he was told to stop, and now they build iron buildings from twenty-two to twenty-five stories high, and of course that gives to the land an artificial value. In 1870, when a man went to buy a plot of ground on Broadway he had in mind that he might possibly erect a five-story building. When you buy a piece of land now you are confronted with the possibility of a building twenty-two stories high; that is what accounts for the increase in the value of land between the points that you have mentioned. The natural increase that has come to us has kept us pretty busy.

MR. HUBBARD:

It has kept New York so busy that, with all the increase and all the buildings, running from four to twenty-two stories high, are still filled, and the people must seek other localities. It is most desirable that we should have them in Brooklyn, so that they will help pay the taxes of the greater municipality, instead of going to New Jersey and paying their taxes there. It is much better for us if we can keep them here, and I think we are keeping them here by that course. New York, also, is the natural, financial and business center, and we want to do everything that we can to assist

New York in that direction, and we can do it by furnishing residences for her business men. We also have a water front which New York requires, and which New York must have to maintain her commercial supremacy, and in order to do that she must have control of the government of this city. In reference to all such matters we should be one. We also have advantages for manufacturing, and we also have a large acreage of land in the suburbs of Brooklyn, where manufacturing establishments that can not be established in New York can locate. We can build up her power and keep New York in the front rank, because we have the facilities here for doing it. Look at our magnificent water fronts. We want to bring money here to increase our opportunities for business advancement, which will surely follow consolidation. It seems to me that consolidation should come at once; the people voted on it two years ago. We should have it, and have it at once. Pass the act and then determine upon the minor details of administration for the two cities. You have plenty of time to do that between now and January 1, 1898. Between now and then a commission can arrange a satisfactory plan for governing the two cities in all detail.

Referring to the question of resubmission to the people. The matter has been submitted. Not only was it submitted, but so confident were the people in favor of consolidation that they simply rested upon their oars and waited for the verdict of the people. The matter was thoroughly discussed; every newspaper in the city of Brooklyn was discussing the question of consolidation, and they were all opposed to consolidation. Those that felt it was the interest of the community that consodidation should be had voted for it, and they carried the day. Those that failed to vote were the people that had no interest here, and were utterly indifferent to consolidation or anti-consolidation. Now, if because the majority of the people have not voted at an election it is necessary to resubmit the question, you never can do anything. People might stay at home; because one-quarter, or about twenty-five per cent. of the total number of registered voters have failed to vote upon this question is not a sufficient ground for a resubmission of a question that has once been decided by a vote of the people. They say a majority of the voters did not vote, and that, therefore, you should resubmit. What is the use of submitting a question to the people for their determination unless you abide by that determination? But my impression from talking with many people is that the great majority of the people to-day is in favor of consolidation and believe that it will be for the best interests of the whole community as well as their private interests.

MR. BRUSH:

Of course, we are all working for the best interests of our city. Now I may ask this question; from the arguments of some of the gentlemen that Brooklyn is not prospering: Do you know how rapidly the city has increased in population in the last fifty years?

MR. HUBBARD:

I don't know the percentage, but I know the increase has been very large.

MR. BRUSH:

I can tell you that our population has increased 600,000 in fifteen years. In the last ten and a half years the increase in the assessable value of property is $113,000,000; so that it does not seem that we are going backward.

MR. HUBBARD:

Many of the people are not the owners of property in the city of Brooklyn. Aside from that question we have an increased assessed valuation, but are you aware that that increase is made by way of new buildings, very largely by simply adding so much assessment each year? And that has not been a natural increase, but it was done because we were near the limit of our bonded indebtedness, and we had to issue bonds to make necessary improvements.

Mr. Brush:

I think that has been done too much in the past, but we are increasing very materially. There is a natural increase from this number of people.

Mr. Hubbard:

The percentage and increase has been very much greater since the establishment of the Brooklyn bridge; but Brooklyn needs more bridges and she is not in a position to pay two-thirds of the expense of additional bridges. She can not bear the burden.

Mr. Brush:

This argument in favor of building more bridges to New York is not paying the cost of building the East river bridge.

Mr. Hubbard:

Consolidation will put Brooklyn in a position where she will receive aid from New York and be able to build the additional bridges that we need.

Mr. Brush:

In view of what has occurred in three years, don't you think that we can go on and build another bridge?

Mr. Hubbard:

No, sir. Don't you know that we are now within a very small amount of the limit for the issue of bonds of the city?

Mr. Brush:

I know that we are two and a half million more outside of the limit than we were two years ago.

Mr. Hubbard:

If you will go back to the time before this bridge was built, you will find that while our expenses were less and the population less, that we were very near the limit then. We have approached the limit notwithstanding the increase in our population. This shows the utter inability of the city, without assistance, to build more bridges.

MR. BRUSH:

I do not dispute the fact that we are very close to the limit; but it seems to me in view of the prosperity of the last year and the improvements that have been carried on under the last administration that there is good prospect for the future.

MR. HUBBARD:

Unless I am mistaken as to the information given me by the mayor of the city within the past week the bonds necessary to be issued and called for now will bring us within half a million dollars of our limit.

MR. BRUSH:

That is not my information.

MR. HUBBARD:

That is my information. I think that you will find that I am correct in that statement.

MR. BRUSH:

You say that the bonds have not been issued but are called for; if you use the same argument for New York, you will come to the conclusion that her underground transit scheme would bring her as close to the limit as we are.

MR. LEXOW:

We are not obliged to build the rapid transit.

MR. HUBBARD:

I am speaking of obligations already incurred and which must be met. We need two or three more bridges and we have no money with which to build them.

MR. BRUSH:

I agree with you that we need more bridges.

Mr. Lexow:

The vote taken in 1894 was a vote of the people and distinct from a political vote, and if a resubmission is had a political issue would be raised.

Mr. Hubbard:

At the previous election it was a vote of the people. Of course it is impossible for me—I have the misfortune not to be a politician—but I think it would be decided on political lines.

County Court House, Brooklyn, N. Y.,

January 25, 1896.

Mr. Lexow:

The committee will hold one more continuous session unless it is necessary to elucidate new points, and we request the speakers to confine themselves, as nearly as possible to new points.

Mr. Redfield:

I desire to file with the committee for its consideration to-day, issues of the Real Estate Record and Guide, of New York city, and have marked the articles which I desire the committee to consider. I will also hand to the stenographer several other documents which I desire incorporated in the record.

S. V. White:

Mr. Chairman and Gentlemen of the Committee: I propose to abide by my time and not be greedy. I am limited to ten minutes, and you will not be burdened long with what I have to say. I shall confine myself to answering questions asked by the Hon. Mr. Coombs.

Mr. Lexow:

I want to know if the vote on consolidation in 1894 was not binding.

MR. WHITE:

It is not binding, because it was given out that that vote was not to be binding. Without charging deliberate fraud, public servants, in giving out the statement that the vote was not to be binding, were guilty of making a grave mistake. When the question first came up it was said everywhere that the people of Brooklyn were to be given an opportunity to vote on the terms. There were but 33 1-3 per cent. of the voters who voted on the question in 1894. Give us a chance to vote on it now, and we guarantee you shall have 90 per cent. of the voters express their views on this subject. The weather will not interfere with us then, I promise you. We shall be out with our umbrellas and mackintoshes, too, if necessary.

When you say that a vote of 33 1-3 per cent. is to be considered as binding, it is not only the case of the tail wagging the dog, but it is a very miserable stump of a tail wagging the dog. In regard to the bill, I don't know very much about making laws, and I certainly do not want to criticise this bill in the presence of the father of it, when I am trying to win his favor. It seems to me, however, that it is a very remarkable bill, for it is a case of suspended animation. Some of the sections of the bill are to go into operation immediately, while others do not take effect until 1898. The consolidation committee is to be continued in power and it is to prepare bills from time to time to effect the consolidation of the two cities. It is not possible, then, to get through with the details of the change immediately. The bill says that consolidation is to be effected completely on January 1, 1897.

MR. LEXOW:

On January 1, 1898, Mr. White.

MR. WHITE:

Then I have a misprint in my copy, and I shall not, therefore, need to make my point.

Mr. Lexow:

The two cities are to elect mayors to take office in 1898, when the change could be effected more easily.

Mr. White:

Very well, then my next proposition is that as you are the representatives of the people, you should not ask these men to frame a law for this important transaction. You will not gain anything if you do. You are not able to bind a succeeding Legislature which will have to adopt the law so framed. Why not take it upon yourself to frame a charter and let us vote upon it. It may be that New York will favor that law — it may be that the country towns will not want it. Why should New York and Brooklyn want to take in Tompkinsville and South Oyster Bay, except to create jobs for laying sewers and other purposes? Let New York and Brooklyn vote on the plan. No man here wants to take in the cabbage and potato lots; let us keep politics out of the way; Democrats and Republicans are in earnest here in wanting to be heard on this thing which affects millions of dollars worth of property and a million people.

Mr. Lexow:

That is why we are here.

Mr. White:

That is what I am here talking for. An aphorism of Horace Greeley was to the effect that when the common people get mad they get ——— mad. We are in the condition of the common people. No party or set of men can frame for us an alien government that will turn us over, bound hand and foot, to New York.

Mr. Lexow:

The consolidationists say they must have consolidation at once. The resubmissionists say the question must be voted upon again, and the referendum advocates want to vote upon the bill. It places us in a dilemma.

MR. WHITE:

I am sorry for your dilemma, but you go on the theory of permitting the people of each locality to have a voice in their own government and you will make no mistake.

RICHARD S. STORRS, D. D.:

Mr. Chairman and Gentlemen of the Committee: I desire to speak briefly and to confine myself wholly to the one question of resubmission, because on that my views are distinct and positive. On the question ulterior to that, of consolidation, I am not finally committed in my own mind to any determinate position. I see arguments for it and I see arguments against it. But on the question of resubmission I am as solid as the court-house. It seems to me very difficult to understand fully the views of those who oppose it. For as far as I am concerned, and those who sympathize with me, we have never accepted the so-called result in November, 1894, as giving an expression of the public thought and feeling in Brooklyn even at that time. You are familiar, of course, with the details of that vote. It was under very confusing circumstances, as has been indicated in the note of Mr. McWilliams. There were a great many ballots and the time was very limited, and it was for something in the air — for consolidation or against it, not for any formulated proposition whatever. The law itself stated that the object of it was to get an expression of the wishes of the people of the different localities affected. It was no suffrage, no vote in the way of accepting the law or rejecting it, in the way of accepting or electing an officer. If it had been a vote then according to our impression of things it would have been satisfactory in its result and final, if it had been five in the majority or ten in the majority instead of 277, or one in the majority. In the old commonwealth of Massachusetts, when I a lad not yet of voting age, Marcus Morton, not a relative, I believe, of Levi P. Morton, was elected over Edward Everett, the accomplished statesman and scholar by a single vote. Nobody questioned the absolute finality of the election when the majority of one vote had been ascertained. But this was not a vote at all. It was an expression of the public desire and wish. Then there came out 193,000 registered voters, 64,000 and a fraction for it; 64,000 and a fraction against it; 62,000 and a fraction voting neither way, and a majority on the whole of 277. In the city of Brooklyn as it was when the act was passed, and as it was when contemplated by that act, there was a majority of more than a thousand against consolidation. New Utrecht and Gravesend, under inspiration which we may conjecture the source of without affirming, voted heavily enough for consolidation to overcome the majority in the city of Brooklyn. But it was in no sense a vote; it was the expression of a desire, simply, and that was fifteen months ago. Now since that, what you want is the present judgment of the city of Brooklyn on this question of consolidation; many have died who voted then; their opinions are not to be counted now. Many have moved away from the city and others, more numerous, have come to live in it; they have a right to their opinion and to the expression of it. Many who were not then of age for voting have come to be of age, many hundreds certainly, probably 2,000, probably thousands, at any rate more than a thousand in this vast voting force of Brooklyn of more than 200,000, more than one-seventh of the voting power of the State. A great many have come to be of age, and they desire an expression of their opinion, and you have no right, in our opinion, to refuse them that expression. Then we want to know how long this thing is going to hold on. This expression was made, as I say, fifteen months ago and the Legislature took no action upon it. That Legislature has passed out of existence, another Legislature has come in, differently constituted and under a different organic law of the State. If this Legislature can go back to that former, as we think, nebulous and fantasma expression of popular opinion, and base legislative action upon it, then the next Legislature can do the same, and the next and it may go on into the next century, and our children's children may come here to find that a legislative action affecting them is to be based upon this expression of opinion, so-called, in November, 1894. Where is the end to the thing? We affirm that the only way is to take a new vote. Let the dead past bury its dead and let us start fair with a new expression of the popular feeling of Brooklyn. That is rooted in our minds, that is a fire in our breasts. We are not to be content unless the present voting population of the city of Brooklyn, as it now is, shall agree to have measures of consolidation submitted to the Legislature and afterward, of course, submitted to the people. But I have not got to that point. Now, observe, if you gentlemen of the committee and of the Legislature go on passing acts of consolidation without taking the present opinion of the people of Brooklyn on the subject what are you doing? Well, you are involving us by your own authority which is novel, unknown and apparently to us very great, which you can not measure and sound and which we certainly can not. Here is a city which has been in existence sixty years and more, a city of eleven hundred thousand people probably, very nearly that at any rate, of more than 200,000 voters, as I said the seventh part of the voting power of the State, and you undertake to put this city into the municipality across the river, larger in numbers, and determine its corporate existence. Well, there are great hazards in that. There is a hazard in regard to government. No precedent has ever been established. No such measure has ever been adopted anywhere, and we do not know what the future of government in this city is to be. We can take care of ourselves as a separate community. We have had a good government for the last two years. We have a good government now; we will take care to have a good government in time to come. But if we are to be controlled by the municipality of New York, we have no guarantee of that government at all. We have had troubles of our own on this side, frauds, no doubt, and conspiracy, but in comparison with the frauds and conspiracies, which you, sir, so largely contributed to unearth and bring to the light two years ago ours have been a mere transient, innocent pimple on the face compared with a plague ulcer. Well, we do not want to come into any connection which will subject us to unknown hazards. We may waive it. We may say when all the arguments on the other side are in that we will take the chances; but for you of the Legislature to expose us without our free, present, deliberate and decided consent to hazards of that sort — well, I do not wish to use any strong words, but I say it is tyranny. It seems to me to be absolute, presumptuous arrogance, to take this large population, which has grown as it has, and to subject it to another municipal power without its own consent. I would say, to speak with all honor of the Legislature of the State of New York, in which I have lived so many years, that it seems to me that while you may have the power to do it, that is for constitutional lawyers to decide, you have no more equitable right to do it than you have to authorize the looting of one of our warehouses because a window was left open casually a year and a quarter ago. Well, then you call upon us to give up all the presumption in our favor which has arisen from our past history. We can do that if we choose, but you have no right to require us to do it. You must submit the question first to the popular vote and make that vote decisive. Brooklyn has a presumption in favor of its continuance. It has been a city all these years. It has grown. I don't regard myself as an old man, but in my public life in Brooklyn it has grown from 60,000 to more than eleven hundred thousand, certainly to more that a million, multiplying eighteen times, multiplying four times faster than the population of New York and with more desirable average population. Now, we have built noble institutions here, done it ourselves, not called upon the State or the other city or any other city to help us. And you will find all these institutes of charity, of religion and of culture, crowning the town, built by the town, itself. We have developed a good government. We have one of the best charters in the world for city government, a model to other cities. We have developed a high and generous public spirit. All the presumption is in favor of going on in our city corporate life. We, as I say, can give up that if we choose, and, when we go to the polls, can say: "Yes, I will let that pass, too." But the Legislature can not constrain us to give that up, in our judgment. They ought to accept it as we accept it, and allow us to go on until we have ourselves definitely decided that we are willing to terminate this which has been really an illustrious career. Well, then you require us to quench our own affection, to surrender our affection for the city that we love. Now, gentlemen, do not say this is sentiment. Sentiment is a power, and this is our sentiment. I know there are a great many who sneer at it and say, " Oh, well, this is all gas." Gas is illuminating and gas is sometimes explosive, and we want it distinctly understood that this sentiment of ours is a deep and energetic sentiment. Of course, I know a great many gentlemen share it, they take Brooklyn as a convenience just as much as they take a horse car or trolley car. They have no affection for it, because they never worked for it. They never did service and sacrifice that others have been doing here for fifty years, and therefore it is to them a dormitory or a restaurant — nothing else. They have no more affection for it than they have for a lamp-post or a door-mat; not so much as they have for an old coat of last year. Well, we say that this affection is something that you can't trifle with. We can put it out of our way if we please, but you can't control it or compel us to surrender it. It looks like a harmless thing. Well, dynamite, I believe, is a harmless looking thing, if I understand about it, but it don't bear much pounding. Men say, sometimes — I have heard them say — " Oh, offer a man a thousand dollars extra for his lot and house and his affection for the two will disappear." You understand, each of you gentlemen understand, that affection is not something that can be measured by a yard stick. It is not something that can be put into a dealer or grocer's scales and measured against the coin of the realm; it is a power with us. Now, we may put all this aside and say, " Well, I love Brooklyn, but I give it up now because the general sentiment seems to be against it." But if you constrain us without our free assent to give up and stifle this affection, fond and proud, which has been born in us and nutured in us for fifty years towards the city of Brooklyn, you do yourselves no good. You gain no peace, and in my impression and conviction, you will do us an inestimable injury and harm. Then observe, further than that, that you require us to submit in this case to that which is irrevocable, and that is a very important matter for all to consider — for us and for you. You may make changes in our local law, in our local policy, submitting them perhaps or not to local option. You may impose them upon us. You may make modifications of our charter, which shall be minor modifications, imposing them upon us, and we may regret it, but we shall not energetically, probably oppose or resist. But here you propose to terminate our municipal life. Well, a man may be cured of many diseases and be as well afterward as before. He may be healed of many wounds and be as well afterward as before. But if you cut off his head an entire college of surgeons can't set it on again. Well, that is what you propose to do with the municipality of Brooklyn, brand it, stifle it and bury it—and bury it beyond the power of resurrection. There is no resurrection coming to this municipality of Brookyln if you once pass these consolidated acts, and you can't disentangle it hereafter from the great floor of population all over the territory any more than you can disentangle the waters of the Hudson out a hundred miles beyond Sandy Hook. It is impossible. Now, we may say, "Very well, we are agreed to all that," but I insist upon it that for the Legislature to impose that on us without our free, present, general assent, is simply preposterous arrogance. I do not think it would be held possible in any other country in the world. Well, then there is no president in this country. Certainly I do not know of any in any other country on the earth. Then remember, for my time is passing rapidly away—remember that in doing this, in any resubmission to the people you get exactly what you are understood to have come here for, that is, information as to the present wish of the people of Brooklyn. You can't get that from thirty or forty gentlemen. You can't get it from Mr. White or from myself, or from Mr. Redfield. We probably look at things through spectacles which our minds color very lightly. I do not know at all how the ultimate vote would go. I know that many who voted for consolidation a year and a quarter ago are now against it. I think that many, some certainly, who voted against it are now distinctly in favor of it. Which way the general set of public feeling and opinion has gone I do not know at all, and I do not know, as I said before, when the question comes up how I shall vote, myself. But that we must have resubmission is unquestionable in order to ascertain the judgment and wish of the people here. You might just as well try to get it by going out and stopping a trolley car and inquiring of the passengers in that car as to try to get it by coming here and hearing on one side and the other advocates of one opinion or another, and judging from the general atmosphere of the place. Give us the vote; then you will understand whether Brooklyn wants consolidation or does not want it, and the legislature will understand it, and the Governor will understand it and every power in this city and in this State will understand it, and that is the only way to get a full and final expression of the popular judgment without bringing upon yourselves opprobium, without exciting a storm here that will not die or pass away. Give us the resubmission. And remember, if you please, Mr. Chairman and Gentlemen of the Committee, that there is more than the municipal life of Brooklyn involved in this question. The honor of the Legislature is involved in it. We certainly do not desire after this fifteen months of interval to count November, 1894, as if it were February or March, 1896. The honor of the State is implicated in this thing. Every city of the State which respects itself ought to make common cause with us and to fight and protest to the last against the hopelessly merging of the municipal life of one great corporation and community in that of another without its own free assent. My deliberate judgment is that, if you refuse us resubmission, then you strike a blow, an astounding blow, at the judgment and the conscience of every fair-minded man in the land.

MR. LEXOW:

Doctor Storrs, do you take the position that the vote of 1894 has spent its force?

DR. STORRS:

It was worthless at the beginning and is invalid now.

ST. CLAIR MCKELWAY:

Mr. Chairman and Gentlemen of the Committee: Until this morning I did not intend or expect to take part in these discussions. I do so only at request of members of your body. My respect for them and for the principle and for the substance of authority which they represent, makes their desire an obligation and my appearance a duty. I trust, however, none will misunderstand my original purpose to take no part here in the debate. It was not due to want of interest in the subject, or to want of appreciation of this committee. It was due to the fact that I have a medium in which my own views can be expressed contemporaneously with the publication of the views of others, and to the fact that that pleasure and function leave to me little time, personally, to interpose in controverted subjects.

The compliment and invitation of some of your members, however, acquit me of intrusion and afford to me opportunity to say that I support the sentiment of those Brooklynites who ask for a resubmission or a referendum of the matter of consolidation to the voters of this city by the Legislature of the State. The preferment of this request by a considerable number of the people affected and concerned should, it seems to me, be an impressive fact in itself. It should be a fact which others should be desirous of granting, not quick to resent or glad to deny. I could not comfortably contemplate a proposition to refuse such a request if the decision of it rested on me. I should feel that I have deprived a man or a city of something akin to a natural right. There is only one thing more strange to me than a spectacle of any one calling themselves Brooklynites opposing such a request, and that is that any outsiders to Brooklyn should oppose it. The action of the first is unfilial. The cause of the second is not easy to explain, except on the theory of meditated spoliation. Brooklyn can bear with, check and forgive her unnatural sons. Brooklyn can be trusted to deal with her external foes.

In this city, as on a hinge, political destinies have turned, and the future can be made as significant with successes and with funerals here as the past has here been made for statesmen and for parties. All moral revolutions in this State have had their initiative in Brooklyn. Here was the first school for general free education established in this country — not a block from where I stand. In this city now is the second academy founded and chartered in this State by the Board of Regents in the interest of higher education. That board itself was created by the authorship and effort of Ezra L'Hommedieu, this island's representative in the State Senate 112 years ago. Here, by victorious defeat and aggressive retreat Washington's army saved the Union's life and afterward were able to beat the consolidation attempted against American liberty by the Hessians in New Jersey and the English in New York. Trenton and Princeton became a resubmission of man's right to be, and Stony Point a referendum of the fate of freedom to the breast of freeman. From this island came the first Governor whose election in 1856 ranged this State against the advances of slavery. Here was spoken by our great Cullen the judicial word that lighted the crime of Maynardism to an immortality of fame and of fire. Here were organized the rebellions of conscience politics, which, in 1882 and 1892, 1893, 1894 and 1895, proved that neither party can put machinehood above manhood in this country or in this commonwealth.

I ask for resubmission or for referendum, because it is a time-honored American recourse. Slavery was abolished only by repeated resubmission of the essential question in issue from the candidacy of Van Buren and Adams, in 1848, to that of Lincoln and Hamlin, in 1860. Twelve years of resubmission or of referendum, none the less real because informal was had; the effect, even then, far outran the intent. The intent was only to confine human bondage to prescribed limits. The effect was the freedom of a race; the emancipation of labor and the rebaptism of the republic into the glory of human rights. All the war amendments to secure the political and moral results of the war rejected by a sufficient number of legislators to compel the repeated resubmission of them to such Legislatures. If I mistake not, such States as Ohio, New York and New Jersey voted to retain the word "white" as a race restriction on suffrage in their Constitutions, but had to vote it out at last under the force of resubmission of the question to their voters. Our friends, the women suffragists, have been repeatedly voted down by Legislature after Legislature, only to resubmit their plea to the last Legislature with success, and it is to be resubmitted to the present Legislature on its way to the people, if this Legislature sends it down. Does anyone suppose, if the women are defeated, they will give up the contest? He little knows the better half of human nature, if he does. If an expression on constitutional changes is not a finality surely an expression on problematic absorption is not. It is a part of history that the issue of the Declaration of Independence by the convention which adopted it was only reached by a resubmission of the informally negatived proposition to issue it on the demand of Dr. Witherspoon, of New Jersey. Resubmission or referendum is an immemorial habit of high civilization. England repeatedly refused recurrence to arbitration on the Alabama claims on the northwestern boundary and on the Vancouver channel matter, as well as on the Behring sea fisheries. Her government, on a resubmission of the questions to it by ours, did consent to arbitration just as her statemen and ours, let us hope, will do on the Venezuelan matter. Wherever there is a wrong there is a remedy. Wherever there is a grievance there is a hearing. Wherever there is a misrepresentative result, there is a resubmission. It is only a local question now. Therefore, better grant it, for the locality affected covets not, yet will not reject the duty of making it a question decisive of State and National contentions.

I shall oppose no verdict if the people of Brooklyn shall pass on their own destiny. I shall respect none that is passed without their consent. It is inconceivable that a Legislature will do violence to the views of the solid delegation from this county on a Brooklyn question. The Legislature that did violence to the will of the people of Buffalo on a Buffalo question was revolutionized out of existence. The functionaries who did violence to the will of the people of Troy on a Troy question bequeathed to their successors the murder of Ross and the fate of Shea. It is a perilous thing to oppose the will of a city, more perilous when it has changed its mind and desires so to record it. That Brooklyn has changed its mind I am unable to doubt. The consolidationists would hardly oppose a vote that they did not believe would go against them. The paper I edit receives more letters from its readers than any other two papers in the world. It prints all that are not libelous or immoral. It prints them promptly. Over eighty-two out of every 100 on consolidation urge resubmission or a referendum. No one who knows the bonds between that paper and its constituency can doubt what preponderance of sentiment here that means.

Gentlemen, the plain people of Brooklyn love it and wish to preserve it. They represent the manhood, the labor and that admirable middle class who are the salt of the earth. They sell what they own. They own what they buy. They are, therefore, not real estate speculators who neither own nor hold what they sell or buy, but are all hyphenated vibrators, for a commission or for a consideration, between the property of actual owners and the money of intending purchasers. Neither are these plain people legal or other users or usurers of the money of others. They earn their own money and when they deposit it in banks or trust companies they do not lay down a mortgage on their manhood with it, and they do not recognize the right of bank officers to sign away their sentiments, when those officers merely sign their own names. A man's a man for all that, and every man is in Brooklyn the political peer of every capitalist or of every lot boomer. These plain people prefer a government that costs them a modest sum per capita to one that cost its citizens twice as much. They prefer reasonable rents to high rents, homes to tenements, and many houses to a few mansions. Our million plain people outnumber our ten or twenty millionaires, and, singular to say, they outvote them, and they do not fear them.

This people do not believe in a charter or a measure devised by a commission appointed by executives whom the people have repudiated at the polls. They do not propose to let the men whom they have buried rise out of their graves, galvanized into a semblance of life, to bury the city that put them under ground. Our people think it disorderly that institutions that owe to Brooklyn all the prosperity they have received should lead in a movement to extinguish Brooklyn. They do not believe that New York will pay our debts or bear our burdens, and they know of no manly man and of no manly city that sell their rights or dodge their responsibilities for dirty money, no matter how high it is heaped. Manhood counts for more than moneyhood here, and whether we be poor or rich we are neither for conquest or for sale. As I said on another and in a lesser crisis of Brooklyn's life, when Brooklyn magnificently responded to my words: "Brooklyn for the right and the right for Brooklyn," so will I now confidently add: "Brooklyn for and by Brooklynites forever."

W. H. Maxwell:

Mr. Chairman and Gentlemen of the Committee: My statement will be brief, but before making it, it is only right for me to say that I appear before you to-day, not bearing any commission from the board of education, not representing, as far as I know, the school teachers of the city. I appear here simply as a citizen who has given some twelve or fifteen years — the best years of his life — in building up the school system of the city of Brooklyn, to give my judgment upon this question, of how consolidation will affect the Brooklyn schools. I have heard it stated that the city of Brooklyn can not build school-houses to accommodate her children, and the inference has been drawn that in case Brooklyn is consolidated with New York, we shall then be able to build school-houses. They claim that when consolidation is effected we shall have school-houses for all our children, a seat for every child. Before we reach any such conclusion as that I think it may be well to compare the present condition of Brooklyn with reference to school accommodations with the present condition of New York; and I have been to some trouble in ascertaining, exactly, the condition of our affairs. I find that according to the health board records of the two cities that the present population in New York is 1,310,395; the present population of Brooklyn, 1,100,000. The registry of pupils on the 3d of October, 1895, in the New York schools showed an attendance of 187,422; the register in the Brooklyn schools on the same day 119,251. What do these figures mean? They mean that one in ten of the entire population in that city is in the public schools; whereas, in the Brooklyn schools the ratio of registration was one in every nine, showing that the Brooklyn schools afford very much better accommodation to-day than do the schools of the metropolis.

MR. GRADY:

Do you leave out the parochial schools?

MR. MAXWELL:

I am speaking about the public schools. As a matter of fact, there are more children in the parochial schools in proportion to the population in Brooklyn, than in New York. I make that statement without fear of contradiction.

MR. GRADY:

Every superficial circumstance is against the statement.

MR. MAXWELL:

We have no superficial circumstances against it, because the census was taken and it proves my statement. This means, sir, that in New York city only 10 per cent. of the entire population of the city are in the public schools; whereas, in Brooklyn 11 per cent. are in the public schools. Now, I further make a statement which will be borne out by facts: I believe that our schools are better built in Brooklyn; take the average of the school buildings of Brooklyn, they are better situated and better in every way than the school buildings in New York.

MR. GRADY:

Are you aware that New York is now extending her school system by the acquisition of new sites for new school buildings?

Mr. Maxwell:

I am aware of that fact. Also, that in 1895, the city of Brooklyn built more school-houses and better school-houses than in any previous year of her existence, almost twice as many as any previous year of her existence, and we are prepared to do the same thing this year and the money had been provided to do it. If Brooklyn be consolidated with New York, it being the larger, the wealthier, and the stronger city, we expect but one thing, so far as our school system is concerned, and that is that the New York city system of school administration will be extended to Brooklyn. I think, sir, that among the educators there is but one opinion with regard to the New York system of school administration, and that is that there is no worse on the continent. The system in New York is radically different from the system in Brooklyn. In the city of New York there is a central board of education with very little power; and there is a board, called the board of trustees, in every ward of the city, that control these several members one from each of the wards — they really hold all the power with regard to schools, the board of trustees have the appointing power, the power to appoint the teachers; and the appointing power in a system of school administration has the power that really controls the system.

Mr. Grady:

They are not supreme bodies?

Mr. Maxwell:

But the fact remains that they have the appointing power.

Mr. Grady:

They have a veto power.

Mr. Maxwell:

It is never exercised. The result has been that the New York school system has been dominated by political influences. That is the system that will be extended to Brooklyn.

MR. GRADY:

I wish to say that there is no system of education so thoroughly divorced from politics as the system of New York. The appointment of its commission is in the very same hands that has it in Brooklyn, and the board of trustees are men who are appointed by the board of education and they have never undertaken to make their office in any way political. Where have you seen anybody turned out of office, by this body? The distinction is, that Brooklyn has a central board while in New York the local authority, the subdivision of local authority is intrusted to deputies selected by the central authority.

MR. MAXWELL:

There is another important difference between the two systems. The city of New York has established two colleges, one is called the College of the City of New York, and the other the Normal College. These are colleges, so called. They are in the view of the educator four-fifths high school and one-fifth college. Be that as it may, the effect of establishing these colleges with the great expense of maintaining them has heretofore prevented New York from establishing high schools. What is the result? Only one-third of all the girls who graduate from the grammar schools are admitted to the Normal College. Only about one-third, or perhaps less, of the boys who graduate from the grammar schools are admitted to the College of the City of New York. Two-thirds, at least, of all the girls, and two-thirds of all the boys cannot find admission to those two colleges. The result is that New York has established, in connection with its higher education, a purely aristocratic idea, admitting only selected pupils to these two colleges. Brooklyn, on the other hand, so far as its higher education is concerned, has gone in exactly the opposite direction. It has adopted the democratic idea, which is that every boy and girl who graduates from the grammar schools should have an opportunity to go on. Are we to have that system of New York introduced into Brooklyn?

Is the opportunity to obtain a higher education which is now given to every child, the poorest in the city, to be cut off by the adoption of the New York system?

MR. LEXOW:

That matter is in the hands of the Legislature.

MR. MAXWELL:

If we may judge of the future from the past, we can arrive at but one conclusion, and that is that the Legislature having failed in the past to reform the New York school system will fail in the future.

Now, Mr. Chairman, there was a law passed by the Legislature in 1895, affecting the entire school system of the Empire State that has elicited nothing but the highest praise and the highest encomiums throughout the length and breadth of the land. I was present at the great meeting of the National Educational Association in Denver, on May 20th. Thousands of teachers, ranging in rank from the kindergarten teacher up, were in attendance. I heard there a statement made by one of the foremost educators of the country, that not since Horace Mann secured the establishment of his normal school in Massachusetts has so beneficent a statute been passed. That great body of teachers passed a formal vote of thanks to the Legislature and the Governor for this splendid law. That is the law which declares that after January 1, 1897, no teacher shall be licensed or employed in any city of this State who has not graduated at least from a high school or from a school for the professional training of teachers. There is one blot on the records of New York, with reference to that law. It proves what I said a moment ago, that it is impossible, apparently, to reform the New York school system. The city of New York is excepted from the operation of the bill.

MR. LEXOW:

That was by request of the representatives of the city of New York?

MR. MAXWELL:

That is what we may expect when they get control of Brooklyn's educational affairs.

MR. GRADY:

The Superintendent of Public Instruction has decided that we are not exempt.

MR. MAXWELL:

But the law says you are.

MR. GRADY:

The first section says that; then in the second section there is a general provision which he has decided, includes the city of New York.

MR. MAXWELL:

I shall be most happy to hope that the State Superintendent will be able to force New York city into doing something. I sincerely hope that he will. If Brooklyn should resist the operation of this law it would be his duty to force Brooklyn and he would very properly do so.

MR. GRADY:

If Brooklyn was exempt you would not want anybody to enforce it.

MR. MAXWELL:

No, sir; and I imagine that New York will make a big kick before it will allow it to be enforced.

MR. LEXOW:

It is only fair to say that there were a number of general schemes for the correction of abuses before the Legislature, during the past two years, and numerous reforms were suggested, but of all the bills that came up they could not agree upon one, and for that reason the bills were not passed.

Mr. Maxwell:

The politicians of New York have always succeeded in defeating any provisions for school reform.

I have but one word to say in conclusion: Supposing we should get consolidation; supposing we should obtain from the additional taxation all that these gentlemen have claimed for it, my position is that the people of Brooklyn would pay very dear for it, if it results, as I believe it will, in a serious deterioration of your public school system, which now is our greatest pride.

Mr. Lexow:

Another act was passed by the Legislature of New York last year with reference to the extension of a temperance education to the public schools. I saw in a paper yesterday, or the day before, that Brooklyn might lose all the State school moneys contributed for this purpose, for the reason that she has been unable to provide the necessary appropriation to buy the text-books required under the terms of the act. Is there any truth in that?

Mr. Maxwell:

If you saw that statement I did not see it myself. It is simply untrue.

Mr. Lexow:

I am glad to hear it. You don't mean the books have been purchased?

Mr. Maxwell:

They will be.

W. A. Short:

Mr. Chairman and Gentlemen of the Committee: I feel that I have no right to take up the time that has been granted to the city of Brooklyn. I propose, therefore, to say nothing about the legal questions involved or the constitutionality of the measure, or about the various plans which you have under consideration.

I desire, however, to say that there is unmistakable evidence of a very strong change of opinion in Richmond county which voted very largely in favor of consolidation in 1894. I appear here at the request of a number of gentlemen from that county, some who are in favor of consolidation and some who are not; they reflect every shade of opinion, but are all in favor of resubmission of the question if it be the desire of this committee to determine what the feeling is. The evidences of this change of sentiment are too varied and too long and too complicated to present to you, and I shall not undertake to state them before you. I will only say that since 1894 one very important consideration has come into the minds of the people of Richmond county, which has, more than any single cause, operated to change their sentiment and feeling, and the evidences of which are, perhaps, by those who come up and down on the boats with a long journey of twenty-five minutes in conversation with the residents of that county. I say, without any hesitation, that in view of such conversations, had not only with myself but with other friends, that there is an unmistakable change of sentiment of a very important character with regard to this question, and the chief ingredient lies in the fact that the people of Richmond county, having heard the matter thoroughly discussed, do not expect to receive the benefits which the consolidation has led us to believe that we would receive. The residents of Richmond county believe there is no possibility of bridges; there is no possibility of a thousand and one other things that have been offered; at least, the people of Richmond county, after considering the question, have reached this conclusion. I do not think it is possible to ascertain the correct feeling without resubmission of the question. Then, again, that their interests lie in the granting of a charter to the county of Richmond which will consolidate it into one municipality; and in view of that feeling, that local pride, sufficient change of sentiment has taken place to overcome the mere superstitious reasons which induced them to vote in favor of consolidation in 1894.

Mr. Redfield:

Mr. Chairman: It has been stated to you that the opposition to consolidation consisted chiefly of the wealthy men of the Heights, and that the plain people of the city of Brooklyn were in favor of consolidation. It has also been stated to you that seventy-five per cent. of the workingmen of the eastern district desired, and were in favor of, consolidation. I now wish to introduce to you my friend, Mr. J. T. Koehler, who comes from as far away in Brooklyn as you can go and still be a Brooklynite — the extreme end of Greenpoint. This gentleman has been a Republican and has voted the Republican ticket since the days of Freemont. He was also a sailor on Commodore Perry's expedition to Japan. He is a workingman and will speak for the workingmen of his district.

J. F. Koehler:

Mr. Chairman and Gentlemen of the Committee: I do not desire to detain you very long. I am a workingman, one of the sons of toil, and am not able to make speeches. I am employed in a factory where 500 men are employed daily, and I have a great opportunity to listen to the sentiments of the workingmen. The workingmen who voted for consolidation in 1894 — two-thirds of them did not know what they were voting for. In my own family I have two boys, one aged 24 and the other 29; they went up to the polls to vote, and when they came home I asked them if they voted for those amendments. One boy said, "I really do not know whether I voted the amendments or not;" the other boy said he cast a straight ticket, but didn't know whether he voted the amendments or not. Both voted the Republican ticket; they said the leaders of the district asked them to vote for the amendments and everything else, and they did so. They now say that if they had an opportunity they would vote against consolidation. But to come back to the workingmen. I am living in the fifteenth ward, but in going to and coming from my work I pass through three wards — the fifteenth, the seventeenth and the eighteenth. I am known to everybody in both wards, and this absorbing question of consolidation has been on their minds; and through my travels I have talked with several people and asked them what they thought about the consolidation question; they would generally say that they were for Brooklyn. Gentlemen, if you give us resubmission you will find that among the working class they are decidedly in favor of resubmission and will vote against consolidation. That is the opinion and the sentiments of the working classes who reside in the district I have referred to. We are not real estate agents; we are not contractors; we are not lawyers; we are not capitalists; we are men who work for a living. It took me many years to raise my little two-story frame house, but as sure as there is a Supreme Being above, I think more of that house than John Jacob Astor thinks of his palace in New York, or Vanderbilt of his palace in Newport. I live in peace and quietness and I want to call Brooklyn my home; it is Brooklyn for me; I have always lived in Brooklyn. I believe in a man's speaking out. I was born in Germany, and I came here to the United States as a boy, at the age of 15. I joined Uncle Sam's navy and was honorably discharged. Of course I have no doubt but you were all born to work and may be some of you gentlemen have done the same honest work that I have done. No matter whatever happens to Brooklyn she will always be Brooklyn to me, whether consolidated or not. I think four out of every five of the working class will vote against consolidation. I will be a Brooklyn man and remain a Brooklyn man all my life.

FRANK WOODRUFF:

Mr. Chairman, and Gentlemen of the Committee: I appear here to-day to state my views against the consolidation of Brooklyn with New York, unless the question is resubmitted to the people to vote upon. I was one of those citizens of Brooklyn having had a long residence here, and having been somewhat active in politics, I voted when the question was before the people in 1894, in the affirmative upon the proposition. I then understood, and have always understood, clearly, that the final plan, when it was consummated, would be submitted to the people of Brooklyn to vote upon it. And it seems to me that it is only fair that it should be. I understood that the vote of 1894 was only to test the feeling of the people — to get at public sentiment. I was in favor of consolidation. I do not believe that if the people had understood that vote was to be a finality that there would have been 15,000 votes cast for it. I am frank to state to you, sir, that since the election of last fall I have changed my views, and am now a pronounced anti-consolidationist. I have considered the question carefully and from many standpoints. They say it is not a political question. I beg to differ with the gentlemen who make that statement. You can no more divorce politics than you can stop the mad rushing of waters over the Niagara. If this act is passed it will be passed by a Republican Legislature and signed by a Republican Governor, and the people of Brooklyn will hold the Republican party responsible. It does not seem to me that it is fair to crowd this thing upon Brooklyn without letting the people vote upon it, without letting the people know what they are voting for; and I do not believe that you will. I believe that if consolidation is forced upon this city, far better it would be if you should declare war against England over the Venezuelan question than to force consolidation upon this great people without their consent. They will remember it in the future against any candidate in this State running for an official position, and I believe that candidate will be beaten by 50,000 Republican votes, and I will be one of them.

Mr. Lexow:

Don't you think that a legislator who would be guided by any such threat would be a coward and would merit the opprobium of the people?

Mr. Woodruff:

I am not making any threat; I am simply stating my views on this question, and if you do pass this act I think you will find my statement prophetic. I am giving you my views; I am expressing my opinion, and I really believe, sir, with all due respect to the chairman and gentlemen of the committee, that in the future, that if this question of consolidation is put upon the people of Brooklyn without a resubmission, that you will find that my words are true. That is simply my judgment, and I believe that I am right in saying that you will see the worst if this thing comes to pass. I expect there is a political side to this question. You have seen the political course of Brooklyn in the past and you will see it again in ten-fold more force, in my judgment. What right have you to take this city and unite it with New York, without the people voting upon it. I do not believe, sir, that you will be a party to do that against the will of the people.

There is also a business side to this question. The city of Brooklyn has natural advantages for becoming a great commercial center, greater than that of any other city in the country. She has sixteen miles of magnificent water front and a good depth of water. Three-quarters of all the heavy commerce comes to Brooklyn, and to her warehouses; she has the finest warehouse system in this country. New York is absolutely dependent upon Brooklyn for her facilities for transacting her commercial business. Does New York propose to give Brooklyn any return if this consolidation is materialized? Is she going to come here and build up our water front, our piers and our warehouses? Who knows whether Greater New York will come over to Brooklyn and spend any of the money they collect from taxation? I have been taxed all my life. I have paid a large amount in the aggregate because I have long been a resident of this city and the money I have paid has gone into the parks and school-houses and public buildings. It is true that our city is not as well off, financially, as it might bė, but this is partially because of Democratic mismanagement. We are now under Republican administration, and I want to see a Republican administration continue in power. I want to see a Republican rule, not only in this city, but in the State and all over the land; and when the Republican party has control in the nation the real estate dealers who are advocating this wrong will find a market for their real estate, and not until then. At present there are too many men out of employment. There will be no appreciable boom in real estate until there is a change in the National administration; this is their only remedy. Until the people have employment we can not expect prosperity in this country.

I appeal to you, Mr. Chairman, to give us a chance to vote upon this question, to vote on it honestly, and it does seem to me that you ought to require nothing more than that every representative in the Legislature from this city is in favor of resubmission. The Republican Club of Brooklyn the other night unanimously voted against consolidation. There has been a very great change of public sentiment, and it is growing rapidly. It seems to me that it should be resubmitted. The voice of the members from this city should be heard — they should be recognized by the Legislature.

MR. LEXOW:

Do you think it is good judgment to make this question a political one?

MR. WOODRUFF:

I do.

MR. LEXOW:

Do you think it is good judgment on the part of the Republican organizations of Kings county to express themselves officialy on a question that simply concerns the well being of the city of Brooklyn?

MR. WOODRUFF:

I think it is well for them to express the opinion, because there is a sort of feeling that we are going to be consolidated whether we want to or not. It seems to me right that all good citizens should express themselves.

MR. LEXOW:

My criticism is passed upon the resolution adopted by the Republican associations in this city. I ask you whether you think the question of the existence or non-existence of consolidation feeling in this city which applies to the material interest of this city should be made a political question.

MR. WOODRUFF:

You can not stop; politics will enter in.

MR. LEXOW:

Did politics enter into the vote of 1894; and if we have resubmission would not we have a political vote?

MR. WOODRUFF:

I do not think that it was discussed politically in 1894. It was understood that the vote would not be a finality. If it had been declared that we were passing upon the question finally I believe that it would have been made a political question. If we have another opportunity you will find that politics will enter it.

MR. GRADY:

You remember that New York was not always dependent upon Brooklyn for warehouses. Before the bridge was built the warehouse business here was not so good. In your experience you of course know that New York city was not all the time dependent upon Brooklyn for warehouse facilities.

MR. WOODRUFF:

Pretty much all the time; back as far as I can remember.

MR. GRADY:

I can remember that it increased considerably after the erection of the bridge.

Mr. Woodruff:

I beg to differ with you.

Mr. Grady:

Don't you know that there are large number of vessels that can not pass under the bridge?

Mr. Woodruff:

There are no vessels that can not pass under the bridge. It is simply a matter of taking down the top mast.

Mr. Grady:

But at great expense.

Mr. Woodruff:

Only fifty or seventy-five dollars. The largest ships that enter and pass under the bridge by taking down their top masts.

Mr. Grady:

I desire to call your attention to the fact that the Republican Legislature when the Democratic representatives from the city of New York were unanimous against giving up their dock for private corporations, the members from Brooklyn voted to turn over their docks.

Mr. Woodruff:

I do not know how Brooklyn's representatives have voted in the past, but certainly New York has no standing, commercially, in the warehouse business, she has but one railroad elevator, nearly all her heavy freight is cared for in Brooklyn. Nearly all the transatlantic steamers that come here are cared for in the Brooklyn warehouses, nearly all of their merchandise is landed here in Brooklyn. There are but two large elevators on the Jersey side. If Brooklyn had a Merchants' Exchange, a Produce Exchange, Coffee Exchange and Stock Exchange, their great businesss would be on this side of the river, and the people from

Brooklyn would not be going over from New York every morning for the purpose of transacting their business. All the sugar is landed on our water front. It is manufactured and refined on this side of the river and then carted over to the wholesale grocers in New York, and they sell it to the retailers. If Brooklyn had the facilities that New York has in addition to her own magnificent water front, do you believe she would lack public spirit and allow the business to go to Boston and Baltimore. It is a great misfortune that Brooklyn has not asserted herself in the commercial world. She has the best wharf facilities in the country.

MR. MATTHEWS:

Is it not a fact that since the vote was cast in favor of consolidation you have sold your interest in the warehouse business to the New York Storage Company?

MR. LEXOW:

There should be no personalities.

DAVID HEALEY:

Mr. Chairman and Gentlemen of the Committee: I did not expect to be called upon to speak and I am too busy to present any prepared or collected facts in the shape of an argument. In what I have to say I shall be very brief. As has been intimated, I have some familiarity with the feelings of the working people of this city and among them I have many friends who made up the small majority for consolidation in 1894. I cast my vote in favor of that bill, but I had no idea whatever that it would wipe out the identity of the city of Brooklyn; I had no idea whatever of favoring any proportion to consolidate with New York upon any other than a business basis, or under any arrangement that would be injurious to the city of Brooklyn or unsatisfactory to the voters of Brooklyn. I believe at the time the vote was taken nobody believed that it was to be a finality? Since that vote was taken there has been a change of sentiment and I have been surprised at the growth of the opposition to the proposition. Amongst the associations of workingmen with whom it has been my privilege to mingle in discussions during the recent campaign, I have found it an absorbing question, especially since it has been introduced in this new form. It was understood that the vote of 1894 was merely an expression of opinion, and it was specifically stated that it would have no binding effect. In an association of which I was one, about two weeks ago, a vote was taken upon the question of consolidation as now presented. The vote of five to one was for resubmission. A friend of mine who was present here this morning and was also a member of this association canvassed one block of his neighboorhood in this city largely inhabited by wage earners and could not find one advocate of the proposition submitted in the form of the present bill. Nineteen were in favor of resubmission and only one was non-committal.

The gentlemen of the committee before whom we are presenting our arguments in opposition to this measure have the official knowledge of the feeling on this question by the fact that the united delegation from this county in the Legislature, is in favor of resubmission. A year ago there were many advocates of consolidation representing this city in the Legislature; now there is not one in either house. This is because the feeling has grown so intense and the representation of this city in the Legislature is about one-seventh of the representation of the entire State. We feel confident that your committee will give us another chance to vote upon this question. If the vote of your committee shall be adverse to the proposition, to the wishes of Brooklyn it would engender some feeling in the approaching presidential campaign. The simple expression of the opinion of the people in 1894 should not bind the wishes of the people of Brooklyn at this time. If these cities are united against our wishes we will take steps to appeal from your verdict. Let us work out our own destiny; we have taken a leading part in the cause of good government, in the work of honest representative government and we want to continue in that way. In saying what I have said I feel that I represent the sentiment of the large proportion of the wage earners of this city.

MR. MATTHEWS:

How do you know that every representative in the Legislature is in favor of resubmission, or against consolidation?

MR. HEALEY:

Because at a meeting at the Academy of Music, a statement was made from the platform and I have not heard that statement contradicted nor its truth questioned from that day to this; and I think it will not be denied to-day.

MR. LEXOW:

Do you not think that the representatives of Brooklyn in Albany were coerced into taking the position they do on this question, when the anti-consolidationists appeared before the candidates from this city and threatened them with political extermination unless they favored resubmission?

MR. HEALEY:

I am very glad that the chairman has brought this question to my mind; I would be the last person in the world to attempt to influence the members of the Legislature in that way. The people simply made known to them their wishes upon this question and that is a proper and logical and natural result of American institutions. When the people vote to send representatives to the Legislature they have a right to make known their wishes.

HENRY HENTZ:

Mr. Chairman and Gentlemen of the Committee: I will not detain you long. I am an old resident of Brooklyn and have lived here since I became a voter. During the same period I have been a merchant in New York, but I have great love for Brooklyn, and have been considerably interested in the welfare of Brooklyn, doing my duty in every particular, I think as regards political work. I wish to say that in voting upon the question of consolidation in 1894 I voted against it; I thought it was merely an informal vote and nothing more. Why, on the Cotton Exchange floor we have frequently taken such a vote when an important question would come before the Exchange; in order to ascertain the opinion, we would take an informal vote so as to avoid the work of getting up rules and altering the by-laws; when the informal vote was taken it frequently led to the adoption of rules.

I do not think consolidation would help this city in the least. I think we are doing very well at present, and I think that we can continue to do well. I am very sorry, indeed, to know that there are so many detractors of Brooklyn living here. I was not aware before that it was such a poor place to live in. We have started many reforms here that have spread throughout the country, and I hope you will permit us to continue the good work; I hope, sir, that the Legislature will not make us unwilling citizens of the great municipality. Do not put us in a position similar to that of Alsace-Lorraine under the German empire. I was in Europe last year and I was told there that many of the French residents were so embittered and so dissatisfied living there as German citizens that their young men went over the border so that if they were compelled to give military service, they would give it to France in preference to Germany. I hope, gentlemen, that you will not make us captives. Give us another chance to vote on the question and if it goes against us we will abide by the decision. I sincerely trust, gentlemen, that you will do so. I have heard from the other side one of the chief reasons for consolidation, that is that our taxes will be lower. I am a fair taxpayer myself, and none of my property is productive. I am willing to continue to pay the taxes if you will permit me to do so. I do not want to be an object of charity to New York city. That seems to be the position you are taking. If we were joined to New York, we would get some crumbs from the table, that is all. I have not seen or talked with any merchants in New York that think that consolidation with Brooklyn would do for us what is claimed. They have hardly considered it on that side at all. Very little interest has been shown on that side. I hope, gentlemen, that you will comply with our request and give us another chance to vote on the subject. As American citizens we ask only what is fair, and I sincerely hope that you will not report in favor of consolidating us without giving us a chance to vote.

January 25, 1896.

Arguments in Favor of Consolidation.

SILAS B. DUTCHER:

Mr. Chairman and Gentlemen of the Committee: When I came to Brooklyn nearly thirty-five years ago I looked carefully over the situation; I became a unionist or consolidationist, from that day. Consequently, I feel that I am one of the oldest annexationists, unionists or consolidationists or whatever you may term it, that there is in the city. I look upon the city of Brooklyn as a city of homes without corporative capital and other things necessary to make a great city. Why not be united to New York and get the benefit of the corporative capital of New York. I realize as I look over the record that New York property is assessed for only one-half of its value. In Brooklyn it is assessed for about 70 per cent. of its value. In New York they pay less than 2 per cent. on a 50 per cent. valuation; here we pay nearly 3 per cent. on a 70 per cent. valuation; and we know that a large part of New York capital is owned by Brooklyn men; a large part of the wealth of New York has been accumulated by men who reside in Brooklyn, but who have their places of business in New York city. It seems to me, so far as I can gather, that there is no politics in this question; in the thirty years that I have considered the question I have never known of either party to look at it from a political standpoint, but purely from what would tend to advance the best interests of the city of Brooklyn. We have increased the assessment of our property year by year, all it will bear, and I think a little more. Property in some parts of the city to-day is asessed for more than it can be sold for. I have in mind a piece of property that can not be sold for its assessed value. Now, I am not one of those who fear the overwhelming power of New York when Brooklyn is consolidated. During the forty years that I have been a resident of the two cities, I have said again and again, that I believe we can trust the people, absolutely. If you can so arrange your municipal government that the terms of the legislative and executive bodies begin and end at the same time, so that when the people desire to make a revolution, they may make it complete, the people will meet their obligations and responsibilities and we will have good government. I have absolute trust in the people and believe that Brooklyn will be benefited by this union. The benefit will come from the corporative capital which Brooklyn is without. I have no fear of the influence of Tammany Hall. I feel confident that we can take care of them at the ballot box, we can right every wrong through the ballot box. I have always favored taking in the outlying districts of the city of Brooklyn and in every instance the city has been benefited. I do not think any person here would say that the eastern district of the city of Williamsburgh was not benefited by consolidation with the city of Brooklyn. I do not think that any one here will say that the country towns have not been benefited by consolidation with Brooklyn. I am very heartily and very earnestly in favor of consolidation. If you are consolidated you will not need any additional police to protect your property, but if you extend Brooklyn six, eight or ten miles and spread out over a large territory you will require more police to protect your property. By all means let us have consolidation. I have studied this question for more than thirty years and I feel very certain great good will come of it. I feel confident that it will be a great boom for Brooklyn; there will be a revival of business.

James T. Lynch:

Mr. Chairman and Gentlemen of the Committee: Although I feel confident beyond the possibility of a doubt that a vote now taken to get the sense of the voters of Brooklyn would show a larger majority in favor of consolidation than was cast in 1894, still I oppose resubmission, because it would be un-American. A majority, large or small, always decides according to our form of government. Besides, politics would enter into the vote. I oppose referendum, because I know the Legislature must and will give Brooklyn justice, including equal taxation. To the plea made that the vote is stale, because it was not acted upon by the last Legislature, comes rather ungracefully from those same individuals who prevented the passage of a consolidation bill last year. I think the owners of the large office buildings around this court-house, who have spent so much money to defeat consolidation, need not fear that their tenants will vacate; this will continue to be one of the business centers long after consolidation. The little civic pride among Brooklyn people is shown by their well-known habit when visiting hotels in other cities of registering themselves as coming from New York. The Westchester people think that consolidation with New York is a good thing for them, but not for Brooklyn. I shall read a short extract from a letter from Senator Guy to the New York World:

"During the last session of the Legislature I was largely instrumental in bringing about the annexation to our city of the lower part of Westchester county. I believe additional territory in the same direction can be added the coming session with great advantage to our city, and I contemplate introducing bills with that object in view."

What are the practical questions? Will consolidation benefit New York and Brooklyn, and how should it be brought about? are to be considered. The grand tax-list in New York, like, say, $50,000,000, in Brooklyn something like $12,500,000, about four to one.

Property is assessed in New York on an average of about fifty per cent.

Property is assessed in Brooklyn on an average of about seventy per cent.

The tax rate in New York is 191, in Brooklyn 261, and upward where special assessments are included in the tax bills. Equalization of these assessed values and rates might reduce Brooklyn taxes about thirty per cent., and increase New York taxes about seven and one-half per cent., because thirty per cent. on $12,000,000 is only equal to seven and one-half per cent. on $50,000,000, consequently the Brooklyn man whose tax bill last year was $100 would find it become seventy dollars, and the New York man's tax bill, which last year was $100, would be $107, less the amount saved by discontinuance of unnecessary offices. The great advantages to real estate in Brooklyn, which pays over nineteen-twentieths of the whole taxes, would be increased confidence in buyers, and particularly in money lenders, as explained by Mr. Bailey, who is the vice-president and Brooklyn manager of the Title Guarantee and Trust Company. That Mr. Redfield did not understand his subject when he undertook to discredit what Mr. Bailey said is fully demonstrated by Senator Grady's questions as to whether he had not omitted to separate second from first-class mortgages, and his confusion at other questions. I have never heard of Mr. Redfield in the financial world, whereas many people think, I certainly do, that Mr. Bailey is the ablest financier of his age in Brooklyn. The Title Guarantee and Trust Company has loaned much larger amounts than any other institution in Brooklyn during the last twelve months, and every one of these loans which were on Brooklyn property had to be approved by Mr. Bailey. Mr. Redfield said no one discredited the petition for resubmission. I should have been less surprised if he had said no one seriously considered it — the man who secured those names must have been paid, and your imagination will suggest the rest. Mr. Carman, one of those whose names were signed to the call, explained his position. I remember Cyrus W. Field told me that when Mr. William Waldorf Astor was in the Legislature and worked to pass the five-cent fare bill on the elevated railroad, Mr. Field caused a remonstrance to be circulated, and Mr. Astor's father unwittingly signed the remonstrance. Now, consider what the lack of confidence in the money-lenders means to the man of moderate means, who owns a piece of property. He lives in constant dread that the mortgage on his house may be called, that he can not borrow money to replace the loan, and he may lose his property, and to the poor man who wishes to build or buy a house, he can not do so if he can not borrow liberally. To the gentleman who says that six per cent. could be borrowed on Brooklyn property, I say he is mistaken — to prove it, I say that the Title Guarantee and Trust Company, to overcome the difficulty of getting capitalists to take mortgages on Brooklyn property, was obliged to organize the Bond and Mortgage Guarantee Company, with $1,000,000 capital, to guarantee the payment of both prinicpal and interest of bonds and mortgages, and this company will guarantee the payment of mortgages on Brooklyn property only in the choicest location and to about fifty per cent. of the value. I know, for I am one of the directors and a member of the finance committee of each of these companies. If consolidation is effected with New York, taxes will be lowered in Brooklyn, and as I have said, over thirty per cent., then capitalists will have confidence and loan on Brooklyn property; this will encourage the construction of thousands of small houses and increase the assessable value proportionately by the new additional structural improvements and cause the man who hires a house in one of the suburbs of New Jersey to be willing to come to Brooklyn, because after consolidation taxes here will be lower and money can be more freely borrowed on real estate. So that if a mortgage be called another loan can be easily procured. Again, the consolidation of these cities will remove sectional prejudices and make it easier to carry on public works for the common good, particularly bridges. Some anti-consolidationists have asked, "Why don't the Greene and Stranahan commissioners bring in a charter (meaning a complete set of bills for the government of the greater city) instead of this declaratory measure?" The answer is, there is no money to pay for such elaborate work and, while it discontinues no offices, it, and this bill give to the commission $25,000 with which, at a future time, to formulate bills for equal taxation and other purposes, and to present them for consideration. Of course each one of these bills when presented will be discussed in the Legislature, and perhaps altered before being passed, or perhaps rejected, the Brooklyn representatives will always be there to see that their districts are not injured. It is remarkable that while the Lexow bill contains these words, New York, as by this act enlarged, and, among other things, for attaining an equal and uniform rate of taxation, and of valuation for the purpose of taxation throughout the whole of the territory of the said municipal corporation so enlarged. The Brush bill contains no words about equal taxation. I have listened to every speech made during these four days' hearings. I have given much thought to this matter ever since the movement was started several years ago, and am firmly convinced that the plan of the Lexow bill is the best. It would be very unwise to longer delay the consolidation of New York and Brooklyn; for uncertainty and delay are most detrimental to business interests. I think it is not right to permit these men, inexperienced in business affairs, to have much consideration alongside such a large proportion of the bank presidents, merchants and mechanics and large real estate owners of the city.

Mr. Brush:

Do you know that there are 8,000 more dwellings in Brooklyn than there are in New York?

Mr. Lynch:

What's that got to do with the matter? If these people who are living around this city and getting their figures from sources, as evidently you do; they say figures can't lie, but the man who puts them down can.

Mr. Brush:

Excuse me. I got my figures from the census. How do you explain that?

MR. GRADY:

I can. In New York they build their houses twenty stories high, in Brooklyn they are content with two.

MR. BRUSH:

But isn't it desirable to have the smaller house?

MR. GRADY:

Yes, but the woman wants everything on the same flat and she rules there as she does in everything else.

MR. LYNCH:

I am against the Brush bill, because it does not say a word about equal taxation. I have confidence in New York city and I have confidence in Senator Grady.

MR. GRADY:

That is the first time I have had a compliment paid to me during this hearing.

JOHN D. KEILEY:

Mr. Chairman and Gentlemen of the Committee: On sentimental grounds I, and the three voting members of my family, voted against consolidation when that question was before the people in 1894. Since that time I have changed my views, and I am now greatly in favor of consolidation. In the course of my official duties as city treasurer of Brooklyn it became agreeable for me to study the financial conditions of both New York and Brooklyn. I approve of the sentiment here expressed by men who are fond of Brooklyn. I, too, am fond of Brooklyn. I am not one of those who signs himself as a citizen of New York when he goes on a journey. The hotel registers of St. Louis, New Orleans and other distant cities will testify to that fact. It is because I love my city and anxious for it to continue in its course of prosperity that I am here to urge consolidation with New York.

Let me present for your consideration a few figures. On December 31, 1895, Brooklyn was within $2,199,208 of her debt limit. The next day she received by the annexation of Flatlands property assessed at $2,340,000, or added to her borrowing capacity one-tenth of that sum, $234,000. She is, therefore, at the present time, $2,500,000 of her debt limit. In no way can the city of Brooklyn borrow more than $2,500,000 without increasing the assessed valuation, and that cannot be done until next August, when the assessors are empowered to meet and make another assessment.

Brooklyn may well feel favored in being allowed to build a new bridge from the foot of Broadway at a cost of only one-half as against two-thirds paid for the present bridge. But had we been consolidated under wise conditions this city would need to pay only less than one-fourth of the cost of that new bridge. The consolidationists and the anti-consolidationists are all anxious to have provided means to cross the East river and reach the metropolitan city quickly. The present bridge added more than $200,000,000, to the assessed valuation of this city. After the construction of the new bridge it is reasonable to expect that a like amount will be added to the assessed valuation in the annexed districts.

I was opposed to the consolidation of Gravesend beause then I knew it would mean the consolidation of Brooklyn with New York. But the anti-consolidationists who favored it, did not think so. We didn't ask Gravesend if she wanted to come in, but annexed her without giving her an opportunity to be heard. It seems to me it comes with bad grace on the part of the anti-consolidationists now to say that the vote in favor of consolidation, 277, came from the town of Gravesend in view of the manner in which that town was annexed to Brooklyn.

During the administration of Mayor Schieren — and, I believe, he was the best mayor Brooklyn ever had — the city received the full measure of value for moneys spent and yet during that time it was necessary to expend $17,000,000. Over $5,000,000 was raised by issuing county bonds for park purposes, because we were so near the debt limit. I am sorry that we were not able to have the bonds for our new bridge issued in the same way, for with them we are forced dangerously near the debt limit. Already, as the superintendent of public instruction has told you, $1,250,000 of bonds are to be issued for the public schools. The schools must be provided for and then if it is necessary to issue that amount of bonds, we have only $1,250,000 left for other improvements. How can we expect to increase the valuation of our property in the outlying districts, to pave the streets there and lay sewers with that small amount? The entrance of the trolley cars into these sections is not alone sufficient to increase the valuation of property in order that the assessed valuation will be adequate. We are now carrying bonds that extend through forty years. In the first instance, when the city issues bonds she must give her credit. Do you want to see the city of Brooklyn retrograde? The argument to preserve the name of Brooklyn is not enough. I am fond of that name. I think it would be hard to obliterate it. It is a name that has cut too much of a figure in history to be easily obliterated. We all, however, are proud of the Empire State and we are all anxious to have the imperial city of the world here. It is shown that the Empire State has reached the zenith of her power, that London, in ten or twenty years, will yield the palm as the centre of the financial world and the commercial world and that it will come here to New York. Consequently we have interests here. The police and fire departments of the consolidated city might easily be placed under one general government and the officers governing the different sections might be termed mayors, or anything you choose. The name of the whole city might be Manhattan, and the different sections might be given the names they now hold.

Shall we stop? In the period between 1880 and 1890 the assessed valuation of the city increased $20,000,000, per annum, and in the period between 1890 and 1895 it fell over $12,000,000, and had it not been for the fact that the annexation of the country towns brought in $30,000,000, enabling us to increase our bond-issuing capacity $3,000,000, we would have been unable to issue our school bonds and carry out our plans.

MR. LEXOW:

Did the fact that the property in Brooklyn did not increase in value justify an increase in the issue of bonds?

MR. KIELEY:

Under the Constitution it was permissible.

MR. LEXOW:

In other words, the increased valuation was forced?

MR. KIELEY:

Exactly.

MR. GRADY:

What was the difference between the bonded indebtedness at the beginning of Mayor Shieren's term and at the end of it?

MR. KIELEY:

The bond and tax certificates issued during Mayor Shieren's term amounted to $11,379,361.01; and there was paid off $6,568,-682.73; the net income, therefore, from those sources was $4,810,-678.28.

MR. GRADY:

Are the tax certificates similar to the revenue certificates of New York city?

MR. KIELEY:

They are the same. The tax certificates do not count as additional indebtedness as affecting the constitutional limit, except, when they are five years old. The gross city debt is $58,583,521.94. Of that amount there is in the sinking fund $5,746,521.94. And in tax certificates, $700,000. From this I figure the net debt to be, $51,827,000. The borrowing capacity, allowing for the sinking fund, is, therefore, $2,198,261.

MR. GRADY:

I wanted to know what two years of economical government would add to the debt limit? There was no humor intended in that remark. Every city that makes progress must spend money for improvements.

MR. KIELEY:

Certainly, sir. I understand you. The net debt in 1893, was $48,034,214.45 and at the close of 1895 it was $52,037,000, showing a net increase of about $4,000,000 in two years and that does not include the $5,000,000 devoted to the parks. Every dollar of it was well spent, too.

MR. LEXOW:

According to your argument, then, Mr. Kieley, Brooklyn could continue in its present course for about one year?

MR. KIELEY:

That is about all, if it were to make needed improvements. It might continue for many years, if it did not make these improvements.

MR. BRUSH:

Is it not a fact that the assessed valuation of Brooklyn on new property has increased every year at the rate of $13,000,000, and that we are, therefore, able to carry on the necessary improvements?

MR. KIELEY:

I do not know that the increased assessed valuation is reckoned on what you call new property. From 1880 to 1890 we were ahead of the constitutional limit. In the next five years instead of continuing onward we went back.

Mr. Lexow:

Your argument is that these assessed valuations are not natural, but forced?

Mr. Kieley:

That is correct. The increased assessed valuation as I understand it is on my neighbor's property and mine.

Mr. Lexow:

It is usual to increase it all along the line, is it not?

Mr. Kieley:

I believe it is.

Mr. Brush:

I don't so understand it. Do you say that the assessed valuation showing an increase of $13,000,000, is not altogether a new property?

Mr. Kieley:

The tax levy of 1893 showed that the total assessed valuation was $486,531,506, and in the three towns of Flatbush, Flatlands and Gravesend it was $24,816,895. The increase in 1894 was $19,419,024. The debt limit of the county towns is higher now than it was before annexation, because the Constitution which permitted us to assume their assessed valuation as we might fix it, did not compel us to assume the liabilities of those towns. They have, beside our taxes, therefore, some debts of their own.

Mr. Grady:

Is that the kind of equal taxation the people are clamoring for?

Mr. Kieley:

No, but I am clamoring for an equal taxation. The assessed valuation of the property in the county towns in 1895 was $25,333,778; the president of the board of assessors knew at that time how necessary it was to strain every point, and the result is that we have the old wards assessed at $509,851,331, an increase over 1894 of $8,833,582, while the increase in the assessed valuation in the county towns is $5,170,577. The assessors in those towns who, perhaps, favored their own interests, made the assessed valuation show an increase of only $500,000, as against our sum of over $5,000,000. While we did get an increased valuation of $13,000,000 in 1895, we got it by saddling $5,000,000 on those county towns. Our borrowing margin at the present date is $2,434,000. We are over $4,000,000 behind hand. I refused to honor the drafts of the comptroller until I had received a note from the law department authorizing me to do it. You know how lawyers are about these matters, they do not want to go on record, but I remained firm, until I got an opinion. We used some of the money levied in 1895 to meet the current expenses of 1894. To-day this city is $3,000,000 or $4,000,000 behind hand. We carry as an asset the account of a bank that broke twenty years ago. We also carry $85,000 due from a defaulting city treasurer.

MR. GRADY:

How do Brooklyn bonds sell as compared with those of New York?

MR. KIELEY:

Brooklyn bonds sell well. They are as good as New York bonds for estates, but not so good for commercial purposes.

MR. GRADY:

What is the distinction between the bonds?

MR. KIELEY:

There is the same difference between them as there is between United States bonds and those of New York State. Your New York city bonds sell at a premium, allowing three per cent. interest, and ours, three and thirty-five-one hundredths. That was the condition before our present financial troubles. Of course, these rates might not prevail now. It is because of my love for my city that I favor consolidation. I don't want to see the city stop, but I want to see it go on. I am glad to find that Senator Grady favors the plan of consolidation. I think that Mr. Lynch rather exaggerated when he said that consolidation would increase the assessed valuation of the city seven dollars on every $100. I certainly should not want to pay taxes on $107 for every hundred dollars worth of property that I own. If the increase were so great it would afford landlords an excuse for raising their rents. To be fair, we ought to spend all of the $5,000,000 levied on the county towns for improvements there, but we can't possibly do it. New York can well afford to help us build more bridges. They say we have 8,000 more houses in Brooklyn than there are in New York, but I am sure a great many of them are empty. What we want is more people in Brooklyn. We want to keep the people in the Empire State instead of permitting them to go over to New Jersey to make their homes. I thank you, gentlemen, for the courtesy you have shown me, and for your kind attention.

Russell Parker:

Mr. Chairman and Gentlemen of the Committee: I appeal to you in the interest of consolidation, not as a real estate boomer, real estate speculator, officeholder or politician, but as a plain business man, and in order that you may weigh my few remarks, I will state that I am interested in a manufacturing corporation in the city of New York, having an actual capital invested of $450,000. I am president of the company, and I will clearly state that all my associates, therein interested, are in favor of consolidation and reside in Brooklyn. I am president of the Montauk Theater Company, of Brooklyn, although I do not claim to represent that company concerning the issue of consolidation; however, I know that many stockholders favor it, possibly more than a majority of the stockholders — in fact I do not know any that disapprove. Yet there may be some. I have interests in five insurance companies in Brooklyn and New York. I own the house where I live in Brooklyn — and, by the way, it is free and clear. I keep it so as an investment, believing that I am benefited more by saving the high rate of interest that I would probably have to pay on a mortgage on said property, rather than I would be by raising money in that way to invest elsewhere. I believe this statement of my personal interests, as distributed in New York city and Brooklyn, will convince you that my opinions on consolidation are clearly of a business nature, and I do not discard my right to exercise sentiment, for I was born in New York city and have lived in Brooklyn for over forty years.

Now, as to the vote of 1894. I understand it is as follows: Sixty odd thousand positively favored consolidation; sixty odd thousand positively disapproved consolidation, and the remaining sixty odd thousand did not disapprove consolidation. Now, to capitulate, what do we find? It clearly establishes the fact that sixty odd thousand disapprove consolidation and that one hundred and twenty odd thousand did not disapprove consolidation, all having an equal right and opportunity to express themselves. Our friends, the Antis, may say, but the sixty odd thousand that did not vote, did not express themselves favorable to consolidation and therefore we can not couple them on our side. I contend that we should couple them with us. I contend that we should couple them with us, as they are on our side and did express their opinions by silence that they did not object to consolidation, as silence gives consent the world over. Were it possible to ascertain, you would, no doubt, find that every one that voted on the consolidation matter voted on consolidation, and that twenty odd thousand or more, in addition, voted on the consolidation matter, that were probably influenced by the solid press against us — and even against such forcible opposition, we won the day, not by any hard work on our part but by simply leaving it to the good judgment of the people, and yet we are now told that there has been no fair or intelligent expression on this subject by the people. I further contend, gentlemen, that the result of the vote on this matter, by sections in 1894, has entirely wiped out the issue as applying to sections, and is now and was made so by the vote of 1894, a matter of the whole as one. Therefore, if there is to be another vote on this subject, it must be by the voters of the whole section; but, gentlemen, do not misunderstand me. I do not advocate another vote, not because I am afraid of such vote, as I believe we would get an overwhelming majority in favor of consolidation, but because I would not care to insult the voters of the section involved by inferring that they were lacking in intelligence; and also, in my judgment, it would be a very bad precedent to establish. I believe that the whole section interested would be greatly benefited by consolidation. In fact, I have heard none and know of no good argument against it. It is unnecessary for me to burden you with my opinion on details that have already been so ably presented favorable to consolidation, therefore I close by saying, that I am satisfied with the bill known as the Greater New York commission bill, and enter my protest at this time against any and all unnecessary delay in the passage of the same.

Mr. Matthews:

I have received a telegram: "Impossible to leave. Tell the committee I favor consolidation, with equal taxation. No vote necessary. Darwin R. James."

Mr. Lexow:

The president of one of the exchanges in New York?

Mr. Matthews:

Yes. I now have the pleasure of introducing to you Joseph Hendricks, president of the Union National Bank of New York, and also ex-Congressman.

Joseph H. Hendricks:

Mr. Chairman and Gentlemen of the Committee: I am very sure I can add nothing to the argument which has been presented to your committee, and I simply offer myself in evidence here for what little I may be worth, to favor my belief as a business man, and as a lover of the city of Brooklyn, that it is for the best interests of this city that it should be consolidated with the city of New York. I have reached this conclusion, Mr. Chairman, by reversing very much in my own mind the grounds of both parties of this controversy. I share fully the feeling which inspires the gentlemen who oppose this question from sentimental grounds. I love the city of Brooklyn, its social atmosphere, its literary institutions, its libraries, its school systems — all that make a part of its life; and while I am susceptible to all those impressions, at the same time, as a student of the city of Brooklyn, from the standpoint at various times in my life of postmaster of this city, of a member and the president of the board of education and of an association in its financial operations, my judgment is clear that the best interests of this city are to be conserved in every way by this forward movement; and I can not understand, Mr. Chairman, how a committee representing the great legislative power of this State can consider for one moment the reversal of the judgment which has been recorded by this community upon this question. You, gentlemen in the Legislature, are custodians of the public policy, and there is a principle in statesmanship — there is a high command in the responsibility which is invested in you that, when the only monarch that we know in this country registers its edict there is nobody to say it nay; that in the league which this city entered with the other cities about us here that they should pass upon the question among themselves for or against consolidation. When this community passed upon it for consolidation, that stands, sir, as the dictum of this community and the commands to the Legislature to move forward. Any review of the public judgment would be a reversal of the fundamental principles under which we all live. We could not go forward in a republican form of government with any success, or with any surety, if we felt that a vote registered by the people to-day might be picked to pieces, turned over, strained, evaded and reversed under legislative influences, or under political or associational influences at some succeeding time. Is this vote attacked? Is the purity of the intention of the majority of the people of this city who registered their judgment in favor of consolidation open to question here or anywhere else? I believe the argument turns simply upon the smallness of the majority.

Mr. President and Gentlemen, you have nothing to do with that. The battle has been fought, and the verdict has been rendered, and a malingering troop of people on the battlefield of Waterloo might as well discuss what they could have done or might have done under certain circumstances; but the battle is ended, and it has entered into history, and it is the command of the Legislature of the State of New York. It is important to the city of Brooklyn that this question should be settled. How are you going to settle it in any other way than by moving forward along the lines pointed out to you by the people of the city of Brooklyn? Are you going to halt as between two courses? Are you going to say to the people of the city of Brooklyn, "You must express your opinion a second time upon this question before we know exactly what you mean." Can you afford to say to the people of the State of New York when they vote upon a constitutional amendment or upon any great question which is submitted to them, "Gentlemen, the majority is small. We must come back to you and see what you think about it the next time." Where would the world's progress be if we had to halt the great machinery, which has struck in this case definitely and clearly; and I can not explain how any man can for a moment think a Legislature can sit anywhere that will be guilty of a violation of public policy which would be involved in the reversal of a popular verdict of that kind. But while the question is in the air it is a cloud upon the future of the city. Are we going to be consolidated, or ought we not? Can a capitalist come here with certainty and buy the property and develop it with the expectation that the city will grow and become greater; or must capital look upon the unfortunate financial condition of the city, must he consider how much it is now eating up of its own capital, how very much embarrassed it is at its own affairs, and stop and hesitate, or go off elsewhere.

It is to the interests of the city of Brooklyn that the question should be settled. We belong to New York. We are all in one community. We want the metropolitan spirit which blows through that great centre of finance and commences to come in through our atmosphere and fill up our veins; we want to draw on its nourishing wine, which it has in abundance, and which belongs by right to the people of this city who either directly or indirectly help to make up the great commercial depot there. The commerce of the nation comes down there to meet the tonnage of the world; and our dome is here—a string of village extending over many miles of territory, lacks that metropolitan spirit—fails to get out of the commercial surroundings here that to which it is entitled. Any one who has studied the city of Brooklyn has seen that it has responded like an enfeebled invalid to every bit of good nourishment it has ever received. When any improvement is mentioned in transportation, when any new ferry is secured the city has felt the thrill of it. When the bridge was opened the city bounded forward, and we felt as though now we begin to get more of the fine breeze of the metropolitan spirit; but the moment we grow up to the advantage which we have attained the city waits and hesitates, and does not go forward until it gets a new stimulus. We have no place to draw from except the great city of New York. We have no transient population filling our streets. We have no great trunk lines coming here bringing people from all parts of the world. We have an incident in the great growth of this metropolis here; and it is important that there should be no constriction of any artery which could bind the two members of the two bodies together; but that the nourishment and circulation tending to growth and development should be perfectly uninterrupted, and perfect according to their own mission. Now, unless we can get this question settled, Brooklyn is going to be like a great magnificent oak tree which is rotting and decaying around the trunk, and showing a little sprout here and there at the end of some extreme branches; and is it to go on that way for the next generation? It is time, it seems to me, that this question should be taken up by your body along the lines of instruction from the people; the next thing, sir, is the act of consolidation. That follows the command which you have received from all of these communities, and it is a larger question than questions of statistics, than questions of Brooklyn, than questions of that nature. It is the edict from a great community entering into a league of cities to pass upon this question; and from this point the command, it seems, to you gentlemen, is, go forward.

Mr. Chauncey:

I would like to make a statement in regard to the evasion of taxes in Brooklyn by large corporations. I make this statement now, and have it from the assessors' office. The large corporations of Brooklyn for years have in every possible way tried to dodge the collection of personal taxes; and they now pay their taxes, very many of them, at their principal office, which they have a right by law to choose, and in almost every case that principal office is in New York city, where the tax rate is the least. I will instance the Union Ferry Company. Until four years ago, they paid personal tax on three million dollars of capital, for many years and are now paying in New York. I will also instance the DeKalb Avenue railroad, that now pays personal taxes in New York city; and I will instance the Brooklyn Wharf and Warehouse Company, which owns every foot of property on the water front from Catherine ferry to Red Hook upon two miles, every warehouse, every dock, every bulkhead. Before Mr. Franklin Woodruff changed his mind, in regard to the subject of consolidation, that property was owned almost exclusively by the people of Brooklyn. To-day that has been bought by the great corporation, which pays this personal tax in the city of New York. Its capital is $30,000,000; and from the day the sale took place, Mr. Woodruff changed his mind. He had no further interest in it. I merely call you attention to the changes taking place to make Brooklyn poorer and poorer every year.

Mayor Gleason, of Long Island City:

Mr. Chairman and Gentlemen of the Committee: I do not know why I am here to-day to address this committee upon the consolidation of both cities convenient to New York. I was going to ask, however, of this committee, if it was their intention that a hearing should be held in other cities that are equally interested with Brooklyn. I intended to write the committee a letter asking that question of the committee; but as I am here to-day I will give my views and the people that I represent. The people of Long Island City have voted and declared their intentions to become a part of the Greater New York; and they have not changed their mind, and they do not desire to change their mind upon that question. We consider that we have always been a part of the city of New York, for perhaps one-half of the population resided with us in Long Island City and in Queens county. I have listened with great interest here, on two occasions, upon the question of Brooklyn, in regard to its bonded indebtedness and its taxation; and I have made up my mind that Long Island City is a prosperous city, after I have heard the argument. I believe that we are the richest city in the State. I know it. I know the bonded indebtedness; I know the floating indebtedness of it and I know the value of the property; but if we are called upon to pay any of the debt of Brooklyn, or any of the debt of New York, I should oppose the consolidation; but I know there is a just committee upon this question. I know the Legislature intends to do justice to all parties. I know there are wicked corporations in both of those cities, and more especially in my own city, that they evade the taxes, the personal taxes especially, because the law requires and states that the corporation shall pay taxes where they have their office, and they have all got their offices in New York city. Very many of them swear off their taxes. They say they have paid in Long Island. That is not so; and when I called the attention of New York to it, the Long Island railroad made their principal office in what they call their "Round House" in Jamaica to evade the other taxation. Those are the benefits that Brooklyn and Long Island City will get the benefit of; and I add to the people of Brooklyn here, that the people of Long Island City do not require another vote on it, and I do not myself; but if you come to Long Island City and request me to give you a statement of our bonded indebtedness and what we have, I will present it to the committee at Albany, so that that committee can act for our little city, and we will throw ourselves into your hands.

MR. SNOOK:

Mr. Chairman and Gentlemen of the Committee: I had the honor of presenting this petition partially the other day, and it was not completed and I will now read it. (See copy of petition attached to Mr. Snook's previous remarks.)

MR. LEXOW:

Have you any more speakers?

MR. MATTHEWS:

Any more? I do not know where to shut them off. We have on our list thirty speakers, and they have come in as we expected they would. I have announced them and have received communications from Andrew G. Brady, Henry Batterman, James McMahon, James Meserole, Nelson Beach, Donaly Ayers, Rufus L. Griggs, Frederick Ullman, Henry A. Meyer and James Gascoigne. They are coming in all the time. We are ready to submit our case at any time in closing. We can keep on and use all the hours the committee might give.

MR. LEXOW:

You have, in order to divide the time equitably, fifteen minutes more. If you want to abandon that fifteen minutes we will be pleased to have you do so.

MR. MATTHEWS:

I know the gentlemen coming here are coming here under stress of business, and we are perfectly satisfied by leaving it by submitting this letter:

ABRAHAM & STRAUS,

BROOKLYN, N. Y., *January* 25, 1896.

My Dear Mr. Matthews:

I am sorry I can not be with you this afternoon. A matter of importance will prevent my attendance at the hearing.

Mr. Redfield, in his argument yesterday, stated that I was wrong in claiming that New York city would add $8,000,000 to its tax revenue this year, and that but $4,000,000 would be added. My information was derived from such a reliable source that I was justified in quoting the amount. As the budget is not yet made out for publication nor passed upon, neither of us can give official figures, yet time will show that I am right and Mr. Redfield wrong.

The slurs Mr. Redfield cast on a number of merchants who signed the petition favoring consolidation by impugning their financial standing and credit was irrelevant and mean. Among the 120 signers of the petition are the firms of Fred'k Loeser & Co., A. D. Matthews & Son, Henry Offerman, Liebman Co., Brooklyn Furniture Company, Henry Batterman, Wm. Batterman, Joseph O'Brien, Joseph Weschler Sons, Wechsler Bros., J. McCormick, Henry Rothschild, Harding Manufacturing Company, Sam'l Koch & Son, Alfred F. Wise, Theodore Ovington, P. F. Cassidy and Abraham & Straus; if these are not the leading firms of Brooklyn I would like to hear who Mr. Redfield thinks are. I will further add that the canvasser stated that not five per cent. of the firms he solicited refused to sign the petition. One dry-goods firm would not sign because it was a stock company. From this result I am justified in claiming that easily seventy-five per cent. of the entire mercantile community of this city is in favor of consolidation and would sign the petition were they solicited. I saw in this morning's Tribune that Senator Brush made a statement that there are 10,583 manufacturing establishments in this city, valued at nearly 20,000,000. The many millions annually produced from these factories I do not know, but does Mr. Brush realize that the city of New York reaps the result of all this brawn and brain? In other words, New York is the clearing-house for all we do. We help to fill her storehouses and offices, which produce so much revenue to New York. They sell the products and wares we produce, receive the money, which enriches her banks and trust companies, etc. Now, why should not New York give us back in part what we help her to acquire?

I am glad that the committee visited Brooklyn. The debate is educational and results in much good to this city.

Sincerely yours,

A. ABRAHAM.

MR. LEXOW:

As I understand this, by mutual agreement and acquiescence on both sides, the hearings in Brooklyn will now be declared closed.

JAMES A. SKILTON:

Mr. Chairman: I wish to present a communication here.

MR. LEXOW:

Mr. Skilton, this is your communication. I notice that it is quite lengthy, and probably covers all the points that you would dwell upon in making a public address.

MR. SKILTON:

No; not as long as I would like to make it.

MR. LEXOW:

Sometimes we reach better conclusions by taking a condensed form.

MR. SKILTON:

This is a large subject, and can not be very well condensed.

MR. LEXOW:

I think, Mr. Skilton, that your letter here, when read before the committee, will convey to them all that you might possibly say by way of further elucidation of it, and we are all fairly intelligent and understand the argument that you make here. I will take pleasure in presenting it at the next meeting of the committee, if you hand it to me.

MR. SKILTON:

Nevertheless, I suppose the chairman and committee will allow me to add to that statement in writing.

MR. LEXOW:

Certainly.

MR. SKILTON:

I don't care to take the time to read at present what I say in writing here in this paper and later on.

MR. MATTHEWS:

I wish to present to the committee this extract taken from the New York Tribune of to-day:

"But even aside from past sins and present necessity for improvements there are reasons why Brooklyn can not hope for taxes as low as New York's. It extends over a wider territory and has fewer people. Long stretches of streets must be cleaned, paved, lighted and policed where the adjoining property has not a tenth of the value of property in New York which requires the same public expenditure. Consequently the cheaper property has to pay taxes at a higher rate for the benefits conferred upon it. Then, too, Brooklyn has not the vast taxable wealth of New York. Its citizens, in fact, contribute largely to New York's treasury. They live there on comparatively inexpensive property, while their business is here and they own real estate in the downtown district of great value. From this the residence regions of Brooklyn get no benefit, while the residence regions of New York are cared for from the taxes on the business of its citizens, aided by those levied on Brooklyn men's investments here. This condition results from Brooklyn's situation and character, and no administration can change it. Honest officials can in time pay off its debts and give it its money's worth in improvements, but only consolidation will give Brooklyn its fair share of the revenue levied in the metropolitan district and relieve it from paying for the conduct of a vast city without the real estate values which make the burden light."

Mr. Lexow:

Before this committee takes final action, the probabilities are that it will hold at least one session in the city of Albany, and if any citizens, who have not been heard, desire to speak before the committee, they will be heartily welcome, especially if they can throw any light on the subject.

Mr. Grady:

Before the hearing of the speeches close, I would move on the record that there be made a minute of our thanks to the officials of Brooklyn, for the kind treatment they have extended to the committee during our sessions here.

Mr. Lexow:

It is ordered unanimously.

Mr. Matthews:

In addition to the letter of Mr. Abraham, which I presented, I also have one from Mr. Parker, representing a large moneyed interest, which he asked me to read, and which I do not care to take the time of the committee in reading it.

Mr. Lexow:

Is there anybody further who desires to be heard?

Mr. Skilton:

I desire to ask one question. Can we send communications and petitions to the committee at Albany, that will be observed the same as if we spoke on the floor here?

Mr. Lexow:

Certainly; if those communications are addressed to the chairman of the committee, or to the committee by names.

MR. SKILTON:

I want to make a communication and will send it in a day or two.

MR. LEXOW:

I understand, by general consent, approved by all, both on the one side and on the other side of consolidation, we have given a full hearing to the subject down here and will now take an adjournment.

The following address was presented by Mr. James A. Skilton:

NEW YORK, *January* 25, 1896.

Hon. Clarence Lexow, Chairman, and the Honorable Gentlemen Members of the Subcommittee on Consolidation, now in session in the city of Brooklyn:

Gentlemen: On the sixteenth of January I sent a letter to the chairman asking "the opportunity of appearing before your committee in this matter of consolidation."

I received no reply to my communication, have attended several meetings of the committee, always to find the time of the committee fully engaged, and from the announcements in the newspapers I am led to believe that the time so far allotted for hearings in Brooklyn will expire without my having the desired opportunity.

I beg now to renew my request, and with that renewal to make as brief statement as possible of the subject-matters that it seems to me very desirable that the committee should have presented before it takes action and before the Legislature and the Governor of the State shall take action upon this most important subject of consolidating Brooklyn with the greater New York.

As legislators of the greatest and wealthiest State in the union, and competent for the high duties imposed upon you as members of this committee, I must assume that you are aware that there is a most instructive and illuminating history of attempts to destroy great charters by the government and authorities of New York, more than 200 years old.

You are aware that under the royal authority of Charles II, and the Duke of York, his brother, subsequently James II, of England, an attempt was made to take away the charter of the Colony of Connecticut; that the attempt was successfully resisted by the sturdy colonists of Connecticut for more than twenty years, and that the charter was finally saved, notwithstanding all the powers of royalty and of New York brought to bear for its destruction or abrogation.

You are also aware that after more than three generations of men had lived and wrought and prospered under the charter, it became the model, not simply of the Constitution of the United States, but of the American system for the protection of human freedom and for the enlightenment of the world."

We can now see and rejoice over the results as they could not, of the work of the sturdy men who protected that charter, who threatened to put the daylight through a Governor of New York who proposed to abrogate home rule under it, and who finally, when the charter was about to be taken away, blew out the lights, concealed the charter in the charter oak, and preserved not only that charter but liberty for their prosperity and for us.

I desire the opportunity to recall to you and to all those whom you represent, but particularly to the citizens of the city of Brooklyn, the historic fact, that during those twenty years and more of effort to destroy the charter of the Connecticut colony, the men who made that effort were walking and living over an abyss of revolution which finally destroyed them, theirs and their successors root and branch forever, until now. I wish also time and opportunity to show that similar influences and impulses under a new form of imperialism is, in seeking to destroy the charter of Brooklyn, endangering the foundation and fabric of American institutions and jeopardizing the hope of western civilization.

Prof. Bryce, speaking in the city of Brooklyn a few years ago, said that when he first came to America he found America Europeanized as far west as Buffalo; that on his second trip he found it Europeanized as far west as Chicago; and that on his then third trip he had found it already Europeanized beyond the Mississippi river. I would like the opportunity to show that in one respect Prof. Bryce was mistaken; and that owing to a variety of circumstances and conditions, including topography and various other matters, Brooklyn had been passed by in the swirl of Europeanization, and was left, not only an American, but practically a New England city, but seriously threatened by a European city lying across the East river. I wish to show in this connection that the attempt to unite these two cities is as unseemly as it would be to unite any American city with any of the great cities of Europe; that the salvation of American institutions is wrapt up in the solution of the municipal problem; that it is a problem from the attempted solution of which Washington, Jefferson, Madison, Hamilton and their associates might well shrink, if they were now living, and was beyond their contemplation or grasp in the foundation and construction of our institutions; and to add to this that Brooklyn is the one city in the United States, and the only one, in which at the present time, and, so far as we now can see, for future time, that municipal and American problems can be dealt with with any prospect of success and salvation. This, in part, because it has been isolated from New York and the continent, surrounded and indented by sea water and the great, free ocean, and therefore peculiarly protected as the locus of the great experiment, yet to be made, with an extensive island behind it, in every way adapted by hygienic, economic and other characteristics. I should like the opportunity to show that only recently have the great inventions making possible the building of a city in which its citizens can have not only fresh air, pure water and the other necessities of life, but also purity in politics, in all sociological relations and in all the requirements of American life, been made, and that this is peculiarly not the time in which to destroy the opportunity of Brooklyn, the State and the States, forever.

In this connection I should like the privilege of showing that politics and politicians have absolutely and finally broken down and failed as saviors of American institutions, broadly and generally; that we have come upon a sociological age, and upon the co-ordinate necessity and duty of studying anew the organization of society, especially in great cities, which have heretofore been the destruction of all civilizations, even the strongest and most hopeful.

There are many other matters that I should like to present, but which time does not permit me to mention; and if those already mentioned are not sufficient as a basis for my request, then probably nothing that I could add would give my request sufficient weight to secure a favorable answer.

Perhaps you will ask, and it would be quite proper if you should ask, on what personal grounds this request is made.

My first reply would be that now nearly thirty years ago I selected Brooklyn as my place of abode, because I found that it was an American city, the home of native Americans and Americanized Americans, discarding and spurning New York as not American, and the home of and controlled by un-Americanized Americans. This selection of Brooklyn and spurning of New York I have renewed daily for seven days in every week throughout the subsequent years, until now.

My further reply to the question would be that more than forty years ago, and before people in America had discovered that there was any such thing as a great municipal problem, I had the privilege of studying, for the better part of the year, the great city of London, and have for all the years since that great year, 1851, watched with interest the Londonization of American cities, great and small, much of the time aghast because of the threatening perils, all too little recognized, and nowise remedied either by the citizens in general, its victims, or by the leaders, teachers and guides of the American people.

And now I find that the one citadel city of American municipal citizenship left in the country, wherein we might yet be saved, is besieged by the enemy, in danger of capture, and, most pitiable of all, that many of its citizens, at least one of them a former president of the New England Society, are endeavoring to persuade its people to accept as a gift of the gods to the pious, the Trojan horse of consolidation.

Further, I discovered, on looking up the matter anew in connection with the attempts now being made to destroy the charter of Brooklyn, a fact and a duty; that I am descended from three at least of the original grantees of the original charter of Connecticut, one of them then, and the other subsequently, Governors of that colony, from John Allyn, known as the Great Secretary, into whose custody the duplicate charters of the colony were placed for safe-keeping, and who faithfully to the end of his life carried out that trust, and also from many of their associates and successors, who for several generations lived under and had to do with the administration and support of that charter and system of government, which, as has been before stated, became a model later for our American system; and that I ought not to allow the charter of Brooklyn to be taken away without protest, on my part, and without making some effort to call the attention of those of whom there must be many in Brooklyn, who are the descendants of some of the same ancestry which saved the charter of Connecticut, and the attention of others, public-spirited citizens, to the fact that under the circumstances the successful abrogation of the charter of Brooklyn, of home rule and a right to decide its own fate, fully and fairly presented, face to face with destiny, would be a political and social crime for which there is no parallel in history, ancient or modern, and to which there should not be a single instant of contemplated submission — except *resubmission.*

If you and your committee should ask how much time I desire in which to prepare, develop and present the subject-matters above mentioned and indicated, my reply would be, not less than ten days, but ten weeks if possible. And my general contention would be that a commission of the most learned experts in the land should be appointed to consider the whole subject during the period as long as that in which the Connecticut charter was in peril — something over twenty years — and, at the end, that consolidation and greater New York be abandoned in favor of greater Brooklyn, the great American city and sample of many great American municipalities.

Awaiting your early reply, I am very respectfully yours.

JAMES A. SKILTON.

THE CONSTITUTION STANDS IN THE WAY — DANGERS AND DIFFICULTIES OF THE "GREATER NEW YORK SCHEME."

(*Editorial in New York Times, May* 8, 1895.)

AN IMAGINARY OBJECTION.

Opponents of the Greater New York bill are in desperate straits for some ground for their opposition when they set up the constitutional bugbear of the right of every county not identical with a city in its boundaries to have a board of supervisors. There is nothing in the Constitution to prevent the Legislature from changing the boundaries of counties in any way that it may see fit.

When some of the towns of Westchester county were annexed to New York over twenty years ago, they were added to the county as well as the city. There is nothing to prevent the addition of more of them. If a part of Westchester county can be added to New York, so can a part of Queens county. If a part of Westchester county can be added to New York, so can a part of Queens county. If a part of a county can be set off and attached to an adjoining county, what is to hinder annexing the whole of it? The fact that the Constitution provides, in connection with the subject of apportionment, that the Legislature may abolish the county of Hamilton and annex its territory to other counties raises no presumption that it can not abolish any other county. It is only a qualification of a provision that Hamilton shall elect a Member of Assembly with the county of Fulton until its population shall entitle it to a member of its own. There is a proviso in another section of the apportionment article that nothing therein contained "shall prevent the division at any time of counties and towns" by the Legislature.

If the Legislature sees fit to make one county as well as one city of the area which it is proposed to consolidate, there is no constitutional bar to its doing so, and we see no reason why it should not do so. There is no occasion for two systems of administration covering the same territory any more in the case of the extended municipality than in the case of the present municipality of New York, or that of Brooklyn after it shall include all of Kings county. Doubtless when the consolidation shall have been effected the boundaries of the city will be the same as those of the county and there will be no occasion for boards of supervisors.

But all this is irrelevant to the pending bill, which provides practically for nothing but a commission to devise the legislation necessary to effect the proposed consolidation. In the meantime all the existing "bodies politic and corporate" are expressly retained with their administrative functions unimpaired. What shall be done with county lines and the functions now exercised by boards of supervisors hereafter is among the thingsto be considered by the commission. The Legislature will do nothing in regard to them until measures affecting them have been proposed, and then it will be time enough to raise questions on that score. They have nothing to do with the pending bill. It is not unlikely that the commission may devise a system of government involving subdivisions of some kind for local administrative purposes, but whether it does or not, there is nothing in the way of any change in county boundaries that may be found expedient.

(*From the New York Times, May* 9, 1895.)

GREATER NEW YORK QUESTIONS — ROBERT D. BENEDICT ON THE PROVISIONS OF THE CONSTITUTION CONCERNING COUNTIES AND JUDICIAL DEPARTMENTS.

To the Editor of the New York Times:

I see in the Times of this morning an editorial on the Greater New York bill, in which the objection that the bill would result not in one city with one municipal government and one debt —

contracting power, but in a city the five parts of which would be subject to the government of five boards of supervisors, with a city government imposed upon them, and with a debt-contracting power up to twice the constitutional limit, is spoken of as a " constitutional bugbear," and the reason for calling it so is stated to be that " there is nothing in the Constitution to prevent the Legislature from changing the boundaries of counties," and further that, " if the Legislature sees fit to make one county as well as one city of the area which it is proposed to consolidate, there is no constitutional bar to its doing so."

I think your epithet of " bug-bear " was used without full consideration of the provisions of the Constitution bearing on the question, or of the provisions of the bill. The bill proposes to constitute the city of New York out of the territory of the county of New York, the county of Kings, part of Queens, part of Westchester county, and the county of Richmond. It also, in its fifth section, provides as follows: "Nothing in this act contained shall be construed as attempting or intending to affect in any way the government, rights, powers, duties, obligations, limitations or disabilities of any county, or officers thereof, as fixed by the Constitution, or to obliterate any county lines."

It follows, therefore, inevitably, that by the bill as at present proposed, the Greater New York would be composed of five different parts, subject to six different governments, as I have said above. That this is very objectionable I understand to be conceded.

But, it is said that the question now is, only the framing of a charter for the Greater New York, and that by the charter, when framed, this difficulty may be avoided, by making, as you suggest, " one county as well as one city of the area which it is proposed to consolidate." It is certainly a grave question whether a commission appointed under the act would have the power in view of the fifth section, which I have quoted above, to provide a charter which should so seriously affect the government, etc., of these several counties, as would be done by making one county as well as one city of the area in question.

But if the commission did frame a charter, which should make one county as well as one city out of the territory of New York, could the Legislature enact it?

Possibly the Legislature could change the boundaries of Westchester county and Queens county and of New York county; for the Constitution, article III, section 5, expressly provides: "Nothing in this section shall prevent the division at any time of counties and towns, and the erection of new towns by the Legislature."

But when we come to the question of abolishing the county of Kings and the county of Richmond a very different question is presented.

If there were no provisions of the Constitution, excepting the provisions of section 5, article III, the power to abolish a county could hardly be claimed to exist, for that section has the following language: "Every county heretofore established and separately organized, except the county of Hamilton, shall always be entitled to one Member of Assembly. * * * But the Legislature may abolish the said county of Hamilton and annex the territory thereof to some other county or counties. * * * Members of the Assembly shall be apportioned to the several counties as follows: * * * Kings county, twenty-one members; * * * New York county, thirty-five members; Richmond county, one member. * * * Nothing in this section shall prevent the division at any time of counties and towns."

Could it be held under these provisions, which expressly authorize the abolition of Hamilton county alone, and expressly provides for the division of counties alone, that the power to abolish any county but Hamilton was implied? No rule of constitutional construction that I am familiar with would allow it.

And, again, if Richmond county is by the Constitution to have one Member of Assembly, and Kings county by the Constitution is to have twenty-one Members of Assembly, can either of those counties, constitutionally, be abolished? And if New York county can constitutionally have only thirty-five members of the Legislature, can the Legislature, by wiping out Richmond county and

Kings county and consolidating those two counties and parts of Westchester and Queens counties into one and calling it the county of New York, provide that the people residing in that Greater New York shall have a representation of only thirty-five Members in the Assembly, whereas they are now entitled to fifty-seven, besdes those apportioned to the parts of Westchester and Queens counties? Is the suggestion that the people can not thus be robbed of their constitutional right of representation a mere "constitutional bugbear?"

But the words of the Constitution relating to Members of the Assembly are not the only ones to be considered.

The same article provides that the State shall be divided into fifty Senate districts, and that the first district "shall consist of the counties of Suffolk and Richmond." Can the Legislature abolish Richmond county? If there is no Richmond county, will the first Senate district, consist of Suffolk county alone? The third to the ninth district are each to be "Part of the county of Kings." Can Kings county be abolished?

And, again, article 6, section 2, of the Constitution provides as follows: "The Legislature shall divide the State into four judicial departments. The first department shall consist of the county of New York. The other shall be bounded by county lines. * * * There shall be an appellate division for the Supreme Court, consisting of seven justices in the first department, and of five justices in each of the other departments."

Can the Legislature by abolishing the county of Kings and the county of Richmond, and including them in the county of New York, provide that the Greater New York, shall still be the first judicial department, with only seven justices in its appellate division for its doubled population?

Again, can the Legislature, under the Constitution, change the first department by taking into it, parts of Westchester and Queens, in the face of the provisions that the other departments shall be "bounded by the county lines?"

In the case of Lanning vs. Carpenter (20. N. Y. p. 447), the Court of Appeals discussed the questions arising, under the Constitution of 1846, out of the formation of Schuyler county. In that opinoin it is said:

"It is parcel of the requirements of the Constitution that the several judicial districts shall always be composed of counties and never of parts of counties. True, the Legislature has power to create new counties out of the old ones. Whenever this can be accomplished without deranging the limits of districts it may, perhaps, be done at any time. And when it is deemed advisable to constitute a new county out of parts of several districts it may be done at a time when the Legislature is empowered by the Constitution to reorganize the districts, but not at any other time."

Whether these words are applicable under the present Constitution, which provides for departments instead of districts, may possibly be a question. But if they are, can the Legislature change the boundaries of a county so as to transfer part of it from one judicial department to another?

What about the county courts of these counties which it is suggested can be abolished? What about their clerks, their surrogates, their sheriffs? If the questions involved in the above considerations are in the view of the Times "constitutional bugbears," the Times idea of bugbear is very different from mine.

These considerations have certainly not been presented to the public mind as they should have been. In view of them I say, without hesitation, that the only proper foundation for the building of the Greater New York must be an amendment to the constitution.

Very truly,

ROBERT D. BENEDICT.

NEW YORK, *May* 8, 1895.

BROOKLYN, N. Y., *January* 18, 1896.

Thomas H. Loomis, being duly sworn, says: I live at 288 Quincy street, Brooklyn, N. Y. On election day, November 6th, 1894, I was a canvasser in the ninth election district of the twenty-third ward. I saw an intelligent looking German who became so confused about his ballots that after once asking for instructions he finally refused altogether to vote any of the ballots. I also saw two other men who refused to vote any of the amendments or consolidation ballots, because they were confused about them. Also that the inspector of election was so intoxicated that he put all the ballots in one box.

THOMAS H. LOOMIS.

Sworn to before me, this 18th
day of January, 1895.
GEO. W. GATEHOUSE,
Notary Public, Kings County, N. Y.

STATE OF NEW YORK,
COUNTY OF KINGS, *ss.:*

John P. Morey, being duly sworn, says that he acted as ballot clerk in the twenty-seventh district in the sixth ward in the city of Brooklyn at last election and states that to the best of his knowledge that about three-quarters of the people who voted in his district did not know what they were voting for when they voted the amendments and the consolidation ballots, and some wanted to vote for and against the amendments not knowing what they were, and further this deponent says not.

JOHN P. MOREY.

Sworn to before me this 18th
day of January, 1895.
GEO. D. GELMORE,
Com. of Deeds, City of Brooklyn.

STATE OF NEW YORK,
COUNTY OF KINGS, *ss.:*

Patrick McGinniss being duly sworn, says that he acted as inspector of elections in the twenty-seventh district in the sixth ward of the city of Brooklyn at the last election, and states that the majority of the voters in that district did not know the difference between the consolidation ballots and the amendment ballots and got so confused that they refused to vote them and further this deponent says not.

PATRICK McGINNISS.

Sworn to before me, this 18th
day of January, 1895.
GEO. D. GELMORE,
Com. of Deeds, City of Brooklyn.

STATE OF NEW YORK,
COUNTY OF KINGS, *ss.:*

Augustine M. McHale being duly sworn, says that he acted as ballot clerk in the sixth district in the sixth ward at the last election and states that about one-third of the people in that district did not know the difference between the amendment and the consolidation ballots, and a great many asked him what they were for, and if they should vote them or not. And further this deponent says not.

AUGUSTINE M. McHALE.

Sworn to before me, this 18th
day of January, 1895.
GEO. D. GELMORE,
Com. of Deeds, City of Brooklyn.

STATE OF NEW YORK,
COUNTY OF KINGS, *ss.:*

Chas. H. Callahan, being duly sworn, says that he acted as ballot clerk in the second district in seventh ward in the city of Brooklyn at the last election, and states that more than one-third of the voters in his district did not understand the amendments and the consolidation ballots, and asked him for instructions in regard to voting the different ballots. He also states that, owing to the confusion, that a great many people who originally intended to vote against consolidation, through confusion, voted for it. And further, this deponent says not.

C. H. CALLAHAN.

Sworn to before me, this 22d
day of January, 1895.

GEO. D. GELMORE,
Com. of Deeds, City of Brooklyn.

STATE OF NEW YORK,
COUNTY OF KINGS, *ss.:*

Dominick Byrne, being duly sworn, says that he acted as inspector of election in the first district in the eleventh ward in the city of Brooklyn at the last election, and states that more than one-third of the voters in his district did not understand the amendments and consolidation ballots and asked for instructions in regard to voting the different ballots, and also states, owing to the confusion, that a great many people who originally intended to vote against consolidation, through confusion, voted for it. And further, this deponent says not.

DOMINICK BYRNE.

Sworn to before me, this 21st
day of January, 1895.

GEO. D. GELMORE,
Com. of Deeds, City of Brooklyn.

STATE OF NEW YORK,
COUNTY OF KINGS, *ss.:*

David J. Scanlon, being duly sworn, says that he acted as ballot clerk in the fourth district of the sixth ward in the city of Brooklyn, and states that more than one-third of the voters in his district did not understand the amendments and the consolidation ballots and asked him for instructions in regard to voting the different ballots. He also states that, owing to the confusion, that a great many people who originally intended to vote against consolidation, through confusion, voted for it. And further, this deponent says not.

DAVID J. SCANLON.

Sworn to before me, this 18th
day of January, 1895.

GEO. D. GELMORE,
Com. of Deeds, City of Brooklyn.

STATE OF NEW YORK,
COUNTY OF KINGS, *ss.:*

George O. B. Weaver, being duly sworn, says that he resides at 375 Cumberland street in the city of Brooklyn, and states that at the last election, held November 6, 1894, in the city of Brooklyn, that, owing to the large number of ballots to be voted for he got so confused that instead of voting against consolidation, as he intended, he voted for it. And further, this deponent says not.

GEORGE O. B. WEAVER.

Sworn to before me, this 21st
day of January, 1895.

GEO. D. GELMORE,
Com. of Deeds, City of Brooklyn.

STATE OF NEW YORK,
COUNTY OF KINGS, *ss.:*

Frank J. Tynan, being duly sworn, says that on last election day, November 6, 1894, he was a ballot clerk in the twentieth district in the sixth ward in the city of Brooklyn, and states that a large number of very intelligent men became so confused about the amendment and consolidation ballots that they finally refused to vote any of them. The number of ballots was so great that many voters could not distinguish between them. And further, this deponent says not.

F. J. TYNAN.

Sworn to before me, this 18th
day of January, 1895.

GEO. D. GELMORE,
Com. of Deeds, City of Brooklyn.

STATE OF NEW YORK,
COUNTY OF KINGS, *ss.:*

Chas. A. Scott, being duly sworn, says that he served as inspector of election in the sixteenth district in the fifth ward in the city of Brooklyn at the last election, and states that about three-quarters of the voters in his district asked for instructions in regard to the different ballots and wanted to know how to vote them, and that a great many of the voters who intended to vote against the amendments and consolidation, through the confusion caused by the number of ballots, voted for them. And further this deponent says not.

CHARLES A. SCOTT.

Sworn to before me, this 19th
day of January, 1895.

GEO. D. GELMORE,
Com. of Deeds, City of Brooklyn.

STATE OF NEW YORK,
COUNTY OF KINGS, *ss.:*

Joseph S. Stone, being duly sworn, says that he resides at 1621 Fulton street in the city of Brooklyn, and served as a ballot clerk in the twenty-sixth district of the twenty-third ward at the last election, and states that more than one-half of the voters in that district asked him for instructions in regard to voting the different ballots, and also states that some voters who intended to vote against consolidation informed him that they did not know how they voted. And further, this deponent says not.

Sworn to before me, this 21st

J. H. STONE.

day of January, 1895.

JOHN F. FOLEY,

Notary Public, Kings County.

STATE OF NEW YORK,

COUNTY OF KINGS, *ss.:*

John F. Ryan, being duly sworn, says that he acted as a ballot clerk in the last election and that he noticed that the majority of the people were confused and got rattled over the amendments and that they asked the ballot clerk if they would have to fold the ballots the same as the regular ballots and that a great many voted for them not knowing what they were voting for. And further this deponent says not.

JOHN F. RYAN.

Sworn to before me, this 17th

day of January, 1895.

GEO. D. GELMORE,

Com. of Deeds, City of Brooklyn.

STATE OF NEW YORK,

COUNTY OF KINGS, *ss.:*

Wm. B. Powell, being duly sworn, says that he resides at 27 Brevoort place in the city of Brooklyn; that he acted as Republican watcher in the thirtieth district in the seventh ward of said city, at the election on November 6, 1894; that at least one-third of the voters in said district were sent back to the booths to rearrange their ballots properly, among these being many men of more than average intelligence; that the number of ballots was such (19) that many voters became disgusted and voted only the ballots for candidates, tearing up those for amendments and consolidation and throwing them away. And further this deponent says not.

W. B. POWELL.

Sworn to before me, this 22d
day of January, 1895.
Geo. D. Gelmore,
Com. of Deeds, City of Brooklyn.

The Brooklyn Club, *January* 24, 1896.

Hon. Clarence Lexow:

I regret that I can not speak in favor of consolidation of Brooklyn and New York as I sail for the West Indies to-morrow. I am heartily in favor of the movement.

Yours truly,
E. W. BLISS.

Brooklyn, *January* 25, 1896.

James Matthews, Esq., *Chairman:*

Dear Sir.— My engagements in New York prevent my being present at the meeting to-day to speak in favor of consolidation. I, therefore, desire to say, that after having given the subject long and careful thought from every point of view, and while the bill under consideration is not entirely to my liking in its present form, I am forced to the conclusion that the consolidation of the two cities into one greater city is for the best interest of all concerned, I am fully persuaded that no further obstacle ought to be placed in the way of immediate consolidation, but that it should be secured at the earliest possible moment.

Yours very truly,
JOHN GIBB.

BROOKLYN, N. Y., *January* 24, 1896.

GEORGE M. CHAUNCEY, ESQ.:

My Dear Sir.—Business of importance compels me to visit Boston to-day, and in making necessary arrangements previous to leaving, my time will be fully occupied, to the extent which will prevent my appearing before the committee. I wish to reiterate a fact which is well known, that I am thoroughly in hearty support of consolidation. I doubt if I could say anything more than has been said. Our friends have touched upon all the vital points. I believe the matter could be safely left with the people's representatives in the Legislature. The people of Brooklyn and New York have passed upon the matter, and the malcontents who desire a new election, remind us very much of the action of some of the candidates in the recent election in Brooklyn, but happily for the city and State the majority rule will continue to prevail, and the sentiments and desires on consolidation, as expressed by the people will receive proper recognition at the hands of the people's representatives.

Very truly yours,
(Signed.) EDWIN KNOWLES.

---

195 WASHINGTON PARK, BROOKLYN, *January* 24, 1896.

TO CHAIRMAN LEXOW, *Legislative Joint Committee, Room 23, County Court House, Brooklyn, N. Y.:*

Dear Sir.— Permit me to vote before your committee most heartily in favor of consolidation. It is more than thirty years since I moved to Brooklyn — I am a property-holder there. I love Brooklyn, but I love Greater New York more.

It seems clear to me that a number of contiguous towns consolidated in one body can be governed more cheaply and more wisely than as separate organizations. I live every summer on Staten Island. The county of Richmond has a number of small municipalities. Nothing could be more corrupt than the political rings that rule some of those villages. Neither the Tammany nor the

McLaughlin ring compared in wickedness with the ring that ruled Gravesend.

The moral sentiment, whether in small or large communities, must be pure and assertive and controlling, or there will be corruption. It is no more true of a large than of a small community that "an indifferentist in politics is an enemy of the government that protects him." All communities must learn this lesson, and I believe that it is easier learned in a great community than by the same number of people broken up under small municipalities. You will remember that the argument that was most frequently urged against the combination of the colonies under one government was the unwieldiness of so large a territory. The same was urged against the consolidation by Bismarck of the German principalities under one rule. But we now see successfully governed under "Old Glory" the thirteen colonies grown to forty-five, and never could Germany have so prospered as under one rule.

I am so strongly persuaded of the desirability of consolidation that I feel like Sumner felt when asked to listen to the other side of the slavery question. He replied, "There is no other side."

All I ask is, that you see to it that the basis of union is equitable.

Respectfully.

I. K. FUNK.

Brooklyn, N. Y., *January* 24, 1896.

W. C. Redfield, Esq., *President League of Loyal Citizens:*

Dear Sir.— Enclosed find list of some of our merchants and business men who are in accord on the subject of resubmission.

I find at the Kings County Savings Bank that five-sixths of our mortgages are at five per cent., and one-sixth at four and one-half per cent. Not a dollar in mortgages at six per cent.

I notice, on statement of William Burgh Savings Bank, January 1, 1895, over $14,000,000 on mortgages at five per cent. and $159,000 at six per cent., and I assume that if any of the latter asked for five per cent. they would be told to look elsewhere.

because of the narrow margin in value for security of bank — a wise thing to do.

They have many mortgages now at four and one-half per cent. Your friend Biley, of the Indemnity Company, is a little bit off. J. C. Lowdon, of 161 Keep street, and Geo. F. Yates, of 431 Bedford avenue, voted for consolidation, and are now against it, and will vote that way if opportunity offers.

Yours truly.

JOHN S. McKEON.

List of names of merchants enclosed in letter from John S. McKeon to W. C. Redfield, president League of Loyal Citizens:

Frederick Loeser & Co.

W. H. Bullard.

James Harkness, 692 Fulton street.

Geo. B. Lewis, 660 Fulton street.

S. P. Willetts, 71 Layfayette avenue.

Benjamin Rosenzweig, 624 Fulton street.

D. Maguire, 703 Fulton street.

Peter Flynn, 701 Fulton street.

Brooklyn Hardware and Sporting Goods Company, 601 Fulton street.

Wechsler Bros., 538-540 Fulton street.

Johnston Bros., 8-12 Nevins street.

P. W. Taylor, 521 Fulton street.

M. Rosenberg, 481-483 Fulton street.

Isaac Mason, 860 President street.

Thomas Thompson, 101 Park place.

Walter B. Shipman, 123 Myrtle avenue.

Joseph J. McIntyre, 1278 Putnam avenue.

P. M. Dale & Son, Myrtle avenue and Gold street.

Armstrong Bros., 339 Myrtle avenue.

F. C. Joslin, 404 Myrtle avenue.

Joseph Wechsler Sons, Bedford avenue and Fulton street.

H. W. Bach, 345 Myrtle avenue.

Longmore & Warwick, 382 Myrtle avenue.

Isaac Knee, 442 Myrtle avenue.

N. F. Green, 455 Myrtle avenue.

David Jacob, 623-627 Myrtle avenue.

Henry J. Leach, 1103 Fulton street.

John Doyle, 1099 Fulton street.

Samuel Downing, 1095-1097 Fulton street.

The Long Island Brewery, Third avenue and Dean street.

Ernest Nason, 601 Fifth avenue.

T. L. Murphy, 66 Richmond street.

John McCormick. Fifth avenue and Ninth street.

J. W. Kimball, 450 Fifth avenue.

C. S. Stephenson, 577-579 Fifth avenue.

M. J. Maxwell, 550 Fifth avenue.

Morris Nason, 601 Fifth avenue.

H. B. Monahan, 503-509 Fifth avenue.

January 22, 1896.

To the Committee of the Loyal League:

Sirs.—At a meeting of the Brooklyn Woman Suffrage Association held January 21st, the following resolutions were adopted to be presented to your committee:

Truly yours,
CORNELIA K. HOOD.

21 First place, Brooklyn.

Resolved, Whereas the women of Brooklyn are homekeepers and taxpayers, and as vitally interested in the question of consolidation as the men, we, the Brooklyn Woman Suffrage Association, respectfully ask the committee of the Loyal League to include in their resubmission bill a request that the women of Brooklyn be allowed to express their opinion on this subject at the polls by ballot.

Signed: On behalf of the Brooklyn Woman Suffrage Association.

CORNELIA K. HOOD,
President.

Resolved, That we, the Brooklyn Woman Suffrage Association, urge upon the members of the Legislature from Brooklyn to vote for the bill introduced by Mr. Brush, providing for the resubmission of the question of consolidation to the popular vote.

Signed: On behalf of the Brooklyn Woman Suffrage Association,

CORNELIA K. HOOD,
President.

NEW YORK, *January* 23, 1896.

HON. SENATOR LEXOW:

Dear Sir.— I am in favor of consolidation and can see no reason against it. We are really one now, but not in name. Our interests are one. We own property in New York and Brooklyn, and have been served by New York government fully as well as the Brooklyn government. We own considerable in both Brooklyn and New York, and all our family are in favor of consolidation. There are George Vernon, Harold, Paul and myself of this firm, voters in Brooklyn, and five more voters in the family owning property in both cities; nearly all were born in Brooklyn. We voted for consolidation and are opposed to resubmission, as we see no necessity for it. We all vote the Republican ticket, but do not see any question of politics in this question. Interested parties alone are against it. The moneyed interests I find are for it and the plain people. It will help New York commercially. I know that people like to live in the biggest place. I traveled many years through the west, and buyers like to buy of the biggest place and to visit it. I trust, as we voted for it once, you will have it speedily accomplished.

Very truly,
T. ALFRED VERNON.

256 Clinton avenue.

BROOKLYN, *January* 17, 1896.

To the Chairman of the Legislative Joint Subcommittee on Consolidation:

Sir.— Unless the majority of this committee have been misreported, they have declared that the question of consolidation has been settled, and that the only thing now to do is to find the best and most feasible plan for accomplishing that purpose.

Against such a proposition I most earnestly protest. We have never had a settlement of this question by the people of Brooklyn. True, there was a vote upon the subject in 1894, but the people of this city did not regard it as a "settlement." Neither did the friends of consolidation regard it as a settlement before the election. Their committee put forth a circular upon the subject in which they declared: "Electors will please observe that a vote amounts to nothing more than a simple expression of opinion on the general subject of consolidation. If every ballot in the city were in favor of consolidation there would be no finality about it," etc.

The people of Brooklyn looked at the question in this indifferent way, and but one-third of the registered voters of Brooklyn voted in its favor; and of those who favored it, we know of a large number of persons who voted for it under a misapprehension. There were a large number of constitutional amendments to be voted on, and Republicans urged upon their followers to vote for all the amendments. Many Republicans voted for consolidation thinking it was a constitutional amendment, as the ballots were similar in form. This is a fact, however much it may go against the intelligence of the voter. And now, forsooth, with less than one-third in favor, and many of them voting under a misapprehension, we are told that the question of consolidation has been settled by the people of Brooklyn in its favor, because there was a paltry majority of 277 votes out of 129,000 voting, and 62,000 who did not feel interest enough in the subject to vote at all. To take this view of the matter and to annihilate the autonomy of a great city of over a million on such a pretext, will be the most infamous outrage of the nineteenth century.

But, for argument's sake, let us for a moment grant that the vote of 1894 was valid and binding; but the Legislature did not act upon that vote when the opportunity was presented. And I claim that because of that failure to act then, Brooklyn is entitled to another vote on consolidation. Are we to be told that that vote is to be always binding? Can a great people not reverse its opinions?

In 1888 the people of the United States elected a Republican President and a Congress in favor of the McKinley tariff by so great a majority that many said the Democrats would never be heard of again, not in at least a quarter of a century.

In 1892 the people of the United States elected a Democratic President and Congress in favor of the Wilson tariff by a majority so great that Democrats said the Republicans were dead, and they bade them an everlasting good-bye, as they thought.

Two years later the Republicans were again on top in Congress, with a greater majority than the Democrats had in the former Congress; and nobody doubts the election of a Republican President next fall, unless he is defeated by the stupidity and foolishness of Republicans in the New York Legislature in cramming consolidation down the throat of Brooklyn at a cost of 30,000 to 50,000 Republican votes in our city.

I speak of these things to show that a great people not only have the right to reverse their opinions, but that they do reverse them. Suppose that either Congress had said to the people in 1888 or 1892, you have voted for the McKinley tariff or the Wilson tariff, as the case might be, and that question is settled, as our legislators at Albany now say to the people of Brooklyn on the consolidation question. Well, suppose they had? I need not discuss the result.

Now, if Brooklyn was for consolidation in 1894, she had a right to reverse her opinion, especially as the Legislature did not act upon that opinion at its following session; and Brooklyn has reversed that opinion; and now she has a right to give an expression of that reversed opinion by a resubmission of this important question to her voters. She asks, nay, she demands this right from this Legislature. If that right is granted and the vote is for consolidation, you will never hear a word again from any present Brooklynite. But if that right is denied us, and consolidation is forced upon us without resubmission, and, as we know, against the will of a large majority of the voters of this city, then all I have to say is, God help the Republican party in

Brooklyn and in the State next fall. On the 14th day of January, 1896, the Brooklyn Eagle said editorially:

"There are 100,000 votes in this town to make things and to smash things, and they can be wielded as a unit, to make or to smash things and men, according as the things or the men are the friends or are the enemies of Brooklyn's right to determine Brooklyn's destiny.

"Mr. Morton would like to be President. It is a commendable ambition. He would lose New York State by more votes than Harrison lost it in 1892, if he wrote his name under a bill to abolish Brooklyn without Brooklyn's consent. Hamilton Fish would like to be Governor. But he could no more be elected Governor of New York, even if he received the nomination of both political parties with a record for the effacement of Brooklyn without Brooklyn's consent to score against him, than he could be elected Pope of Rome. Brooklyn means business, and the Eagle means business, on this thing, and when both mean business on the same thing, events prove that business is effectively done."

Gentlemen, without any thought of boasting, but simply to show that I have a right to speak as a Republican, let me say that I have been a staunch Republican, since the 7th day of August, 1854, when the first Republican convention was held. I was a member of that convention. I have never flinched from Republican doctrines. I have always worked faithfully for the party. I wrote a book on the tariff, of which 3,000,000 copies have been circulated. I know something of the party and its teachings and its doctrines. I love the party for what it has done and is doing, and for what it will do if wise counsels prevail; and I know something of the temper and feelings of the Republicans in Brooklyn; and I say to you in all earnestness and sincerity, that the Eagle is right, and that if you compel us to take consolidation without resubmission, or at least a referendum, there will be no longer a Republican party in Brooklyn. They will never again trust or support a party that has deliberately robbed them of their dearest rights and privileges, and turn them and their property over to the spoliation of Tammany Hall and its vile crew, with its Republican attachment, equally vile. One of the fundamental doctrines of Republicanism is home rule, and on this doctrine we also demand resubmission.

The chairman of this subcommittee was in Brooklyn at the Republican judiciary convention, last October, and was then asked how he stood on the question of consolidation. He answered in my presence: "Gentlemen, that is a question that you ought to settle in Brooklyn." We have settled it in Brooklyn. We have now a legislative delegation that is unanimous for resubmission; we have a common council that is unanimous for resubmission; our mayor and ex-mayor are both earnest for resubmission; and the people of Brooklyn are for resubmission.

I entreat you, give the people of Brooklyn another chance to vote on this all important question, and thus let it be forever settled in the only just, right and righteous manner.

(Signed.) D. G. HARRIMAN.

SHRINKAGE OF LOCAL VALUES — CONSOLIDATION WITH NEW YORK AS A REMEDY FOR IT.

To the Editor of the Brooklyn Eagle:

Permit me to say a few words relative to the several editorials that have appeared of late in your influential paper as regards the depopulation of and shrinkage of values in Brooklyn. In my opinion this condition of affairs will prevail until ample facilities of travel are provided for the people now residing in Brooklyn and the multitude of those who would reside here if proper means of travel were at hand. To bring this about large expenditures will be necessary, the greater part of which should be borne by New York city, and not, as in the case of the Brooklyn and New York bridge, one third by New York and two thirds by Brooklyn; nor, as in the case of the contemplated East River bridge, half by each city. To arrive at the proper proportion that Brooklyn should bear, I advocate consolidation with New York under equal taxation. Consolidation with New York, I advocate, also, for many other reasons, too numerous to mention in this letter, knowing how valuable space is in your paper. I must mention a few, however. First, to fully develop Brooklyn and vicinity. Second, to make sure that the metropolis of this continent remains where it is. Third, this is really the most important and probably should have been mentioned first — the people so decided it by vote when the question was submitted to them. Of course, I understand your paper's position on this question; that it was a light vote, that the question was not thoroughly understood, etc. I am fully aware, also that the mayor elect and many other late candidates for office have expressed themselves in favor of resubmitting the question to popular vote. But what has this, I ask you, to do with the question that has been decided by the people whose servants the aforesaid candidates were willing to be and many of them soon will be? It would, in my opinion, be a dangerous precedent to set aside the question of consolidation with New York that has been decided in the affirmative by the people. And, for one, I do not understand how the people's representatives at Albany during the last session dared to ignore the will of the people. Mr. Grout, the late Democratic candidate for mayor, has as much, if not better right to have the question of who is or who should be mayor of this city for the term beginning January 1, 1896, resubmitted to the people because of the vote cast. Mr. Wurster was elected by a very much smaller majority than was given for consolidation. Perhaps the people did not understand fully. Mr. Grout does not advocate resubmission. Is it because he is not a loyal Brooklynite? I realize that I will be put down as a traitor to Brooklyn by certain people, but I would have them understand that I am a resident of Brooklyn for more than thirty years, have done and am ready now to do everything in my power to influence and advocate the material prosperity of Brooklyn, and that I represent large interests, all of which are located in Brooklyn, and my love for Brooklyn is second to none. I might and could say much more, but dare not encroach further on your space.

CONSOLIDATIONIST.

BROOKLYN, *December* 24, 1895.

CONSOLIDATION ARGUMENTS ARRAYED AGAINST THOSE OF THE LOYAL CITIZENS.

To the Editor of the Brooklyn Eagle:

Since writing you my letter of the twenty-fourth ult. and which in your impartiality and desire to air all sides of a question you published in one of your issues I have noticed and read quite a number of opinions also printed in your paper, emanating from so-called "Loyal Citizens" of Brooklyn, many of who are, and rightly so, highly honored gentlemen and citizens and who are opposed to consolidation with New York for various and what seems to be valid reasons, among which and the most prominent are these: First, a pride in the municipality of Brooklyn. Second, a desire not to see Brooklyn effaced from the map of this country. Third, a wish to know the conditions or terms of consolidation, and to have them submitted for approval to the vote of the people. Fourth, a desire to have the question of consolidation resubmitted to the people of Brooklyn on the ground that it was not properly and fully understood when voted on before, because of the fact that at the time nineteen questions or ballots had to be considered. So far as the first reason is concerned, and to show an inconsistency, I will merely refer to the well-known fact that when the municipality of Brooklyn wanted to restore the city hall tower after the fire, the first thing the authorities did was to invite New York architects to submit designs, Brooklyn's architects being silently and successfully ignored. Mr. Schieren, during his term as mayor, accomplished a great deal of good for which he is and ever will be honored by the people of Brooklyn, and because of which a considerable degree of civic pride has been inculcated in their hearts, but, to my mind, not sufficient to overcome the advantages of consolidation with New York. It is stated that the Republicans of Brooklyn are against consolidation, because of the fact that there seems to be a possibility of their party permanently getting control of affairs in this city, and they do not want to sacrifice the chance by consolidating the two cities of Brooklyn and New York. I fail to see what bearing this has on the matter. Have they the best and honest interests of Brooklyn at heart, or are they merely out for spoils? Mr.

Schieren's administration was a very creditable one, but, strictly speaking, not Republican. The present administration, as I understand, is to be purely and religiously a Republican one, and I am glad of it; but if that is all there is to recommend it and no good is to be accomplished, the people will and should make short work of it. In municipal affairs, give me good men first and if Republicans so much the better. I have full and undoubted faith in the virtue of the people to believe that they will relegate Tammany to the same oblivion that has been meted out to the old ring of Brooklyn, with the aid of your valuable paper. As to the second reason how do these gentlemen know but that the consolidated city will not be called Brooklyn. It is certain at this time that the name New York should be changed, as it is very difficult for foreigners, and for that matter many natives, to distinguish the difference in relation as understood by New York city, New York county and New York State, Some ephonious name should be adopted, and I know of none more so than Brooklyn. As to the third reason: To submit the conditions of annexation to the average voter is not feasible, especially when it is claimed that these same voters did not understand the question of for and against consolidation. A competent body of men, such as would be capable of framing the laws under which the consolidated city should be governed, should determine the conditions and Brooklyn should be ably represented by men of well known standing and ability, and possessing the full confidence of its people. As to the fourth question: If this question should be resubmitted why should not the other eighteen be resubmitted as well? If the vote on consolidation had been in the negative instead of the affirmative would these gentlemen be so ready to have it resubmitted to popular vote on the same grounds as now set forth by them? Many of those who have expressed themselves as opposed to consolidation and whose reasons for being so you have published at different times, as well as those gentlemen, twenty, I believe, who attended the meeting at the academy assembly rooms on the seventh inst. I recognize and know them to have large interests in New York city. It is true they reside in Brooklyn and are widely and favorably known because of their philanthropy and furthermore, of benevolent enterprises, but it is, nevertheless the fact that far their greatest investments are in New York city, both in real as well as personal property. Is it, perhaps, that these gentlemen fear an increase in taxes in New York city if Brooklyn were annexed to it? However this may be, it is true, none the less, that the wealth of Brooklyn is invested in New York, and being so is subject to taxation there. This in the nature of things will always be so and, therefore, Brooklyn should have the benefit of taxation on this enormous capital, the amount of which can not be computed. To reach this capital for the purpose of taxation so that Brooklyn should have her due share of it I know of no better way than by consolidating the municipalities of Brooklyn and New York.

CONSOLIDATIONIST.

BROOKLYN, *January* 11, 1896.

BROOKLYN, *January* 25, 1896.

HON. CLARENCE LEXOW, *Chairman Joint Committee on Consolidation, Court House, Brooklyn, N. Y.:*

Dear Sir.— Inclosed I beg to hand you for your perusal clippings from the Brooklyn Daily Eagle, being copies of letters from myself to the editor over the signature of "Consolidationist." These letters appeared respectively, in the issues of the Eagle of December 26th and January 16th.

My excuse for troubling you in this matter is primarily because I am thoroughly interested in the welfare of Brooklyn and New York city, and I am too modest a man and too little of a public speaker to weary you with any talk on the subject. I want to write you in the matter, however, because I notice that frequent reference is made at the meetings held by your honorable body to the fact that all, or nearly all, of the representatives from Brooklyn at Albany, who were elected last fall, were pledged to resubmission, or against consolidation. This is a fact, but how it occurred I think was as follows: The anti-consolidationists having nothing to lose desired a resubmission of the vote taken on consolidation and therefore "the Loyal League" took it upon themselves to interview all candidates for offices for which an election was held last fall and obtained their pledges to vote for resubmission. Those in favor of consolidation, so far as I am aware, took no such steps and because of the fact that they considered that the question had been definitely settled the year previously. I, personally, so understood it. Now, the anti-consolidationists, or the "Loyal League," having pledged all candidates, is it to be supposed that those in favor of consolidation should refrain from voting altogether because if they voted at all they must vote for a Republican, a Democrat, or any other individual who was already pledged against consolidation or for a resubmission of the question?

The honorable representative from New York has frequently propounded the question to persons speaking in favor of consolidation as to whether it is a fact that the taxes of what is now New York city would increase proportionately to the reduction, and which I thoroughly believe will take place in the taxes of Brooklyn. To this I would answer, yes, and New York city can well afford to pay the ratio of increase over and above what is paid on the assessment now prevailing in New York city, and have what is now Brooklyn a part of the greater city, being, as it is, the most convenient to the heart of commerce of the present New York city, and be the means of diverting the population which is naturally overcrowding New York to Brooklyn instead of obliging them, as now, to seek residence in New Jersey, which, aside from Brooklyn, is the nearest point to the marts of New York city. If it were not for the fact that the land west of the North river is under the jurisdiction of another State, I would be heartily in favor of consolidating New York city with that portion of it westward to the extent of at least fifteen miles. As this is impossible, however, it is then the more necessary that Brooklyn should be consolidated with New York city.

Respectfully submitted.

H. C. BECK.

120 LEXINGTON AVENUE, *January* 6, 1895.

MR. GRIFFITH:

Dear Sir.— My niece has asked me to write you about the Duffield street property. On inclosed slip you have an account of it and its indebtedness.

As I can not take care of this kind of property I should be willing to sell it for whatever I can get over and above the indebtedness. I am told that the houses are worth, at lowest valuation, $10,000. Three years ago they were officially valued at $12,000 each. The question of what they are worth does not concern me; it is what I can get for them, as I do not want tenement-house property, or, indeed, any real estate.

Please get the best offer possible for me and greatly oblige,

Yours truly.

CATHERINE G. FOOTE.

THE PACKER COLLEGIATE INSTITUTE,
BROOKLYN, N. Y., *January* 23, 1896.

MR. EDWARD BARR, *Secretary the League of Loyal Citizens, Brooklyn, N. Y.*:

Dear Sir.— My engagements out of town will prevent my attendance upon legislative subcommittee on consolidation this week.

I am informed that one of the speakers before the committee on Friday afternoon of last week, urged consolidation as a means for providing better public school instruction for neglected children of this city. Such a statement, if unrefuted, would have great influence upon the thoughtful members of the committee. I hope that Superintendent Maxwell, who stands at the head of his special line of educational work, will be called before the committee to give authentic information showing the proud advance which the Brooklyn public schools have made during the last ten years. There is nothing in the city's history more stimulating to civic pride than knowledge of the generous appropriations of money, and, in the main, economical and wise use of such funds for the development of the public school system. The teaching force of the city has been greatly strengthened. We have the largest and in some respects the best high schools of the country, and our new school-houses are admirably planned and beautiful buildings. Do not fail of having the facts in this particular brought to the attention of the committee.

Very truly yours.
TRUMAN J. BACKUS.

BROOKLYN, *January* 20, 1896.

MR. R. D. BENEDICT:

Dear Sir.— Pardon me for asking a portion of your valuable time in an examination of the decisions of Judges Dykeman and Patterson, and the affirmation of them by the Court of Appeals in the question of consolidation of the Westchester towns, under the act passed last winter. I am confident that you are perfectly willing to correct an error if its justice can be demonstrated, and I am as firmly convinced that the records of the decisions rendered in July last, and later, will furnish ample proof that county lines are no bar to consolidation. Under these decisions the towns referred to are a portion of New York city, and enjoy to-day the benefits of equal taxation.

Very respectfully,
GEORGE W. CHAUNCEY.

BROOKLYN, *January* 21, 1896.

GEO. W. CHAUNCEY, ESQ.:

Dear Sir.— I have received your letter of the 20th inst. You are quite correct in judging that I would be willing to correct any error which I had made, and I am equally confident that you have the same willingness.

I am acquained with the cases you speak of, which arose out of the transfer of some of the towns of Westchester and joining them to the city of New York. But I think you had not adverted to the fact that in that legislation no question of abolishing a county was involved. The county of New York and the county of Westchester both exist to-day, as they did before that act was passed. The only change that has been made has been a change of the boundary between them. You are mistaken, therefore, in supposing that the case "furnishes ample proof that county lines are no bar to consolidation." It furnishes proof that existing county lines can be changed, so as to transfer a portion of one county to another. But it has no bearing whatever on the question of whether a county can be abolished.

If you will read what I have heretofore in my speech before the legislative committee and elsewhere said, in reference to this matter, you will see that what I have said was first, that county lines can not be abolished and that the consolidation bill which has been introduced expressly provides for the continued existence of the counties involved; second, that as in each county of the State the Constitution requires the existence of a board of supervisors, it follows that in the consolidated city the board of supervisors of the county of Kings and the board of supervisors of the county of New York must be each re-established by the passage of a bill which brings both those counties within the boundary of a city. I have urged that no man that was in favor of good government could believe that it would be promoted by the establishment of a city, five parts of which would be governed as to its financial concerns by five boards of supervisors, with a municipal city government extending over the whole territory in addition, and with the limit of the debt-contracting power extended to twenty per cent. instead of confined, as the Constitution now confines it, to ten per cent. of the assessed valuation. I can not believe that you would desire the establishment of such a complex and grotesque form of government. If you would, you are the first man that I have met to express such a desire.

But it occurs to me that it is possible, in view of your reference to the act of last year, that you might think that the existence of Kings county, as a county, might be preserved, although, let us say, nine-tenths of it was consolidated and made part of the city of New York; that, for instance, to put an extreme case, all of Kings county, except Barren island, might be declared to be part of the city of New York, thus leaving Barren island as being the county of Kings. Such an act would be a somewhat similar one to the act which was passed last year, differing in the extent of the territory annexed. But there are many difficulties which would arise in the case of such legislation. Under the Constitution the county of New York is entitled to thirty-five members of the Assembly, and the county of Kings to twenty-one members. The effect, therefore, of such legislation would be to give Barren island, then the county of Kings, a representation in the Assembly of twenty-one members and to give to the territory, which is now the city of New York and to all the territory which is now the county of Kings, except Barren island, the same representation of thirty-five members only, which New York county alone, under its present administration, is entitled to.

Such a result of itself is alone sufficient to show that no such legislation could be adopted.

Furthermore, under the Constitution, Senate districts Nos. 3, 4, 5, 6, 7, 8, and 9 are required by the Constitution to consist each of certain specified parts of the county of Kings. This provision could not possibly be complied with if all the county of Kings, except Barren island, were made a part of the county of New York. Furthermore, Senate districts Nos. 10 to 21 are required by the Constitution to consist of certain specified parts of the county of New York. District No. 21, by the Constitution, is required to consist of a certain specified part of the county of New York, "and all that part of the county of New York not hereinbefore described." The result of such legislation, therefore, would be to put the whole of the county of Kings, except Barren island, in to district No. 21, and to give to that district but one Senator.

I think you will see that no legislation which should produce such results is possible.

The act of last year of which you speak, in my judgment established great injustice to the inhabitants of the annexed district, and to the inhabitants of the Senate and Assembly district to which the annexed district was necessarily joined. It diminished the proportionate right of representation of every inhabitant within the district affected.

The case to which you referred decided that the Legislature had power to work that injustice, but I think no man will be found hardy enough to suggest that the Legislature should so exercise that arbitrary power as to deprive the citizens of Brooklyn of their fair proportionate representation in the Legislature of the State.

If the above views which I have expressed commend themselves to your judgment as reasonable, it would seem to me that, unless you are in favor of such a consolidation of the cities of Brooklyn and New York as would deprive the city of Brooklyn of such fair representation, or are in favor of a city which would be governed by five boards of supervisors, as well as a municipal government, with a double tax limit, you would have to concede that you are in error in supporting the present consolidation bill. And, if so, I am sure you are willing to correct that error.

I remain your obedient servant.

R. D. BENEDICT.

We, the undersigned real estate brokers in the city of Brooklyn, are in favor of resubmission:

Ruston & Robbins, real estate, 44 Court street.

W. G. Rushmore, real estate, 186 Remsen street.

C. J. Bisbee, real estate, 73 Flatbush avenue.

Hermann Roeker, real estate, 118 Prospect place.

G. H. Barnsdall, real estate, 286 Flatbush avenue.

J. O. Cleaveland, real estate, 186 Remsen street.

We, the undersigned real estate brokers engaged in business in the city of Brooklyn are in favor of resubmission of the question of consolidation:

Thomas W. Story, 76 Broadway.

E. C. Macchuchey, dealer in real estate, 392 Broadway.

Henry Fettel, real estate and insurance, 896 Park avenue, Brooklyn.

D. G. Campbell & Son, real estate and insurance, 1147 Myrtle avenue.

We, the undersigned real estate brokers in the city of Brooklyn, are in favor of resubmission:

Edmund R. Terry, conveyancer, 12 Remsen street.

Wm. O. Sumner, 166 Pierpont street.

Isaac H. Cary, 200 Fulton street.

George D. Gilmore, 44 Court street.

John W. Pierce, Boulevard and Neptune avenue, thirty-first ward.

Chas. A. LaRuesue, 371 Fulton street, Brooklyn.

Hiram G. Bedell, 375 Fulton street.

Francis E. Heron, 1149 Third avenue.

J. B. McQuillon, Fifty-second street, Third avenue, Brooklyn.

Wm. H. Mayband, 1562 Fulton street.

The undersigned business men of Brooklyn, believing our interests at stake, do hereby protest against consolidation and respectfully demand that this important question be resubmitted to the voters of this city:

F. H. Chandler, 300 Fulton street.

John Segelken, 371 First street.

H. C. Segelken, 314 Hicks street.

Casper Segelken, 314 Hicks street.

Charles A. Packard, Jr., 601 Evergreen avenue.

Michl. O'Connor, 55 Atlantic avenue.

Patrick Dunnigan, 39 Atlantic avenue.

John Loughlin, Atlantic avenue, Brooklyn.

Francis Hayward, 635 Carroll street.

Theo. J. Grunewald, 25 Canton street.

Henry F. O'Neill, 65 Columbia place.

S. H. Liddle, 66 Atlantic avenue.

Wm. T. Liddle, 291 Columbia street.

Wm. T. Hagan, 291 Columbia street.

Thos. G. Splint, 77 Atlantic avenue.

J. E. Carroll, 91 Atlantic avenue.

Frank Berry, 89 Atlantic avenue.
Robert Milne, 116 Atlantic avenue.
Henry A. Olsen, 113 Atlantic avenue.
John P. Johnson, 117 Atlantic avenue.
Wm. H. Short, 119 Atlantic avenue.
Augustus C. Vaennams, 145 Atlantic avenue.
H. J. Brunton, 171 Atlantic avenue.
Peter Becker, 173 Atlantic avenue.
Byrne Brost Co., 183 Atlantic avenue.
Wm. Xeller, 187 Atlantic avenue.
J. J. Rife, 193 Atlantic avenue.
C. G. Schwitter, 193 Atlantic avenue.
Joseph Dahlbender, 98 Court street.

We, the undersigned merchants and business men of the city of Brooklyn, respectfully petition the Honorable Legislature, through its joint sub-committee on consolidation, to take no final action of any kind on consolidation until the matter shall have been submitted to the people of Brooklyn for a further expression of their opinion.

Edward J. Ovington, 38-42 Flatbush avenue.
Hardenburg & Co., 42-44 Flatbush avenue.
William Wynn, 496 Fulton street.
Smith, Gray & Co., Fulton and Flatbush avenue.
James C. Hughes, 376 Clermont avenue.
George Rockitts Sons, 5130 Fulton street.
Thomas P. Blankley, 518 Fulton street.
F. M. Horton, 394-396 Fulton street.
C. W. Brindley, 453 Fulton street.
C. W. Kienan, 447 Fulton street.
Balch, Price & Co., 376 Fulton street.
L. Schwager, 325 Washington street.
L. Levyson, 325 Washington street.
Slee & Longstreet, 504 Fulton street.

Harry Bristow, 500 Fulton street.

C. F. Case, 498 Fulton street.

Henry J. Bladger, 478 Fulton street.

Cushing Adams, 417 Fulton street.

Edward D. Burt, 446-448 Fulton street.

James McCullough, 364 Fulton street.

William Arthur Chutrugh, 467 Fulton street.

J. W. Peek, 110 Fulton street.

J. Chobot, 449 Fulton street.

John A. Dietz, 433 Fulton street.

D. B. Powell, 69 Lefferts place.

John W. Kissam, 423 Fulton street.

Bome, Crawford & Co., 419 Fulton street.

Aaron Sherk, 451 Fulton street.

J. Franklin Bowie, 589 Fulton street.

Jackson & Cowenhoven, 639 Fulton street.

J. Fred Windolph, 564 State street.

Louis S. Earll, 272 First street.

Theo. H. Sommers, 580 Atlantic avenue.

Adolph Schwartz, 511 Atlantic avenue.

Moerstaller Hartmann, 502 Atlantic avenue.

Elias Johnson, 494 Atlantic avenue.

H. A. Dahl, 290 Schermerhorn street.

T. J. Bennett, 31 Pond street.

L. Lippmann, 12 Hanover place.

M. McNamee, 342 Fulton street.

We, the undersigned merchants and business men of the city of Brooklyn, respectfully petition the Honorable Legislature, through its joint subcommittee on consolidation to take no final action of any kind on consolidation until the matter shall have been submitted to the people of Brooklyn for a further expression of their opinion.

John S. McKeon, Broadway and Bedford avenue.

J. Henry Huhn, 49 William avenue.

D. R. Banks, 95 Broadway.

Chr. I. Wolf, of Kings Co. Fire Ins. Co., 97 Broadway.

A. Fahey, 128 Broadway.

Henry W. Allers, 446 Bedford avenue.

Theodore Wolcott, 84 Norman avenue.

J. H. Fountain, 397 Bedford avenue.

William Vincent, 139 Broadway.

Thomas A. Christopher, 381 Bedford avenue.

M. J. Hayden, 153 Broadway.

B. G. Latimer & Sons' Co., Broadway and Driggs avenue

A. G. Brown, 420 Bedford avenue.

George F. Yates, 431 Bedford avenue.

Arthur Rifenburgh, 417 Bedford avenue.

Edward Cooper, 107-109 Broadway.

Isaac Reynolds, superintendent Geo. W. Coger, 124 Broadway.

H. Steinicke, 122 Broadway.

H. B. Parham, 91 Broadway.

M. E. Sutton, 141 Broadway.

William Lewis, 408 Bedford avenue.

Frank B. Anderson, 369 Bedford avenue.

Fred. G. Anderson, 369 Bedford avenue.

S. B. Anderson, 369 Bedford avenue.

R. F. Thompson, 254 Division street.

George W. Swain, 429 Bedford avenue.

John Hoerle, 201 Broadway.

James S. Rearns, President Kings County Savings Bank, 80 South Tenth street.

Frank J. Manier, 625 Willoughby avenue.

We, the undersigned, merchants and business men of the city of Brooklyn, respectfully petition the Honorable Legislature, through its joint subcommittee on consolidation, to take no final action of any kind on consolidation until the matter shall have been submitted to the people of Brooklyn for a further expression of their opinion.

John W. Woltmann, 121 Macon street.

W. B. Clark, 9 New York avenue.

J. W. James, 176 Herkimer street.

McElhenie & Marsland, 259 Ryerson street.

Wm. C. Anderson, 318 Lafayette avenue.

Frederick Wilkins, 344 Classon avenue.

Wm. P. DeForest, 392 Classon avenue.

R. Schurenbeck, 248 DeKalb avenue.

Bernard Rasler, 73 Lafayette avenue.

T. Clark, 90 Fort Greene place.

W. B. Dayton & Son, 647 Fulton street.

Y. V. Corvenhoven, 639 Fulton street.

W. & H. Mumford, 390-392 Fulton street, per H. M.

A. Clinton Bird, foot of Montague street.

Marston & Son, 21 Water street.

Chas. W. Davidson, 84 Montague street.

Herzog & Erbe, 83-87 Washington street.

Thos. R. Almond, manufacturer of machinery, 85 Washington street.

Frank J. Schenck, 124 Pearl street.

Aaron Levy, wholesale butcher, 256 Hudson avenue.

We, the undersigned, merchants and business men of the city of Brooklyn, respectfully petition the Honorable Legislature, through its joint subcommittee on consolidation, to take no final action of any kind on consolidation until the matter shall have been submitted to the people of Brooklyn for a further expression of their opinion.

A. J. Haff, 402-404 Nostrand avenue.

W. H. Bemdery, 406 Nostrand avenue.

A. W. Totten, 277-279 Quincy street.

Wm. Cabble & Sons' Manufacturing Company, Union avenue and Ainslie street.

Chas. B. Paul, 467 Keap street.

Brooks, Mack & Peace, 479 Keap street.

Alex. R. Harris, 430 Keap street.

Charles Kloeffer, 452-460 Keap street.

We, the undersigned, merchants and business men of the city of Brooklyn, respectfully petition the Honorable Legislature, through its joint subcommittee on consolidation, to take no final action of any kind on consolidation until the matter shall have been submitted to the people of Brooklyn for a further expression of their opinion.

Joseph A. Osborne, 88 Fifth avenue.

W. H. Webster, 117 Fifth avenue.

Hermann Witte, 188 Fifth avenue.

Wm. J. Brown, 156 Fifth avenue.

J. Solomon, 154 Fifth avenue.

M. Grace, 70 Fifth avenue.

F. D. Hadjes, 64 Fifth avenue.

Henry T. Vail, 46 Third avenue.

George Boyle, 74 Third avenue.

George A. Duke, 109 Third avenue.

Chris. Gatz, 120 Third avenue.

Walter Galpine, 129 Third avenue.

Martin Wohlgement, 130 Third avenue.

Edward F Woods, 129 Third avenue.

Geo. K. Walters, Third avenue and Douglass street.

Frank C. Willett, 192 Third avenue.

Dennis Russell, 254 Third avenue.

Thomas W. Woods' Sons, Gowanus canal and Third street.

William Nungann, Third street, near Third avenue.

George House, 358 Fifth avenue.

Andrew Jenkins, 386 Fifth avenue.

Henry Jochens, 43 Sumpter street.
C. W. Veith, 390 Fifth avenue.
Charles Bemmhes, 390 Fifth avenue.
William Brereton, 373 Thirteenth street.
Samuel Lusk, 288 Fifth avenue.

Persons who voted for consolidation in 1894, and who now desire resubmission.

(List No. 1.)

Silas P. Wirsley, 467 Tompkins avenue.
G. M. Schmidt, 101 Macon street.
C. A. Borrow, 284 Quincy street.
Jno. E. Burns, 529 Greene avenue.
Henry Taylor, 102 Conselyea street.
Wm. Storms, 439 Graham avenue.
T. W. Spear, 497 Gates avenue.
Edward McCann, 289 Park avenue.
J. dePalos, 177 Sand street.
L. M. McNaughton, 589 Pacific street.
Edward Holloway.
Wm. Pond, Gates, near Bedford avenue.
G. Froland Johnson, 619 Washington avenue.
W. M. Marshall, 858 Atlantic avenue.
Howard Fleming, 860 Atlantic avenue.
David Healy, district attorney's office.
C. W. Miller, 298 Fifth avenue.
Bernard Fowler, 679 St. Mark's avenue.
Isaac H. Hodgdon, 267 Nassua avenue.
E. R. Terry, 12 Remsen street.
Jos. D. Stone, 794 Greene avenue.
E. K. Robbins, 604 Madison street.
G. H. Richards, 295 Decatur street.
Franklin Woodruff, 106 Remesen street.
Wm. O. Miles, 101 State street.

A. E. Smith, 303 Nostrand avenue.
Jas. E. Byrene, 450 Grand avenue.
J. W. James, 176 Herkimer street.
R. Schierenbach, 284 De Kalb avenue.
James M. Meade, 139 Myrtle avenue.
Henry A. Phillips, 15 Willoughby avenue.
P. Barrett, Johnson, corner Navy street.
P. Barrett's first son, Johnson, corner Navy street.
P. Barrett's second son, Johnson, corner Navy street
P. Barrett's third son, Johnson, corner Navy street.
Frank A. Baltz.
Lincoln M. Adams.
A. R. Stevenson, Market, near Magenta.
Geo. S. Abell, Seventh avenue and First street.
Wm. J. Logan, Atlantic, corner Crescent.
G. W. Brush, 2 Spencer place.
H. B. Brush, 90 Hathorne street.
F. W. Kristeller, 419 Pulaski street.
R. S. Kristeller, 419 Pulaski street.
J. C. London, 161 Keap street.
Geo. F. Yates, 431 Bedford avenue.
Aug. Donohue, 5 Hanson place.
G. Johnson Froland, 619 Washington avenue.
Geo. P. Fiske, Montague street.
John G. Hudson, 364 Sixth avenue.
Geo. A. Booth, 116 Verona street.
J. Horton, 381 Fourth avenue.
J. A. Hardner, 213 Manhattan avenue.
George C. Gledhill, 184 Franklin street.
James Dewey, 163 State street.
Robert Caset, 255 Reid avenue.
R. Auerbach, 112 Third place.
C. Seibert, Fifteenth avenue and Coy street.
J. S. Scanlon, 80 Tompkins avenue.
Wm. H. Powers, 760 Grand street.
F. Fay, 129 Third avenue.

W. H. Livingston avenue, 202 Columbia street.
M. C. Helfrich, 123 Fifteenth street.
Charles Clark, 420 Fifth avenue.
Thomas Dove, 122 Twelfth street.
Hans Larsen, 671 Third avenue.
D. F. Farley, 477 Third avenue.
John E. Close, 198 Tenth street.
George Ellis, 148 Eleventh street.
Nelson M. Hedges, 362 Tenth street.
S. Ellis, 148 Eleventh street.
Frank J. Blessington, 159 Prospect avenue.
Frank Neiman, 112 Fifteenth street.
Jesse D. Frost, 482 Eleventh street.
John G. Thomson, 442 Eleventh street.
John Rodgers, 361 Twelfth street.
S. J. Plummer, 224 Eleventh street.
Herman T. Smith, 244 Sixth avenue.
C. G. Duflon, 208 Fifth avenue.
W. W. Morton, 449 Eleventh street.
George P. Boxold, 273 Twenty-first street.
Robert M. Noble, 368 Eighth avenue.
F. J. Creighton, 456 Sixteenth street.
W. R. Smith, 612 Sixteenth street.
Thos. Ford, 1345 Third avenue.
Charles W. Miller, 298 Fifth street.
Herbert R. Churchill, 362 Throop street.
James Donovan, 157 Second avenue.
C. J. Bode, 542 Fourth avenue.

We, the subscribers to this instrument, declare that we voted "For consolidation" in the election of 1894. We further now declare that we favor resubmission and respectfully urge it.

Charles A. Bradley, 201 Myrtle avenue.
Sylvester Blume, 190 Myrtle avenue.

G. Schulze, 256 Myrtle avenue.
F. W. Kunzinger, 270 Myrtle avenue.
Charles W. Senior, 713 Myrtle avenue.
Noah Otton, 709 Myrtle avenue.
Charles E. Farman, 720 Myrtle avenue.
William Hilz, 730 Myrtle avenue.
Thomas A. Kennedy, 80 Sandford street.
William Garlick, 723 Myrtle avenue.
Edmond Angeline, 109 Spencer street.
M. Walsh, 725 Myrtle avenue.
James A. Todd, 566 Willoughby avenue.
Henry Wollman, 736 Myrtle avenue.
M. Pass, 729 Myrtle avenue.
R. Hoppen, 725½ Myrtle avenue.
Richard A. Ward, 721 Myrtle avenue.
P. J. Sweeney, 332 Myrtle avenue.
Hugh Conolity, 106 Sandford street.
Edward Doran, 738 Myrtle avenue.
Ben Freen, 810 Fulton avenue.
Henry Morris, 140 Nostrand avenue.
Marcus Morris, 145 Nostrand avenue.
Peter Snyder, 52 Vernon avenue.
Frank R. Tenk, 384 Madison avenue.
John Wogart, 126 Nostrand avenue.
John H. Stamm, 114 Nostrand avenue.
Daniel Cooney, 109 Nostrand avenue.
Thomas Dailey, 507 Marcy avenue.
William Sander, 239 Floyd street.
Alfred G. Wood, 788 Myrtle avenue.
William Hoehn, 217 Central avenue.
John Prenderville, 85 Nostrand avenue.
Harry Lill, 746 Park avenue.
George Gebhardt, 138 Nostrand avenue
Christian Gebhardt, 98 Union avenue.
Joseph Menelle, 742 Myrtle avenue.
John Becker, 740 Myrtle avenue.

James Lawrence, 740 Myrtle avenue.
Louis R. Goabowsky, 595 Park avenue.
Morris Marks, 58 State street.
David Ferris, 163 South First street.
M. Minden, 999 Atlantic avenue.
M. Abrahams, 884 Myrtle avenue.
Edward J. McGlynn, 66 Heywood street.
Thomas J. Lynch, 44 Stockton street.
David Mendes, 187 Classon avenue.
John A. Cambel, 178 Nostrand avenue.
S. Abrams, 125 Sandford street.
S. R. Seymour, 125 Sandford street.
B. Davis, 182 Nostrand avenue.
P. Benjamin, 144 Hart street.
A. Nohert, 44 Willoughby avenue.
J. Hertzog, 732 Myrtle avenue.
W. Powerman, 735 Myrtle avenue.
A. Kagel, 735 Myrtle avenue.
F. O. Kane, 470 Koscinaka street.
John B. Donovan, 134 Eckford street.
George Henhum, 703 Myrtle avenue.
Augustus Roupp, 717 Myrtle avenue.
Peter Hyppart, 788 Myrtle avenue.
W. S. Hammond, 22 Lawton street.
J. J. Hiffans, 703 Gates avenue.
Thos. Hiffins, 65 Floyd street.
D. Jacobs, 737 Myrtle avenue.

BROOKLYN, N. Y., *January* 15, 1896.

To His Excellency, the Governor, and the Legislature of the State of New York:

The undersigned, merchants of the city of Brooklyn, respectfully urge the passage of a bill consolidating Brooklyn city with New York city, providing among other things, for attaining an equal and uniform rate of taxation and uniform valuations for the purpose of taxation.

Frederick Loeser & Co.

W. H. Bullard.

Joseph Wechsler's Sons.

James Harkness, 692 Fulton street.

Morris Nason, 601 Fifth avenue, corner Prospect.

George B. Lewis, 660 Fulton street.

S. P. Willets, 71 Lafayette avenue.

Benjamin Rosenzweig, 624 Fulton street.

D. Maguire, 703 Fulton street.

Peter Flynn, 701 Fulton street.

Brooklyn Hardware and Sporting Goods Co., 601 Fulton street; H. H. Nudough, President.

Weschsler Bros., 538 and 540 Fulton street.

Johnston Bros., 8, 10 and 12 Nevins street.

P. W. Taylor, 521 Fulton street.

M. Rosenberg, 481 and 483 Fulton street.

Isaac Mason, 860 President street.

Thomas Thompson, 101 Park place.

Walter B. Shipman, 123 Myrtle avenue.

Joseph J. McIntyre, 1278 Putnam avenue.

P. M. Dale & Son, Myrtle avenue and Gold street.

Armstrong Bros., 339 and 339½ Myrtle avenue.

F. C. Joslyn, 404 Myrtle avenue.

John Flynn, 137 Carlton avenue.

Henry M. Bach, 345 Myrtle avenue.

Longmore & Warwick, 3182 Myrtle avenue.

Isaac Knee, 442 Myrtle avenue.

N. F. Green, 455 to 461 Market avenue.

David Jacobs, per H. J., 623 to 627 Myrtle avenue.

Henry J. Leach, 1103 Fulton street.

John Doyle, 1099 Fulton street.

Samuel Downing, 1095 and 1097 Fulton street.

The Long Island Brewery, J. W. Brown, President; Third avenue, Dean and Bergen streets.

Ernest Mason, 601 Fifth avenue

Thomas L. Murphy, 66 Richmond.

John Mc Cormick, 448 Fifth avenue.

John W. Kimball, 450 Fifth avenue.

H. V. Monahan, 503 to 509 Fifth avenue.

C. S. Stephenson, 577 and 579 Fifth avenue.

M. J. Maxwell, 550 Fifth avenue.

To the Honorable Members of the New York State Assembly:

The following resolutions, passed by the "Unity Republican Club," of the city of Brooklyn, were ordered to be sent to you:

WHEREAS, A bill has been introduced into the Legislature, looking to the consolidation of certain territory, to be known as "Greater New York,"

Resolved, That we, the members of the "Unity Republican Club," of the city of Brooklyn, representing, as we believe we do, the voice of the people of the eastern district of said city, heartily denounce said consolidation as being a real estate scheme, pure and simple, to rob the masses of their born rights.

We do not believe that an expression of opinion favorable to the incorporation of a "Greater New York" is obtained when but one-third of Brooklyn's registered voters vote in the affirmative, and we appeal to the Governor of our State and to every right-minded member of the Legislature to vote for the bill introduced by Senator Brush and Assemblyman Audett, for a resubmission of this all-important question, believing that two-thirds of the people of the city of Brooklyn would vote against consolidation had they the chance.

During the last municipal election, Mayor Wurster, Republican, who agitated the question of resubmission, was elected over Mr. Grout, a consolidationist, by 2,500 majority, the first time in many years that the affairs of our fair city have been presided over by a Republican mayor without the aid of the independent organizations. We sincerely believe that a party in power when such a bill goes through will lose Kings county at the following election by at least 25,000 majority.

Resolved, That a copy of these resolutions be sent to the Hon. Levi P. Morton, the State Senate, State Assembly, and the Hon. O. L. Forrester, Assemblyman from the thirteenth district.

E. A. CONNOR,
President.

T. K. FRENCHARD,
Secretary.

The following was handed to the commission by Mr. Matthews:

There did a party call on me at my house, begging me to sign the call for resubmission; that he was getting five cents a signature. It was at night, and he said he was out of work. A great many signed it to help this poor fellow.

H. L. BRYANT.

105 Butler street.

We, the undersigned members of the Union League Club of Brooklyn, are in favor of consolidating New York and Brooklyn into one city:

Howard M. Smith, ex-President Union League Club.
Benjamin Russell.
Austin Kelly.
J. W. Harman.
Ira Preston Taylor.
Russell Parker.
Adolphus G. Bailey.
George B. Jones.
E. C. Fuller.
M. J. Cooney.
George P. Chappell
J. G. Dettmer.
J. S. Nugent.
A. G. Perham.
C. Washington Colyer.
William H. Lyon.
Nelson J. Gates.

Louis J. Seitz.
J. D. Carpenter.
C. D. Rhinehart.
D. P. Darling.
W. H. Biggam.
M. S. Hayes.
T. G. Christmas.
O. W. Ingersoll.
E. C. Moore.
S. H. Benton.
Chester Pell.
Alexander H. Doty.
Theodore Corning.
B. C. Miller.
F. J. Ashfield.
Joseph L. White.
John H. Donnelly.
R. O. Sherwood.
S. S. Voshell.
George H. Squire.
W. A. Porter.
J. L. Voshell.
T. E. Quinn.
Edward H. Hobbs.
E. W. Scarborough.
James H. Taft, Jr.
Thomas Bishop.
S. B. Holt.
H. E. Jacobs.
W. H. Pierson, M. D.
George I. Jackson.
James G. Stevens.
William Cooney.
Frank L. Bartley.
Owen E. Houghton, M. D. S.
Thomas L. Wells, M. D.

James H. Stearns.
W. H. Irwin.
A. S. Haight, 8 Spencer place.
Abel E. Blackman, ex-president,— if with equal rights.
William A. Barnum.
Charles E. Newton.
James Rice, Jr.
Henry C. Larore.
Marshall T. Davidson.
Ethan Allen Doty.
Jon. V. Jewell.
Frank L. Coon.
T. B. Keppy.
F. H. Sellman.
D. M. Munger.
T. H. Taylor.
David Thornton.
Montrose W. Morris.
Benjamin Estes.
John A. Schmidt,— provided equal taxation
F. E. Barnard,— with equal taxation.
Herbert S. Ogden,— no commission.
L. F. Silva,— on equal taxation.
William C. Pate.
Stephen H. Hand.
Charles H. Reynolds, Jr.
H. H. Gates.
J. W. Hussey.
William H. Coon.
F. H. Wilson, ex-president.
B. L. Houghton.
F. H. Cowperthwaite.
C. W. Prankard,— for equal taxation.
John Nash.
W. M. Matthews.
T. G. Garner.

Henry C. Alger.
J. F. Hamilton.
Welcome S. Jarvis.
E. H. Warren.
A. H. Romeyn.
John R. Crum.
William H. Reynolds.
M. L. Bowen.
R. W. Gleason.
W. E. Edmister.
Roho Lundell.
Ysindo Pendas.
William P. Gill, 24 Brevoort place.
J. Hamilton Gill, 24 Brevoort place.
J. Culbert Palmer, 14 Breevort place.
James M. Cromwell, 29 Brevoort place.
Edgar O. Pearce, 1092 Dean street.
William H. Sterling, 1086 Dean street.
Seth T. Stewart.
Bennett E. Fettman.
George N. Robinson.
Hugo Hirsh.
James Webb.
William Degbie.
A. Abraham.
Edward Lyons.
George H. Conklin.
E. G. Blatchford.
Charles H. Macklin.
John Ditmars.
W. B. Mead.
Thomas J. Washburn.
William Jeremiah.
Charles J. Sands.
Arnold Cooper.
G. W. Connithies.
S. W. Milligan.

Andrew Mercer.
A. H. Carleton.
E. M. Cragin.
Frederick H. Pouet

ASSEMBLY CHAMBER, ALBANY, N. Y.

WEDNESDAY, *January* 29, 1896.

Meeting of subcommittee of joint committee on cities of Senate and Assembly, for a continuation of hearing on "the Greater New York bill."

PRESENT.— Senators Lexow, Brush and Grady; Assemblymen Austin, McKeown and Keenholts.

MR. LEXOW:

The committee is now ready to listen to further argument on the Greater New York question. I understand that Senator Brush has a communication to present, in the first instance, to the committee.

MR. BRUSH:

Mr. Chairman and Gentlemen: I received this telegram a short time ago from Mr. Redfield, the president of the League of Loyal Citizens of Brooklyn:

To Senator George W. Brush, Assembly Parlor, Capitol, Albany:

We do not think necessary to trouble your committee by appearing in Albany after full hearing here. Are working actively for Brooklyn, however, and shall be glad to furnish any information desired or to come when needed.

WILLIAM C. REDFIELD,
President League of Loyal Citizens.

MR. LEXOW:

Will you kindly file that with the stenographer, Mr. Brush?

I believe the introducer of the resubmission bill in the Assembly was Assemblyman Wilson, and inasmuch as we first hear arguments against the bill pending in the Senate, which would mean by an advocate of the resubmission bill in the Assembly, we would like to hear if Mr. Wilson has anything to say upon the subject of resubmission.

MR. WILSON:

Mr. Chairman and Gentlemen: I thank you for the compliment of being called on before your honorable body, but it occurs to me that, inasmuch as we shall sit as judge and jury in this case, that it would not be right for me at this time to present my views upon the subject. In fact, what I would say has been reiterated time and time again by the different papers of New York and Brooklyn and elsewhere; but I must say, with all respect to the committee, that we are wholly unprepared on such short notice. As far as I am concerned personally, with all respect to the committee, I think that we ought to have had more time for consideration, to mature our plans, so that our friends who understand our side of the question of resubmission could present their views intelligently, quietly and conservatively.

MR. LEXOW:

(Interrupting.) Excuse the interruption — but a telegram is on file now to the effect that the friends of resubmission do not desire to have any further argument upon the question.

MR. WILSON:

Very good, sir — but I merely wish to say that, of course, they have no desire to have them, for the reason that they have not had time to prepare them —

MR. LEXOW:

No — that was in the telegram — that the matter has been fully presented by their side, and that they do not care to present anything else.

MR. WILSON:

Well, so I understand it now — because they have not had

time — even if there were time — So, Mr. Chairman, thanking you for the honor, I beg to be excused from further remarks.

MR. LEXOW:

Is there anybody here who desires to speak against consolidation? (Pause.) Then the side in favor of consolidation will be heard; but I assume the same principle will apply, namely, that the ground has been fairly thoroughly threshed over, so far as both sides of the question are concerned, and relating only to the city of Brooklyn; and we would ask any speakers on the consolidation side of the question to apply themselves to new arguments, if they have any, and to present new speakers upon the question and not those that have been heard before — unless Judge Tenney will give us an oration — I think we would all make an exception in his case.

MR. MATTHEWS:

Mr. Chairman: As I have individually no new argument to present, I will introduce to you General George W. Wingate, who, I think, will present some arguments.

GENERAL GEORGE W. WINGATE:

Mr. Chairman and Gentlemen: I am somewhat embarrassed in addressing you in regard to — in view of the suggestion of the Chairman. So much has been said already upon this proposition that it is almost impossible to say anything that is new.

I congratulate the committee that after the storm of talk to which they have been subjected they are now coming into a position where they can seriously consider the weight of the arguments which have been addressed to them and the weight of the people who have brought forward those arguments.

When you take the testimony, as I have done, and weigh it through, you will be pleased to find — and what?— how few arguments have really been presented to you in opposition to this plan. They are simply these — I propose to be very brief on this matters; and simply sum up the arguments which have been brought against this plan. The burden is, as the committee has decided, on behalf of those who oppose the bill.

The arguments are: First, that the people of Brooklyn were not aware when in 1894 they voted at the election, on the subject of whether or not there should be a consolidation with New York, what they were doing.

That some of them who might have voted did not vote. In other words, that the majority was not sufficiently large to be satisfactory.

That the Brooklyn people have such a high idea of the sanctity of their positions as citizens of that great — village — because that is about all it is, as Mr. Depew said — that they go out and have fits in the public squares whenever anybody suggests to them that they should be annexed to New York. That the majority of the people of Brooklyn have not yet changed their minds and are opposed to consolidation. That under — not this bill, but under some legislation which comes, I suppose, in carrying out the bill — there will be difficulty in connection with the board of supervisors, and other legal difficulties.

That the law is an experiment, and the Legislature should not try any experiments.

That it is possible — as Jesse Johnson argued — for great cities to be governed by imperial government, but it is not possible to govern great cities under republican form of government.

That Brooklyn will not be able — that Brooklyn is able to raise all the money she desires for her future needs and that if she was annexed to New York, New York would not assist her.

And, finally, that there ought to be a referendum.

Now, those are all the arguments, boiled down, which have been produced to this committee.

Now, I suggest, Mr. Chairman, in considering this question — in view of the fact that there was an election; in view of the fact that the voters of the city of Brooklyn are all men over the age of twenty-one and not women, children and ministers, entirely; and that a vote is to be considered as being conslusive unless those who are opposing the vote and those who are opposing the bill can show, not by mere argument, not by oral statements, but by overwhelming evidence, that the bill — the vote — was not a fair one or that there has been such a change in the sentiment of the people that that vote should be disregarded. On this question I say, without hesitation, that instead of the opponents of this bill being able to demonstrate that, the contrary has been proven to you. The gentlemen who have appeared before you in opposition to this bill are undoubtedly eminent and respectable citizens of Brooklyn, but they represent a comparatively few interests. All the interests of Brooklyn which make it what it is; all the people who represent all this business, these interests which depend for their prosperity upon the development, are in favor of this bill. All the railroads, the elevated railroads, and the surface railroads, have signed petitions in its favor. What class of the community is there whose very life depends upon Brooklyn being prosperous and populous as the railroads? All the great merchants have been in favor of this bill. They are dependent upon the same things. The banks, the trust companies, the real estate dealers, all the people who are business men, who make it their business to study what is good for Brooklyn, because what is good for Brooklyn is good for their pockets, those men have all come to you and addressed you in favor of the bill. The other gentlemen, largely, I think, are sentimentalists, and largely who bring theoretical arguments; but they are not entitled to the weight as practical men which the supporters of this bill have.

Now, the argument that the people of the city of Brooklyn, or most of the people of the city of Brooklyn, have any particular affection to this place, because it is their birthplace, because their children have grown up there, is the merest nonsense. The average ciizens of Brooklyn knows how to perambulate about a circle over about a mile from his house, and he knows how to come to New York, and that is all he knows about Brooklyn, and pretty much all that he cares. All of the great measures which have been introduced in Brooklyn, as the railroads, the manufactures, the great stores, etc., have been introduced by the people who have come from the other side of the river. As far as the sentimental question of the thing is concerned, it is not entitled to any consideration which is worthy of your thought.

Now, the law — it is said that nobody ever had a city of this size before, and, therefore, you should not pass a law which establishes it now. Is not this Legislature every day passing laws which are experiments? Is not the whole theory of the government such that we should constantly develop? Is it not an experiment to annex to Brooklyn the county towns? Was it not an experiment to annex to Westchester the annexed districts, and have not those experiments been successful? What right has anybody to say that it is going to be — that we are not going to be able to carry out the administration of the great city? They have been able to carry out the administration of the present cities, where New York has grown from what is was when I was a boy to its present condition, and Brooklyn has grown to its present immense population — why, my father told me a few weeks ago that when he first came from the east to settle in New York city, he was a teacher in Flatbush. At that time Flatbush was a bigger place than Brooklyn; he settled there because he thought the prospects would be better than they would be in Brooklyn. Brooklyn has grown to be a great city and Flatbush is a little village. But Mr. Johnson says — and that is the fair type of the inconsistency of the arguments which are brought against this bill — it is an instance of the desire of those who are opposing the thing, for different reasons, to clutch at anything which looks like an argument against it — Mr. Johnson says that you should not pass this bill because, while great cities may be governed by imperial authority, it is not practicable to do that under popular suffrage. If that is the case, then our government is a failure, and you might as well recognize the fact, and instead of introducing bills for consolidation, bills should be introduced for disintegration and distribution. It seems to me that the argument, on its face, is clearly entitled to no weight.

Now, as to the question as to whether or not Brooklyn is in such a financial condition that it is for her interest to be annexed to New York, that is the question of the day. On that you have been overwhelmed with figures; on that you have heard many speakers address you; and it seems to me that there can be no question but what, at the present time, while the people who live in Brooklyn build up New York and make it rich, because they do business there, because they pay office rent there, that, on the other hand, Brooklyn, being a city of homes, is not able to increase its taxation, is not able to issue bonds which are necessary for the improvements which were required; but if the two cities are united, as they ought to be, there will be plenty of money for all the purposes, and then you will have a true city, the business city which New York will be, and the city of homes which Brooklyn will be. The taxation in New York will be increased to a very slight percentage, the taxation of Brooklyn will be reduced to such an extent that the poor man will be able to obtain what he can not now, and that is, a loan of money upon his house at a moderate rate of interest. It is for this reason, to attract, to make the little homes of Brooklyn — to reduce the taxation upon the little homes of Brooklyn, so that they will attract the workers in New York who now live in tenement-houses to come over there and buy them, and in this way build up the population of Brooklyn and stop the stagnation which now crushes it, is the main object of the supporters of this bill.

But, the great argument here is referendum. Now, Mr. Chairman, I would like to inquire of you and the gentlemen of the committee, who ever heard of the principle in a republican form of government that after a grave question of legislation, such as the annexation of Brooklyn with New York, was, after three years of discussion, deliberately submitted to the people and was adopted by a majority vote — whether that majority was large or small makes no difference — that thereafter it was the duty of the Legislature when they proceeded to frame legislation to carry out the will of the people thus expressed, that the details of that legislation should be submitted to a popular vote? Nothing of the kind was ever heard of in our political history; it is not practicable to do anything of the kind, and the argument in favor of referendum is brought forward by those who seek in that way to kill the bill. They all admit it, if I am not mistaken, every single one of them admits it, when asked by the chairman, that that was the opposition to the bill, and they hoped if it was again submitted that by the division — not upon the general subject of whether or not there should be annexation — but by the division of sentiment which might take place in regard to the details of the bill, that they could crystalize and concentrate such an opposition to it as would enable them to defeat it, thus seeking to do unpractically what they have failed to do practically. Now, no such effort and no such purpose should be permitted. It is not possible for this commission of the Legislature — or, perhaps, even at the next session of the Legislature — to prepare a proper and a detailed bill which will cover all matters, the thousands of matters which have to be thought out and considered on such a problem as the charter for the Greater New York. The bill provides, as it should, that annexation is declared and will take effect on the 1st of January, 1898, and that the principle upon which this annexation is to take effect is equality of taxation and equality of valuation — those are the two things, the two special propositions; all the rest are matters of detail. Now, to carry out these details will take thought. They should not be put in a single charter. They should, as the bill well provides, be prepared one by one, each great interest being taken by itself, discussed by itself and voted by itself, and then thus, one by one, a harmonious and symmetrical edifice may be constructed, which will be a credit to all concerned.

In deference to the suggestion of the Chairman, I will be brief; and I assure you that there can be no question in the mind of any unprejudiced man — that laying aside any particular "fads" which some gentlemen may have in regard to loyalty to Brooklyn, laying aside any particular enmities which some gentlemen may have in regard to this person or the other person, and laying aside some particular interests which some gentlemen may have in regard to the effect of consolidation making a fall in their real estate property around the city hall, laying aside all which is merely for personal ends, and looking at it in the general interest of the city of Brooklyn as a whole, there can be no doubt whatever in the mind of any reasonable man that seventy-five to eighty per cent. of the people are in favor of the consolidation which is contemplated by this bill; consolidation, to take effect in 1898, upon equal taxation, equal valuation, and the details to be discussed, one by one, as the emergency arises.

MR. LEXOW:

I understand that Senator Wray has something to say to the committee. Is Senator Wray present? (He must have left.)

MR. MATTHEWS:

I have a few telegrams. I do not know that you wish to have the time particularly occupied. I will read just one or two.

I will state to the committee that we did not know of this meeting until about four o'clock yesterday afternoon; and I sent out some words for friends of consolidation to come up; and I received quite a number of telegrams stating the reasons why they are not present. (Reading)

James Matthews, Esq., Chairman Consolidation Committee, Kenmore Hotel, Albany, N. Y.:

Am detained by important engagements. You can not over-estimate the importance of consolidation. Should the opponents defeat it they will realize their great mistake when the people become fully conversant with the subject. Our citizens will not forget such disregard for their interest and such a contempt for their will.

DAVID A. BOODY (Ex-Mayor Boody.)

Russell Parker, Kenmore Hotel, Albany, N. Y.:

Detained. Record us as in favor of consolidation; no referendum.

WILLIAMS & ADAMS.

MR. MATTHEWS:

And then comes another — shall I present the names?

MR. LEXOW:

I think it unnecessary. I assume consolidation has some friends in Brooklyn.

Mr. Matthews:

Well, they are names of those to whom I sent. I have a letter which I would like—

I have received this letter Mr. Chairman, which is from Henry Batterman, one of the new bridge commissioners, who expected to come with me, and Mr. Andrew D. Baird, the president of that commission, but they have a meeting this afternoon to settle upon the four or six tracks to go over the bridge. He says:

Office of H. Batterman,
Broadway, Graham and Flushing Avenues,
Brooklyn, N. Y., *January* 28, 1896.

Mr. James Matthews, 208 Berkeley Place, Brooklyn, N. Y.:

My Dear Sir.— I regret exceedingly that a meeting of the East River Bridge Commission on Wednesday will prevent me from going to Albany with you. It seems to me that no further arguments are necessary to convince the Senate Committee that the consolidation of the cities of New York and Brooklyn is not only very desirable, but an absolute necessity. I desire to call the attention of the committee to the fact that every man, who is doing business in Brooklyn, and who is interested in the growth and progress of Brooklyn as a city, commercially, is heartly in favor of consolidation; whereas the opponents are those who desire to keep Brooklyn as a quiet abiding place. So far as this section of the city, the Eastern District, is concerned, I am safe in saying, that ninety per cent. of the people are in favor of consolidation, for the reason that they are largely engaged in local enterprises. Sentiment is not to be considered here.

I was born and have always lived in Brooklyn, but I realize that the unity of those two cities, means prosperity to the people, who are actively engaged in the development of the city.

The two factions to this question are: Progress and anti-progress. Consolidation means progress; anti, the contrary.

I sincerely trust that the will of the people, as expressed by their vote, for consolidation, will be consumated by our legislators.

Yours very truly,
H. BATTERMANN.

MR. BRUSH:

Mr. Chairman, I want to answer that letter, in the presence of the committee, by saying that I represent the district in which Mr. Batterman lives or has his business and the district which he mentions in his letter, a large portion of it I may say, and that district gave 500 against consolidation in 1894. He says ninety per cent. of the people are in favor of it. I simply make that statement to show how much truth there is in his letter.

Mr. Matthews filed with the committee the following telegrams received by him:

JAMES MATTHEWS, ESQ., *Kenmore Hotel, Albany:*

Regret not seeing you before you left Albany. In my judgment the best interests of Brooklyn demand immediate consolidation.

HOWARD GIBB.

MR. JAMES MATTHEWS, *Kenmore Hotel, Albany:*

Brooklyn's welfare necessitates a speedy enactment of the Senator Lexow bill for consolidation.

ABRAHAM & STRAUS.

RUSSELL PARKER, *Kenmore Hotel, Albany:*

Short notice will prevent attendance. Heartily in favor of consolidation.

BENJAMIN F. SUTTON.

87 Halsey street.

JAMES MATTHEWS, *Kenmore Hotel, Albany, N. Y.:*

The building interest of Brooklyn is almost a unit in favor of consolidation. The Brooklyn chapter of the American Institute of Architects on Saturday last passed resolutions unanimously favoring it.

GEORGE L. MORSE.

Russell Parker, *Care Kenmore, Albany:*

Notice too short to attend, but strongly favor consolidation.

H. C. BURTON.

615 St. Mark's avenue.

Russell Parker, *Kenmore House, Albany, N. Y.:*

Short notice will prevent attendance. Heartily in favor of consolidation.

JAS. H. STEARNS.

585 St. Mark's avenue.

Russell Parker, *Care Kenmore, Albany:*

Notice too short to attend, but strongly favor consolidation.

F. D. SOPER.

615 St. Mark's avenue.

Russell Parker, *Care Kenmore, Albany:*

Notice too short to attend, but strongly favor consolidation.

A. H. DOTY.

615 St. Mark's avenue.

Russell Parker, *Kenmore House, Albany:*

Can't attend on such short notice. Positively favor consolidation.

W. G. BUTON.

Mr. Lexow:

Let us hear your next speaker, Mr. Matthews.

Mr. Matthews:

I now take pleasure in presenting to you Hon. Asa W. Tenney, a gentleman whom you would like to hear, I think.

Mr. Tenney:

Mr. Chairman, and Gentlemen of the Committee: I hardly think I had better speak to you this afternoon, because after the suggestion of the chairman, to select new questions to talk about in this matter — that is, an absolute impossibility. There are really but two questions, it seems to me, now before this committee, and they are — whether resubmission or referendum.

When I was before the committee in Brooklyn I did not expect to speak upon referendum. I did say something upon resubmission. And if the committee will indulge me, I will take a moment or two upon the subject — upon both of those subjects, because they seem to me to be very important in this matter; especially so after the speeches that were made against consolidation and against the bill now before this honorable body, at your last hearing in Brooklyn. A great deal was said, gentlemen, of learning and of thought and of high consideration; said that resubmission was a part of our government, and that the thirteenth, the fourteenth and the fifteenth Constitutional Amendments had been resubmitted again and again and again, and I believe the newspapers have gone so far as to say that I had traveled the country advocating the resubmission of those questions, these amendments. Now, gentlemen, this is what one of the speakers before you said: "All the war amendments to secure the political and moral results of the war, were rejected by a sufficient number of Legislatures to compel the repeated submission of them to such Legislatures." Now, bear in mind, gentlemen of the committee, which you doubtless have already done, these measures, these war amendments were rejected until it became necessary for a resubmission — that is right. I make no issue upon that. That is true. They were rejected by these Legislatures, and they were voted upon again until they were adopted; but there is a great difference, gentlemen of this committee, between rejection and adoption. I challenge any man who spoke before this committee in Brooklyn, I challenge any man upon this committee to name me a single instance in the history of this government, from its commencement until the present moment, that an amendment or a proposition or a question that has been submitted to the people and adopted and approved has ever been submitted a second time for adoption and approval. An instance does not exist; it can not be done; it is only when the amendment, the proposition and the question is rejected that it is to be resubmitted. Hence, we claim that the vote in Brooklyn was final. It was final. There is no question about it; and it is about time, gentlemen, that we brushed away words and sentiments and ideas and got down to the law and to the fact in this matter. The election in 1894 was based upon an act of the Legislature which, perhaps, some of you gentlemen were instrumental in creating. It was the act of 1894, and it has never been referred to as I have seen in any of the arguments that have been made before this honorable body.

Now, let us see what that says, and what is the title of the act. Men say this was an informal vote. One gentleman said to this honorable committee that it was no vote at all. And yet, it was based upon a law that grew out of the Legislature of this State, known as chapter 64 of the Laws of 1894, "An act providing for the submission of the question of consolidation of the city of New York with certain territory under a single municipal administration to a vote of the people." Now, that goes on and says, speaking about how the ballots should be formed: " One-half of the number of said ballots shall read ' For consolidation ' and the other half of the number of said ballots shall read 'Against consolidation,' and the indorsement on said ballots shall read ' Consolidation.' Each elector shall be provided, in addition to the other ballots furnished at said election, with two ballots, one of which shall be for and the other against consolidation." That is what the law says. He is furnished with the other ballots at the election, and then he has two other ballots, one for and one against consolidation. And now, what is the provision of this law, gentlemen, which, to my mind is exceedingly important in disposing of this question, and it is this: All the provisions of said chapter 680 of the Laws of 1892, relating to the submission of a constitutional amendment or other propositions or questions to a popular vote, shall, in all respects, be followed, complied with and applied to and carried into effect in the submission of said proposition or question of consolidation to a popular vote as therein provided. Now, I ask you, have we ever in our State asked for a resubmission upon any constitutional question that has been adopted in the State or any question or any proposition since our State had existence. Hence, I repeat what I said before your honorable body in Brooklyn, to attempt to resubmit this question is un-American; it is unconstitutional; yea, more, it is the overthrow of the very principle upon which our government exists; for one of the greatest statesmen of our country said, within the last ten or fifteen years, that the law of this country was the supreme will of the people, honestly and fairly expressed at the ballot box.

Now, they say that it is no vote; that it is simply a guess; that it is a wish or a desire. Let us see what the law says about this: "The ballots cast shall be deemed and taken as an expression of the voter, as the case may be, in favor of or against the consolidation with the city of New York." That ends the whole question. They may say it was no vote; they may say it was a guess or a wish or has become stale; the law that this body enacted and put into the statute books of this State and under which we live, says that the ballots so cast shall be deemed and taken as an expression of the voters.

MR. BRUSH:

Mr. Tenney, may I ask you a question? Do you contend that that act laid any legal obligation upon the Legislature to act upon it?

MR. TENNEY:

Any legal obligation? I don't understand your question.

MR. BRUSH:

Any binding obligation — I will change my question — any binding obligation upon the Legislature?

MR. TENNEY:

I don't understand it now.

MR. BRUSH:

Well, hasn't the Legislature full power to enact laws without the vote of the people, without any vote upon the question by the people?

MR. TENNEY:

To enact — full powers — in what regard?

MR. LEXOW:

Consolidating the cities without the expression of the voter, Senator Brush means.

MR. TENNEY:

Within the Constitution — well, I suppose they may have, but the fact that you passed a law — I am speaking upon this act — which is to control this body and control the entire community.

MR. BRUSH:

Yes; but the feature of it that I was trying to get was, did that act ever have any binding effect upon the Legislature?

MR. TENNEY:

The fact that that act was passed?

MR. BRUSH:

Yes.

MR. TENNEY:

Most certainly; just as much binding effect upon this Legislature as the adoption of our Constitution last fall.

MR. BRUSH:

I don't see it.

MR. TENNEY:

Just as much binding effect — no; I know you don't see it. That is the trouble. (Laughter.)

MR. TENNEY:

(Continuing.) If you did see it, we would not be here, perhaps. (Laughter.)

MR. BRUSH:

No; I am afraid you don't get my meaning, now.

MR. TENNEY:

I get your meaning, now. I say that that vote of 277 majority in the city of Brooklyn, cast as it was, is as final, is as certain, is as obligatory upon this committee and upon this Legislature as though the majority had been 277,000.

MR. BRUSH:

Then the Legislature of last winter did not do its duty?

MR. TENNEY:

I am not criticising that Legislature; I have personal views about that, but it is not here.

MR. LEXOW:

It tried to, Mr. Tenney.

MR. TENNEY:

I am not here to criticise. I hope this Legislature will do its duty. Let this Legislature do its duty and the last Legislature will take care of itself. I claim that that majority of 277 votes — my dear friend, Senator Brush, as you are my friend — I say that that vote is final, from which there is no appeal, and you have to act upon it and accept it absolutely.

MR. BRUSH:

I do not wish to take your time, Mr. Tenney, but the point is here —

MR. TENNEY:

Provided you ask a question.

MR. BRUSH:

The point is this: The vote, as I understand it, of any locality upon any question has no actual binding effect upon the Legislature; the Legislature has full power, in other words to enact those laws without any reference to the vote of the locality?

Mr. Lexow:

No doubt of that.

Mr. Tenney:

Mr. Senator, the trouble with that position is that this law is here.

Mr. Brush:

I admit that; that is all right.

Mr. Tenney:

This law is here, and it your duty as a Senator to stand by that law that stands upon the statute books until it has been repealed. It is my duty, it is the duty of every man; and when they say that that shall be an expression of the voters it is the end of it until — so long as the law stands upon our statute books and is unrepealed.

Mr. Lexow:

It is only fair, Mr. Tenney, that the chairman from personal experience should say that the Legislature last year attempted to do its duty; that the Assembly did its duty and passed the bill (if it was a duty), and that the Senate tried to pass the bill and was obstructed in so doing by a failure to receive the constitutional majority for the bill, failing by one vote to do so.

Mr. Tenney:

I know —

Mr. Lexow:

(Continuing) — and that the reason it failed was that the gentlemen who are opposing the bill to-day obstructed the passage of the bill last year.

MR. TENNEY:

Yes; I do not want to be considered in the slightest as making any criticism upon the Legislature in doing that; I am not doing that at all. I simply say this: That the town of Westchester defeated — cast 220 votes for consolidation and 221 against it. Now, if they want resubmission, let them go right up there and apply there arguments to the town of Westchester; it was not voted there, it was not ratified there, but it was in Brooklyn.

MR. LEXOW:

And they are annexed to-day?

MR. TENNEY:

They are annexed to-day, as I understand it, or part of them.

And I want to say a word more. I intimated, when this honorable body was in Brooklyn, that it does not make any difference, gentlemen, in my view of this case, what your opinions may be; you may be against consolidation or for consolidation. (To Senator Brush:) I don't know — only my friend, I know how he stands; but it does not enter into this matter at all. I do not see how it is possible for any man to escape the conclusion that I have come at, whether for consolidation or against consolidation, namely, that he must accept the vote as passed in the city of Brooklyn — that that vote was final and at an end.

Now, I come to one other question. Much more could be said upon that, but it has been reviewed again and again and again. The point I made is this, with my friends on the other side, that when a measure is approved by a popular vote it ends it and is final. But when rejected, as our constitutional amendments were by many Legislatures, then it may be resubmitted; but the instance is not in existence when once accepted and once adopted it has gone back to the people for a second adoption.

Now, I desire to call your attention, gentlemen of the committee, to one other matter, upon which I have not said yet one word, and that is referendum. It is claimed by some of our friends on the other side — the number is few — that the charter should be adopted here, created here in the lawmaking power, and then go back to the people to be voted upon by them. Now, this, gentlemen, to my mind, is as absurd and inconsistent a request as the question that we should resubmit the question to the people. The only reason given for that is, as my friend General Wingate, has said, that the bill may be defeated. Now, suppose for a moment that you refer this matter back to the people. You can not — you can not amend the charter by the vote of the people. You can not enlarge or abridge the charter by the vote of the people. You can not make a suggestion to the Legislature by the vote of the people. You can simply reject or accept or approve the charter; that is all you can do. If the charter is rejected then it comes back to the Legislature the next session for another charter. Now, who ever heard of a city charter being referred back to the people for their ratification? There never was an instance in this State to my knowledge. There never was an instance in any city in this land, to my knowledge, where that was done.

Now, the first thing to be done is this: The charter is here to be created, and in getting at this matter directly you have to bear in mind, gentlemen of the committee, that a city is nothing but a corporation. It is just the same as a bank, an insurance company or a railroad company. It is the creature of the Legislature, of the statute; that is what a city is. It is born right here in Albany, in the Legislature; it grows by the sea. You might, with the same propriety, refer the charter of a bank to the people as a charter of a city to the people. You can, with the same propriety, refer the charter of a railroad to the people, to the community through which it runs as to refer back the charter of a city to the people. The present charter that we have in the city of Brooklyn was never submitted to the people of that city, nor was the charter of the great city of New York submitted to the people. It was made here in Albany. Brooklyn came to her present magnificent charter by a journey of forty years in the wilderness, over briar and thorns and pitfalls, until she has one of the best charters now known in the world; but the people of Brooklyn did not do it. Her representatives in Albany, the representatives all over the State did it, and they did not make the charter perfect first; during —

MR. BRUSH:

(Interrupting.) We are trying to preserve the charter now.

MR. TENNEY:

Yes — well, all right. They did not make it perfect first and it is not perfect now.

MR. BRUSH:

Well, it is the best one we have in the country and we are trying to preserve it.

MR. TENNEY:

Two or three bills are before this Legislature now to make that charter better. Now, you will not make a charter that will be perfect.

MR. LEXOW:

You do not see any difficulty in extending that charter so that it shall cover the greater city?

MR. TENNEY:

None whatever.

MR. LEXOW:

If that charter is perfect —

MR. TENNEY:

I do not say it is perfect —

MR. LEXOW:

Then the greater city should get the benefit of it?

MR. TENNEY:

Certainly, get the practical benefit. When people say that you can not make a charter that will cover these two great cities they are talking in the air. It is just as easy to make a charter to cover these two great cities, or three great cities, when consolidated, as it is to make a charter for the city of Brooklyn. It is as easy to make a charter for three millions of people as it is for one million of people. As a citizen of the city of Brooklyn, I am perfectly content, perfectly willing, to leave this charter making to this committee or any other committee that may be selected in this Legislature. I believe I have confidence in the Legislature, and I think it is a very poor compliment to the lawmakers of our State when people will say, "We won't trust them but we want it to come back to us." Now, I tell you, gentlemen, I had rather — and I think I touch the heartstrings of every man on this committee — I had rather have seven men make a charter for me, bright, intelligent, experienced men, than to have seven hundred or seven thousand. Submit that charter back to Brooklyn! Who will read it and who will know anything about it? It will amount to absolutely nothing. Bring about you gentlemen, here the best influence and the best means you can from the two cities. Frame your charter the best you can, you will not get a perfect charter, as I said before, at first. It will be after years of experience, after testing, after trial; you will get a good charter, that will cover all the exigencies of the times and meet every requirement and every demand.

I do not understand why it is — I do not understand why it is that they want a referendum — a referendum is something for the defeat of this charter. The charter should be made here, and applied to the great city the best that can be done, and then under experience we can perfect that charter, if it should need perfecting, as we go along in time and experience.

Now, gentlemen, I do not want to detain you, and I am not going to. But I am a New Yorker as well as a Brooklyn man; and I tell you, gentlemen, I want a big city by the gates of the sea! I have a little civic pride in this matter; that is not controlling by any means, for I believe, as I believe I said before you gentlemen, that Brooklyn can only be saved by consolidation. But we want here a great city! We want here a city which every American will be proud of, outside of the city of Chicago. We want here a city like the city of London, occupying both sides; London, as you know, occupies both sides of the

Thames; Paris occupies both sides of the Seine; Rome occupies, as you may know, both sides of the Tiber; Vienna both sides of the Danube; St. Petersburg both sides of the Neva; Berlin both sides of the Spree. Now let us have the great city on this continent occupying both sides of the East river; and let us have, as I said to you when in Brooklyn, let us have a ship canal reaching across the outer part of the island, linking Flushing bay on the north with Jamaica bay on the south, so that the heavy tonnage from out of New York harbor can be taken there, relieving the harbor of its now over congested condition. And let us remember this, men of New York, that these two great cities belong to our State. They are part of New York. They pay allegiance to the same laws, pay taxes into the same treasury. They are nearest to the commerce, admit of the same weather; they lie upon the same bay, they have the same custom-house and the same clearing-house. They have the same stock exchange, produce exchange, and oil exchange and cotton exchange. The princely merchants of Brooklyn unite with the princely merchants of New York in the same chamber of commerce and in the same board of trade. And it has been the muscle and the brain and the capital and the thought of these two great cities, each working in harmony and together, that have builded these magnificent cities by the sea. They are joined together in wedlock to-day in fact, if they are not in law.

Gentlemen of this committee, I beg of you not to hesitate in this matter, but to act and act promptly, and lift this great question out of politics. There should not be a particle of politics in it — and if there was politics in it, I would not be addressing you to-day. It is a question of citizenship. It is a question for the well-being of these two great cities. It is a life and death struggle for the city of Brooklyn. Give us consolidation! Put your bridges across the river. Settle the riparian rights of the East river between these two cities by consolidation. Tunnel the East river, and the years are not many before the population on the east side of the East river will outstrip by thousands and tens of thousands the population on Manhattan island.

We can not delay longer. If you do delay, gentlemen, if you do delay, politics will get into this question; there is no doubt about it — and the next Legislature — it will be a political question. Now, it is not a political question; the people who voted for this question voted as citizens, not as politicians. They voted for the welfare of Brooklyn, not as partisans, but as citizens, and I beg of you, therefore, gentlemen, to act and act promptly in this matter, that we may know where we stand.

Gentlemen of the committee, there are other things I might say, but I will not. But I want to thank you personally, as a citizen of Brooklyn, for the magnificent consideration you have given this question. It is a great question. It is a question that reaches beyond persons, beyond individuals; it is a question that concerns millions of people and millions of money — it should be carefully and thoughtfully considered. You have come to Brooklyn and heard us there. You have invited us here. You have treated the citizens of Brooklyn magnificently, and as a citizen of that town I return you grateful thanks.

MR. BRUSH:

Mr. Chairman, I would like to ask Mr. Tenney one or two questions, just to get his opinion. You spoke of London, the government of London, Mr. Tenney —

MR. TENNEY:

No, I did not speak of the government of London.

MR. BRUSH:

Of the government of the city of London.

MR. TENNEY:

No.

MR. BRUSH:

Did you not?

MR. TENNEY:

I spoke of London occupying both sides of the Thames.

MR. BRUSH:

You, of course, know that London is governed by nineteen different municipalities?

MR. TENNEY:

I know, sir, that the old city of London covers only one square mile; I know that the present city of London occupies 122 square miles.

MR. BRUSH:

And that it is governed by nineteen different municipalities?

MR. TENNEY:

I know that London — I do not know that fact, but I know that London is a set of villages. And I know another fact, that within a year and a half or within two years the city of Vienna has taken into her borders her entire outlying suburban districts.

MR. BRUSH:

You recognize the fact, Mr. Tenney, that this problem of municipal government is the question for this generation to solve?

MR. TENNEY:

I do, sir; one of the greatest questions we have ever had to do.

MR. BRUSH:

I agree with you there. Then, do you not think — you say to us that we should act and act speedily.

MR. TENNEY:

I do.

MR. BRUSH:

Do you not think —

MR. TENNEY:

I want this Legislature to take care of this question.

Mr. Brush:

Do you not think that it would be rather rash for this Legislature to go to complete this question, when it is so important a question?

Mr. Tenney:

No, sir.

Mr. Brush:

And consolidate this district?

Mr. Tenney:

No, sir. We have been discussing, as you ought to know, this question of consolidation in Brooklyn, for twenty years. It is no new question with us. I made a speech, myself, in 1892, I think, years ago, with Judge Gaynor, Mr. Greene, Mr. White, in the Real Estate Exchange, on this very identical question. It is no new question with us; it has been the liveliest question we have had in Brooklyn for the last five or ten years. There is no question about it. The great question has not been precipitated on us, as full discussion has been had in the newspapers, and full discussion in the Consolidated League.

Any more?

Mr. Brush:

I am much obliged to you.

Mr. Lexow:

Senator Wray, do you desire to address the committee?

Mr. Wray:

Mr. Chairman and Gentlemen of the Committee: I had not intended to occupy your time at all in talking to this subject, as I shall expect to say something in the Senate concerning it.

The purpose of the appointment of this committee, I believe, was to obtain information from the people at large, rather than through their representatives in this body. But I have here a telegram from the secretary of the Brooklyn Young Republican Club requesting me to come before the committee and say to it that that club had adopted resolutions favoring a referendum. That I do.

The Brooklyn Young Republican Club is a club having among its membership no officeholder, no political officeholder, by constitution of the club. It is a club which reaches into every ward in the city of Brooklyn; and it has had for its president Mr. Low, who was afterwards mayor of the city of Brooklyn, and is now president of Columbia college. It has had that eminent civil service reformer, Mr. Deming, as its president. It has had as its president, ex-Mayor Schieren; and I had the honor to be in a humble capacity an officer in the organization myself, some years ago, having been chairman of its advisory committee at the time the work of reorganizing the Republican party in the county was undertaken.

MR. TENNEY:

Mr. Chairman: I would like to ask if the gentleman knows how many were present of that club at that meeting?

MR. WRAY:

I do not, Mr. Chairman; I do not. Possibly, Judge Tenney can tell me, better than I can tell you, probably; and I would ask him if he knows to state to the committee.

MR. TENNEY:

I do not know, personally. I know it is a club originally, or until lately, of about three thousand members. Some of the grandest men in our city belong to it. And I know by hearsay about its meetings, and I would simply say, in parenthesis, "Do not put too much support in this." (Laughter).

A brother of our chairman, Mr. Matthews, who is not here, is a member of that club, and informed me all about it.

MR. WRAY:

The telegram speaks for itself, and is my only authority. I attend to my business here, and the gentlemen in Brooklyn are attending to theirs, I suppose. The secretary of this club requested me to make this statement to this committee to-day. I do it.

Mr. Lexow:

Senator Wray, I think the committee regrets very much that political bodies should take any formal action upon a question that the committee have desired to keep out of the range of politics, so far as we could.

Mr. Wray:

That suggestion is very well as a positive proposition. The Brooklyn Young Republican Club of the city of Brooklyn, as Mr. Tenney has said, has been one of the strongest organizations in that city for a long time, having a membership of about three thousand; it is not so strong now, as he intimated in what he said; that is true in part. All things considered, I believe the Young Republican Club is very strong in the city of Brooklyn.

Mr. Tenney:

(Interrupting) Once a year.

Mr. Wray:

Never mind how often. It has had as its presidents and officers men who have met the commendation of the people repeatedly, time after time, and do to-day, Judge; they do to-day. So, that the Young Republican Club, while it is a Republican club, is not a political organization alone, but represents the thought and the manhood and decency and the honesty of the people of Brooklyn, where we have thousands and thousands of that kind of people. For that reason, I personally place some little significance in the action of the Young Republican Club, more than I do in the ward organizations, which are purely political bodies; that is to say, they are partisan political bodies, whereas this Young Republican Club has not always been a strongly partisan Republican body.

I should have contented myself with merely making this statement had it not been for the fact that the bill drawn and introduced by me relating to the referendum of the charter has been spoken of by Mr. Tenney; and I was requested by a gentleman in attendance on the committee to explain the nature of that bill. I presume the gentlemen of the committee have read and considered the bill, although it has not been printed long; but I should like briefly, in order to correct any error that may have been lodged in the mind of the committee by the remarks of Mr. Tenney concerning it — I should like briefly to state the provisions of the bill.

It seems to me that as it was distinctly and well understood and could not be properly — if the Legislature would intend it to be so — that the bill passed in 1894 submitting this question to a vote of the people was merely for the purpose of obtaining an expression of opinion; as it declares by itself — the bill itself says that the vote shall be taken and deemed as an expression of opinion of the voter for or against.

MR. LEXOW:

Do you understand, Senator Wray, the reason of the bill of 1894?

MR. WRAY:

Why, certainly; a commission — they have been years — Mr. Tenney has said this has been before the people for a good many years; it has been agitated day after day, day after day, time after time — and I believe in consolidation; I believe in it. I believe if we did not consolidate the cities, they would consolidate themselves.

MR. TENNEY:

That is the talk!

MR. WRAY:

I believe in it.

MR. LEXOW:

The question then before the Legislature was whether we should decree consolidation without a vote of the people, or whether we should first ascertain the desires of the people of Brooklyn on that subject; I was in the Legislature at the time.

MR. WRAY:

Ah! — Now in the provision —

MR. LEXOW:

(Continuing) I know that the same gentlemen, the same associations, the same that are arrayed against consolidation, arrayed even against the bill submitting it to popular vote down there, and it was only after a controversy of about two months in the Legislature that we finally succeeded in passing a bill submitting the question to a popular vote.

MR. WRAY:

And I made a hearty, strong fight to have included in the provisions of that bill a further provision that any charter — that this vote should be taken with at least this much of knowledge on the part of the voter as to what should be done and what consolidation meant, that the bill when drawn, or at least, that the question when submitted as to whether they wanted to have consolidation of those cities or this territory with a uniform rate of assessment and taxation. I wanted them to understand that, but the friends of the bill said that that would probably defeat it. As a Brooklyn man, having every interest in Brooklyn, I felt that we must have some sort of security that the people would understand what they were voting for, and not vote at random for some proposition.

The question assumed this form in my mind. Suppose that two men, A and B, agree to enter into partnership, each having a certain amount of capital or a certain amount of experience. A says to be B, "Let us go into partnership;" B replies, "All right; I am satisfied; let us begin at once." And A says, "No, I want to be in partnership with you; but let us go to Senator Lexow, who is a good lawyer, and get him to draw our writings of copartnership agreement, so that we will each understand exactly where we stand in the division of profits and bearing of losses."

Now, wherever there is power lodged in any body of people and there is an unequal distribution of power, one body of people concerned having more than another, it has been the universal history of the human race that the strong has held down the weak, and where occasion offered, rather than give up their own rights, they have oppressed the weak; and as a friend of Brooklyn, one of her sons, I do not want to see Brooklyn, which is in this case the weaker one, the weaker for her having not the same numerical strength, borne down or overslawed by the great vote of New York.

MR. LEXOW:

I understand that, and I admit the proposition, excepting that the weakness is here, that the very Legislature passes upon the charter and not the representation of the city of New York.

MR. WRAY:

Very true; but if the proposition which is before that Legislature to-day, take it, with a solid delegation lacking only one from the county Republican, what can we expect from another Legislature in the way of consideration of what we ask. We ask to-day — a united solid delegation in this Legislature, to have either one of two things done for us in this matter, that the people — we ask — and those of my friends who agree with me in my view of the matter who are for and have been for consolidation all through consistently — we ask that a charter be drawn and submitted to the people. On the other hand, there are some gentlemen who say, "Let us submit the question of whether a charter be in fact drawn; that is, whether we would have consolidation." Now, it seems to me that we can come together on that proposition. But on the one proposition we are all together, and all say to this Legislature — the twenty-nine representatives of the city of Brooklyn come here in a solid body, and say to the Legislature, "Do not force this proposition upon us." Now, if they do not listen to that request, Mr. Chairman and gentlemen, what can we then expect from the Legislature when this weaker power shall ask to be protected from the stronger?

I would like to say — and I hope I am not trespassing upon the time of the gentleman — I will ask his pardon for taking so much of his time — in answer to the chairman's question, I want to say, this consolidation plan has been a question which has been agitated in New York and Brooklyn, as to the territory mentioned in the terms of that bill, Mr. Chairman, for a good many years. There was a growing and strongly growing feeling that consolidation would be a good thing and would cure many evils existing in both cities. After a time, the Legislature was induced to take that view of it, and a commission was appointed for the purpose of granting information and ascertaining whether or not it would be a wise thing to consolidate the cities. That commission was at work for years before the matter ripened, and finally it came to a position where the Legislature submitted the question of consolidation or not. The old commission having then performed its work, as I regard it, it having ascertained the condition of the public mind, having worked up public sentiment to take hold of it at all, and the Legislature submitting this question in 1894, got an expression of the will of the people, which some contend was not a fair one. If a vote under such circumstances as this was taken is to be considered as conclusive then it was a conclusive vote; if not, then it was not a conclusive vote. I do not question that.

But here, then, comes the other question. This matter has been before us; it is before us. People are taking sides on it; people are looking into it. They are informing their minds as to what there is in it, for and against it. After examining the question, I am of the opinion that consolidation will benefit us all.

Now, as a friend of consolidation, as a man who believes in it certain, as sure as the people live on Manhattan Island and as sure as the people live on Long Island, I believe that the manifest destiny of those two cities, make it very, very unwise for us to force an issue upon them which may result disastrously to us. Why should not we take as much time in considering the question of a partnership interest between these two cities owning billions of dollars of property, as we should in forming a partnership among ourselves where we would invest ten or fifteen or twenty-five thousand dollars?

Now, in this referendum if this charter is drawn — not drawn by this Legislature — Judge Tenney, we have no time to draw charters here — my bill provides that this Legislature shall — that the mayor of New York shall appoint three property-owners of that city, the mayor of Brooklyn shall appoint three property-owners of that city, the Governor of the State of New York shall appoint three property-owners from the territory affected outside of those two cities, making nine; and that the two mayors shall themselves be members of the commission, making eleven. They shall employ counsel, buy maps, prepare maps, and employ all necessary help, and between now and the 15th day of September, 1896, they shall prepare a plan or scheme of the consolidation of the two cities — of this territory, rather — and file that in the form of a report to the Legislature in the Secretary of State's office. He shall have a hundred thousand copies printed and have them delivered to the commissioners for distribution in the territory affected, for my very eloquent and able friend to study in order to inform the voters in our town, for lawyers to study in order to inform their clients, and for other people, laymen, who have the time and interest in it, to study to inform themselves. That the commissioners shall prepare in this way, then, the synopsis of the charter and have that published daily in the newspapers, at least five in each city. Then, the people shall vote for or against that charter; and if the charter is fair, and I believe it would be drawn fairly under such circumstances, and the people want the charter — want consolidation — they will vote for it and they will take it. And if they do not want it, they will vote against it. Now —

MR. LEXOW:

Another word, Senator Wray — suppose that if any large proportion of the people objected to some insignificant detail in connection with that charter, then all that work, all that trouble and the general plan of consolidation itself shall be defeated by a trivial mistake of judgment on the part of this committee preparing the charter.

Mr. Wray:

This is so, exactly, Mr. Chairman. And that is the fundamental law of the State of New York, as contained in its Constitution; and we have just seen the State doing it in this State, in holding a constitutional convention for the purpose of finding out whether we wanted any amendment to the Constitution, and then we might submit it to the people, the vote on that Constitution, running the risk that on any proposition contained in it if it met with the disapproval of a majority of the people, the whole Constitution should be swept away.

Mr. Lexow:

I beg your pardon — that is in order —

Mr. Wray:

Except in the three — in the fact that there were three separate propositions. But the main bulk of the Constitution was contained in one amendment.

Mr. Lexow:

I understand, but there were separate divisions, and three separate divisions for the express purpose of not permitting the defeat of the entire revised Constitution, because one or the other elector of this or the other place disagreed on a particular feature or some part of it.

Mr. Wray:

Exactly. But the main — all the main propositions contained in our Constitution were submitted in one body, one body. So that if any one of these provisions had met the disapproval of enough people to have them vote against it, we would have run the risk of having the whole Constitution defeated. This has been so right along, every time; it must be so. But, Mr. Chairman, the very fact that that was so made it absolutely impossible for a man, considering his dignity as a voter, as an elector in this State, considering the importance to himself and the other electors in this State, to allow some trifling thing contained in that Constitution, that proposed Constitution, to affect his vote so as to endanger all these vast interests. Now, wouldn't it be so with consolidation? We have in the consolidation act of the city of New York a charter. We have in the Brooklyn consolidation act a charter, the Brooklyn charter. The main provisions of those charters would apply, with but very little change.

Now, then, comes the main question — these main questions upon which the charter should be based which would in reality be the facts the people wanted to know, the main points of the union — as to a uniform rate of assessment and taxation, and that the city of Brooklyn would be taken care of in its public works department, so that when we wanted a street paved or a lamp set or a street flagging set or a sidewalk laid, or some such thing, the people of the outlying districts would be sure that somebody was charged with the care of these, so that they would not have to go to the city hall in Brooklyn and encounter an adverse vote because — and in New York encounter an adverse, vote because somebody else having the majority of the men in power should vote it.

MR. LEXOW:

Now, Senator, a vote on the charter would not be a vote on the question of union. The great trouble is that you would have — against union would be arrayed all those people, for instance, who have incumbrances upon the sidewalks, with reference to which the charter says something — every one interfered with by authority would organize against the charter because it says that restrictions shall be enforced on the sidewalks; and so you could go into every community where such government interferes with the personal rights and liberties of the individual. There would not be a vote taken on the great question of consolidation; but a vote would be taken as to whether or not the law would be too stringent in one respect or too lenient in another.

Mr. Wray:

Do you think, gentlemen of the committee — do you think that on a question involving so much of real interest to the people, that a matter of an incumbrance on the sidewalk — I know that is only one instance mentioned by the chairman — or that any other interest which does not go so deeply into the question of the rights of the individual and affect him so nearly in his person and his property — do you think that these questions would defeat the great question?

Mr. Lexow:

Why, Senator Wray, the gentlemen who argued against consolidation before this committee substantially stated that the people had taken absolutely no interest in the matter at all — so little interest that after five years' work the people of Brooklyn were absolutely unable to tell who their particular representatives were upon the consolidation commission.

Mr. Wray:

Well, it is quite possible, because they did not regard the consolidation commission as being consolidation, but the work of the commission was entirely aside from the commission itself.

But it seems to me that the main proposition which this committee will have to consider, could well be met by adopting the suggestions contained in my bill, and I wanted to say — I have no pride of authorship in it — while I drew it last year, while I had it in mind the year before, because I had to settle the question of where I should stand, when I came to go before the electors in 1894. Now, I had to settle it in 1893. And I have maintained an absolutely consistent course in the matter from the beginning to the end up to this present moment, and I expect to maintain the same course all the way through.

Now, if we prepare such a charter as the wise men who would undoubtedly be selected by the mayors and the Governor employing the counsel, if they would prepare a plan of consolidation, I truly believe that the people, after seeing what they were getting (not buying a pig in a poke), would be in a position to make a vote upon that charter a finality, either that they would have consolidation, or that consolidation would be put to sleep, the sleep of Rip Van Winkle possibly, not to wake up in twenty years.

MR. TENNEY:

I would like to ask Senator Wray, if you will permit me, Mr. Chairman, if he does not consider that the vote taken in 1894 in the city of Brooklyn was not a finality?

MR. WILSON:

Can I answer that?

MR. WRAY:

Oh, Mr. Chairman, not by any means; not by any means! In the first place, if the vote were intended to be a finality — if one Legislature could submit a question which could bind the answer to which would bind another Legislature — it can not do it by any possibility absolutely. By no possibility can this Legislature do a thing which binds the next one, recommend a thing. If that had been —

MR. TENNEY:

I would like with the permission of the chairman, to ask the gentleman if he does not consider that the canal improvement vote, that was submitted, is binding upon this Legislature?

MR. WRAY:

The canal improvement submitted was not binding on this Legislature, any more than the work of the constitutional convention was binding on this Legislature, until its adoption and ratification by the people, and then it became governing

MR. TENNEY:

Exactly that is it.

MR. WRAY:

Now, that was a totally different thing. "Here is the canal appropriation," was the question submitted to the people — "If you ratify this then it becomes a law." This was merely a question which said: "Do you want consolidation or not?" And the answer, "Your vote shall be to this effect; it shall be recorded as an expression of opinion on your part; the vote for consolidation will be regarded as an expression of opinion that you want consolidation; and a vote against it an expression of your opinion that you do not want it."

MR. BRUSH:

And not binding upon the Legislature.

MR. WRAY:

Oh, how can one Legislature bind another? It is utterly impossible. The Constitution binds us; not the former Legislature. I do not believe that Judge Tenney or any one else will claim that we are bound in fact by it — bound to the people —

MR. LEXOW:

How can it have any effect if that final vote on the question has no moral legislative obligation on the question as a legal binding —

MR. WRAY:

Now, then, when we come to the other proposition — That has been settled, I believe, Judge, has it not?

MR. TENNEY:

(Testily) Oh, anything is settled — so far settled —

MR. WRAY:

Then we come to the next proposition, as that Legislature could not bind this, then the question is, did they want to bind the Legislature in this way. Was there such an expression of opinion as will put a moral obligation upon this Legislature to heed the voice of the people?

Now, as to that I did not intend to speak at all, if it were not for the questions asked me by the Judge. In a community where they have nineteen ballots handed them, under the old ballot law — which was a nuisance aside from the nineteen ballots — and five propositions to amend the Constitution among the things to be voted on, and the question of whether or not the voter wanted consolidation also to be voted on. When the voter went into the booth with nineteen bollots in his hand from which he was to select the ballots he would vote, he was told by the leaders of his party, if he happened to be a Republican, that he must vote everything that had "For" on it that was handed him by the ballot clerks; and if he were a member of the Democratic party that he must vote everything that had "Against" on it, and where that man — and unfortunately there are people in this world who are not fully educated and up to the highest standard — where that man, we will say, was in some fear, not understanding the position or understanding comparatively little, and having got these confusing ballots and having these different instructions given him, when he finally struggled through this mass of stuff and picked out things, I fully believe that I am justified in the statement that of the 63,000 or 64,000 men who voted for consolidation, I believe that 20,000 of them there were who did not fully understand what they were doing at all; and there were at least 60,000 people who did not vote on the proposition at all; I believe that of the 63,000 people who voted against it, at least 20,000 did not understand what they were doing.

MR. WILSON:

Will the Senator allow me to read a short extract?

MR. WRAY:

I am not sure, Mr. Chairman —

MR. LEXOW:

What is it?

MR. WILSON:

It is in reference to what the consolidation commissioners officially stated, in a pamphlet published October 15, 1894, over their own officers' signatures, that this vote was to be only an expression of opinion, merely to get at the sentiments of the electors; also, adding in the same pamphlet, that if every ballot in a city or town were cast in favor of consolidation, there would be no finality.

Mr. Lexow:

Nobody disputes that; and it is a fact, there is no finality about it until the Legislature puts its final touch to the bill.

Mr. Wilson:

That is how the people voted, Senator.

Mr. Parker:

I attended the sessions of this committee in Brooklyn, not because I was a resident of Brooklyn, but because I drafted the bill and was anxious to see whether any criticism, any substantial criticism, was made upon its form or substance. I waited there during four sessions, four days' sessions of the committee, and went away, having heard really no plausible objection to the bill whatever. It is practically the same bill that was submitted to the Legislature last year, and with very slight changes, and whatever objection the anti-consolidationists had to it were then urged. However, I took from the lips of the speakers the objections as they were uttered; and although I shall not refer to every one of them, since some are so trivial, really so desperate that they need no answer, yet, some of them I shall answer, simply because the average man conceives an unanswered objection is a formidable one.

Mr. Benedict referred first to the fact that if New York city is extended under this bill, it would present the anomalous feature of a city partly in one county and partly in another. I do not believe that is anomalous, sir. So far as a city can be in one county partly, and partly in another, has it not been observed that New York city is to-day in that condition? At the last Legislature part of Westchester county was, as it was said, "annexed," and the Court of Appeals has decided that that annexation has taken place as far as it ever can take place, for certain purposes that territory remains in the county of Westchester and for certain purposes it is in the county of New York; still returns are made to the county canvassers in Westchester in the election, but the New York city officials count the votes. Mr. Chairman, under that law, you have had a tax levied, you have had a vote counted. I am referring now to the board of supervisors. Has anybody declared that that tax was invalid or that the canvass of that vote was illegal? We have got away from that objection a great deal — I simply want this to go upon the record that it may be answered — on the committee's record — we have got away from that practically by the fact that we have postponed the vote and effect of the first section until January 1, 1898.

His next objection was, that under this bill the city and county of Brooklyn — of Kings — could each contract ten per cent. indebtedness. I think if he looks at the constitutional provisions he will find that that is not tenable at all but by reference to the bill — I may refer first to article eight, section eleven, of the Constitution, which provides the debt-raising or debt-contracting power of the county, which restricts it — and to article twelve, section one, which provides that the Legislature may at any moment restrict the debt-contracting power.

It was asked who is to be the mayor and act on the bills submitted to him? The answer is so simple that I should think it would occur to anybody. Until consolidation takes place, the same mayors we have always had, with power. When consolidation takes place, the mayor who shall take the place of those mayors.

It was said by Mr. Benedict that they had an insuperable objection. That it would take ten years to complete this process. Nobody has exaggerated the size of this problem. It has not been overstated. It is almost the building of an empire! But, as I believe with many who have appeared against the bill, that consolidation is inevitable, so I believe that the only way to solve that problem is to grapple with it and not to shirk it.

As to the argument against increased jurisdiction — you will notice that I am replying to these very briefly — the argument against increased jurisdiction has been made over and over again. It was said, How can you concentrate power so as adequately to rule the immense territory, with its tremendous official interests? That is the sole argument that has been made against every increase of jurisdiction, municipal, State, national, from the beginning of our history. It must be met sooner or later. We can not, as London is — we can not remain in this seggregated condition — and I may say to Senator Brush that one of the most imminent and pressing problems that London has been confronted with for now twenty years is the problem of unifying these separate municipalities.

MR. BRUSH:

You are right.

MR. PARKER:

(Continuing): Commission after commission has been appointed The privy council has insisted upon the absolute necessity of unifying these separate municipalities, if London would become the economic government they want her to be. The abuses of the seggregation have been dwelt upon over and over again. In the time of Dickins the costliness, the corruption, the foulness of the parish and the vestry governments had already become a by-word.

MR. BRUSH:

The commissioners have not been able to solve the problem.

MR. PARKER:

We have surpassed them in that, as we have in many other things. We have not had all the obstacles they had. That is hardly an argument.

MR. BRUSH:

It is a fact I am stating; that is all.

MR. PARKER:

Oh, yes; still, you intended it as an argument.

MR. LEXOW:

Their difficulty arose from the fact of having over thirty independent municipal governments that they have brought into one — they have consolidated into one —

MR. PARKER:

That is it.

MR. LEXOW:

While we have to treat with substantially only two. The interests of those are so small, comparatively, that there is no difficulty in unifying them. The only difficulty arising here is the unification of the two great interests, Brooklyn and New York city.

MR. PARKER:

That is about all, sir. But one word upon the much-mooted point that the vote was an opinion, not a determination. It was as much a determination as anything ever can be, submitted to the people. It need never have been submitted. It was submitted as an act of mere grace, if I may say so. It is without precedent that a charter should be submitted to a people —

MR. WRAY:

(Interrupting) Mr. Chairman, will the gentleman give way for one moment? Judge Tenney made that statement also, and I meant to have answered it. There are cases reported in our own New York State reports where the Legislature has submitted a charter after it was passed by the Legislature, to be approved by the people, and the Court of Appeals held that such a submission was unconstitutional. For that reason I prepared my bill for the submission of the charter to the people before the Legislature should adopt it. So, I should say that the question has been submitted to the people time and time again in this State.

MR. LEXOW:

But as I understand it, Senator Wray, a submission of that kind is entirely without constitutional precedent and is entirely unconstitutional, for this reason, that any number of cases in this State hold that unless there is something in a law which goes absolutely into effect without the expression of the popular will, the law is unconstitutional. We had that question in the rapid transit matter.

MR. WRAY:

Your statement of the law, as I remember it, is exactly correct; but the point is this: The Legislature has seen fit here to submit this to the people for their approval. The Court of Appeals said that was wrong because they were of no effect; after having been passed by the Legislature, they were either laws or no laws. Now, if they have submitted these charters to the people before this, that establishes a precedent for us to submit a charter in such a form as a matter of submission.

MR. LEXOW:

You mean as an opinion and not as a legal finality?

MR. WRAY:

It has always been so — yes, that is all it is.

MR. PARKER:

I had not quite concluded as the gentleman interrupted me — perfectly, properly. I say it is without precedent that a charter has ever been submitted to the people in this state, for them to declare whether or no the Legislature shall enact it into law. Now, I think I am correct on that; and the unconstitutional precedent to which Senator Wray refers does not touch that. In those eases the Legislature had passed upon it and it was said to be wrong.

Now much has been said, as to whether any one Legislature can bind another. Absolutely not; except where the action of the first Legislature takes the shape of a contract protected by the constitutional provisions of the United States Constitution; in no other way, as I take it. In other words, there could be no more binding, final decisive way in which the people could speak what they wanted and preferred.

Now, I do not touch upon resubmission or referendum, because that has been dwelt upon ad infinitum almost. I pass to Judge Reynolds at the time — and the only new thing he brought to the discussion was that this was a stale vote — and I took these notes from his remarks — that the people of Brooklyn understand that the Legislature of 1894 only meant that the vote taken in pursuance of its act should be taken for the guidance of the Legislature of 1894; and when the vote was taken the Legislature on of 1894 had adjourned sine die. Now he must have said that without thinking; because he could not have meant, speaking for his friends, that the Legislature of 1895 before you came up here to Albany and before your committee declared it was already no — as I said — declared it was already stale. So much for that.

Mr. Johnson rose, and thought that he saw a "mare's nest" in the fact that the word "Charter" was omitted. As you recollect, Mr. Chairman, last year you empowered the commission to get a charter and such other bills as should be necessary for the government of the greater city. This year the word "Charter" was omitted; and you personally are aware of the reason, a very simple and innocent reason. In olden times the king granted charters, he made the corporation, and his court revoked the charter if the corporation abused it in their opinion. Now, no king grants them now; the Legislature makes the law, and erects the corporation by the same machinery as it does any other corporation, and a charter means nothing to-day, apart from any other bill. Where, pray is the charter of New York to-day? The Dongan charter, the Montgomery charter have passed away, since this has become an independent commonwealth, and the Legislature has made the charters in the same way as any other bill. Look for the charter of New York to-day. Look even for the fundamental general act, to which Mr. Johnson so generally refers as the contract of incorporation. Where is it?

Embodied in a tremendous volume of law known as the consolidation act. Look similarly for the charter of Brooklyn. It is perfectly innocent; we should have done it last year, if it had not been that having two gentlemen on the commission who supposed that this same suspicious criticism would take place that has now. Moreover, its surprising that Mr. Johnson should raise the objection because in section 14 of article 3 of the other constitution, which he was so prominent in revising here, occurred these words: "No law shall be enacted except by bill," which was not only our authority and almost our controlling one, that a bill, it alludes to the presenting of the bill. It is a merit, not a vice. Dr. Johnson once apologized for writing a long letter because, said he, "I have had no time to write a short one." There has been more labor compensated in that bill, sir,—which should declare all the wider outlines, and still would simply cover a page of the statute books — than there might have been if we had added to it ten thousand words; no merit would have been added to it.

He says it is a bill not for consolidation but for annexation. That is merely a matter of words; the whole population will have a chance to do what it pleases about it. It is a bill of annexation, of consolidation of municipal corporations. Brooklyn will always play her part in the greater city, you can place her upon that, she will always —

Mr. Lexow:

(Interrupting) Call her name.

Mr. Parker:

(Continuing) Call her name.

Mr. Johnson asked, to my surprise, "How many corporations will there be here?" Until consolidation takes place, as many as ever there were. When the consolidation takes place, one. He asked, "Who owns the property?" — the same answer; until it takes place, the same corporation; when it takes place the new corporation. Those are such axioms I hardly think them worth dwelling upon. He says we have not got down to the provisions by which the bills are referred — of course we haven't — the Constitution won't allow us — the bills will be referred if necessary; if not, they won't.

Well, heeding the request of the chairman I won't read all these things — I am taking them only once. He speaks of the terrible complications in the problem —

MR. LEXOW:

(Interrupting) We have got all of this.

MR. PARKER:

(Continuing) Of course, there are complications that have got to be met. Now, ex-Mayor Schieren wants to have this thing submitted — ex-Mayor Schieren wants to have this thing submitted to the people of the cities, because the people of the United States voted on the Constitution of the United States. That is not so. They did not. Mayor Schieren ought to know that the Constitution of the United States was voted by conventions of representatives, as to whether or no that should be the Constitution. I think it was at Poughkeepsie that Alexander Hamilton carried it by only three votes — carried New York, if I am not mistaken. Now, those are the only questions. I think that touch the bill as a bill.

I want to say but one word for the commission. There has been only one allegation, that the commission of which Mr. Greene is chairman has been insincere, and that is, that in a leaflet, a printed leaflet, issued over the name of the president and the vice-president, the statement was made that if every vote in Brooklyn was for consolidation that would not be a finality — and the chairman — you chairman, has said, certainly, that is very true. Now, to dispose of that, I will not say that if it were a finality, you would not be talking about it all, it would have gone into effect at once.

Now, one word as to the bill itself. It is absolutely as provisional, as harmless, as open and ingenious a measure as could be devised for the first step in this tremendous process. In the first place, in its first section, it simply announces that consolidation shall take place. Could we do less than that? It puts it off two years in the next place; it holds all things in statu quo, meanwhile, and unless seriously changed by the Legislature. In the third place it provides who shall go ahead and approve those measures to be submitted to you. Everything is left open for consideration. Brooklyn can come here and object; every part of the State can come here and object. The slow and careful process of discussion in committee and in the House and Senate can go on always; the most intelligent discussion — not the discussion that will follow up sending copies of huge charters out to people of all kinds, illiterate and literate, but the most intelligent, careful discussion by educated, interested and qualified men, will take place, the only discussion contemplated by the constitution. We could not do less. The following and last provision simply supplies a small amount of money necessary to pay for this work.

Now, allusion has been made to the age of two members of the commission. They are aged, and they have grown old in the service of these cities and of this State. I am not their apologist nor their champion; they need neither an apologist nor a champion. You could not find two men who by a consensus of opinion would more quickly, promptly and indisputably — two such men — conduct an operation of this sort to success.

Now, I have no feeling against the gentlemen who have opposed this matter, who have fought it from end to end; I think we are indebted to them for the extreme clearness in which this issue has been brought forth. I consider them in a good many ways about as good advocates of consolidation as you could have found; but in view of the harmless character of this measure, in view of its extreme provisionality, I do not think that they can be regarded as little more than obstructionists, salutary obstructionists it may be, but obstructionists; for I believe that consolidation must go through in one shape or another.

It has been said that behind the scheme of consolidation lie opportunities and purposes of political interest and faction purposes. If that be so it is my belief that they will recoil upon the party or faction which makes use of it. I believe it will hang about them like a cloud for a generation, if they do. I believe, on the other hand, if carefully and safely carried through it will redound in equal degree to their credit for that length of time. But ultimately I do believe it will go through.

You can read in the Rabbinical writings, Mr. Chairman, that when the first lines of Solomon's Temple were laid they were laid among the twitteringsand noisy protests of ten thousand sparrows, who entered an indignant opposition to the disturbing of their retreats (Laughter). They twittered when the lines were laid, they twittered as the walls were raised, they twittered as the rafters were put in place, they twittered when the roof tree was finished. But at length, when every detail was complete they sought shelter beneath the broad eaves, in every bit of ornamentation upon the cornices and the entablatures, and it declares they and their descendants bless the name of the prophet whom they had just reviled. And, so, Mr. Chairman, when we have at length filled out the immense detail which we now simply outline, when the influence of this troubling has become nothing more than a dim tradition, and when the descendants of these opponents, prominent in the great city as they are in the less, when they look back to this day, I believe they will thank Heaven for nothing more fervently, than for the failure of the well-meaning, but shortsighted efforts of their ancestors.

MR. BRUSH:

I am one of those who, like Senator Wray, believes in consolidation having time. But do you think it unreasonable for us in Brooklyn, who believe in consolidation, and fitting out this beautiful temple — that we should see the architect's specifications before you ask us to pay for it?

MR. PARKER:

No, I do not; we do not propose you should.

Mr. Brush:

That is my point.

Mr. Parker:

We do not propose you should. Following out the gentleman's smile, sir, we have simply proposed that certain gentlemen heretofore engaged in making estimates, shall continue to lay before you the ground plan of the temple, and every specification can be objected to by this Legislature; it will take some years before the process is completed.

Mr. Brush:

You used the words — you said the bill said "shall be." I notice the bill reads, "are hereby consolidated;" look at the last section and you will see that section don't take effect until January 1, 1898.

Mr. Parker:

Yes, but the first clause reads, "are hereby consolidated"— why not later on?

Mr. Brush:

You make that "shall be."

Mr. Parker:

Well, why will it? I may ask you.

Mr. Brush:

Simply that they conform to each other then.

Mr. Parker:

Oh, no, I beg your pardon; pardon me for contradicting; if that shall be consolidated on January 1, 1898, we should then alter the last section and say, "This act shall take effect immediately," so that it would be simply the substitution of one charter for the clean-cut scientific way of drawing an act, if I may say so;

we drew it as that is drawn, and then in the section which declares that the different parts shall take effect, prescribe those duties. That was done deliberately, sir.

MR. BRUSH:

Now, I want to ask you one question more. I didn't hear you answer the question. A great deal has been said about the revival of the board of supervisors, both in Brooklyn and in New York. Now, we have just gotten rid of a board of supervisors in Brooklyn, and we would rather keep them out of office; we don't want any more of that kind; and I would like to ask you as to your judgment on that point.

MR. MCKEOWN:

(To Senator Brush) You ran for that office, didn't you, once?

MR. BRUSH:

No, sir; I did not — a good many years ago —

MR. MCKEOWN:

Oh, I know that — it is a good many years ago, but nevertheless you ran.

MR. BRUSH:

I had forgotten it.

MR. MCKEOWN:

Well, I didn't.

MR. BRUSH:

But nevertheless, it is——

MR. PARKER:

The answer to that, and the same answer that was made last year, is this — this bill — assuming for a moment that it is imperative to create a board of supervisors, in case the boundaries of this city are extended beyond New York county, assuming that it be granted for the moment this bill is unconstitutional. When you say a bill is unconstitutional —

Mr. Brush:

No, I did not say that it was unconstitutional.

Mr. Parker:

You mean that there will be hereafter created a necessity for —

Mr. Brush:

Yes, I mean under the constitution — that the constitution says, in such counties as are not identical in territory there shall be boards of supervisors. Now, does that revive the board of supervisors?

Mr. Lexow:

I think Senator Brush means this: That while the city of Brooklyn is able to elect good officials in every other office in the city of Brooklyn, the reappointment of that board would lead again to a discreditable board.

Mr. Brush:

I did not — excuse me — I do not make any criticism nor intend to be understood as making any adverse criticism upon the board of supervisors. I said that we had gotten rid of the board of supervisors and we did not want to revive it; the reason is that it saves us some seventy-five thousand dollars a year, for that board of supervisors.

Mr. Parker:

Well, I will answer your question very simply upon that. The same question was presented in 1874 in New York city. Charles O'Connor drew an act of that nature, and that act was a very short one, which consolidated the city and county governments. There was between the passage of that act, in the spring of 1874, and the enactment of the constitutional amendment, to which you now refer, an interregnum of several months. During that time things went on just the same as before; there was a tax levied, a vote counted, and both declared valid; never anybody ever thought of contesting them. Then, in 1874, came the present form of the constitutional amendment. Now, the reason I refer to the tax and the vote is this — the canvass of the vote — is this: That in New York county, little by little all the power of the board of supervisors was taken away form them. There was a popular distrust of the board of supervisors and of the board of aldermen as such, until at length, practically all that was left, practically all that is left to-day with the board of aldermen as a board of supervisors, are those two powers — and they were — existed through those few months; that is very important to recollect. The principle upon which that was sustained by the best lawyers in New York — and Charles O'Connor stood at the head of the bar, concededly at that time — was this: That no matter whether or no a duty is imposed upon a Legislature and no matter how imperatively, their mere neglect to perform that duty and to provide the agency for the carrying out of a great and extensive governmental function, can not, therefore, kill that function.

MR. BRUSH:

Your interpretation of it is, then,— whether a board of supervisors — providing the Legislature did not take action —

MR. LEXOW:

(Interrupting) A single act, the board of aldermen would act?

MR. PARKER:

Would act absolutely. Whenever a great governmental power — I want to go further, because I want this to go on the records now, as long as we have come to it.

Your Constitution provides, in the most imperative way, that the Legislature should apportion this State every twenty years. The Legislature did not do it. The Legislature, if I may say so, violated its duty in omitting to do that. Year after year, year after year great regions of people were unrepresented in the Legislature, but who ever contended that a legislator holding his seat under the wornout apportionment had no title to it, and so — I had a reference here, I will supply it to you later on — I recollect in New York in the corporation counsel's office — there was a new tax law passed and the old tax law repealed, conferring upon the board of tax commissioners new powers, but omitted inadvertently one particular preliminary to levying the tax to which they had been accustomed; the comptroller, at that time, Mr. Kelly, held that the tax, under certain columns of the tax book — unless that could be done you could not levy the tax. Well, they did it; they took the responsibility, upon the corporation counsel's opinion of doing it, and thereupon John Stranahan — whom probably you know, you remember him — who was an acute lawyer — carried that vote to the Court of Appeals, and submitted that because there was no provision, that there was no place to put that power; that the only place where it was lodged could not go on, could not do it; they had to have specific power. The Court of Appeals said, "They have got to levy a tax and they have got the power to do so;" and the Court of Appeals, the highest court of the State, located that just where it was. Now, does that sufficiently answer. Another thing I may say, that you have two years — if you take the other view — you have two years in which to erect a board of supervisors. We do not want any more than Kings.

Mr. Chairman and gentlemen, in order to have the records correct, I would like to answer some statements that I read in the daily press.

I read in most of the Brooklyn papers, last evening, that all the delegation from Brooklyn, in both the Senate and Assembly, are in favor of resubmission or referendum. I know that is not so. I wish also to offer in evidence a paper, which I handed one of your committee, as you will remember it, as an evidence or partial evidence of why so many of our delegations from Brooklyn are in favor of either referendum or resubmission. Prior to the election I was approached by some anti-consolidation people and asked how I stood upon this question. I answered that I had been a member of the Consolidation League ever since it started. I was then informed that except I would sign a paper handed me or sent me that they would beat me in my election. I answered them, calling their attention to the Senators' oath, that when he takes office he swears that he has made no promise. By referring to that paper you will find, I think, these editorials directed against me, the first one of which will read, "The duty of the hour is to defeat McNulty for election as Senator." Knowing the feeling that paper engendered, in my canvass, speaking three or four times a night, for four or five nights, I frequently would ask the audience in different wards wherein I spoke, in a district numbering 26,000 voters, "All those in favor of consolidation with resubmission or referendum, will please hold up their right hands or stand up; and those for consolidation under equal taxation and equal valuation will please signify their assent;" I am prepared to say that I would be false to a constituency running through the heart of Brooklyn from the center of it — I should not represent them correctly if I favored either resubmission or referendum.

MR. WRAY:

In view of the fact that I have made a statement here that all of the members of the Kings county delegation, except one were for consolidation, I would like to ask the gentleman whether he speaks for himself alone or for any one else whom he knows.

MR. MCNULTY:

This gentleman will speak for himself.

MR. WRAY:

I would like to ask Senator McNulty if he speaks for anybody else.

MR. MCNULTY:

I know of some other gentlemen, yes, one more.

A. Ebbets:

Mr. Chairman and Gentlemen: I have the honor to represent the twelfth Assembly district of Kings county. At no time and under no circumstances have I ever said that I was against consolidation and in favor of resubmission or referendum. I have heard it stated several times that all or all but one were so in favor of it. I wish to deny that, and while I am about it I would like to give my reasons: In 1894 the people of my district voted very strongly in favor of consolidation. I think I am in honor bound to respect that vote, which I shall do, unless on the final passage of the charter I think that Brooklyn is not being treated fairly, or unless it strikes me that there should be too much politics in it. That is all I have to say, Mr. Chairman, and I thank you.

Mr. Lexow:

You do not know as to whether you will be here when the charter is passed.

Mr. Ebbets:

Well, Mr. Chairman, this is my first attempt at legislative duties; I do not know whether I will be here or not, but if I will be that is my feeling.

Mr. Heneshel:

Mr. Chairman and Gentlemen of the Committee: I believe it is proper for me to call attention to the fact that Senator Wray in referring to the referendum bill that he has introduced has practically answered the question in regard to it, when he stated that one Legislature can not bind another. Is it not clear that if we go to the trouble of presenting a proposed charter to the people to vote upon it, and if succeeding Legislatures should pass favorably upon that charter, and enact it into a law, that thereafter another Legislature could violate all that had gone before, the referendum would not be worth anything, and the Legislature assuming again its constitutional powers could alter, amend or modify that charter which had been referred, and consequently there would be a circumlocution of no practical use. Why not go directly at the thing? Of course, there would be no harm, excepting the harm of delay — delay which every defendant wishes who believes that he is beaten in his suit.

I would like to refer briefly to a few points that presented the submission of this question to a vote. In 1889, Mr. Andrew H. Greene, the father of this present movement of consolidation, presented a bill to the Legislature asking that a commission be appointed to determine the expediency of consolidation. Those who opposed consolidation immediately got together and said, "We do want any such commission. We do not want the question examined." But, in 1890, a law appointing such a commission was created. Then after this commission had discussed the subject, sought information, giving public hearings, and had come to the determination and had so reported, that consolidation was advisable, those who opposed from Brooklyn said," It is not fair to empower this body with the right of preparing a charter without knowing whether the people in the communities really desire to be consolidated." Thereupon they said let us vote. What did we do? We immediately prepared a bill allowing the people to vote; and when these people who had demanded a vote said, "There is not enough interest in the subject to submit it. It ought not to be submitted." Finally, after stripping the bill of all other matter, a law was enacted, Governor Flower having in his message favored it, and Mayor Gilroy at the time in his message also favoring the mere fact that this question which had created such an agitation should be submitted to the people. Thereupon it was so submitted. Now, after the vote had turned in favor of consolidation, they say to us that the submission was no submission, and that they would like to have it submitted again. Now, I claim that under these circumstances existing heretofore this question is not a new one. It is as old as the existence of the city of Brooklyn itself. And permit me briefly to allude to the remonstrance which was made by the city of New York against the city of Brooklyn securing a separate charter for itself apart from the city of New York, in 1834. The remonstrance in part is as follows: "That it is impolitic, as well in respect to the interests and welfare of the applicants themselves as of the inhabitants of the city of New York that the former should be incorporated as a city except in connection with the city of New York upon just and equal principles." This is the language of the city of New York in 1834, remonstrating against the establishment of a rival city right on the other side of the East river. They continue, "That the same can not be otherwise done with any substantial advantages to the inhabitants of Brooklyn, without materially intrenching upon the vested rights and necessary immunities of the city of New York. That from the peculiar situation of the city of New York, its commercial character and importance, and the inseparable connection existing between its prosperity and that of the whole State, it is for the interests of the people of this State, as a political body, to second your memorialists in their efforts to preserve and protect the right and privileges of the city of New York in their full integrity, and to defeat all attempts to establish a distinct and rival commercial community, which, by exercising a divided or concurrent jurisdiction over the waters which now constitute the harbor of New York, must inevitably interfere with regulations already established in respect to its navigation, embarrass the commercial pursuits of this ancient and flourishing city, and lead to a state of hostility and bad feeling between parties whose contiguity and peculiar location indicate that they should be united as one body, to participate in and enjoy with mutual security and benefit the advantages with which nature has surrounded them." There is a great deal more literature on this subject tending in the same direction, and which is a sufficient index thereof. There is only one other point I desire to call your attention to and that is to the great advantage in securing improvement in the governing of municipalities which it is believed in this country of ours has been very largely to a very large extent a failure. How is that municipal government to be improved by the proposed consolidation? Mr. Andrew H. Greene, in a document which I propose to present for the archives of this committee, has said among other things upon this point: "If the lines of division between city and country be drawn upon the same lines which divide dense city populations from sparce rural populations, we accentuate by artificial boundaries the antagonisms which it is the part of prudence to moderate. A large city can with advantage be so extended as to have within its own lines the modifying element of rural space and rural population, thus broadening and shading off differences which become difficulties only when sharply defined." In another place he says, and this shall be my last quotation — and it goes to the very ethics of securing a beneficial improvement and progress in our city affairs — Mr. Greene says: "It is an unwritten presumption of our political code that a citizen is a voter in the neighborhood of his work, and that his work is in the neighborhood of his home. It is this presumed arrangement which is supposed to inspire the voter with discretion in exercising the voting privilege. Yet there are very many thousands of persons earning a livelihood here who vote elsewhere, and very many who vote here who have the tie of merely transient domicile and whose prospective homes are situate in other jurisdictions. It thus happens that actual conditions are at variance with our theories, and as a result there is produced a character of citizen who is a drudge in his field of work and a dummy in his sphere of citizenship. Whatever mischief there is in absenteeism is to be found in this."

Now, I claim if we have the good people, that good, honest class of citizenship of Brooklyn, exerting in behalf of good government their power and their voice in our municipal elections, the judgment of the people, in the place where they work, where they live as a united city, will be potent in improving city affairs. What is the fact? We have in the city of New York a large body of men who occupy our factories, our mercantile establishments, or stores, our colleges and our schools, who have no voice in the condition of city affairs; the place where they spend most of their days, the place where their life is practically spent, there they must suffer whatever inconvenience results from bad government, if there is any; and although they are largely taxpayers, although they are practically dwellers in the city of New York, they can not raise a finger in the affairs of that city without the charge of being intermeddlers or of concerning themselves with matters they ought not to have anything to do about. Now these same citizens become half-hearted citizens in Brooklyn. They are only half citizens in Brooklyn; they sleep there; and they can not be expected to exercise that vigilance, exercise that power and care which it is the duty of a citizen to exercise in observing the affairs of a city and seeing that the management is proper. Now I say, make these people citizens of one city and you will bring to bear upon this government, upon the nomination and election of its officers, an amount of public influence, and in the direct office of its real citizens there could not be but a large step in favor of purer and better city government.

One more point. Senator Brush has referred to the fact that city governments in this country are largely failures. Now I believe I can state a circumstance which will lead probably to the solution of that problem. Our United States, under the United States Constitution and that form of government, dividing the functions of government as nearly as possible into executive, legislative and judicial, is a pretty fair government. In our State governments we have a fair example of republican institutions, working successfully under that same arrangement of dividing up the sphere of government into natural divisions which have been outlined and determined by the fathers of the republic. It is only in city governments that that arrangement, that that system of republican government, is violated, that the Constitution of republican government is violated, that I claim that in the formation of this charter, which I expect will be a model of a charter for the government of cities, there will be this following of the federal Constitution in the arrangement; and if we do that I believe that with consolidation and with a specific arrangement of the functions of government properly divided among the officers, I believe that you will find a great improvement; and while we do not expect a perfect charter at once, the gradual process of amelioration and the amendment of modifying law will go on until in ten or twenty years hence we will have a charter which will be the wonder of the world.

I take pleasure in presenting the document I referred to, and also a little pamphlet on the subject embodying my views, that I have here.

MR. LEXOW:

File them with the stenographer.

MR. CLEVELAND:

I will say I am one of the two gentlemen that interviewed Senator McNulty, and I wish to say in answer to what he said, that I worked every hour during the campaign for his election, both because I believed with him politically and also from what I could learn of the character of the two men running for the office I thought that it would be better represented by the major; and so far as the statement is made that the league of which I am a member did anything to make this a party question or to work against a man during the campaign, I do not think it fair to say so. If gentlemen of the opposite political faith have done anything to make this a political question why that is their affair. It certainly was not made by the League of Loyal Citizens — and I would say one word and close — I believe that I fairly represent nine-tenths of the members of that league when I say that primarily the reason why we oppose consolidation is because we believe that the problem of the government of great municipalities in this country is the most serious one that confronts us, and that until it is better solved it is very unwise to make that problem a greater one by increasing the size of these two cities.

MR. LEXOW:

Do I understand that that is the fundamental objection of nine-tenths of the members of the league, and not that objections —

MR. CLEVELAND:

(Interrupting.) I think it is.

MR. LEXOW:

(Continuing.) That have been stated before this committee at its hearings in Brooklyn.

MR. CLEVELAND:

I think that has been stated very clearly by every Brooklyn man that addressed this committee.

MR. LEXOW:

I would like to get on the record, Mr. Cleveland, inasmuch as you say you represent nine-tenths, as to whether or not that is the objection —

MR. CLEVELAND:

(Interrupting.) I said that in my opinion —

MR. LEXOW:

(Continuing.) That they make; that is characteristic of their position?

MR. CLEVELAND:

I stated to you, in my opinion, that primarily that was the reason that influenced nine-tenths of the members of the League of Loyal Citizens.

MR. LEXOW:

That, therefore, the sentimental question does not influence the citizen of Brooklyn or any of those other subsidiary questions that have been dragged into the argument —

MR. CLEVELAND:

I hardly think so.

MR. NEWMAN:

I represent the seventh district of Kings county. Unfortunately I have been sick since the Assembly organized, so that I know very little of what is going on. I do not know how Kings county stands on Greater New York; but I want to put my district and myself on record as being heartily in favor of consolidation, and against anything that would block the wheels of progress.

MR. LEXOW:

Is there anybody else who desires to be heard? If not, the chair is authorized to state that while it was the judgment of the committee that this should be the final hearing, on the request of the representatives of the city of New York on this committee—I may add their very earnest solicitation—that the city of New York shall be extended the courtesy of a hearing, although it is not known that anybody desires to speak at it.

This committee will stand adjourned, when it does adjourn, to meet in New York, on Saturday, at half-past 10 o'clock, for the purpose of holding a hearing there, in Part I of the Supreme Court, Criminal Division, in the Criminal Court building.

NEW YORK, *February* 1, 1896, 10.30 A. M.

Proceedings held in Part I, Supreme Court room, Criminal Court building, New York city.

PRESENT.—Chairman Lexow and the remainder of the committee.

MR. LEXOW:

A quorum of the committee being present, we will now proceed to hear any arguments against the Greater New York bill, and incidentally in favor of the resubmission bill or the referendum bill. The same procedure will be followed here as was followed in Brooklyn, viz., those opposed to the bill will receive two hours' attention and then those in favor of the bill, if they desire to speak any further, will be heard for two hours on the question. Who appears against the bill?

Mr. Benjamin F. Romaine:

Mr. Chairman: I represent the New York Taxpayers' anti-Equalization League, and individually, and of counsel of my own right, I have to make a formal application in behalf of the signers of the pamphlet which has been circulated, and which only came from the printer's hands yesterday, for an adjournment of one week, and that meanwhile the process of this committee, by way of subpoenas issued to the persons named in our applications for the further information of the committee on this subject, and for such further issuance of the process of the committee as the investigation undertaken by your honorable committee may develop. Mr. Chairman, we have had but forty-eight hours' notice of the intention of the committee to come to the city. Our movement, while it began practically with the pamphlet issued by a committee of our association, Mr. Deering and Mr. Doremus, in the fall of 1894, before the New York referendum, our movement practically, in its present phase, commenced only with the beginning of the commission of the present legislative session hearing. It was clearly demonstrated that the bill last to be brought in implied an equalization of taxes and valuation in the whole of the consolidated municipality. I wish to have it distinctly understood that we are not opposing political consolidation.

Mr. Lexow:

Then it would seem to me as though this appearance before this committee was premature. The bill that is now before the committee proposed political consolidation — actual political consolidation, as you suggest. It then enabled this Greater New York commission to frame bills for the actual consolidation of the Greater New York area, and, among other requirements, imposes upon them the duty to bring in bills that will equalize taxation, assessment and valuation throughout the district.

MR. ROMAINE:

That is precisely it, Mr. Chairman.

MR. LEXOW:

Therefore, your opposition does not go to the merits of this bill, but will go to the merits of any bills brought in afterwards in favor of actual consolidation.

MR. ROMAINE:

But we object to the commission being given any authority to bring in a bill like that. What consideration is this committee entitled to at the hand of taxpayers of New York? We object to their being given authority for anything of that kind, in behalf of the taxpayers of New York. We are only the advance guard that will throng the sessions of this committee.

MR. LEXOW:

I understand, Mr. Romaine, but do you not think the thronging ought to be when the vital question you have under consideration is under discussion. This committee, appointed by the two houses, this joint committee is charged with the duty of only considering this one question of political consolidation. I think that is a very apt phrase to use, and used for the first time — "Political Consolidation;" but if they should come to the conclusion that "Political Consolidation" should be had, then they are charged with the further duty of ascertaining the terms and conditions. If this committee should report in favor of political consolidation, and therefore the passage of a skeleton bill, making the political consolidation a fact, then they will give hearings upon the terms and condition upon which that consolidation shall be had; and if, then, you have any reason to oppose the general equitable proposition of equal taxation and assessment, it would seem to me, if you are in favor of political consolidation, that you should then make any argument you please upon the question of this taxation.

Mr. Romaine:

Will the chairman allow me to read, from what I understand is a bill now before the Senate?

Mr. Lexow:

Certainly.

Mr. Romaine:

Mr. Chairman, Senate bill No. 12, in its third paragraph, states this: "The commission appointed under chapter 311 of the Laws of 1890, is hereby authorized and directed to prepare such bills as will, upon their enactment into laws, provide a government for the municipal corporation, the mayor, aldermen and commonalty of the city of New York, as by this act enlarged, and among other things for attaining an equal and uniform rate of taxation, and of valuation for the property's tax." We ground our opposition, sir, at this hearing, on that clause.

Mr. Grady:

What system of taxation do you favor?

Mr. Romaine:

Well, sir, that is hardly now before the commission; we do not see any reason for the departure from our present method of governing the present municipality of the city of New York.

Mr. Grady:

That is on the basis of equal taxation.

Mr. Romaine:

Excuse me, sir, regarding the methods now in vogue respecting the territory of the city of New York.

Mr. Grady:

I say the present territory of the city of New York is under precisely that system of taxation. You do not distinguish as between the annexed district of the city of New York?

MR. ROMAINE:

No, sir; we do not.

MR. GRADY:

That provision is that you shall not distinguish in the Greater New York, as between the territory of New York and the present territory of Brooklyn.

MR. ROMAINE:

That is what I am proposing now.

MR. GRADY:

Then I ask you what system instead of the fair and equal system you oppose, do you propose?

MR. ROMAINE:

That will be disclosed by testimony we will offer.

MR. GRADY:

We can not take testimony on one provision of the bill, unless there is some plan offered to us on which you will take testimony.

MR. ROMAINE:

That will be disclosed at the hearing, which we ask. Now, after reading this pamphlet, Mr. Chairman, one of my associates will undertake to explain that phase of it to you, if you so desire.

IMPORTANT TO EVERY CITIZEN AND TAXPAYER IN NEW YORK CITY—ABOUT "GREATER NEW YORK" — HOW THE PROPOSED SCHEME TO EFFECT AN "EQUAL AND UNIFORM RATE OF TAXATION AND OF VALUATION FOR THE PURPOSE OF TAXATION THROUGHOUT THE WHOLE OF THE TERRITORY" OF GREATER NEW YORK, AS PROPOSED BY THE COMMISSIONERS' BILL, WILL RETARD THE PROGRESS AND IMPROVEMENT OF THE CITY OF NEW YORK AND INCREASE ITS TAXATION FOR THE BENEFIT OF KINGS, QUEENS AND RICHMOND COUNTIES, WITHOUT COMPENSATING ADVANTAGE.

The bill introduced in the Legislature by the "Greater New York" commission provides in its third section as follows:

"The commission * * * is hereby authorized and directed to prepare such bills as will, upon their enactment into laws, provide * * * among other things, for attaining an equal rate of taxation and of valuation for the purpose of taxation throughout the whole of the territory of the said municipal corporation as so enlarged."

The expressions above quoted are the same as those which the consolidationists of Brooklyn have uniformly employed. They frankly admit that the mere sentimental argument of size of the enlarged city proposed has no weight with them, but that it is the opportunity to divert the surplus moneys raised by taxation of New York property to the improvement of Brooklyn which makes them so eager for "Greater New York."

How this is proposed to be effected may be seen from an address issued by the Consolidation League of Brooklyn just prior to the last municipal election, which we quote in full, so that the taxpayers of New York may judge of the merely selfish motives which the advocates of consolidation of Brooklyn openly avow. It is difficult to see from the standpoint of New York taxpayers just where the New York "comes in":

The Consolidation League of Brooklyn has favored the union of the two cities. It has favored such union on a basis of uniform taxation and a uniform rate of valuations, as provided in the Lexow bill. How important these provisions are to Brooklyn is evident from the construction of a few figures. From simple arithmetical calculation we are able to make three distinct statements which we challenge any one to controvert:

First. We declare that with consolidation and a uniform rate of taxation on the valuations as given in 1894 in the two cities, the rate of taxation in the consolidated city would be less than $2 on $100.

Second. We declare that with consolidation and a uniform rate of taxation with the valuations in New York raised to seventy per cent. of real value as in Brooklyn, the rate of taxation in the consolidated city would be less than $1.56 on $100.

Third. That with a tax levy of $2.62 on $100 — being Brooklyn's tax rate in 1894, on the valuation of the two cities at seventy per cent. of the real values, there would be more than $35,000,000 raised beyond the sum necessary to meet the whole budget of the consolidated city. Here are the figures:

Brooklyn's valuations, including Kings county, 1895, at seventy per cent....................	$549,469,412
New York county's valuations, at eighty per cent..................................	2,003,332,037
Total..................................	$2,552,801,449

BUDGET.

Kings county..............................	$14,500,000
New York..................................	37,500,000
Total..................................	$52,000,000

To raise $52,000,000 on the above valuations it will be seen by a simple process of division that the rate will be $2 and a fraction on $100. This is giving no credit for the several millions of dollars annually paid into the treasury of New York from its ferries and water fronts and other sources, nor for less cost of government.

Raise the valuations of New York to seventy per cent. as in Brooklyn, and we have a valuation in New York of $2,804,664,857, and a total of $3,354,134,263.

To raise $52,000,000 on such valuations it would make the tax rate $1.56 on $100.

These figures are based on the former tax rate and valuations. We call attention to the fact that the bonded debt under Mayor Schieren has increased $3,000,000, and that the average tax rate for 1895 will be $2.77 on every $100, an increase of over fourteen points.

These figures prove that the only financial salvation for the city of Brooklyn is through consolidation.

Consolidation means more bridges, more facilities for travel, more improvements in our streets and avenues, more schools, more investments in real estate for rental purposes, and less shifting and uncertain rentals, more activity in all kinds of business, and more civic pride in what is destined to be the great metropolis of the world, with all the attendant advantages.

Briefly stated, the argument of these Brooklyn gentlemen is that valuations in New York should be increased from fifty per cent. to seventy per cent., so that the tax rate of Brooklyn may be reduced from $2.62 per $100 to $1.56.

Our Brooklyn friends naively conclude: "These figures prove that the only financial salvation for the city of Brooklyn is through consolidation." We, on the other hand, propose briefly to consider how the "salvation" of the present city of New York, considered in the light of its future progress and improvement, will be affected by the proposed scheme of uniform taxation and valuation. As the figures below given show, New York had on December 31, 1895, a limit within its constitutional power of indebtedness (ten per cent. of valuation) of say $55,000,000, while Brooklyn was within $2,000,000 of its limit.

The following admirable presentation of the relative financial conditions of New York and Brooklyn is from the Record and Guide of January 18, 1896:

"Notwithstanding the great improvements made and contemplated in New York, the city can show a clean balance sheet, while keeping within the statutory limits of its debt, for the next five years. As the debt now stands it could still spend $54,000,000 on a rapid transit railroad and not exceed the ten per cent. limit of the assessed valuation on real estate. It is estimated that it will have to issue bonds for various works outside of the rapid transit railroad in the next five years amounting to $61,794,000. The income of the sinking fund amounts to about $8,500,000 and there is no reason to suppose that it will fall off, but rather that it will increase. Allowing that that will be the income for the five years, it will make a reduction in the debt of $42,000,000, leaving the net increase of the debt at $19,294,000. The increase in the assessed valuations based on the increase for the past five years, is estimated at $247,971,450, which if realized will increase the legal limit of the city debt by $24,797,145, leaving a further margin of about $5,000,000. Moreover, New York has immense latent resources to meet the cost of necessary improvements in the low valuation put on real estate for purposes of taxation. It is impossible to estimate what the actual proportion is. Some good judges put it at fifty per cent., and this is always used for the purpose of making favorable comparisons. The commonly accepted idea of sixty per cent. is certainly a very high one. In Brooklyn the tax department admits that the assessed valuation is quite up to seventy per cent. If New York's assessments were made on that basis it would give the city to-day an additional borrowing power of $16,000,000, and in five years of $18,000,000. The following is an authoritive estimate of the bonds to be issued in the five years 1896-1900, inclusive, and the estimated resources to meet them:

Balance from bonds authorized to be issued for pending work, but not yet actually issued....	$3,500,000 00
Additional Croton water stock..............	1,320,000 00
Additional water stock	10,500,000 00
Additional water stock (sanitary protection)...	1,500,000 00
Third avenue bridge.........................	500,000 00
Willis avenue bridge	1,883,000 00
East river bridge	3,500,000 00
Dock bonds..................................	7,500,000 00
Repairing....................................	1,400,000 00
Repairing, twenty-third and twenty-fourth wards..................................	115,000 00
Site and building, College City of New York....	1,128,000 00
Metropolitan Museum of Art................	1,000,000 00
Riverside Park improvement...............	384,000 00
School-house bonds.........................	5,000,000 00
Fort Washington Park......................	1,000,000 00
St. John's Park..............................	300,000 00
Parkway, twenty-third and twenty-fourth wards,	300,000 00
Concourse, one-half estimate cost...........	5,000,000 00

Change of grade damage....................	$1,000,000 00
Miscellaneous purposes, authorized and to be authorized..........................	15,000,000 00
Total..............................	$61,794,000 00
Estimated surplus revenue sinking fund $8,500,000 a year......................	42,500,000 00
Estimated net increase city debt............	$19,294,000 00
Net December 31, 1895......................	109,885,509 45
Estimated net debt December 31, 1900........	$129,179,509 45
Estimated assessed value of realty, 1900......	$1,894,000,000 00
Ten per cent., limit of debt, 1900............	$189,400,000 00
Estimated debt, 1900......................	129,179,509 00
Estimated surplus......................	$60,220,491 00

If we make a summary of these figures and a similar calculation for Brooklyn, which will be purely arbitrary, of course, and only reliable for illustration, some idea may be got of the relative credits of the two cities. If for Brooklyn we allow that the increase of debt will be five times what it was in 1895, and that the increase in real estate valuation will, in the coming five years, be equal to what it was in the past five years (the same allowance as was made for New York in the figures previously given), we shall have about the following comparison:

	New York.	Brooklyn.
Assessed valuation real estate....	$1,646,028,655	$540,608,346
Legal limit of indebtedness.......	164,602,865	54,060,834

	New York.	Brooklyn.
Present indebtedness, less sinking fund........................	$109,885.509	$52.037,000
Estimated net increase of debt in five years (Rapid Transit railroad not included)...............	19,294,000	9,640,000
Total estimated debt December 31, 1900...............	$129,179,509	$61,677,000
Total estimated valuation of realty, 1900.................	$1,894,000,000	$632,414,222
Margin of debt limit.............	$60,220,491	$1,564,422

These figures suggest, at least, if they do not prove, that Brooklyn will have much difficulty in carrying on needed improvements in the next five years and keeping within the constitutional limit, with her assessed valuations based on seventy per cent. of actual value; while New York will have no such difficulty even on a fifty or sixty per cent. basis of valuation. If it were proposed that consolidation be effected by conditions that would keep the burdens on property where they now belong, the objections to it that are found in these figures would not hold good. But as it is, on the contrary, proposed that the basis shall be equalization of valuations and of taxes, they have force. Brooklyn has a tax rate varying in the older and new portions of the city, but the average in 1895 was 2.62; in New York it is 1.91. If the valuations are to be equalized it can easily be seen that the cost of administration and of the improvement of the consolidated city can only be met by an increased valuation in New York or a higher tax rate. A competent authority has estimated that consolidation means an increase of fifteen per cent. on the tax rate of New York city. Such an increase would bring the tax rate up to 2.19, and the addition would be equal to a new permanent charge on a $10,000 investment of about twenty-nine dollars a year, or the interest on $580 at five per cent. How far the property would depreciate under the affliction of a new burden like this it is hard to say.

As an example of the several degrees of efficiency the two cities are in, the following table showing their mileages of streets and the nature of the paving is applicable It should be noted that the figures do not relate to the new portions of either city. The superiority of New York would be brought out in much greater prominence if the twenty-third and twenty-fourth wards had been included. The number of miles of unpaved streets and of streets paved with the antiquated cobbles in Brooklyn is a startling evidence of the necessity for large expenditures in the near future in order to bring the condition of the city to respectability at least. It should be noted that New York's unpaved streets are graded and curbed, while those of Brooklyn are not, and that the Brooklyn departments have no record of street mileage or paving in the towns recently annexed:

	22 wards.	28 wards.
Miles of streets	449.86	666.20
Miles of streets laid in granite	184.19	106.60
Miles of streets laid in Belgian block or trap	111.88	41.30
Miles of strets laid in cobble	.58	269.04
Miles of streets laid in asphalt	69.97	26.10
Miles of streets laid with wood	.56	......
Miles of streets laid with macadam	20.68	2.80
Miles of streets laid with brick	......	.30
Miles of streets unpaved	62.00	219.70

If a comparison be made of the taxable resources of Long Island City, another of these towns clamorous for "equality of taxation and valuation," with New York city, the result is still more astounding

From the latest figures available it appears that on January 1, 1894, the net debt of Long Island City was $2,301,205, while its assessed valuation was but $16,717,677, thus showing that it was considerably beyond its constitutional limit.

It is notoriously bankrupt — in arrears to its very policemen and its public officers, without ability to collect their salaries.

To summarize our objections to any plan of consolidation involving " equality of taxation and valuation " we submit the following:

1. The outlying territory is composed very largely of lands unimproved. Any municipal improvement in this area of necessity, from the figures shown, must be made at the expense of the taxpayers of the city of New York, since all these towns or municipalities are now staggering under debts closely up to their constitutional limits — Brooklyn within one per cent. thereof and Long Island City already beyond it. What New York taxpayers will acquire from these corporations will be the heritage of debts, the result of many years of misgovernment.

2. New York city has entered upon a period of large public expenditures for improvements within its present area. Its powers of taxation should be retained for the benefit of its present inhabitants and not expended for distant districts. Its constitutional power of indebtedness should be carefully guarded, so that it may avoid the embarrassment of applications to the courts whenever new issues of bonds are proposed, as has been the case lately in the city of Brooklyn.

3. It is not too much to say that all projected improvements in this city, including a municipal system of rapid transit, must be abandoned if the proposed scheme of consolidation on the basis of equality of taxation and valuation be carried into effect. The comptroller of the city of New York, Hon. Ashbel P. Fitch, in testifying before the Supreme Court Rapid Transit Commission, said:

" Having regard for the constitutional limitation (ten per cent.) to the debt of the city, we have, therefore, a margin now of about $55,000,000."

This margin is, however, only a theoretical one, as Mr. Fitch proceeded to show, for besides the amount of bonds which would have to be provided for in the immediate future.' The first of these is for work that has been authorized by law and is actually under way. The second is where expenditures have been authorized by law and can be estimated upon, and part are authorized by law, but are beyond any one's power to calculate the cost of.

Of the first kind, he said, there was a total of $4,069,303.56 in bonds which he had been legally ordered to issue, and that would be issued whenever the proper call was made upon him for the money. Of the next lot, where the expenditures were authorized by law but not yet by the municipal authorities, he had made a calculation. These included such items as the Carmel and Jerome Park reservoirs, which would cost $16,800,000, and were to be completed respectively in 1902 and 1903. It would take $2,000,000 a year probably to pay this. Then there was $500,000 a year authorized to spend for the protection of the Croton watershed. The entire sum had been used in 1895, and it was fair to assume that the entire half million would be used in each year for some years to come. Then there was an estimated $500,000 for land for the approaches to the new Harlem bridge at Third avenue, $1,833,000 for another Harlem bridge to be spent within the next three or four years, $1,250,000 authorized for a bridge at One Hundred and Forty-fifth street across the Harlem, and one-half of the $14,000,000 or $16,000,000 which the new East River bridge will probably cost.

The dock board has a right to call for $3,000,000 a year. Last year it got $1,190,000, but the improvements now going on at West Eleventh street to accommodate steamship lines, and some other work, is likely to call for the whole $3,000,000 this year. Repairing streets will make another demand. Then there is a little sum of $1,175,000 for the new site and buildings of the College of the City of New York, likely to be called for soon; an addition to be built to the Metropolitan Museum of Art at a cost of $1,000,000; new small parks, $3,000,000; new schoolhouses, $5,000,000; land damages at Fort Washington Park, $1,400,000, and at St. John's Park, $533,765; $100,000 for parkways in the twenty-third and twenty-fourth wards, and a few more little items of about that size. Leaving out of consideration such uncertain items as the Grand Concourse in the Boulevard, which is variously estimated at from $5,000,000 to $15,000,000; a new park west of Ninth avenue, between Twentieth and Thirtieth streets; the Colonial park; damages for the change of grade in the Twenty-third and Twenty-fourth Wards, which may cost $2,000,000; St. Nicholas park, a park at One Hundred and Eleventh street and the East River, and one at Dykman street; the Harlem driveway and the rapid transit scheme of $50,000,000. Mr. Fitch said he had estimated that during the next five years the city is likely to be called upon to issue $61,794,000 up to and including the year 1900.

The income from the sinking fund averages about $8,500,000. This would make $42,500,000 in the five years leaving a net increase of estimated positive debt of $19,294,000 in 1900. Taking the increase of assessed valuation upon the basis of recent increases, Mr. Fitch said that on December 31, 1900, the real estate in this city would be rated at about $1,894,000,000.

"This would leave a margin for the increase of the debt at that time to the extent of $60,220,491," said Mr. Fitch; "but this is based upon estimates for the accuracy of which no man can vouch. The results may be very different. I am a great friend of the rapid transit scheme, but if its cost were to be much more than $50,000,000 I should be very much afraid it would get us into serious difficulties. I am much afraid of the consolidation scheme for the same reason, for Brooklyn has about reached the legal limit of her debt; her tax rate is 100 points higher than ours, and property there is taxed at eighty per cent. of its real value, while ours is only rated at fifty per cent."

4. All the outlying territory proposed to be annexed on this basis of "equal taxation and valuation" has both higher tax rates and higher valuations than those of New York city.

We challenge a denial that all the advocates of annexation in Brooklyn in their public utterances and publications have favored consolidation solely upon the sordid financial consideration that their taxes may be reduced at the expense of New York and that local improvements may be made and paid for from the same source; in other words, that the resources of this city shall be frittered away among overgrown villages and cities to pay for improvements which the law will not permit them to make at the expense of their own taxpayers.

5. New York city has within its present corporate limits ample accommodations for an increase of more than a million people. If rapid transit be accomplished, as without consolidation it can be, such increase will inure to the lessening of the taxation of New York. But this increase will of necessity be drawn largely from these outlying debt-burdened communities, and the advocates of equal taxation and valuation know this but too well.

Whether a city composed of such diverse communities, of widely distinct areas, is likely to insure economical and efficient government is certainly at least very doubtful. Certainly the local history of New York in the past gives us very little assurance that it can be. On the contrary every local improvement proposed would meet with little favor from districts not interested, and the result in all probability would be such as is witnessed in the national legislature every winter over the "river and harbor bill," i. e., a log-rolling combination certain to invite municipal corruption and scandals far exceeding the shameful annals of the most corrupt period of our local history.

The vote which was taken on consolidation is not an answer to any of the considerations against "equalization of valuation and taxation." It is certain that very few persons, either taxpayers or rentpayers in New York city, would have voted in favor of the proposition if such a condition had been annexed. If taxes are increased by consolidation, rents will necessarily be raised; if improvements are obstructed, values in New York will either remain stationary or decline. In either event, both taxpayers and rentpayers will suffer.

If either or both "equalization of valuation and taxation" is to be a condition of consolidation, those questions should be submitted to the taxpayers and rentpayers of New York. The submission of the naked question of consolidation gave no notice whatever to the electors of New York that their taxes would be increased or their property interests affected. To impose such a scheme as a prerequisite of consolidation is a grave political blunder, certain to react most disastrously on any party or individuals responsible for it.

CYRUS CLARK,
CORNELIUS DOREMUS,
R. H. L. TOWNSEND,
BENJAMIN F. ROMAINE,
AUGUSTUS A. LEVEY,
JAMES A. DEERING.

NEW YORK, *January* 29, 1896.

AUGUSTUS A. LEVEY:

Mr. Chairman and Gentlemen of the Committee: As counsel and individual and on behalf of the Anti-Equalization League, as counsel and as an individual taxpayer of New York, I propose to direct myself particularly against this provision, which makes it mandatory upon this commission to be appointed under this act, which, having been introduced by the chairman, may be called the Lexow bill. It provided "a government for the municipal corporation, the mayor, aldermen and commonalty of the city of New York, as by this act enlarged, and among other things for retaining an equal and uniform rate of taxation and of valuation for the purpose of taxation. That same expression is contained in the similar bill, which is before you, introduced, I think, by Mr. Gray, if I am not mistaken; and the same expression has been continuously used by the advocates of consolidation in the city of Brooklyn; and they explain, in their publications and circulars, just what they mean and what they intend to have carried into effect by your committee, under this expression, "Equal Taxation and Valuation." What they mean is, that there shall be a uniform assessment through this district, and that the percentage of valuation to the real values of the property shall be uniform all over the district; and that is what we particularly object to, as taxpayers of the city of Brooklyn, because, sir, the values in this district differ in every section of it. In Brooklyn, the assessed values are about eighty per cent. — from seventy to eighty per cent. on the real values. In the city of New York, they are about fifty per cent. Now, what these Brooklyn gentlemen propose and what we more specifically refer to in the pamphlet, which I shall lay before you, is that this equal taxation of values necessarily involves raising the valuations that the taxation of the city of Brooklyn may be reduced and we considered that, however valuable the political consolidation of these towns and municipalities may be, that it is possible to effect that consolidation at too high a price, and that this will be too high a price. We have shown you, sir, and it may be proved, and we propose to prove it, if you give us an opportunity to do so, by subpoenaing the witnesses here, which we have named in our application before you, and which motion, I understand, you are now entertaining. We propose to show this will increase the taxation of every taxpayer in the city of New York about twenty-nine dollars for each $10,000 of assessed valuation. Now, the effect of that must necessarily be to impair the value of all real estate in New York so taxed. It will necessarily involve an increase in the rents of the people who pay rents in the city of New York, for by increasing taxation, you increase rents. It affects the value of real estate. There is not a single taxpayer in the city of New York, with whom I have had an opportunity of conversing on this subject since this committee proposed to give us, on a two days' notice, — and, by the way, here the lowest motion in the city of New York is on a notice of eight days; and now you propose on a notice of two days to require us to answer —

MR. LEXOW:

That criticism has already been passed once.

MR. LEVEY:

I propose to pass it repeatedly here.

MR. LEXOW:

It was not taken notice of, for this reason: We first stated that we would give hearings in Brooklyn on two occasions, that the next week we would come to New York. During the three weeks that have intervened, with the exception of one telegram received by the chairman of this committee the day before yesterday, there has not been a single individual in the city of New York who has asked for a hearing here.

MR. LEVEY:

Well, sir, that is only more disgraceful to the inhabitants of the city of New York. They do not know whether their interest is impaired; and they have got so accustomed in the city of New York to be treated by the Legislature of the State of New York, as if the city of New York was a kind of province, as ancient Rome treated their provinces. They have got so accustomed —

MR. LEXOW:

Unless you restrain yourself within parliamentary limits, the committee will not hear you.

MR. LEVEY:

I am speaking in a parliamentary manner. I have not made any individual assertions whatever. The language, I suggest, I could use in any court room.

MR. LEXOW:

You can not use it before the legislative committee.

MR. LEVEY:

I propose to use it. It is not contempt of the legislative committee. I do say it is shameful that upon a notice of merely two days, with these enormous millions and millions of dollars interest in the city of New York, that you propose upon an ex parte application here in one city to dispose of these questions, which affect vitally the interests of every taxpayer and rentpayer in the city of New York. No, you can not do it. The Legislature of the State of New York can not do it. The Governor of the State of New

York is an honest man, and he, sir, brought you down here, and you know he will not permit this legislation to go through, without carefully considering all the suggestions that may be made by the taxpayers and rentpayers in the city of New York.

Mr. Lexow:

What do you mean by the statement that the Governor sent us down?

Mr. Levey:

I meant what I said. I mean that if it had not been for the Governor of the State of New York you would not be here now. I mean to say that he will not permit this legislation to go through without careful consideration.

Mr. Lexow:

I mean to say that the Governor of the State of New York made absolutely no suggestion, in reference to this matter at all, and I call on you again to restrain yourself, within the limits of the proprieties of argument, and not go outside of it

Mr. Levey:

I am doing that.

Mr. Lexow:

Unless you do so, your privileges will be taken from you.

Mr. Levey:

I am doing that, and when you get ready to take my privileges away from me, you can do so. If you think I have made individual aspersions on any individual member of this committee, I have not.

Mr. Lexow:

Address your argument to the chairman.

Mr. Levey:

I am addressing myself to your body.

MR. GRADY:

It is fair for the committee to state that the first information they had that there was on Manhattan Island one man who desired to appear before the committee, they immediately provided for a hearing; and the statement that they ever proposed to deny to anybody to give anything germain to the subject to a hearing is entirely gratuitous and against the action of the committee. We never heard, until it was announced that there was to be no hearings in New York, because no applications had been made for one — we never heard that there was a man who desired to be heard; and just as soon as there was the slightest evidence that we could come here and find any one to talk to us, the committee dealt with New York city, precisely as they dealt with other localities. Now, isn't this a shame that the committee do not provide for a number of extended hearings in New York, a shame that all these millions of dollars that wanted to speak and did not speak, so as to give the committee an opportunity to provide for their being heard.

MR. LEVEY:

I agree with you entirely, sir.

MR. GRADY:

I want to say, for my associates on the committee, those from New York city, and those from out New York city, that as soon as Mr. Austin, the chairman of the committee of the Assembly, suggested that there were people in New York, who were making some criticism upon the committee for not meeting in New York city, that was immediately provided for by this meeting, and they put no limit as they appointed the time to be occupied, the number of hearings to be had, or the number to whom they would listen. It is under those circumstances, and not only those that you appear before the committee.

MR. LEVEY:

Then I will say that this committee is attended by many taxpayers of the city of New York, and will be attended by many more before they get through; and this large assemblage is an intimation that if they have an opportunity to be heard they will appear before the committee in large numbers, but certainly, they have had their opportunity to appear before you. But now in regard to the question to which I addressed myself, particularly in the first instance. We have shown you, in reference to that pamphlet, that to equalize the tax rates and valuation in the city of New York will be detrimental to the taxpayers in the city of New York. What we propose is this, and there is no difficulty whatever in undertaking this, and this is what we desire to prove by the witness we shall ask your committee to subpoena: That the taxes and valuation in each of these districts shall remain under any political consolidation that you effect just as they are now; that the tax rates in the city of Brooklyn as they exist now shall be expended in the city of Brooklyn; that the taxes in the city af Long Island shall be expended in Long Island City; that the tax rates in the towns of Richmond county, as they exist now, shall be expended in those towns; that the taxes raised in the city of New York, as it exists now, shall be expended in the city of New York; that no alteration shall be made either in valuation or in taxes. There is no more practical difficulty in effecting that than there is in the present tax system in the city of Brooklyn, in which they have a different tax rate in every ward of Brooklyn. That is what we have directed ourselves towards, and that is a simple proposition for which we appear before you to-day, to see that the interest of the taxpayers of the city of New York are safeguarded; that the moneys received in the city of New York shall not be diverted to the improvement of Bensonhurst or Far Rockaway or towns in Richmond county.

Mr. Grady:

Mr. Levey, why not extend that. Let us provide that the money raised in each ward in the city of New York be applied in that ward?

MR. LEVEY:

No, sir, because the situation is an institution existing to-day. If you look in the city of Brooklyn, you will find that they have a tax for every ward. You can continue it.

MR. GRADY:

If you are going to subdivide as to the existing lines of division, why not make it entirely fair, why not have the money raised in New street, spent on Riverside drive; why not keep the appropriation within the ward?

MR. LEVEY:

You are making an absurd argument.

MR. GRADY:

I am not making an argument ad absurdum, unless the argument is absurd. You propose a division, which the bill proposes to obliterate. Why not keep up the old lines? You and I know, that New York has not always embraced the territory embraced to-day. Why was not the proposition made when we annexed Westchester county, that the money received in New York should be spent in New York, and the money received from West Farms should be spent in West Farms. Does the water make a difference?

MR. LEVEY:

As a practical matter, those twenty-third and twenty-fourth wards did just get about what they received in taxes.

MR. GRADY:

I know at one time they gave more money than they got in taxes, when they were annexed.

MR. LEXOW:

You do not propose uniform taxation throughout. You do not dispute that there is uniform taxation and valuation throughout the city of New York, including the taxes of the annexed district last year?

Mr. Levey:

I think there is, but I do not know anything to the contrary.

Mr. Jefferson Levy:

I addressed you as chairman last week, when I first heard you proposed to go ahead in the annexation of the Greater New York, without the city of New York being heard. I myself addressed you as chairman, and I believe you have called this meeting to-day at my request as one of the taxpayers of New York. I believe you desire to treat us fair, but the position to look at is this: I do not think we have a large attendance here to-day, and I would like to call your attention to the reason why you do not have them. Many people think you hold them in the County Court house; it is mixed up between two court houses, where the meeting is to be. Many do not think this is new Supreme Court house of the Supreme Court chambers, part one. I would like to state this: In 1892, there was 335,000 votes cast in the city of New York; there was 98,000 cast in favor of it and 68,000 against it; that made about 170,000 votes virtually that opposed this annexation. We New Yorkers, as a whole, I do not think, oppose annexation of the Greater New York; but they most decidedly oppose annexation on the ground of uniformity of taxation. This is a most stupendous affair. Mr. Green, himself, will tell you in the laws of 1894, this adjudication was that the Greater New York have annexation upon fair taxation. We are all proud of Brooklyn, with its million of inhabitants; the citizens of New York are proud of it, we are willing to receive it; but are willing to receive it upon fair and equitable ground. What right have you to put upon the city of New York the taxation of the city of Brooklyn, with its enormous debt, with no comparison — with the exception of taxation — in income. The city of New York has a vast sinking fund, as the comptroller can tell you, amounting to millions of dollars, receipts every year amounting to millions.

I will answer the Senator, Mr. O'Grady, from New York, when he says, "Why divide up?" Why, it is a common practice. In the great cities of Paris and London they have taxation there by districts and municipalities, you may say. It has mayors of different districts. Why shouldn't we tax it that way? Take, for instance, the city of Brooklyn. Why, to-day their bonded indebtedness outside of Kings county, from what statistics we have in our hands, amounts to over fifty millions; and I am sure the comptroller of that city can not say to-day positively what their indebtedness is. I verily believe it amounts to sixty millions. They have gone recently and bought enormous tracts of land. I myself, and the late mayor of the city, Mayor Ely, own some property in the city of Brooklyn. We could not sell it. The city of Brooklyn said: "We are going to take this as a highway." We laughed at them, and said: "What do you want of it; you can not pay for it." And they said: "We are going to buy it." We said: "You can take it at your valuation; we don't want you to condemn it." And when we came to pay the taxes and assessments they could not tell us what the assessment was in that particular district. They can not tell to-day when you put in a search there what the assessment is. I hold in my hands a piece of property which I own in the city of Brooklyn. You can not sell it to-day for the amount of its assessment, for under that bill the tax rate is some twenty-seven dollars a thousand. It runs up in some wards of the city to $101 a thousand. The city of Brooklyn can not go on as it is going on to-day. What will be the upshot of it? If we take in the city of Brooklyn I and every other property holder in the city of Brooklyn shall demand that the taxation values shall be fair. The law of the Supreme Court states the valuation of real estate is sixty-six per cent. of its real value. Here is a case where it is valued for as much, and in fact what you can not receive for it. That is the situation of affairs in Brooklyn. They have recently passed a law to build a bridge for $25,000,000. They are to pay half of it. Their limit is extended and does not amount to over $2,000,000. How are they to raise this indebtedness? It is to be raised in the city of New York. If you carry out this proposition the taxes in New York will be three dollars and fifty cents instead of about two dollars and ten cents the coming year. I hope the Legislature will only listen to the citizens of New York. You should look into it, because it is becoming very important — this enormous debt that is heaped upon us. We hear every year of legislative increase of salaries for court officers we do not need.

Mr. Lexow:

If that is true, why is it that in the two years that I have been a member of the Senate, with all these bills coming before us, there has not been a single property owner from the city of New York who has taken enough interest in the subject apparently to even send a letter or circular?

Mr. Levy:

I admit that, Mr. Chairman. That is the great people of New York. They will not take any interest in anything until it is thrust upon them. When it is thrust upon them they come like a whirlwind. Why, if this proposition goes through — outside of politics — throw politics aside and ignore it — if this proposition goes through, the party in power that carried the bill would be wiped from existence all over the Union; for whatever we do in New York, it affects the whole nation. That is the situation here. Now, I admit what you say is perfectly correct. The citizens of New York are very dilatory. Then there is another thing I want to call your attention to. There was an announcement here that you were going to give a hearing. That was the first I heard to any extent that uniform taxation would go into existence. Think of it! In some wards in Brooklyn it it $101 per thousand; and think of it, that the valuations are the full valuations of the property! They can not go on that way. It has got to stop. I do not blame the people of Brooklyn coming in and saying, "Give us uniform taxation and we will go in." Why, their taxes would be reduced. If you had a piece of property in New York worth $5,000 the fair valuation would be assessed for about $3,000 taxes. Now, that is the way the great uniformity of our taxes is here. If a piece of property is valued at $20,000 it is assessed here for probably $13,000, but in Brooklyn the full valuation is put on it. Now, there is nothing to prevent the Legislature from saying to the city of Brooklyn and each one of these great municipalities, "You can do as they do in Paris, make up your own tax budget." It could be taxed against their own property, and then we can go on and be the Greater New York. Now, they have no docks in the city of Brooklyn; they have no large receipts. While I believe you have a right in the Legislature to pass any laws for annexation purposes, I do not believe if any bond holder in New York comes in and restrains you in the courts that you could succeed with this policy, because the sinking fund of New York is pledged for the security of these bonds. Now, you must go into another thing, and I would like to call your attention to it here, that to some extent in the future you would consider these enormous expenditures as to New York, the increased taxation, the increase of the tax-list, the amount of money collected for taxes. The amount of money going into bonded indebtedness in the city of New York since 1894 amounts to over $19,000,000; and if we keep on in New York I do not know where we will land. Now, the pamphlet here of Mr. Deering shows very plainly —

MR. LEXOW:

This is the pamphlet you refer to?

MR. LEVY:

Yes.

MR. LEXOW:

Sent out by a committee of six, I think.

MR. ROMAINE:

Yes. I think if you allow me, the committee should have the pamphlet of 1894, which was sent by Mr. Deering.

Mr. Lexow:

I was just going to ask for that. Now, is it not a fact that this question was before the people when they voted in 1894, upon the question of consolidation?

Mr. Romaine:

No, sir.

Mr. Levy:

No, sir. The statement was made that that business would be settled afterwards, that New York would be treated fair; that the taxable properties of each district would pay their own. Now, that is not a foreign thing in our ideas; it is not an improper thing to be done. The city of Brooklyn can raise its own budget. as Paris does it. The city of London does the same thing. Why shall we not have it here. Here is this enormous sinking fund of ours. Why shall we give it to the city of Brooklyn? The next other important thing I would like to call the Senator's attention to, is one thing referred to by the Senator from New York. He stated that in the twenty-third and twenty-fourth wards more money was expended in those districts than they ever received from taxation. I desire to say that he is incorrect in that statement.

Mr. Grady:

You do not give my statement as I made it. I say, immediately after the consolidation of New York with what is known as the annexed district the expenses of the city government were far in excess of any money received from that district.

Mr. Levy:

I disagree with you, Senator. I was a property owner at that time in 1871, and for several years the city of New York did not expend the money they collected there for taxes. In fact the district lay dormant, and no money was expended there. We have now an extraordinary state of affairs in the new districts of

Westchester county. This year no tax is paid in those districts at all to the city of New York, by reason of lax legislation of last year and the year before in regard to those annexed districts. Those districts pay no taxes at all. That is the most extraordinary state of affairs. But in these districts of the twenty-third and twenty-fourth wards for many years the property was, in fact, very low before annexation. People thought it was going to go up. It went immediately down. Of course there might have been a panic, or some other reason; but for four or five years they did not expend any money for improvements in those districts; and I am quite confident the moneys raised there were more in excess than the amount expended in those districts.

MR. LEXOW:

Mr. Levy, I would like to ask you a question. I believe you are posted in real estate values in the city of New York as well, perhaps, as any man living. Don't you think the material welfare of New York would be subserved so largely by consolidation that a small difference of taxation possibly the first year, would be very much more than equalized by the additional value gained here by the effects of consolidation within a year or two?

MR. LEVY:

I verily believe it will really hurt the city of New York, although I am individually in favor of annexation on the ground that each district pay their own taxes; but I tell you for several years it will not benefit New York. We have a vast territory here that we ought to improve. We do not expend the money. These new wards have no taxes this year. We spend very little in improvements even to the present day compared to what they are entitled to. They need a great deal more to be expended there, that is, the districts in Westchester which may be hurt materially. We ought to include the roads and highways there. They are in bad condition; and the city of Brooklyn will absorb all this, and take it away from the real interest of New York. While New York feels a feality towards the city of Brooklyn, I think a great deal more than other people feel towards us, at the same time we want Brooklyn to make us a greater New York, provided our taxes and our sinking fund are not affected. This will put our taxes up. It can not put it up less than three per cent. unless we issue bonds.

Mr. Lexow:

I have a letter from the president of the Emigrants' Industrial Savings Bank, Mr. James McMahon, and in his letter he says: "I regret that I can not appear before your committee to give my views upon subject matters of consodidation. I do not flatter myself that I could add anything to the information already possessed by your committee, for it seems to me that the ground has been gone over very thoroughly; at the same time I think the testimony of representative citizens — those who are in a position to feel the pulse of the people — should put themselves upon record for, or against legislation deciding this question, although it would seem unnecessary for citizens to give their views, when the people as a whole have already manifested their decisions by ballot.

"I am an old New York merchant, and have lived in Brooklyn thirty-five years, and believe the sentiment favoring consolidation of these two cities is very general in both cities. With few exceptions, I find that the opposition to it springs from interested motives; especially is this the case in Brooklyn, where the press are a unit in opposition to the movement. I heartily favor consolidation, because I believe it will be of the greatest possible good to both cities, and for very different reasons respecting each — Brooklyn needs a helping hand to enable her to accomplish her destiny successfully. New York needs a population and the area which she would acquire by having Brooklyn annexed, to forever secure to her the prestige of being the great city, and the commercial and moneyed heart of this continent. No matter at what cost — Brooklyn would be for New York a most desirable acquisition.

"But would New York suffer any material loss in this connection.

I claim it would not, because the very act of consolidation would tend to strengthen and increase values in Brooklyn to such an extent that in the near future, Brooklyn upon her merits, would be self-sustaining, and New York would be a great gainer, because the two cities could work in unison in so many directions for their mutual benefit.

"I could say a great deal upon this subject, having given it my careful study and attention for many years, but from what I have read in the papers of matter given to your committee, it seems to me I would be only wasting your time by giving you matter of which you are already in possession."

MR. LEVY:

That is very well for Mr. McMahon, who resides in the city of Brooklyn, to write such a letter. He is in favor of Brooklyn, of course. I am informed he resides in the city of Brooklyn.

MR. LEXOW:

He is president of one of the largest banks in this city.

MR. LEVY:

He is president of the Emigrants' Industrial Savings Bank, but he resides in Brooklyn, and Brooklyn must have some relief. It is impossible for Brooklyn to go on as they do. They must raise the tax. They can not tell from their own statements or accounts there what their indebtedness is. It is a most extraordinary statement. If you go over there to-day you can not ascertain the exact amount of assessment in some of those districts, and they do not know the exact amount of their bonded indebtedness. Now here comes the bridge which will cost $12,500,000. They have gone out of the way and made a bill to build a railroad on a bridge which was intended for the public benefit. Why? Simply because the elevated railroad in Brooklyn can not pay without this bridge. They have got about fifty millions of dollars of debt now, and with the buying of these parks there must be sixty or sixty-five millions of dollars; but the property is assesed so high as to valuation that when we come to the great city of New York, and when we find a piece of property here is only assessed at sixty per cent. of the value they will insist that their property shall be reduced in that same way, and we shall have our taxes increased; so, putting the facts together as to tax rates, which I am informed will be about $2.20 in the city of New York next year, with an increased valuation over what we have already had and it will make the tax $2.50.

MR. LYNCH:

I think Mr. Levy has made a very bad mistake. I understand the taxes in Brooklyn will be $3.50.

MR. LEVY:

No; I say in the consolidated district. It would be less in the consolidated district than in Brooklyn.

MR. LEXOW:

It would be upwards of $3.50 according to your remarks.

MR. LEVY:

No; in the city of New York it will be two dollars and twenty cents.

MR. LEXOW:

What will it be in Brooklyn?

MR. LEVY:

Where it is now. In some cases it ran from two dollars and seventy-nine cents to three dollars and one cent. Here is your own bill.

MR. ROMAINE:

Now we read there are thirty-one wards in Brooklyn; twenty-eight of them are the main part of Brooklyn, the other four are only country towns that have been added. In none of the twenty-eight wards can you find where the rate runs as high as three per cent.

MR. LEVY:

I stated they ran from two dollars and seventy-nine cents to three dollars and one cent.

MR. ROMAINE:

I want to state the fact.

MR. LEXOW:

I think Mr. Levy wants to be fair. I think he is a fair man.

MR. ROMAINE:

The fact is that a great bulk of the property is in the twenty-eight wards. The other four wards are very small and are known as the Kings county wards, added by annexation in the last four years. The assessment is by special assessment. Here is a sample of the taxes in Brooklyn for 1895:

DEPARTMENT OF COLLECTION,
MUNICIPAL BUILDING.
Collector of Taxes and Assessments.

To City of Brooklyn, Dr.

Tax, 1895. Confirmed November 15, 1895. Due and payable December 15, 1895.

R. ROSS APPLETON,
Collector.

HICKS. EAST SIDE.

WARD.	Tax roll index.	Block.	Lot.	Street number.	Des.	Val.	Tax.
First ward........	633	41	2	23	H. & L.	$5,00	$13,979

Received payment,

....

Collector of Taxes and Assessments.

The following is on the back of this bill:

RATE OF TAX, 1895, PER $1,000.

WARDS.		Dollars.	Cents.	Mills.
1		27	95	8
2		28	01	1
3		27	98	6
4		27	96	9
5		28	10	7
6		27	98	5
7		27	97	0
8		27	98	9
9		27	97	4
10		28	00	8
11		28	00	0
12		28	00	5
13		26	15	1
14		26	18	9
15		26	22	8
16		26	17	9
17		26	15	1
18		26	23	1
19		26	14	6
20		27	97	7
21		27	97	8
22		27	96	1
23		27	95	5
24		28	00	1
25		27	98	0
26		28	45	4
27		26	18	1
28		26	14	3
	School districts Nos. 1 and 2	31	24	9
	School district No. 3	31	89	7
29	School district No. 2 of Flatlands	31	24	9
	School district No. 1, in sewer district	35	22	4
	School district No. 1, outside	30	31	0
	School district No. 2, exempt	30	15	1
30	School district No. 2, outside	30	32	8
	School district No. 3, exempt	30	44	2
	School district No. 3, outside	30	61	9
	School district No. 4	29	60	7
	School district No. 2 of Flatbush	29	60	7
	School district No. 1, outside	27	46	2
	School district No. 2, in sewer district	101	61	9
31	School district No. 2, outside	27	46	2
	School district No. 2, sewer only	74	15	7
	School district No. 3	29	87	3
	School district No. 4, in sewer district	101	61	8
	School district No. 4, outside	27	46	2
	School district No. 5	27	46	2
	School district No. 6, in sewer district	89	63	9
	School district No. 6, outside	31	23	5
	School district No. 6, sewer only	58	40	5

WILLIAM E. RODGERS:

I appear, Mr. Chairman, as representing some considerable real estate in this city belonging to others, and also to myself. I did not intend to say anything; but it seems to me that in consequence of the question of Senator O'Grady, perhaps a word may clear up what seems to be a misunderstanding. The point of the thing in a nutshell, so far as I see it, is that, whereas in the city of Brooklyn — we will take the year 1894 — the rate of taxation, as shown by the documents submitted to you to-day, average about two dollars and sixty-three cents on a hundred dollars, upon a valuation averaging about seventy per cent. of the cash valuation; whereas, in New York, at the same time, the rate of taxation was one dollar and ninety cents on an assessed value of fifty per cent. on cash valuations. Well, it is perfectly evident that if these two cities come together and taxation is equalized over the whole area, that New York must be raised or Brooklyn must be lowered. Now, the documents submitted to you to-day, in reference to which there is an application to have witnesses called to substantiate under oath, show, that in case of this consolidation, and in case of this equalization of the taxation, the result will be that New York will have to pay $6,000,000 more upon an expenditure equal to that of 1894, and Brooklyn will have to be permitted to pay $6,000,000 less. That is where the injustice comes in to the taxpayers of New York.

MR. GRADY:

There is no misunderstanding on that point, Mr. Rogers.

MR. ROGERS:

Now, let us get to the motive. The Brooklyn Consolidated League frankly state as the reason for consolidation that the rate of taxation will be lowered in Brooklyn and will be raised in New York. I congratulate them upon their frankness; but I confess that is rather a strange way to bring about New York's consent.

MR. GRADY:

The suggestion is that with that very evident proposition in view New York voted for consolidation; and that this inequality and apparent injustice to the city of New York, at the moment and time of consolidation, will be remedied and will be atoned for by the future increase in values in Brooklyn, which will make it a more than self-supporting city. The difference in income and outlay under consolidation is much more marked when you take in Staten Island than when you take in Brooklyn; and yet the people voted at the election that they would consolidate, not only with Brooklyn, but would even consolidate with Staten Island.

MR. ROGERS:

It is true, Mr. Senator, that in the referendum of 1894 they did so vote; but it was simply a sentimental vote; and I think almost everybody is agreed that the reference of the question of an economical character, somewhat complicated in its form, to universal suffrage, is not a success. The conclusion derived therefrom is not one that carries a great deal of weight. I do not think the average man in New York who does not pay taxes appreciates that the increased taxation is a detriment to him. The so-called "poor man" who does not draw his check or come to the taxpayer's office and pay his money, does not appreciate that an economic law decreases his taxes to be paid. Higher taxes mean higher rents. Higher rents means higher prices paid for everything the poor man eats or wears. The poor woman who gets her peck of potatoes or scuttle of coal at the grocery has to pay to the grocer the pro rata of the taxation in order to pay his rent. They do not appreciate that.

MR. LEXOW:

Is not that equalized by the fact that consolidation will add to the population and will increase the taxable area.

MR. ROGERS:

I fail to see how consolidation with a territory separated by such natural boundaries as Staten Island, and Brooklyn, and

Long Island have — I fail to see how consolidation can have much effect upon population one way or the other. I have read the arguments that have been set forth. The only one that I have seen other than the selfish one of saddling on New York the taxes, has been a purely sentimental one: Because we live in the greatest country in the world we ought to have the biggest city in the world. The next we will hear will be the obligation to take in additional territory in New York, including perhaps Hoboken and Newark, and we won't be the biggest city unless we take in up to the classic shades of Nyack.

MR. LEXOW:

I believe we are agreed as to consolidation up there.

MR. ROGERS:

Then, so far as this referendum is concerned, remember Mr. Senator, that there was not a word said in the law authorizing it, or in the ballots when the vote was taken, as to the terms upon which consolidation should take place. It was a mere expression of opinion. It was not mandatory; and it was merely an expression of opinion, and in my opinion a very false one. Then, in regard to people representing property in New York not appearing before your committee. It is perfectly true. I was in Albany nine years, and I constantly saw economic questions involving the taxation of New York in regard to which nobody ever came, unless the corporations were interested in it, until it was too late to come. I do not think it is fair. I know it is not fair to assume that the majority of the people are in favor of consolidation in New York in consequence of that vote in 1894.

MR. LEXOW:

Mr. Rogers, you were aware, were you not, that this same bill in words as this, verbatim ad literatum, so far as its principles are concerned, was in the Assembly, and passed by the Assembly, and failed in the Senate, by not securing the constitutional majority necessary to make it a law. In other words, that this question that has now suddenly been objected to has been before the Legislature practically two years, and that no objection has been made until within one week.

Mr. Rogers:

I saw, sir, that it was there, and I plead guilty with the rest of the million of inhabitants of New York to neglect and laches in not appearing before.

Mr. Romaine:

I will say for myself and associates, with the possible exception of Mr. Deering, who is so busy that he is not able to be here, that we were not aware of that bill.

Mr. Lexow:

The debates in the Assembly and Senate turned very largely on that expression.

Mr. Romaine:

It seems very strange, because I have had the honor to appear in Albany every year in behalf of the New York Tax Association, that I had not heard of it. It seems to me, if you will pardon the allusion, that the political confusion of last year probably obscured the horizon of the New York taxpayer, and therefore it was not noticed in the Legislature, for which the chairman of this committee was responsible, and the other legislators of last year. I think you will find New Yorkers are slow to take up economic questions. Some of you gentlemen may remember the avalanche of opposition to the Speedway, and the measures taken to secure the Speedway repeal; and you may also remember — I make now no criticism on any present member of the Legislature, because I think none of them are responsible for it — there was an aqueduct measure introduced in the year 1891, that sought to deprive the city of New York of the benefit of trial by jury in the immense claims for extra work made by the aqueduct contractors. The gentlemen at Albany, in their wisdom that year, in their first hearing, gave three-quarters of an hour to the counsel for the aqueduct contractors, and then told two of the aqueduct commissioners and the assistant corporation counsel that the city of New York would have five minutes. Now, this committee, I know, will do nothing of that kind with the New York taxpayers. Now, sir, what has been said by us is simply introductory to a formal application which we have the honor to make to your committee, and it is seconded by a former member of the Legislature, Mr. Alfred R. Conkling, setting forth that we have had practically but two days' notice that the committee intended to sit here. Shall I read it, Mr. Chairman?

MR. LEXOW:

An application by whom?

MR. ROMAINE:

It is a formal application by a committee of taxpayers and their counsel. I think it had better be read to you. It is entitled in this proceeding.

27 EAST TENTH STREET, NEW YORK, *February* 1, 1896.

HON. CLARENCE LEXOW, *Chairman, etc.:*

Dear Sir.— I am confined to my house by a severe cold, so I can not attend your hearing to-day. I fully concur in the statements contained in the pamphlet of the Anti-Equalization League, signed by Mr. Cyrus Clark and others, and I think they are entitled to an adjournment of at least one week to present their case and to produce the attendance of witnesses. As a freeholder and trustee of property of great value I respectfully request a hearing against the proposed tax equalization involved in the consolidation of the two cities.

Yours respectfully,

A. R. CONKLING.

ANNEXATION AND TAXATION.

At a special meeting of the West End Association, held on

Monday evening, October 22, 1894, at its rooms, No. 167 West Eighty-first street, New York city, it was ordered that the communication of Mr. James A. Deering and the remarks of Mr. Cornelius Doremus, relative to the proposed "Greater New York," be printed and circulated.

CYRUS CLARK,
President.

MR. CYRUS CLARK, *President of the West End Association:*

Dear Sir.— I regret exceedingly my inability to attend the special meeting of the association called for this evening, to consider the "Greater New York" and "Rapid Transit" propositions, which are to be submitted to the taxpayers and citizens of New York city, for their approval or disapproval, at the approaching election. I therefore take this means of presenting to the association, through you, some of the reasons which in my judgment should induce every citizen of New York to vote against, and use his utmost endeavors to defeat the proposed consolidation or the annexation of 279 square miles of additional territory to be known as "The Greater New York."

Why is it that the promoters and advocates of "The Greater New York" have never informed us, but on the contrary have studiously avoided giving any information as to what the effect of annexation will be upon the taxation and indebtedness of this city and the several municipalities to be annexed?

Does the proposition to annex Brooklyn and the outlying towns and villages mean anything more than to compel the taxpayers of the present city of New York to contribute largely to the annual support of the government of these localities, and provide the means for their development and permanent improvement? If this be so, and no other conclusion is possible, after investigating the history of the movement and the financial standing of the several localities favoring the proposition, consolidation will be the greatest check to the improvement and growth of New York city that it is possible to conceive of. Not only will the annual taxes for the ordinary purposes of government be at once increased fully $6,000,000 per year, and the rate to more than two per cent. but the margin it now holds within the constitutional limitation for the creation of a funded debt to meet the cost of permanent improvements, which are not paid for by yearly taxation, be applicable to (as it certainly will be devoted to) meeting the cost of public works and improvements in these outlying districts, which their present indebtedness forbids them to incur.

The scheme is permanent to say the least. No possible present or future advantages can outweigh the immediate and permanent loss which New York will sustain.

For a better understanding of the situation it may be well to state the procedure for raising public moneys by taxation and otherwise.

The ordinary expenses of government in each locality are paid by annual taxation. These ordinary expenses are such as its share of State taxation, the interest on its own funded debt, the salaries of police, fire, school, and health officers, etc., and the annual supplies for all departments.

But for permanent improvements, such as furnishing a supply of pure water, public parks, boulevards, water front extensions, etc., the money is raised by the issue of bonds or stocks payable at some future time, usually after twenty years, the annual interest by taxation, and the principal, either from a sinking fund raised by annual taxation or by the issue of other bonds.

There is another class of improvements the cost of which is payable in whole or in part from the proceeds of bonds, namely, ordinary street improvements; but these bonds are usually issued for a short time and redeemable from the special assessments levied upon property immediately benefited, but until so repaid they constitute part of the funded debt.

The Constitution (article VIII, section 11.) places a limit upon the debt which may be thus created, as follows:

"No county containing a city of over 100,000 inhabitants, or any such city, shall be allowed to become indebted for any purpose or in any manner to an amount which, including existing indebtedness, shall exceed ten per centum of the assessed valuation of the real estate of such county or city on the last assessment for State or county taxes prior to the incurring of such indebtedness."

But the practice of New York city and Brooklyn in respect to the creation of an indebtedness in the last two classes has been widely different. In New York, bonds and stocks have rarely been issued otherwise than for improvements of a permanent character, and of benefit to the entire city, such as its water supply, its parks, water front improvements, etc. For the new parks and the new aqueduct since 1887, bonds to the extent of $28,000,000 have been issued. But in Brooklyn, the city at large has, in many cases, assumed the cost, or a great part of the cost, of street improvements of an ordinary character and of value only to the property adjacent thereto and specially benefited thereby. Hence we find that the net funded debt of New York on September 30, 1894, was but $103,888,589.48 against an assessed real estate valuation of $1,613,057,735, leaving a margin under the constitutional limitation of $57,417,184.02, while the net funded debt of Brooklyn on October 1, 1894, was $49,164,000, against an assessed real estate valuation of $500,752,349, leaving a margin of only $911,234, and if the valuation of Flatbush, New Utrecht and Gravesend, which were annexed in 1894, be added, a total valuation of $525,762,827, the margin is but $3,412,282. From the latter, however, should be deducted the outstanding bonded indebtedness of these new districts, the amount of which I have not been able to ascertain on inquiry at the comptroller's office in Brooklyn.

It may be well also to bear in mind Brooklyn's financial standing prior to the recent annexation of these outlying towns. In 1892 its real estate valuation was $467,112,182, and its net funded debt $46,513,111.95, leaving a margin of but $198,106.25, and in 1893 the valuation was $486,531,506, and its net funded debt $48,034,214.45, leaving a margin of $618,936. By the annexation of these towns it has increased its valuation so that it has now apparently a margin of over $3,000,000. Evidently this annexation of 1894 has secured to it a substantial ability it did not before possess to incur further expenditure. Does it propose to annex to New York for the same reason?

To meet or provide for the payment of their respective funded debts when they shall fall due, New York has a sinking fund of $68,990,795.25, while Brooklyn's sinking fund is but $5,398,521.94. New York's sinking fund, with its rapid accumulations will fully and promptly meet every dollar of its present liability, but could not possibly, with the slight increase it would receive upon annexation, meet the combined obligations of both cities. That this would injuriously affect the value of our securities in the hands of all present holders is equally clear.

While it appears, therefore, that the present New York city has sufficient power, *but not more than sufficient,* to meet the obligations which may be incurred, possibly within a short time, for much needed permanent improvements, such as a municipal rapid transit system, the completion of the "New Aqueduct," which will require new reservoirs and supply systems in the upper part of the city, and in the twenty-third and twenty-fourth wards, the laying out and improvement of these wards, as recently planned, new docks and piers on the North and East rivers; the small parks laid out within the last few years, and others much needed in the lower part of the city, as the committee of seventy has pointed out, Brooklyn has neither the power nor desire to incur, on its own credit, such expenditures for similar improvements within its own limits, much needed as they may be.

To the owners of property and residents of the west side of the city, the results of annexation would be especially disastrous. For more than ten years we have been agitating and urging additional rapid transit facilities, and these, it is now conceded, can only be obtained by municipal aid, by extending thereto the city's credit, the acquisition of the water front adjacent to Riverside park, and the completion of the park itself. From year to year these admittedly urgent improvements have been postponed mainly for the reason, or upon the pretense, that the expenditure involved would unduly increase the city debt. It is safe to say that should the proposed annexation be carried, the immediate demands upon the public credit by Brooklyn, and of the 297 square miles of annexed territory, would postpone indefinitely the possibility of the realization of these to us most important and necessary undertakings.

The question, therefore, upon which the people of New York city are to pass at the coming election is not only whether they will assume annually a very substantial part of the ordinary expenses of these outlying cities and towns, but whether they will surrender their ability to incur an indebtedness for permanent improvements which are only needed at the present time but demanded by the progress of the city. And that they are asked to surrender this and assume the cost of improvements outside of it, in which they are in no way interested, is very apparent from the legislation of last winter, and the recent public utterances of the advocates of annexation. See chapter 758, providing for a park and parkway in Brooklyn, apparently a water front boulevard to Coney Island, to be paid for by the issue of city bonds.

In the address issued by the Municipal Consolidation Commission it is said: "Consolidation means no more than the formation of a partnership between an established and prosperous firm and the younger members of the family." The present area of New York city is 38.85 square miles. The proposed "Greater New York" will contain 317.77 square miles. The "established and prosperous" 38, whose resources are scarcely sufficient for their own immediate wants, are called upon to at once assume all the obligations and assist and establish the younger and additional 279 "members of the family," who have no resources whatever.

At the public meeting held at the City Hall, Mr. Green, among other things, said, referring to the necessity of building a great drain along the valley of the Bronx river from Westchester County: "New York has no authority to enter upon the Westchester side even to make surveys. Much less have the towns of the Westchester side the willingness to contribute their share of the expense of this great main drain so essential to the development of both sides."

A comparison of the most recent financial statements of New York city and Brooklyn (I have been unable to obtain within the brief time allowed, any information from the other smaller cities, towns and villages), will sufficiently illustrate the result upon future taxation in, and the ability of, the "Greater New York" to institute and carry out public improvements payable by the issue of bonds and stocks.

First. Comparative ability of New York city and Brooklyn to incur indebtedness for public improvements within the constitutional limitations.

NEW YORK CITY.

City debt September 30, 1894	$172,879,384 73
Less sinking fund	68,990,795 25
Net funded debt	$103,888,589 48
Total valuation of real estate	$1,613,057,735 00
Constitutional limit of indebtedness	161,305,773 50
Excess of constitutional limitation over indebtedness	57,417,184 02

BROOKLYN.

City debt as represented in bonds and stocks on October 1, 1894	$54,562,521 94
Less amount held in sinking fund	5,398,521 94
Net city debt October 1, 1894	$49,164,000 00
Total valuation of real estate, including Flatbush, New Utrecht and Gravesend, annexed in 1894	$525,762,827 00
Constitutional limitation, ten per cent	52,576,282 70
Excess of constitutional limitation over debt	3,412,282 70

From this should be deducted the indebtedness of three annexed towns.

Second. Annual taxation as affected by the annexation of Brooklyn.

NEW YORK — TAXATION FOR 1894.

The assessed valuation (real and personal) of New York city for 1894 is	$2,003,332,037 00
Total taxes for 1894	35,659,026 78

Or equal to rate of $1.779 per $100. But owing to the difference in rate of taxation of personal estate of corporations, joint-stock companies, upon personal estate and real estate, the rate is: Upon personal estate of corporation, $1.58 per $100; upon real and personal estate generally, $1.79 per $100.

BROOKLYN — TAXATION FOR 1894.

The assessed valuation for Brooklyn for 1894 is,	$506,054,676 00
Total taxes for 1894	14,466,271 90

Rate of taxation, $2.86 per $100. As taxes are assessed in Brooklyn by wards, at different rates, the rate runs from $2.71 for the nineteenth ward to $2.91 for the tenth ward.

NEW YORK AND BROOKLYN ANNEXED.

If Brooklyn should be annexed to New York the result would be:

Valuation New York city	$2,003,332,037 00
Valuation Brooklyn	506,054,676 00
Total valuation	$2,509,366,713 00
Taxation New York city	$35,658,026 78
Taxation Brooklyn	14,468,271 90
Total	$50,127,298 58
Or equal to rate of $1.997 per $100, of which New York city's proportion would be $2,003,332,037 at $1.997	$40,018,360 24
Of which Brooklyn's proportion would be $506,054,676, at $1.997	10,108,897 60
Or New York city's taxes increased by	4,359,334 36
Brooklyn's taxes reduced by	4,359,374 30

Third. A further increase of New York taxation to equalize salaries.

The principal items of annual expenditure in both cities, exclusive of State taxes and interest on the city debt, and for the redemption of the city debt, are:

	New York.	Brooklyn.	Total.
Police department. .	$5,139,147 64	$2,027,650 00	$7,166,797 64
Fire department. . .	2,240,397 00	1,259,030 00	3,499,427 00
Board of education,	4,634,137 27	2,331,924 00	6,966,061 27
Total.			$17,632,285 90

Of these amounts there was expended for salaries:

	New York.	Brooklyn.	Total.
Police department. .	$4,506,570 00	$1,916,000 00	$6,425,570 00
Fire department. . .	1,467,280 00	710,900 00	2,178,180 00
Board of education,	3,684,470 00	1,772,268 00	5,456,738 00
Total.			$14,060,488 00

Upon annexation the equalization of salaries (raising the same to those now paid in New York city) would result, taking the average of the salaries now paid in each department, as follows:

Police department, 5,368 officers and employes, at $1,232.47.	$6,115,898 96
Fire department, 1,679 officers and employes, at $1,376.20.	2,310,639 80
Board of education, 7,812 officers and employes, at $771.13.	6,024,067 96
Total.	$14,950,406 72
Making increase of taxation to equalize salaries in those departments.	$889,918 72
To this may be added for similar increase to equalize salaries and wages in all other departments.	500,000 00

To which also add additional amount required to equalize salaries of policemen under chapter 741, Laws of 1894, increasing salaries of patrolmen and roundsmen.................	$1,143,750 00
Making a total increase of taxation to equalize salaries and wages.................	$2,533,668 72
This added to present amount raised by taxation,	50,127,298 68
Making total taxation..................	$52,660,967 40
Making rate of taxation, $2.098.	
New York city's share in proportion to valuation,	$42,128.774 32
Present taxation of New York city...........	35,659,026 78
Increase in annual taxation of New York city,	$6,469,747 54

If New York desires to extend its limits at all, such extensions should be to the northward and take in the towns and villages close to its present northerly boundary, and extending to Long Island Sound. The Sound and the East river are at present the natural boundaries of all our important city interests. Even this at present time would be premature, and may be well laid aside until we have secured municipal rapid transit and additional school accommodations, the completion of our public parks, large and small, and of the new aqueduct, its reservoirs and system of distribution, the laying out and improvement of the twenty-third and twenty-fourth wards, and the renovation of our pavements and sewerage system. Providing for these, even with the utmost economy, will exhaust our ability under the Constitution, and increase the burthen of annual taxation.

Very respectfully yours,

JAMES A. DEERING.

NEW YORK, *October* 22, 1894.

MR. DOREMUS:

Mr. President and Gentlemen: By the last Legislature an act was passed intended to elicit at the election to be held on November 6th next, an expression of opinion by the inhabitants of the counties of New York, Kings, Queens and Richmond on the question of annexing to the present city of New York the territory contained within the three counties last named.

While the opinion thus expressed by the inhabitants of the proposed "Greater New York" will accomplish nothing practically, it will surely lead, if the majority of votes be in the affirmative, to an act of consolidation by a subsequent Legislature, which act will most likely not be submitted to the people for ratification or rejection.

With Chicago pressing New York so closely in the number of her population it is natural, perhaps, to desire that our boundaries be extended to take in as much territory as Chicago to-day does, and thereby show a population double that of the latter city.

It is, however, very necessary that voters inform themselves thoroughly as to what is involved by the proposed annexation.

The question of taking Brooklyn into our municipal limits is the main factor and a matter of most serious import.

The debt of New York city is about $100,000,000 on an assessed valuation of $2,000,000,000, or 5 per cent. The debt of Brooklyn is about $50,000,000 on an assessed valuation of $500,000,000, or 10 per cent.

This comparison, however, does not by any means show the relative situation financially of the two cities, because while New York real estate is not assessed for purposes of taxation at more than one-half its value, in Brooklyn it is assessed for fully three-fourths, and I frequently find instances where the assessment for purposes of taxation is greater than the value of the property.

Take the following instance of Brooklyn assessments for the purpose of taxation.

	Value of property.	Assessed at
1.	$14,000	$11,000
2.	7,000	5,700
3.	9,000	6,500
4.	9,000	6,500
5.	27,500	25,000
6.	11,400	8,400
7.	9,000	7,000
8.	8,000	5,800
9.	13,000	12,300
10.	7,000	7,500
	$114,900	$95,700

Showing total value of these ten properties to be $114,900, while they are assessed for purposes of taxation by the city of Brooklyn, $95,700.

On these excessive valuations for purposes of taxation, the rate in Brooklyn is almost three per cent. per annum, while in New York, on a much lower assessment, it is considerably under two per cent.

No public improvement, such as our new bridges, viaduct, speedway, thousands of acres of parks, can be made in Brooklyn, because she is in debt to-day up to the constitutional limit, and every dollar extorted from taxpayers on the scale shown above is either used in payment of interest on the existing debt or absorbed by the ring by which she is governed.

A couple of years ago, after years of effort in that direction, the Brooklyn Congressmen got an act passed selling to the city part of the navy yard land for market purposes, at a price of $1,000,000. The transaction could not be carried out, because the city had no money to pay for the land, and the Constitution of the State properly debarred her from incurring further indebtedness, so that Mayor Boody made an arrangement with the then Secretary of the Treasury to give a year or more of time for the payment.

Whereby by still further increasing their already enormous tax valuations it was made possible to issue bonds and pay for this land from the proceeds of them, or whether the land be not paid for yet to-day I do not know.

It is no wonder that, in Brooklyn, a most active consolidation league has been formed, with branches in every ward, to further this scheme to foist a city practically bankrupt into partnership on equal terms with the prosperous metropolis.

It is a matter of easy calculation to ascertain to what an enormous extent the annual taxes on New York city realty will be increased, as things stand to-day, if this scheme of consolidation be consummated.

And when we consider that Brooklyn, in everything that pertains to the making of a city, has been starved for generations; that half of her streets to-day are paved with cobble stones and boulders, many of them the size of a flour barrel; that her water supply is entirely inadequate to her population; that Prospect park is the only park worth mentioning within her borders, and that in almost every respect she is lacking in everything which goes to make a large city attractive, we can faintly imagine what a scramble there would be on the part of her population immediately after her annexation to New York to have all these things supplied to her at the expense of the New York city of to-day.

It behooves every one who has the interest and further progress of New York city at heart, not only to vote against consolidation, but to see that all whom he can influence, and who may not be aware of the evil effects of consolidation, do the same.

MR. ROMAINE:

In explanation, Mr. Chairman, of the last clause, I will say that I do not now personally represent any one from the twenty-third or twenty-fourth wards, although Mr. Levey has appeared here as the individual representative of his own interest, and ex-Mayor Ely's interest, and they have several associations up there which now desire to have a full hearing on this subject, because they are convinced that it means the practical cessation of the appropriations for that district if we have any so-called equalization of taxes and valuation.

Mr. Lexow:

It means more, does it not? It means those upper wards of New York city are opposed to consolidation as a principle; that their representation in the Senate last year are opposed to consolidation.

Mr. Romaine:

It may be, sir.

Mr. Lexow:

It means that the consolidation will redound to the benefit of Brooklyn, and take from them the natural increment of the population they will get if Brooklyn is not annexed or consolidated with New York.

Mr. Romaine:

That I understand is their view, but they are in the habit of being heard very distinctly when they are given an opportunity. It is a long distance from here to the Harlem river, and I know one of their counsel could not get here to-day, as he is out of town; and they will undoubtedly be present and ask of your committee a day on which their side of the case can be heard; therefore, I have purposely refrained from including the name of Mr. Haffen, the commissioner of street improvement for that district, and the concourse commissioners, and possibly certain others connected with the immediate development of that locality, and I have omitted to include in the general development of the city of New York the aqueduct commissioners, and the tenement-house commission that are applying to the Legislature, I believe now, for an expenditure of $5,000,000 a year for certain purposes. Mr. Chairman, that my own position may be clearly understood, I state I own neither dock property or tenement-house property, so I am not here in the position of a pleader for condemnation proceedings on the part of the city of New York. I would not be affected by the expenditure of all these moneys which, largely by mandatory legislation, has been put on the city of New York. They would not affect my individual property in the slightest degree. We therefore respectfully ask for an adjournment of the meeting for that purpose.

MR. LEXOW:

Have you any further argument to make to-day, or would anybody here like to be heard?

MR. SETH LOW:

I would like to be heard as a New York merchant.

MR. ROMAINE:

I would like to ask, as a taxpayer, that any citizen and taxpayer in the city of New York who appears here in advocacy of the scheme of equal taxation, may hereafter be held amenable to the process of this committee, so we can have his testimony under oath. We are not asking for testimony at present from gentlemen in Brooklyn, or Long Island City, or Staten Island; but I would simply like to reserve that right, Mr. Chairman, to the league which I represent, that we may hereafter call these gentlemen, if we see fit, and examine them; or that you may call them, Mr. Chairman, under oath hereafter; and that we may have the opportunity to cross-examine.

MR. GRADY:

Mr. Romaine, you can see the granting of the application made by you would put the Legislature practically in arrears.

MR. ROMAINE:

We only ask for time for a hearing.

MR. GRADY:

Yes; but you wish these gentlemen to be subpoenaed at such time as you suggest; and the time for hearing would depend on the time you might set. There would be a good deal of cumulative testimony if we only subpoenaed those gentlemen named.

MR. ROMAINE:

That may be so, quite largely. The comptroller has already testified before the Supreme Court Commission in the matter of rapid transit that the vote of 1894, taken at the same time, as the expression of the opinion of the citizens of New York that fifty million dollars should be spent, could not be carried out by the city in his opinion, with the other expenses passed by mandatory legislation. Rapid transit could not be carried out, if this thing went through in its present form.

MR. GRADY:

I understand that to be the result attained by all the testimony taken. Of course we could not disturb the fact, that is, of New York city if consolidated with Brooklyn and the other territory under the terms of fair and equal taxation, will certainly at the inception of the consolidation be subjected to greater burdens of taxation than it now bears, and that Brooklyn and other localities will be to the same extent relieved. Would the inquiry go any further than that.

MR. ROMAINE:

I think it would go further. I think it relates to the legal status of the sinking fund of New York, whether it cân, or shall be diverted by legislation.

MR. GRADY:

There is not in this question now before the committee any possibility of at all interfering with the sinking fund or determining its legal status, or disturbing it.

MR. ROMAINE:

You are aware that the question of the status of the sinking fund went to the Court of Appeals.

MR. GRADY:

I am; but here is the position of this committee: We are now hearing those who are in favor of the consolidation of New York and the adjoining territory upon the ground that the people have voted for it upon the one hand; and those who believe that notwithstanding that vote, for some reason that political consolidation should not take place. Then there is the other element to which our attention is called, if the political consolidation is decided upon, shall it be on lines of fair and equal taxation. I am, in my personal judgment and opinion, an anti-consolidationist; first, for all the reasons that have been stated, that I think New York will have enough to do to take care of itself. I am opposed to it upon the political ground that the Constitution provides that this great community shall never have more than one-half of the representation of the Senate, even if it has three-quarters of the population.

MR. ROMAINE:

Those matters we have not touched on.

MR. GRADY:

I want to say on both of those grounds I am opposed to it myself; but how is any man who holds his commission by reason of a public vote going to get from under the vote that instructed the Legislature that in the opinion of all these localities, consolidation should be had. Now that is a point to which I think all legitimate discussion before this present committee should be directed. How can you get from under this vote? You say there were circumstances attending it that do not make it a finality. What vote can you get that will be so relieved from circumstances that affect it that it will be considered a finality? What objection can be urged to that vote that can not be urged to the vote on a constitutional amendment? How is any man who is appointed under representation of that vote to get from under that vote? That disturbs the committee. There are others who think they see their way clear to avoiding that question.

Mr. Romaine:

We will present our side on that question at length at the proper time; and if you will allow me, Mr. Chairman —

Mr. Lexow:

That was the very reason why I suggested to you at the beginning, that this argument of yours and this testimony you seek to take here would be more properly addressed to this committee if this committee reported in favor of political consolidation at all, and then upon the terms and conditions, and ways and means whereby actual and final consolidation can be secured, this argument you now make can be more properly addressed. Here we have to deal with the simple consolidation or carrying into effect the popular vote of 1894; and the argument about Brooklyn, although it did go into the question of taxation and subsiduary questions, were mainly addressed to the committee to show that on the part of the anti-consolidation commission that that vote had some point, and some reason behind it why it should be disregarded.

Mr. Romaine:

This is New York and not Brooklyn, and we believe we have cogent reasons; we believe we can show them to you.

Mr. Lexow:

We will hear you on other reasons, then.

Mr. Romaine:

Will the committee, if the chairman please, be in a position to announce that it will remit all those questions to a future day to discussion on taxation, and will address itself solely to the political union; that it will cut off debate on the other side of the East river, who claim that they stand on the foundation of a reduction of taxation for Brooklyn? No, sir; you have not done it radically.

Mr. Lexow:

I think it is perfectly proper for you to bring that into debate in debating the motion proposed, but not to make an issue or point here which will distract the committee from the main proposition, which is, "Shall this committee report back to the Legislature its belief that the popular vote of 1894 should be adhered to?"

MR. ROMAINE:

I think we would greatly desire to be heard to-day on that point.

MR. A. A. LEVEY:

Mr. Chairman: I would like the privilege of a few words in addition to what I said before directed particularly to this question, and what you yourself and the Hon. Senator Grady said, as to the effect upon your committee as published on this referendum vote which was taken in 1894. From the published statements of the proceedings in Brooklyn I understand that you, yourself, Mr. Chairman, repeatedly asked the question whether that vote might not be considered as an estoppel upon the Legislature on the main question of consolidation. Now as matters very properly bearing on that question, I hold in my hand here a publication which appeared in the New York Sun, October 26, 1894, which was a reprint of a publication issued by the commission, of which Mr. Green was chairman. I will read the whole of it. This was just prior to the vote of 1894: "At the coming general election the question will be put before the people of this city, of Brooklyn, and of a considerable surrounding territory on the northern and eastern boundaries of these two cities, whether, in their opinion, it will be better or not to make this whole territory one great municipality. It is an important question and one which should be thought about and carefully discussed so that by the time election day comes around, a little more than a month hence, all the electors may be prepared to cast their ballots upon this subject with an intelligent purpose.

"In this article it is not proposed to enter into the merits of the consolidation scheme, but to put before the reader a clear idea of what he is about to be asked to vote upon.

"For many years efforts have been made to bring New York city and Brooklyn under a single government. Each city has had territory added to it in the meantime until New York city has absorbed the county that it stood in and taken in a lot more of land to the north of it, and Brooklyn under the action of the recent laws by which it has acquired Coney Island and other places, will soon include all of Kings county.

"The Consolidation League of Brooklyn and Mr. Andrew H. Green and his associates in this city, who believe that it wiil be of advantage to go on with such work and bring the two cities and some of their surrounding towns into one compact municipality, got the Legislature last winter to pass the following bill:

"Chapter 64.— An act providing for the submitting the question of consolidation of the city of New York with certain territory under a single municipal administration to a vote of the people. Chapter 64 of the Laws of 1894. And publishing that bill which provided that at the next general election held in this city there should be submitted to a vote of the duly qualified electors of the said territory the question of consolidation under one municipal government. Now, that was the whole extent of the notice that was given to the voters of the territory affected as to the question that was to be brought before them for the exercise of their franchise: 'The question of its consolidation under one municipal government.' That was all the notice the electors had. That was the question upon which they voted; nothing more, nothing less. Now, after publishing this act, this circular of this commission prints a map of the territory, and winds up with these remarks: 'The accompanying map shows just what territory it is proposed to include in the new city, and it is the electors living within these limits that will be called upon to decide whether they will cast the ballot which reads for consolidation or the one against it.'

"The questions which the voters will naturally ask now are:

"What will be the outcome of this if there is a majority vote for consolidation?

"If one great city be erected in place of the two big ones and the surrounding towns and village governments, what form of government is to succeed these?

"Will New York also absorb the others and take them under the wing of its present city government, or will an entirely new organization follow?

"The present vote will settle none of these questions. The voter need not bother himself at all about them. Whether he votes for or against his ballot, either singly or aggregated with all the others cast, will not have a particle of legal weight. If every vote were cast in favor of consolidation the only thing that would be accomplished would be to furnish the advocates of the Greater New York with a cogent and perhaps overwhelming argument to prove to the next Legislature that the necessary laws should be passed to carry out their demand.

"This is the whole purpose of the vote. The friends of the Greater New York have arranged this in this manner purposely. Had the law made it obligatory for the coming Legislature to pass laws to carry out the consolidation of this territory in case of a favorable vote, it would have been a grave question as to whether such an enactment, seeking to bind the action of a future legislative body, would have been constitutional.

"All the questions, therefore, which might arise as to how the Greater New York is to be governed, will be fought out in the Legislature. What you are to decide is whether you want a Greater New York or not, and whether you wish to become a part of it."

Now, Mr. Chairman, in view of that statement published by this Consolidation League it is very clear that neither the Legislature or your committee is at all estopped by the question of the vote of 1894 from considering the entire question of consolidation in its details as res nova.

MR. LEXOW:

Then any suggestion I made or you made on the first argument before the committee was that when the question of detail was reached, it should more properly be addressed to the committee after we have decided the main proposition as to whether consolidation shall take place.

MR. LEVEY:

Mere inchoate consolidation, without any details whatever. Without affecting the office or tenure of office of any office holder in any part of this district, a mere expression of opinion. Have you got no further than that. Then I say you should follow the mandate of the people in this vote; but I say after that vote it is impossible that you can consider yourself estopped from anything more than a mere declaration by the Legislature that these territories shall be consolidated. Your bill makes it mandatory upon this commission to enact a system of equal and uniform taxation; that is the expression.

MR. LEXOW:

They propose bills to the Legislature, they can not enact any thing.

MR. LEVEY:

You suggest whether it is desirable that the bill shall be proposed. You should consider the question or you should not have come saying that you are estopped by the legislation passed, which compels you to say the taxation shall be uniform.

MR. GRADY:

It may raise the question whether you shall have consolidation at all. If you are not going to have consolidation upon the line of fair and equal taxation, I do not think there can be any difference of opinion about this committee being able to decide that you can not have consolidation at all.

MR. LEVEY:

I rather agree with the Senator myself on that point.

MR. GRADY:

Why not face the question.

MR. LEVEY:

If the chairman takes the view that this vote of the people of 1894 is a mandate compelling the Legislature to make a report in favor of consolidation and leave the details afterwards to be considered — which I should consider very absurd legislation — why, I can not object to it; but it goes on further.

ANDREW H. GREEN:

Allow me—

MR. LEXOW:

You are in favor of consolidation, I suppose?

MR. GREEN:

I believe I am.

MR. LEXOW:

I want to ask a question. I want to correct a statement made by the gentleman. It speaks of the Consolidation League. Did you mean the Consolidation League, or the consolidation commission?

MR. LEVEY:

I simply read what is in there.

MR. GREEN:

This is an article in the newspaper, not published by any consolidated league.

MR. LEVEY:

It is contemporaneous.

MR. GREEN:

I do not wish to interrupt, as it is taking up the time of the other side.

MR. LEVEY:

That statement has considerable value as contemporaneous evidence.

MR. GREEN:

It is a newspaper statement.

MR. LEXOW:

I think, however, Senator Grady is stating the position of this committee with absolute accuracy; that is, that every location shall be treated fairly.

MR. ROGERS:

May I say this one word; fair and equal taxation has a very plausable sound; but when two partners come together in the way of business, one putting in ten thousand dollars, and the other putting in fifty thousand dollars, should the one putting in ten thousand dollars receive a greater proportion of benefit than the one who puts in fifty thousand dollars? I think not.

A VOICE:

That depends on the amount of brains contributed.

MR. ROGERS:

I think so. Fair and equal taxation would be to let the city of Brooklyn pay its share of expenses and the city of New York pay its share; that would be fair and equal taxation.

MR. GRADY:

What I desire to be understood as saying is that from my experience it is not practicable to attempt to pass nor is it profitable to discuss any bill that will provide for a consolidation, unless we provide that all of the new territory should be treated alike in the matter of assessment and taxation.

MR. ROMAINE:

I would simply state that the former comptroller of the city of New York is of the opinion — Mr. Theodore W. Meyer — that consolidation is practicable having taxable units, as it has now.

MR. GRADY:

It is practicable?

MR. ROMAINE:

Yes.

MR. GRADY:

The practicability that I am discussing is the practicability of getting seventy-six votes in the Assembly.

MR. ROMAINE:

I understand you. He says as a financial problem it is quite practicable.

MR. GRADY:

I understand that; but I say the question is not an advisability question, as you might think that while you do not appear opposing political consolidation, but appear here only opposing the equal and uniform taxation of all the new territory, in case a bill should pass that that is one and the same question. You might as well not attempt to pass a bill that would provide political consolidation without all the territory was treated alike in the matter of assessments and taxation. I am not one of the majority of the Legislature, and perhaps I ought not to speak for it, except as an old and intimate friend has a feeling on that subject.

MR. ROMAINE:

I will ask the committee if they will be kind enough to rule on our committee's application for an adjournment.

MR. LEXOW:

The committee will take that into consideration in executive session.

MR. ROMAINE:

Will we have an announcement of it?

MR. LEXOW:

I can not say. We will probably consider it immediately after this session, and probably announce the decision. That will rest with the majority of the committee. Is there anybody else who desires to speak against consolidation?

MR. LOWE:

I desire to speak against it. I desire to protest, Mr. Chairman, against any action being taken by the Legislature of New York, or by this committee, on the basis of the vote of 1894. Now, while it may be admitted by some that from a view taken in accord with the letter of the law we are committed to the question of consolidation, when we take the spirit of the law into consideration we are committed to nothing whatever of the kind; and I also protest, Mr. Chairman, against a vote which is called a vote of opinion before election, without any finality about it whatsoever, being called the will of the people after election. Now, I think the people of Brooklyn know the difference between their opinions and their will; and when they voted on this question they did not express their will. The act which was passed by the Legislature of the State of New York said nothing about the will of the people; it merely said "an expression;" so it is idle talk. It is un-American talk to speak of the people of Brooklyn expressing their will on the subject of consolidation; and I call you to witness, gentlemen, that the papers and the hostile press had in every direction since the election spoken of the opinion of the city of Brooklyn as the will of the city of Brooklyn. I need not say that the people of Brooklyn know the difference between an expression of their opinion and an expression of their will, and so I believe of every American citizen. Now, I am opposed to consolidation because I have honest convictions on the subject, that it is much better for New York, and much better for Brooklyn not to consolidate. I speak from the standpoint, of course, to-day as a merchant of New York; and I also speak more or less directly as a resident of Brooklyn; and I am sure that I have as much the interest of the one at heart as I have the other; and I do not feel that this all-important question has received the consideration that it ought to have. A question of this magnitude, affecting the entire interest of the whole country to an extent which perhaps no one realizes. The metropolis of the United States is something more than a big city. It means that it affects every man and woman in the United States in the same degree; and I say that it is a question of the very first magnitude, for every American citizen, as well as for every resident of New York and Brooklyn; and I say that I welcome the hearings which have been given to the citizens of Brooklyn and New York, for the reason that they let in a great deal of light upon this important subject; and I feel that even with the best intentions in the world — and I think you will find in the city of New York as good people as you will find anywhere in the world — it is foolish to suppose that the people living anywhere else are better or worse in any respect, but with the best intentions in the world, I do not believe it is in the power of New York to do justice to the people that of necessity should have it really at arms length. It is, therefore, that I urge and respectfully pray that this question receive more and thorough attention. When the city of London was consolidated the matter was considered most exhaustively. They had meeting after meeting, and thousands of individuals were invited, and thousands and thousands of reports were sent in; but it has been our experience in that respect that the matter has been in charge of a commission of inquiry. Now, Mr. Chairman, may I ask to what extent this commission of inquiry has inquired? Has it consulted, for instance, in Brooklyn, the men who occupy the most responsible positions there, who are most interested there? Has it called any public meeting? I saw a statement the other day to the effect that it had not held a meeting there for twelve years.

Mr. Green:

May I answer the question?

Mr. Lowe:

I am very happy to have Mr. Green answer it.

Mr. Green:

You alluded to a statement made in the paper that we had not had a meeting for twelve years. We have not been in existence longer than six years, so it would not be possible to have it in twelve years. This thing started in 1890. We had meeting after meeting and public hearings advertised in the paper for four or five years, and men from Brooklyn and New York appearing before us, gathered all the statistics of debt and taxable areas; and therefore, I want to make public that fact in the newspapers, as I have no doubt the gentleman speaks with fairness.

Mr. Lexow:

You refer to your memorial setting forth all those facts.

Mr. Lowe:

I am glad to know that statement in the paper is not correct. The gentleman who has spoken, I think, refers to the time of the appointment of the present commission. I am not sure whether there was not another commission prior to the present one. At any rate this question has been talked about, of course, for a long time informally; but nevertheless, speaking of the report of that commission, after the vote of 1894, I tried in vain to procure a single report of that commission. I sent to Albany to get this report; and finally, in order to get what there was to be had, I sent to Mr. Green's office, and I received a small pamphlet on the subject. Now, Mr. Chairman, I repeat that I do not think that this question has received the consideration to which it is entitled; and I think it is only fair that a committee should be appointed to investigate the commission itself, and to find out to what extent it is an inequality for the citizens of Brooklyn and for the citizens of New York, and find out exactly what it has done. Now, Mr. Chairman, I believe that the work of this commission has been mostly voluntary. Under those circumstances I can easily see that they would be limited in their belief to do the question justice; and I think that it is only fair that you should have ample means and ample facilities placed at your disposal in order that a proper investigation may be made; but I do say that I think when the investigation of the committee is made that it will be found that they have had no facility for giving the matter proper attention, and therefore, I respectfully protest against any action being taken by the Legislature of the State of New York until this matter has received the consideration to which it is entitled.

MR. LEXOW:

Does anybody desire to speak further against consolidation?

MR. CLARENCE WINTHROP BOWEN:

I desire to say a word.

MR. LEXOW:

The first hearing is against consolidation. Are you against it?

MR. BOWEN:

Yes, I think so; a word on that. I have been asked to come here and say a word on the subject, and I wish to say this, if you will kindly allow me to, that inasmuch as a number of hearings have been given to the citizens of Brooklyn, that an equal number should be given to the citizens of New York, and that we should be in no hurry to close this matter to-day or Monday; but that we should take ample time to consider it in every respect. I was born in Brooklyn, and have lived there most of my life, but at present a citizen of New York; and I believe the citizens of Brooklyn, as well as the citizens of New York, wish consolidation; but they wish it in a way that will be honorable to both cities, and fair to both cities, and certainly there can be no harm in the fullest discussion. I would suggest — perhaps the suggestion has already been made — that the mayor of this city, and the heads of the different departments and some of the leading members in this city be especially requested to come here and give their views. Certainly there can be no harm in that. I would, therefore, repeat, viz.: That the fullest hearing be given, and the fullest investigation be made before your honorable committee make its recommendations at Albany.

Mr. Lexow:

Does anybody else desire to be heard against consolidation? If not, the hearing for to-day on that branch of the subject will be closed, and those who are in favor of consolidation will be heard, if they desire it.

Mr. Romaine:

At what time does the committee sit?

Mr. Lexow:

That will depend on whether those in favor of consolidation wish to do any talking. We will sit two hours if those desiring consolidation wish to be heard.

Mr. Grady:

We can arrange, Mr. Romaine, to notify you and your colleagues of the decision of the committee on the point you raised.

Mr. Romaine:

I simply want, if the committee overrules me, to be on record.

Mr. Lexow:

You probably would like to hear the argument on the other side.

MR. ROMAINE:

I would only ask, on behalf of the taxpayers of New York, that if any citizen of New York appears before you in advocacy of the equalization of taxes involved in consolidation, that we be allowed the privilege, in case we have an investigation under oath, that we may examine them under oath, and that the subpoena of the commission issue to them. I desire to place on record one communication on the subject that is about to be closed; and if you will allow me, I will hand that up to the desk. I wish to present to you the two articles in the Record and Guide of February 1, 1896, and also a letter signed by Mr. Alfred T. White, of Brooklyn. The articles are as follows:

"A correspondent, writing to us from Brooklyn asks: 'Where do you stand on the question of consolidation? Are you for or against? The Record and Guide is as much a Brooklyn as a New York journal — in fact, isn't it the representative of real estate in Greater New York?—and it should lean to the interests of Brooklyn as well as to those of Manhattan Island.' This extract exhibits the working of the ordinary mind; upon every vexing question under the sun one is to take at once a definite stand at either extreme of the problem. The middle ground, where thought and self-instruction is possible, is never for a moment considered tenable. It is this middle ground, however, that the Record and Guide occupies at present in reference to consolidation. We desire to have the subject intelligently treated. Up to the present moment we have had very little except newspaper gush, 'politics' and 'hurrah,' and we believe that to rush through so serious a matter upon this stupid impetus is to create for ourselves certain confusion and a number of harassing problems. So far, the creation of a Greater New York has received scarcely as much real sober consideration, downright careful 'figuring,' as would be given to the formation of a partnership between two peanut stands. The vital matters of taxation, finance, administration, development of the proposed municipality, have scarcely been dealt with at all. Indeed, from the marked absence of rational discussion as to the many problems that lurk under these details, it might be imagined that consolidation involves nothing but a legislative creation of a geographical expression — a sort of baptism, over which everybody can make merry, and then proceed with business as before. Once establish our larger city, however, and people will promptly discover that the difficulties and problems which they previously and blindly ignored will thrust themselves imperatively to the front for solution. New Yorkers have been strangely apathetic about consolidation. Will they be as indifferent when they find themselves burdened with taxes for needed municipal improvements in localities across the East river, the proposition of which they are profoundly ignorant of? There is no dodging the fact that New Yorkers will have to pay something for consolidation. If they are willing to foot the bill, well and good. Anyone is entitled to what he will honestly pay his cash for. But New Yorkers ought not to order goods and kick afterward when the legitimate charges are demanded. Moreover, consolidation involves the abandonment of a long tradition and the substitution of a new policy. New York hitherto has regarded the north as the natural direction for civic expansion, and has annexed beyond the Harlem a very vast territory, a great part of which is yet undeveloped. All the superfluous resources of the city for years to come will be needed to improve that district and advance it to the condition of even many New Jersey suburban towns. Under consolidation, is the capital of the city henceforth to be deflected in part from the betterment of this section in the north to the improvement of the outskirts of Brooklyn in the east? The question is not, where does the Record and Guide 'stand' upon these matters, but where do the people of this city, the real estate owners and taxpayers, stand?

" Messrs. Cyrus Clark, Cornelius Doremus, R. H. L. Townsend, Benjamin F. Romaine, August A. Levey and James A. Deering, on behalf of the Taxpayers' Anti-Equalization League of New York, have issued an address to citizens and taxpayers of New York city pointing out the probable effect upon property interests and public improvements in this city if the consolidation of the various cities, towns and outlying villages to constitute 'Greater New York' be carried into effect upon the basis proposed by the Consolidation Commission — the equalization of taxation and valuation. The statement is one that must interest every citizen and particularly such as are property owners. Those who desire to peruse it and join in the work of the league should communicate with its secretary pro tem., Mr. Levey, at No. 20 Nassau street, room 65.

"The joint committee on consolidation has announced from Albany that it will give a hearing on the subject of consolidation in this city to-day. Presumably the place of hearing will be the City Hall and the time 11 A. M."

The following is the letter from Mr. White:

COMMISSIONER'S OFFICE,
DEPARTMENT OF CITY WORKS, MUNICIPAL BUILDING,
BROOKLYN, N. Y., *January* 31, 1896.

MR. WILLIAM C. REDFIELD, *Garfield Building, Brooklyn:*

Dear Sir.— I received your letter yesterday morning and it is now 6 o'clock P. M., and I have not yet had the opportunity to look over Mr. Kieley's statement which you sent me. I read it at the time he made it and have a general recollection of it. I do not remember that Mr. Kieley opposed "Resubmission," which I take it is the issue of the hour. The statements he made could, with great propriety be discussed during a campaign prior to a vote, but they seem to me of little account now when the main issue is the right of citizens of Brooklyn to determine their own future.

I think I recall that Mr. Kieley said there would be no additions to the sinking fund prior to August, and, therefore, no opportunity to issue bonds for improvements beyond the $2,300,000 on hand January 1st. If he said this, he must have forgotten the items of surplus water revenue, interest on sinking fund, etc., etc., which will increase the margin between January and August some seven or eight hundred thousand dollars, I think. I speak of this because people generally imagine that our only increase in resources is by new buildings or increased valuations, which is an error. I remember, too, that he said something of public schools, in which matter Brooklyn is far ahead of New York to-day that it would be retrogression for us to fall to her level. Nothing that Mr. Kieley said has altered, in the least, my opinoin that Brooklyn can go right along in a moderate way with all needed improvements and that they will be made more rapidly and more wisely without consolidation than with it. Of course, this is a matter of opinion and I respect Mr. Kieley's judgment to the contrary, while I differ from him. I have never seen anything in the treatment of any annexed territory by any city, even our own, to warrant the faith which he seems to have that a "Greater New York" would spend more money on schools, pavements, parks, etc., in Brooklyn, than we shall spend by ourselves, but as I said before, these are questions to be discussed when the opportunity for discussion is given by another vote.

I regret not to be able to oblige you by a reply in detail, but you know something of the strain of closing up two years' work in this department to leave it in clean shape for my successor.

Sincerely yours,

ALFRED T. WHITE.

ERASTUS WIMAN:

I desire to appear as an advocate for consolidation, for the advantages that it will offer to New York in three things: That it will check a decline of foreign commerce, which, at this moment, is menaced to a great degree; second, by the proposed absorption of Staten Island, it will check the decline in manufactures, which New York is rapidly losing, and which, because of the disabilities under which it suffers, enables cheap towns, such as Bridgeport, New Haven, Paterson, Newark, Scranton, Reading, and even Philadelphia, to compete most successfully against them; the third, that by the proposed consolidation homes will be created for the workingmen which are now impossible in New York. In relation to ocean commerce, it is a fact that the disabilities which it suffers in the harbor of New York are the most astonishing in the history of the commerce of the world. The absorption of Staten Island by consolidation would supply the three great needs that New York now feels most acutely, that is, a place for receipt, for storage, and for shipment. Because New York lacks what Staten Island alone can supply, her foreign commerce is rapidly declining; she can no longer compete with other near-by towns in other States in manufactories, and worse than all, no workingman within the city limits has the hope of a home. I maintain that the hope of property is one of the strongest incentives of good government, and to deny to the wage-earner the hope of a home of his own is to defeat the idea of perfect citizenship. By the acquisition of Staten Island all these three acquisitions to a perfect city could be placed within the city limits. When they are united there is a perfect terminal furnished to receive the commerce of the world. Now, we receive the commerce from .the world in Jersey City, store it in Brooklyn, and have it transferred to New York; and if the devil had wished to exert a malign influence to divert the ocean commerce from New York and make it costly, that is the plan he would have recommended. That New York is not accessible to the trunk lines is a fact of extreme importance to it, because it implies a system of lighterage from New Jersey to New York which is the most costly expenditure for the purpose of any in the world.

The decline in ocean commerce, I maintain, can be checked by making available under consolidation the wide stretches of water front on the west shore of the commodious harbor of Staten Island, and which, under consolidation, would be immediately improved. This portion of the new city is the only portion of the harbor within the State reachable by all the trunk lines west of the Hudson,, which handle three-fourths of all the exports and imports of this great center. New York, as she is to-day, is completely isolated from this most important trunk line connection, and equally with Brooklyn, nothing can come or go from either of them except at an expense for water communication by floats or lighters. This involves a tribute so great that it has driven the commerce of the port away. On the Staten Island shore the ships and the cars can come side by side, and here alone in the harbor can the three great purposes of a terminal be perfectly performed, namely, receipt, storage and shipment. We are now receiving nine-tenths of our products in Jersey City, storing them in Brooklyn and shipping it in New York. Hence, you can ship a barrel of flour from Baltimore or Newport News from the dock to Liverpool for less than it takes to handle it in the harbor of New York. The figures presented show a decline so great that if continued for ten years the foreign commerce of New York would cease to exist.

The tribute levied on New York on its foreign commerce is simply suicidal, and amounts to a vast sum. Thus the drayage system which results from the absence of storage on the water front cost no less a sum than thirty-five millions a year. The number of drays are so great that stretched in a line west from New York the oaths of the drivers could be heard between each other all the way to San Francisco. This vast tax added to lighterage, which amounts to fifteen or twenty millions more, make an annual tax on commerce of more than fifty millions a year. Thus a million of dollars a week is taxed upon a commerce largely for the interior and to avoid which it is going in other directions. I will adduce the following figures to show the result of this system of tribute:

FOREIGN COMMERCE OF NEW YORK.

	Total.	Increase.	Decrease.
Fiscal year ending June 30, 1895	$934,290,314	....	$27,028,077
Fiscal year ending June 30, 1894	961,318,391	....	73,047,013
Fiscal year ending June 30, 1893	1,034,365,404	....	26,855,474
Fiscal year ending June 30, 1892	1,061,220,878	$61,328,243	....

Thus it will be seen that the total decrease in three years, 1892 to 1895 inclusive, was $126,000,000. This vast sum is full of significance to any thinking man.

The chief element in the foreign commerce of the port of New York is the export of breadstuffs. If the tonnage that reaches this port can not get a return cargo from this broad continent of its products that the world requires of it, then shipping will cease to come to this port. Hence, the true test of foreign commerce are the figures as to the receipts and exports of flour, wheat and corn. With this in mind note how startling are the following figures, indicating a decline so great that, if it continues at the same ratio, ten years will witness an almost total obliteration of the traffic.

Receipts at New York average for five years, of flour, 7,000,000 barrels. For 1895, they averaged only 6,400,000. Receipts of wheat, for five years ending with 1894, averaged 43,000,000 bushels. Last year these receipts fell to 28,000,000 bushels, a most startling decline. Of corn, the receipts for five years averaged 30,000,000 bushels. Last year they reached only 25,000,000.

The same starling decline appears also in the exports from New York. Thus for five years exports of flour were 5,219,000 barrels, while for last year the export reached only 4,400,000 barrels. The exports of wheat for five years averaged 34,000,000 bushels, while in 1895 they attained only 24,000,000, a loss of 10,000,000, and a loss of over three million bushels in the exports of corn.

The decline in the grain trade of New York in 1895, as compared with that of the five preceding years, will approach twenty per cent., a percentage so startling and so significant as to set every one thinking. For the last week, even, the movement in corn is full of significance. Thus while New York received 280,000 for distribution over the most densely populated area, the one-horse port of Baltimore received 639,000, and far away Newport News no less than 477,000 bushels, New Orleans receiving nearly one-half the total movement, 1,107,000. This total movement amounted to 2,757,000 bushels, out of which the great port of New York received the beggarly quoto of only 280,000. These figures speak in trumpet tones and indicate conditions here that consolidation with Staten Island alone can remedy.

This remedy, that Staten Island once within the city can afford, is that by the great railway bridge across the Staten Island sound all the trunk lines west of the Hudson can be brought into immediate touch with the water front of such ample dimensions as will permit storage at the cheapest shipment by the largest class of steamers without cost of lighterage. No boom to the commerce of the port would be so great as to effect a perfect union between railway and ship, impossible either to New York or Brooklyn, and equally difficult to Jersey City from want of room. The astounding statement was made that cars loaded with flour waiting for storage and shipment to the extent of thirty miles now were occupying tracks outside of Jersey City. Think of it! A train thirty miles long loaded with a costly article like flour waiting for shipment, tying up equipment, stopping transportation by a car famine in the west, while miles of water front within the harbor are available on the Staten Island shore, and if once within the limits of New York would be used for the growth and permanence of the commerce of the port. No contribution to the continued supremacy of the port of New York would be so great as to place within her control ten miles of fore-shore with the deepest water available for the largest shipping, and immediately reachable by the greatest system of transportation the world has ever seen making the great point of transfer for the products of the continent to meet the tonnage of the world.

Mr. Wiman then proceeded to show how serious were the disabilities for manufacturers in Brooklyn and New York. No sane man would enter either of these cities expecting to compete successfully with such cheap towns as Bridgeport, New Haven, Newark or Paterson, Reading, Scranton or even Philadelphia. Raw material and coal cost more to get from the wharf to the factory than elsewhere for an equal distance in the world, while finished products for distribution over the country could only be conveyed to points for diffusion at a cost that handicapped every manufacturer within the limits of either city. As against this, Staten Island offered access by the sea for raw material from all parts of the globe; for coal by train direct from the mine into the bunker of the boiler; while for distribution of finished products it would give a switch into the back yard to trunk lines from every factory. No region could be imagined better adapted for manufacturing facilities than Staten Island affords, and New York will bitterly rue the day if she does not include it within her borders and possess herself of advantages which alone can arrest the decadence of her manufacturing interests.

As for the workingman and his home the statement that ninety per cent. of the populace within New York paid tribute to the other ten per cent. for the privileges of shelter, shows how impossible it is that within the city limits he could have a house of his own. The hope of a home of the average wage-earner is the most hopeless of hopes. If it was a fact that the perfection of civilization was found in the character of the home, then in New York the home of the workingman shows that civilization is a failure. The hope of property is the strongest incentive of citizenship, its noblest ambition and its strongest basis, yet to nine-tenths of the wage-earners of New York this hope is utterly denied. By the acquisition of Staten Island this vast mistake could be remedied. With its area of fifty-eight square miles of most diversified topography, and reachable from the Battery for a five cent ferry fare, a region for workingmen's homes would be added to the city limits by consolidation that would be of the highest importance morally, physically and financially and make it continue to be the greatest city of the greatest country under the sun.

MR. ROMAINE:

I would like to know from the gentleman if he voted for the referendum in Richmond county.

MR. WIMAN:

The gentleman is a British subject, and is not entitled to vote, but has done more for the harbor of New York than any other gentleman.

Mr. Brush:

He made the statement that there were no manufactories in Brooklyn.

Mr. Wiman:

No; but they are far less than they ought to be.

Mr. Brush:

I would like to read from a memorandum I have taken from the United States census: In men's and women's clothing in Brooklyn, there are employed 14,240, and the value of the output is $13,000,000.

Mr. Wiman:

I did not mean to state that there was no manufacturing in Brooklyn, because that would be very wide of the mark; but I say they suffer from a disability, from a separation from the point of distribution and the point of receipt of raw material, which is mostly costly in coming to them, for which reason I projected the tunnel under the bay.

Governor Roswell P. Flower:

I came here to-day rather unexpectedly, but I came here to say that I, in my message of 1894, asked the Legislature to pass a bill to give the people of New York and Brooklyn, and these outlying places, a chance to vote on consolidation. I understood from the papers that they voted for consolidation. I would not be in favor of consolidation unless the people were; but if they were in favor of it in these several great cities I could see great advantage to flow from a consolidation under a home rule charter and an honest government, and that is the only way the people of these great cities can live under; and if they have any other they will throw it off in time. So, therefore, I am in favor of the consolidation of these great cities. The results to flow from it, as Mr. Romaine has said, are very great as far as your terminal facilities are concerned — the cheaper you can make your terminal facilities, the cheaper you can get your railroads and canals to bring freight to this market, the greater will be the volume of business in exports from abroad and imports to this city. The manufacturing industry always, under the shifting scenes in the tariff, will naturally seek the best place in which to manufacture. The less crowded, and the less freight they pay the better will be their facilities. New York to-day is the greatest manufacturing city in the world, and Brooklyn runs up pretty close to it. If you can give them the proper facilities, if you can give them the proper mode of getting to and from their homes quickly, if you can give them cheap freight, and cheap truckage you can still retain in this great city this great manufacturing interest for all time to come. To-day it is reaching out to Long Island City, it is reaching out to Newark, New Jersey, and all along among these Jersey villages. It will soon reach out to Staten Island; but give us clothes large enough to stretch around this great body of people, and there are good citizens enough in this city, in Brooklyn, in Staten Island, in Long Island City to make this government what it ought to be. It can not run itself. You may all be interested in it to-day; you may stir it up all you have a mind to; but after one election they all go to sleep. That is not the way to run this great city. It has got to be run by active, vigilant, intelligent citizenship the year around; and when that is done this great city can be run more economically than it is now, with a Greater New York and Brooklyn and Staten Island and Long Island City, and all combined.

Mr. Romaine has touched upon one more point, that is, the home of the poor. Any historian will tell you the more sparsely settled the country the less it is subject to revolution. If you can take the densely populated places of this city and scatter it over the great flats in Brooklyn where the streets are made, the sewers are made, and everything complete for houses; if you can take this tenement-house population and put it into little homes where they can own them, and where they can buy lots for $100, or two or three hundred a piece, if they can buy the house, if they can go to those homes, anybody can tell you who has had anything to do with labor, if they got their own homes there would be but few strikes.

If you can scatter the population in a line you have accomplished a great betterment for the people and this city, and this commonwealth. I do not worry about the taxes, as a New Yorker being larger in this great city as compared with Staten Island, and Long Island City and Brooklyn. Take their tax rate, where they have spent money for the last ten years in building good streets; as fast as you fill it up your taxes will go down. When you fill up the upper end of New York you have added to the taxable property in this city; and I think the cheapest city in the State of New York to live in, with all its taxes, will be New York city. Again, I do not believe that Staten Island is going to take all this great overflow when it comes. I believe that the Erie canal when once equipped with electricity as I saw the actual experiment made last fall and winter, and you get that for one-fifth the cost of horses and mules — with electricity you can get double the speed to bring your freight down here.

I have the idea that you should build this city to-day for all time to come. Remember that the lowest population of Europe is that of France, and that is 180 people to the square mile; the highest is Belgium, 485. We have less than twenty and seven-tenths for a square mile in this country. Haven't we as good government as they have? Why do they flock from the old world if we have not? Then, believe this, that the time will come when New York and Staten Island is going to be all built up, when we will have ten or fifteen million people, and will be as densely populated as France. To do that, and to keep the people happy, you have got to get bridges across from Jersey City; you have got to have terminals from Staten Island, and got to have bridges from Brooklyn, four or five of them; and you do not want to change your cars in going from Brooklyn to San Francisco any more than you do going from here to Albany. Within thirty years, in going to Albany, you had to change on to a ferry boat; you are doing it now. To-day, as to expressage, the man in Brooklyn and the man in New York can employ a hundred wagons to run around your streets and deliver goods all over. You will have, some time or other, the streets given to the railroads, who will be doing that express business and getting rid of the wagons, except on the streets where you want to deliver; and they will simplify that system of charges that are now so exorbitant in this city. All those things will come together under consolidation; and I want to have this city with a great big government, big enough for the whole of it, and strong enough to protect us in our rights; and the way to get the strength is to spread it out and take these crowded tenements and put the people in the different places that are isolated and give them some ground to work. When they get a part of the ground they will feel that they are a part of this country. We assimilate the peoples of the whole world in this city; our civilization is different from that of any in the world, and it ought to be stronger, and I believe it is stronger. We may have different ideas about licenses and religion; but all these in time in this great city will be made to work together for good, because, if we are a little bit rapid in our ideas about this thing we must give away to our neighbor and try to live in unity, and in that way; I believe now is the time to pass the Greater New York bill, and then in your Legislature in 1898 frame your proper charter for it. I believe the question of personal taxation will not enter into it much.

MR. LEXOW:

Does anybody else desire to address the committee in favor of consolidation?

The following was presented to the committee:

January 30, 1896.

To the Legislature of the State of New York:

We, the undersigned hotel proprietors, respectfully urge the passage of a proper bill for a "Greater New York."

J. H. BRESLIN & BRO.,

Gilsey House.

GEO. C. BOLDT,

The Waldorf.

WM. G. LELAND,

Grand Hotel.

THOMAS GUNNING (custom tailor):

Mr. Chairman and Gentlemen of the Committee: I am a workingman, and a few of us came here this morning to give our opinion on this question. Our opinion is that it is already decided by the vote which the working people cast, when the people at large cast their vote on this question; and after the last speaker, I think there is nothing more that I can say. I am in favor of what he has said.

MR. GRADY:

Do you come here in your working capacity or as a committee of an organization?

MR. GUNNING:

From the organization of the custom tailors.

JOHN BOGERT:

I appear here also as one of this delegation of workingmen. I have not been specially credentialed to appear here to-day on this subject; but I should say that it fair to assume that of the thirty-six thousand majority cast in favor of this scheme, the greater portion are workingmen and it is safe for me to say that the workingmen are in favor of it. I have ascertained that in conversation with workingmen. I am at present a representative, but not appearing here as such at this time. I have been recently elected as an organizer of a state branch of the American Society of Labor, and I mean that as being qualified to speak on behalf of workingmen. I have noticed a growing feeling among workingmen, that they have not heretofore shown a proper interest in these public questions, and I think the tendency is now that they should express themselves as an organized force in the community; they should have something to say as to these great projects, which are safe-guarded for the benefit of the people; and we have noticed, I think, that in many instances where undertakings have been authorized, great public works authorized, there has been unnecessary delay; and we felt that if we could come here to-day and say to our representatives in the Legislature, represented here by a committee of the Senate and Assembly, that we feel as though this project ought to be pushed, and that there ought to be no unnecessary delay in the work, as in some others, that we would be doing a proper work for our constituents. It may be that if the workingmen guarded the enjoyment of their functions, that there would be an extension of franchise privileges, and that in such extensions workingmen might expect to get some concession, which they do not have now, in the way of cheap affairs, and larger accommodations, etc. I think that that is a point it is fair to speak of. Of course, we have not the details of the scheme in any shape for discussion, and it is only upon general lines that we speak. The indications are that in the enjoyment of the jurisdiction of the city government, we may have also a distinct benefit for the labor organizations, which are doing a great work for the wage-earners of the State. I think myself all the large unions will have to be in favor of us extending their jurisdiction, and therefore the benefits of the work they are doing now.

MR. LEXOW:

Do you represent any large body of workingmen?

MR. BOGERT:

Well, sir, as an organizer for the State branch of the American Federation of Labor, I represent about ninety thousand workingmen in that official capacity.

MR. GRADY:

You do not appear in your official capacity?

MR. BOGERT:

I do not. I have not been specially credentialed, but I have no doubt if the matter had come before our convention two weeks ago in Albany, that we would have been willing to take a stand in favor of this project.

Mr. Grady:

A State organizer of the American Federation?

Mr. Bogert:

Yes.

Mr. Grady:

Of course, you have more or less discussion and conversation with various representatives throughout the State?

Mr. Bogert:

Yes, sir; I should say that it is because of that experience of twenty odd years with labor organizations and other work that I have been connected as an organizer of other unorganized workingmen.

Mr. Lexow:

Do you understand that you represent the sentiment of the workingmen of the city here, while not officially representing them, that that is their opinion?

Mr. Bogert:

I should say as far as I have spoken, I do represent the sentiments of workingmen. Heretofore, they have not had the proper public interest in great works; that they propose to have more interest in them; and that the only way to do it is through their organized movement, and that very likely the extension of this government would need many changes in the franchises from which we might expect some benefit. I have no doubt about that. I offer this resolution:

Whereas, By a majority vote of 36,979, the people of the city of New York voted in favor of the consolidation of the territory commonly known as Greater New York; and,

Whereas, We believe that such a consolidation would be for the common good; and,

Whereas, It is evident that delay and uncertainty in deciding the matter are prejudicial to business interests in general; therefore,

Resolved, That we, the undersigned, respectfully recommend the enactment of such legislation as is needed to carry into practical effect the sovereign will of the people thus formally expressed at the polls.

HERMAN ROBINSON,
MAYER SHOENFELD,
T. J. CROUCHLEY,
HENRY WHITE,
Members of the General Executive Board, United Garment Workers of America.

JOHN N. BOGERT,
State Organizer, A. F. of L.

G. W. JONES,
Clothing Cutter.

G. E. SCHULTE,
Clothing Trimmer.

LOUIS SCHWAB,
Clothing Cutter.

JULIUS SAMUELS,
Clothing Cutter.

JULIUS FRANKEL,
Clothing Cutter.

WOLF MARKS,
Clothing Cutter.

B. J. HAWKES,
Printer.

HENRY MALKER,
Bookseller.

G. TOMLINSON,
Gilder.

THOS. GUNNING,
Gilder.

CHAS. G. BLOETE,
Gilder.

Mr. George Tomlinson (Gilders' Union):

I do not appear here as a delegate to represent anybody, but owing to the fact that it had, as in the case of the last speaker, been brought before our organization; but I believe I voice the sentiment of the majority of the workingmen of this city and of Brooklyn when I say we are in favor of consolidation. A gentleman, a little while ago, alluded to the hardships or the impossibility of a workingman getting a home in New York. I might apply an old remark that is frequently made and put it this way: That it would be as easy to drive a camel through the eye of a needle as for a workingman to get a home in the city of New York, as it is now; but we hope in consolidation that we may possibly reach that point. The workingmen feel that if consolidation goes into effect, that it will increase the work; it will make more work for the people, and for that reason and many other benefits that they feel would accrue from it, they are in favor of consolidation. They have already cast their votes, and they hope it will not happen that that vote will be put aside. With these few remarks, Mr. Chairman and gentlemen, I think that I might say that I express the sentiment of the workingmen generally on this question of consolidation; and I hope it will become a positive fact in the near future.

Robert Winston:

I represent the New York hackdrivers. Mr. Chairman and Gentlemen of the Senate and Assembly, I thought that when the votes were taken at the election on the referendum clause, that such a question as this would not occur, especially to the workingmen; but as the Legislature thought it necessary to make inquiries of the condition of the people's mind on that vote, I thought it wise to talk to my fellow-workmen. I am a journeyman hackdriver. I want to say that the feeling of the hack trade is in favor of having consolidation. I want to say we took an active part in the question of the referendum clause in the various organizations, and especially in the New York Hackdrivers' Association, known as the Labor Dawn Association. I find, Mr. Chairman, that one side of the house has been very strongly represented for and against the bill, and I also know that one of the speakers made a remark in regard to the situation, that the general run of the people were not in favor of consolidation. If that is what is meant that is not true. When the municipal bill was first introduced in 1874, that bill was placed before the people the same as the referendum clause was put before the city of New York. I took a very active part in that amendment; and before I came to this country; and after the bill took a very particular turn, and the very same people who oppose this measure to-day are the very same people who opposed the bill in those days. The property owners who did not desire to see that bill made the law, from the very fact that it took away a great deal of power, that they could send their representatives to the board of guardians, and did not represent the people. Now, that bill is one of the greatest success. The government was one of the most corrupt before the bill. Now, after the bill of the Greater New York, I claim the consolidation of New York with Brooklyn means a brotherly existence between New York and Brooklyn. I claim there is a sectional opinion existing to-day. I assure you the sooner we get together and form a brotherhood in this gigantic city, the sooner we can get together as brothers and travel across that chasm. What we want is the consolidation. The people, Mr. Chairman, will have a chance then. Now, they are living in ramshackle, rackrenting, tumble-down houses in some district unfit for residences, and then the people will be able to go across the bridge ten years from to-day, and travel just as quick as they travel now from Harlem to the City Hall. It is necessary often to live in the city, and we can then enjoy the good atmosphere of the city in the suburban districts. That is our work in London. Thousands of workmen travel night and morning, after working hours, fifteen miles out of London and live in small houses with gardens back and front. Why? Not because they want to favor consolidation, but the consolidation wiped away all the little obstacles.

MR. LEXOW:

Will you address the Senate and Assembly committee?

MR. WINSTON:

Excuse me, I feel somewhat warm on this question.

MR. LEXOW:

We are much interested in your remarks if you will address them to the committee.

MR. WINSTON:

I felt so warm about it that I made up my mind, after I came in, to say a few words in regard to consolidation. I heard one of the speakers remark, in regard to wages in New York, that they were about fifteen dollars a week or sixty dollars a month; that is a glorious state of affairs, if it is true; but it is not so. The average workers, take skilled artisans, get seven dollars a week. You can imagine, Mr. Chairman and gentlemen, what a remarkable state of affairs it is, when a man is compelled to pay fifteen dollars for three small, poky rooms in the city. These are living figures and you can understand how necessary it is for the workmen in New York to live further out in Brooklyn and have the glorious haven of rest in Staten Island. They could also travel to Yonkers on a cheap, tariff system, provided the consolidation is brought about and made a fact. The question of commerce has been very scientifically put, and I am sure everybody knows the condition in New York, the peculiar surroundings which apply to New York, to have to stretch out our wings and take in everything around us to make the greatest city of the world. Even Chicago will get ahead of you. You are in the very worst condition to spread your wings, worse than Chicago; nevertheless, this narrow rock, as it were, does not give the chance and the same scope as if you were connected with the mainland, but it is necessary that we should make the most use of all that we have. Why not have it now. You might as well let me have some of those blessings and let my children see some of those blessings; and I think I have touched very closely, at least, upon the fact; but 36,000 votes are a large majority of the very popular vote; and, of course, we understood that it was going to be passed and agreed that there would be no trouble; but evidently there has been some hitch in the arrangement. As far as the hack trade is concerned, we are unanimously in favor of consolidation. The present system of the hack trade in New York is not what it ought to be. A new consolidation would mean a new licensing system. It would bring about a man's reputation being above par, and the examination would be an examination of a good citizen. To-day we have in New York some of the very worst characters known to represent the hack trade in New York, and for that alone, we would desire to bring about a new licensing system for New York and Brooklyn; and I am sure you gentlemen, who ride at night from the various hotels and theaters, — I know the gentlemen I carry, I see them, I know the class of men; and at night, from theaters and hotels, you find you have a different class of men altogether than you do early in the morning. We want, Mr. Chairman, to have this bill passed on purpose to make a new license system, and have the same character of men at 9 o'clock at night as we have at 9 o'clock in the morning.

MR. ROGERS:

Is the gentleman a naturalized citizen?

MR. WINSTON:

Yes.

J. P. COHEN:

I want to come before you as a member of the Manhattan Single Tax Club, to speak upon this question of consolidation. The physicial surroundings of the city of New York make it so that the people who own the land here keep the population of the city like a lemon-squeezer keeps a lemon within it, and they squeeze, squeeze and keep on squeezing until the lemon is almost dry, and has not the virtue and hardihood to get up here and speak for their rights. The gentlemen from the other side represent the squeezer. I represent the lemon. They fear that the lemon will probably have a chance through this consolidation to get across the river, and if planted over there may grow into a sightly tree, and more lemons may come to the tree. I am one of these people who have been disappointed in getting a home on Manhattan Island. I am a graduate of your public school and college here, and it has been the hope of my life to establish my house for my wife and children in this greatest city of this continent and of the world. I have lived outside New York for many years, and I felt I was only camping out, and New York was the city of my heart, and where I wanted to live. We can only get rid of these people who are manipulating the squeezer by spreading ourselves across on the other side of the river. I do not own any land over there. I do not own any land here. I do not own any land on Staten Island. I do not want any commerce to be sent down there to increase my property. I come as a representative of the poor woman who goes to the store and pays her price for these little goods which, as the gentleman says, she pays for with a portion of the rent, and therefore she is a taxpayer of the city of New York. Out of our population of nearly two millions now there are about thirteen to fifteen thousands owners of the land. That is about one in one hundred and twenty-five. Now the other one hundred and twenty-four have voted upon this question, and they think that vote should be final. They can not understand how you can get from under the votes that announced their intention for more light, and more air and a better mode of living. I can imagine somebody at the bottom of the "Black Hole in Calcutta" crying out against the opening of the ventilators at the top of it. These gentlemen would knock anybody down that offered fresh air in the Black Hole of Calcutta; and these people want now to keep them living in cellars and in the sweat-shops. They do not want them to have a chance to go across the Brooklyn bridge in from two to twenty minutes on foot; but to carry them further, I would spread this city across the North river. I would include a part of Jersey to Newark, and make it one grand city, easy of access, so that people would work here as bookkeepers and bank clerks, and lawyers and go out there and get a little bit of land, and fresh air and a garden. That can all be brought about later on. But there are representatives here from the upper end of the island. They are afraid these people are going to increase their assessments. They have been speculating in land up there, and they hold it vacant. Now if the bridges are built, and the city is extended across to Brooklyn, there will be vacant land coming in competition with their holdings, and they do not want the people of this city to go upon that land. They have stated that the increase of taxes increase rents. As a matter of fact the increase of taxes can not increase rents. The rents are as high to-day as they possibly can be under the conditions existing. They have stated here that the increase of rent will fall upon the tenant. They can not possibly saddle any increased rent upon the tenant. When a vacant lot stands alongside a building, the man who owns that building, knowing that the vacant lot is not his competitor, and he can increase his rent; but as soon as a vacant lot contains a building, he knows he has a competitor, and the rent will come down. We have on the island forty thousand vacant lots. We have enough lots to populate the entire east side; but they do not want to have it so. They want to have the people down here, where they can keep them, and squeeze them, and get forty times the amount of rent out of them that they ought to pay. I am in favor of consolidation; not on the ground that it will make it the most glorious city on the globe, not on the ground that it will make the commercial center like London; but because we can have God's fresh air, because we can get a chance to go out and dig in our garden, and cultivate our brains with contact with another; not to meet hard brick walls and sodden streets, but get a little bit of God's blessing; and we can get that by consolidating these cities. We ought to have perfect autonomy and home rule. We ought to have bath-houses all over the water front. We can have those things. We can spread our facilities for transportation, more playgrounds, more parks, and more blessings of every kind; but particularly and above all we can have better homes for our workingmen, and the hope of having a home will then become revived in the heart of the men that are working for a thousand or fifteen hundred dollars a year, because he can be a New Yorker and go down and have a bath within walking distance of his own house. I say this, not as an owner of real estate, not as the owner of any interest that will be promoted by the consolidation of these cities; but as a person who desires to be an honest citizen of the United States. It has been touched upon that the home owners are the best citizens. The greatest miracle to-day is that there is not more crime in New York than there is. It is not that crime has been increasing, as it has been alleged, but it is that it has not increased fifty times more than it has increased. I can not understand how men with families to support, who sit down to empty tables, do not go out on the streets and clutch men to get money to support their wives and children; and yet your landlord would try to prevent consolidation. We will get them by the throat. I say you can not possibly recommend to the Legislature that these cities can not be consolidated. You can not, in the face of that justice that reigns above; you can not in the face of the demand of these people who want these homes, and light, and fresh air; and if you do, your names will go down in ignominy because it will be a century before they have a chance to vote on the question of consolidation again, if they ever have it.

Mr. Lexow:

Does anybody else desire to be heard on the subject of consolidation?

Edward F. Linton:

Since you have asked if there was anybody else to be heard, and I waited to see if somebody would rise before I took your time. Nobody having risen, I want to say a very few words. Perhaps it would be as well to say that I have the honor to belong to the Consolidated Inquiry Commission. Next it might be proper to say that I have the honor to live in Brooklyn. I do not wish to take up the time here as a commissioner, nor necessarily as a resident of Brooklyn. I do want to say two or three things in answer to two or three points that have been made here, and notably by the gentlemen who appeared first, various gentlemen calling themselves counsel, and appearing here as opposed, and more particularly referring to the limited notice that they have had of this hearing, etc., and words to that effect. I want to say another word about the confusion of those people as to the Court-House and some other building as the Court-House. I want to say that this commission held a meeting in the City Hall of New York once, prior to the vote, and publication was made of that meeting, more than any meeting the commissioners ever held, and there were not in that City Hall twenty people to hear or take any part in the matter at all. I only speak of that in reference to the commission itself and the opportunity offered those people then. Another thing, I am glad to have been in this hall to-day and heard a wider scope of treatment of this great question than was heard in the four hearings in my own city. I am glad to come over here to-day and hear the breadth of treatment of this question and not a puny narrow treatment of the question. It has been better said than I can speak here in regard to the home; and I can say there is no human tribute that outranks the hope of home. It outranks the hope of salvation. The hope of salvation is a personal and selfish hope; but the hope of home is broad and covers one's offspring; so I am glad to hear that thing brought up here as bearing upon this question. I am not going to enlarge upon it; but I do say that there is more in this question of consolidation bearing upon the ultimate achievement of the hope of home, that it outranks all the other questions pertaining to it. Now I am going to close with these very brief, few further words: We had a vote upon consolidation in 1894. Prior to that vote, for a long time in this city there was a bridge from this city to Brooklyn. New York paid one-third, and Brooklyn paid two-thirds towards the erection of that bridge; and I have heard many eminent men in New York, occupying many different branches of life — legislators and others — who have said New York will never pay another dollar towards any bridge to Brooklyn, and that has been the cry and announcement all along the line for years. The point I want to make upon that is that in connection with the vote for consolidation, carried by a majority of more than 40,000, within the entire district, that a bill was introduced in the Legislature last year, two months after that vote, to build another bridge across the East river; and that that bill went through the Legislature, I think, easier than any other bill ever went through that was given wide publicity, involving such an expenditure; and I was present in Albany at the hearings on that subject, and never heard a dissenting voice on the proposition for the new bridge; and if you please, Mr. Chairman, New York, instead of refusing to pay a dollar, is going to pay half the cost of it. Now, I want to make a point of that fact, and of the bill, and of the bridge, in this way, that it was the very best evidence of good will. In Brooklyn it was asked, what evidence that Brooklyn is going to be treated fairly. I say, the first evidence was in Albany in that very bridge bill, without a dissenting voice from New York. New York has answered your vote by saying, "Here, we will give you half the money to build the bridge." That is a response and an evidence of what New York's disposition is towards a part of its suburbs; and so I say, and I believe that our people of Brooklyn would not have got that bill and that bridge, which is absolutely on the way to construction to-day, except by reason of the vote on consolidation; that the New York legislators, representing this city, voted affirmatively on that bill, on the ground that they were not building a bridge to Brooklyn any more, but building a bridge between one part of New York and another part. Now that is about all I have to say. I could not help getting up here. I would not have spoken if there had been other speakers taking your time; but I felt like expressing myself just as I have done.

Mr. George J. Greenfield:

While I do not wish to detain this committee at all, I deem it very important that I should refer to what I consider some misstatements probably made at the time in good faith, which have been presented with reference to the county of Richmond, which I understand from the newspapers has recently been presented to this committee by the corporation counsel of this city, Mr. Scott; and as this seems to be quoted from his communication to you, I presume it is correct as it is stated. He says: "Without at present expressing any opinion as to the desirability of consolidating the cities of New York, Brooklyn and Long Island City, may I not beg your committee to take into very serious consideration the question whether they should not, at the outset, eliminate that portion of the proposition which contemplates the inclusion of Richmond county in this consolidated city. That county, as you are aware, comprises an island situated in New York bay, many miles distant from the present city of New York, too far to even permit of the erection of a bridge between the two, and while not so far from the city of Brooklyn, yet separated from it by the ship channel, which itself will probably render the erection of a bridge impracticable for many years to come.

The county is, for the most part, sparsely settled, there being no considerable towns or villages upon it, and its inclusion into the consolidated city would necessitate the attempt to apply metropolitan methods and appliances to a large territory which is now purely country, which will be separated from the other parts of the city by water, which will be accessible otherwise than by water transportation only by going through an adjacent State, and which has no geographical or logical reason for annexation to the city of New York." Now, Mr. Chairman and gentlemen, I must say that is the most extraordinary manifestation of ignorance upon the part of a gentleman of intelligence whom I have known for many years, and living in the city of New York; but, gentlemen, I do not believe he ever could have been on Staten Island, at all events, not within the last two or three years, or I might say ten years, and then have come and presented deliberately to this commission statements of that description. The county of Richmond, or Staten Island, contains within its boundaries three important villages. The village of New Brighton is, I believe, either the second or third largest village in the State of New York, and contains to-day, at least I have been informed so, 20,000 inhabitants, enough to create a city of the third class. The village of Edgewater, which immediately adjoins it, contains at least 15,000 inhabitants, if I am not misinformed; and the village of Port Richmond contains five of six thousand; and then they have a new village of Tottenville opposite Perth Amboy. The total population of the county of Richmond is to-day at least 60,000, which would entitle it to be placed as a city in the second class. It takes in all cities over fifty thousand inhabitants; and yet, gentlemen, that is the community of which Mr. Scott says, "it is sparsely settled. No considerable town or villages in it, and its inclusion in the consolidated city would necessitate the attempt to apply metropolitan methods and appliances to a large territory which is now purely country, which will be separated from the other parts of the city by water and practically inaccessible." Now, gentlemen, as to the accessibility of Staten Island, we know this, that it is not distance, but time, that is the question which constitutes inaccessibility or separation. Staten Island is really practically, and should be to-day, within fifteen minutes of the Battery by transportation, and at the time the present boats were built they were guaranteed to make that distance in fifteen minutes, and it is practical to do it, if the distance is only five miles, but at all events in twenty minutes, which would not be unreasonable in any way; and with the trolley car system which has been introduced on Staten Island, any part of Staten Island within five or ten miles of the shore front would be accessible to New York city within thirty or thirty-five minutes, and into the very heart of the business section of New York in at least thirty-five or forty minutes. Now, look at the outlying districts of New York city. How long does it take to get from Harlem and the annexed district? You know it takes an hour at least. From the remotest part it is more, and they can only get less time by express trains. Now, by the reasonable traffic between New York and Staten Island I can vouch for it that, after consolidation, there will not be three years or five years after it goes practically into effect before you will find fast ferry boat transportation and cheap ferry boat transportation that will give homes to any of the working people in the city of New York, that will bring Staten Island an income in the neighborhood of $5,000,000 and bring the people within a distance of thirty-five or forty minutes of the places they have got to work in. Is not that a boon, gentlemen? You may say, "Why is it not done now?" I will tell you why it is not done now; because the attitude in the city of New York has been and is hostile to the increase in facilities that is going to include Staten Island, as they say, at the expense of New York city; and it was because of that that one of our mayors said that he did not propose to build any golden bridges from Staten Island to New York city. To-day we are taxed as I understand people are taxed in some of the eastern countries, for every man that passes from Staten Island to New York city. They have to pay toll to New York city for the privilege of entering its borders. The ferry companies are taxed so much per passenger, and, of course, gentlemen, that makes the cost of traffic greater. It is like putting up a Chinese wall around New York — and I do not speak now with reference to Staten Island, but with reference to New York city — I say that is a suicidal policy that will make it hard for any one to reach New York city and to reach their business, even if he lives outside its borders.

MR. LEXOW:

You do not mean there is any tax imposed against residents of Staten Island beyond the selling of the franchise to the ferry?

MR. GREENFIELD:

Yes, sir; I say it was sold in this way: So much percentage upon the ferry proceeds they receive, besides the rental of the docks.

MR. GRADY:

They get so much of the gross.

MR. GREENFIELD:

It comes from each individual passenger, and is in fact a tax on the passenger himself.

MR. GRADY:

Do I understand that New York should give its franchises away?

MR. GREENFIELD:

No, sir; I say if we were a part of New York city that reason would be gone; and I say further that I do not believe in the principle that New York city has a right to tax the waters of the bay of New York at all. It ought to be free to every passenger, free to the world; and that is a tax not only by the rental of the dock and ferry, but it is a tax upon the right to enter New York city from any place outside of its borders.

MR. GRADY:

New York city should not tax any of the waters of its bay; but she ought to get every dollar she can for franchises. I do not see anybody granting New York anything; and when we come to talking about New York city property that ought to be looked after first, nations next and civilized communities all over the world afterwards. You put the proposition as though New York city was maintaining some injustice at the present time. It is fair for the city to say that she should get all she can for the franchises she grants.

MR. GREENFIELD:

I was going to say that this franchise originated under the Montgomery charter at the time New York city was a small village as compared to what it is to-day, when it was struggling for existence; but if that was to be presented to-day I warrant you there would be no such charter ever granted again, which was putting a tax on the people doing their business in New York city, because there was no home within it where they could live. As a general principle, you are right. So long as New York city holds that franchise as a property, she has a right to enforce it. I am not disputing that. I am not saying it is wrong, but I say as a matter of policy I do not believe it is a good policy for New York city. The small amounts it acquires in that way is not a matter that should be considered by the great commonwealth of the city of New York.

MR. LEXOW:

You mean it is a restraint on the city and on the citizens of New York itself.

MR. GREENFIELD:

Yes, I do. I know it is on Staten Island. I know the feeling there; and consolidation will remedy that feeling; and that is one reason we feel strongly about it, without hurting New York either. And I was going to say one more thing to show how small a matter this opposition to New York taking in Staten Island is: It can only be because of the increase of taxation. I can not see anything else why the city of New York should object because they are afraid, as Mr. Scott says, that it is going to cost them a great deal to develop this "purely country district." Now, Mr. Chairman, the total levy, county levy on Staten Island — and it is the largest one, I think, we have had for some years — was $300,000 last year, and that included the interest on our bonds, the maintenance of the county roads, the interest on the county road bonds, and every other debt and every other expense that could be covered. What, gentlemen, would that be in the levy of New York city? I do not believe the whole expense, if it were put on New York city, as it is now without any added territory, would raise it to one-tenth of one mill; and yet, gentlemen, that is the reason, that is the outcry, that we ought not to be brought within the city of New York. And then, if we take in the addition of the expense of village government, and other matters in connection with it, it certainly would not exceed six hundred thousand dollars all told, the total expense for the municipal government of Staten Island; and I say these are considerations, these facts which I state, which it seems to me show that there ought to be no real opposition on any ground whatever to having Richmond county in the great consolidation.

MR. LEXOW:

There being apparently nobody else who desires to be heard, the hearing now will be adjourned, and the committee will decide in a few minutes whether to grant any further hearing in the city of New York.

MR. GREEN:

I do not wish to detain the committee, as the time is up that they allowed to New York. I have quite a large number of letters here which I think had better be read.

H. H. BREWER & CO.,
33 NASSAU STREET,
NEW YORK, *January* 31, 1896.

HON. CLARENCE LEXOW, *Chairman:*

Dear Sir.— We are in favor of Greater New York; the people voted for it and should have it.

Delay will be detrimental to the interests of the city.

Very truly,
H. H. BREWER & CO.

THE MUTUAL LIFE INSURANCE CO. OF NEW YORK,
32 LIBERTY STREET,
NEW YORK, *January* 31, 1896.

HON. CLARENCE LEXOW, *Chairman, Greater New York Committee:*

My Dear Sir.— The people voted for Greater New York and I urge you to pass a proper bill for that purpose as soon as possible.

Yours respectfully,
H. R. FREEMAN.

HENDERSON & COMPANY, BANKERS,
\ 64 CEDAR STREET,
NEW YORK, *January* 31, 1896.

HON. CLARENCE LEXOW, *Chairman:*

Dear Sir.— Regarding the "Greater New York" bill it would seem to every fair-minded man that as the people voted in favor of the measure, that their will should be respected and in due time the consolidated consummated.

Yours faithfully,
CHARLES HENDERSON.

JOHN B. WATKINS,
213 PEARL STREET,
NEW YORK, *January* 31, 1896.

HON. CLARENCE LEXOW:

My Dear Sir.— Regretting my inability to attend the hearing Saturday, February 1st, I trust that the action regarding "Greater New York" will be urged to the utmost.

Respectfully yours,
JOHN B. WATKINS.

TITLE GUARANTEE AND TRUST CO.,
55 LIBERTY STREET,
NEW YORK, *January* 31, 1896.

HON. CLARENCE LEXOW, *Chairman, Joint Committee on Greater New York:*

Dear Sir.— I regret that I am unable to be present at the hearing before your committee on Saturday. I desire, however, to urge the committee to carry out the will of the citizens of the community interested, as expressed by their vote in favor of consolidation.

There is no other way known to us of getting at the general judgment and executing it, except by ballot. There seems to be much special pleading before your committee, and it would be possible to occupy many sessions in listening to arguments in favor of the measure by those who think they would be benefited by it, and against it by those who think they would be injured by it; but it would seem as if it were the duty of your committee to consider only the general good of the whole territory and if the inhabitants of it have decided by a majority vote that it is best for them to come together, to carry out that will.

It has not been the practice in the United States to try a ballot over again if those who have lost are not satisfied. In my judgment, the measure now before the Legislature proposing to enact consolidation and call the territory and community one city, will itself make easy of solution all the other problems.

Business interests will be benefited by prompt and decisive action. Politics should have no part in the settlement of the question, and any political party which attempts to use this Greater New York movement for partisan ends will be injured thereby.

Respectfully yours,

C. H. KELSEY.

AUDOBON PARK,
NEW YORK CITY, *January* 31, 1896.

HON. CLARENCE LEXOW, *Chairman, Joint Committee on Greater New York:*

Dear Sir.— I am a citizen of New York, with considerable interest in land in this city.

I believe it to be the duty of the Legislature to obey promptly and without taking a new vote of the citizens, the will of the people of New York and Brooklyn, already expressed in favor of consolidation. No difference of opinion as to details or temporary municipal arrangements should delay a step that is essential to the welfare of the metropolis.

Very respectfully,

HELEN G. PAGE.

AUDOBON PARK,
NEW YORK CITY, *January* 31, 1896.

HON. CLARENCE LEXOW, *Chairman, Joint Committee on Greater New York:*

Dear Sir.— I am a citizen of New York, with considerable interests in land in this city.

I believe it to be the duty of the Legislature to obey promptly and without taking a new vote of the citizens, the will of the people of New York and Brooklyn, already expressed in favor of consolidation. No difference of opinion as to details of temporary municipal arrangements should delay a step that is essential to the welfare of the metropolis.

Very respectfully,
WILLIAM MIBEE GRINNELL.

AUDOBON PARK,
NEW YORK CITY, *January* 31, 1896.

HON. CLARENCE LEXOW, *Chairman, Joint Committee on Greater New York:*

Dear Sir.— I am a citizen of New York, with considerable interests in land in this city.

I believe it to be the duty of the Legislature to obey promptly and without taking a new vote of the citizens, the will of the people of New York and Brooklyn, already expressed in favor of consolidation. No difference of opinion as to details of temporary municipal arrangements should delay a step that is essential to the welfare of the metropolis.

Very respectfully,
LAURA GRINNELL MARTIN.

SMITH & MARTIN,
7 NASSAU STREET,
NEW YORK, *January* 31, 1896.

HON. CLARENCE LEXOW, *Chairman, Joint Committee on Greater New York:*

Dear Sir.— I am a citizen of New York, with considerable interests in land in this city.

I believe it to be the duty of the Legislature to obey promptly and without taking a new vote of the citizens, the will of the people of New York and Brooklyn, already expressed in favor of consolidation. No difference of opinion as to details of temporary municipal arrangements should delay a step that is essential to the welfare of the metropolis.

Very respectfully,
NEWELL MARTIN.

MARTIN KALBFLEISCH CHEMICAL CO.,
39 LIBERTY STREET,
NEW YORK, *January* 31, 1896.

HON. CLARENCE LEXOW, *Chairman, Joint Committee on Greater New York:*

Dear Sir.—As president of the Martin Kalbfleisch Chemical Co., I venture to express the hope that the consolidation of New York and Brooklyn may soon be an accomplished fact.

I believe such political union to be to the interest of my company as well as to that of the cities themselves.

Respectfully yours,
GEO. W. KENYON.

SMITH & MARTIN,
7 NASSAU STREET,
NEW YORK, *January* 31, 1896.

HON. CLARENCE LEXOW, *Chairman, Joint Committee on Greater New York:*

Dear Sir.— I desire to urge upon your committee the wisdom

of carrying out as speedily as possible the will of the citizens of New York and Brooklyn, as expressed by the ballot already taken.

As a citizen of Brooklyn, doing business in New York, I feel that I have a vital interest in this question. With considerable interests in New York, and paying taxes there equal to those that I pay in Brooklyn, I am in a position where my New York taxes scarcely benefit me and where I have no voice or vote whatsoever in their disbursement. This is the condition of at least 100,000 citizens of Brooklyn to-day, and the result is that taxes so paid in New York by Brooklyn citizens are diverted from Brooklyn, and the largest industry that any city can have, that of the building trade, with all its ramifications, is practically paralyzed in the city of Brooklyn.

The two cities are essentially one, geographically, but their political separation has resulted in doing an injustice to the business interests of Brooklyn and is doing an equal injustice to the political interests of New York by preventing a participation in its management of that large and confessedly intelligent vote which exists in Brooklyn.

Very respectfully,

CHAS. ROBINSON SMITH.

WILLIAM T. MEREDITH & CO.,

48 WALL STREET,

NEW YORK, *January* 31, 1896.

HON. CLARENCE LEXOW, *Chairman:*

Dear Sir.—There ought to be but one opinion in the mind of every citizen who is anxious for the prosperity and happiness of the cities of New York and Brooklyn, and that is, that the attempts that are being made to delay the steps towards a final consummation of the complete joining of the two great cities under one Greater New York are practically attempts to dwarf the growth and the prosperity of the two communities.

Yours truly,

WILLIAM T. MEREDITH.

THE NATIONAL BANK OF NORTH AMERICA,
25 NASSAU STREET,
NEW YORK, *January* 31, 1896.

HON. A. H. GREENE:

Dear Sir.— In reply to your communication, it gives me pleasure to write that I am strongly in favor of the consolidation of New York, Brooklyn and contiguous territory. Such a union is inevitable in the near future, and will, I trust, be successfully consummated within the next two or three years. I am confident that the result will be for the best good and largest prosperity of the communities interested.

Very sincerely yours,
WARNER VAN NORDEN.

DR. EDWARD SEAMAN BUNKER,
178 ST. JOHN'S PLACE,
BROOKLYN, *January* 31, 1896.

HON. CLARENCE LEXOW, *Chairman, Etc.:*

Dear Sir.— I have been a resident of Brooklyn more than forty years. All my interests are here.

Consolidation, I think, would be advantageous to all the communities affected.

Referendum, I do not desire. I am no more competent to pass upon the complexities of the act than is my patient to decide what course of treatment I shall adopt on his case.

Truly yours,
E. S. BUNKER.

Mr. Grout disposed of " resubmission."

SWAYNE & SWAYNE, ATTORNEYS-AT-LAW,
120 BROADWAY,
NEW YORK, *January* 31, 1896.

ANDREW H. GREEN, ESQ., *214 Broadway, New York City.*

My Dear Mr. Green.— In compliance with the request which you have made of me, among others, to examine the bill introduced into the Senate, January 8, 1896, to consolidate into one the local governments of New York city, Brooklyn, and adjacent cities, and then write to you in reply.

No better bill has I think, been framed or easily could be. It first concludes the main fact that such consolidation is to be; a fact which is material, if not necessary, to a right disposition and earnestness on the part of those whose concurrence in matters of detail is part of the general plan.

It then provides time enough before the consolidation is operative, for full consideration and agreement, with no change whatever in the meantime, and with the State, through its Legislature and Executive, as arbiter, upon every aspect the consolidation, when it becomes operative, is to have.

This affords scope for careful, and, if need be, gradually, bringing about "an equal and uniform rate of taxation," and whatever else is found to be requisite to give to the consolidation itself an equitable basis.

Yours very truly,

WAGER SWAYNE.

MR. ANDREW H. GREEN:

I desire to say a few words. The question is, what is before this committee? I understand it is a bill to give effect to a vote of the people, and that is all there is of it, except it authorizes certain bills to be prepared to be hereafter presented to the Legislature. I can not go on with any remarks on this subject, which involves so great a subject, in five minutes time; and if the committee are satisfied with what they have heard, and prefer not to hear any further remarks, I should prefer to submit it now. I have no disposition whatever to prolong the session. The letters which I have presented are from persons in New York who have large interests here and desired to give expression to their sentiments. I have yet to hear one word against consolidation at this meeting, except the gentlemen who spoke over in the corner. Whenever the qustion of establishing any machinery of government in this area comes up then it will be time for them to be heard. This commission has been at work for six years on this question. The press has been full of it. It has been three or four times before the Legislature, and the bill finally passed to submit it to the people, and they passed upon it by a very large majority. Now whenever any bill comes up to set in motion any part of the government within this area, then is the time for these gentlemen to be heard. If they have anything to say about taxation, or any other branch of it, then, when that is brought before this body, they can be heard on it. There has been no want of care or want of entire appreciation of the delicacy of this whole subject, and in communication after communication that has been presented to the public, has been presented the greatest effort to assimilate, with an assurance that no public or private interest will be damaged in any way. Now, Mr. Chairman, if the committee think they have heard enough on this subject I have not the slightest desire to go on.

Mr. Lexow:

I do not think it will be necessary, Mr. Green, to continue the argument, except in so far as you can meet any argument on the other side. As I understand the situation to-day there has been no argument presented by either side against political consolidation. On the contrary, a number have announced in making their remarks, and in premising their remarks, that they were in favor of political consolidation, but that they did not wish the question of political consolidation to be solved excepting upon a more equitable distribution of the taxes and assessment question over the greater area. There is, therefore, really no necessity for argument on the question of political consolidation. So far as New York is concerned it seems to be conceded that they are in favor of that; but some gentlemen appear here to-day opposed to any proposition that lays a foundation for equalization of taxes and assessments over the greater area, and have asked for an adjournment upon that ground; and the committee now will consider that part of the question disembarrassed by the other.

MR. A. A. LEVEY:

I understood Senator Grady to say in his view it was useless to consider the question of consolidation at all if you eliminated from it this question of equalization.

MR. GRADY:

I said one was part of the other.

MR. LEVEY:

In other words you could not get a bill through the Legislature which did not involve in itself the determination of this question of equalization and taxation.

MR. GRADY:

That is my position.

MR. LEVEY:

Yes; and that is my position. Although we do not come here to oppose political consolidation as such, we do not favor it.

MR. GRADY:

Mr. Levey, can't you see that if the committee are agreed upon the question, that if they are to have any consolidation it must be upon fair and equal taxation, as we understand it, and equal assessment — if the committee have agreed that they have anything at all — they must have that; and what is the use of going through an investigation as to an accepted condition of things. That means New York shall pay something to Brooklyn and the other localities for the privilege of consolidation.

MR. LEVEY:

That is where we want to be heard.

MR. LEXOW:

I shall rest the question of hearing you on accepted state of things. You will understand that. The resolution passed by the Senate on Thursday. In all probability the financial statements of all these communities will be before the whole committee before they act, and these statements will show very clearly that if consolidation is had New York will pay a little more than she is paying now, and these others to be relieved will either get more for their money than they get now, or be asked to pay less in the way of taxes. The committee then must address themselves to the question as to whether or not, the people haven't given their opinion as to whether this consolidation should take place or not, shall it take place in the face of the admitted accepted fact that taxation must be uniform, that the assessment must be uniform, and that that means at the present time at all events that it shall be at the expense of New York. Now, is not that the situation?

Mr. Levey:

That is not Mr. Green's theory. Mr. Green says you can consider consolidation without the question of equalization of taxes.

Mr. Lexow:

Mr. Grady says it can not be. Each man voting on this main question has in mind certain propositions outside of the main proposition, and that is one of them. Neither the city of New York nor the city of Brooklyn would want any consolidation except on fair terms as between the two municipalities, and in voting on the main proposition we bear that in mind; but what I want you understand is that this proceeding does not foreclose any New York man in making himself heard on the general question of equalization of taxes and assessments; that this bill is a direction to the commission as to formulating the bill or charter that they shall bring in before the Legislature, a bill which shall substantially provide for an equalization of taxes and assessments throughout this extended area; but it is not absolutely obligatory on them, and New York can be heard on the question; and the resolution under which this committee is now operating will give New York an opportunity to be heard on that question when those bills which are submitted for that purpose are brought before the Legislature; therefore, we want to have this question now disembarrassed of any argument on the question of equality of taxation or assessment, because you will have your day in court when that proposition is reached.

MR. LEVEY:

If Mr. Green will agree that that question is not before this hearing at all, and is eliminated from the question, we can agree.

MR. GREEN:

It is as plain as a pike-staff in the bill that, for all, this consolidation takes effect on the 1st of January, 1898; and for all the legal purposes of the territory all the functions and all the government remains precisely the same. The taxing power remains the same in Brooklyn and New York until the Legislature, in its wisdom, thinks it best to act on that subject or fifty other subjects that may come up. That has been published in the newspapers, and I have said it over and over again. The only argument that was made on that subject that seemed to have some place, with all deference to the speakers, was that a passage of this bill would, in a sense, foreclose the Legislature; and that having passed the bill for the main question of consolidation, coupled with the bills which indirectly declare an intention to equalize taxes and assessments over the greater area, that they could substantially be foreclosed from taking any future action which would be at variance with the direction in the bill itself. But all legislation proceeds upon the fundamental basis of justice and fairness and equality to all interests; and this main proposition should not be, now in the eleventh hour, embarrassed by something which is subsidiary and auxiliary to the whole, and not connected with the main proposition at all.

MR. BRUSH:

May I put in a question which has been bothering me some; that is this, you pass a bill and suggest in the bill equalization of taxation, but perhaps the bill is prepared to equalize taxation and assessment and that bill is not passed, does that question prevent the consolidation?

MR. GREEN:

Not at all.

MR. BRUSH:

You may not pass a bill for equalization of taxation, but for consolidation you do.

MR. LEXOW:

The bill places itself on an equality of taxation, and that is the only fair adjustment as stated by Senator Grady. It is a self-evident fact, however, that if future hearings upon this question should disclose a dishonest situation, one that would work such an injustice to the city of New York, that an absolute basis of equality of taxation and assessments could not be reached excepting by being a gross injustice to the city, then it would be for future legislation to consider that subject, unembarrassed by any comprehensive declaration in the bill. I think that is very plain, and I think every gentleman on this committee agrees with that general proposition; and that being the case, unless there is argument to be made against the main proposition, we see no reason why the time of the committee should be taken up by discussion of a question, the discussion of which will have ample room, the discussers of which will have ample opportunity when we come to consider these subsidiary questions.

MR. LEVEY:

We think the phraseology of the Lexow bill — you can not get away from the fact that when this bill is passed the Legislature and this committee will be committed to the framing of bills, " Directed to prepare such bills as will provide for retaining equal taxation and valuation in this district." And it is that principle we are opposed to, and we appear in opposition to that principle, and even in the preparation of a bill. It prejudices our case.

MR. LEXOW:

I do not agree with the gentleman at all. As I introduced that bill it seems to me my interpretation of that bill should stand. All that bill means is, we are going in this consolidation to treat every part of the annexed territory fairly, and in any consideration of the question the benefits derived by the city of New York in consolidation have got to be taken into consideration. If New York pays a few cents or dollars more in the way of taxes after consolidation than she did before, but derives benefits from consolidation which would enable her to pay that ten times over, certainly then you could not disagree with us in establishing a uniform system of taxation and assessment throughout the district. Now, those are matters properly left to legislation. All this bill does is to declare the political union.

MR. ROMAINE:

We are not here to advocate political union, but we do not oppose it.

MR. LEXOW:

We are simply giving effect to the voice of New York requiring political union, at the same time expressing ourselves as being in favor of absolute justice towards the sister cities or places that are annexed.

MR. ANDREW H. GREEN:

I would call attention of the gentlemen to one or two paragraphs of the communication of the commissioners with the Legislature. This commission was constructed purely on the home-rule principle. Every district in it has its representation on this commission. The State is represented by six persons appointed by the Governor. It has the State Engineer and Surveyor. The city of New York has itself represented by appointees of the mayor; the city of Brooklyn its representatives appointed by the mayor of Brooklyn; and the counties of Westchester, Kings, Queens and Richmond all have their representatives appointed by the supervisors of those various counties. So, the constitution of the commission is strictly a home-rule constitution, and every district proposed to be involved in this matter has its representative members diligently attending to his duties, except the gentleman from Westchester, who has not, but Westchester fortunately came in. I want to read one or two paragraphs here: "To provide, then, the methods and means for the transfer from existing conditions, complicated as they are, to those more simple and direct, without shock or injustice or injury to persons or property, there may well be employed the utmost forecast, the widest experience and the most conscientious and painstaking application. While the commissioners would gladly see this transition promptly effected, they are of the opinion that the details involved in the transfer, so far as they affect the tenure of existing officials, their emoluments, and the scope of their duties, should be left to be worked out without disturbance as time brings fitting opportunity, as the Legislature may direct, and as considerations of prudence and protection of public and private interests dictate." It is to distrust the Legislature and the representatives of the various organizations to say that when these various questions come up before the Legislature, each district having its representative in the representation, Brooklyn having its seven Senators and twenty-one Assemblymen, is to distrust their own representatives to say that anything will get past the Legislature that is not going to be fair and honorable and just to anybody. That is precisely what the bill means, that there shall be an equal and just rate of taxation for all, and that may come by next year or may come about the year after. If this bill has not passed the Legislature — a gentleman made the suggestion that this bill be amended. The committee have full power over this bill, but the simple object of this bill was to effect the consolidation, and put in motion the means of submitting to the Legislature a proper subsidiary bill.

MR. BRUSH:

You say this matter of equalization of taxation might come

about the next year or the year after. Is it not possible it might come about in ten years?

MR. GREEN:

It will come about, sir, in just this way: You and I meet in the street. You and I are in the same line of business. I say to you, "Would you like, Senator, to do away with the double expense and conduct a partnership?" You say, "No;" and that ends it. You say yes, and then we have got to agree upon the terms.

MR. BRUSH:

Consolidation is a fact, and you have got to accept that, and accept the conditions of the fact.

MR. GREEN:

Yes. Let me carry out my figure, if you please. You say yes, and we agree on the terms. The people of these sections say yes, and we want this consolidation. If every man in New York and every man in Brooklyn should say that this consolidation should take place it can not take place under our form of government except through the Legislature. Who is the Legislature? How is it made up? Brooklyn has its representative. Everybody is there to look after the interest of that locality. There is no other authority than the Legislature that can dictate or consummate consolidation. You have asked the advice of the people, and they have said they want it, and it is your business to carry it out, in my judgment.

POLICE COMMISSIONER PARKER:

Mr. Chairman: It seems almost incredible that there should be any question about the meaning of that bill. The partnership has been used as a means of illustration through this discussion. It contains a fallacy. They meet and discuss whether they shall go into partnership, and they, and they alone, decide it. That is not the case here. A and B — New York and Brooklyn — are both suitors before the Legislature. The people as a whole have decided whether two corporations shall be fused into one; and as we said in Albany, "It is a mere act of grace" that they are permitted to voice their sense on that question. It is above all things just, equitable and fair; but still in its essence, an act of grace. Let us thus put the question. Suppose that A and B, not having free will, not having decisive power, were to say, "Shall we go into partnership, and shall we submit to the sole arbiter that there is in existence — C — made our arbiter by law— the question of what the terms shall be." That is the state of affairs. They say, "We shall. We have only one person to decide on what terms we shall join — the Legislature." That is all that is said. In brief the duties of the commission by that provision are that it shall submit, among other measures, a bill providing for "attaining." That word means the sole means by which that is to be done. The provision simply says, if I may put it succinctly, "Go, Commission, draft such a bill as seems to be a fair and equal and just thing. Submit it to us, and we will say what shall be done with it. It practically meant to put this bill before the Legislature so they shall pass on that question; and the next Legislature, if they do not see fit to indorse that view, can repeal it. New York, Brooklyn and the whole State can elect delegates against it. Senator Grady has pointed out what, in my opinion, is the only way ultimately to rule that greater city — by equality of taxation. You may take as many steps to avoid it as you please, that is the only escape in the end from the anomaly of different burdens upon different sections of the same population. Not a right but is preserved by this bill. It will take years of discussion, years of fight, years of obstruction, years of labor to settle that whole affair. I only put this as one last word to the gentlemen on the other side who object to that provision and see great trouble in it. Let them formulate, if they can, some clause that shall indicate at once the term towards fairness that the Legislature of this State has all along extended to these constituent municipalities, and will preserve the rights of the municipalities to any better degree, and I have no doubt this Legislature will accept it.

MR. LEVEY:

I would like to reply to a few of the arguments Mr. Parker has just made on a legal standard. Mr. Parker is evidently of the opinion that a corporation of the city of New York and its franchises depend upon the grace of the Legislature of the State of New York? Now, I differ with him as to his law. I think that under the last Constitution of the State of New York, the Legislature of the State of New York has no power to interfere with the county of New York; and I think we will find when he comes to the Court of Appeals that the Court of Appeals will agree with me rather than him. But that agress with the difficulties that we begin to see on the horizon of this question, that this question has ultimately to be decided in the courts, and will be there so decided. We see here, in the course of this discussion, that it is impossible to eliminate this proposition from the question of taxation and valuation. The discussion has brought it out. It is clear that it is impossible to decide this question of consolidation under this bill of yours here without considering this question, and we see that we should, to go on with this examination under the motion that we have made, examine our witnesses, and show you the financial condition of the city of New York, and the financial situation of these other municipalities that desire to be brought in here, and then see exactly what would result if a uniform tax were to be put on all these communities, show you what would be fair to the communities to be brought in. Otherwise the discussion of this question and drafting a bill making political consolidation, without interfering with any department of this Greater New York, without disturbing a single office holder, would be a mere vox praetoris magnun. Now, for instance I am a property owner in the town of New Utrecht which is a portion of the county of Kings now. If I had an opportunity to examine the officials of the county of Kings on the condition of the former town of New Utrecht I could show that the city of Brooklyn to-day is up to its constitutional limit of taxation, and beyond it; in other words, the city of Brooklyn is to-day bankrupt.

MR. GREEN:

That has nothing to do with it.

MR. GRADY:

So it is. Now go on. Its financial statement will show how near the financial responsibility is.

MR. LEVEY:

It does not show how much that is in these bonds.

MR. GRADY:

We can not go into that. If you are going to have this committee decide on the validity of the bonds, suppose we did adjourn for a week, suppose we summoned the officials here, would not the result of all the investigation resolve itself into the financial statements of these several localities?

MR. LEVEY:

It would be necessary to examine what amount of revenue bonds are issued. For instance a mere financial statement would not cover the rights of Long Island City.

MR. GRADY:

Why not?

MR. LEVEY:

Because the deeper you go into the finances of Long Island City the more inexplicable they are. It has no way of paying its public officers and police. It is a disgrace and shame to the State of New York.

MR. LEXOW:

Does it not come to the proposition that we can admit here that every one of these municipalities are not in the best financial condition, that their financial condition does not compare with the city of New York, and we will start an argument that, admitting all these facts, and you can not paint them any blacker than our imagination can paint them; but it don't interfere with the main proposition that the committee shall pass the consolidation bill, making a consolidation bill, without considering the question of taxation at all.

MR. ROMAINE:

To the extent that we feel we are prejudiced by your committee bringing in such recommendations I think we ought to record our protest with you.

MR. LEXOW:

Suppose we put in the body of this bill that, among other things, this commission shall report bills provided for a single-headed police commission in the greater area, do you mean to say that we foreclose the Legislature, at the next Legislature when it comes to pass upon that particular bill, from putting in a bi-partisan commission, or any other commission it deemed wise?

MR. ROMAINE:

It might; but it would prejudice the taxpayers of New York if they do not lend their opposition.

MR. LEXOW:

This is the conclusion at which the committee has arrived:

MR. GRADY:

Let me say before the Chairman reads that conclusion that I have not read it, and I will dissent from it before I read it.

MR. GREEN:

I think the appointments of the gentlemen here by the mayor of New York are quite as competent to protect the taxpayers of the city of New York as these gentlemen are. I do not choose to sit here and see a man say he appears here to defend the taxpayers of the city of New York. I attend to that business myself.

MR. LEVEY:

Who constituted you their protector?

MR. GREEN:

The mayor of the city of New York. If you look at the laws you will see that.

MR. LEXOW:

Inasmuch as the ground of application for adjournment is confined to the question of tax equalization and valuation, and as ample opportunity will be had for the discussion of the subject after the committee makes its report on the main proposition; and inasmuch as the information required and suggested by those asking for the adjournment will be procured by the committee without formal postponement of this hearing, the application for a week's adjournment will be denied.

MR. BRUSH:

I wish to go on record as dissenting from that decision. I wish to get all the light I can on this subject; and I would like to hear everything we can hear that will give us any light; and I would be in favor of these gentlemen having the extension of time.

MR. ROMAINE:

In the sense that we feel prejudice by the ruling, we present this protest:

Subcommittee of the Joint Committee on the Affairs of Cities:

The undersigned citizens and taxpayers of the city of New York, in their own behalf and as counsel for the Taxpayers' Anti-Equalization League of New York, and of all citizens or taxpayers of the city of New York, who may now or hereafter signify their approval of the course of the undersigned, hereby except to and protest against the denial of their application for an adjournment of this hearing, and for process by way of subpoena to the proposed witnesses named in said application dated February 1, 1896, as an infringement of the rights guaranteed to them by the Constitution of the State of New York, and of the United States.

JAMES A. DEERING,
AUGUSTUS A. LEVEY,
BENJ. F. ROMAINE,
Individually and of Counsel.

Dated February 1, 1896.

The following memorial was then submitted to the sub-committee: Consolidation by Hon. Chauncey M. Depew, at the dinner of the New England Society, December 21, 1894, and the memorial to the Legislature by the Consolidation Commission.

The second speaker was Chauncey M. Depew, whose toast was "Municipal Consolidation." He said: Mr. President and Gentlemen: Under ordinary circumstances it would be a hazardous undertaking for a New Yorker to invade Brooklyn in the interest of consolidation. I come here to-night, however, not as a soldier, a conspirator or a missionary, but as a wooer. So experienced a lass as Brooklyn, ought to be besieged by the usual process which reduce a beleaguered city. Her heart should be surrounded with ditches and earthworks, her supplies cut off, her avenues of communication intercepted, and finally the citadel stormed in the hope of a surrender at discretion. But Father Knickerbocker, whose ambassador I am, adopts no such militant procedure. He bids me lay his heart, his fortune and his future at fair Brooklyn's feet. He appreciates that he is rather mature, and relies upon the fact that can be stated with bated breath that Brooklyn is at least old enough to know her own mind. Ever since the fair Priscilla bade John Aldine speak for himself, the Puritan maiden has known well how to bring the bashful, halting or uncertain lover to the altar.

Puritan Brooklyn, following the traditions of the Mayflower, has not been backward in coming forward, and I am here to-night on her invitation, and she also invited me to make this proposition. I know that the Rev. Dr. Storrs, than whom there is no higher intellectual, moral or spiritual authority in this community, has declared against the union, and on lesser and narrower lines the local critics have also been heard. These opinions embarrass the situation, but nothing can stop the inevitable.

All arguments against Greater New York are based upon the experiences or the lessons of the past, and of the distant past. It is the privilege of our glorious period that it exists because of revolutions and upheavals which have destroyed the value of the past and precedents. The ancient, the mediaeval, the feudal and the independent city are pictures which have value like the canvases of the old masters, portraying saints and martyrdom, but which teach few lessons to the modern student. The Greek city presented in larger and fuller measure than we can hope to reach the elements of the high civilization and civic pride which justify the ardor of the local patriot who would limit the boundaries of his town. In Athens was a population which did not compare in numbers with one of our great cities. Within its walls was concentrated that splendor of intellectual gifts and development which inspired the philosophers of the academy, the orators of the Assembly and the Areopagus, the architects of the Parthenon, the painters of the immortal pictures and the dramatists whose works have survived the centuries. But without its walls was brutish ignorance, and more than half its population were slaves. Its wives and daughters had no proper place in the domestic circle; its superb and cultured intellectuality was confined to a few brilliant men and bad women. The mediaeval city, whether a free town or the seat of royal power, was primarily a fortress. Its industries, its arts, and its learning were subordinate to its castles, its walls, its moats and its drawbridges. It could encourage population only to the point where it could stand siege and feed the people.

Steam, electricity and invention have created conditions in our times where the city assumes new relations to the world. One-third the population of civilized countries are gathered in these busy communities. The farmer and the miner and the sailor still gather from the fruitful fields and the bowels of the earth and the depth of the sea their wealth, but the city works up the raw material in its manifold industries and factories, attracts enterprise and becomes the representative of national life.

It is true that this beautiful city of Brooklyn has a singularly intelligent and homogeneous population; it is true that it possesses characteristics in its Puritan origin and development which lend to it peculiar grace and strength. It is also true that these qualities could be preserved, and the city become infinitely more a matter of pride to its citizens, by being part of the metropolis of the two American hemispheres.

It is seldom that poetry and prose, finance and fiction, sentiment and sense are in unison for a political idea. But they are all in harmony with the idea of the imperial city, which is and shall remain the center and source of the industrial, the financial and the intellectual life of the American republic.

New York, with a million and a half people, and Brooklyn, with a million, are to be easily surpassed in a decade by Chicago, and buffeted by the petty strife of figures and censuses. The Greater New York, with three millions of inhabitants, is easily the empress of the new world and a power in the old.

It can not be claimed that better government is more sure without than with the union with New York, you have not been free from similar circles; if we have found it difficult to break ours, you were for years struggling to escape from yours. Both New York and Brooklyn have furnished the argument against self-government in cities. Both of them have given to the pessimist and to the advocate of State control the illustrations to enforce their ideas; both of them have had periods when the most hopeful of us have despaired, and yet by the resolution of the twelvemonth pessimist and opitmist are united in enthusiasm for popular government in great cities. A trifling accident in each aroused inquiry, and the result of inquiry demonstrated the ever-present power of public opinion and public spirit. I called attention three years ago, at a dinner given to me in this city, to the rumors current of municipal corruption. The mayor, himself, a worthy and respectable man, left the table in a rage. Instantly, not only Brooklyn, but the whole country, began to inquire if it was chaff, why not meet it with chaff; if it was a charge, why not answer it by refutation; if it was false, why not deny it; if it was true, then the people demanded a remedy. And so a mad mayor broke the Brooklyn ring.

A Presbyterian clergyman in New York made charges of which he had no proof, but which he believed from public rumor. He was summoned before the grand jury to be jailed as a slanderer, or laughed out of town as a scandal-monger. Again the community wanted to know whether the rumors and the reports and the charges were true or false. The answer has revolutionized the great city and made a hero of Dr. Parkhurst. The forces which produced these reforms were not on the Fifth avenue in New York, nor the Heights in Brooklyn. They were those whom Abraham Lincoln, loved to call the "plain people" — who live in the cottages and tenements, who toil day and night, but who, when they appreciated the situation, brought to the rescue of the city their intelligent and indomitable courage and civic patriotism. I found the Bowery blooming with peach trees.

Two-thirds of the business men in Brooklyn sleep here at night, but their business, their capital and their energies are in New York. For them and their affairs the stone piers and basins and docks are builded; for them the great warehouses are extended and the granite structures rise to enormous heights to house them; for them the banks and trust companies and the exchanges multiply. New York for them derives the sources of her wealth, the splendor of her trade, the extent of her commerce and the taxable resources which enable her to be lavishly extravagant, and still, so far as taxation is concerned, apparently economical.

It is because there is drawn to New York capital, individual and corporate, and because there is concentrated there such immense wealth, that on an assessment twenty-five per cent. lower than in Brooklyn of real estate values the tax rate is one per cent. less.

New York is jealous of New Jersey across the North river, Brooklyn and Long Island across the East. She does what she can to retain her population within her borders. She does not meet you in your effort to bridge the river on one side and she scorns the proposals of New Jersey on the other. The crowded tenements of a block are torn down and upon their sites rise the sky-scraping buildings of twenty-two and twenty-four stories which would arouse the anger of the gods, if they did not excite their admiration, at the audacity of architect and constructor. The people thus made homeless are crowded into already congested districts until the density of population surpasses that of any other city in the world.

New York frantically seeks to retain its population within its own limits by the panacea of rapid transit, but the difficulties of a transportation problem by which twenty miles are to be covered within as many minutes at a rate of fare founded upon stops and the filling up and discharging of cars every two thousand feet do not tempt the capitalists. The city places its resources in the hands of the individual or corporation who will undertake the task, and yet there is little enthusiasm or confidence in the project. The individual or corporation who undertakes to pay four and one-half per cent. on the city's loan wants to see for his risk a handsome profit. If, however, New York and Brooklyn and Queens county and Staten Island were one, the energies of the great city would not be concentrated upon north and south lines of transit. Bridges would span the East river at half a dozen points of prominence, tunnels would be dug under it and the ferries would increase their capacity. It would be then not a matter of policy but of pride. The congested population finding its way under the river, on the river and over the river, would meet the developed resources for transportation and transit on this side to be carried to cheap and healthful homes.

The pessimist says this is a real estate view. Suppose it is. The history of our municipal development shows that when real estate is solidly advancing the prosperity of everybody is correspondingly accelerated. If there were hundreds of thousands of people a year seeking homes in the suburbs of your city it would mean wealth to the holder of the land; it would also mean that barometer of prosperity — the quick transfer of lots from one to another by enhancing prices. It would mean the employment of a large army of mechanics in the building and equipment of the houses; it would mean the vast distribution of money in the purchase of materials; it would mean local industries and internal commerce, all tending to the employment of labor and the distribution of wealth.

You have the beauties of the situation upon your Heights; in the healthfulness of the ozone of the sea which pervades your streets and your houses; in the natural facilities for drainage and the absence of the conditions which poison the atmosphere, healthful opportunities for a resident population which are offered nowhere in New York. And yet the anxiety to live in New York, to be part of the metropolis, to be a segment, however small, of that imperial power which stands for so much in every department of American life, crowds the avenues of our city so that equivalent situations in New York sell for ten and fifty times as much as in Brooklyn.

You go to London, and you find its Thames spanned by bridges which are historic and by new bridges upon new models and upon new theories in constant course of construction. I was last winter in Rome, to discover that with all the poverty of the country and the city, millions were being expended to unite the older and the newer towns across the turbulent Tiber. The same improvements I discovered in Florence, over the Arno, and the same in Vienna, over the Danube. It was because one government, one municipality, moved by a common spirit, was earnestly seeking to bring all its sections in harmonious and profitable contact.

When the lower towns of Westchester county were annexed to New York the conservative voted against it and dreaded the result. They were ideal communities, not only in their civic conditions and in their neighborhood life, but in invaluable historic associations. No sooner, however, were they united to the great city, than without feeling the additional taxation, the city assumed the opening of streets, the laying out of their avenues, the projecting and building of their parks and their sewer and water systems. None of these things could have been done by the towns without burdens which would have bankrupted them; but with taxes less than those of their town life, they were brought within the full benefit and enjoyment of metropolitan oportunities, development and progress.

The essence of the marvelous development of the nineteenth century is combination. It is the strength, the force and motive power of our age. It crowned the Emperor William at Versailles and created modern Germany. It made Rome the capital of Italy. It is inspiring the Slav and the Scandinavian for government and liberty on broader lines. It has made London, Paris, Berlin, Vienna and Rome, Europe. It has drawn all the surrounding towns to Chicago, Philadelphia and St. Louis. The lesson of Puritan ancestry and experience is for union, and in union strength.

This day of all days in the year is full of inspiration derived from Plymouth Rock for Greater New York. The Plymouth Colony represented the flower and fruitage of the Puritan idea. Persecution had done more than confirm their faith. It gave them a prophetic vision of the future which developed a broad spirituality, which in its declarations and conduct produced that consummate realization of the hope of man — American liberty. Their eleven years in Holland had brought them in contact with the common school and with other sects, under the blessings of toleration and religious liberty in its modern sense. They bore with them, as they sailed from Delfthaven, the immortal message of Pastor Robinson, that God has not revealed the whole of His truth, and therefore it was right to search, to inquire, to speculate and to doubt. They formulated in the cabin of the Mayflower for the first time in the ages the doctrine of man's equal rights before the law. Around them in Massachusetts Colony gathered bigots and zealots, who hung witches, banished Baptists and persecuted Quakers, who would not permit anyone to hold office who did not belong to their congregations, and who formed and exercised a modified sort of Church Tammany. There were 40,000 of these outside, narrow-minded Puritans of Massachusetts bay and 7,000 of the enlightened and developed Pilgrims at Plymouth. But the far-sighted Pilgrim was a State-builder. He realized the power, the influence and the supremacy of concentrated and homogenous populations, and by mutual consent Plymouth was consolidated with Massachusetts Bay. The Pilgrim leaven leavened the whole lump and the fruit of the Pilgrim and the Puritan marriage impressed itself upon the Constitution of the United States, upon the Declaration of Independence, and upon the Constitution of every new State which has come into the Union, and carried the common school, the church and the blessings of equal liberty to the creation, development and conditions of the American Republic as we have it to-day.

One hundred years ago to-day and Philadelphia was twice as large as New York. Ten years from now and Chicago will be a third larger than New York, as circumscribed by Manhattan island and the annexed district. When the World's Fair went to Chicago the world knew her not. To-day she is one of the most celebrated and best known of cities, and her population has increased by reason of this knowledge and the prestige that the great fair gave her more rapidly within two years than any other municipality has ever grown.

There is a national and international power and prosperity of incalculable value, which is accorded to the unquestioned metropolis of a country. As soon as Berlin became the metropolis of Germany she drew from the cities and from the rest of the country their best in every department of life, so that she is not only one of the largest towns in Europe, not only advancing with a rapidity in population and in the construction of houses and in the laying out of streets and avenues equal to that of any booming town in the United States, but she is, by the very aggregation within her walls of the political, intellectual and financial life of Germany, a greater safeguard and strength for German unity than the throne, or parliament, or army or navy. London, with its 5,000,000 of inhabitants, is the capital of the world. A residence there of three months is a liberal education. Its financial institutions control the government and the policies, to a large degree, of South America, Europe, Asia and Africa. Syndicates in parlors on Lombard street, by the results of an afternoon's consultation, affect the destinies of hundreds of millions of the human race all over the world. Meetings and conventions stop massacres in Armenia, ameliorate the condition of the Jews in Russia, or compel action of infinite moment to the civilization of African tribes or the condition of the people of India. Through its drawing-rooms pass all that is most eminent in statesmanship, in literature, in art, and in genius of every land, our own being always well represented.

So impressed is the European mind with the representative character of cities that it judges countries by their society, their business and their government. I was in London one year, and met there American Governors, United States Senators and Congressmen. Said Mr. Gladstone to me: "I had a conversation last evening with a most interesting countryman of yours." I ran over the list of Governors, United States Senators and Congressmen then in the city, and he said: "No; he held a much more important position than any of those. He was once mayor of New York." I was very glad that the Grand Old Man met with such a worthy representative of all that is best in New York, as ex-Mayor Abram S. Hewitt.

With the Greater New York an accomplished fact, the metropolitan center of this republic and of these two hemispheres is fixed forever. In the future, as in the past, only in a larger degree, the banking-houses of the world will have their agencies in New York. The thrift and energies of the country will concentrate in New York. New York will continue to be the greatest manufacturing city in the United States. Wall street will remain the financial heart, whose throb-beats are felt by the miner in Colorado, the fruitgrower in California, the sheepraiser in Texas, and the farmer, manufacturer and laborer all over the country.

The metropolis will stand, as a metropolis always does, for sound currency, for wise finance and for stability of credit. In a larger measure than ever before, great calamities like the Chicago fire and the Johnstown flood will be relieved by the millions of dollars gathered from New York. In national crises the government will appeal with confidence to the city which floated the national debt in the Civil War, in 1863, and took in an afternoon the fifty millions of bonds required to meet the demands of the Treasury in 1894. Scientists and educators in every department will make the city the university of the country. The intellectual life of the nation will concentrate here upon magazines, books and publications which make the fame and name of the century. The artists in stone or in metals, or with the brush, or upon the dramatic or lyric stage, will seek reputation in New York. The grandeur of the city, the rapidity of its growth, the majesty of its power, the splendor of its civilization, the prosperity of its people, and the intelligence of its citizens will compel honest government and pure administration. In twenty years the office next to President of the United States in the eyes of the world will be that of mayor of Greater New York.

THE COMMISSION'S REPORT.

The consolidated bill, as introduced by Senator Lexow, was drawn up by the Greater New York Commission, which also sent the following report to the Legislature:

To the Honorable the Legislature of the State of New York:

The commissioners appointed under chapter 311 of the Laws of 1890 to inquire into and report upon the consolidation of certain areas about the port of New York into one municipality, respectfully report: That during the nearly five years that have passed since their appointment they have given much time and attention to the work assigned to them. It was only at the session of 1894 that the passage of the act to submit the question of consolidation to the arbitrament of the electors was secured. These electors, availing themselves of the provisions of this act, have given their verdict in favor of union.

The Secretary of State certifies the official result of the ballot as follows:

VOTE OF CONSOLIDATION.

New York County.— Total vote cast, 166,505; for, 96,938; against, 59,959; defective and blank, 9,608.

Kings County.— Total vote cast, 129,466; for, 64,744; against, 64,467; defective and blank, 255.

Queens County.— Total vote cast, 12,453; for, 7,712; against, 4,741.

Richmond County.— Total vote cast, 7,041; for, 5,531; against, 1,505; defective and blank, 5.

Town of Eastchester.— Total vote cast, 634; for, 374; against, 260.

Town of Westchester.— Total vote cast, 1,241; for, 620; against, 621.

Town of Pelham.— Total vote cast, 404; for, 251; against, 153.

It will be seen that every municipality proposed by the commissioners for union has declared in its favor, with but two exceptions, the towns of Flushing and Westchester, the vote in the former of these towns being 1,144 for and 1,407 against, and in the latter there appears a majority of one against. Taking the total vote throughout the area of the greater city, there stands a decided majority of 44,188 in favor of consolidation, and it is not to be left unobserved that the great municipality that offers the chief advantages of union is unmistakably in favor of it.

The popular will having been thus expressed, it remains for the Legislature to determine the terms and conditions upon which effect shall be given to it.

The great diversity of civil jurisdictions established by law — legislative, executive and judicial, each at work in its own way — within the area proposed for the greater city is but rarely understood and their respective functions are often ill-defined and imperfectly comprehended.

A few statistics are subjoined to give some idea of the complexity of affairs with which we have to deal:

NAME OF COUNTY.	Amount of State tax for 1894–1895.	Population, census of 1890.	Percentage of assessed to actual value as shown by State assessors for 1893.	The assessed value of real estate for 1893.
New York	$4,186,119 96	1,801,739	63.0	$1,562,582,393
Kings	1,114,886 36	995,276	68.4	518,501,441
Queens	154,100 51	*117,982	50.0	50,672,429
Richmond	58,344 88	53,452	50.0	19,750,376
Westchester	242,119 41	†29,412	51.0	82,802,083

NAME OF COUNTY.	The assessed value of personal estate for 1893.	Area, square miles.	Area, acres.	Debt value of municipal property.
New York	$370,936,136	38.85	24,864.00	$105,784,549 12
Kings	19,704,920	77.51	49,606.40	Not authentically ascertained.
Queens	2,377,860	*123.98	79,347.20	
Richmond	162,950	57.19	36,601.60	
Westchester	2,277,956	†20.24	12,953.60	

* Includes the whole town of Hempstead.
† Includes only the whole towns of Eastchester, Westchester and Pelham. Sinking fund deducted. State, $9,253,702.88. Entire State tax for the whole.

As things now are, counties, towns, incorporated villages, school districts, officers and boards, with their varied powers and duties, wheels within wheels, issue their mandates, contract debts, devise and execute each of its own plans.

Were this complicated condition confined to the preservation of order and peace, and to affairs not involving physical undertakings, the untoward consequences might pass away with the lapse of time, leaving no traces other than great expense and discomfort.

When, however, it comes about that the numerous agencies employed in this confused condition are applied to, and act upon material works, it will readily be seen that the results, becoming fixed, are projected into the future, with continuous cost and discomfort to succeeding generations.

To fuse these multifarious powers, duties and functions, involving as they do, the conveniences, the necessities, the nearest interests of 3,000,000 people, into a unit of govermental care and control is a task of no ordinary dimensions.

The suspension or disturbance of the varied machinery of administration now operating within the area to be united, until other agencies are provided, will inevitably bring confusion, litigation, and possibly further damaging consequences.

To provide, then, the methods and means for the transfer from existing conditions, complicated as they are, to those more simple and direct, without shock or injustice or injury to persons or property, there may well be employed the utmost forecast, the widest experience and the most conscientious and painstaking application.

While the commissioners would gladly see this transition promptly effected, they are of the opinion that the details involved in the transfer, so far as they affect the tenure of existing officials, their emoluments, and the scope of their duties, should be left to be worked out without disturbance as time brings fitting opportunity, as the Legislature may direct, and as considerations of prudence and protection of public and private interests dictate.

What is at present proposed is the enactment of a simple declaration by the lawmaking authority that the territory concerned, its people and its property, shall thereafter be one city, under one government, with one destiny; and the bill herewith submitted to the Legislature is framed in consonance with these views.

That the administration of the affairs of the enlarged city should be continued under the same corporate name, "The Mayor, Aldermen and Commonalty of the City of New York," seems too clear to admit of serious discussion. The city of New York is known the world over, and it appears quite inexpedient to attempt a change of its name.

In any thorough consideration of this subject there occur three prominent conditions that must sooner or later be dealt with — namely, debt, taxation and valuation.

It seems but reasonable, that those intending a partnership

should each bring some contribution towards the accomplishment of the ends for which it is formed.

The indebtedness of the divisions proposed to be united differs widely, as thus the rate of taxation and the percentage that the valuation for taxations bears to actual value.

In the city of New York the debt of the city and county are practically the same; and though this debt differs in detail as to maturity and rate of interest, it is one debt, and its volume easily ascertained. There is also but one rate of taxation and one standard for valuation.

In Brooklyn it is very different. There are some fifty odd rates of taxation, each higher than that of New York, and there exists both a county and a city debt. Compared with the simpler condition of New York, this is confusing; and it would seem that the sooner the situation is simplified the better it would be.

However desirable it may be, it is very obvious that the diversity in the financial affairs of the various municipalities can not at once be replaced by a system less intricate and more simple. It also must be left to be adjusted by time and the equitable provisions of future legislation, and in such wise that ultimately within the whole area of the greater city but one standard of valuation for taxation, one equal rate of taxation, and one debt-contracting authority only, shall exist.

There appears to be no insurmountable obstacle to the vivifying of the frame work of the proposed unification, by the immediate setting in motion of the executive departments of police and health.

The appropriate functions of these two bodies, which are to be exercised in the common field, are admittedly essential for all, and, in the interests of all can be neglected in none.

Should your honorable body deem it wise to put these particular agencies at work at an early date, the appointment of commissioners of police and of health, with jurisdiction over the whole area of the greater city, might well be left to the joint action of the present mayors of the two principal cities, with the provision that such of the subordinates of these commissioners as are to act in divisions outside of these cities should for the present be made upon the nomination of the existing authorities of these divisions respectively.

The existing forces to remain as now with their duties and emoluments until these beneficial changes are made, which it is quite too apparent are imperatively demanded.

It is perhaps as well to call to mind the fact that the commission that has for nearly five years been devoted to this work, was constituted on the basis of the home rule idea. The State, the parent of all its subdivisions, has among the members of the commission the State Engineer and Surveyor and a representation of six members appointed by the Governor; the cities of New York and Brooklyn each has its representative designated by their respective mayors; and the counties of Kings, Queens, Richmond and Westchester each has its representative, designated by their respective boards of supervisors, so that the commission is distinctly representative of the various localities.

The commissions are also of the opinion that among the earliest and most essential movements for administration of the contemplated union should be the constituting of an elective local legislative body, with adequate power and sway to give to it dignity, respect and importance. This is the solid and only permanent basis of local self-government — home rule.

In this body the elected representatives of each locality should have a large voice in the determination of the improvements to be made and the moneys to be expended in their respective districts, preserving local influence with local central authority, which latter should be relieved of administrative details when its intervention is not necessary, and the local representatives intrusted with such duties as they can conveniently discharge, care being taken to respect the natural desire of the citizens of various localities for the preservation of memorials of historic achievements and local traditions.

Every year that passes brings with it new complications, fixes those existing more firmly, greatly increasing the obstacles to union, while rendering its desirability more manifest.

In London, the subject of amalgamating its congeries of subdivisions, jurisdictions, powers and authorities has claimed attention for more than fifty years. Commissioners after commissioners have addressed themselves to the task.

As late as March, 1893, a Royal Commission issued "To Consider the Proper Conditions under which Amalgamation of the City and County of London can be effected, and to make specific and practical proposals for that purpose."

The following is an extract from the text of this appointment:

"And for the better effecting the purpose of this our commission, we do by these present give and grant unto you, or any three or more of you, full power to call before you such persons as you shall judge likely to afford you any information upon the subject of this our commission; and also to call for, have access to and to examine all such books, documents, registers and records as may afford you the fullest information on the subject, and to inquire of and concerning the premises by all other lawful ways and means whatsoever.

"And we do further by these presents, authorize and empower you, or any three or more of you, to visit and personally inspect such places in our United Kingdom as you may deem it expedient so to inspect, for the more effectual carrying out of the purpose aforesaid."

With no "feeble" or shrimped authority, but supplied with those ample powers so evidently essential for the intelligent performance of the great work entrusted to them, these London commissioners proceeded, and in August last submitted a report bearing signs of patient investigation, judicious discrimination, and an experienced and informed statemanship.

Reading its pages, one can but feel an anxious desire that the unification of the cluster of municipalities about our port may not be postponed to be entangled with increasing obstacles, but that it may be now resolutely and disinterestedly met and consummated.

With a climate that contributes and favors the beauties and the bounties that come with the ever varying seasons, with a diversity of topography that responds to the amenities and the requirements of a great city, with a population of similar pursuits and interests, with capacious waters that bear to its marts the commerce of nations, nothing beyond the approval of the expressed wish of the electors by their representatives in the Legislature remains to insure the permanent establishment at this port of a city that shall in its institutions and in its administration stand as a type and an example.

If we would secure in this most important undertaking the best and broadest advantages, conveniences and economies for the present and the future, it needs that we look to those whose vision is equal to taking a wider horizon, rather than to those whose apprehensions, however groundless, naturally incline them against that union which is so manifestly desirable and which whole communities are looking with confidence to your honorable body to see perfected.

While neither expecting nor desiring any pecuniary advantage from their employment, which indeed they are by the law of their creation expressly prohibited from receiving, the commissioners respectfully suggest the necessity of a moderate appropriation to meet the expenses of clerical and technical service that obviously will be required in the discharge of the responsible duties committed to them.

The commissioners submit the accompanying bill as an initiative measure, to be supplemented by such further bills for legislative action as may be required for public convenience or demanded by its necessities.

ANDREW H. GREEN,
President.
J. S. T. STRANAHAN,
Vice-President.

Dated, NEW YORK, *December* 31, 1894.

MR. LEXOW:

We will now stand adjourned without date, unless there are others who desire to be heard on the main proposition. There being no others, we stand adjourned without date.

CONTINUATION OF GREATER NEW YORK HEARING.

SENATE LIBRARY, CAPITOL, ALBANY, *February* 5, 1896.

MR. SCOTT:

I think I ought, perhaps, to apologize, in the first place, for having asked you to give me this hearing, because, strictly speaking, I suppose I should have appeared before the committee at the time you sat in New York, but I thought there were so many gentlemen who were anxious to be heard that realized it would be night before you could get to me.

I think it is proper to say to the committee before I start in on what I have to say, that I am not and never have been an ardent advocate of the scheme of consolidating the municipalities in the lower part of the State into a greater New York. I have always had a great deal of doubt as to the wisdom and expediency of that course, and for that reason that I had and that I voted against the proposition, I am inclined to think that I should vote against it again if I had another opportunity.

My feeling, however, upon that subject has been actuated not by reason of the difference in taxation, as to which so much has been said, but because I had a serious doubt as to whether it was a practical proposition, at all events, to provide in a proper way for the government of so large a city as you contemplate creating. If the consolidation of these municipalities should tend to better government and better conditions of living, I should consider that it made very little difference whether, as a result of that, the city of New York paid a little less or a little more taxes than the city of Brooklyn, or paid a little less.

But I had a great deal of doubt as to whether or not this consolidation would tend to good administration and toward better conditions of living. I felt for a long time — I think, perhaps, we will all agree to that — that the most difficult unsolved problem that we have to do with is the question as to how to govern, how best to govern, portions of our State which are thickly populated, as cities are. And I felt that when — where we arrive at the question of attempting to decide how to govern so large a city as this, we shall be met with a great many problems.

Up to the present time, the general concensus of opinion appears to have been that the most satisfactory way of arriving at the government of a great populous city has been to center, so far as possible, responsibility and power, and at the same time to limit the exercise of that power and responsibility by strict legislative lines. Whether or not that system could be applied to so great a city as you contemplate seems to me to be doubtful; and it seems to me probable that you may have to apply for something like a Federal system of administration, similar to that which is now in operation in London.

Now, I know that the answer to all that is that the bill proposes to appoint a commission which will provide for all that, which will consider that and report to the Legislature. And yet I can not help feeling some apprehension that even such a commission as that, with the limited experience which any commission organized here must have upon a subject of that sort, might, perhaps, not reach the wisest conclusion. And therefore, as I say, I have been in a great deal of doubt, and am still, as to whether the whole plan is a wise plan; because it seems to me to be a very momentous, far-thinking proposition, the end of which I can not see; momentous and far-reaching, too, because the history of this State is that the cities increase in population, and the country in proportion apparently decreases; and if you create this Greater New York which is contemplated by the bill, it seems to me that we may look forward with reasonable certainty that within a time, perhaps, during the lifetime of some of those here present, it will arrive that a majority of the Legislature in both branches may be representatives of this Greater New York that you propose to create; and I confess I do not know what the result upon the State of New York would be if —

MR. LEXOW:

(Interrupting) — Under the Constitution, it can not be, Mr. Scott.

Mr. Scott:

Under the Constitution, Mr. Chairman, it can be for this reason — the only thing that the Constitution prohibits is that at no time shall the representatives — shall there be more than half of the members of the Senate or Assembly represented in two counties in the State or the territory — now, then, on the 1st of January, 1894, comprises in two counties of this State — you propose to consolidate in this bill three counties and a little over —

Mr. Parker:

(Interrupting) — Oh, no; I beg your pardon. We do not propose to consolidate the counties at all —

Mr. Scott:

(Interrupting) — I beg your pardon, but upon the law —

Mr. Parker:

Simply the municipal corporations.

Mr. Scott:

(Continuing) — I mean the territories — what the Constitution says is this: "That no two counties or territory now comprising two counties shall ever hereafter have more than half the Senators and Assemblymen." Now, in that bill it is proposed to create a city which shall include a portion now included in three counties and a little over; and therefore the constitutional prohibition would not prevent that city electing more than half of the Senators and Assemblymen. I think if you look at the Constitution you will see I am entirely right about that.

However, I do not suppose — and I do not come here for the purpose of making an argument against consolidation.

I think that there are a great many cogent reasons that you have suggested for the question, though a new one, but I assume that from all that I have seen and heard, that it is the intention of the majority of the Legislature to pass some measure, at least, upon this subject; and therefore, although not being an advocate of that measure, I have come before you to-day, striving earnestly and honestly to make to you some suggestions toward the improvement, as it seems to me of the bill that you now have before you. And I want the committee to feel that while I do not pretend — I am not undertaking to masquerade in false colors — while I do not pretend to be an advocate of consolidation, yet, if you decree that some bill upon that subject shall be passed, I feel it to be a duty that I owe to the committee, and to the community to attempt to offer to you such suggestions to making this a more perfect bill before it is permitted to be advanced.

Now the first suggestion that strikes me is that, as Mr. Parker has just suggested, you propose to create a city which is to be composed of three, and a little over, counties in this State. And you provide for that in the first section of the bill and in the fifth section of the bill, in the most positive terms that nothing in this consolidation contained shall — the language of the statute is, I think, to be entirely accurate —"Nothing in this act shall be construed as attempting or intending to affect in any way the boundaries, government, rights, powers, duties, obligations, limitations, or disabilities of any county or officer thereof, as fixed by the Constitution or otherwise."

That means that you are going to produce as I have said an entirely novel state of affairs in this city and which are not contained in any city we have had. We have had cities which are co-terminous with the counties in which they are located. We have had and we have to-day many cities in this State which comprise only a portion of the counties in which they are located. But never before has it been suggested that we should have a city which comprised within itself three whole counties and a part of another county. And the proposition embodied in this bill is that you shall have a municipal corporation known as the city of New York, which shall comprise the whole of the county of New York, the whole of the county of Kings, the whole of the county of Richmond and a portion of the county of Queens.

Now, the first result that follows from that proposition is, that you will at once revive in each one of these counties separate boards of supervisors. The constitution provides that they shall have in every county in this State except those counties the boundaries of which are the same as a city, a board of supervisors. Under that provision of the Constitution we have had no board of supervisors in the county of New York, they have had no board of supervisors in the county of Kings, although until the first of January they had a board of supervisors. There is a board of supervisors in the county of Richmond. And under the bill as drawn, as this greater city will not be bounded the same as any county, there will necessarily be in each county a board of supervisors. Now, I can not tell how other cities in the State may feel, but I know that in the city of New York we have gone through a bitter experience arising out of the dual government of a common council and a board of supervisors. And I think I can speak for the inhabitants and taxpayers of the city of New York when I say that we have no desire to repeat that experiment. You know, gentlemen, upon this committee — know better than I do — are more familiar than I am with the great powers that are vested in the board of supervisors as to this State. And you will from that very familiarity be able to appreciate in an instant the confusion and the trouble that is to be ours, if you have a great municipality and within that great municipality three or four separate and distinct boards of supervisors, passing resolutions, incurring debt, obligating their separate counties in various ways. That is the first obstacle which appears to me to stand in the way of the scheme in this bill as it is now before this committee.

In addition to that it will be necessary, I take it, under the Constitution, if this plan goes through that now is before you — it will be necessary to have four different surrogates exercising concurrent jurisdiction over different parts of this great city, and four different district attorneys exercising jurisdiction over different parts of this great city; for the Constitution appears to clearly contemplate that surrogates and district attorneys, and other officers, but those are the principal ones, shall be elected by the counties and upon county lines, and subject to county limitations.

But perhaps the most serious difficulty, the most serious

result, which is likely to flow from the inclusion of three or four counties within a single city is, that you are going to open the floodgates of municipal and county extravagance in a way that I am quite sure this committee has not yet considered. It was held by the Court of Appeals in the case of Adams against the East River Institution that the ten per cent. limitation which the Constitution provides against the incurring of debt by counties and cities — that is that enactment that no city should issue bonds to an extent exceeding ten per cent. of the assessed valuation of the real estate contained therein — that that limitation applied to counties and cities distributively. It appeared in that case that the city of Brooklyn contained within its boundaries ninety-six per cent. of all the assessed real estate in the county of Kings, and that the city of Brooklyn had issued up to the full extent of the ten per cent. of assessed value of the real estate contained in it. Then it was proposed to issue, and there were issued, bonds of the county of Kings — which added to the bonds already issued by the city of Brooklyn exceeded ten per cent. of the assessed valuation of all the real estate in the county. And it was objected by the purchaser of those bonds that they were invalid. The Court of Appeals held that this was not true, saying that the power of the county, or of the city, as the case may be, is restricted only by the amount of its own debt, and for the purpose of creating a disability against the one or the other the debts of both can not be aggregated. As a consequence it was held that the county of Kings might issue bonds to the full extent of ten per cent. of all the real estate contained within its limits. And the city of Brooklyn, comprising ninety-six per cent. of all the real estate within the county of Kings, might go on and issue another ten per cent — bonds to the extent of another ten per cent — on that ninety-six per cent. Now the reasoning of that case, and it appears to be very strong reasoning, in that case, as applied to this great city that you propose by this bill to create, would be that the great city could issue bonds to the extent of ten per cent. of the assessed value of the real estate contained within its limits, and then that each of these separate counties which is contained within it could in turn issue bonds to the extent of ten per cent. of that portion of the real estate which was included within the limits of the county. Therefore, this benevolent and most useful check which the Constitution has set and imposed upon municipal extravagance and municipal debt-incurring, would be swept away at once, and it would be entirely possible — I fear it would be probable — that there would be issued bonds to the extent not of ten per cent. of the real estate comprised within this great city, but of twenty per cent. as could easily be done by the device of issuing city bonds on the one hand and county bonds on the other.

Now, it does not seem to me that all those objections are serious objections to the scheme of this bill, which provides that the counties shall preserve their autonomy and remain distinct, and I can see no reason why they should do so.

The first suggestion I have to make, sir, is that, if the committee favorably consider this bill, and propose to report it, that they shall strike out from it all those provisions which forbid the consolidation of counties, and that you should add to the city of New York not only the city of Brooklyn and the city of Long Island City, and these towns and villages which are mentioned in the bill, but that you should also add to the county of New York the county of Kings, the county of Richmond, and those portions of the county of Queens that are to be included within the bill.

Mr. Lexow:

How can that be done constitutionally?

Mr. Scott:

I see no possible difficulty in doing that constitutionally, Mr. Chairman. Last year the Legislature passed an act, as you will recollect, annexing to the county of New York a portion of the county of Westchester. The validity of that act was promptly and ably contested, and it was argued — and the question as to its validity was exhaustively argued—before the Court of Appeals by as able counsel as there are in this State. After due deliberation that court unanimously held — and I quote now almost the exact words of the decision — that the only limitation — that the erection of counties in this State was a branch of the legislative power — (sotto voce to Commissioner Parker, "147 N. Y. State Reports") — that the only limitation upon the power of the Legislature to erect new counties and the creation of old counties into new ones was the requirement that each county should have a population sufficient to entitle it to one Member of Assembly; and if that decision decided anything, to my mind, it clearly decided that it was within the power of the Legislature to make new counties, to re-establish county lines so far as it chose, providing that it should not interfere with those of the Senatorial — would not interfere with the several district lines.

MR. LEXOW:

Well, Mr. Scott, if that were applied to the county of Queens, would there be sufficient left of the county of Queens to entitle them to a Member of Assembly?

MR. SCOTT:

I don't know anything about that, about the application of that; that I couldn't tell you.

MR. LEXOW:

I rather think we take in about two-thirds.

MR. SCOTT:

That could be easily evaded by taking in less of the county of Queens, or by taking in all of it.

MR. LEXOW:

Yes.

MR. SCOTT:

Now, as to the power of the Legislature, I do not think there can be any difficulty. It seems to me that the act gives power to erect a city, and under that decision of the Court of Appeals that they considered very carefully, that I think is conclusive upon that subject. If that were not so, I think you would find in the Constitution itself an intimation, a very clear and direct intimation, that it is within the power of the Legislature to unite these counties, because in that very section to which I referred a moment ago, in the legislative article of the Constitution — I think it is the third article — and various sections, where it is provided, as I had said, that no two counties shall have more than a majority, more than half of the Senators and Assemblymen, the framers of the Constitution were careful to use these words, that no two counties, or the territory now comprising two counties, shall hereafter be entitled to one-half the Members of Assembly. Now, it seems to me, that the inclusion of those words, " or the territory now comprised in two counties " clearly foreshadowed in the Constitution the attempt by the Legislature to create a Greater New York out of the counties which are situated in the lower part of the State, at the close, itself clearly foreshadowed — carried out the idea that the Legislature had the power to do that. And I feel quite sure, sir, that I risk nothing in saying that if you will take the trouble to look at the decision of the Court of Appeals in the People on the relation of Henderson against the Board of Supervisors of Westchester County, you will be convinced that the court has there held that the Legislature has absolute power as to making and remaking counties in this State.

MR. BRUSH:

Do you know the section on the subject of the Constitution?

MR. PARKER:

Section four of article three.

MR. LEXOW:

Mr. Parker, have you looked that up?

MR. PARKER:

I have, yes. I did not want to interrupt —

MR. LEXOW:

That is right. I only wanted to suggest to you to answer that, if there is any answer to it.

MR. PARKER:

I think so, yes.

MR. SCOTT:

Well, of course I have not come here for the purpose — I have no desire to enter into a polemic or legal discussion as to what the Legislature can or can not do. If the members of this committee should be of the opinion that they can not do this thing, why of course, that is all I have got to say.

MR. LEXOW:

Of course — I will say that was my opinion up to this time.

MR. SCOTT:

Precisely, sir, and it has been the impression of the people — it was the impression of a good many people until the Court of Appeals decided in the Henderson case. I know it was the impression of all my antagonists in that case (Laughter).

But what I do want to impress upon this committee is this, that if upon the consideration of that case and the consideration of this Constitution, you should be of the opinion that it is within your power to combine these counties as well as combine the cities, then I beg you to consider whether or not that would not be a wise and judicious thing to do.

Now, the next subject to which I wish to call your attention is the question of taxation. I am by no means one of those who contend, as I heard contended before your committee on Friday last — that there should be no general taxation. As I understood the argument the proposition was that if there was a consolidation each city should be assessed and be taxed in the same proportion in which it is now assessed and taxed. I do not believe in that view at all. If we are to have a municipal marriage, then I believe that we should have a municipal marriage for better or for worse. If it is a good thing to consolidate the county of New York with other counties, then it is a good thing in general, I think, to distribute taxation over all parts of the county, in an equal and uniform way. But I think there is a distinction to be made between taxes and taxes. There are certain classes of taxes, taxes for certain purposes, which I think it is entirely clear should be distributed over the whole of this new city in equal ratio, and in proportion to the value of the property. And I thing that any plan of taxation for the general administrative purposes, for the support of the police department, for the support of the fire department, for the support of the health department, for the support of the law department, for the expenses of the — that come entirely under general administrative expenses — I believe if are going into this thing at all — that those should be clearly divided throughout the country. But on the other hand there is another class of taxes which I believe it is not for the benefit of any one that they should be equally distributed throughout all members of the Greater New York. And I refer to that class of taxes which has especially to do with the improvement and development of communities and the maintenance of public works. It would be manifestly unfair, I think, for instance, that the land that comes within the county of Richmond should be called upon to contribute any taxes to the payment of debt which has been incurred by the county of New York for the establishment of its Croton water system, a system which has already cost some thirty millions of dollars, and the bonds issued for which have, under the law and the Constitution, to be paid out of taxation. The only county at the present time, at all events, which derives any benefit from that water is the county of New York; and it seems to me that it would be manifest injustice to the county of Kings and the county of Richmond that they should be compelled to contribute by their taxes to the payment of those bonds, the only benefit from which is derived by the county of New York. In the same way, it would be equally unfair to the county of New York and the county of Richmond, that they should be called upon to contribute by their taxes to pay the bonds which have been issued by the county of Kings, or of the city of Brooklyn, for the water supply which they have in that county and in that city. Those are some of the kinds of taxes that it appears to me should be laid and distributed. And in making that suggestion I am speaking very much for the benefit of what may be termed the outlying and undeveloped portion of this Greater New York, than I am for the thickly populated and developed portion. We have had in our county an experience in that direction which teaches us a great deal. Many years ago we annexed to the county of New York that portion of the present city of New York which is known as the twenty-third and twenty-fourth wards, and there was no provision made for the distribution of taxes, and all taxes were to be levied equally. Naturally enough the people who were to determine how much taxes were to be levied and how those taxes were to be paid out and distributed, were people who were elected in, and were especially interested in the thickly populated portions of the city, and for years they retarded the development and advancement of what we then knew as the annexed district, because the representatives of the city who lived down town were unwilling to vote to extend the city's money derived from general taxation in the development and advancement of this outlying district of our city. It may be an alluring prospect to the inhabitants of Richmond county, to the inhabitants of Hempstead, to the inhabitants of Flushing, to the inhabitants of Jamaica, to think that they are going to have their territory, their home territory, developed at the expense of New York and Brooklyn. But if they think that this is going to happen, they are buoying themselves up with a false hope. That will not happen for a great many years. If taxation is made equal over the territory, because whatever board or body of men, in the development of the scheme for the government of this city — whatever board or body may be charged with the duty of determining where and how the taxes are to be paid — will inevitably be controlled by the representatives who come from, and who represent the thickly populated and the richer portions of this city, and they will not vote for the expenditure of their money in the development and improvement of the outlying districts, which have neither a large population, nor any political influence in the government of the city. Therefore, I contend, sir, that the proposition that there should be some difference made in certain classes of taxes, is one which is made for the benefit of the outlying undeveloped portions of this new city, and not for the benefit of the richer portions which are now thickly populated.

Now that all leads up to the proposition, that this committee and this Legislature should not hamper the commission you propose to appoint by any instructions whatever upon the subject of taxation. You have in the bill a provision for the appointment of a commission who are given the widest possible powers as to the preparation and submission to the Legislature of bills providing for the government of this great city. You have hampered them and restrained them in no possible way by this bill, except only in one, and that in the one way which it seems to me they should be left the freest possible hand. You say they shall report bills providing for the municipal — providing a government for this municipal corporation which is to be made; and among other things for attaining an equal and uniform rate of taxation, and of valuation for the purposes of taxation throughout the whole of the territory of the municipal corporation as consolidated. Now as to that most important matter, a matter which I think needs a great deal of consideration in detail and not only in general, you propose to foreclose and tie the gentlemen of this commission you are about to appoint. Now, sir, let me ask this committee if they can trust this commission to devise and frame laws for the government of this truly novel and anomalous city, can you not trust them to devise and submit to you, for your approval, laws for the regulation of the question of taxation? Is it not better and safer? Are you not likely to have better results in the end if you allow this commission, after having obtained all the light that it can obtain upon the subject — if you leave their hands as free upon the subject of taxation as you have upon any other subject, and allow them to report to you at once a scheme of government and a scheme of taxation? Nothing can be lost by that because you do not pretend you could not extend to this commission power of legislation; the best that you can do to them is to give them the power you propose to give them here, to frame laws and submit them to you for your approval. Nothing that they submit can become a law unless it is approved by you. And with all deference to the committee and the Legislature, I think I may venture to suggest that after that commission has sat and have examined into this subject, have heard the opinions of experts and taken testimony, and have considered it, even the Legislature will be in a better position to determine wisely and justly upon the scheme of taxation for this great city than they can possibly do now with the limited knowledge and informa tion that is at their disposition.

And, therefore, sir, the second suggestion that I wish to make to the committee, is that you shall throw out of this bill all restrictions and limitations which you undertake to place upon the judgment and discretion of this commission you propose to appoint, leaving them as free to report to you a scheme of taxation as you leave them free to report a scheme of government.

Now, sir, there is one other matter, and a matter of real seriousness, to which, I think, every friend of this bill will agree, when the proposition is stated. You propose by this bill to enact that so many cities, towns and villages shall, two years hence, be consolidated into a great city, a great municipal corporation, and pending that actual consolidation, you propose to leave to the town boards, the boards of supervisors, and the village boards all powers and authority that they have at the present time. In other words, you give two years' notice to all these boards that at the end of two years they are to be consolidated with the city and county of New York into a great municipality, and, of course, as must naturally follow that, at the time of that consolidation, this greater municipality will assume all the debts and obligations which have been incurred by these smaller municipalities. We have had in the city of New York some experience with that kind of legislation. Last year, as I have said, the Legislature passed an act providing for the consolidation with the city of New York — for the annexation to the city of New York — of a few towns and villages in the lower part of Westchester county, a small, sparsely populated territory, and it did not seem as if there was any particular import in the annexation to the city. There was much doubt up to almost the last moment whether or not that act would become a law. It was sent to the city of New York, and after considerable hesitation and argument it was accepted by the city and was returned to the Governor and met his approval. Only a few days elapsed between the acceptance of this act by the city and its signature by the Governor, and yet within that time, within those few days — I can not venture to saw now how many contracts were awarded, how many franchises were granted, how many schemes were put into operation designed to ultimately extract money from the treasury of the city of New York. It is currently reported — I do not know that it is true — it is currently reported that most of the officers in those towns and villages sat up all night and every night from the time of the approval of that bill by the mayor until its signature by the Governor, in order that all these plans and contracts and schemes should be consummated. I am not prepared to say, sir, that those schemes and plans were fraudulent, but I am prepared to say, and prepared to establish it if necessary, that they were wildly extravagant. That it is almost true, as has been said of some one, that electric lights were put upon every stump in the district. Now, sir, if those things could be done in a small district, and in a few days, what can not be done in this great territory that you propose to annex to the city of New York in two years? What schemes can not be concocted; what contracts can not be entered into? What franchises can not be granted, if the Legislature does not take some steps in this bill which they now have before them to prevent the incurring of these enormous obligations. And, sir —

MR. LEXOW:

(Interrupting.) I understand, Mr. Scott, Brooklyn must be excepted from that general remark, because she has already reached her debt limit.

MR. SCOTT:

Well, Brooklyn is one of those cities, sir, that nobody could ever suspect to go into a scheme of that kind, but I was specially referring to the other —

MR. BRUSH:

(Interrupting.) Thank you.

MR. SCOTT:

But it is perfectly safe to say that it is not necessary in order to grant contracts for work and make agreements for putting down sidewalks and roads and for all of these cases — it is not necessary you should have power to issue at present investment— issue bonds. It would be quite sufficient for the people who, I imagine, may be entering into these schemes, if they had an agreement that at some future day when the Legislature has consolidated the cities, that bonds will be issued.

At all events, it seems to me to be, and I think it will appeal to the members of this committee when I say that, if possible, some restriction should be devised — if you are going to give two years' notice of this consolidation — that some restriction should be devised and put into this bill which will provide against that, that every contract entered into in some parts of this city in these two years should be noticed in some shape.

Now, sir, these are the principal suggestions that present themselves to me as requiring some action upon the part of this committee. And I submit them to you, as I said at the outset, with a view not to criticise, with a view not to embarrass or retard your action, but simply with a desire, if possible, to assist you, in framing a bill with which you may yourselves be satisfied hereafter if it shall become a law.

There is only one other thing that I want to say before I close. I want again to urge the committee, as I have already urged them by letter, to seriously consider whether they should not restrict the limits of the city especially whether they should not exclude from all consideration that piece of country which lies far away from our borders and which is wholly uninhabited, known as Richmond county. (Laughter.) Nobody, so far as I can learn, desires the inclusion of that county, except a few gentlemen who own real estate there, and expect their property will be increased in value. We have heard a great deal of its vaunted water front, but we have not been told always that that water front is now wholly in the hands of private individuals, and that if it were developed so as to be a mart for foreign commerce that that would be no advantage to the people or to the city of New York, but that that would simply assist the Baltimore and Ohio railroad, which is a foreign corporation, to run things out of the State of New York, into New Jersey. There is no argument that I can see, except a purely sentimental argument, a geographical argument, arising from the desire of drawing straight lines on a map rather than crooked ones, which have ever led to the inclusion of Staten Island into this scheme at all — and I feel quite confident that my friend Parker who drew this bill — if you can persuade him to put his hand upon his heart and tell us what he really thinks — will say that he did not think himself that Staten Island ought to be added to New York.

I am not at all sure that that same proposition does not extend, perhaps in a minor degree — or rather the same thing does not extend to those outlying towns, now chiefly celebrated for their hunting facilities, which you propose to annex out of Queens county — Flushing, and Jamaica, and Hempstead, and Cedarhurst, and all of those places down there. It seems to me that if we are to have a Greater New York, if we are to have a consolidated city, if we are to consolidate into one municipality these three cities, which now stand at the threshold — at the outlet of the State of New York — that there should be some degree of moderation and reason exercised in doing it; and that that will be best exercised if you limit this bill to the three cities of New York, Brooklyn, and Long Island City, which are already cities in name, the inhabitants of which have become as it were used to being governed by civic methods, and which logically, geographically, historically and in every other way, are the proper component elements of a great city, if you desire a great city at the mouth of the Hudson river.

Now, I am quite aware that it will be said by some people that this whole proposition, including Staten Island, was submitted to the people at the end of 1894, and that they voted in favor of it. That referendum vote, certainly so far as the city of New York is concerned, does not seem to me to be of any value whatever, it certainly does not seem to me that it should be of controlling value upon that subject, and upon this Legislature, if upon mature consideration you think the proposition submitted about that was to be made. So far as the city of New York is concerned I think that every one will agree with me, and you, Mr. Chairman, perhaps more than any one else, that the vote upon the referendum should be given but slight attention, because, as you are well aware, the citizens of New York in that year had many other things of more pressing and immediate importance to attract their attention than this idea, which was then largely in the air, of annexation. Some developments had taken place in the city, with which you, yourself, had something to do, which had attracted such a measure of public attention, and which had created so much public excitement that I am confident that I speak the exact truth and keep within mention, when I say that the attention that was given to the question of Greater New York was a very slight attention of any one; that it obtained a large majority of the votes, I think was due to the fact that in the election everybody was in favor of voting for the affirmative of every proposition. They voted for the new Constitution, they voted for the referendum and for the Greater New York. I think they voted for the people who were making the affirmative fight against those who were making the defensive fight. There was a feeling in the air arising not out of any consideration of the Greater New York, but out of other considerations altogether, and whatever was suggested was a good thing, and that whatever was new must be better than what was old. And I therefore think that the vote was — certainly so far as the details of the scheme is concerned — should not be considered as binding or conclusive upon this Legislature, if upon mature consideration you think that other provisions in your judgment ought to prevail.

I want to thank you, sir, for the courtesy and attention the committee has given me, and the kindness of listening to me.

Mr. Lexow:

I think the committee are pleased, Mr. Scott, to have heard you, and have been very much instructed by your remarks.

Mr. Brush:

One question I would like to ask, if the chairman will permit, and that is this: We have adopted an amended Constitution since this referendum vote — is it in your judgment, or should it — should this vote of 1894, which was purely a vote of sentiment, be considered as binding upon this Legislature when this Legislature has not authorized that vote at all — upon the Legislature of 1894 — which authorized it.

Mr. Scott:

Well, sir, that is a question of legislative ethics more than — and that Legislature — that is, these men who are elected for that purpose legislate, and the legislation went over this vote, upon the supposed expression of opinion by the people in a somewhat irregular way, and one which is not provided for in any system of government that we have. That is my idea about that. I don't know that the amended Constitution has much to do with it one way or the other. If it has, I think it is fair to say that there is a provision in the new Constitution which foreshadowed and looked forward to a consolidation of cities, and indeed I think it is perfectly fair to say that there is no doubt that the framers of the Constitution did have in mind the possibility advanced that there would be a consolidation of this sort attempted, and that they made certain provisions which point in that direction.

MR. LEXOW:

It was open to debate at that time — if you remember the proceedings of the Constitutional Convention —

MR. SCOTT:

Oh, yes; that was before —

MR. LEXOW:

(Continuing) making these various propositions having in mind the creation of the greater city.

MR. SCOTT:

Yes; there is no question about that. There is no doubt that it has been in people's minds for a great many years, as a public question.

MR. BRUSH:

But as I understand you, Mr. Scott, you do not consider that you would be morally bound by the vote of 1894 having been for consolidation?

MR. SCOTT:

I should not consider it so, if I had a vote on it.

MR. BRUSH:

Well, argument has been made here by some of the gentlemen that there was no obligation laid upon the Legislature.

MR. SCOTT:

I should always feel that referendum was an easy way to get rid of the responsibility (laughter).

MR. MATTHEWS:

I take pleasure in presenting the following list of members of the Union League Club of Brooklyn.

BROOKLYN, N. Y., *February* 4, 1896.

HON. CLARENCE LEXOW, *Senate Chamber, Albany, N. Y.*

Dear Sir.— I take pleasure in presenting the following list of members of the Union League Club, of Brooklyn, who have subscribed in favor of consolidating New York and Brooklyn into one city.

This list was started Saturday, February, 1, 1896, four days ago, and I desire to state that I have devoted but a small portion of the said four days to such purpose, and that during such time I have interviewed 148 members, without a prior knowledge of their views, and have secured the signatures of 131, a percentage of 88 19-37, favoring consolidation, among the 11 18-37 per cent. who might be understood as opposing consolidation. I find many who say that they favor the matter but object to signing for reasons peculiar to themselves.

We, the undersigned members of the Union League Club, of Brooklyn, are in favor of consolidating New York and Brooklyn into one city:

Howard M. Smith, ex-president Union League Club.
Benj. Russell.
J. W. Harman.
Russell Parker.
Geo. B. Jones.
Jno. J. Cooney.
J. G. Dettmer.
A. G. Perham.
Wm. H. Lyon.
Louis F. Seitz.
C. D. Rhinehart.
W. H. Biggam.

T. G. Christmas.
E. C. Moore.
Arthur Pell.
Theo. Corning.
F. J. Ashfield.
John H. Donnelly.
S. S. Voshell.
W. A. Porter.
F. E. Quinn.
Austin Kelley.
Ira Preston Taylor.
Adolphus G. Bailey.
E. C. Fuller.
Geo. P. Chappell.
J. S. Nugent.
C. Washington Colyer.
Nelson J. Gates.
J. O. Carpenter.
D. P. Darling.
M. S. Hayes.
O. Ingersoll.
G. H. Benton.
Alex. H. Doty.
B. C. Miller.
Joseph L. White.
R. O. Sherwood.
Geo. H. Squire.
J. L. Voshell.
Edward H. Hobbs.
E. W. Scarborough.
Thomas Bishop.
N. E. Jacobs.
Geo. I. Jackson.
Wm. Coone.
Owen E. Houghton, D. D. S.
James H. Stearns.

A. S. Haight, 8 Spencer place.

A. E. Blackmar, ex-president of Equal Taxation.

Wm. A. Barnum.

James Rice, Jr.

Marshall T. Davidson.

Jno. V. Jewell.

F. B. Keppy.

D. M. Munger.

David Thornton.

Benj. Estes.

F. E. Barnerd (with equal taxation).

Herbert S. Ogden, no commission, and with equal taxation.

L. F. Silva.

Stephen H. Hand.

H. N. Gates.

Wm. H. Coon.

B. L. Houghton.

Jas. H. Taft, Jr.

S. B. Holt.

W. H. Pierson, M. D.

James G. Stevens.

Frank L. Bailley.

Thomas L. Wells, M. D.

W. H. Irwin.

Chas. E. Newton.

Henry C. Larowe.

Ethan Allen Doty.

Frank L. Coon.

F. H. Sellimar.

W. L. Tyler.

Montrose W. Morris.

John A. Schmitt, provided equal taxation.

William C. Pate.

Chas. H. Reynolds, Jr.

J. W. Hussey.

F. H. Wilson, ex-president.

F. H. Cowperthwait.
C. W. Prankard, for equal taxation.
Jno. Nash.
T. J. Garnes.
J. F. Hamilton.
E. A. Warren.
William H. Reynolds.
R. W. Gleason.
Robert Lindell.
William P. Gio, 24 Brevoort place.
J. Hamilton Gill, 24 Brevoort place.
J. Culbert Patmer, 14 Brevoort place.
James W. Cromwell, 29 Brevoort place.
Edgar O. Pearce, 1092 Dean street.
Wm. H. Sterling, 1086 Dean street.
Seth T. Stewart.
Geo. N. Robinson.
James Nibb.
A. Abraham.
Geo. H. Conklin.
Chas. H. Macklin.
W. B. Mead.
William Jeremiah.
Charles Cooper.
S. W. Milligan.
H. A. Carleton.
W. M. Matthews.
Henry C. Allard.
Welcome S. Jarvis.
John R. Crum.
M. L. Bowden.
W. E. Edmister.
Ysidno Pendas.
F. Pelletman.
Hugh Hirsh.
William Degler.

Edward Lyons.
Eugene G. Blandford.
John Ditmars.
Thos. J. Washburn.
Chas. J. Sands.
G. W. Carruthers.
Andrew Mercer.
E. M. Cragin.
Fred H. Pond.

Mr. Brush:

The Union League Club is composed of over a thousand members — and he says that was the result of his labors — that only shows that consolidation —

Mr. Lexow:

Mr. Parker.

Mr. Parker:

I should like to ask Mr. Scott one question. Mr. Scott, I believe, advocates consolidation, into one county, of the three counties — the three whole counties named in this bill. That is correct, is it not?

Mr. Scott:

Yes, that is my idea.

Mr. Parker:

I wish to call his attention to this clause in section 4 of article III. of the Constitution: "No county shall have more than one third of all the Senators," and to direct his attention to the fact that Kings county at present has seven, and New York, has at present twelve, which together make nineteen, and which is more than one third of all the Senators — and simply ask how that could be avoided.

MR. SCOTT:

Well, I don't know.

MR. PARKER:

Well, then, that settles that, I rather think. That is the only thing which at the very outset, laying aside every other objection, that might have been urged, determined the proposed consolidation of municipal corporations, expressly excepting counties. And there stand those words just ahead of the constitutional provision, that no two counties or a portion thereof as now organized, which are adjoining counties, or which are separated only by public waters, shall have more than one half of all the Senators. Now then that is decisive of it, it appears to me. Here is that thing you are running against in a moment — take even these two counties, you run over the constitutional prohibition — Suffolk and Richmond comprise another Senatorial district, and Queens another, and so you see, there you are.

MR. LEXOW:

That is twenty-one — now adding —

MR. PARKER:

Well, leaving out the argument of growth, you see that Richmond itself is not a whole district. I mean even taking those where there can be no question. It takes nineteen, anyhow.

Certainly Mr. Scott's argument, I may say at the outset, and his statements here, have been made in so moderate and so friendly a spirit to this whole scheme that, although many of his arguments have been heretofore touched upon, and in my opinion practically exhausted, that we cannot but thank him at this time for his suggestions, and it is in that friendly and temperate spirit that I propose briefly to speak of them now. I will take them up in the order that he did. He spoke at the first of the magnitude of the problem. Mr. Chairman that has been conceded and dwelt upon at meeting after meeting, and we admit that absolutely. I believe personally that it will be a decade before the process of consolidation is completed. It will be more than a decade before the full assimilation has taken place of all the diverse circumstances and interests throughout this territory. There are different degrees of interest and different natures of obligations and different rates of taxation, all these to be fused into one great aggregate, but, as has been heretofore said, the way to grapple with that problem, inevitable and soon necessary to be referred, is to grapple with it, not to avoid it. We realize the magnitude of that. For five years it has been dwelt upon. Representatives and delegations from all parts of this territory have been summoned before the commission and their opinions taken pro and con, and as a result the magnitude of the problem has been impressed more and more deeply upon the minds of the commission.

Now I think that this clause of the Constitution to which Mr. Scott very particularly admits that there is no answer disposes —

Mr. Scott:

I only want to say this. The answer is this. One answer is this: That the Court of Appeals in the same Henderson case decided that the present apportionment could not be disturbed— they would not interfere with the present apportionment.

Mr. Parker:

I have read the speeches, and read word for word, sentence for sentence, the opinion of the court on the cases cited. It does just this—and I have it here—it does just this: That for all the county purposes enumerated in the Constitution the apportionment of the Assembly district, the election of a Senator, for all that theretofore inhered in the county of Westchester as an integral community of the State recognized in the Constitution, that county must still live in every way. As to purely — as to purposes of the election of an alderman and I think of a district judge — I am not — I don't remember about that — it proposes as to those it should be a part of the city and county of New York. I know very well that the Legislature by the change of boundaries — as Senator Brush exhibited some curiosity as to that, or some inquiry — there is no doubt about that. I have not spoken of these things until they have arisen. There is no use of pouring out upon this committee the crude processes by which we have arrived at our results.

MR. BRUSH:

My thought was whether the Legislature had the power to abolish the county. I have no doubt you can take a piece of one county and add it to another.

MR. PARKER:

Well, it is abolition in one degree or another, whether you cut a county up, or whether you totally parcel its territory out among other counties. For instance, on the question of annexation, on taking in the towns of Westchester and Williamsburg — I think it is — that act of 1895, that is taken away from the county of Westchester and annexed and made a part of the county and city of New York, and of the twenty-fourth ward. Here is the text of it, and there is no doubt about that; in the Constitution there is no express provision that that can be done, but the Legislature — the court alludes to it here and says, when there is no provision in the Constitution, but there are allusions that plainly point that way, and the general power of the Legislature is not expressly prohibited, the necessities of the case give it to the Legislature.

Now, I shall be very brief about these matters. As to the taxation clause, Mr. Scott's suggestion is that it be aboslutely taken out of the act, out of the bill. The language of the bill is that the commission which is to be, and through which the bill shall be transmitted to the Legislature, that the commission shall submit to the Legislature bills for the government of this greater city, and which shall provide, among other things, for attaining an equal rate of taxation. We arrive at that as an ultimate result. Now, Mr. Scott has argued that in the interest of outlying districts — he says, while it is perfectly just and proper that he should do so, no doubt — but I do not think that they will argue that themselves — he says that you have hampered the commission by that. I beg to differ from him; we have not hampered the commission at all. The commission is directed to submit that one, among, perhaps, a thousand bills, as it chooses; if it chooses, it may at some time submit to this Legislature a strong disapproval of that bill, or it may at some time submit one together with it, one looking to the conservation of the present conditions, and strongly approve that. It is not hampered in any way. It is not hampered any more than when, Mr. Chairman, the commission had been directed as a contingent experimental reaching toward a result, directed to submit to the Legislature a bill providing for the government of that greater city by a city council of two houses, or something of that kind, something in the Federate way. And these questions, as I have said before, as we have said right along, these questions will come up before the Legislature at some time.

MR. LEXOW:

Well, all that the commission intends to imply from this provision in the bill is that they start out with a desire to do the fair, square, just and honorable thing by every one of these districts they propose to be annexed.

MR. PARKER:

Yes —

MR. LEXOW:

(Continuing.) And they put the Legislature in passing this bill upon the platform of fairness and equality, so that the Legislature in years to come can take against any one of the various localities, whether New York city or otherwise, any position that is hostile to the intent of the bill, without going back upon this record as established in this bill. Is that the proposition?

MR. PARKER:

Well, that is even more fully than I think, sir. I do not believe the Legislature is in any way estopped whatever in fairness from adopting another policy.

MR. LEXOW:

It is intimated that every locality shall be fairly treated.

MR. PARKER:

Fairly treated — and as you have said —

MR. LEXOW:

And by that you mean that there shall be equal taxation throughout the entire district when that, in fairness, can be consummated?

MR. PARKER:

Can be consummated. We are well aware — here is the municipality of New York with between eleven and twelve millions of dollars — I think the figures are about that, something of that kind — nobody proposes that there shall be any injustice done to any one of those municipalities. And if the outlying districts expect they are going to get any undue advantage, it is rather good than otherwise that these advantages should be gradually filtered out to them. It is a very good thing.

Now, the last proposition — the last suggestion that Mr. Scott made — was that there should be included in this bill something to restrain the outlying municipalities from contracting debts and from flooding the city of New York with debts contracted improvidently. Well, that can be done in any bill at any moment if it is considered well. I can not see a way to do it very clearly. I do not think Mr. Scott can; and I think if you ask him to put his hand on his heart, and he will tell you that it will be a very difficult thing to do — to restrain these — to oversee and restrain and restrict these outlying municipalities from contracting debts, to watch them, and determine that this or that thing is improvident —

Mr. Scott:

(Interrupting.) I think if you were to provide that they could make no contract obligation extending more than two years, that might do it.

Mr. Parker:

They could not make a contract — it would be very improbable, that would not extend over two years.

Mr. Scott:

They are all of them up to their debt-issuing capacity.

Mr. Parker:

Well, then, if they are, there is not very much danger.

Mr. Scott:

Yes there is for new obligations. There is no danger of their increasing the present debt.

Mr. Parker:

After the two years?

Mr. Scott:

Yes, I should allow them two years. That thing may be done.

Mr. Parker:

There is no objection that I can see to it, if it can be devised in any way; it can be done in fairness to them; I am sure there is no objection to that; if they will stand it the city of New York will have nothing to say on that.

Mr. Scott:

Well, they ought to be thankful to get in out of the rain (laughter).

MR. PARKER:

Well, I think so, too.

Now as to the question of including Richmond county; and as to the question possibly of leaving out a part of Queens county that is provided for. I do not believe in limiting it entirely to the three cities mentioned by Mr. Scott. You want something of latitude for expansion from consolidation. It is something — you know when we took in the twenty-third and twenty-fourth wards there were rocks and groves and streams, and pieces of land there that looked almost as if they were in the Adirondacks. You go to the Bronx park and you can hardly believe that you are in the city of New York — you would make a tremendous mistake about that; Chicago and Boston include many country districts in their proposed consolidation. As to Staten Island, I will frankly say that at the outset of this argument I had considerable doubts as to the desirability of including it. I do not think anybody can have any doubt of the wisdom upon a broad policy of including that territory after having heard the arguments before this committee from Saturday last. I heard Mr. Wiman's arguments there, and I never heard a more solid, substantial, forcible argument than that. I am well aware that Mr. Wiman is a large property holder there, and the improvement of that property may enrich him, and I thought of that as I listened to him, but what has that got to do with it? Whether it was John Smith, or James Brown, or William Jones that would be made rich by it; the question is, what is the proper thing, what is the policy that is going to make a rounded, perfect whole? That is hardly a question of law, and perhaps it is not within my province to advert to it, since I simply wish to answer questions of law. But I submit that to the consideration of the committee as to whether or no those things, likely to develop in the near future, do not make it very politic, very desirable, to include the tremendous advantages that Staten Island offers. If I were asked to throw my vote one way or the other, as to whether it should be included, I should say decidedly, yes.

Mr. Scott said what I can not quite understand. He was asked about this restriction of less than one-half of the Senators to two counties. He said that two counties can not elect more than one-half the Senators. But this proposed one county — I do not think he could have meant that — how could the city, if it could not elect as a county, how could it elect as a city? You might, with equal logic, declare that a city after you have taken the entire county, elect more Senators than the county.

Mr. Brush:

(To Mr. Scott) — One of the questions I want to ask is this: You say that you have come to help to elucidate this latter, or that is, as I understand it. Have you thought of some such plan as the subdivision of this district into certain districts and each one of those districts preserving it local form of government and a representative or representatives from each local form of government to be selected to represent it in the central government?

Mr. Scott:

No, sir; I have not. I have not thought very much about details of the government. I have assumed that you would have to take some such plan as they have adopted in London; have a central council.

Mr. Brush:

So far as Brooklyn is concerned, I think we are anxious to preserve our local form of government, that is preserve our charter; and the proposition to swallow us up, and make us in a certain measure serfs, we seriously object to.

Mr. Scott:

The difficulty appears to be that you do not want to be swallowed up, and New York don't want to swallow you up, and yet we have got to.

MR. PARKER:

I will say to Senator Brush that the commission has in time past given not a little attention to the form of local legislature of this great city. We have refrained from discussing it heretofore, because it is a large subject. The question has come to our minds, to the minds of the commission, should it be a legislature of two houses, should it be one house, should the representatives in one house, which ever you choose, from a given locality, have a peculiar vote, a peculiar power and weight in that house, as to expenditures over the other; shall we form it on the scheme of the London county council; or what shall we do. A good deal of thought has been expended upon that, but we have thought it premature to dwell upon it at this time. And I should be very glad with Senator Brush, to show him all the things and talk to him about all the alternatives we have dwelt upon.

MR. BRUSH:

Why not give us a skeleton of the scheme, if there is any such scheme, in the minds of these gentlemen. Why not give us the skeleton of the scheme as it is laid out and then we shall have something to work on.

Now I think I can say for Brooklyn, and I certainly can for myself, in this matter, that we do not care to stand as the obstructionists; what we do want is to preserve the charter of the city of Brooklyn, and our own form of local government. If it is proposed to divide this district into subdivisions, I can conceive in that being done and the local government of each district being preserved, and a representative body organized, coming from each one of these subdivisions, that shall preserve the principle of home rule and still preserve the local autonomy of each one of the districts. And I believe that such a scheme as that, if it was worked out, and we were given the skeleton, I could properly swing in with the position which this bill as it it now stands has. We do not know what you ask of us; it is a leap in the dark; and we want something that is tangible, and that we can depend upon.

MR. PARKER:

The Senator of course understands that every movement, at every stage of what is to be proposed, is to be submitted to the Legislature, to be published, to be argued upon in the clearest manner, and that all that he requests is that that submission be made now, rather than a few months later on.

MR. BRUSH:

Excuse me — what we want in Brooklyn, is to know what you ask us to go into. This bill provides for consolidation; consolidation is had before we know what is back of it, and we do not want to be asked to take a leap in the dark.

MR. PARKER:

You know what is back of it, and you do not have to accept it until the State says so. In other words, this bill passes, and whatever may come thereafter, whatever may be proposed, whatever may be prepared by this or any commission, does not take —

MR. BRUSH:

No — excuse me, Commissioner Parker — this bill passed, and consolidation is effected.

MR. PARKER:

Yes.

MR. BRUSH:

If it becomes a law?

MR. PARKER:

Yes.

MR. BRUSH:

Then we have got to take what follows whether we like it or not.

MR. PARKER:

No; I beg your pardon — you have not. You have not, sir — and it seems to me strange that we should have to dwell upon that. Let us take for instance the making of a health department. Suppose we say that is the first thing it is to be extended over. What is done? A bill is drawn. It don't become a law at once. It comes up here, delegations come from Brooklyn to protest against this or that feature, commend this or that other feature, and it goes through the same slow process of fight or repulse and advance that any other bill in this Legislature does.

MR. BRUSH:

Yes.

MR. PARKER:

(Continuing) And so on bill after bill goes through the Legislature. Now what more — what can you ask any fairer than that?

MR. LEXOW:

Even that affecting the police department — you don't seem to be at all nervous about it.

MR. PARKER:

Even that, I presume sir, will take that same slow, tentative way.

MR. BRUSH:

No what we ask for is your frame work now. Give us your frame work, and let us know what you are going to build on.

MR. PARKER:

We build on this bill.

MR. LEXOW:

I am glad to see that Dr. Brush has become so good a consolidationist. By slow stages I think we will have him.

MR. PARKER:

This is an illustration of the slow tentative way in which the process goes on (indicating Dr. Brush.)

MR. BRUSH:

I beg your pardon; Dr. Brush is no consolidationist on the lines which are here proposed. Dr. Brush is open to any reasonable scheme for the welfare of the district, that is right; but he don't propose to stand as an obstructionist, and he does propose to stand for the rights of the people that he represents and for the charter of the city of Brooklyn, and to preserve its local autonomy until the last ditch.

MR. LEXOW:

But suppose Doctor, that we take that magnificent charter of the city of Brooklyn, and spread it over the whole district

MR. BRUSH:

We want to preserve our own local autonomy there in Brooklyn; that is what I shall contend for. I give due notice of that.

MR. LEXOW:

I believe some members have requested copies of the charter of Brooklyn, and have not been able to get them; are they guarded so sacredly?

MR. BRUSH:

I think I can furnish them.

MR. SCOTT:

You will find them in the laws of 1888.

MR. LEXOW:

Were the bills forming the charter consolidated in 1888?

MR. SCOTT:

They passed the consolidation act of Brooklyn in 1888.

MR. BRUSH:

We have new copies that have just been issued by the —

MR. LEXOW:

(Interrupting) And I may say from personal experience of two years or over, covering the period from 1888 down to the present time that they have been tinkering with that charter ever since — and that a very large proportion of the time of the Senate and Assembly of the two last years has been given to making improvements upon that charter, or changes.

MR. BRUSH:

There has been issued this year a copy of the charter, a new copy, down to the present time.

MR. LEXOW:

If there is anybody else to be heard on the subject of consolidation, or no consolidation, the committee will be glad to hear them. If not the hearing will be declared closed.

EXHIBITS.

EXHIBITS.

New York, *January* 22, 1896.

Hon. Clarence Lexow, Chairman Joint Committee on Consolidation, Senate Chamber, Albany:

Sir.— I venture to address you upon the subject of the duties imposed upon the committee of which you are chairman:

First. Because, if I recollect aright, by the resolution under which your committee is acting, you are authorized to consult with the counsel to the corporation of this city; and

Secondly. Because there are some matters which will require the careful attention of your committee, and as to which an early opportunity to obtain information should, as it seems to me, be sought.

The proposition touching the proposed legislation is to consolidate into one municipality all the territory now composing the city of New York, the city of Brooklyn, Long Island City and Richmond county, comprising all of Staten Island and certain outlying towns and parts of towns on Long Island adjacent to the present city of Brooklyn.

To pass an act saying that these territories shall be consolidated into and hereafter shall form one city, is apparently a simple proposition, but to legislate intelligently upon the subject, and to treat all portions of the proposed consolidated city fairly and equitably will require the knowledge of certain facts which I think can only be ascertained by your committee, acting in its official capacity and with the power vested in it to compel answers to its inquiries.

As you are doubtless aware, the existent municipal corporations, which it is proposed to consolidate into one corporation, differ widely from each other as to the amount of their bonded indebtedness; as to their capacity for issuing bonds under the provisions of the Constitution, as to their revenues, as to the assessed valuation of property for purposes of taxation and its proportion to the actual value of property assessed, as to the rate of taxation upon the assessed value thus fixed, and as to the present state of efficiency of the several instruments of municipal administration.

For instance, the city of New York has at the present time a margin of debt issuing capacity, under the limitation fixed by the Constitution, amounting to some sixty millions of dollars.

The real estate in this city is currently reported to be assessed for purposes of taxation at an average rate not much exceeding sixty per cent. of its real value in the market. Upon this valuation the tax rate has for a number of years fallen below three per cent. and the city has, by virtue of its ancient charters and for other reasons, large revenues from various sources aggregating nearly or about twelve millions of dollars per annum.

As opposed to this state of affairs, the city of Brooklyn, if I am correctly informed, has pretty nearly, if not quite reached its debt issuing capacity. Its real estate is said to be assessed for purposes of taxation at an average rate approaching very nearly and in many cases quite reaching its real value in the market, and upon this valuation the average tax rate is about one per cent. larger than that of the city of New York upon its smaller comparative valuation; and the city of Brooklyn, as I am informed, has no considerable sources of revenue other than that which is derived from taxation.

I apprehend that similar discrepancies would be found to exist if a careful examination were made of the financial condition and resources of each of the other municipalities which it is proposed to consolidate with New York into this large city.

The arguments and discussions which your committee are now engaged in hearing in Brooklyn, and expect hereafter to listen to in New York, may be and doubtless will be instructive to some extent as to the wishes and desires of the inhabitants of those two cities upon this important question; but after you shall have ascertained those wishes and desires, if you deem it proper to proceed with the subject and recommend consolidation, you will find it necessary to carefully consider what adjustment and arrangement should be made as to the assumption of present indebtedness of the several existent municipalities; of the disposition hereafter to be made of such revenues as each municipality may now have; and of the disposition hereafter of the burdens of taxation.

The suggestion that I desire to make to you is that your committee should, as soon as practicable, address a circular letter to the proper officers of each of the municipalities proposed to be included in the consolidation, asking for formal and accurate statements as to the condition of each of such municipalities in the particulars to which I have referred, and in such other particulars as will doubtless occur to your committee upon consideration of the question.

It will probably take some little time for the preparation of these statements, and it would therefore seem that the sooner such a request is made the sooner will you committee be in a position to consider the matter with that full comprehension which I am sure you desire to possess.

I suggest that such an inquiry should be made by your committee, because it is very difficult to obtain this information except in some manner such as I have suggested. Some time ago I made an effort to obtain this information myself and found that so far as concerns certain localities it was impossible to obtain a satisfactory statement of their financial condition.

Without at present expressing any opinion as to the desirability of consolidating the cities of New York, Brooklyn and Long Island City, may I not beg your committee to take into very serious consideration the question whether they should not at the outset eliminate that portion of the proposition which contemplates the inclusion of Richmond county in this consolidated city. That county, as you are aware, comprises an island situated in New York bay, many miles distant from the present city of New York, too far to ever permit of the erection of a bridge between the two, and while not so far from the city of Brooklyn, yet separated from it by the ship channel, which itself will probably render the erection of a bridge inpracticable for many years to come.

The county is for the most part sparsely settled, there being no considerable towns or villages upon it, and its inclusion into the consolidated city would necessitate the attempt to apply metropolitan methods and appliances to a large territory which is now purely country; which will be separated from the other parts of the city by water; which will be accessible otherwise than by water transportation only by going through an adjacent State, and which has no geographical or logical reason for annexation to the city of New York.

As you will recollect, the Legislature of last year annexed to this city a small piece of territory formerly comprising a part of Westchester county, which compares very closely as to the density of its population and its general characteristics to the present county of Richmond; and, even as to that small territory, it has been the experience of the officers of the city that the annual expenses necessary to be incurred for the purpose of bringing it in some degree up to the metropolitan standard of efficiency has largely swelled our budget for this year.

It seems to me that whatever may be the final conclusion to which your committee may arrive as to the consolidation of the city of New York with the cities adjacent to it, you will readily see that there is no sufficient reason for the attempt to bring Staten Island into this municipality.

I hope to be able to consult you personally upon this subject before very long, but in the meantime ask you to consider this communication, and lay it before your committee.

Yours very truly,

FRANCIS M. SCOTT,

Counsel to the Corporation.

BROOKLYN, N. Y., *January* 16, 1896.

To the Committee on Consolidation:

The statement made yesterday by one of your committee, Dr. George W. Brush, that those in favor of consolidation were mostly real estate speculators, was intended, no doubt, to cast discredit upon those engaged in real estate business who see that consolidation alone can save owners of real estate from disaster. I regret that so estimable a gentleman as Dr. Brush should make such a statement over his own signature. The firm with which I am connected has never engaged in real estate speculation, and I have therefore a right to be heard, by communication, at least. We represent hundreds of men and women who are not real estate speculators, but whose little all is invested in realty from which they look for an income to keep body and soul together. They see, as we see, only disaster in the near future where a city having only realty from which to derive an income is constantly piling up indebtedness of millions year after year.

I beg to assure your honorable committee that the cry about real estate speculators should not deceive your committee. There are no real estate speculators in Brooklyn. They have all been wiped out long since or have passed to Westchester county or Montauk point. Our friend, Dr. Brush, knows this as well as his neighbors, and he knows that the Brooklyn realty market has long since been abandoned as a field for speculation.

If another election is insisted upon and the will of the people is to be set aside, how can there be any certainty that innocent and well-meaning people may not rise up and ask for a third election to make sure that people have not again changed their mind. If it takes two elections why should our Senators refuse the people an opportunity to say whether they have not changed their minds as to who should represent them.

Yours truly,

C. AUGUSTUS HAVILAND.

BROOKLYN, N. Y., *January* 15, 1896.

To his Excellency the Governor and the Legislature of the State of New York:

The undersigned, representing the railroad companies of the city of Brooklyn, respectfully urge the passage of a bill consolidating Brooklyn city with New York city, providing, among other things, for attaining an equal and uniform rate of taxation and uniform valuations for the purpose of taxation.

THE KINGS COUNTY ELEVATED RAILWAY CO.,
THE BROOKLYN AND BRIGHTON BEACH RAILROAD CO.
By James Jordan, President.

THE BROOKLYN ELEVATED RAILROAD,
By Elisha Dyer, Jr., Treasurer.

VAN BRUNT STREET AND ERIE R. R. CO.,
By Michael Murphy, President.

CONEY ISLAND AND BROOKLYN R. R. CO.,
By W. Van Derhoef, Treasurer.

In case the provisions of the "Cantor Railroad Act" do not apply to the territory of Brooklyn.

THE NASSAU RAILROAD CO.,
By P. H. Flynn, President.

BROOKLYN, N. Y., *January* 18, 1896.

Senator Clarence Lexow, Chairman of Committee:

Dear Sir and Senators.— You asked me at the hearing of the committee yesterday if I had "changed my opinion that the bill would be unconstitutional." I think you will remember when I recall it to you, that my argument of unconstitutionality last year was directed against the bill of last year on the ground that it practically was an attempt to abolish county lines, which could not be done under the Constitution. That view has been adopted in the preparation of the bill of this year, for it in express words provides that the county lines shall not be disturbed.

That being so, I think you must agree with me that the only consolidation that is possible is one that would reinstate the county boards of supervisors in New York and Kings county and would make of the Greater New York a city, the government of whose affairs was divided between five boards of supervisors and a municipal government, with the debt contracting limit twice as high as it was intended to be by the Constitution.

Now, I am sure that we all agree that the construction of a good form of government for such a city as the Greater New York would be is one of the most gigantic works of legislative architecture of the time; and it seems to me that all must agree that a governmental structure with such a division of authority and responsibility as I have indicated would be faulty in design and would be not only incommodious but dangerous.

Mr. Senator, it is not of so much importance that consolidation shall take place in one year, or five or ten, as it is that if it takes place it shall be upon a plan which shall not increase the difficulties of good government and discourage the exercise of good citizenship.

The only sure foundation of a wise constructive legislation is a change in the Constitution of the State, which shall enable the Legislature to make one municipal government for the greater city.

And, if you, accepting the force of the positions above expressed should determine no longer to proceed in a way whose results can not possibly be such as all friends of good government desire, and should lead off in what seems to me the only way to accomplish a satisfactory result, viz.: that of amending the Constitution so as to enable our legislators to deal freely with so gigantic a plan involving such enormous interests, the judgment of reasonable and well-informed men must be that it was a course dictated by a far-reaching statesmanship and not by hand-to-mouth politics.

I earnestly beg your thoughtful consideration of these suggestions. I remain,

Your obedient servant,

ROBERT D. BENEDICT.

BROOKLYN, N. Y., *January* 21, 1896.

Senator Lexow:

Dear Sir.— I am in favor of the Greater New York. I, however, see no serious objection to a "referendum." If the terms of the union are made just and equitable I am confident that a bill for consolidation would be endorsed by a large majority of the voters in the city of Brooklyn.

Yours truly,
TIMOTHY PERRY.

BROOKLYN, N. Y., *January* 22, 1896.

To the Hon. Clarence E. Lexow, Chairman of the Legislative Consolidation Committee, Albany, N. Y.:

Dear Sir.—As a citizen of Brooklyn and a large taxpayer, I take the liberty of writing to you in relation to resubmission to the people of Brooklyn of the question of consolidation.

From my knowledge of the feeling of the people, there would be seventy-five per cent. against consolidation when put to a vote.

I am president of one of the prominent corporations in Brooklyn and director in many others and have a general interest at stake.

Politically, the Republican party, of which I am one, would feel the injustice that would be done to Brooklyn.

Yours respectfully,
CLEMENT LOCKITT.

NEW YORK, *January* 22, 1896.

Mr. Lexow:

Dear Sir.— I am a resident of Brooklyn and a taxpayer, and very much in favor of consolidation; and any representation by our representatives in the Legislature that there is a change in sentiment in regard to this matter is not true.

While it is true that I live in Brooklyn, yet every dollar that I spend in that tax-ridden and cobble-stoned town is made in New York. And, therefore, anything that contributes to the prosperity of New York city is of great interest to me.

Trusting that you will carry out the expressed wishes of the citizens of Brooklyn in regard to this matter, and pay no heed to the threats of our mis-representatives,

I am yours, etc.,
JOHN L. SHEPPARD.

BROOKLYN, N. Y., *January* 25, 1896.

Hon. Clarence Lexow:

Dear Sir.— I desire to say in reference to the matter of consolidation now before your committee, I voted against consolidation in 1894, not that I was opposed to it, but did not think it wise at that time on account of the condition of New York city, and I know many more like myself. My office is located at the foot of the elevated station. I called in the first hundred gentlemen who passed my door that I knew personally, the morning previous to your first visit to Brooklyn, to sign a petition if in favor of consolidation; out of the hundred called in four refused (three were opposed and one said it made no difference to him, so he would not sign). I do not claim there is such a large percentage all over the city, but I do claim there is a large majority of Brooklyn people in favor of consolidation, and what I have stated is my experience and hope you will use your best influence to bring about such a result. I can refer you to Senator Brush.

Very respectfully yours,
JOHN PULLMAN.

NEW YORK, *January* 29, 1896.

Senator Clarence Lexow, Albany, N. Y.:

Dear Sir.— I do not hesitate to say that a large majority of the people of Staten Island are in favor of consolidation with the city of New York. At the election held in 1894, the vote for consolidation was 5,531, against 1,505. The people stand to-day where they stood at that time. The taxpayers and most of the voters are for consolidation. I am a taxpayer both in the city of New York and in Richmond county, where, thank God, I reside, and have resided for many years — a most beautiful island, situated upon New York bay — needed by the greater city because of its many miles of deep water front. Corporation Attorney Scott puts us many miles removed from the city, yet, nevertheless, I comfortably pass over those "many miles" in a ferry boat in a few minutes. What is the matter with Scott, anyhow? A look at the map will prove that Richmond county is nearer to the City Hall than is Central park. " Sparsely settled! " says Mr. Scott, yet we have one village with 20,000 inhabitants, and a total of about 70,000, a vast majority of whom desire consolidation and look anxiously for a favorable report of your honorable committee. I send you a copy of my remarks before the Staten Island chamber of commerce, a majority of whom promptly laid the resolution seeking a separate charter upon the table.

Grant this boon of consolidation and the greater portion of the people of our Empire State will hail you and your honorable committee as blessed.

Yours truly,

READ BENEDICT.

BROOKLYN, N. Y., *January* 29, 1896.

Hon. Clarence Lexow, Albany, N. Y.:

Dear Sir.—At a large meeting of the Twenty-second District Republican Association of the Seventh Ward, the following resolution was unaminously adopted, with instructions to forward you a copy of the same:

Resolved, That this association most earnestly protest against the enactment of any bill by the State Legislature having for its object the consolidation of our city with the municipality of the city of New York, without first submitting the same for the approval or disapproval of the citizens of Brooklyn.

Very respectfully yours,
JOHN J. WALKER,
President.

N. K. EVERETT,
Secretary.

WHEREAS, A bill has been introduced into the Senate of the State of New York, by Senator George W. Brush, providing for the resubmission of the question of consolidation with New York to our voters, therefore

Resolved, That we, the Republican Association of the Sixth Ward of the city of Brooklyn heartily favor such a bill. We urge the members of the Legislature from Kings county to do their utmost to secure its passage and commend it to the favorable action of legislators from other parts of this State.

Resolved, That a copy of this resolution be sent to each member of the Legislature from Kings county, the Speaker of the Assembly, the President pro tem. of the Senate, the Hon. Clarence Lexow, chairman of the joint subcommittee on consolidation, Lieutenant-Governor Saxton and Governor Morton.

(A true copy.)

C. J. TEEHAN,
Secretary.

BROOKLYN, *January* 21, 1896.

At a meeting of the First Ward Republican Committee held

this date, the following preamble and resolutions were adopted as the sense of this body:

WHEREAS, A bill has been introduced into the Senate of the State of New York, by Senator George W. Brush, providing for the resubmission of the question of consolidation with New York, to our voters; therefore,

Resolved, That we, the Republican Committee of the First Ward of the city of Brooklyn, heartily favor such a bill. We urge the members of the Legislature from Kings county to do their utmost to secure its passage, and commend it to the favorable action of legislators from other parts of the State.

Resolved, That a copy of this resolution be sent to each member of the Legislature from Kings county, the Speaker of the Assembly, the President pro tem. of the Senate, the Hon. Clarence Lexow, chairman of the joint legislative committee on consolidation; Governor Morton and Lieutenant-Governor Saxton.

WM. T. SHARP,
President.

WM. R. FLEMING,
Secretary.

BROOKLYN, N. Y., *January* 23, 1896.

Senator Clarence Lexow, Albany, N. Y.:

Sir.— Acting in accordance with the expressed wish of the Seventeenth Ward Republican Committee of the city of Booklyn, assembled Tuesday evening, January 21, in the Kerasmos Building, this city, we beg leave to transmit to you, enclosed herein, copy of the resolutions adopted at that meeting, asking their earnest consideration at your hands.

Very truly yours,
THOMAS J. PERCIVAL,
President.

EUGENE A. AMELI,
Secretary.

BROOKLYN, *January* 21, 1896.

At a meeting of the Eleventh Ward Republican Committee held this date, the following preamble and resolutions were adopted as the sense of this body:

" WHEREAS, A bill has been introduced into the Senate of the State of New York, by Senator George W. Brush, providing for the resubmission of the question of consolidation with New York to our voters; therefore,

" *Resolved*, That we, the Republican Association of the eleventh ward of the city of Brooklyn, heartily favor such bill. We urge the members of the Legislature from Kings county to do their utmost to secure its passage, and commend it to the favorable action of legislators from other parts of the State.

" *Resolved*, That a copy of this resolution be sent to each member of the Legislature from Kings county, the Speaker of the Assembly, the President pro tem. of the Senate, the Hon. Clarence Lexow, chairman of the joint subcommittee on consolidation; Governor Morton and Lieutenant Governor Saxton."

JOHN E. THORNE,
President.

WM. F. ABBOTT,
Secretary.

WHEREAS, A bill has been introduced into the Senate of the State of New York by Senator George W. Brush, providing for the resubmission of the question of consolidation with New York to our voters; therefore,

Resolved, That we, the Republican Association of the twenty-sixth ward of the city of Brooklyn heartily favor such bill. We urge the members of the Legislature from Kings county to do their utmost to secure its passage, and commend it to the favorable action of legislators from other parts of this State.

Resolved, That a copy of this resolution be sent to each member of the Legislature from Kings county, the Speaker of the Assembly, the President pro tem. of the Senate, the Hon. Clarence Lexow, chairman of the joint subcommittee on consolidation, Lieutenant-Governor Saxton and Governor Morton.

The foregoing resolutions were unanimously adopted at a regular meeting of the above ward committee, on January 21,1896.

F. W. CODDINGTON,
President.

W. M. FRANSECKY,
Secretary.

BROOKLYN, N. Y., *January* 23, 1896.

Dear Sir.— You are hereby respectfully notified that at a regular meeting of the Twenty-seventh Ward Republican Association, held on Tuesday evening, January 21, 1896, the following was unanimously adopted:

WHEREAS, A bill has been introduced into the Senate of the State of New York by Senator George W. Brush, providing for the resubmission of the question of consolidation with New York to our voters; therefore, be it,

Resolved, That we, the Twenty-seventh Ward Republican Association of the city of Brooklyn heartily favor such bill. We urge the members of the Legislature from Kings county to do their utmost to secure its passage, and commend it to the favorable action of the legislators from other parts of this State.

Resolved, That a copy of this resolution be forwarded to each member of the Legislature from Kings county, the Speaker of the Assembly, the President pro tem. of the Senate, the Hon. Clarence Lexow, chairman of the joint subcommittee on consolidation, Lieutenant-Governor Saxton, and His Excellency, Levi P. Morton, Governor of the State of New York.

Very respectfully yours,
GEORGE SCHLAGENHAUF,
President.

GEORGE SENN,
Secretary.

January 23, 1896.

We, the undersigned, citizens of the city of Brooklyn, desire to put ourselves on record as in favor of a resubmission of the question of consolidation:

Collins & Day, 138 Livingston street.
Charles Meyer, 94 Livingston street.
James S. White, 109 Livingston street.
Robert J. Wilkin, 105 Schermerhorn street.
A. J. Foren, 40 Boerum place.
E. W. Meek, 83 State street.
G. A. Dessart, 42 Boerum place.
T. B. Sidibotham, Jr., 85 Schermerhorn street.
William A. Butler, 67 Schermerhorn street.
John Wilson, 197 State street.
T. H. Doheney, 78 Livingston avenue.
W. B. Willicott, 78 Livingston street.
Edward Devos, 78 Livingston street.
E. C. Airla, 356 State street.

BROOKLYN, *February* 10, 1896.

Hon. Senator Lexow:

WHEREAS, The members of the Bushwick Republican Club, of the eighteenth ward, of the city of Brooklyn, believing that, on the last popular vote of the people relating to the question of annexation with New York, the matter was not thoroughly understood by them as to their interests, whereby they might be benefited or otherwise by the carrying or rejecting of the same, and thereby insuring an intelligent vote on the question; be it

Resolved, That we, the members of the Bushwick Club, endeavor to have the respective Senators and Assemblymen representing the people of Brooklyn in the Legislature of the State exert themselves to the utmost of their power to secure the enactment of laws to enable the people of the districts interested in such annexation having another popular vote on the question; and, further, be it

Resolved, That a copy of these resolutions be forwarded to the Governor of the State of New York and each of the said Senators and Assemblymen for their consideration.

JACOB MAURER,
Secretary.

Brooklyn, *January* 30, 1896.

Hon. Clarence Lexow, Albany, N. Y.:

Dear Sir.— By direction of the executive and advisory committees of the Brooklyn Young Republican Club, I hand you herewith a copy of resolutions adopted by the club Monday evening, January 27, 1896, and for which I ask your kind consideration:

Resolved, That, without expressing any opinion in favor of or adverse to the consolidation of Brooklyn with New York, this club is strongly opposed to the passage of any charter or other legislation consolidating the two cities which shall not be subject to ratification by the voters of Brooklyn.

Resolved, That copies of this resolution be forwarded to his excellency, Levi P. Morton, Governor of the State of New York; to each Senator and member of the general Assembly and to the press.

Respectfully,
JUDSON G. WALL,
Secretary.

Flushing, N. Y., *February* 13, 1896.

Hon. Frederick Storm, Albany, N. Y.:

My Dear Sir.— At a well attended meeting of the Republican Club of Flushing, last night, the following was adopted:

Resolved, That this club is opposed to consolidation.

It might be well to state that the passage of this resolution was well night unanimous, but two votes being cast against it. The club also wishes me to state that no previous action in this matter has ever been taken by this club.

Very truly yours,

G. W. HILLMAN, Jr.,

President.

Whereas, It is contemplated by a Republican Legislature to enact what is known as the Lexow Consolidation Bill, merging the city of Brooklyn into the Greater New York, without any knowledge or information as to the conditions upon which such consolidation is to be effected so far as it relates to our city;

Whereas, The Republican party in Kings county for the past two years has demonstrated renewed vitality and fealty to true Republican principles, by its reorganization on the election district system, by its active and successful participation in the great work of redeeming the city government from corruption and misrule, by its victories in county, State and Congressional campaigns, and by its united and aggressive action again securing a Republican control in municipal affairs, which gives every indication of force and permanence;

Whereas, This organization is to-day still united and loyal to the principles of the party and is looking forward with eagerness to the larger duties of, and still greater achievements in, the national campaign of this year, and

Whereas, The contemplated legislative action in passing a consolidation act without a referendum, threatens to take from this city and county the results of the achievements of this party organization, without any satisfactory indication that the interests of our municipality and citizens will be properly safeguarded; be it

Resolved, That we, the representatives of the Republican party organization of the county of Kings, earnestly and emphatically declare with all the force, power and influence of a united party, that we disapprove any and all attempts to consolidate our city with any other, unless full and complete information be obtained of the terms and conditions upon which such consolidation be based.

G. H. ROBERTS, JR.,
ALEX. ROBB,
M. B. CAMPBELL.

BROOKLYN, N. Y., *January* 31, 1896.

At a regular meeting of the Republicans of the nineteenth district of the sixth ward, held Tuesday evening, January 28, 1896, the following resolutions were unanimously adopted:

Resolved, That we, the enrolled Republicans of the nineteenth district of the sixth ward, are most emphatically opposed to the passage of any charter or any other legislation consolidating the two cities, until the question shall have been referred to the voters of Brooklyn.

That copies of the above resolution be forwarded to His Excellency, Levi P. Morton, Governor of the State of New York; to Senators Lexow, Brush, Gallagher, Wray and Assemblyman Cullen, and to The Standard Union, Eagle and Times.

HENRY H. HANTON,
Secretary.

I, Robert Seabury, clerk of the board of supervisors of Queens county, do hereby certify that the annexed is a true copy of a resolution duly passed by the said board of supervisors, at a regular meeting thereof, held at Long Island City, in said county, on the 20th day of January, 1896.

In witness whereof I have hereunto set my hand and affixed the official seal of said board of supervisors, this 22d day of January, 1896.

ROBERT SEABURY,
Supervisors' Clerk.

WHEREAS, By a concurrent resolution of the Senate and Assembly of the State of New York, the corporation counsel of the cities of New York, Brooklyn and Long Island City were specifically named in said resolution as counsel to aid the joint committee of the Senate and Assembly in the investigation relating to the Greater New York; and

WHEREAS, A large portion of the county of Queens, outside the limits of Long Island City, is included in said Greater New York, and the board of supervisors of this county is deeply interested therein; therefore,

Resolved, That the said joint committee of the Senate and Assembly be requested to add the counsel of the board of supervisors of Queens county to the said joint committee; said counsel to be paid by Queens county.

At a regular meeting of the Thirteenth Ward Republican Committee (Brooklyn), held January 21, 1896, on motion of Hon. Stephen B. Jacobs the following were unanimously adopted:

WHEREAS, A bill has been introduced into the Senate of the State of New York by Senator George W. Brush, providing for the resubmission of the question of consolidation with New York to our voters; therefore,

Resolved, That we, the Republican association of the thirteenth ward of the city of Brooklyn, heartily favor such bill. We urge the members of the Legislature from Kings county to do their utmost to secure its passage and commend it to the favorable action of legislators from other parts of this State.

Resolved, That a copy of this resolution be sent to each member of the Legislature from Kings county, the Speaker of the

Assembly, the President pro tem. of the Senate, the Hon. Clarence Lexow, chairman of the joint subcommittee on consolidation; Lieutenant-Governor Saxton and Governor Morton.

F. J. LE COUNT,
President.

WM. A. MARINUS,
Secretary.

January 17, 1896.

To Hon. Clarence E. Lexow and Gentlemen of the Legislative Consolidation Committee:

I regret exceedingly that a most urgent business engagement at the very hour at which you are to meet prevents my being present in person at your hearing, but that my voice may not be entirely unheard I take this method of presenting briefly my views on the subject of consolidation of the cities of New York and Brooklyn.

I shall not waste your time by going over the arguments that others who will be present can more effectually lay before you, but say to you as a Republican, desirous of the continued success of my party in city, State and national elections, that if consolidation is brought about without referring the matter to the citizens of Brooklyn, the party guilty of such legislation may expect and will receive such a condemnation at the polls at the next election as will seriously affect the chances of their candidate for the presidency carrying this State.

Kings county went against Folger by upwards of 45,000 majority. Governor Morton, or whoever is the standard-bearer of the Republican party this year, will lose the county by over 50,000 if this unwise legislation is brought about, which, added to New York county's Democratic majority, will wipe out the Republican majorities in the other counties and give the State to the Democrats.

Very respectfully,
WM. C. BRYANT.

BROOKLYN, *January* 20, 1896.

To Hon. Clarence E. Lexow and Gentlemen of the Legislative Consolidation Committee, Albany, N. Y.:

It does not appear that the moral phase of the question of consolidation was presented at the recent sessions of your committee in this city. I would therefore respectfully submit for your consideration the following questions, viz.:

Is not the moral phase of the question of consolidation more vital to the future welfare of the city of Brooklyn than the matter of speculative real estate values and the glory of rivaling other great cities in population and grandeur?

Do not the facts in regard to great cities all through the ages make it important that we should carefully consider this question from a moral standpoint before uniting New York and Brooklyn under one municipality?

How do the records of New York and Brooklyn compare as to morality?

Does any intelligent person familiar with the past and present history of the two cities, question that the moral status of Brooklyn has been and is higher than that of New York?

What will be the effect upon Brooklyn from a moral standpoint should consolidation take place?

Would not it be a great injustice to all intelligent citizens of Brooklyn to force consolidation without first allowing a full and fair discussion of this and other phases of the question?

I would also ask, has not Brooklyn, "The City of Churches," a higher reputation morally throughout this country and the civilized world than New York? If this is so, I ask shall we surrender this reputation? I say no! emphatically, no!

Respectfully yours,

A. A. ROBBINS.

BROOKLYN, *January* 17, 1896.

To the Chairman of the Legislative Joint Subcommittee on Consolidation;

Sir.— Unless the majority of this committee have been misreported, they have declared that the question of consolidation has been settled, and that the only thing to do now is to find the best and most feasible plan for accomplishing that purpose.

Against such a proposition I most earnestly protest. We have never had a settlement of this question by the people of Brooklyn. True, there was a vote upon the subject in 1894; but the people of this city did not regard it as a "settlement." Neither did the friends of consolidation regard it as a settlement before the election. Their committee put forth a circular upon the subject, in which they declared: "Electors will please observe that a vote amounts to nothing more than a simple expression of opinion on the general subject of consolidation. If every ballot in the city were in favor of consolidation, there would be no finality about it," etc.

The people of Brooklyn looked at the question in this different way, and but one-third of the registered voters of Brooklyn voted in its favor; and of those who favored it, we know of a large number of persons who voted for it under a misapprehension. There were a large number of constitutional amendments to be voted on, and Republicans urged upon their followers to vote for all the amendments. Many Republicans voted for consolidation thinking it was a constitutional amendment, as the ballots were similar in form. This is a fact, however much it may go against the intelligence of the voter. And now, forsooth, with less than one-third in favor, and many of them voting under a misapprehension, we are told that the question of consolidation has been settled by the people of Brooklyn in its favor, because there was a paltry majority of 277 votes out of 129,000 voting, and 62,000 who did not feel interest enough in the subject to vote at all. To take this view of the matter, and to annihilate the autonomy of a great city of over a million on such a pretext will be the most infamous outrage of the nineteenth century.

But, for argument's sake, let us for a moment grant that the vote of 1894 was valid and binding; but the Legislature did not act upon that vote when the opportunity was presented. And I claim that because of that failure to act then, Brooklyn is entitled to another vote on consolidation. Are we to be told that that vote is to be always binding? Can a great people not reverse its opinions?

In 1888 the people of the United States elected a Republican President and a Congress in favor of the McKinley tariff by so great a majority that many said the Democrats would never be heard of again, not in at least a quarter of a century.

In 1892 the people of the United States elected a Democratic President and a Congress in favor of the Wilson tariff by a majority so great that Democrats said the Republicans were dead, and they bade them an everlasting good-bye, as they thought.

Two years later the Republicans were again on top in Congress with a greater majority than the Democrats had in the former Congress; and nobody doubts the election of a Republican President next fall, unless he is defeated by the stupidity and foolishness of Republicans in the New York Legislature in cramming consolidation down the throat of Brooklyn at a cost of 30,000 to 50,000 Republican votes in our city.

I speak of these things to show that a great people not only have the right to reverse their opinions, but that they do reverse them. Suppose that either Congress had said to the people in 1888 or 1892, you have voted for the McKinley tariff, or the Wilson traiff, as the case might be, and that question is settled, as our legislators at Albany now say to the people of Brooklyn on the consolidation question. Well, suppose they had? I need not discuss the result.

Now, if Brooklyn was for consolidation in 1894, she had a right to reverse her opinion, especially as the Legislature did not act upon that opinion at its following session; and Brooklyn has reversed that opinion, and now she has a right to give an expression of that reversed opinion by a resubmission of this important question to her voters. She asks, nay, she demands, this right from this Legislature. If that right is granted and the vote is for consolidation, you will never hear a word again from any present Brooklynite. But if that right is denied us, and consolidation is forced upon us without resubmission, and, as we know, against the will of a large majority of the voters of this city, then all I have to say is, God help the Republican party in Brooklyn and in the State next fall. On the 14th of January, 1896, the Brooklyn Eagle said, editorially:

"There are 100,000 votes in this town to make things and to smash things, and they can be wielded as a unit, to make or to smash things and men, according as the things or the men are the friends or are the enemies of Brooklyn's rights to determine Brooklyn's destiny.

"Mr. Morton would like to be President. It is a commendable ambition. He is well fitted for the office. He would lose New York State by more votes than Harrison lost it in 1892 if he wrote his name under a bill to abolish Brooklyn without Brooklyn's consent. Hamilton Fish would like to be Governor. But he could no more be elected Governor of New York, even if he received the nomination of both political parties, with a record for the effacement of Brooklyn without Brooklyn's consent to score against him, than he could be elected Pope of Rome. Brooklyn means business, and the 'Eagle' means business, on this thing, and when both mean business on the same thing, events prove that business is effectively done."

Gentlemen, without any thought of boasting, but simply to show that I have a right to speak as a Republican, let me say that I have been a staunch Republican since the 7th day of August, 1854, when the first Republican convention was held. I was a member of that convention. I have never flinched from Republican doctrines. I have always worked faithfully for the party. I wrote a book on the tariff, of which 3,000,000 copies have been circulated. I know something of the party and its teachings and doctrines. I love the party for what it has done and is doing, and for what it will do if wise counsels prevail; and I know something of the temper and feelings of the Republicans in Brooklyn — and I say to you in all earnestness and sincerity that the "Eagle" is right, and that if you compel us to take consolidation without resubmission, or, at least, a referendum, there will be no longer a Republican party in Brooklyn. They will never again trust or support a party that has deliberately robbed them of their dearest rights and privileges, and turned them and their property over to the spoliation of Tammany Hall and its vile crew, with its Republican attachment, equally vile. One of the fundamental doctrines of Republicanism is home rule, and on this doctrine we also demand resubmission.

The chairman of this subcommittee was in Brooklyn at the Republican judiciary convention last October, and was then asked how he stood on the question of consolidation. He answered in my presence, "Gentlemen, that is a question that you ought to settle in Brooklyn." We have settled it in Brooklyn. We have now a legislative delegation that is unanimous for resubmission; we have a common council that is unanimous for resubmission; our mayor and ex-mayor are both earnest for resubmission, and the people of Brooklyn are for resubmission.

I entreat you, give the people of Brooklyn another chance to vote on this all-important question, and thus let it be forever settled in the only just, right and righteous manner.

Truly yours,

D. G. HARRIMAN,

Police Justice, Second District.

BROOKLYN, N. Y., *February 4*, 1896.

Hon. Clarence E. Lexow, Chairman of Joint Subcommittee:

Dear Sir.—The public hearing to the citizens of Brooklyn on the question of consolidation having been closed, I beg as a citizen of that city the privilege of addressing you in relation to the late vote on consolidation. This vote was authorized by the Legislature.

A vote upon the question without such authorization would have been entirely without effect. Hence, any commanding or limiting effect which it might have upon the Legislature, was derived from the act of the Legislature authorizing it. The vote either did or did not positively or morally bind the Legislature authorizing it to legislate in accordance. If an affirmative vote bound the Legislature so to act, a negative vote would likewise have debarred them from so acting (otherwise the proposition would have been, Decided by your votes, whether or not Brooklyn, New York and other districts shall be consolidated. If your vote is an affirmative one, the Legislature will act in accordance; if it is in the negative it *will* or *will not* so act, but will act at its discretion).

If an affirmative vote in any way bound the Legislature to legislate in accordance, or had a negative vote forbidden the Legislature to sanction the project, the authorization of such commanding or limiting vote was a delegation of legislative power. The Legislature could not pledge itself to carry into effect an affirmative vote without limiting the freedom of two-thirds of its members to override a possible gubernatorial veto.

If the vote had any binding or commanding effect upon the last Legislature, was not that command fully satisfied by the last Legislature by the introduction and urging of the bill which failed?

If the present Legislature is in any way, morally or positively, bound by the vote, they are so bound by the act of a previous Legislature, and if this Legislature is so bound will not all succeeding Legislatures be similarly bound?

Had the consolidation bill been passed by the last Legislature and approved by the Governor, the present Legislature would have power to repeal it and the Governor to approve such repeal. Can it be consistently held that this Legislature holds the right and power to repeal or reverse an act of the last Legislature carrying into effect a majority vote, and yet be bound to remedy the failure of the last Legislature to pass such an act?

Whatever commanding or limiting effect, direct or moral, the vote may have had upon the last Legislature it became such by the delegation of its powers. And whatever effect it may have upon the present Legislature is in the line of a restraint or a limitation of its free action by the act of a previous Legislature.

Viewing the vote as an expression of popular feeling at the time it was certainly within the province of the previous Legislature to authorize such a vote as a test of the sentiment of the citizens of the localities which were to be affected. It would be equally within the province of the present Legislature to call for a second expression, and it would be of far more use as a guide and aid in the wise performance of its legislative duties.

During the hearings in this city it was affirmed that the call for a resubmission or a new vote placed the Legislature in a dilemma, that if the last vote was admitted to be indecisive and another should be authorized, that vote so authorized might also be claimed to be indecisive, and so on *ad infinitum*. The dilemma disappears if it is recognized that the vote was a more or less imperfect expression of the sentiment at the time and not of binding force upon the Legislature, but an aid to it in the fulfillment of its legislative functions.

This vote differed widely from a vote for public officers or for a constitutional amendment, in either of which cases the votes are cast for the decision of a clearly marked and definite action to be taken, or are a definite and positive expression of a choice of individual representatives.

The vote on consolidation was different in this, that it was an expression in favor of a complex project involving countless modifications, none of which had been formulated, and fixed no date either for beginning or for completion. As no date was fixed it certainly could not be construed as a demand for immediate legislative action, and this fully justifies any reasonable postponement for consideration and final deliberate action or inaction.

To argue that the vote was an assent to an agreement between the cities and sections, the terms of which agreement were unknown and at the time unknowable, would seem an absurdity. As an expression of the sentiment of the people at the time it was certainly entitled to the respectful attention of the last Legislature. As such an expression of opinion it has far less force to-day. A resubmission to-day would give expression to a far more enlightened and deliberately formed opinion, and afford a safer basis for legislative consideration.

As a measure of public opinion the simple rule of majority is in no sense conclusive, nor is it to be relied upon as a safe guide.

On the contrary, as respects important measures of vital interest, a nearly even division of opinion should suggest caution, and act as a warning against precipitancy of action not to be disregarded with safety.

Very respectfully,
JNO. L. DIBBLE.

NEW YORK, *February* 1, 1896.

Hon. Clarence Lexow, Chairman Joint Committee on Greater New York, New York:

Dear Sir.— When the subject of consolidation was put to the public vote, something more than a year ago, I voted against it. Since that time I have had more opportunity to study the question and I am now of the opinion that it is decidedly for the material, moral and political advantage of both cities to be united.

In expressing this view I know that I express the feelings of my associates in the Sackett & Wilhelms Lithographing Company.

Respectfully yours,
C. WILHELMS,
Treasurer.

STATEN ISLAND SOLID YET FOR CONSOLIDATION.

To Senator Clarence Lexow, Chairman Investigating Committee Regarding Greater New York:

Dear Sir.— As a member of the Staten Island chamber of commerce, and known here as an advocate of public improvements, I desire to state that all reports coming through certain parties, who would like a little penny municipality of their own down here, to whistle on, according to their own sweet wills, setting forth that a " change " has come over the people who voted for consolidation, is absolutely false and unauthorized in my opinion, so far as the people are concerned. I am in daily touch with many of the most wide-awake and energetic citizens of this place, on my way to my office in New York, and have not found one who objects to consolidation where I find ten in favor of it. A few penny whistle advocates undertook to get the chamber of commerce here to indorse their views and declare against the Greater New York by resolution of the chamber. Notice was given one month before hand, but when our regular monthly meeting came, with the members prepared to defeat the resolution, the propounder thereof, having found that general sentiment was strongly against him, simply withdrew the part declaring against consolidation and instead substitute a resolution that " we prepare a city charter, in event of this consolidation not being settled within a short time, and instruct our Richmond county representatives at Albany to apply for power to incorporate now with a view to consolidation when the time might come for it." But this clear back down substitute was not acceptable as an equivalent to the original resolution — did not give ample scope for ranging against it a few even of the many broadsides lined for a volley — and after a farcical debate in the air by a lonely few in favor of it, and more against it, as a substitute, some adroitness being used to suppress one or two who were well handed with shot destructive to the resolution, the whole thing was " ingloriously " placed on the table, where it belonged, in the majority vote opinion.

There are some here who are afraid that they will lose their individuality as leaders on the island if absorbed into a Greater New York; but the real active, far-seeing men, here, who have the respect of the whole county for their patriotism in public matters of magnitude, and who take into consideration the near future result to the whole grand scheme, with its immense possibilities, are all in favor of immediate consolidation. With the North river bridge once and for all time a fact, it will, in my opinion, only be a comparatively short time when Staten Island will be also connected at Constable Hook by bridge, and a railway to New York via the Hudson Suspension bridge lines into New York's center. Millions of dollars already have just been capitalized, as your books there at Albany show, incorporating for active operations in Staten Island, and this at once. The trolley has just begun to branch in various directions also, and new concerns in manufacturing have begun to apply for sites, one such already having located and now setting up their plant. This capital is largely from outside, and more is even now nucleating for a project with which all others here combined will pall in comparison, I sincerely have reason to believe.

It is the larger, fuller, grander view, of the prospect as a whole, which inspires us when we look upon the map of the Greater New York, and reflect upon the possibilities that are before us. The miles upon miles of deep water frontage for our commerce — now cramped and taxed so heavily at the nucleus, or present New York — will be utilized on Staten Island comparatively soon; the western products, loading at both places direct into foreign ships without the present enormous lighterage cost, will come this way instead of seeking outlet from other ports in the country north and south of us in the United States. Perhaps the antis of Brooklyn storage-house owners, for instance, are afraid of Staten Island for the above reason.

As it is impossible for me to be present to give these views and statements in person before your honorable committee and publicly, I take the liberty to address your board by letter, hoping it may be read by you publicly, as an expression or statement of facts and opinion concerning the real expressed attitude of the people of Staten Island, and as a direct contradiction of the statement made quite recently before your board in public by a Staten Islander, who says there has been a change since the vote in favor of consolidation, and who would make it appear as though our whole people were doing nothing else, while riding to and from

New York daily on the boats, but talk about this so-colled change of heart and anti-consolidation. I think that man must be a lawyer unwisely talking in the interest of a client in Brooklyn who pays him for this particular kind of talk; otherwise I can not conceive of anyone spending the time that would be necessary to canvass the entire or even major part of the vote which declared for consolidation, and without which canvass he can not have authority to say that the people of Staten Island "have changed their minds," if the papers report him correctly. Without such a canvass, or even with it, in absence of the public's expression of the same, it is in my opinion a libel and an infringment upon our rights. But we have no fear of losing them.

Truly yours,
J. W. MOULTON.

BROOKLYN, *January* 29, 1896.

To the Hon. Members of the Commission on the Consolidation of New York, Brooklyn and Surrounding Cities and Towns:

Gentlemen.— Kindly allow me as an American citizen, a resident of the city of Brooklyn, N. Y., for over twenty years past, a Republican in political principles, and because I have been requested by a number of prominent citizens to say what I think would be for the best interests of Brooklyn in matters of consolidation with New York and other surrounding cities and towns, based upon my experience as a resident of the city of London twenty-five to thirty years ago and my observations of the changes there and here since that time.

In introducing this subject I would like to say that I fail to see how any sensible and independent person who has the present and future good and prosperity at heart can in honor oppose the consolidation of these places except through certain kinds of hollow sentimentality which has no weight as against common sense.

E Pluribus Unum is one of our principal mottoes and if this be true, as it has so often proved itself in conflicts of opinion, in times of peace and even when such opinions had to be carried to the force of arms, we found that our forefathers succeeded by such union as in 1776. I would ask what could have Boston or Massachusetts have done without the twelve sister States than in union with them, as against the old Tories of these colonies and the mother country of these days, who as to-day were obstructionists and fought against the development and progress of the masses of the common people. In looking back at the pages of history it will be found that there was not a place in the colonies where the old Tory spirit was more obstinate than within the precincts of the present city of Brooklyn. Remember the battle of Long Island; then look back through more recent years and see who has been the parties to oppose nearly every improvement that has been introduced into this locality of Brooklyn, and you will see the spirit that induced them to do so was simply the sentimental fear of loosing their personality or sovereignty as popular and public individuals.

Be it remembered that the cry made against land sharks and speculators as being the only ones who want consolidation is a false alarm, and that most of the men who now cry aloud we want to be left alone in our dear circumscribed Brooklyn and to bask in its quietude, are men whose forefathers owned the farms and lands on which Brooklyn now stands and have grown rich, some with their millions, through sales and investments made by cutting up lands into town lots and selling them at prices as high as procurable. Then lending their money to those so-called speculators, but really builders and developers of cities, at large rates of interest or profit, keeping all power in their own hands in a legal ways, that when the proper time came they could crowd these poor fellows into submission and sometimes poverty, and it seems to the writer that this to a great extent is being done now. What means these large New York institutions, who are some of them controlled by our so-called Brooklyn leading men, in refusing to loan one dollar on real estate security in the city of Brooklyn?

They know and it is for the public to find out. In this is the principle of some of the men who come out with the strong language and say, "We don't study the public," and when their vacillating arguments will hold together no longer they then get enraged and use their financial forces to bring about their own nefarious schemes with the destruction of their opponents whose desire it is to advance the interests of their fellow men and develop their city so that it shall be second to none in the whole world, not excepting the great city of London, England.

Why is it that there should be such difference in values of real estate between the city of New York and the city of Brooklyn? Why is it I ask that twenty-five hundred square feet of land in New York at one end of the present bridge should be valued at one hundred dollars a square foot, and the same amount at the other end of the same bridge should only be valued at five dollars a square foot when it it only six minutes ride or twelve minutes walk between them? We answer it is for want of union of interests or consolidation.

Why is it there are millions of dollars lying in New York banks and trust companies for investment that the city of Brooklyn can have no interest in? It is because that money has been devised for investment in New York city and for want of consolidation all these millions must stay on the other side of the East river although it could find investments more secure and safer on the Brooklyn side of the river than on the New York side.

Why is it that mechanics in Brooklyn are compelled to work at from fifty cents to one dollar a day less than mechanics in the same trade get in New York? We answer it is because Brooklyn property owners can not afford to pay more; therefore the employers can not pay New York wages for want of consolidated interests.

Why is it that Brooklyn's water front has never developed to the same extent as New York? We answer it is New York owns the whole of the East river to low water mark and Brooklyn people who want dockage have to pay to New York annual taxes, etc., which ought not to be the case, because they are paying taxes to a corporation in which they have no rights to representation. We claim this to be unconstitutional.

Why is it that a piece of property in Brooklyn is not worth more than one half of a similar piece in Harlem? It is we answer for want of consolidation and more bridges and closer communications by railroad connections. With them we should be nearer to the commercial center of New York than Harlem is to-day.

Why is it that hundreds of our Brooklyn manufacturers whose interests are all on this side of the river are compelled to have warehouses and offices in New York? It is simply because of the prestige of New York as a city known all over the world as one of the principal ports of entry in the United States, and they therefore find they are forced to identify themselves with New York, which would be unnecessary if Brooklyn and New York were one.

The writer has noticed among other and many improvements in the city of London, England, and its citizens that land on the Surry side of the river which sold for one pound one shilling per square yard before the union has since that time sold (and directly after) at an advance of from four to ten pounds per square yard and in some choice sections for more than that. All this of course was brought about because of union of interests and concert of purposes. As every person felt that his interest could be protected as well on one side of the river as the other; being under the same municipal laws he had the same security.

As a matter of history, before the so-called consolidation there were only seven public and two railroad bridges and most of those were toll or pay bridges in those early days, but now there are over three times that number and all free because they are the property of the people, except the railroad bridges, and there is no reason whatsoever that there should not be at least six bridges over the East river — one over Hell Gate and another over the Narrows, within the next ten years — because the people of these United States know how to build bridges about as well as any people in the world, and it is no more trouble for us to build bridges than it is to make other gigantic city improvements which are found necessary and profitable for the people and it is a fact that all the money required for such vast improvements would be forthcoming without any trouble.

Referring again to the increase of values of property through consolidation we would call your attention to certain matters which are facts of record of property in Harlem and above in the year of 1871-1872 and 1873, when lots were sold at from one to three hundred dollars each and in some cases less than those prices that since the annexation some of those very lots have sold at from three to twelve thousand dollars each, and gentlemen, we contend that this is the possibility and probability of the increase when we get consolidation as a Greater New York.

And all this prosperity means so much more work and better wages for our mechanics, so much more trade for our storekeepers, so many more orders for our merchants, and so much more prosperity for our industries.

Consolidation is the one thing needful in this city at this time. Although there has been an increase in the population since the building of the present bridge of about four hundred thousand, but this increase in numbers has not been a financial improvement to the city but rather a drawback than otherwise, as it demanded an increase in buildings which has been no encouragement to the builders, who would often have to dispose of his property for less than it cost him, because he could not realize, as in New York, a fair value for his labor, trouble and expense; now, therefore, the values of properties have been put down, city improvements have been compelled to go on, and on account of a low valuation of property taxes have always seemed to be very much higher than they ought to be, and this would not have been the case if we had been part of the city of New York as we ought and demand to be.

In conclusion, allow me to say that I have had a long and varied experience in the city of Brooklyn, being a large employer of labor and a consumer of manufactured goods, I therefore know in the foregoing whereof I speak.

I know that in the natural course of events Brooklyn property ought to have increased in value per ratio with other parts of the same distance of New York City Hall, and would have done so if it had been called New York and under the one bonded interests.

But where interests are divided there is nothing in common, therefore, I pray and beseech you to make the consolidation of these two cities your one grand effort this session, putting aside resubmission, as this would be an insult to the intelligence of the present city of Brooklyn; also referendum, as this, we think, would be unconstitutional and cause a precedent which would be a disaster to the commonwealth of this State.

I am, gentlemen, your obedient servant,

J. C. METCALFE.

BROOKLYN, N. Y., *January* 20, 1896.

Hon. Clarence E. Lexow, Chairman Investigating Committee:

Honorable Sir.— I am in favor of consolidation of New York and Brooklyn.

Brooklyn can not stand the increased rate of taxation that will be absolutely necessary to make the necessary public improvements.

The owners of Brooklyn, those who pay the money to carry on the government, are in favor of it.

Who is Brooklyn anyway, but those who furnish the money.

The few people who appeared before you in Brooklyn against consolidation were from what is called Brooklyn Heights, a certain aristocracy of high literary and aesthetic character, and act on sentiment, but know little of the burdens of taxation, but think they are Brooklyn, but really have not seen as much of Brooklyn in years as you saw in the short time you were here. The building in which I write now is three miles from Brooklyn Heights, and I guarantee that most of them have never seen it. Although it is the finest banking building in the world (I mean it), but they know nothing of this section of the city. I believe three-quarters of the voters are in favor of consolidation, and the women, a large number of them having considerable property interests (45,000 women depositors in this bank), I believe are in favor of it.

If there had been no East river there would not have been two city governments here.

Give us the Greater New York, the greatest city of the world, that to say " I live in New York," will be as great an honor as of old to say, " I am a Roman citizen."

Yours truly,
J. V. MESEROLE.

To the Cities Committee of the Senate and Assembly of the State of New York:

WHEREAS, The public press reported on February 21, 1896, that your honorable committees had decided to leave the town of Flushing out of the proposed Greater New York; and,

WHEREAS, The public press to-day reports that such determination has been reconsidered, and that said town is to be included in the bill providing for the Greater New York; and,

WHEREAS, This mass meeting of citizens of the said town of Flushing was called to protest against the exclusion of our town from this beneficial legislation, and to repudiate the statements of that member of Assembly who claimed that the residents of this town are opposed to consolidation with New York; be it

Resolved, That this mass meeting of residents and voters of the town of Flushing heartily approve of the action of your joint committees in restoring their town to the Greater New York bill, and urge the members of said committee to use every honorable effort to keep the town of Flushing in said bill.

Resolved, That your committees be requested to present these resolutions to the Senate and Assembly, and to impress upon the members of both branches of the Legislature the fact that the residents of the town of Flushing, irrespective of party affiliations, are heartily in favor of the Greater New York, and that the sentiment on that question is rapidly increasing.

Resolved, That the chairman and secretary of this meeting sign these resolutions and forward them to the chairman of the Senate and Assembly committees on the affairs of cities.

Adopted by unanimous vote at the mass meeting of voters of the town of Flushing, held in the village hall at Whitestone in said town, Tuesday, February 25, 1896, in accordance with the annexed placard and accompanying typewritten resolutions.

T. D. GODLEY,
Chairman.

ALFRED MITCHELL,
Secretary.

A MASS MEETING

Will be held in the Whitestone village hall, next Tuesday, February 25, 1896, at 8 P. M., to protest against the exclusion of Whitestone from Greater New York. All favoring consolidation with New York city as voted by Whitestone, College Point and the town of Flushing in 1894, are urged to attend the above meeting in order to devise methods to carry out the vote of the people for Greater New York. The small but active minority against Greater New York have suddenly succeeded in striking our town out of the bill reported to the Legislature last Thursday, and unless immediate effort is made by the sleeping majority we shall be left out altogether. Come. Come.

By order of
EXECUTIVE OF PROVISIONAL COMMITTEE.

WHITESTONE, *February* 22, 1896.

PETITION OF CITIZENS OF TOWN OF FLUSHING FOR GREATER NEW YORK.

Resolved, Whereas, after protracted discussion by the people concerned, the Legislature submitted to the legally qualified voters thereof, at the election held in November, 1894, the question of consolidation with New York city as part of the Greater New York; and

WHEREAS, At the said election the said question was decided in the affirmative by the emphatic vote of the said territory, including the almost unanimous vote of Whitestone, of the town of Flushing, and whereas the said question having been thus decided, and thus finally settled by the said vote, the said inhabitants contentedly relied upon the Legislature carrying out the wishes of the people it had itself obtained at the said polling; and

WHEREAS, The opinion of Whitestone as expressed at the said voting has undergone no change but continues, remains and constitutes the well-considered and emphatic expression of the strong desire of a very large majority of the voters and also of the inhabitants aforesaid; and

WHEREAS, It now further appears that the minority opposed to the said consolidation, after their complete defeat at the said polling, has continued its opposition to the present time and has, in defiance of the said vote, at last temporarily succeeded in excluding Whitestone from the Greater New York, to the great disappointment and disgust of the said people generally; and

WHEREAS, The said exclusion, being so regarded and being highly injurious to the best interests and lasting welfare of the said place generally, depriving it of the advantages certain to flow from the more closer union with the great American metropolis, of which the town of Flushing is already to a large extent practically a part and portion; and

WHEREAS, Such defiance of the people's will, as expressed at the ballot-box, is a dangerous and unprofitable proceeding, certain to weaken respect for law and order, discouraging to peaceful people and gratifying only to political schemers and wire-pullers seeking to serve personal purposes without regard to the general benefit; and

WHEREAS, No good reason has been advanced by any one why

the town of Flushing should be deprived of the great benefit it was invited to share;

Therefore, this mass meeting of inhabitants of the town of Flushing, now held in the village hall at Whitestone, in said town, without respect to party affiliations of any kind whatever, does hereby, in the name of fairness, reason, justice and law, most sincerely and emphatically object and protest against the proposed exclusion of the town of Flushing and particularly of the village of Whitestone, from the proposed Greater New York city.

It is also further submitted and averred in support of the foregoing protest that the town of Flushing is not a rural district nor its inhabitants a rural population, as alleged.

That by far the larger part of the male population goes daily as commuters to New York city or Brooklyn, being employed therein in law, banking, manufacturing, mercantile and other business houses, to a much larger relative proportion than are the inhabitants of Brooklyn, similarly engaged in the city of New York.

That a large proportion of the now vacant land of Flushing town was once farming land, but is now abandoned by agriculturists and is being cut up into streets and graded, paved, curbed, guttered, sewered, supplied with water, gas and electricity, and rapidly being sold off in building lots, or dwellings erected thereon for lawyers, bankers, merchants, clerks and workmen, who simply sleep in the town of Flushing with their families, and daily go and return between New York city Brooklyn and Flushing town, by trolley car, railroad, steamer or ferry boat, to earn their livings in one of the two said cities, just as the same daily exodus prevails between the upper and lower parts of the county of New York.

That agriculture in the town of Flushing is a rapidly dwindling pursuit, which is being crowded out by the natural growth, extension, increase and overflow of and from the great American metropolis, and it is estimated that something like ninety-five per cent. of the population of Flushing town is in the villages of Flushing, College Point and Whitestone, in which three said incorporated villages, the foregoing condition altogether prevails.

That it is a fact that the vote of 1894, of Queens county, was relatively very many times greater, in favor of consolidation than that of Brooklyn. Yet Brooklyn is included and we are at present excluded. The actual figures were, Kings county, 129,211 votes, giving a majority of 277 for consolidation, whilst that part of Queens county in question gave 12,453 votes with 2,971 majority for consolidation.

In other words, we who are now excluded gave relatively many times a greater vote in favor of consolidation than those who are now included. Our majority vote for consolidation was, in fact, relatively greater than that of New York city itself. The total vote was given for the inclusion of the whole of the district voting, and being carried by a large majority there is now no authority for leaving out any district simply because a portion of it voted in opposition. Odd districts can not now be left out unless majority rule is to be an unmeaning sham. As a matter of fact Whitestone had a very large majority in favor.

Wherefore, your protestors respectfully petition and pray that the Legislature of the State of New York will not allow the outrage of exclusion to be finally consummated against your dutiful citizens, but will in its wisdom restore the said territory to the said bill as originally arranged, so that the people's mandate, as cast by them, at your request in 1894, may be faithfully enacted into law.

That a copy of the foregoing be sent to each member of the committee of the Legislature in charge of the bill, and that a delegation of citizens be appointed by the chair, to go to Albany to interview the said committee in the interest of the object of this meeting generally, that it have power to add to its number and to invite the corporation of Flushing and College Point.

Delegation, if Needed.

Sanders Shanks.
Judge McKnight.
Alfred Mitchell.
Moses Worms.
James F. Taylor.
S. H. Wessells.

Stephen Poey.	H. B. Niles.
Lawrence Collins.	D. A. Harrison.
R. S. Munson.	Joseph Winkler.
D. L. Godley.	Rev. J. J. Moffitt.
Joseph H. Titus.	Robert Blissert.
Louis Fromer.	John Morrison.
W. S. Overton.	Oliver Taff.

ALFRED MITCHELL,
Secretary.

WHITESTONE, *February* 25, 1896.

Debts of Queens County and Towns and Villages in Queens County, January 1, 1896.

Total debt, Queens county	$1,121,500
Total debt, Long Island City	3,456,000
Total debt, Jamaica town	109,000
Total debt, Flushing town	338,500
Total debt, Newtown town	387,500
Total debt, Hempstead town, about 1-10 to be apportioned	490,000
Total debt, College Point village	231,000
Total debt, Far Rockaway village	12,000
Total school debt of Jamaica town	325,000
Total school debt of Flushing town	250,000
Total school debt of Newtown town	175,000
Total school debt of Hempstead town, about 1-10 to be apportioned	30,000

TOTAL ASSESSED STATE VALUES.

	Real.	Personal.	Totals.
Newtown	$8,232,961	$58,500	$8,291,461
Hempstead	9,915,834	319,200	10,235,034
Jamaica	11,746,934	710,000	12,456,934
Flushing	8,851,963	79,050	8,931,013
Long Island City	21,199,922	232,500	21,432,422

(*Queens County Herald, December* 28, 1895.)

The County's Valuation — Long Island City Gets a Heavy Dose as Usual.

The board of supervisors completed the annual audit, with the exception of the sheriff's bills, on Thursday morning. The amount of real and personal valuation in the county as returned by each town and by Long Island City is as follows:

	Real.	Personal.	Totals.
Newtown	$6,472,658	$58,500	$6,531,155
Hempstead	7,795,730	319,200	8,114,930
Jamaica	9,488,020	710,000	10,198,020
Flushing	6,959,320	79,050	7,038,370
Oyster Bay	4,335,768	476,950	4,812,718
Long Island City	16,667,132	232,500	16,899,632
North Hempstead	3,423,950	474,150	3,898,100
Total	$55,142,575	$2,350,350	$57,492,928
Amount of State valuation			72,168,015
Deficiency			$14,675,087

The supervisors made the following apportionment among the towns and Long Island City to make the aggregate equal the State valuation:

	Real.	Personal.	Totals.
Newtown	$8,232,961	$58,500	$8,291,461
Hempstead	9,915,834	319,200	10,235,034
Jamaica	11,746,934	710,000	12,456,934
Flushing	8,851,963	79,050	8,931,013
Oyster Bay	5,514,688	476,950	5,991,638
Long Island City	21,199,922	232,500	21,432,422
North Hempstead	4,355,363	474,150	4,829,513
Total	$69,817,665	$2,350,350	$72,168,015

The State tax for 1895 is as follows:

For schools	$67,837 93
For care of insane	72,168 02
For general purposes	67,837 93
For canals	25,980 49
For stenographers, etc	2,880 43
Total	$236,704 80

Of the above amounts the following sums are apportioned to Long Island City:

For schools	$20,146 47
For care of insane	21,432 42
For general purposes	20,146 47
For canals	7,715 67
For stenographers, etc	855 34
Total	$70,296 37

The county is credited with $150,268.72 in the State Comptroller's office, and of this su[m] the county has given Long Island City credit for $101,138.92 for taxes paid in 1894, making the amount of State tax to be raised $135,565.58, and this sum has been apportioned as follows:

Newtown	$15,575 32
Hempstead	19,226 26
Jamaica	23,400 03
Flushing	16,776 70
Oyster Bay	11,255 17
Long Island City	40,260 25
North Hempstead	9,072 15

The following is the increase in the valuation of real estate in the county in 1895 over 1894:

Newtown	$407,200
Hempstead	358,982
Jamaica	673,260
Flushing	378,992
Oyster Bay	42,821
Long Island City	201,955
North Hempstead	71,325
Total	$2,134,135

Population of Queens County, 141,805 — District to be taken about 100,000.

	Bonded debts.	School district debts.	Number of officers in each town.	Number of trustees in each village.	Number of school trustees in each district.	Tax rate.	Value of personal property.	Per cent. of assessed to actual value.
Jamacia Richmond Hill } * Jamacia Valley } Richmond Hill	$109,000	No. 1 to 3 } $160,000 No. 5 to 10 } No. 4 100,000 65,000	27 to 30	7 to 9	1 to 9	Gen. 1.38 School 1.00 2.38		50
Flushing Flushing Village } * College Point } Whitestone Village }	Flushing $338,500 College Pt. 231,000	$250,000	27 to 30	7 to 9	1 to 9	Gen. 1.70 School 1.00 2.70		40
Newtown	$387,500	$175,000	27 to 30	7 to 9	1 to 9	Gen. 2.48 School 2.00 § 4.48		20
Hempstead † Far Rockaway*	$490,000 12,000	$30,000	27 to 30	7 to 9	1 to 9	Gen. 1.76 School 1.00 2.76		40
Long Island City	$3,456,000				5 wards, 3 in each.	Cities 3.10 State 56 Ward 28 3.94	$500,000	40
Queens County	$1,121,500		‡			4.21		
	$6,145,500	$780,000						

* Incorporated villages. † About one-tenth of Hempstead is in consolidation district. ‡ 28 county officers. § Assessed value only 20 per cent of actual value.

Department of Finance and Receiving of Taxes and Assessments.

LONG ISLAND CITY, *October* 19, 1895.

To the Honorable, the Common Council:

GENTLEMEN.— In compliance with the requirements of the city charter the undersigned herewith submits to you account of the receipts and expenditures, from the time of my entering upon the duties of the office to the 1st inst., with exhibit of the state of the treasury on October 1, 1895, as follows:

STATEMENT FROM JANUARY 1, 1895, TO OCTOBER 1, 1895.

RECEIPTS.

January 1, 1895. From ex-Treasurer Bleckwenn as the full amount of moneys in his custody belonging to Long Island City, as per his report accompanying the transfer thereof to me	$149,305 01
May, 1895. From Queens County Bank, credit of balance due city and not set forth in ex-Treasurer Bleckwenn's report	830 00
	$150,135 01
City taxes for the year 1895	308,953 76
Ward taxes for the year 1895	53,358 17
State and county taxes, 1895	110,859 60
Percentages	5,213 38
Interest on city and ward taxes	3,088 64
Interest on State and county taxes	1,262 26
Water taxes, with interest	27,643 76
Extra water rates	26,638 33
Taxes with interest of levies previous to 1894, and not for the year 1895	187,694 86
Redemptions from tax sales to sundry persons	1,374 02
Redemptions from tax sales to Long Island City	29,506 52
Redemptions from assessments, first ward improvement	51 80

From Union College, under chapter 973, Laws of 1895	$5,000 00
From interest on deposit in banks	4,757 29
From department of public works, for street openings	105 00
From fire department, sale of horse and old hose	151 75
From city clerk, license fees	3,035 40
From board of excise, license fees	15,600 00
From board of education, State funds	124 11
From board of plumbers, filing fees	158 00
From clerk of justices' court, fines	778 75
Assessments for the improvement of Jackson avenue, Vernon avenue and the Boulevard	30,663 60
Assessments for the Grand avenue and Main street improvement	1,917 49
Assessments for Fulton avenue and Main street improvement	480 84
Assessments for Flushing avenue improvement	7,121 74
Assessments for Steinway avenue improvement	1,921 81
From sale of refunding survey and map bonds	8,500 00
From sale of refunding water debt bonds	15,000 00
From sale of revenue bonds, 1895	50,000 00
From sale of general improvement bonds	274,000 00
From accrued interest on sale of bonds	4,442 47
From premium received on sale of bonds	1,442 75
From water supply bonds, to James Stevenson	2,500 00
From mayor's office, enclosed with statement of delivery of water bonds by his honor directly to snow steam pump works and F. W. Miller, independent of this office	116 34
Credited to special surplus funds as overpayments, etc.	228 98
From general improvement commission to credit of Jackson and Vernon avenues and Boulevard improvement fund	12 00
	$1,333,838 43

PAYMENTS.

On account of new school, fourth ward	$23,098 57
New school building fund	112 47
Fifty thousand dollar school fund	665 86
Board of education fund, 1894	11,385 44
Board of education fund, 1895	71,916 56
Salaries fund, 1895	15,367 20
Salaries fund, 1894	100 00
Police department fund, 1894	2,046 93
Police department fund, 1895	36,714 13
Water department fund, 1895	56,022 93
Water department fund, 1894	4,248 01
Fire department fund, 1894	4,126 35
Fire department fund, 1895	30,821 17
Health department fund, 1895	6,922 83
Health department fund, 1894	2,111 43
Contingent fund, 1894	8,134 95
Contingent fund, 1895	21,189 41
Poor fund, 1895	8,076 04
Poor fund, 1894	9,760 45
Judgment fund, 1894	782 85
Judgment fund, 1895	3,496 00
Ex. and Sup., board of plumbers, 1895	1,550 75
First ward road and street fund, 1894	442 50
First ward road and street fund, 1895	3,810 34
Second ward road and street fund, 1894	467 50
Second ward road and street fund, 1895	2,042 53
Third ward road and street fund, 1895	2,526 65
Third ward road and street fund, 1894	276 66
Fourth ward road and street fund, 1894	68 25
Fourth ward road and street fund, 1895	888 73
Fifth ward road and street fund, 1895	956 26
Fifth ward road and street fund, 1894	97 92
First ward lamp and gas fund, 1894	3,024 68
First ward lighting fund, 1895	6,036 62
Second ward lamp and gas fund, 1894	3,003 90

Second ward lamp and gas fund, 1894	$3,033 90
Second ward lighting fund, 1895	5,025 19
Third ward lamp and gas fund, 1894	3,132 18
Third ward lighting fund, 1895	5,422 15
Fourth ward lamp and gas fund, 1894	5,126 34
Fourth ward lighting fund, 1895	9,584 77
Fifth ward lamp and gas fund, 1894	2,413 15
Fifth ward lighting fund, 1895	5,508 96
County treasurer, on account taxes, levy 1893	105,000 00
Expenses, Blissville bridge	1,013 79
Redemption, Newtown debt bonds	20,000 00
Redemption, survey and map bonds	12,000 00
Redemption, water debt bonds	20,000 00
Public dept aand interest	45,120 00
Interest on general improvement bonds	21,687 80
On warrants of general improvement committee	275,206 29
Jackson avenue, Vernon avenue and Boulevard assessment fund	15,020 53
Jackson avenue, etc., improvement fund	20 00
Redemption from first ward improvement sale	51 80
Surplus from sale for first ward improvement assessment, per order of Supreme Court	420 49
Redemptions from sales, 1886	538 87
Redemptions from sales, 1888	96 57
Redemptions from sales, 1890	19 52
Redemptions from sales, 1892	33 69
Redemptions from sales, 1894	125 73
To Sheridan Post, G. A. R.	269 50
To Ringold Post, G. A. R.	130 00
From excise fund	2,276 94
From licenses	662 65
From justices' fines	834 50
From sinking fund (judgment)	1,119 89
From special surplus fund, overpayment of taxes	10 81

From special sinking fund, return of interest charged and collected in excess of two per cent. and part of allowance under provisions of same act relating thereto	$846 12
Purchase of revenue bonds	10,000 00
Interest and premium on revenue bonds	19,573 27
Interest on funded debt bonds, 1893	1,090 20
Interest on Grand avenue, etc., improvement	5,232 25
Interest on Fulton avenue, etc., improvement	570 00
Interest on Flushing avenue improvement	1,857 00
Interest on Steinway avenue improvement	1,053 90
Total payments	$941,350 95
Total receipts	$1,333,838 43
Total payments	941,350 95
October 1, 1895, cash balance on hand	$392,487 48

ANALYSIS OF CASH BALANCES.

Sinking funds, for public debt, and interest, etc	$28,703 20
Sinking funds, for redemption of revenue bonds, etc	261,945 18
Improvement funds	37,346 34
Improvement funds, first ward	8,530 73
Tax sale and surplus funds	1,247 13
Trust funds	2,567 51
Hospital fund	29 53
Judgments fund	2,007 06
School funds	19,744 20
County funds	5,859 60
Ward funds and Flushing avenue repair funds	13,363 10
Charter and special funds	11,143 89
Total	$392,487 48

STATEMENT OF BONDED INDEBTEDNESS.

Seven per cent. Newtown funded debt bonds	$101,500 00
Seven per cent. Newtown refunded debt bonds	64,000 00
Six per cent. Newtown refunded debt bonds	112,500 00
Four per cent. Newtown refunded debt bonds	16,000 00
Seven per cent. funded debt water bonds	170,000 00
Five per cent. refunded water debt bonds	75,000 00
Four per cent. refunded water debt bonds	45,000 00
Six per cent. water debt bonds	47,000 00
Three and one-half per cent. water debt bonds	34,000 00
Seven per cent. survey and map bonds	12,000 00
Five per cent. refunded survey and map bonds	66,000 00
Seven per cent. fire department bonds	20,000 00
Four and one-half per cent. fire department bonds	35,000 00
Four and one-half per cent. public school bonds	220,000 00
Four and one-half per cent. public school bonds, new	122,000 00
Five per cent. engine-house bonds	16,000 00
Five per cent. station-house bonds	15,000 00
Four and one-half per cent. funding debt bonds, 1893.	112,000 00
Four and one-half per cent. street improvement bonds	573,500 00
Four and one-half per cent. general improvement bonds	790,000 00
Revenue bonds, 1883	106,500 00
Revenue bonds, 1884	53,000 00
Revenue bonds, 1885	77,000 00
Revenue bonds, 1886	44,500 00
Revenue bonds, 1887	6,500 00
Revenue bonds, 1888	39,000 00
Revenue bonds, 1889	29,500 00
Revenue bonds, 1890	28,500 00
Revenue bonds, 1891	50,000 00
Revenue bonds, 1892	80,000 00
Revenue bonds, 1893	50,000 00

Revenue bonds, 1894	$60,000 00
Revenue bonds, 1895	50,000 00
	$3,321,000 00
Water bonds delivered by mayor as per resolution of common council:	
To Snow Steam Pump Works	3,000 00
To F. W. Miller	3,000 00
Total bonded indebtedness	$3,327,000 00

Respectfully,

LUCIEN KNAPP,

City Treasurer and Receiver.

Taxes of 1895 — Levied by the Common Council, December 30, 1895 — Approved by the Mayor December, 30, 1895.

INFORMATION FOR TAXPAYERS.

ASSESSORS' VALUATIONS.

First ward	$5,314,160
Second ward	2,083,680
Third ward	2,622,772
Fourth ward	3,945,310
Fifth ward	2,933,710
	$16,899,632

STATE AND COUNTY TAXES.

State and county purposes	$85,224 91
Expenses, Blissville bridge	1,510 20
Surplus	1,237 56
Interest	3,956 20
Support of county poor	2,709 07
	$94,637 94

CITY TAXES.

Public debt and interest	$104,658 42
Interest on general improvement bonds	43,015 63
Support of schools	112,000 00
Salaries	36,120 00
Police department	58,650 00
Fire department	40,000 00
Health department	9,000 00
Contingent fund	37,500 00
Poor fund	8,000 00
Judgment fund	69,937 50
For board of examiners of plumbers, etc	2,100 00
Public library	3,000 00
	$523,981 55

TOTAL OF TAXES.

State and county	$94,637 94
City	523,981 55
Ward	76,112 00
	$694,731 49

SUMMARY OF RATES ON $100.

	City.	Ward.	State	Agg.
First ward	3.10	.28	.56	3.94
Second ward	3.10	.55	.56	4.21
Third ward	3.10	.54	.56	4.20
Fourth ward	3.10	.55	.56	4.21
Fifth ward	3.10	.50	.56	4.16

The interest of $21,707.50 for the year 1895 on water bonds is not included in the tax levy, but will be paid out of the receipts of water taxes.

The interest on bonds for the improvement of Jackson and Vernon avenues and the boulevard for the year 1895 is $25,807.50, of which there is included in the levy $10,372.50 and the balance, $15,435, is to be paid from the collections of the assessment.

SPECIAL NOTICE.

City and ward taxes may be paid within thirty days before the 4th day of March, 1895, free of charge; during the next thirty days 1 1-3 per cent. will be added. After such sixty days said taxes will be levied and collected in the manner provided by law, together with interest thereon at the rate of eight per cent. per annum from the 1st day of February, 1895.

The State and county tax may be paid with the addition of one per cent. fees thereon, within thirty days before the 4th day of March, 1895. After the 3d day of March, 1895, five per cent. will be added; and if not paid within the prescribed time, such tax will be collected by distress and sale of the goods and chattels in the manner provided by law, together with interest thereon, at the rate of eight per cent. per annum.

Tax bills will be furnished on application (personally or by mail), subject, however, to such additions to the items of "Percentages" and "Interest" as the lapse of time may render necessary to comply with the law. Applicants must state ward, block and lot numbers, or give an exact description of their property.

N. B.— Communications must be accompanied by return postage.

Bonded Indebtedness of Towns in County of Richmond.

MIDDLETOWN.

Two bonds of 1891, $1,000 each, interest 6 per cent.—$2,000, one-half payable June 1, 1895, and June 1, 1896.

Four bonds of 1892, $2,500 each, interest 6 per cent.—$10,000, one-quarter payable Sept. 1, 1897, one-quarter annually thereafter.

Four certificates issued Nov. 24, 1894, amounting to $1,064, interest $12.97—$1,064, payable March 1, 1895.

NORTHFIELD.

Four bonds of 1894, $1,500 each, interest 6 per cent.—$6,000, one-quarter payable May 1, 1895, June 1, 1895, April 16, 1896 and May 1, 1896.

One town certificate, $250, May 15, 1894, interest 6 per cent.—$250, payable May 15, 1895.

SOUTHFIELD.

Thirty-eight bonds of 1891, $600 each, and six bonds same issue, $1,000 each, interest 4 per cent.—$28,200. One bond of $600, payable Dec. 1, 1894, and annually thereafter with the last bond payable Dec. 1, 1932.

WESTFIELD.

No bonded indebtedness.

CASTLETON.—(Village of New Brighton.)

By charter the power to issue moneys is wholly and solely vested in the trustees of said village.

The above is a transcript of a statement filed with the board of supervisors in February, 1895, and furnished to us by Mr. F. C. Vitt, clerk.

Bonded Indebtedness of Richmond County.

Date.	Series.	Amount each.	Total.	Rate interest.	Law.	Purpose.	Payable.	When payable.	Remarks.
Aug. 1, 1879	1 to 15 1 to 8	$1,000 5,000	$55,000	5 1-2 per. ct.	Ch. 75, 317 L. 1878 and acts amend. thereto.	To retire mat. bonds.	Co. treas.	Aug. 1, 1899	Coupon.
April 30, 1883	A 1 to 57	1,000	57,000	4 do	do	do	do	April 30, 1898	Coupon.
April 30, 1884	58, 107 B 108, 115 116	1,000 10,000 9,400	139,400	4 1-2 do	do	do	do	April 30, 1899	58 & 107 reg. 108 & 116 reg.
July 31, 1884	117, 118, 120.25 B 119 126	10,000 11,000 8,000	99,000	4 1-6 do	do	do	do	July 31, 1900	Registered.
July 31, 1885	C 1 to 63	1,000	63,000	3 1-2 do	do	do	do	July 31, 1905	Coupon.
Jan. 31, 1886	1 to 5 D 6 7	10,000 5,000 3,000	58,000	3 1-4 do	do	do	do	Jan. 31, 1901	Registered.
April 1, 1887	E 1 to 40	1,000	40,000	3 1-2 do	do	do	do	April 1, 1902	do
April 1, 1888	F 1 to 4	10,000	40,000	3 1-2 do	do	do	do	April 1, 1908	do
Aug. 1, 1889	G 1 to 10	5,000	50,000	3 1-2 do	do	do	do	Aug. 1, 1904	do
Aug. 1, 1889	H 1 to 10	5,000	50,000	3 1-2 do	do	do	do	Aug. 1, 1906	do
Aug. 1, 1889	I 1 to 10	5,000	50,000	3 do	do	do	do	Aug. 1, 1909	do
Aug. 1, 1889	J 1—11 12	5,000 3,000	58,000	3 do	do	do	do	Aug. 1, 1910	do
Aug. 1, 1890	A 1 to 20	5,000	100,000	3 1-2 do	Chap. 555, Laws 1890	Improved county rds.	do	Aug. 1, 1915	Road bond, registered.
Aug. 1, 1891	B 1 to 30	5,000	150,000	4 1-2 do	do	do	do	Aug. 1, 1916	Road bond, registered.
Nov. 1, 1892	C 1 to 45	1,000	45,000	3 1-2 do	do	do	do	Nov. 1, 1917	Road bond, registered.
June 1, 1894	D 1 to 75	1,000	75,000	5 do	do	do	do	June 1, 1919	Gold rd. bond, registered.
June 1, 1894	E 1 to 15	1,000	15,000	5 do	do	Maintaining co. rds.	do	June 1, 1919	Gold rd. bonds, reg. main.
June 1, 1894	1 to 95	1,000	95,000	4 do	Chap. 68, 576, Laws 1892.	Funding debts not rep. by bonds	do	June 1, 1914	Gold bonds, coupon.
June 1, 1895	F 1 to 35	1,000	35,000	4 do	Chap. 555, Laws 1890	Maintaining co. rds.	do	June 1, 1920	Gold road bond, mainten.
Aug. 1, 1895	G 1 to 100	1,000	100,000	4 do	do	Improving co. roads	do	Aug. 1, 1921	Gold road bond, mainten.

Compiled for the committee Oct. 8, 1895, from the records of the board of supervisors, by F. C. Vitt, *Clerk*.

School Districts Bonded in Richmond County.

AUGUST 31, 1895.

TOWNS.	When bonded.	Amount.	Payments made	Indebtedness.	Last payment due.
Castleton........No. 2	1889 1890	$60,000 00 8,000 00	$32,600 00	$35,400 00	1899 1900
" 4	1895	32,000 00		32,000 00	1911
" 5	1889	7,500 00	4,500 00	3,000 00	1899
Middletown ....No. 2	1895	98,000 00		98,000 00	1944
Southfield ....No. 2	1895	12,000 00		12,000 00	1915
" 4	1889	3,700 00	2,200 00	480 00	1899
" 5	1890	5,500 00	3,000 00	2,500 00	1900
" 6	1894	4,500 00	225 00	4,275 00	1914
Northfield.......No. 1	1890	2,000 00	1,000 00	1,000 00	1900
" 4	1894	4,300 00	430 00	3,870 00	1904
" 5	1895	25,000 00		25,000 00	1920
" 6	1891	30,000 00	12,000 00	18,000 00	1901
" 7	1895	3,500 00		3,500 00	1905
" 8	1895	2,100 00		2,100 00	1905
" 9	1891	4,000 00	2,222 22	1,777 77	1899
Westfield........No. 6	1895	11,875 00		11,875 00	1914

This statement was furnished to our committee by Mrs. Julia K. West, school commissioner.

The assessed valuation of Richmond county as equalized by the board of supervisors December, 1895:

Castleton	$8,615,287 48
Northfield	4,054,253 40
Middletown	3,142,046 38
Southfield	2,533,908 38
Westfield	1,925,770 36
	$20,271,266 00
The county budget	$387,397 59

Yours very truly,

JOHN B. PEARSON, *Chairman.*

New York Tax Levy, 1895.

VALUATION.

Real estate	$1,646,028,655 00
Personal estate	288,575,587 00
Shareholders of banks	82,343,420 00
	$2,016,947,662 00
Amount of tax	38,403,761 18

Rate, 1.91 per cent.

Rate on personal estate of certain corporations, 1.7278 per cent.

Confirmed at 1.40 P. M., Tuesday, August 27, 1895.

Finance Department—Abstract of Transactions of the Finance Department for the Week Ending February 1, 1896.

DEPOSITED IN THE TREASURY.

To the credit of the sinking fund	$79,012 34
To the credit of the city treasury	910,647 94
Total	$989,660 28

BONDS AND STOCK ISSUED.

Three per cent. bonds	$520,360 04
Three per cent. stock	5,000 00
Total	$525,360 04

WARRANTS REGISTERED FOR PAYMENT.

The mayoralty:		
Salaries and contingencies, mayor's office		$2,024 98
The common council:		
City contingencies	$100 00	
Salaries, common council	7,191 44	
		7,291 44

Item	Amount	Total
The finance department:		
Cleaning markets.	$778 43	
Salaries, chamberlain's office.	2,083 33	
Salaries, finance department.	18,886 88	
		$21,748 64
Interest on the city debt.		1,020 29
The aqueduct commission:		
Additional water fund.		18,211 01
The law department:		
Contingencies, corporation attorney's office.	$142 00	
Contingencies, law department.	1,250 00	
Salaries, counsel to commissioner of street improvements, twenty-third and twenty-fourth wards.	516 66	
Salaries, law department.	11,561 54	
		13,470 20
Bureau of public administrator:		
Salaries, bureau of public administrator.	. . . .	1,083 32
The department of public works:		
Additional water fund.	$1,044 20	
Aqueduct, repairs, maintenance and strengthening.	2,838 10	
Boring examinations for grading and sewer contracts.	73 50	
Boulevards, roads and avenues, maintenance of.	1,353 99	
Bridge over Harlem river, between First and Willis avenues.	371 66	
Bridge over Harlem river at Third avenue.	561 66	
Bridge over Harlem ship canal at Kingsbridge road.	853 83	
Bronx river works, maintenance and repairs.	201 62	

Croton water fund	$7,109 46	
Fire hydrant fund	266 33	
Free floating baths	321 70	
Lamps and gas and electric lighting.	90 00	
One Hundred and Fifty-fifth street viaduct, maintenance and repairs,	35 12	
Public buildings, construction and repairs	322 60	
Public buildings, Seventh District Police Court	7,426 50	
Public building, twenty-third and twenty-fourth wards, in Crotona park	24 00	
Removing obstructions in streets and avenues	82 00	
Repairing and renewal of pipes, stop-cocks, etc	3,011 59	
Repairs and renewal of pavements and regrading	1,530 27	
Repaving, chapter 475, Laws of 1895,	67,590 40	
Repaving streets and avenues	4,655 00	
Repaving, chapter 35, Laws of 1892,	2,291 76	
Restoring and repaving, special fund, department of public works	1,854 12	
Roads, streets and avenues, unpaved, maintenance of and sprinkling	142 87	
Salaries, department of public works,	21,445 89	
Sewers, repairing and cleaning	1,652 25	
Street improvement fund, June 15, 1886	19,100 32	
Street improvement, for surveying, monumenting and numbering streets	24 00	
Supplies for and cleaning public offices	5,725 67	
Water-main fund	534 00	
		$152,534 41

The department of public parks:

Aquarium	$108 71	
Cathedral parkway, improvement and completion of	31 50	
Corlears Hook park, construction and maintenance of	21 00	
Harlem river bridges, maintenance and repairs	141 97	
Improvement of parks and parkways, chapter 11, Laws of 1894	1,523 22	
Maintenance and construction of new parks north of Harlem river	570 19	
Maintenance and government of parks and places	9,358 91	
Riverside park and drive, construction of	4,300 00	
		$16,055 50

The department of public charities and corrections:

Public charities and corrections		11,186 36

The department of street improvements, twenty-third and twenty-fourth wards:

Bridges crossing the New York and Hartford railroad depression in the twenty-third and twenty-fourth wards, etc	$20 06	
Bronx river and other bridges, repairing and maintenance of, etc	19 12	
For making rock soundings, borings, etc	183 00	
Maintenance, twenty-third and twenty-fourth wards	2,919 92	
Monumenting avenues and streets, twenty-third and twenty-fourth wards	36 00	

Sewers and drains, twenty-third and twenty-fourth wards	$305 50	
Salaries, office of commissioner of street improvements, twenty-third and twenty-fourth wards	1,989 98	
Street improvement fund, June 15, 1886	4,738 91	
Surveying, laying out, maps, plans, etc., twenty-third and twenty-fourth wards	153 00	
Telephone service and contingencies,	65 00	
Williamsbridge sewer fund	28 00	
		$26,513 99
The department of public charities:		
Department of public charities		4,396 62
The department of correction:		
Department of correction		12,966 05
The health department:		
For bacteriological laboratory	$2,112 42	
For burial of honorably discharged soldiers, sailors and marines	175 00	
Fund for gratuitous vaccination	300 00	
Health fund, for disinfection	1,280 00	
Health fund, for payment to board of police	5,733 33	
Health fund, salaries	22,062 88	
Hospital fund, hospital supplies	135 00	
		31,798 63
The police department:		
Contingent expenses of central department and station-houses, etc.	$916 66	
Police fund	467,471 02	
Police fund, salaries, clerical force, etc.	11,053 33	
Police pension fund	75,000 00	
Police station-houses, alterations, etc.	2,916 66	
Supplies for police	9,583 33	
		566,941 00

The department of street cleaning:

Cleaning streets, department of street cleaning...		$64,919 83

The fire department:

Fire department fund..............	$61,332 47	
New York fire department relief fund,	18,206 00	
		179,538 47

The department of buildings:

Department of buildings, special fund...........		101 25

The department of taxes and assessments:

Salaries, board of assessors........	$1,733 33	
Salaries, department of taxes and assessments....................	10,685 93	
		12,419 26

The department of docks:

Dock fund....................................		22,298 42

The board of education:

College of the City of New York.....	$10,567 36	
School-house fund.................	6,910 00	
Public instruction.................	5,653 40	
		23,130 76

The board of excise:

Commissioners of excise fund..................		10,787 72

Printing, stationery and blank-books:

City Record, salaries and contingencies...........................	$824 98	
Printing, stationery and blank-books,	473 69	
		1,298 67

Municipal civil service examining board:

Civil service of the city of New York, expenses of,		1,778 15

The coroners:

Coroners, salaries and expenses.................		3,474 96

The commissioners of accounts:

Salaries, commissioners of accounts.............		5,987 46

The sheriff:		
Furniture, keep of horses, etc......	$50 00	
Incidental expenses of sheriff's office and county jail..................	148 90	
Salaries, sheriff's office.............	8,912 18	
Salaries, county jail...............	1,470 96	
		$10,582 04
The register:		
Salaries, register's office........................		9,223 66
The bureau of elections:		
Election expenses.............................		14,107 38
The judiciary:		
Salaries, city courts...............	$27,291 33	
Salaries, judiciary.................	94,729 89	
		122,021 22
Charitable institutions:		
Babies' wards of the Post Graduate Hospital......................	$1,288 96	
Mothers and Babies' Hospital......	885 00	
New York Medical College and Hospital for Women................	1,763 81	
New York Post Graduate and Medical School and Hospital..........	5,000 00	
New York Society for the Relief of the Ruptured and Crippled......	6,203 01	
The Babies' Hospital...............	1,408 28	
		19,500 31
Miscellaneous purposes:		
Advertising......................	$738 40	
Armory fund......................	217 00	
Armories and drill rooms — wages of armorers, engineers, laborers, janitors, etc....................	456 00	
Assessment commission, awards....	97 69	
Benjamin Brewster and Richard M. Hoe, as executors and trustees of David Dows, deceased...........	25,395 83	

Block tax assessment map fund....	$774 98
Board of street opening and improvement	166 66
Board of estimate and apportionment, expenses of...............	250 00
Bureau of licenses................	1,045 83
Change of grade damage commission, twenty-third and twenty-fourth wards..................	1,208 33
Contingencies, district attorney's office	6,551 37
Examining board of plumbers......	85 00
For removal of old gate-house at Tenth avenue and One Hundred and Ninteeenth street...........	1,037 20
For the preservation of public records	2,781 18
Fund for street and park openings..	22,190 12
Jurors' fees, including expenses of jurors in civil and criminal trials	9,584 00
Judgments.....................	3,594 30
New East river bridge fund........	1,887 13
Rents..........................	3,625 00
Refunding taxes paid in error......	28,335 70
Revenue bond fund — Furnishings for Appellate division of the Supreme court..................	24 00
Revenue bond fund—Compilation of Arrears of taxes and assessments.	924 96
Revenue bond fund, county clerk's office........................	566 65
Salaries, board of revision and correction of assessments (salary of the recorder)..................	83 33
Salaries, commissioner of the sinking fund (salary of the recorder),	83 33

Salaries, inspectors and sealers of weights and measures...........	$450 00	
Trustees of the Seventh Regiment armory......................	8,000 00	
Unclaimed salaries and wages......	16 51	
		$120,170 50
Total..................................		$1,492,527 00

Suits, Orders of Court, Judgments, Etc.

Court.	NAME OF PLAINTIFF.	Amount.	Nature of Action.	Attorney.
			Notice of motion to confirm reports of commissioners in following matters:	
Supreme	Opening Tiffany st., from Longwood ave. to East river.	....	....	F. M. Scott, corporation counsel.
	Opening 141st st., from Third to St. Anne's ave., and from center of Cypress ave. to Locust ave.	....	....	F. M. Scott, corporation counsel.
	Opening Brown place, from East 132d st. to East 138th st.	....	....	F. M. Scott, corporation counsel.
	Opening Hall place, from East 165th st. to Intervale ave.	....	....	F. M. Scott, corporation counsel.
Supreme	George W. Cook.	$125 00	Summons and complaint, for salary as assistant clerk to the Board of Coroners for month of Dec., 1895.	J. A. Donegan.
Supreme	James W. Fellows.	1,679 55	Transcript of judgment	J. A. Deering.
Supreme	Max Gombossy	382 74	Transcript of judgment	Goldfogle & Cohen.
Supreme	In the matter of opening Decatur ave., from Kingsbridge road to Brookline st.	829 91	Certified copies of orders confirming report and taxing costs of commissioners in said matter.	F. M. Scott, corporation counsel.
Supreme	In the matter of establishing permanently, the location and boundaries of the Fort Washington Ridge road.	....	Certified copy of order confirming report of commissioners in said matter.	F. M. Scott, corporation counsel.
Supreme	William Kelly	8,100 00	Transcript of judgment	Kellogg, Rose & S.
Supreme	Dodge & Bliss Co. (a corporation), against The Mayor, etc., Joseph Moore, and others.	441 50	Notice of pendency of action and summons and complaint. To foreclose lien upon contract of said Moore for furnishing materials for fitting up north end of the arsenal building in Central park.	J. Kearney.
Supreme	In the matter of the petition of Jacob Lorillard and others, for appointment of commissioner of appraisal, under chapter 249, Laws of 1890.	20,000 00	Certified copy order entered at a Special Term of said court fixing compensation of David Leventritt for services rendered as special attorney and counsel to the corporation in said proceeding.	H. Nathan.

CLAIMS FILED.

Date.	NAME OF CLAIMANT.	Amount.	Nature of Claim.	Attorney.
1896.				
Jan. 27..	Henry Otto	$1,500 00	For damages for personal injuries	E. F. Bullard.
Jan. 27..	Mrs. Grace D. Kane	5,000 00	For damages for personal injuries	G. F. Boyd.
Jan. 27..	Ellen T. C. Fallon, ex'x, etc.	227 30	For return of amount paid for an assessment for opening 12th avenue from 59th to 153d street.	E. H. Hawke, Jr.
Jan. 28..	Selina M. Brien	1,503 00	For return of amount paid for an assessment for regulating, etc., 1st avenue from 92d to 109th street.	E. H. Hawke, Jr.
Jan. 28..	John Dunbar	274 75	For return of amount paid for an assessment for regulating, etc., Worth street.	E. H. Hawke, Jr.
Jan. 28..	Townsend Wandell, as ex'r, etc.	152 00	For return of amount paid for an assessment for opening 12th avenue.	E. H. Hawke, Jr.
Jan. 28..	James Slattery	1,761 00	For return of amount paid for an assessment for regulating, etc., West 87th street.	
Jan. 28..			Claims and demands. For furnishing transcripts of testimony of cases tried in General Sessions:	
	Frank S. Beard	492 30		
	Thomas W. Osborne	135 10		
Jan. 29..			Claims and demands of the following named persons for extra services and duty as keepers in the prisons on Blackwell's Island, for the years 1889 to 1895:	
	Peter Miller	2,753 00		J. I. Green.
	Joseph McQuade	8,488 50		J. I. Green.
	John J. Shea	5,660 00		J. I. Green.
Jan. 30..	Jane Curry, adm'x, etc.	20,000 00	For damages for death of Thomas Curry, caused by being thrown from a truck.	Weed & Story.
Jan. 30..	New York News Publishing Co.	227 45	For balance claimed to be due for advertising the official canvass on December 23, 1891.	M. J. Stein.
Feb. 1..	McCarthy & Baldwin	1,565 41	Notice of lien for professional services on award made for damage Nos. 1 and 2, made to Gabreil Nuoffer, or wife, in matter of opening Cromwell avenue, from Jerome to Inwood avenue.	McCarthy & Baldwin

Statement of the City Debt as Represented in Bonds and Stocks Outstanding January 31, 1896.

	Classification of Bonded Debt.	Outstanding December 31, 1895.	Outstanding January 31, 1896.
	Funded Debt.		
1....	Payable from the Sinking Fund, under ordinances of the common council..	$2,512,100 00	$2,500,600 00
2....	Payable from the Sinking Fund, under provisions of chapter 383, section 6, Laws of 1878, and section 176, New York city Consolidation Act of 1882.	9,700,000 00	9,700,000 00
3....	Payable from the Sinking Fund, under provisions of chapter 383, section 8, Laws of 1878, and section 192, New York city Consolidation Act of 1882, as amended by chapter 178, Laws of 1889	69,832,221 12	69,875,721 12
4....	Payable from the Sinking Fund, under provisions of chapter 79, Laws of 1889	9,810,100 00	9,812,100 00
5....	Payable from the Sinking Fund, under provisions of the constitutional amendment adopted November 4, 1884	33,670,000 00	33,977,000 00
6....	Payable from taxation, under provisions of chapter 490, Laws of 1883..	445,000 00	445,000 00
7....	Payable from taxation, under the several statutes authorizing their issue.	49,598,246 05	49,598,046 05
8....	Bonds issued for local improvements after June 9, 1880	9,355,429 91	9,430,429 91
9....	Debt of the annexed territory of Westchester county (chapter 329, Laws of 1874)	490,500 00	490,500 00
10....	Debt of the annexed territory of Westchester county (chapter 934, Laws of 1895)	175,000 00	234,009 64
	Total funded debt	$185,588,597 08	$186,063,406 70
1....	Deduct Sinking Funds for redemption of debt (investment and cash)	75,703,087 63	75,838,935 92
	Net funded debt	$109,885,509 45	$110,224,470 78
	Temporary Debt—Revenue Bonds.		
1....	Issued under special laws	$1,406,910 78	$1,453,269 72
2....	Issued in anticipation of taxes of 1995.	1,157,600 00	1,150,000 00
3....	Issued in anticipation of taxes of 1896.	....	7,600 00
	Total revenue bonds	$2,564,510 78	$2,610,869 72

Cash—City treasury account	$1,840,628 97
Sinking Fund for the redemption of the city debt	2,260,815 32
Sinking Fund for the redemption of the city debt, No. 2	1,327,823 87
Sinking Fund for the payment of interest on the city debt,	485,550 57
Total cash	$5,914,824 73

City of New York, Finance Department,
Comptroller's Office, *February* 1, 1896.

I. S. BARRETT,
General Bookkeeper.

Municipalities of New York and Brooklyn.— The Logic of the Figures.—They Tell Their Own Story.

NET PUBLIC DEBT AND OFFICIAL CITY VALUATIONS FOR TAXABLE PURPOSES, JANUARY 1, 1895.

	Assessed Valuation. Real estate.	Personal.	Total.	Per cent. of real value on real estate.	Real value.	Tax budget for 1895.	Tax rate.	
BROOKLYN: All of Kings Co., except Flatlands,	$527,008,427	$22,460,985	$549,469,412	70*	$775,330,166	$14,500,000	$2.638 per $100	
NEW YORK	1,613,057,735	390,274,302	2,003,332,037	50	3,616,389,772	37,500,000	1.872 "	
	$2,140,066,162	$412,735,287	$2,552,801,449		$4,391,719,938	$52,000,000	$2.037 equalized.	
FLATLANDS	2,180,810	53,000	2,333,810					
	$2,142,246,973	$412,788,287	$2,555,035,259					
If the tax rate only were equalized, Brooklyn's share for budget of 1895 would be at				70	to produce	52,000,000 at 2.037		$11,192,692—$3,307,308= Saving to Brooklyn tax-payers, say 22.80 per ct. of present budget.
Valuations equalized at 50 per cent	$1,989,492,325	$412,735,287	$2,402,227,612	50	to produce	52,000,000	2.170 would be the rate equalized.	
BROOKLYN	$376,434,590	$22,460,985	$398,895,575					
NEW YORK	1,613,057,735	390,274,302	2,003,332,037					
If valuation and tax rate were both equalized, Brooklyn's share for budget of 1895 would be				50	to produce	52,000,000 at 2.170		$8,656,034—$5,843,966= Saving to Brooklyn tax-payers, say 40.30 per ct. of present budget.

* Mr. R. A. Bishop, accountant, Comptroller's office, Brooklyn, who has given especial attention to equalizing valuations throughout the State for twenty years past, in relation to the State tax, for the Kings county board of supervisors, claims that the assessed value of all real estate in Brooklyn was, in

1880—70 p. ct. of its current purchase price.
1883—75 " " " " "
1890—79.23 " " " " "

N. B.— In the above computation each city assumes interest charges on its own personal obligations.

THE DEBT OF EACH MUNICIPALITY.†

Brooklyn county and town debt, net	$62,000,000 =	11.76 per cent. of present real estate valuation, and 16.44 per cent. of equalized real estate valuation.
New York	104,000,000 =	6.45 per cent. of present real estate valuation.
Combined	$166,000,000 =	7.75 per cent. of present real estate valuation.
Combined	166,000,000 =	8.35 per cent. of equalized real estate valuation.

† For the debt limitations of cities, see article VII, section 10, of the new State Constitution.

TO OFFSET NEW YORK'S INCURRED DISADVANTAGE OF $3.00 PER $1,000 IN HER ANNUAL TAX RATE, SHE WOULD RECEIVE THE FOLLOWING ASSETS, OVER AND ABOVE BROOKLYN'S DEBT OF $62,000,000, VIZ.:

	Estimated value.
Water works and reservoirs	†$20,294,000
Prospect park and East Side lands	15,510,000
(a) Other parks	3,160,493
School houses	8,500,000
(b) Fire department—houses, horses and equipment	1,659,700
(c) Police department—houses, horses and equipment	1,288,100
Public market	2,000,000
Brooklyn bridge (cost to Brooklyn)	15,845,431
Real estate (bought in under arrears act)	471,079
Arrears of taxes and water rates	3,561,222
(d) City buildings and other property	2,767,000
(e) Uncollected general assessments	364,376
(f) Uncollected special assessments	779,537
Penitentiary and county buildings, Flatbush; Kings park (St. Johnland)	4,000,000
(g) Special assessments not yet levied	1,899,000
(h) County buildings, Brooklyn	1,701,815
(i) Armories	2,773,617
Parade grounds, Kings county	175,000
	$86,750,370
Brooklyn, county and town debt, net	62,000,000
Surplus assets, over liabilities	$24,750,370

ESTIMATED VALUE OF BROOKLYN'S ASSETS, JANUARY 1, 1895.

(See table above.)

(a) Other parks:

City park, 7½ acres	$150,000 00
Tompkins, 7¾ acres	250,000 00
Carroll, 1 8-10 acres	390,000 00
Washington, 30 1-16 acres	1,500,000 00
Winthrop, 7½ acres	133,678 00
Bushwick, 27th ward	105,308 00
Sunset, 14¾ acres, 8th ward	164,604 00
Ridgewood, 45 acres, 26th ward	184,025 00
Bedford, 24th ward	150,133 00
Twelfth Ward park	132,745 00
	$3,160,493 00

†Represented by present bonded indebtedness of $15,946,000.

(*b*) Fire department:

Real estate and houses	$783,900 00
Horses, engines, fire boats, telegraph, etc	675,800 00
Firemen's insurance fund, mortgages and cash	200,000 00
	$1,659,700 00

(*c*) Police department:

Real estate and station houses	$1,099,000 00
Horses, police boat, patrol and telegraph	127,100 00
Police pension fund, bond and cash	62,000 00
	$1,288,100 00

(*d*) City buildings and other property:

City hall and grounds, 1½ acres	$700,000 00
Municipal building	280,000 00
Municipal building, additional site	265,000 00
Truant home and school, Jamaica road	75,000 00
Kent avenue basin improvement	464,000 00
Wallabout Bay improvement	913,000 00
Court of Special Sessions, Myrtle and Vanderbilt avenues	35,000 00
Plot of ground, First avenue, 43d and 44th streets	35,000 00
	$2,767,000 00

(*e*) Uncollected general assessments:

November 30, 1894.

Gas lamps and posts	$3,667 75
Grading and paving	285,092 45
Repaving	40,579 34
Sewer	31,705 99
Opening and widening	3,330 74
	$364,376 27

(*f*) Uncollected special assessments:

November 30, 1894.

Prospect park, twenty-two yearly instalments	$736,780 00
Widening North Second street	42,757 18
	$779,537 18

(*g*) Special assessments not yet levied, for which bonds have been issued:

Eighth ward improvement	$650,000 00
Twenty-sixth and adjacent wards, sewers	999,000 00
Sewerage fund bonds, act of 1892	250,000 00
	$1,899,000 00

(*h*) County buildings, Brooklyn:

Court house—land and building	$543,746 13
Hall of Records—land and building	787,210 61
Jail—land and building	370,858 12
	$1,701,814 86

(*i*) Armories:

13th Regiment old armory—site and building	$183,617 15
13th Regiment new armory—site and building	700,000 00
14th Regiment new armory—site and building	650,000 00
23d Regiment new armory—site and building	650,650 00
32d Regiment old armory—site and building	140,000 00
47th Regiment new armory—site and building	180,000 00
47th Regiment, Co. "I," Greenpoint armory	10,000 00
47th Regiment old armory hall, North Second street	50,000 00
3d Battery, old armory, 23d Regiment	160,000 00
3d Battery, old armory, Dean street	50,000 00
	$2,773,617 15

IN 1895 THE INTEREST ON BROOKLYN, COUNTY AND TOWN DEBT IS AS FOLLOWS:

	Principal.	Interest.
City—Net debt	$50,184,000 00	‡$1,409,934 83
County	7,641,216 00	363,297 35
Flatbush	987,000 00	say 48,350 00
New Utrecht	1,077,447 94	say 53,872 40
Gravesend	1,825,083 02	say 91,254 15
Flatlands	43,984 64	say 2,189 23
	$61,758,731 00	$1,968,897 96

‡ While the net debt of Brooklyn is relatively much greater than New York, it is to be noticed that in Brooklyn, including the county towns, the interest charge raised by taxation for 1895 is a little less than $2,000,000 while the interest charge similarly raised in New York is about $5,000,000, which is exclusive of the amount payable from the Sinking Fund, say $2,000,000 more. In Brooklyn the water revenue, amounting to $1,813,000 in 1894, pays the interest on the water debt of $15,946,000, amounting to $722,000 in 1894, whereas in New York the water revenue, say $3,500,000 annually, is credited direct to the Sinking Fund, for the payment of interest on all city debt.

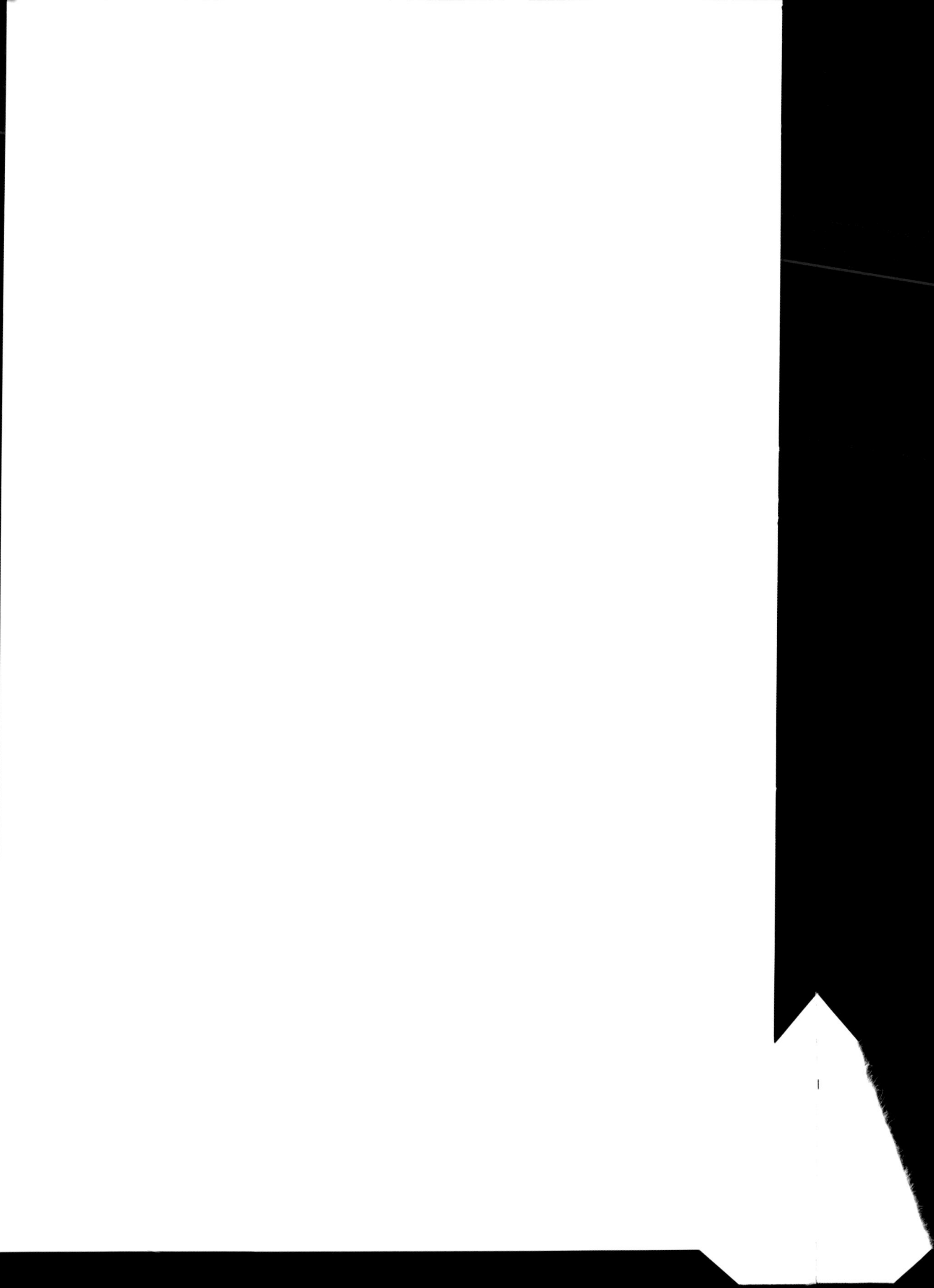

www.ingramcontent.com/pod-product-compliance
Lightning Source LLC
LaVergne TN
LVHW021051110826
845150LV00001B/44

* 9 7 8 1 4 2 5 5 6 8 2 2 1 *